P9-DHM-566

Ethnicity, Crime, and Immigration
Comparative and Cross-National Perspectives

Ethnicity, Crime, and Immigration

Comparative and Cross-National Perspectives

Edited by Michael Tonry

Crime and Justice
A Review of Research
Edited by Michael Tonry

VOLUME 21

The University of Chicago Press, Chicago and London

This volume was prepared under grants awarded to the Castine Research Corporation by the Research and Statistics Department of the Home Office of England and Wales, the Dutch Ministry of Justice, the Max Planck Institute for International and Comparative Penal Law in Freiburg, Germany, the Swedish National Crime Prevention Council, and the National Science Foundation of Switzerland, and to Michael Tonry by the Harry Frank Guggenheim Foundation. Points of view or opinions expressed in this volume are those of the editor or authors and do not necessarily represent the official position or policies of the sponsors.

The University of Chicago Press, Chicago 60637
The University of Chicago Press, Ltd., London

Printed in the United States of America

ISSN: 0192-3234

ISBN: 0-226-80827-0
00 99 98 97 96 5 4 3 2 1

ISBN: 0-226-80828-9 (paper)
00 99 98 97 96 5 4 3 2 1

LCN: 80-642217

Library of Congress Cataloging-in-Publication Data

Ethnicity, crime, and immigration: comparative and cross-national perspectives / edited by Michael Tonry.
p. cm.—(Crime and justice, ISSN 0192-3234; v. 21)
Includes bibliographical references and index.
ISBN 0-226-80827-0 (cloth).—ISBN 0-226-80828-9 (pbk.)
1. Crime. 2. Immigrants. 3. Ethnicity. I. Tonry, Michael H. II. Series: Crime and justice (Chicago, Ill.) : v. 21.
HV6001.C672 vol. 21
[HV6181]
364.3′4—DC20 96-27347
CIP

The paper used in this publication meets the minimum requirements of American National Standard for Information Sciences—Permanence of Paper for Printed Library Materials, ANSI Z39.48-1984. ♾

Contents

Preface

Members of minority groups are overrepresented among crime victims, arrestees, pretrial detainees, convicted offenders, and prisoners in every Western country. This is true in countries in which the largest affected groups are black or Afro-Caribbean, as in the United States and England, in countries in which the most affected groups are aboriginal occupants of colonized lands, as in Australia and Canada, in countries in which the most affected groups are of North African origins, as in France and the Netherlands, and in countries in which the most affected groups are mainly of European origins, as in Germany and Sweden. Whatever the explanations for these consistent patterns, and there are many, they encompass much more than racial or ethnic animus.

This volume presents the fruits of an effort to establish what is now known in Western countries about group differences in offending, victimization, and justice system case processing, and about the reasons for those differences. So far as I, and others involved in the effort, know, the essays in this volume together constitute the most comprehensive examination of the subject that is now available. The essays were commissioned to a common outline although, for reasons of the differing research traditions and data availability in the countries covered, they vary substantially in the detail in which some of the included topics are discussed. Initial drafts were discussed at a conference attended by the writers and others at All Souls College, Oxford. Later on, the more general set of theoretical, methodological, substantive, and policy issues the essays raise was discussed at a second conference at Kappel Monastery outside Zurich. Essays underwent an extensive vetting process, and most were substantially revised to incorporate lessons learned at the two conferences.

"Race and crime," "ethnicity and crime," "minorities and crime," or "immigration and crime," slightly different phrases that describe the same core set of empirical and policy issues, are high on the political agendas of most Western countries. Perhaps because of this, but most unusually, agencies in a number of European countries awarded grants to Castine Research Corporation, a small nonprofit research firm based in Castine, Maine, that made the project and this volume possible. We are most grateful to the Research and Statistics Department of the Home Office of England and Wales, the Dutch Ministry of Justice, the Swedish National Crime Prevention Council, the National Science Foundation of Switzerland, and the Max Planck Institute for International and Comparative Penal Law in Freiburg, Germany, for their support. In addition, a much appreciated grant from the Harry Frank Guggenheim Foundation made my work on this project possible.

Other thanks are due. The Warden and Fellows of All Souls College made the facilities of the college available for the project's first conference, and Roger Hood of All Souls was our gracious and painstaking host. The welcome could not have been warmer or the surroundings more conducive to a promising beginning. The second conference, in Kappel, was organized by the School of Forensic Science and Criminology of the University of Lausanne. Martin Killias was our solicitous and remarkably efficient host. In each of the sponsoring countries, a participant in the project served as an indispensable liaison with the funding agency: Gunther Kaiser in Germany, Roger Hood in England, Josine Junger-Tas in the Netherlands, Martin Killias in Switzerland, and Per-Olof Wikström in Sweden. The project and the papers also benefited from the advice and critical comments of others who attended one or both of the conferences: Benjamin Bowling, Marianne Junger, Hans-Jürgen Kerner, André Kuhn, Patrick Langan, and David Daubney.

Finally, and crucially, the writers of the essays in this volume all deserve high praise for the substantial and insightful glimpses they have provided into the experiences of minority group members with their countries' justice systems. Five of the essays were written by scholars whose first language is not English, and they compare favorably with much scholarly writing in English by criminologists for whom that is their only language. All of the writers with good humor and patience endured a lengthy and persnickety process of reviews and editing. Readers will decide for themselves whether all those efforts were worthwhile. For myself, I have no doubt and am immensely grateful to the nine essays' eleven talented writers for the instruction they have given me.

Michael Tonry

Michael Tonry

Ethnicity, Crime, and Immigration

Members of *some* disadvantaged minority groups in every Western country are disproportionately likely to be arrested, convicted, and imprisoned for violent, property, and drug crimes. This is true whether the minority groups are members of different "racial" groups from the majority population, for example, blacks or Afro-Caribbeans in Canada, England, or the United States, or of different ethnic backgrounds, for example, North African Arabs in France or the Netherlands, or—irrespective of race or ethnicity—are recent migrants from other countries, for example, Yugoslavs or Eastern Europeans in Germany and Finns in Sweden. Important social policy dilemmas that are seen in individual countries to be uniquely their own, such as race relations in the United States or assimilation of Maghreb-derived guest workers in France or the experience of Aborigines in Australia, are not unique at all but are instead variations on common themes of social structure that characterize many countries.

It is important, however, not to be reductionist. The different offending patterns and justice system experiences of members of different groups in a country are not simply the result of group differences in wealth, social status, or political power. That is why the word "some" is emphasized in the phrase "some disadvantaged minority groups" in the first sentence of this essay. Not all economically and socially disadvantaged groups are disproportionately involved in crime.

In England and Wales, for example, Afro-Caribbeans and migrants from the Indian subcontinent began to arrive in large numbers at about the same time—the 1950s and 1960s—and experienced comparable forms and levels of invidious discrimination. In the 1990s, Bangladeshis in particular are on average poorer and more disadvantaged than Afro-Caribbeans. Yet Afro-Caribbeans in England are as disproportionately involved in crime and the justice system compared with whites, as are blacks in the United States compared with whites. Indians, Pakistanis, and Bangladeshis in England, however, are less involved in crime and the justice system than are whites. (It is possible that crime rates for some Asian groups will rise. Bangladeshis arrived in England later than other groups and are on average younger and poorer. One might also hypothesize that anti-Muslim feelings are rising in England and that this will produce greater alienation and higher crime rates. No evidence to sustain either theory has as yet been reported.)

Similarly, Moroccans and Turks came to the Netherlands as guest workers in the 1950s and 1960s. Many stayed and were later joined by family members after the doors closed to new labor migrants in the early 1970s. By the 1990s, both groups were comparably disadvantaged economically and socially compared with the majority population, but crime and incarceration rates for Turks were not much higher than those of the Dutch, while those for Moroccans were much higher.

The English and Dutch experiences capture all of the themes which the phrases "race and crime," "ethnicity and crime," and "immigration and crime" encompass. The criminal justice system experience of Afro-Caribbeans in England is often seen as a problem of race and crime. The experience of Moroccans in the Netherlands is often seen as a problem of ethnicity and crime. The experiences of minority groups in both countries are often seen as problems of immigration and crime. In all the countries examined in this book, disproportionate crime involvement all too often fosters negative stereotypes of minority groups and both discrimination and xenophobia directed at them and, conversely, provokes passionate arguments and accusations about racial, ethnic, or anti-immigrant bias as a or the primary cause of justice system disparities.

These are not small problems. Race relations and political controversies about immigrants are high on the political and policy agendas of many countries. In an era of rapid social and economic changes in many countries, persistent high unemployment in Europe, and declining real wages in North America, many people feel threatened and insecure and nativist politicians have been quick to blame minority and immigrant groups for much of what seems wrong. Hate crimes are increasingly common and publicized in many countries, and violent attacks against minority groups are more evident in Europe. Members of victimized minority groups in turn are likely to become more alienated from majority populations.

This book, no book, can realistically aspire to affect those powerful social forces, but it can and does aspire to shed light on the narrower question of what is now known about crime and justice system involvement of members of minority groups in nine countries and about the reasons for the differences that exist. Public policy does not always take account of systematic knowledge about the subjects it addresses, but in civilized countries it should. The aim of this book therefore is to establish what is now known about racial and ethnic patterns of crime and justice system involvement in nine Western countries. They were selected because they are among the relatively few countries, Western or otherwise, that have empirical research traditions that have generated research findings or well-maintained official statistics on which credible assertions can be based. The writers of the essays in this book have examined evidence concerning both "minority groups and crime" and "immigration and crime," two subjects that are seldom brought together which, once brought together, can teach more than can either alone.

This introduction, most readers will be relieved to learn, does not summarize and comment on the contents of each of the essays. I have never understood why introductions so often do that; the essays are after all but a few pages away, and if they do not stand on their own and say what they mean should not have been published. Instead, these introductory pages explain why the volume was conceived and suggest some of the things that a look across national boundaries can teach us about "race, ethnicity, and crime" and "immigration and crime." The essays are vertical or longitudinal looks at the experiences of individual countries. This introduction attempts to look horizontally across national boundaries to indicate common findings and ways in which cross-national inquiry on this subject can modify or enrich current knowledge based on the experiences of individual countries.

There are four sections. The first describes some of the difficulties that confront efforts to investigate these issues. Most human beings, including this one, are captives of their own experiences and both more parochial and more ethnocentric than they know. The seemingly straightforward questions that this volume examines are not easy to answer cross-nationally, not only because of differences in criminal codes and legal processes but also because of important cultural differences in views about things as seemingly mundane as compilation of official statistics. The second section discusses racial and ethnic differences in offending, victimization, and system processing, relative to majority populations, and shows that similar patterns occur in every country, whatever the race, ethnicity, or nationality of the overrepresented minorities. The third discusses "immigration and crime" and shows that the widespread conventional wisdom that first-generation immigrants typically are more law-abiding than the resident population, while their children and grandchildren typically have higher crime rates, is true, but for a much smaller proportion of immigrants than is commonly recognized. Very different patterns characterize other groups of immigrants. The fourth, finally, offers suggestions for how genuinely comparative and cross-national research might advance current understanding and provide knowledge that can help policy makers predict conditions and circumstances associated with high rates of offending by minority and immigrant groups and devise measures to ameliorate those otherwise foreseeable results.

I. Impediments to Looking across National Boundaries

Although none of the essays in this volume attempts to compare sentencing severity for particular crimes in different countries, the problems involved in trying to make that comparison provide a good starting point. If the goal were to compare average severity of sentences for burglary of a dwelling, street robbery, and rape in Germany, Sweden, and the United States, a number of important contextual differences would have to be taken into account. Definitions of offenses vary between countries, as do traditions about reporting crimes to the authorities, so it would be necessary to look beyond the formal definitions to make sure that similar criminal behaviors were being compared. In principle, this could be done by use of statistical controls, if sufficiently rich data were available in each country on "actual offense behavior." A second problem, however, is that criminal processes vary substantially between countries. In Germany (Weigend 1993) and the Netherlands (Tak 1994), for example, large percentages of cases are disposed of by means of conditional dismissals in which the defendant acknowledges guilt and agrees to pay a penalty, often a fine, comparable to that which might have been imposed following conviction, in exchange for conditional dismissal of the charges (and thus no criminal conviction). Comparisons of average prison sentences between countries in which conditional dismissals are common and countries in which they are not will suffer from selection bias: all other things being equal, in the former countries the average seriousness of the crimes for which convictions are entered will likely be greater. Comparisons of prison sentences for robbery, for example, would be biased since the comparison would be between a smaller proportion of more serious robberies in one country and a larger proportion of both more and less serious robberies in another. Similar problems are presented by national differences in the use of suspended prison sentences, whether a discretionary parole release system exists and how it is used, and whether nominal sentences include a period, often one-third of the total, of automatic remission of sentence ("good time" in the United States).

Comparisons of sentencing patterns in different countries must, accordingly, be made with caution and evaluated with skepticism. None of the essays in this volume make cross-national comparisons. All of the comparisons between groups are made within countries, and the formal legal context is in effect controlled for. That does not mean that there may not be selection biases within a jurisdiction's legal system that occur when members of some groups are more likely to be arrested or prosecuted or convicted and, conversely, less likely to benefit from informal diversions or gentler sentences. Those selection biases within countries, however, have often been studied and many of the essays in this volume report the results. Nonetheless, the warnings above about the need to be skeptical of cross-national comparisons also apply, if with weaker force, to assessment of writings on countries about which the reader lacks detailed knowledge.

A number of other impediments exist to national and cross-national studies of racial and ethnic disparities. They are described below, and illustrated, but not discussed at length.

A. Measuring Racial Disparities

It is not possible with existing data to make even crude cross-national comparisons of racial disparities in the justice systems of Western countries other than the major English-speaking countries. Partly this is because the social construct "race" has played a larger role in the history of the English-speaking countries, and partly it is because in many countries maintenance of official data on race is forbidden for ethical reasons.

When Americans think about racial bias and racial disparities, they tend to think first about the experience of black Americans. Given America's race relations history and that blacks, at 12 percent of the population, are the largest nonwhite minority group, this is not surprising. Thus, if the subject is disparities in imprisonment, a natural question is whether and to what extent blacks compared with whites are locked up. The answer on an average day in 1990 was that 1,860 per 100,000 American blacks were in jail or prison, compared with 289 per 100,000 whites. That is a difference of 6.44 to 1 (Tonry 1995, table 2-1). Stated differently, the chance that a black American was in prison or jail in 1990 was six-and-a-half times higher than for a white American. Racial disparities in prison have worsened since 1990. According to the U.S. Bureau of Justice Statistics, 2,316 per 100,000 blacks were confined in federal or state prisons on December 1994, compared with 291 whites per 100,000 (Bureau of Justice Statistics 1995). That is an 8 to 1 difference (and ignores jail populations which would make the absolute confinement rates half again higher, but probably not significantly affect the ratio).

The first and easiest international comparison is to look at equivalent data in other English-speaking common-law countries. At least for 1990, when that comparison is made, racial disparities in the United States can be seen to be not unique. In that year the 6.44 racial difference in total incarceration rates in the United States was lower than the corresponding disparities in England (a 7:1 Afro-Caribbean/white difference). Disparities in countries with sizable aboriginal populations are worse: Canada (a 16:1 native/nonnative difference in 1986), and Australia (a 12:1 Aborigine/non-Aborigine difference in 1993) (Tonry 1994).

That, however, is where the international comparisons must stop. No other country retains data in official records on defendants' or offenders' race. Only the United States routinely records and publishes such data in its justice system records; England records and publishes racial data in its prison statistics. Canada, Australia, and New Zealand retain data that permit native/nonnative, Aborigine/non-Aborigine, Maori-Pacific Islander/other comparisons. None of the last three countries, however, records data that permits black/white comparisons.

There are two reasons why black/white racial identification data are not recorded in official records in most countries. First, on ethical grounds, lawmakers in many countries have decided that such data should not be recorded. One rationale is that race is not a morally relevant difference between individuals and that recording such data is to treat it as if it were a relevant difference and thereby to tend to reify it into a relevant difference. Another is that recording such data, especially when minorities are overrepresented among offenders, may create or support stereotypes that are stigmatizing or otherwise damaging to members of minority groups. Still another is that recording such data might make it easier for biased officials to discriminate against minority offenders. Outside the United States, this is an intensely controversial subject. In Canada, for example, in the early 1990s the use of racial identifiers in official records was widely discussed in the editorial columns of national newspapers among other places (e.g., Doob 1991). The conclusion at that time was that racial identifiers should remain forbidden. More recently, Ontario's Commission on Systemic Racism proposed a five-year data collection pilot project using racial identifiers (1995, p. 405), with the caveat that the pilot project follow "guidelines . . . established in collaboration with racialized communities." England's Royal Commission on Criminal Justice (1993) likewise concluded that efforts to reduce racial disparities could not be assessed unless data on racial disparities were collected.

The second reason in most countries for not recording racial identifiers is that the data would be overaggregated and lack social validity. In most countries "blacks" are as heterogeneous a grouping as "whites." In Ontario, for example, where recent allegations of racial bias, especially on the part of police, have been vigorous, many black Canadians have protested that "black" is overinclusive (Commission on Systemic Racism in the Ontario Criminal Justice System 1995). Until thirty years ago, most black Toronto residents were members of families that had migrated from the United States generations earlier. Since then there have been successive waves of immigrants from the West Indies, especially Jamaica, and Africa, especially Ethiopia and Somalia. At least in public stereotype, high crime rates have been most characteristic of West Indian immigrants, and both long-time residents and African immigrants have resented being victims of guilt by stereotyped racial association. (And members of Ethiopian immigrant groups often insist that Tigreans and Amharic-speakers be distinguished.)

In most countries, there is little reason to lump dark-skinned people into one "racial" group. In Germany, as Hans-Jörg Albrecht shows in this volume, at different times in recent years people from Gambia, Nigeria, and Senegal have been active in drug trafficking. In England, the black population includes both a sizable proportion who derive from the West Indies and another sizable group who derive from various African countries. In much of his discussion of racial disparities in England's justice system, David Smith (in this volume) is careful to note that heterogeneity even though English official records do not.

Disaggregation below the category "black" is seldom attempted or discussed in the United States. A large percentage of black Americans are descendants or members of families that have lived in the United States for many generations, so that may not be surprising. Nonetheless, it must obscure important differences between groups such as Puerto Ricans, Haitians, black Cubans, West Indians, recent migrants from many African countries, and descendants of long-time residents. There is, for example, substantial evidence that West Indian migrants to the United States in the middle third of this century assimilated more successfully both economically and socially into the American mainstream than have other groups (Sowell 1983).

B. Measuring Ethnicity Disparities

Cross-national comparisons of ethnic disparities cannot be made. With only a few anomalous exceptions in individual countries, ethnic identifiers are not recorded in justice system data. In Europe especially, widespread aversion to ethnicity classifications by government is one legacy of the horrors of Nazi Germany. If the subject were open to reconsideration, presumably the concerns about stigmatization, reification, and potential invidious use that lead most countries to reject racial identifiers would be among the concerns opponents would urge, but the subject is nowhere open for reconsideration.

As the next subsection notes, some countries record data on "nationality" which sometimes may be a proxy for ethnicity, but only sometimes. Concerning relatively homogeneous countries like Denmark and Norway in which nationality and ethnicity are largely congruent, the categories "Danish" and "Norwegian" might efficiently characterize people who speak the national language as a first tongue and share cultural traditions and customs and, in those respects, share a common ethnicity. For many nationalities, however, that would not be so. In the Netherlands, for example, "Surinamese" include subgroups commonly distinguished by others and themselves as "Creoles," "Hindustanis," and "Asians"; while "Antilleans" may be disaggregated further by particular islands. "Turks" make up sizable minority groups in many European countries, but the category includes both ethnic Turks and ethnic Kurds, two subgroups that in some places differ substantially (and sometimes violently). "Yugoslavs," the world will not soon forget, include Croats, Serbs, Bosnians, Albanians, and Slovenians, among others. And so forth. In the same way that "black" is an overaggregated category in Ontario, nationality is an overaggregated category in many places and for many nationalities.

There are major exceptions to the general aversion to use of ethnic identifiers. Some countries with sizable aboriginal populations, for example, Australia and New Zealand, routinely use Aborigine/non-Aborigine identifiers. Perhaps surprisingly, given the Canadian reluctance to use black/white racial identifiers, Canadian official records have long, and with little controversy, distinguished natives from non-natives (Roberts and Doob, in this volume). Perhaps most surprisingly, although German laws prohibit use of ethnicity identifiers, including "Gypsy," German police have long recorded other euphemistic data that allow them to identify Gypsies (Albrecht, in this volume).

The anomalies, however, are anomalies and are not useful for making cross-national ethnicity comparisons except, possibly, between the experiences of Aborigines in Australia and New Zealand. Anyone who wanted to compare the criminal justice system experiences in different countries of Kurds or (before the breakup of Yugoslavia) Croats would have to look somewhere other than official records.

C. Measuring Nationality Disparities

Some countries do use nationality identifiers, but as many do not. In Germany, many statistical systems record nationality data. For most purposes, French data distinguish only between French nationals (*citoyens*) and foreigners (*étrangers*). Similarly, although nationality is commonly recorded in official records in Switzerland, published Swiss crime statistics distinguish among Swiss nationals, resident foreigners, and nonresident foreigners. Swedish official statistics also commonly distinguish among Swedish nationals, resident foreigners, and non-resident foreigners, and for some purposes report data for geographical regions (e.g., Africa, Nordic countries, South America). In the Netherlands, neither ethnicity nor nationality data is recorded in police or court records, but some use of national origin data is permitted in prison records.

Data systems in the English-speaking countries are even less informative about nationality. At state and national levels, American data typically distinguish only among black, white, Native American, "other," and Hispanic individuals. Australian official data contain only the Aborigine/non-Aborigine distinction (although some systems routinely collect "country of birth" data), and most Canadian data identify only natives and nonnatives. Through the 1930s, U.S. and Canadian data often recorded nationality, but as "crime and the foreign born" declined as a controversial political issue after large-scale immigration stopped in the mid-1920s, use of nationality identifiers stopped.

The prospects for cross-national studies are not as bleak as this summary may suggest. Germany has the richest nationality data and, as the essay by Albrecht (in this volume) shows, permits highly discriminant and informative analyses. In some countries, for example, Sweden, special studies are done that link official justice system records to other records that contain nationality identifiers. In the Netherlands and Sweden, self-report and victimization studies validated against official records provide much useful information.

This is not the place to explore measurement problems in detail, but a few general problems concerning measurement of nationality should be mentioned. They relate to comparisons within countries both between the experiences of nationals and foreigners and between different nationality groups. A major problem is that countries differ in their naturalization policies and in how naturalized citizens are classified. Naturalization has traditionally been readily available to immigrants in Sweden, France, and the Netherlands, which means that comparisons between citizens and noncitizens are weakened; "citizens" include many people who are recent immigrants, and their children, and thus both sides of the comparison include recent immigrants. If individuals sharing a particular national origin have higher crime rates than ethnic Swedes, the comparison will understate the difference. Germany and Switzerland, by contrast, have traditionally been less open to naturalization, and the citizen/foreigner distinction is sharper.

A second complication is that many countries' records do not distinguish between resident and nonresident foreigners (Sweden and Switzerland do). In a country like Switzerland, where annual border crossings exceed the resident population by a factor of thirty (Killias, in this volume), tourists and illegal entrants may commit a large proportion of crimes by foreigners, making it difficult to compare the behaviors of resident citizens and resident foreigners. As Europe continues its movement toward political and economic unification, and as drug and economic crimes become increasingly transnational, this problem will become more important.

This litany of complications is intended only to show that complexity faces efforts to make cross-national comparisons and not that they are impossible. The complications can be overcome by creative analytic techniques and by collection of original data. And, more important, notwithstanding all these problems, as the essays in this volume show, a great deal has been learned within each country which reveals strong similarities in every included countries' experiences with ethnicity, crime, and immigration, which offers hypotheses for understanding other countries' experiences, and which provides a rich foundation on which later research can build.

II. Racial and Ethnic Disparities

Many readers of this volume, I suspect, will be surprised to learn that racial disparities in America's justice system are paralleled by comparable minority group disparities in other countries. Similarly, in most countries in which researchers have attempted to learn whether disparities occur primarily because of group differences in offending or because of bias, the general conclusion, as in the United States, has been that most of the measured disparity appears to be attributable to offending differences. Finally, in every country in which case processing studies have been carried out, similar patterns of systematic adverse effects for minority groups appear as a result of "neutral" policies and practices.

Two prefatory points need making. First, as mentioned earlier, most comparisons of offending or system processing are based on such overaggregated categories as race, aboriginality, and nationality. Substantial behavioral and experiential differences often distinguish subgroups.

Second, countries have distinct research traditions, and the kinds of research findings and official data available to investigate specific questions vary a great deal. On the question of whether invidious bias is a major cause of racial and ethnic disproportions, although large between-group disparities occur in every country, only in a few has there been much research on the subject. There is a vast American empirical literature on justice system bias. There is a smaller English literature. In Australia and Canada, there have been a few studies concerning aboriginal and native disparities; the findings from the first major Canadian study on black/white disparities are reported in the essay by Roberts and Doob in this volume. No studies of this type appear to have been done in France or Sweden and but a few each in Germany and the Netherlands.

Victimization studies offer another example. Victimization studies can be used to compare group patterns in arrests with victims' reports of the identities of their assailants or to investigate the extent to which offending is intragroup. Comparisons of arrest and victim-identification patterns for particular crimes may suggest the presence or absence of police bias. If offending typically occurs within groups, if, for example, black offenders in the United States typically victimize black victims, epithets of racism are less likely to be used to explain high rates of prosecution of black offenders; not doing so would in effect undervalue crimes against blacks, a form of discrimination and insensitivity which is difficult to justify. Here, too, countries vary widely. Long-term national victimization studies exist in the United States and England, and to a lesser extent in Canada and the Netherlands. Occasional surveys with large samples have been conducted in Switzerland (Killias, in this volume). The Swiss and English surveys, like the American ones, find that assailants' ethnic or national background has little influence on victims' decisions to report to the police.

Still and all, for all the differences in data availability and research tradition in various countries, on some subjects the findings are so robust and so consistent across national boundaries that meaningful generalizations can be offered. The essays that follow discuss the evidence in detail.

1. *In Every Country, Crime and Incarceration Rates for Members of Some Minority Groups Greatly Exceed Those for the Majority Population.* Perhaps most important, comparable disparities exist both for racial and ethnic minorities and for national origin minorities who are not visible racial minorities. In England and Wales, and the United States, black residents are seven-to-eight times more likely than whites to be confined in prisons, and the black/white imprisonment disparities in the Canadian province of Ontario are greater (Roberts and Doob, in this volume). In Australia and Canada, arrest and imprisonment disparities affecting Aborigines and natives are even greater than black/white disparities in the other English-speaking countries. In the Netherlands, however, the greatest disparities affect people from Morocco and Surinam (Junger-Tas, in this volume). In Sweden, Finns have higher rates than Swedes, and the highest disproportions in arrests affect immigrants from Arab countries, South America (notably Chileans, of whom those in Sweden are mostly of European descent), and Eastern Europe (Martens, in this volume). In the German state of North Rhine–Westphalia in 1993, Romanians experienced by far the highest arrest rates (nearly 740 per year per 1,000 people, 44 times the German arrest rate) and the most disproportionate imprisonment rate (1608 per 100,000 population, 21 times the German rate) (Albrecht, in this volume). In France, the highest imprisonment rates characterize people from the Maghreb countries of Algeria, Morocco, and Tunisia (Tournier, in this volume).

Too much should not be made of numbers like those in the preceding paragraph. They tell us something important—that stark disparities in arrests and imprisonment exist in many countries, not simply those in which blacks or Aborigines are the most politically and socially salient minority—but they do not tell much more. Most important, they do not indicate what kinds of offenses are being disproportionately committed and sanctioned and why. Albrecht's essay in this volume, for example, graphically shows that the kinds of offenses different groups commit in different countries vary greatly. Romanians have by far the highest arrest rates in the state of Hessen in Germany, but their offenses are mostly minor property and immigration offenses; their arrests rates for violent and drug crimes are lower than those for many other much less often arrested groups. The essays on Sweden and Germany describe relatively high crime rates for people from Eastern Europe, but both describe their crimes as being principally theft and shoplifting, crimes that are arguably explicable in terms of the exposure of materially deprived people moving into wealthy societies to consumer goods that are readily accessible by illicit means. And in many countries, some groups may be recent migrants who are temporarily in assimilation or acculturation phases often afflicted by high crime rates. Finally, at any time groups may differ from others in age and gender composition, wealth and social status, and other social and economic characteristics that are strongly correlated with criminality; apparent differences in behavior between groups may on closer examination reflect nothing more than composition differences between groups.

2. *Minority Groups Characterized by High Crime and Imprisonment Rates Are Also Characterized by Various Indicators of Social and Economic Disadvantage.* This should be no surprise. For as long as social reformers and researchers have studied criminality, the correlation between criminality and disadvantage has been clear. Those correlations were as clear in nineteenth-century England (Mayhew 1861) and early twentieth-century America (Shaw 1929), when the high-crime groups were white, as today in those countries when some of the high-crime groups are black. The essays in this volume on Switzerland (Killias), Sweden (Martens), and the Netherlands (Junger-Tas) discuss the links between disadvantage and crime most fully and all make the relationship clear.

However, and it is a big however, not all disadvantaged groups exhibit high crime rates. In England, as already noted, migrants from the Indian subcontinent were as disadvantaged and as discriminated against as migrants from the Caribbean and Africa; Afro-Caribbeans have crime and imprisonment rates far higher than those for whites, while rates for Indian subcontinent migrants are lower. While, in the United States, it remains unclear whether recent Southeast Asian immigrants will have high crime rates, it is clear that the typically impoverished Chinese and Japanese migrants of the nineteenth century did not. In the Netherlands, Turks and Moroccans first arrived in large numbers as guest workers in the 1950s and 1960s; although labor migrant entry ceased in the early 1970s, the two groups have increased both naturally and as a result of family reunification policies under the immigration laws. In the 1990s both groups are comparably less well-off economically, educationally, and vocationally than the Dutch. Yet the Turks have crime and imprisonment rates much like those for the Dutch while Moroccans have rates that are far higher.

3. *In Countries in Which Research Has Been Conducted on the Causes of Racial and Ethnic Disparities in Imprisonment, Group Differences in Offending, Not Invidious Bias, Appear to Be the Principal Cause.* I have phrased that conclusion in as nontendentious a way as I can. It could be phrased differently. If the critical aim were to demonstrate that racial and ethnic stereotypes and animus influence disparities, the conclusion would be that, all other things being equal, members of racial minorities receive harsher sentences. The hypothesis to be tested is that race and ethnicity matter, and research findings support the conclusion that they do. If the apologetic aim were to demonstrate that stereotypes and animus have little influence, the conclusion would be that, controlling for offense circumstances and criminal histories, race and ethnicity explain little of the variation in sentencing outcomes. The hypothesis is that neutral or legally relevant factors are the principal determinants of sentences, and the data support the conclusion that they are. Put another way, neither proponents of the claim that bias is the sole or primary cause of disparities nor proponents of the claim that bias has no influence on disparities will find empirical evidence to prove their claims.

Whether bias or behavior was the primary cause of racial disparities in arrests and imprisonment was for two decades a highly controversial question in English-speaking countries, and, as a result, much of the relevant research has been in those countries. However, a significant body of German research has also investigated the causes of disparities from police stops through sentencing (Albrecht, in this volume), as has a smaller body of Dutch research (Junger-Tas, in this volume). Relatively little research on the causes of disparities has been done in the other three countries. The writers of the essays in this volume on France (Tournier) and Sweden (Martens) offer informed speculation. The essay on Switzerland (Killias) compares proportions of foreigners among arrestees to those among prison admissions and populations and finds reasonable consistency, but neither detailed case studies on system processing nor sophisticated statistical analyses have been done to buttress that observation.

Much the largest volume of work has been in the United States and has several times been summarized (e.g., Wilbanks 1987; Mann 1993; Tonry 1995; Sampson and Lauritsen, in this volume). There have been case processing studies, both qualitative and quantitative, at every stage of the justice system from police stops to parole release, aggregate statistical analyses of the relations between national crime data and national imprisonment data, and statistical comparisons of victimization data on victims' identifications of assailants with police data on the racial characteristics of arrestees. With only minor exceptions, the evidence, while certainly not showing that bias has no role, indicates that criminality past and present is the major determinant of officials' decisions.

The next largest literature is in England and Wales and, as summarized by Smith in this volume, supports much the same conclusions as in the United States. Work in Australia and Canada is not inconsistent with the American and English findings, but so little work has been done that no strong conclusions can be offered.

Curiously, although much work has been done in Australia in recent years to document Aborigine/non-Aborigine disparities at every stage of the adult and juvenile systems (Royal Commission into Aboriginal Deaths in Custody 1991; Harding et al. 1995; Broadhurst, in this volume), there have been only a few case processing studies to test bias hypotheses, and although one rigorous study found significantly higher arrest risks after controlling for key factors, this was not conclusively or solely attributed to racial prejudice (e.g., Gale and Wundersitz 1987; Gale, Bailey-Harris, and Wundersitz 1990; Duguid 1992).

The first major statistical analyses in Canada to test antiblack bias hypotheses were completed in 1995 under the auspices of the Ontario Commission on Systemic Racism and are reported in the Roberts and Doob essay in this volume. The findings, depending on the starting point, either show that most of existing sentencing disparities are attributable to legally relevant differences or that, after all legally relevant differences are controlled for, some disparities remain that may be evidence of racial bias. In other words, the findings are broadly consistent with American and English findings. Some work has been done on the causes of native/nonnative disparities, and there too differential behavior patterns seem to be the primary explanation (Laprairie 1990).

4. *Seemingly Neutral Case Processing Practices, Especially Pretrial Confinement Decisions and Sentence Reductions for Guilty Pleas, Operate to the Systematic Disadvantage of Members of Minority Groups.* This is a perplexing problem because practices that are justifiable in their own terms, such as detaining those people who seem least likely to remain in the jurisdiction and appear for trial, produce outcomes, greater proportions of minority offenders in confinement, that are widely seen as regrettable.

The pretrial detention problem appears in many countries. The essays on the Netherlands (Junger-Tas), Germany (Albrecht), Switzerland (Killias), England (Smith), Canada (Roberts and Doob), and the United States (Sampson and Lauritsen) discuss the relevant research in each country. The difficulty is that the rational and humane policy of restricting pretrial confinement to those least likely to appear for trial means that those who live the least settled lives—those without permanent residences, or stable family lives, or jobs—will be held. Those traits more commonly characterize disadvantaged people, and many minority groups are disadvantaged. The resulting disparities are especially unfortunate because, at least in England (Hood 1992) and the United States (Blumstein et al. 1983, chap. 2; Petersilia and Turner 1986; Klein et al. 1991), all else being equal, being detained before trial increases the likelihood that a prison sentence will be imposed after trial.

A second, similar problem—rewarding prisoners who plead guilty with sentencing concessions—may be more troubling. There is convincing evidence in the United States (Petersilia and Turner 1986; Klein et al. 1991), England (Hood 1992), and the Netherlands (Maas and Stuyling de Lange 1989; Junger-Tas, in this volume) that members of some minority groups are less likely than other defendants to plead guilty. From a management perspective, it makes sense to encourage defendants to plead guilty, and thereby conserve resources, by providing a sentence reduction. From a sentencer's perspective, it will often seem appropriate to acknowledge a defendant's contrition and acceptance of responsibility, evidenced by a guilty plea, by reducing the sentence that would otherwise be imposed. These phenomena are particularly explicit in England where appellate courts have elaborated a doctrine of "progressive loss of mitigation" under which defendants who plead guilty are entitled to a lesser sentence than if they were convicted after trial, the amount of the discount depending on when the plea is made; the later the plea, the smaller the discount. Hood's landmark study (1992) of sentencing disparities in the English Midlands found that Afro-Caribbean defendants were less likely than white defendants to plead guilty and, when they pled guilty, often did so later in the process than did whites. Thus Afro-Caribbeans lost sentence mitigation under both branches of the progressive mitigation doctrine.

This to many people is more troubling than the pretrial detention disparities because the guilty plea pattern may be shaped by many minority defendants' alienation from the justice system and beliefs that the system is biased against them. Research in many countries, including the Netherlands (Junger-Tas, in this volume), Germany (Albrecht, in this volume), Australia (Broadhurst, in this volume), England (Smith, in this volume), and the United States (Sampson and Lauritsen, in this volume), shows that members of minority groups are more likely to be stopped by police than majority citizens (albeit in most countries there is little evidence of bias in arrest decisions) and to believe that the police are biased against them. If minority defendants are hostile and distrustful toward the justice system because they believe (with some basis) they are treated unfairly, and as a result are less likely to cooperate, including by pleading guilty early or at all, progressive loss of mitigation penalizes them for their (to many people, understandable) alienation.

In both these instances, pretrial confinement based on legitimate criteria that disproportionately characterize minority defendants and sentencing policies that reward defendants who plead guilty, facially neutral policies disadvantage minority defendants for reasons that have nothing to do with their alleged crimes. To detain more minority offenders, or punish them more severely, as a matter of conscious policy would be seen as wrong in all Western countries. To maintain policies which foreseeably have that effect is not exactly the same thing but deserves more hard ethical scrutiny than typically it receives (Tonry 1995, chaps. 1, 8). There is no easy way to resolve this dilemma, but at the very least policy makers should consider whether seemingly neutral, disparity-causing policies can be revised to achieve their express goals in ways that produce fewer disparities.

5. *Subcultural Behaviors and Stereotypes Sometimes Associated with Mi-*

nority Group Members Often Work to Their Disadvantage in Contacts with the Justice System. Two behavioral patterns interact to create special problems for members of some minority groups. First, disproportionately large numbers of members of some groups, including blacks in the United States, Surinamese and Moroccans in the Netherlands, and Aborigines in Australia, commit crimes. Many offenders in particular subcultures share characteristics such as distinctive patterns of dress and speech, places of recreation and residence, and social and economic backgrounds. As a result, justice system officials and many ordinary citizens often assume that individuals who possess those characteristics are likely to be offenders. Social welfare scholars call this statistical discrimination. Psychologists call it attribution. Sociologists call it stereotyping. Whatever it is called, it makes people suspicious of entire groups of individuals. In the United States, young black men are particular victims, as is illustrated by a much-quoted statement by civil rights leader Jesse Jackson: "There is nothing more painful to me at this stage of my life than to walk down the street and hear footsteps and start thinking about robbery—then look around and see somebody white and feel relieved" (Cohen 1993). Stereotyping of this sort is one reason why, as noted earlier, members of minority groups in many countries are especially likely to be stopped by the police.

The second pattern compounds the first. For many reasons, including self-esteem, self-assertion, and peer group expectations, some members of some disadvantaged minority groups behave and act in ways that other people find strange and threatening. Novelist Tom Wolfe in *Bonfire of the Vanities* (1987), a novel that describes the workings of high-volume urban American felony courts as well as any political scientist's case study, describes the "pimp roll," the rolling, loose-jointed walk, which, combined with an off-the-shoulder black leather jacket, blue jeans, gold chains, and untied hightop basketball shoes, were then the fashion for young underclass black men in New York City. In the novel, a black juvenile defendant lost the benefit of a favorable plea bargain when, rather than dress for success in middle-class style as his attorney instructed, he pimp-rolled into the courtroom with two similarly attired friends. To the judge his appearance was that of an incorrigible, antisocial offender, and nothing like the redeemable minor participant in a crime, entitled to another chance and the benefit of the doubt, whom his lawyer had described.

Put together, these two phenomena, widely held stereotypes of minority offenders and distinctive dress and behaviors that evoke the stereotypes, probably explain the consistent finding in many countries that young minority men are especially likely to be stopped by police and, when stopped, to react defiantly and hostilely. Hostility and defiance toward the police are likely to elicit hostility and authoritarian responses from the police. And, in turn again, police aggressiveness is likely often to confirm minority offenders' belief that they are being treated discriminatorily and unfairly. Evidence of this vicious spiral is discussed in the essays on Australia (Broadhurst), Canada (Roberts and Doob), England (Smith), Germany (Albrecht), the Netherlands (Junger-Tas), and the United States (Sampson and Lauritsen). Small wonder then that many minority defendants are not more cooperative when they get to court.

What is most striking about the five findings discussed in this section is that they come from so many countries. They apply to many groups and many countries, suggesting that bias, disparities, and disparate impact policy dilemmas are not uniquely the characteristics and problems of any particular minority groups or countries but are endemic to heterogeneous developed countries in which some groups are substantially less successful economically and socially than the majority population.

III. Immigration and Crime

Although nonimmigrants often attribute many social problems to the presence of immigrants in their midst, especially in periods of high population movement, for at least sixty years there has been a widely shared different understanding among researchers. The popular perception is not surprising; as the essays in this volume show, in each of the European countries examined, "foreigners," who are preponderantly recent immigrants or their descendants, are disproportionately involved in crime. Nonetheless, on the basis of research on the experiences of Western European immigrants to Canada and the United States early in this century, it has often been asserted that first-generation immigrants are typically more law-abiding than the resident population, that their children and grandchildren suffer assimilation problems that produce higher-than-normal offending and imprisonment rates higher than those of either their parents or the resident population, and that subsequent generations have crime experiences indistinguishable from those of the general population.

The first American national crime commission, the National Commission on Law Observance and Enforcement, popularly known as the

Wickersham Commission after its chairman, former Attorney General George W. Wickersham, devoted an entire volume to "Crime and the Foreign Born." Noting that public opinion attributed high crime rates to immigrants throughout most of American history, the commission devoted substantial energies and impressively extensive data collection and analysis to determining whether public opinion was justified. Among other things, the commission assembled data from many jurisdictions (e.g., arrest and crime statistics from fifty-two cities) on recorded crime, arrests, convictions, and prison commitments.

The commission's conclusions were signaled by use of the phrase "foreign born" in the immigration volume's title. The commission observed that there was substantial evidence that foreign born persons committed fewer major offenses, in proportion to their numbers, of the same sex and age, than did native-born persons, concluding that available data "seem to disagree radically with the popular belief that a high percentage [of contemporary crime] may be ascribed to the 'alien' " (National Commission on Law Observance and Enforcement 1931).

Thus the "foreign born" were not the problem, leaving the possibility that their American-born children were extensively involved in crime. Unfortunately, although many official records indicated (however accurately) foreign-born defendants' countries of origin, records for American-born defendants did not, making it impossible for the commission to array much data on the subject and leading it to recommend "a continuing study of a scientific character over a period of at least five years and on a national scale of the subject." (This difficulty in identifying children of immigrants in justice system records exists today in most countries.)

However, there were other sources of evidence. The commission's staff conducted extensive interviews with justice system officials and the commission received formal testimony. Every police officer, prosecutor, probation officer, and judge interviewed on the subject expressed the belief that there was an immigrant crime problem but that it was attributable not to immigrants but to their sons.

This "not the foreign born but their children" conclusion, though contrary to public opinion, probably did not surprise informed people who had previously taken an interest in the subject. Two earlier federal commissions had reached the same conclusions although on the basis of less evidence. The Industrial Commission of 1901 issued a "Special Report on General Statistics of Immigration and the Foreign Born" which discussed crime. That commission observed that foreign-born whites were less criminal than native whites but also that the large proportion of native-born prisoners having foreign parents was "just as strong an argument as to the injurious effect of immigration as would be a high proportion among the foreign born themselves" (Industrial Commission 1901).

A few years later, in 1911, the Immigration Commission, which existed from 1907 to 1911, issued a report on "immigration and crime." Although expressed cautiously in recognition of the limited evidence on which its conclusions were based, this commission reached the same conclusions: "No satisfactory evidence has yet been produced to show that immigration has resulted in an increase in crime disproportionate to the increase in adult population. . . . Such figures as are presented . . . indicate that immigration has not increased the volume of crime to a distinguishable extent, if at all. . . . In fact, the figures seem to show a contrary result" (Immigration Commission 1911). And, although the evidence was spotty, the immigration commission found that for some offenses American-born children of immigrants had higher crime rates than did American-born children of American-born parents.

From the 1920s through the 1940s, crime and immigration was a central interest of American criminologists who continued to observe, and then tried to explain, the broad patterns of findings of the three commissions (e.g., Reckless and Smith 1932; Sutherland 1934). The explanations for the relatively low crime rates of the foreign born are straightforward: self-selected economic migrants who braved an ocean voyage and left their home countries and families thousands of miles away came to America for economic opportunity and to improve their and their children's lives. Most were hard-working, ready to defer gratification in the interest of longer-term advancement, and therefore likely to be conformist and to behave themselves.

Their children, however, were caught between two worlds. Even if life were better in America than in the place their parents came from, the children often were unable to make or find solace in that comparison. What they knew was that their families often were poor, that others were much better off, and that opportunities for legitimate economic advancement were less available to them than to many nonimmigrant young people. Various theories have been offered to explain why the second generations' crime rates were higher than those of their parents or those of children of native-born parents: alienation, blocked opportunities, lack of role models, deviant subcultural values of youth gangs which young people joined as a source of self-identification and self-esteem. Whatever the reasons, the immigration and crime model that distinguishes the experiences of the generations settled into the conventional wisdom of criminology.

Large-scale immigration into the United States stopped after 1924, and, as time passed, the descendants of immigrants assimilated into the American mainstream. "Immigration and crime" attracted less attention as a political issue and other issues attracted American criminologists' attention. Interest first revived not in the United States but in Europe as the result of the migration of guest workers from southern Europe and North Africa into many European countries in the 1950s and 1960s.

Contemporary research in Germany (Kaiser 1974; Albrecht 1988, 1993), France, Switzerland (Killias 1977; Queloz 1986; Kunz 1989), and Sweden (Sveri 1987; Martens 1990; Ahlberg 1996) has attempted to test that model and has to some extent validated it. Killias (1989) has surveyed the German and French research. Earlier Swiss research showed that Italian labor migrants in the 1950s and 1960s had lower crime (conviction) rates than native Swiss males of comparable ages (Neumann 1963; Pradervand and Cardia 1966; Gillioz 1967).

However, from the essays on European research in this volume, we now know that the multigeneration immigration and crime model based on American experience is simplistic and is only partly true even for the self-selected economic migrants whose experience it describes.

1. *Self-Selected Economic Migrants from Many Asian Cultures Have Lower Crime Rates than the Resident Population in the First and in Subsequent Generations.* The traditional model does not take account of Asians: immigrant groups deriving directly (Chinese, Japanese, and Koreans to the United States, Indian subcontinent migrants to England) and sometimes indirectly (e.g., "Hindustanis" from Surinam to the Netherlands, "African Asians" from East Africa to England) from South and East Asia typically have low crime rates in the first and in subsequent generations.

In England, where comparisons have been made between the experiences of Asian immigrants from the Indian subcontinent and black immigrants from the Caribbean and Africa, Asian immigrants typically have lower crime and imprisonment rates than whites' and Afro-Caribbeans' higher ones. The contrast is particularly marked for Bangladeshi immigrants who are as, if not more, economically and socially disadvantaged as Afro-Caribbeans (also though, as noted earlier, Bangladeshis are relatively recent immigrants and their crime rates could rise over time). David Smith's essay in this volume summarizes research that shows that Asians were no less the victims of bias and stereotyping in England than were Afro-Caribbeans but from the outset adapted differently. Most notably, many expected to be discriminated against and organized their lives in ways that depended less on fair treatment than on self-help and ethnic-group networks (as, for example, seeking economic opportunities primarily within their own ethnic communities).

2. *Cultural Differences between Structurally Similarly Situated Immigrants Can Result in Sharply Different Crime Patterns.* The traditional model insufficiently takes account of cultural differences between groups that differentially affect their adaptation: the model would predict that Moroccans and Turks should have similar experiences in the Netherlands, both being economically and socially disadvantaged migrant groups who arrived as self-selected guest workers between 1950 and 1973, augmented by natural increase and by family unification policies; yet Turks have markedly lower self-reported and official crime rates than Moroccans (Junger-Tas, in this volume), and similar contrasts distinguish the two guest-worker groups in other countries (e.g., in Germany: Albrecht, in this volume). The essays in this volume on Sweden (Martens) and Germany (Albrecht) document other stark contrasts between the experiences of different nationality groups. Some of the contrasts may reflect age or class composition differences between groups, or the influence of the behavior of transients (illegals and tourists), but those considerations cannot explain all of the differences.

3. *There Are Grounds for Hypothesizing That, All Else Being Equal, Some Countries' Policies for Aiding Immigrants' Assimilation Can Reduce Crime Rates, Including Those of Their Second- and Third-Generation Descendants.* The traditional model insufficiently takes account of differences in receiving countries' social welfare (and settlement) policies. Martens (in this volume) provides plausible evidence that Swedish social welfare policies have reduced the "second-generation effect" even among economic intra-European migrants. Data covering many national origin groups, developed by Ahlberg (1996), indicate that crime rates for most groups are lower in the second than in the first generation, but that relative crime rate differences between groups remain the same. Overall, however, the second generation's crime rates were higher than those for nonimmigrant Swedes. These findings are striking because they simultaneously suggest that settlement policies can

suppress crime rates and confirm the observation in the preceding paragraph that cultural or other differences between groups are independently predictive of criminality.

4. *The Reasons Groups Migrate Powerfully Shape Criminality and Other Indications of Successful Adaptation.* The traditional model insufficiently takes account of the reasons why groups migrate: Swedish research shows that the adaptation experiences of guest-worker migrants in the fifties and sixties from Croatia and Serbia have been very different from those of demographically comparable war refugees from Serbia and Croatia in the eighties and nineties. The experience of the first wave roughly followed the North American pattern. In the second wave, first-generation migrants had high crime and victimization (and unemployment, welfare dependence, family breakup, and mental health problem) rates (Martens 1995).

A remarkable essay by Peter Martens (1995) gives insight into the special problems refugees face. It has been estimated that between 20 and 25 percent of recent refugees who immigrated to Sweden had earlier experienced physical torture. Many suffer from post-traumatic stress disorder. Angel and Hjern (1992, p. 36) observe that "seeing a close relative being ill-treated, killed or arrested or personally being subject to injustice are examples of mentally traumatic experiences that are common in refugees." Human beings suffer many kinds of traumatic experiences, and sizable psychological and psychiatric literatures document their effects. These include alienation, apathy, lack of trust in personal relationships, reduced ability to plan for the future, irritability, and exaggerated reactions to emotionally charged situations. Martens (1995, p. 287) observes, "Reduced self-esteem and alienation are expressed both in reduced self-control and in social isolation, which increase the individual tendency to commit crime."

Martens's work, and that of other Swedish researchers, forces attention on the reasons why people immigrate. Once the question is recast from "What do we know about the adaptation and criminality of economic migrants?" to "What do we know about the ways people respond to traumatic experiences?" the observation that the reasons why people immigrate are important predictors of their subsequent behavior becomes unexceptionable. It is, however, an observation that is seldom made concerning "immigration and crime."

5. *Many Categories of Immigrants Do Not Fall within Any of the Preceding Generalizations.* The traditional model does not describe the experiences of many immigrant groups that for one or another reason have

economic or social characteristics that fundamentally shape predicted criminality. Large numbers of Hong Kong Chinese have in the 1980s and 1990s either moved to Pacific Canada or purchased homes and made investments that will make it possible to make such a move after the transfer of governance of Hong Kong from Great Britain to China. As a group, expatriate Hong Kong Chinese are likely to be affluent and well-educated, characteristics that are seldom associated with high crime rates. Similarly, thousands of Americans migrated to Canada in protest against the Vietnam War. As a group the American expatriates were by definition politically conscious and are likely disproportionately to have been middle-class and relatively well-educated. For these two groups and for many others, their economic, social, and cultural characteristics are likely to be much better behavioral predictors than is any broadly phrased immigration and crime hypothesis.

IV. Learning More

Unanswered questions leap from the pages of this book. Why do some Asian groups adjust more readily to immigration than other groups? Are there lessons that can be drawn from such groups' experiences and then incorporated into settlement policies to help other groups adapt as successfully? Is it true that Swedish settlement policies have suppressed the second-generation effect and, if so, how? Can a taxonomy of settlement policies be developed that will permit matching of optimal policies to address the distinctive special needs of different migrant groups? Why do some seemingly similarly situated groups, like the Turks and Moroccans in the Netherlands, have such different crime patterns? Are there ways that legal practices and rules can be altered to lessen the adverse effects of some "neutral" policies on disadvantaged minority groups? Does the traditional immigration and crime model provide grounds for optimism that Afro-Caribbeans in England, who until the mid-1970s were not seen as a high-crime-rate group (Smith, in this volume), are simply passing through the second- and third-generation phases, amplified by an age distribution skewed toward young adults? If so, as with many other economic migrant groups in many countries, the problem of race and crime in England is likely gradually to disappear. Less optimistically, are the aboriginal populations of Canada and Australia in effect chronically traumatized peoples whose overinvolvement in crime is not likely to abate until the underlying causes abate, something that has not happened over several hundred years of exposure to colonization?

This book focuses primarily on crime and the justice system, but the focus could be made broader. There are a number of important related, but little studied, phenomena. First, minority group involvement in organized and transnational crime receives much media and policy attention in Europe. Second, similarly, minority groups are at least as likely as majority groups (probably more likely) to participate in black markets and the underground economy. Third, in Europe, at least, members of many migrant groups retain active ties to their home countries and yet intend to remain in their new countries; the effects of these multiple bonds on economic, social, and psychological integration (and crime) remain unstudied. Fourth is the increasing social segmentation of many European countries; members of many migrant groups fall into blue-collar and low-wage strata, which makes them highly vulnerable as semi-skilled and low-paid jobs become less available and economic pressures to survive make both work in the underground economy and crime more tempting.

A great deal can be learned about "race and crime" and "immigration and crime" by looking at the issues comparatively and cross-nationally. What needs to be done now is to move beyond single-country analyses to work that integrates those analyses: comprehensive efforts to combine learning in different countries, comprehensive efforts to establish what data are needed and available in each country to answer the questions that should be asked, development of a comprehensive research agenda that can begin to provide policy makers with the information they need to anticipate and work to prevent or ameliorate the kinds of problems that particular kinds of migrant groups are likely to experience. The political and ethical sensitivities that cause many countries to omit race and ethnicity data from their official records no doubt present a formidable challenge to the kind of projects described here. Unless that challenge can be overcome, however, little more will be learned and governments will have great difficulty improving the justice system experiences of members of minority groups.

Every Western country faces and will continue for many years to face political and policy issues related to race, ethnicity, population migration, and crime. Work like that discussed in this volume promises to provide crucial knowledge for addressing those issues.

The next step is to create a community of researchers and policy makers in many countries who will attempt to establish what is known, what is knowable, and how current knowledge might be advanced through comparative inquiry.

REFERENCES

Ahlberg, Jan. 1996. *Criminality among Immigrants and Their Children. A Statistical Analysis.* (In Swedish.) BRÅ-report. Stockholm: Fritzes.

Albrecht, Hans-Jörg. 1988. "Ausländerkriminalität." In *Fälle zum Wahlfach Kriminologie, Jugendstrafrecht, Strafvollzug,* 2d ed., edited by Heike Jung. München: Beck Verlag.

———. 1993. "Ethnic Minorities: Crime and Criminal Justice in Europe." In *Crime in Europe,* edited by Francis Heidensohn and Michael Farrell. London and New York: Routledge.

———. In this volume. "Ethnic Minorities, Crime, and Criminal Justice in Germany."

Angel, B., and A. Hjern. 1992. *To Meet Children of Refugees and Their Families.* (In Swedish.) Lund: Studentlitteratur.

Blumstein, Alfred, Jacqueline Cohen, Susan E. Martin, and Michael Tonry, eds. 1983. *Research on Sentencing: The Search for Reform.* 2 vols. Report of the National Academy of Sciences Panel on Sentencing Research. Washington, D.C.: National Academy Press.

Broadhurst, Roderic. 1996. In this volume. "Aborigines and Crime in Australia."

Bureau of Justice Statistics. 1995. "State and Federal Prisons Report Record Growth during Last 12 Months." Advance for release, December 3. Washington, D.C.: U.S. Department of Justice, Bureau of Justice Statistics.

Cohen, Richard. 1993. "Common Ground on Crime." *Washington Post* (December 21), p. A23.

Commission on Systemic Racism in the Ontario Criminal Justice System. 1995. *Report of the Commission on Systemic Racism in the Ontario Criminal Justice System.* Toronto: Queen's Printer for Ontario.

Doob, Anthony. 1991. *Workshop on Collection of Racial and Ethnic Statistics in the Criminal Justice System.* Toronto: University of Toronto, Centre of Criminology.

Duguid, A. M. 1992. "Police and Aboriginal Youth—Arrest or Report? Are Aboriginal Youth Treated Differently?" Paper presented to the conference on Measurement and Research in Criminal Justice, Griffith University, Mt. Gravatt, August.

Gale, F., R. Bailey-Harris, and J. Wundersitz. 1990. *Aboriginal Youth and the Criminal Justice System: The Injustice of Justice?* Melbourne: Cambridge University Press.

Gale, F., and J. Wundersitz. 1987. "Police and Black Minorities: The Case of Aboriginal Youth in South Australia." *Australian and New Zealand Journal of Criminology* 20:78–94.

Gillioz, E. 1967. "La criminalité des étrangers en Suisse." *Revue pénale suisse* 83(2):178–91.

Harding, R., R. Broadhurst, A. Ferrante, and N. Loh. 1995. *Aboriginal Contact with the Criminal Justice System and the Impact of the Recommendations of the Royal Commission into Aboriginal Deaths in Custody.* Sydney: Federation Press.

Hood, R. 1992. *Race and Sentencing.* Oxford: Clarendon Press.

Immigration Commission. 1911. *Report of the Immigration Commission.* U.S. Congress, Senate, 61st Congress, S. Doc. 750, Vol. 36. Washington, D.C.: U.S. Government Printing Office.

Industrial Commission. 1901. *Special Report on General Statistics of Immigration and the Foreign Born Population.* Washington, D.C.: U.S. Government Printing Office.

Junger-Tas, Josine. In this volume. "Ethnic Minorities and Criminal Justice in the Netherlands."

Kaiser, Günther. 1974. "Gastarbeiterkriminalität und ihre Erklärung als Kulturkonflikt." In *Gastarbeiter in Gesellschaft und Recht*, edited by Tugrul Ansay and Volkmar Gessner. München: Beck.

Killias, M. 1977. "Kriminelle Fremdarbeiter-Kinder? Strukturelle Determinanten der Delinquenz bei Fremdarbeitern unter besonderer Berücksichtigung der zweiten Generation." *Revue suisse de sociologie* 3(2):3–33.

———. 1989. "Criminality among Second-Generation Immigrants in Western Europe. A Review of the Evidence." *Criminal Justice Review* 14:13–42.

———. In this volume. "Immigrants, Crime, and Criminal Justice in Switzerland."

Klein, Stephen, Patricia Ebener, Allan Abrahamse, and Nora Fitzgerald. 1991. *Predicting Criminal Justice Outcomes: What Matters?* Santa Monica, Calif.: RAND.

Kunz, K.-L. 1989. "Ausländerkriminalität in der Schweiz—Umfang, Struktur und Erklärungsversuch." *Revue pénale suisse* 106(4):373–92.

Laprairie, C. 1990. "The Role of Sentencing in the Over-representation of Aboriginal People in Correctional Institutions." *Canadian Journal of Criminology* 32:429–40.

Maas, C. J., and J. Stuyling de Lange. 1989. "Selectiviteit in de rechtsgang van buitenlandse verdachten en verdachten behorende tot etnische groepen." *Tijdschrift voor Criminologie* no. 1:1–14.

Mann, Coramae Richey. 1993. *Unequal Justice—a Question of Color.* Bloomington: Indiana University Press.

Martens, P. L. 1990. "Criminal Behaviour among Young People with Immigrant Background." In *Crime and Measures against Crime in the City*, edited by P.-O. H. Wikström. BRÅ-Report 1990:5. Stockholm: National Council for Crime Prevention/Allmanna Förlaget.

———. 1995. "Immigrants and Crime Prevention." In *Integrating Crime Prevention Strategies: Propensity and Opportunity*, edited by Per-Olof H. Wikström, Ronald V. Clarke, and Joan McCord. Stockholm: Fritzes.

———. In this volume. "Immigrants, Crime, and Criminal Justice in Sweden."

Mayhew, H. 1861. *London Labour and London Poor.* London: Griffin, Bohn.

National Commission on Law Observance and Enforcement. 1931. *Crime and the Foreign Born.* Washington, D.C.: U.S. Government Printing Office.

Neumann, J. 1963. "Die Kriminalität der italienischen Arbeitskräfte im Kanton Zürich." Law faculty doctoral dissertation, University of Zurich.

Petersilia, Joan, and Susan Turner. 1986. *Prison versus Probation in California.* Santa Monica, Calif.: RAND.

Pradervand, P., and L. Cardia. 1966. "Quelques aspects de la délinquance italienne à Genève; Une enquête sociologique." *Revue international de criminologie et de police technique* 20:43–58.

Queloz, N. 1986. *La réaction institutionnelle à la délinquance juvénile.* Neuchâtel: EDES.

Reckless, W., and H. Smith. 1932. *Juvenile Delinquency.* New York: McGraw-Hill.

Roberts, Julian V., and Anthony N. Doob. In this volume. "Race, Ethnicity, and Criminal Justice in Canada."

Royal Commission into Aboriginal Deaths in Custody. 1991. *Report.* Canberra: Australian Government Printing Service.

Royal Commission on Criminal Justice. 1993. *Report.* London: H.M. Stationery Office.

Sampson, Robert J., and Janet L. Lauritsen. In this volume. "Racial and Ethnic Disparities in Crime and Criminal Justice in the United States."

Shaw, Clifford R. 1929. *Delinquency Areas.* Chicago: University of Chicago Press.

Smith, David. In this volume. "Ethnic Origins, Crime, and Criminal Justice in England and Wales."

Sowell, Thomas. 1983. *The Economics and Politics of Race.* New York: William Morrow.

Sutherland, E. 1934. *Principles of Criminology.* Philadelphia: Lippincott.

Sveri, B. 1987. *Recidivism in Crime among Foreign Citizens.* (In Swedish.) Stockholm: Stockholm University.

Tak, Peter J. P. 1994. "Sentencing and Punishment in the Netherlands." *Overcrowded Times* 5(5):5–8.

Tonry, Michael. 1994. "Racial Disproportion in U.S. Prisons." *British Journal of Criminology* 34(special issue):97–115.

———. 1995. *Malign Neglect: Race, Crime, and Punishment in America.* New York: Oxford University Press.

Tournier, Pierre. In this volume. "Nationality, Crime, and Criminal Justice in France."

Weigend, Thomas. 1993. "In Germany, Fines Often Imposed in Lieu of Prosecution." *Overcrowded Times* 4(1):1, 15–16.

Wilbanks, William. 1987. *The Myth of a Racist Criminal Justice System.* Monterey, Calif.: Brooks/Cole.

Hans-Jörg Albrecht

Ethnic Minorities, Crime, and Criminal Justice in Germany

ABSTRACT

Research on ethnic minorities' involvement in crime is highly sensitive in Germany. Most research is based on official statistics, which indicate that foreign minorities' crime involvement is higher than that of the German population, even when crime data are adjusted to take account of demographic differences (age, sex, etc.) and even if immigration offenses and nonresident foreigners' crime are disregarded. First-generation guest workers have had crime rates comparable to those of Germans. The second and third generations display sharp upward crime trends. Processing of foreign offenders by the justice system has received little attention. Existing research does not confirm hypotheses of discriminatory treatment in police and criminal court decision making, including in sentencing. The proportion of foreigners in the prison population has increased substantially, reaching 25 percent in 1994. In youth correctional facilities, the minority proportion has increased to 50 percent. In pretrial detention the share of foreigners is as high as two-thirds in many places.

The history of ethnic and racial minorities in twentieth-century Germany and research on minorities are overshadowed by the murderous terror regime German fascism created for various ethnic and other minorities in Europe during the thirties and forties. One consequence is the elimination of all variables referring to race and ethnicity from official information systems (and from most questionnaires and interview forms used in criminological research). Official statistics, whether of crime, the judicial systems, or population, cannot account for the racial or ethnic composition of populations. Only estimates are thus available

Hans-Jörg Albrecht is professor of criminal law and criminology at the Dresden University of Technology.

0192-3234/97/0021-0001$01.00

on, for example, the number of blacks or Afro-Germans, ranging between 40,000 and 50,000 (Forbes and Mead 1992, p. 39). Only the variable "nationality" or "citizenship" is used, and it is often a crude proxy.

Postwar Germany has experienced a short history of immigration, beginning with guest workers around 1960 and with significant changes in patterns occurring since the end of the 1970s. Unlike other European countries, Germany has had no significant history of colonialism since the end of World War I, which significantly shapes relations between immigrant minorities and society at large.

Other German experiences with immigrating ethnic and foreign minorities are available from the turn of the century, too, when Polish workers entered in large numbers (Stefanski 1995). This wave did not, however, lead to an extended public discussion on integration, culture conflict, and crime, and Polish immigrants assimilated unobtrusively into mainstream society.

The topics of immigration and immigrant minorities arose in the social sciences in the early 1960s. Research on the concept of culture conflict can be traced back to the mid-1960s, when migrant workers became a subject of concern in German criminology and in the social sciences at large (Kurz 1965). This was due to rapidly increasing numbers of foreign workers attracted through official hiring schemes established around 1960 in southern Europe (then predominantly Italy, Spain, and Portugal). Guest workers were principally viewed from an economic perspective. Problems of assimilation and acculturation of guest workers were not considered to fit within the concept of culture conflict as developed in North American minority research. Concepts of partial and temporary acculturation dominated, stressing the importance of accounting for specific goal-attainment patterns of foreign minorities. From the mid-1960s on, the question has been asked whether crime patterns (and other behavior patterns) of guest workers exhibit signs of cultural conflicts and social disintegration. The debate in German criminology has centered on the effects on deviance and crime of differing value and norm systems and pressures arising from coping with new demands put forward by values and norms of the host society. Research on coping was soon well established in criminology, and the concept of culture conflict thus has been used primarily to account for individual behavior.

The focus of criminological research on foreign migrant workers shifted as the ethnic composition of immigrants, and motivations for migration, changed significantly over the last twenty years. Southeastern European countries (former Yugoslavia and Turkey) replaced southwestern European countries (Italy, Spain, and Portugal) as the sources of the migrant workforce. At the beginning of the 1960s approximately 60 percent of the foreign population came from countries of the European Community (EC). By the 1990s, their share dropped to approximately 27 percent. Immigrants from Turkey and former Yugoslavia now account for almost half of the resident foreign population in Germany. Immigrants from developing countries in Africa and Asia also have constituted substantial proportions of the immigrant population since the second half of the 1980s. At the end of the eighties and after the breakdown of socialist regimes, increasing numbers of migrants came from eastern European countries, thus adding to the ethnic and cultural diversity of immigrant populations in Germany.

Shifts in motives for migration and legal aspects of immigration have been associated with changes in the ethnic composition of immigrants. The status of foreigners in Germany must be differentiated because different legal standards apply to citizens of European Community countries, Turkish citizens (who are in between European Community status and non–European Community status [Beschluss (Resolution) Nr. 1/80, 1993, p. 258]), and citizens of non–European Community states. With respect to motives for entry, the law distinguishes between tourists (or short-term visitors), foreigners joining the labor force (or enrolling at schools or universities), asylum seekers, and refugees (to whom the Geneva Convention applies). Abandonment of schemes for hiring workers abroad and severe restrictions on granting permissions for non-EC foreigners to work in Germany led in the 1980s to larger numbers of foreigners asking for asylum (which, until recent amendments of the German constitution and the immigration law, had the effect of a preliminary grant of entry pending a final decision).

A distinctive German immigration phenomenon concerns ethnic Germans whose ancestors emigrated to Poland, Russia, and Romania and who are entitled to be renaturalized (if evidence of German origin can be provided). Slightly more than two million ethnic Germans were renaturalized between 1968 and 1992, the majority since the second half of the 1980s (Statistisches Bundesamt 1993, p. 92), making them the largest ethnic minority. Although ethnic Germans from eastern Europe form a minority group distinct both from other foreign populations and from the German majority, they have not attracted attention in terms of crime policy or criminological research. Ethnic Germans are not distinct in police or other criminal justice statistics, as they fall under the category of Germans. Some research has dealt with ethnic Germans but principally on the causes of migration, problems of integration, and adaptations of family structures (Wilkiewicz 1989; Bade 1994; Riek 1995). Research so far shows that ethnic Germans from Russia experience ethnic isolation (two-thirds feel that they are not welcome), which is underlined by an elevated rate of intraethnic marriages (75 percent; see Wilkiewicz 1989, p. 59).

Data from the central youth correctional facility in the state of Baden-Württemberg suggest that involvement of young ethnic Germans in crime and criminal justice may be increasing. The proportion of prison admissions of young German offenders born abroad has increased from 2 percent in the late 1980s to approximately 5 percent in 1994 (unpublished data provided by the prison administration of the state of Baden-Württemberg). Crime statistics of the Organization of German Police (Bund Deutscher Kriminalbeamter) from the first half of 1995 suggest that the recent increase in the crime rate among the German population, especially young people, was due to the heavy immigration of ethnic Germans from eastern Europe (*Süddeutsche Zeitung* 1995, p. 6; see also Pfeiffer [1995], p. 102, with some narrative information from several German cities).

Figure 1 shows long-term immigration trends. The increase starts around 1960. These figures underestimate the size of ethnic minorities because they do not count renaturalized Germans from the former Soviet Union, Afro-Germans, German Sinti, Roma, naturalized immigrants, short-term visitors (e.g., with tourist visas), and illegal immigrants. Figure 2 shows that countries of origin of the foreign resident population have undergone significant changes.

Other significant changes occurred with respect to lengths of stay. In 1992, approximately 39 percent of the resident foreign population had been in Germany for more than fifteen years (down from more than 50 percent at the end of the 1980s). An increase in short-term stays of less than one year took place, reflecting the sizable increase in immigration in the 1980s (1982, 4.5 percent; 1988, 7 percent; 1992, 12 percent). As a result, differences are apparent in the demographic composition of various immigrant populations. There are also regional differences in the density of foreign residents; metropolitan areas and the western part of Germany are the places to which immigrants are mainly attracted. Approximately 2 percent of the foreign population in the 1990s live in the "new Bundesländer," that is, the eastern part of

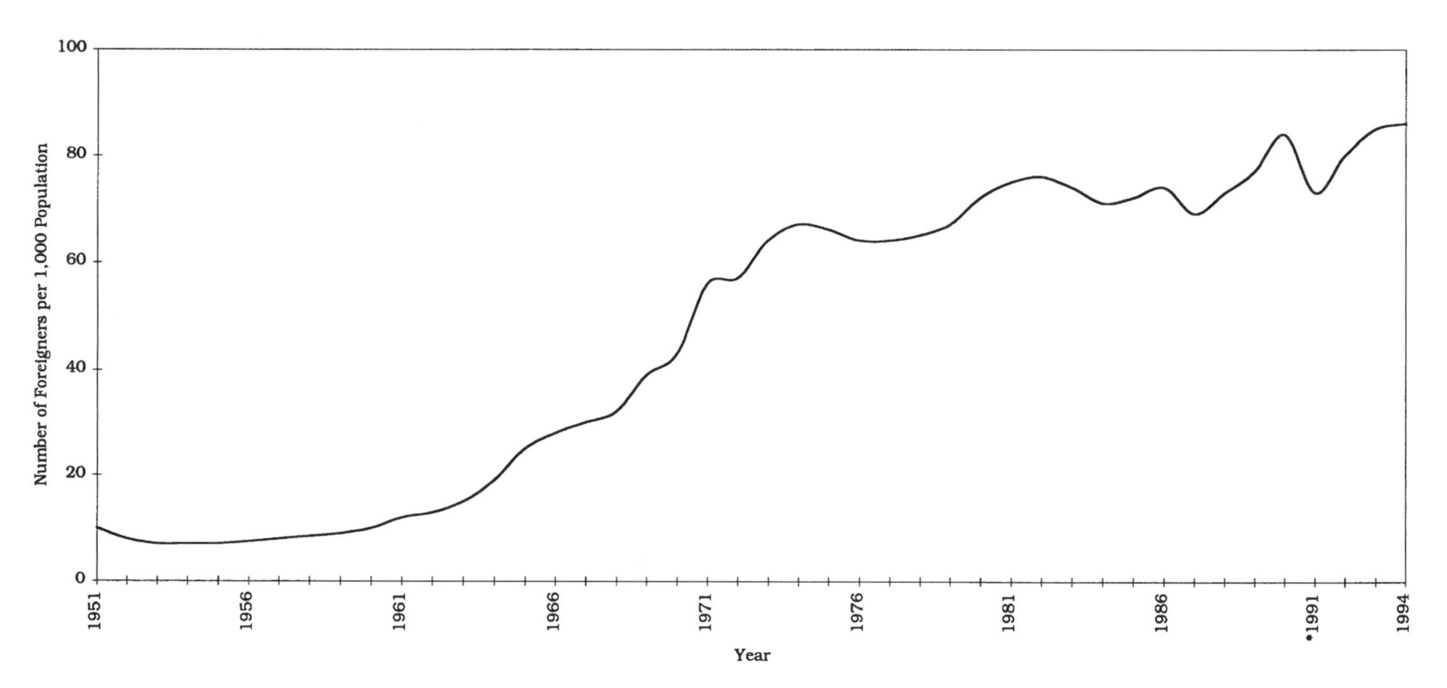

Fig. 1.—Foreigners per 1,000 population, Germany, 1951–94. Note: Data since 1991 include East Germany. Source: Statistisches Bundesamt (1995*b*).

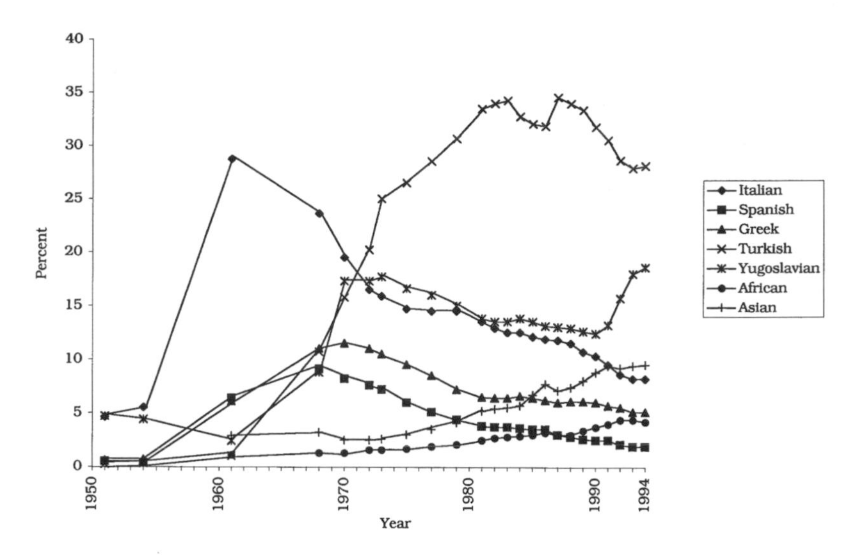

FIG. 2.—Citizenship of immigrants, by place of origin, 1951–94. Note: Not all places of origin are included; percentages shown do not equal 100 in any year. Source: Statistisches Bundesamt (1994*a*).

Germany, which has approximately 20 percent of the total population (Statistisches Bundesamt 1993, p. 72).

Knowledge of ethnic minorities' crime involvement comes almost entirely from official crime data provided by police and justice information systems. Information on immigration and demographic characteristics of foreign populations are available from state and federal statistical departments. The main limitations of police statistics concern the category "foreign citizenship," which does not correspond to concepts of ethnicity or visible minority. Police statistics subdivide foreign suspects into such subcategories as illegals, guest workers, and tourists, which in turn allows for differentiation between various subgroups of foreign minorities in terms of differences in their legal status. Federal prison statistics account for a general category, "foreign citizenship," but do not partition this category into separate nationalities. Some of the data used for the purpose of this essay were received from "Bundesländer" (German states), for example, North Rhine–Westphalia, Hessen, and others. North Rhine–Westphalia, to which considerable reference is made, is the most populous state. Self-report studies and victimization surveys have been conducted in the Federal Republic of Germany since the end of the 1960s and the beginning of the 1970s but only rarely included foreign minorities. This was, and is, due to methodological and financial implications of extending surveys to minority groups.

Information and data available for analyses explain the concentration of studies on foreigners' crimes. As police statistics in this respect are crude (official data do not allow for separate analyses of different age brackets, citizenship, and differences in status), most research dealing with ethnic minorities and crime refers to the general category "foreign citizens." That is why research on ethnic minorities, crime, and justice during the last twenty years improved little but was restricted monotonously to questions that, on the basis of available data, could not be answered: overrepresentation of ethnic minorities in crime involvement or discrimination against minority offenders in crime control.

Apparent overrepresentation of offenders and victims from various ethnic minorities to some extent may be explained by deprivation and control theories. But criminology needs to move beyond such theories. As society becomes segmented along ethnic lines, the lowest segments are increasingly composed of members of immigrant groups that are most likely to be affected by unemployment, bad housing, poverty, and insufficient education and vocational training and are likely to remain in this situation for a considerable time. Research questions that in the 1960s and 1970s highlighted class, crime, and justice issues (and class solidarity and class conflicts) will in the 1990s be replaced by research on ethnicity and crime (in addition to ethnic solidarity and ethnic conflicts). Structural theories should focus on black markets and subcultures in which ethnic and foreign minorities are heavily involved.

System processing in the case of members of minorities is heavily influenced by two characteristics: legal particulars and certain types of crime involvement. Foreign offenders are likely to be handled differently compared with German offenders on legal grounds, as decision making in the criminal justice system in several respects takes account of bonds to conventional society such as place of residence. Participation of some ethnic minorities in black markets, especially drug markets, is likely to lead to disproportionate use of pretrial detention and prison sentences. This reflects concern not for ethnic minorities but for illicit drugs, which continue to provoke massive criminal justice reactions.

This essay is organized as follows. Section I describes a number of contentious issues linking minorities and crime—drug trafficking, trafficking in women and children, and hate crimes—that are associated with increased migration. Section II surveys findings of analyses of official data and case studies on ethnic differences in offending. Section III briefly examines theoretical explanations for elevated offending rates by minority groups. Section IV examines evidence on disproportions at various stages of the justice system and on the causes of those disproportions.

I. European Integration, German Reunification, Organized Crime, and Issues of Mobility and Immigration

Although this essay's primary focus is on disparities in offending and system processing, other issues related to minorities, crime, and justice must be considered too, as they importantly influence social and political construction of foreigners' crime. Among them is growing concern about immigration in Europe, making immigration and immigration restrictions and border controls highly topical political issues. In addition, the fall of the "Iron Curtain" has led to an integration of illegal or black markets and integration of subcultures and "milieus" involved with cross-border crimes, migration, organized crimes, and economic crimes. Organized crime has attracted considerable attention, particularly concerning trafficking in drugs, women, and stolen goods (especially automobiles). Most recently, right-wing extremism and hate violence have been seen as social and political issues associated with immigration and especially asylum policy; these phenomena are widely perceived to be linked with uncontrolled immigration and abuse of asylum laws.

A. European Immigration Policies, Drug Trafficking, and Organized Crime

European integration and abolition of border controls among several EC countries have added a new dimension to the debate on ethnicity, migration, and crime. The Schengen treaties of 1985 and 1990 and the Maastricht treaty have put the focus on coordination of policies toward immigration and asylum, while international organized crime and cross-border crime have become a major point of concern for the European Community (Kühne 1991). Migration and ethnic minorities receive attention concerning organized crime for two reasons. First, organized crime is still conceived as a threat posed by alien groups, for example, the Sicilian (or the Polish, Russian, Chinese, etc.)

Mafia, which according to most official statements is expected to extend its scope of criminal activities to central European countries (Boge 1989). Official accounts of organized crime in Germany suggest that a majority of offenders suspected of belonging to organized crime groups are foreigners (Bundeskriminalamt 1991, p. 14; 1992, p. 21; Ahlf 1993, p. 138; Gewerkschaft der Polizei 1994).

Second, ethnic and foreign communities in western and central European countries are perceived to provide logistic support for organized criminals (Bovenkerk 1993, p. 279). While consideration of such support functions surely is important in analyzing the spread of organized crime, another aspect has received little attention until recently. Within some ethnic minorities, organized crime patterns may have been developed from the very beginning, for example, with respect to drug trafficking and supply of local drug markets, and new immigrants may be pulled into organized crime as such activities can appear to be a promising way to earn a living if other legitimate opportunities are inaccessible (Buiks 1983; Korf 1993). The concept of "ethnic ladders," therefore, might be useful in explaining preferences in criminal offending of certain minorities and corresponding overrepresentation in the criminal justice systems of certain regions. The discussion of ethnicity and organized crime had a precursor in the 1970s and 1980s with concern over terrorism and politically motivated violence among ethnic minorities (Jäger 1984).

Some ethnic minorities have been seen as especially vulnerable to victimization, for example, by racketeering schemes within ethnic groups. While interest in organized crime emerged primarily concerning drug trafficking, in recent years broader policy concerns have been voiced about criminal enterprises and criminal organizations. Special attention has been paid to money laundering and to investments of illegal profits in the Federal Republic of Germany (especially in eastern parts) through foreign organized crime groups. Global estimates of the revenue of drug trafficking are used to demonstrate its financial dimensions and its effect on the social fabric. During recent debates in the German Federal Parliament it was assumed that international criminal enterprises have been investing as much as DM 60–80 billion annually in Germany (Bundesministerium des Innern 1993, p. 17). Fears have been raised that the Mafia will take over honest and respectable businesses, undermine established values, corrupt the political system, and lead to a society based on rules of organized crime. Beyond implications concerning organized crime, the dramatic increase in mobility is associated with changes in general criminal opportunity structures and with the development of black markets (illegal drugs, cars, etc.) linking various countries and regions (Pilgram 1993, pp. 28–29) and serving as important push-and-pull factors in migration processes.

B. Trafficking in Women and Children

Trafficking in women and in children has attracted attention in the social sciences since the 1980s. Trafficking in children has been made a focus of international adoption work and adoption studies (Bach 1986, 1991), while trafficking in women has been taken up as a research topic from a feminist (but not criminological) perspective (Swientek 1988; Tübinger Projektgruppe Frauenhandel 1989). As the demand for children greatly exceeds the number of children of German origin available for adoption in Germany, international adoption from South America, Eastern Europe, and Southeast Asia has become widespread (Albrecht 1994*a*).

Trafficking in women involves the now well-established phenomenon of organized recruitment and transportation of large numbers of women to Germany and other European countries (see Fijnaut 1994) from South America, Africa, Southeast Asia, and Eastern Europe for purposes of prostitution and marriage (Regtmeier 1990; Heine-Wiedenmann 1992; Heine-Wiedenmann and Ackermann 1992; Sieber and Bögel 1993). Demographic patterns among some minorities partly account for this type of migration. Among Brazilian residents of Germany, for example, women outnumber men by 2.3:1. Among Thai and Philippine citizens, the gender ratio is 4:1. Problems in implementing criminal laws on trafficking in women can partly be attributed to the precarious legal position of women being trafficked as prostitutes (Heine-Wiedenmann and Ackermann 1992, p. 198). Affected women are not likely to serve as witnesses in criminal proceedings since they face the threat of deportation once their prostitution activities become known.

C. Hate Violence and Sociological Theory

Police-recorded incidents of violence against ethnic minorities have increased since German reunification (Willems 1993). Violence against minorities may be conceived not only as a consequence of rapid sociopolitical transition and its effects on social disintegration but also as an indicator of cultural disintegration or segregation. Moreover, these developments could be understood as evidencing basic bias in the general population. To explain increased hate crime, few sociological and criminological approaches go beyond xenophobia, discriminatory attitudes, or traditional explanations of youth violence (Bliesener 1992; Rommelspacher 1993, p. 75; Kerner 1994*a*). The prevalent approach in explaining youth violence toward minorities relies on the frustration-aggression hypothesis. Most violent offenses are committed by juveniles or young adults; 70 percent of offenders fall into the age bracket fourteen to twenty years; only 3 percent of the offenders are thirty years or older (Ministry of Internal Affairs 1972–94, p. 83 of 1991 annual report). Seventy-five percent of all bias-motivated crimes recorded by police in Germany between January 1991 and April 1992 were committed by children, juveniles, or young adults up to the age of twenty years (Landeskriminalamt Sachsen 1993*a*, p. 12). Eighty-three percent of all bias-motivated crimes recorded by police in Sachsen in the years 1991 and 1992 were committed by youthful offenders up to the age of twenty years (Landeskriminalamt Sachsen 1993*b*).

New sociological concerns have been expressed concerning these phenomena (Friedrich-Naumann-Stiftung 1993). Outbursts of violence toward foreign and ethnic minorities may relate to a "conscience collective" and "ethnic solidarity" emerging around issues of the nation, the nation-state, and cultural and racial differences and may point to the need to redirect attention to social groups and group solidarity in explaining integration in modern societies (Möller 1993, p. 43). Modern sociological theory has been deplored for failing to account for such developments because of its primary emphasis on describing and explaining integration in postindustrial or modern societies through communicative action (Habermas 1994) and rational choices (Hondrich 1992; Münch 1995, p. 16).

Nationalist ideologies, once seemingly obsolete because of structural changes and concern for rationality in modern societies, are on the rise in most European countries, and these changes are beyond the reach of sociological explanations (Brock 1993). With increasing attention being paid to violence against ethnic minorities, the issues of fairness and nondiscrimination have reemerged, including the general problem of how fairness and justice can be established for foreign minorities in multiethnic areas. Part of this debate deals with explicit antidiscrimination legislation (as called for by the International Convention on the Elimination of all Forms of Discrimination, January 4, 1969), recently again recommended by an European Parliament initiative against "racism in Europe and the dangers of right wing extremism" (European

Parliament 1993). Explicit antidiscrimination legislation has not yet been introduced in Germany.

Studies to date concerning immigrant populations and crime and criminal justice are mostly based on views that assign exclusive etiological importance to social structure and social integration. According to these views, social structures create for immigrant populations the very problems faced by deprived groups of the German population. One consequence has been support for policies aimed at providing better education and employment opportunities and, in general, policies thought to facilitate social integration for immigrant populations (Killias 1989). Only recently have efforts been made to facilitate integration in the cultural and political systems by granting voting rights and extending minority participation in the political and justice systems.

It was commonly thought that prejudices against immigrant and ethnic minorities, general xenophobia, racial attacks, and hate crimes could be reduced by policies aimed at cognitive and moral dimensions that provided information on the need for immigration and the positive benefits of cultural pluralism and cultural tolerance (Brockhaus 1994). This was also true for relations between police and ethnic minorities, where proposals to reduce discrimination concentrated on changes in basic police education, special antiracism training courses, and the need to increase the presence of members of minority groups in police forces (Stork and Klein 1994, p. 294).

All available information indicates that immigrant populations' crime involvement does not pose risks for the social fabric. The effects of dissemination of such information on public views and attitudes, however, may be marginal. Victim surveys reveal that fear of crime is dependent on factors other than objective measures of crime, whether based on the individual's own experiences or derived from scientific sources of information (Albrecht and Arnold 1991). It is not clear how feelings of safety and fear of crime relate to attitudes toward immigration, ethnic minorities, and cultural differences. Victimological research could not find direct links between different measures of feelings of safety and actual experiences of victimization (with the exception of small groups of victims of violent or other serious crime). Victim surveys in Germany have not yet investigated direct links between racial or cultural fears and fear of crime (Boers 1993*a*, p. 71).

Recent surveys show that immigration problems are given low priority by the general public compared with other social problems (Boers 1993*b*). On a bivariate level, fear of different types of crime (general crime, violence, sexual crime) is correlated with concern for immigration, although the size of the coefficients is modest. Coefficients are strongest for the relation between fear of violent crime and immigration (.18 vs. .11 for other types of crimes; see Boers 1993*a*, p. 22). One might conclude, therefore, that fear of social unrest and violent clashes, not fear of ordinary crime, especially property crime, is related to concern for immigration. Public opinion research seems to confirm this view. Survey respondents, when asked for phenomena associated with asylum seekers often refer to hate crimes, riots, and so on, while mention of ordinary crime is low (Noelle-Neumann and Köcher 1993, p. 537). Fears of discrimination and perceptions of discriminatory practices are also largely independent of actual outcomes of decision making in the criminal justice system. Missing links between objective and subjective dimensions of fear of crime and fear of discrimination are likely to create particular problems in designing policies that try to reduce feelings of lack of safety and of discrimination.

The concept of culture conflict can be used to understand the nature and extent of risks to social stability and integration. These risks are the product of collective reactions related to the defense of cultural or national identities. In modern industrialized countries the locus of stability and integration is no longer a culture based on shared values and collective morals (Brock 1993, p. 178). This type of culture has been replaced by a material culture that is not dependent on shared values or cultural consensus but allows for individual choices in lifestyles and orientations. Under the conditions of stable economies, which provide the material basis for this mechanism of integration, the potential of cultural conflicts should in theory be low. But for large proportions of the population that are denied access to the material culture and the pursuit of individual interests, the potential of collective reactions or reaction formation may increase.

People denied access to the benefits of material culture may be especially susceptible to all types of social, religious, and political movements that stress collective values and collective responses to social problems. Such developments may have occurred in German society in recent years. The data on bias-motivated violence point to a sharp increase at the end of the 1980s (see figs. 3 and 4) and at the beginning of the 1990s (Willems 1993, p. 97) followed by a decline after a peak in 1992. Although the reliability of these figures is questionable because motivations are not easily established, inferences about trends may be drawn. However, the proportion of bias-motivated violence among all

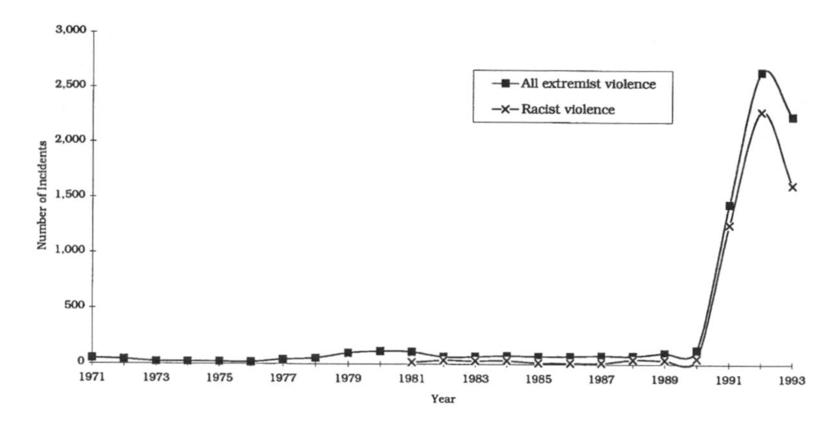

FIG. 3.—Extremist violence, Germany, 1971–93. Source: Ministry of Internal Affairs (1972–94).

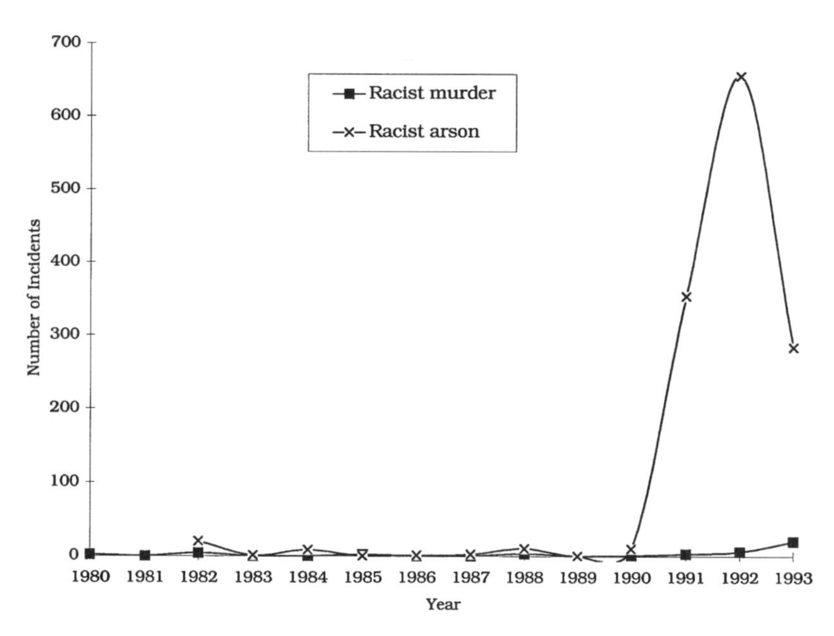

FIG. 4.—Right-wing extremist violence, arson and murder, 1980–93. Source: Ministry of Internal Affairs (1981–94).

violent crimes committed by youth is small. Furthermore, most inter-ethnic violence is associated not with racist or hate motivations but with conventional precipitants (Solon 1994, p. 74).

Analysis of motivations and targets of bias-motivated violence over the past twenty years shows important changes (Brockhaus 1994, p. 5). This may partly involve the exchangeability of targets of youth violence. During the 1980s ethnic minorities became the prominent target of bias-motivated violence. That virtually all violent acts against immigrant populations and ethnic minorities are committed by male, youthful offenders with poor educational and social backgrounds may support the perspective outlined above (Landeskriminalamt Sachsen 1993*a*, p. 12; Willems 1993, p. 110).

The analyses just offered could be said to amount to little more than conclusions that could be drawn also from theories of anomie and subculture. The implications, however, could be different inasmuch as such collective reactions might lead to cultural conflicts between groups and go beyond individual violent acts or other types of deviance (Solon 1994, p. 75). Such processes may reinforce a trend toward ghettoization of immigrant populations (Wiles 1993), which can be observed in some metropolitan areas in Europe. Youth violence has been understood as something resembling a "biological constant" that can be followed through history (Rusinek 1993, p. 83). From this view, it seems important to look at the political and social framework within which youth violence occurs to identify risks embedded in the instrumentalization of violent youth for other, political purposes.

II. Criminology and Research on Ethnic Minorities

Crime, fear of crime, safety, and justice have become central topics in the debate on relations between the majority group and minorities. In German criminology, politics, and the mass media, the terms used to describe minority groups refer to the status of being a foreigner. While in the 1960s and 1970s "guest worker" more narrowly focused on migrating labor forces and on resident foreign populations, the term "Ausländer" (foreigner/alien) includes ethnic and racial differences more generally. However, the concept of "foreign" and "ethnic minority" are vague and flexible. They do not amount to more than a shopping-basket term that neither depicts a homogeneous group of people nor offers theoretical guidance. The concepts of the foreign or ethnic minority include a range of minorities that differ with respect to religion, race, language, citizenship, material circumstances, cultural background, migration motives, and histories of relations between home country and immigration country (Manfrass 1991). Substantial differences occur between and within ethnic minorities. However, most criminological research on immigrant populations and ethnic minorities has been preoccupied with crime. "Gastarbeiter-Kriminalität" and "Ausländerkriminalität" (guest workers' or foreigners' criminality) continue to be favorites in criminology, with "Ausländerkriminalität" now having replaced "guest workers' criminality."

Assumptions of causal links between migration or minority status and crime and deviance point to powerful belief patterns concerning the potential for conflicts and instability associated with immigration and the "stranger." The topic "ethnicity and crime" therefore is most sensitive as it can facilitate social polarization and is susceptible to political exploitation. Indeed, the issue of ethnic minorities' and especially asylum seekers' potential for threatening safety has become a rallying point for authoritarian sentiments in society and for new right-wing political parties and extremist groups (Walter and Kubink 1993). The mainstream political parties in Germany also have linked fear of crime and fear of foreigners during election campaigns. The Social Democratic Party, for example, offered the slogan "Destroy the Mafia" in elections for the European Parliament in 1994. Although explicit references to Sicily, Italy, or Russia were not made, it seems clear that the public mind associates the Mafia with people from Russia and southern Italy.

Content analyses of print media in Germany reveal that two-fifths of articles related to foreigners highlight the topic of "crimes committed by foreign minorities" (Delgado 1972; see also Kubink 1993, p. 87). Drug trafficking and organized crime were the subjects of approximately 60 percent of mentions, outweighing other types of crimes (Kubink 1993, p. 93). Thus the concepts of ethnic minorities and deviance and crime have been separated from their respective theoretical bases and have become available for any association. This is especially true concerning drug trafficking and ethnicity. Problems of immigration and problems of illicit drugs are easily confounded and may reinforce each other. Examples can be found in North America, where control of opiates in the nineteenth century is said to have been motivated by opium-smoking habits of Chinese immigrant workers, and in England, where the national drug law enforcement unit first was located in the Central Drugs and Illegal Immigration Unit (Pearson 1992).

The danger of polarization also emerges in scientific research, including in parts of German criminology. A recent example may be drawn from the *Kölner Zeitschrift für Soziologie und Sozialpsychologie*, with a debate between Mansel (1994) and Reichertz and Schröer (1994). Mansel argues that fear of ethnic minorities and hate crimes committed against members of ethnic minorities are facilitated, even stimulated, by reporting on crimes committed by ethnic minorities. This argument easily can be used to oppose any research devised to test hypotheses on differences in crime patterns of minority and majority groups or on criminal justice decision making involving foreign offenders (other than research premised on assumptions of discriminatory treatment). This last type of minority research amounts to little more than "Gesinnungs-Soziologie" (ideologically motivated sociology) (so argue Reichertz and Schröer [1994, p. 299]).

Analyses sometimes focus on assumptions of disproportionate crime involvement of foreign minorities (Traulsen 1988; Kube and Koch 1990), while hypotheses of discriminatory treatment within the justice system are favored (Mansel 1988, 1990). Sometimes it appears the essential question is, Whose side are we on? (see, e.g., Berbüsse 1992). The debate is fueled by a lack of comparative research designs that could provide reliable and valid data on the contributions of minority and majority members to the overall crime load and by an apparent lack of adequate research on the discrimination hypothesis (which poses the same problems in terms of arranging for sound research designs). Indeed, most past criminological research has emphasized crime involvement of foreign and ethnic minorities during the last three decades and has sought answers to the question of why higher rates of minority suspects and offenders are found guilty. Fewer resources were invested in study of victimization of minorities (Albrecht and Arnold 1991, pp. 25–26) and on relations between minorities and criminal justice agencies, especially between minorities and police (Villmow 1993; Stork and Klein 1994).

Few studies have dealt with victimization, although there is some evidence that members of ethnic minorities are disproportionately affected by criminal victimization (including violence in the family) and other victimization, such as workplace accidents or traffic accidents (Kaiser 1974, pp. 225–27; Pitsela 1986; Albrecht 1987; Sessar 1993). Numerous surveys in the 1990s on victimization and fear of crime after the fall of the Berlin Wall, or as part of community crime prevention approaches, do not include foreign minorities but are restricted to the

German population (see, e.g., Boers, Kerner, and Kurz [1995, p. 1] for three nationwide victim surveys—1991, 1993, 1995; and the surveys discussed in Kaiser and Jehle [1995]; see also Boers et al. 1994; Strobl 1994).

Other surveys have included foreigners, but high nonresponse rates among minorities and a low base rate of foreigners in the general population (not balanced by oversampling) generate too few interviewees for meaningful analysis (see, e.g., Legge [1994], p. 136: 43 foreigners among 426 respondents; Arbeitsgruppe "Strafrechtliche Rechtstatsachenforschung und Empirische Kriminologie" [1995], p. 5: 40 foreigners among 1,308 respondents). Higher victimization rates among minorities should be expected from the high offender rates observed for various ethnic minorities because a significant proportion of personal crime is intraethnic crime. Research in the 1970s showed that approximately 70 percent of all victims of homicide committed by foreign nationals were foreigners (10 percent of victims of homicide committed by German nationals were foreigners [Sessar 1981]). Analysis of police-recorded crime committed by a cohort of persons born in 1970 in the state of Baden-Württemberg reveals that 58 percent of all homicides, 45 percent of all rapes, 38 percent of assaults, and 16 percent of robberies are committed against members of the same ethnic group. (The data were provided by Peter Sutterer from the criminological research unit of the Max-Planck-Institute for Foreign and International Penal Law, Freiburg.)

Although differences in victimization rates between ethnic minorities and majority groups should fall when controlling for other nonethnic variables such as neighborhood type, demographic and socioeconomic background, and routine activities, effects of victimization may be especially severe for some subgroups. When considering, for example, intrafamily violence, vulnerability of minority women and children is likely to be reinforced by their weak legal position as foreigners, which may be adversely affected (in terms of the risk of deportation) by permanent separation or divorce. Furthermore, knowledge about available victim services is not widespread among these groups. Traditional weak positions of females in some groups and language problems may add to the extent of victimization (Hagemann-White 1981).

The tendency for research on victimization to exclude foreign and ethnic minorities parallels treatment of foreigners in justice information systems. Partly from convenience, partly from tradition, German criminology relies heavily on police and other official statistics. Police statistics record the citizenship of suspects but do not record characteristics of victims (although such information is available because victim characteristics such as sex, age, citizenship, and relationship to the offender are regularly entered into police computers). The disregard in criminology for victimization among ethnic minorities reflects the preoccupation with offenders shown in police statistics.

Noncriminal victimization and structural victimization also need to be taken into account (Sessar 1993). Abortion rates among ethnic minority women in Germany exceed by far those observed among the German population (Bärtling 1982). Estimates of accident rates among migrant workers are twice those among German workers (Kaiser 1974). Additionally, migrant workers are more at risk from exploitative employment conditions, with employers hiring immigrants on a noncontractual basis that allows avoidance of social security payments and other social benefits.

Empirical evaluations of the effects of policies aimed at the reduction of discrimination and perceptions of discrimination are virtually nonexistent. This may be explained by a general neglect of research on relations between the public and police or other justice agencies. Likewise, the corrections system and "prison and ethnic or foreign minorities" topics have received only surface consideration. The focus has been merely on the numbers or proportions of foreigners in prison facilities. Research on ethnic or foreign minorities and crime usually ends at sentencing (Kubink 1993). German prison research remains heavily influenced by assumptions about rehabilitation that have not taken ethnic variables into account but have highlighted evaluation problems and theoretical bases of rehabilitation.

The debate on discrimination has been extended to the question of whether variables such as ethnicity or citizenship should be included at all in criminal justice statistics. The variable "citizenship" or "nationality" has been excluded from federal court statistics since 1984. With respect to police statistics, the debate is going on, but it seems unlikely that the variable "citizenship" will be omitted (Kerner 1994*b*, suggesting that police statistics displaying information on the status of nationality should also include caveats concerning proper interpretation of such data).

Besides standard information systems, police authorities traditionally have maintained special files on certain groups of suspects, among whom the Sinti and Roma (gypsies) have been prominent. Special police attention to these ethnic minorities is rooted in past centuries (e.g., Schwencken 1822; for preoccupation with these minorities and associated myths, see Albrecht [1994*a*]). Stigmas attached to gypsies from alleged theft of children were substantial, although nineteenth-century criminological literature and research never documented cases of child theft that could be linked to gypsies. Marginalization of Sinti and Roma climaxed with the systematic terror these minorities experienced in Nazi Germany (Kaiser 1988). After 1945, special attention to gypsies did not change significantly; police continued to maintain special files on the group without special reference to criminal behavior (Feuerhelm 1988, p. 305). This came to an end in the 1970s when political organizations of gypsies exerted pressure, backed up by an increasingly powerful general policy of better protection of privacy and personal data. Instead of maintaining direct information on Sinti and Roma, since the 1970s general police information systems include a variable (with respect to suspects) of "numerous changes of the place of residence," which can be assumed to be a synonym for "gypsies" (Feuerhelm 1988, p. 306).

A. Research on Crime Involvement

A "suspect" is an individual suspected by police of having committed a crime when enough evidence is available to pass the case to the public prosecutor's office for further decision making (for a detailed discussion, see Albrecht and Teske [1992]). In 1993, 33.6 percent of persons suspected of crimes in Germany were foreigners (Bundeskriminalamt 1994; including crimes in the new Bundesländer as well as all criminal offenses besides traffic offenses that are not covered by police statistics). If immigration offenses are omitted, the percentage drops to 26.7 percent (for 1993). In 1953, when police statistics were published for the first time after the Second World War, 1.7 percent of suspects were foreigners. Since 1984, police statistics count suspects only once. Earlier, a suspect was counted separately each time there were grounds to pass the case to the public prosecutor.

Offender rates of police-recorded crime among some minorities are two to four times that observed in society at large (H.-J. Albrecht 1988). Some minorities have below-average offender rates, for example, Spanish and Portuguese (Geissler and Marissen 1990, p. 668; Pichler 1991, p. 16; Walter and Pitsela 1993). Figure 5 demonstrates the enormous differences in crime rates, expressed as the number of suspects per 100,000 same group population, among various foreign

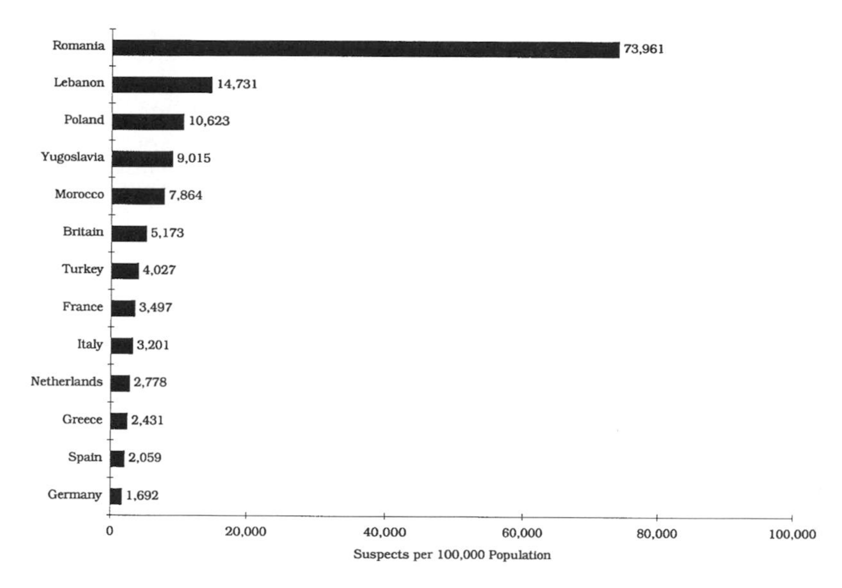

FIG. 5.—Suspects per 100,000 same-group population, North Rhine–Westphalia, 1993. Note: A suspect is any person suspected by police to have committed a criminal offense. Source: Landeskriminalamt Düsseldorf (1994).

minorities in the state of North Rhine–Westphalia in 1993. Such interethnic differences suggest that ethnicity and minority status do not have a uniform and consistent effect on crime rates, whether rates are viewed as indicators of crime involvement or of law enforcement activities (Junger 1990). These differences suggest also that surface analyses that link population figures with police-recorded crime figures may mask underlying processes.

The suspect rate in the Romanian population of 74,000 per 100,000 (of the population registered with the immigration authorities) demands careful inspection. The apparent crime rate among Romanians could mean that nearly all Romanians living in North Rhine–Westphalia are engaged in some criminal activity. Virtually all of the offenses recorded by Romanians involve small property offenses (simple theft) and violations of immigration and asylum laws (see fig. 6). Most Romanians who immigrated to North Rhine–Westphalia (and other German states) are of Roma origin; high involvement in these offenses could point to distinct cultural behavior patterns and to an extremely marginal social position. The basis for calculating crime rates could be misleading and crime rates could be overestimated if significant num-

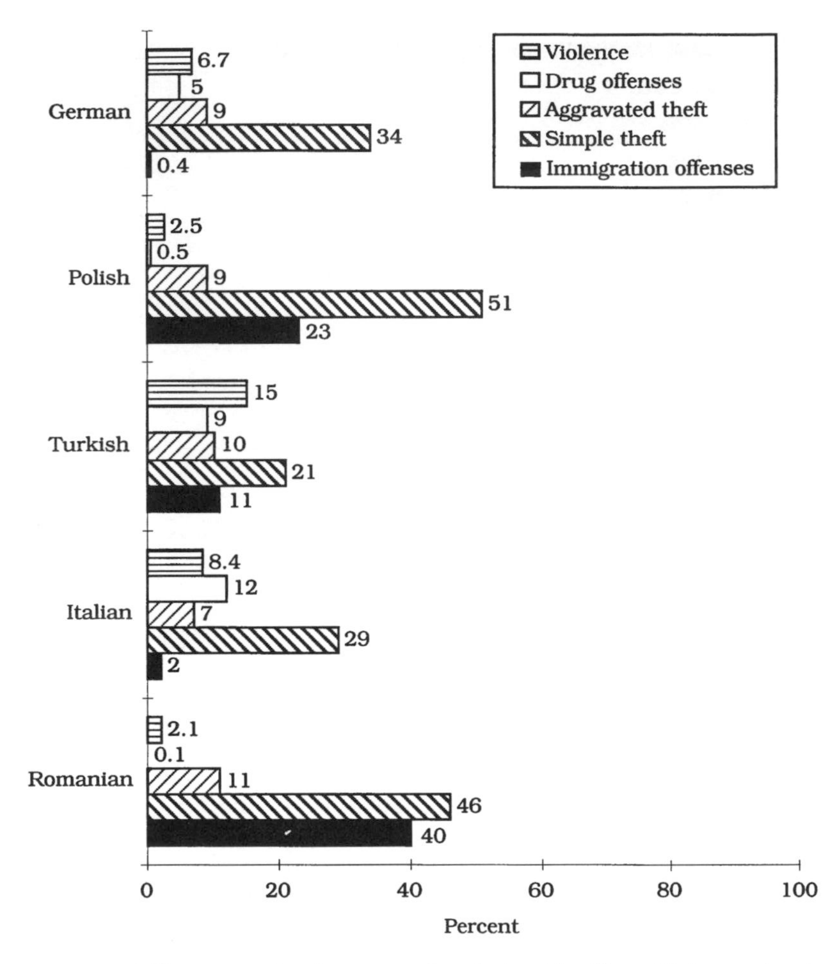

FIG. 6.—Offense categories of suspects, selected minorities. Notes: Violence = homicide, rape, robbery, aggravated assault. Not all offense groups are included; totals for groups do not equal 100. Source: Bundeskriminalamt (1994).

bers of Romanian suspects are not resident in North Rhine–Westphalia but are part of a transient population moving through various regions. (The Roma traveling groups have been estimated to number about 60,000 people at the beginning of the 1990s; see Forbes and Mead 1992, p. 39.)

Police data also allow for a longitudinal analysis of data on crime by minorities. Figures 7 and 8 demonstrate different trends. In figure 7, North Rhine–Westphalia crime rates are presented from 1973 to 1993 for selected foreigners coming from EC-member states. There is a

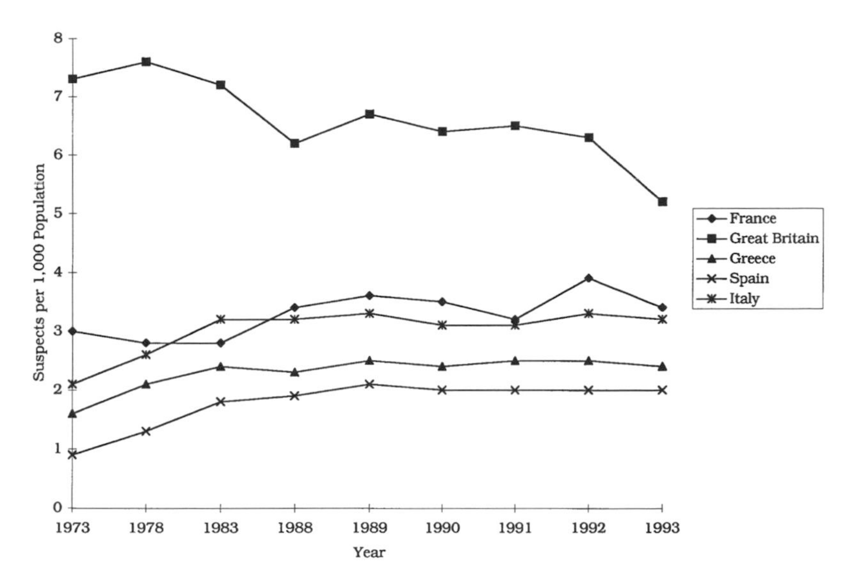

Fig. 7.—Suspects per 1,000 population, selected groups, North Rhine–Westphalia, 1973–93. Source: Landeskriminalamt Düsseldorf (1994).

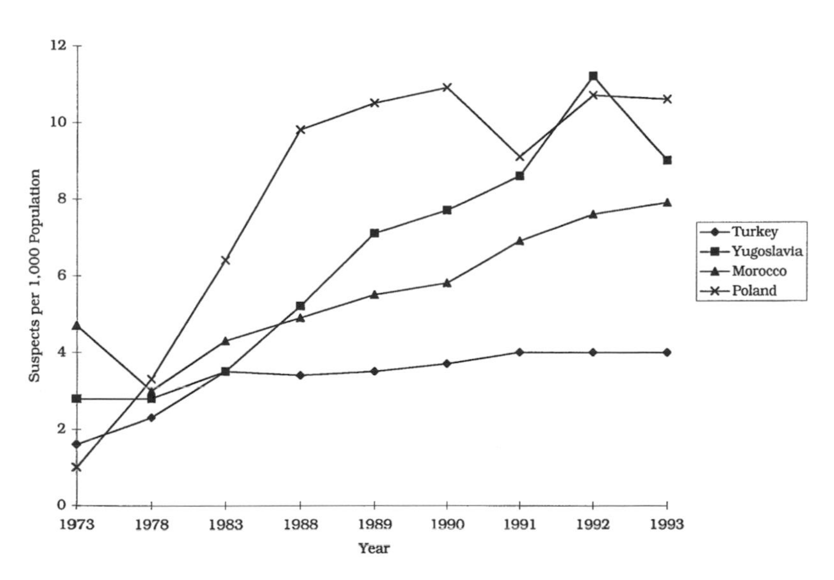

Fig. 8.— Suspects per 1,000 population, selected groups, North Rhine–Westphalia, 1973–93. Source: Landeskriminalamt Düsseldorf (1994).

downward trend in crime rates of British citizens over the 1980s and at the beginning of the 1990s, which is easily explained by the withdrawal of British Army forces, who had been concentrated in North Rhine–Westphalia since the Second World War. The trends for other groups reveal nothing in particular and resemble the general trend in North Rhine–Westphalia. Figure 8 shows crime rates among selected foreign groups from different parts of Europe and North Africa (Poland, Turkey, Yugoslavia, Morocco). The Turkish rate of suspects corresponds to those in figure 7 (though on a somewhat higher level), but the figures related for other national groups rose substantially in the second half of the 1980s. The marked increases coincide with increases in migration activities from Poland, Yugoslavia, and Morocco.

Comparative analyses of different German regions show that large differences in offender rates can be observed among the same minority groups (Mansel 1986). This finding points to the need to look for interactions between crime and law enforcement variables and variables accounting for minority status. Research findings point to significant differences in the degree of crime involvement between generations of immigrants, with the second or third generations born or raised in the Federal Republic of Germany displaying considerably higher offender rates than did the first generations of immigrant workers (Kaiser 1974, p. 228; Kunz 1989, p. 390; Walter 1995, p. 194).

The time series of foreign suspects and population rates demonstrate clear trends that might be interpreted as the combined effects of both changes in behavior patterns of second and third generations and changes in migration patterns (see fig. 9). In the 1960s, both rates tracked closely but separated during the 1970s and thereafter take completely different courses, with suspect rates rising much more steeply. Disproportionate involvement of minority members in police-recorded crimes are especially evident among young suspects. In 1993, almost half of eighteen-to-twenty-year-old suspects (46.5 percent) were minority members, as were 34 percent of all juvenile offenders and 30.7 percent of seven-to-thirteen-year-old child offenders (Bundeskriminalamt 1994).

Demographic characteristics may account for some of these increases, as foreign populations have comparatively high proportions of children and juveniles (see fig. 10; Walter 1995, p. 193). But crime rates per 100,000 of the respective population increased considerably, too, among young foreigners and much faster than among young Germans. In North Rhine–Westphalia between 1984 and 1993 the crime

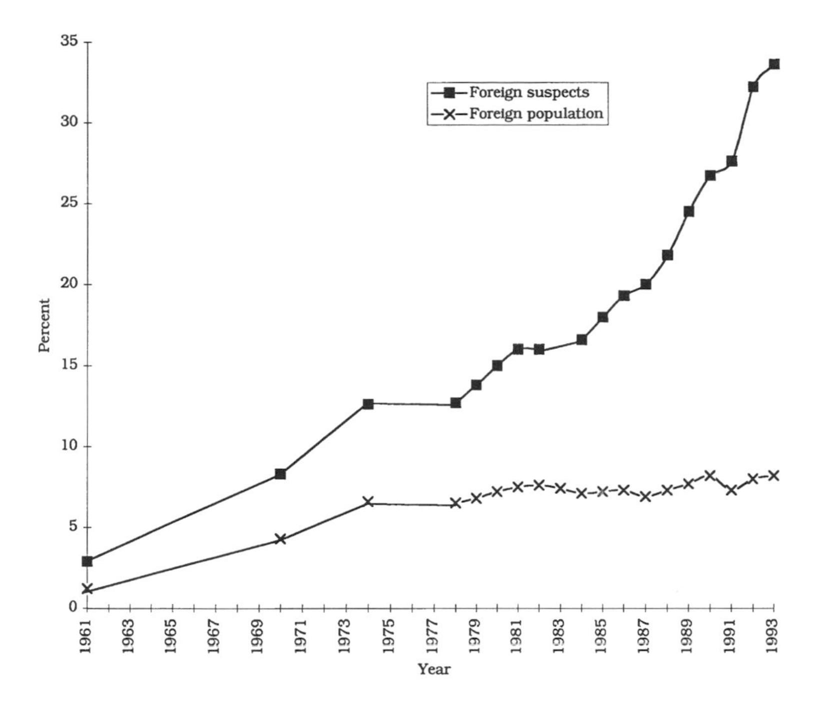

Fig. 9.—Percentages of foreigners in general population and among suspects, Germany, 1961–93. Sources: Bundeskriminalamt (1994); Statistisches Bundesamt (1995*a*).

rate among young foreigners more than doubled (from 6,651 to 13,614), while the increase among young Germans was from 4,075 to 5,038 (Walter 1995, p. 194). Between 1984 and 1993, the crime rate among guest workers, or in general terms, the foreign labor force, did not change much, with rates ranging from 4,246 per 100,000 in 1984 to 4,339 per 100,000 in 1993 (Bundeskriminalamt 1995, p. 124). One possible explanation is that first-generation immigrants experienced first improved living conditions, housing, and medical care, and so on, outweighing remaining differences between minority and majority groups (Kunz 1989, p. 390).

It may be that selection took place through hiring schemes and that the first generations interacted mainly within the ethnic group, with contacts to the majority group confined to the workplace. The second or third generations are more likely to be conscious of relative deprivation and socioeconomic inequality and affected by conflicting expectations presented by traditional values of minority groups and the secular values prevalent in modern societies. With time, interactions with ma-

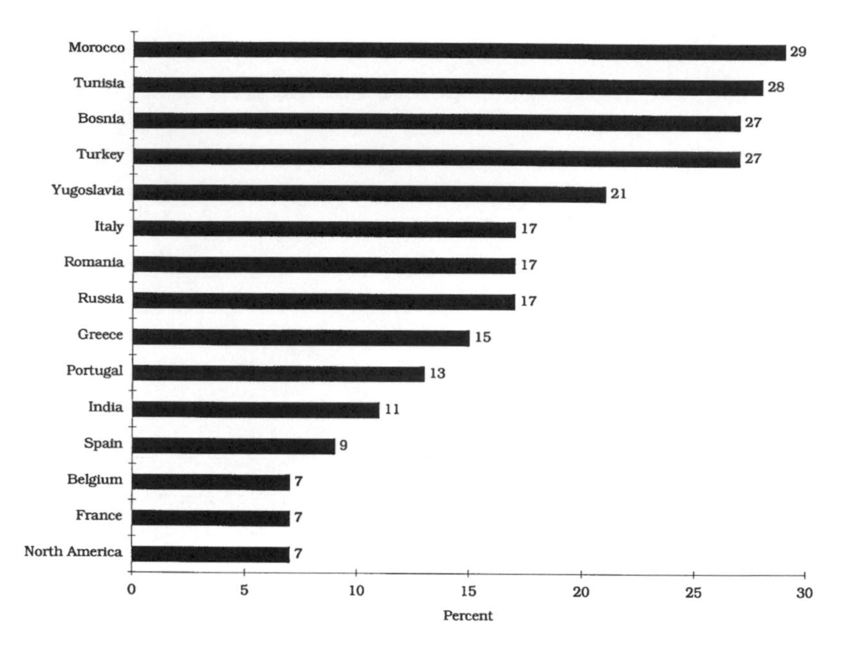

FIG. 10.—Percentage of population under age fifteen, selected groups, Germany, 1992. Source: Statistisches Bundesamt (1994*a*).

jority members increase, and with them, the risk of conflicts. Research on social and economic integration of minorities reveals that the marginal position of Turkish and other minorities with respect to income, general socioeconomic status, and housing conditions did not improve over the last decade and over different generations (Seifert 1991). Differences between the majority group and immigrants in average income, housing, and unemployment remain marked (Headey, Krause, and Habich 1990; Seifert 1991, p. 38). Housing space available for German respondents is approximately twice the size of space available for foreign respondents; furthermore, the risk of falling below the poverty line given a certain employment status and income level is significantly higher for foreigners. Although approximately half of eighteen-to-twenty-four-year-old immigrants express the desire to live permanently in Germany, the vast majority (73 percent) felt strong bonds to the home culture and denied a "German identity" (Seifert 1991, p. 40). In addition, psychological and psychiatric research points to a range of psychological problems and disorders experienced by minority groups (Lajios 1993).

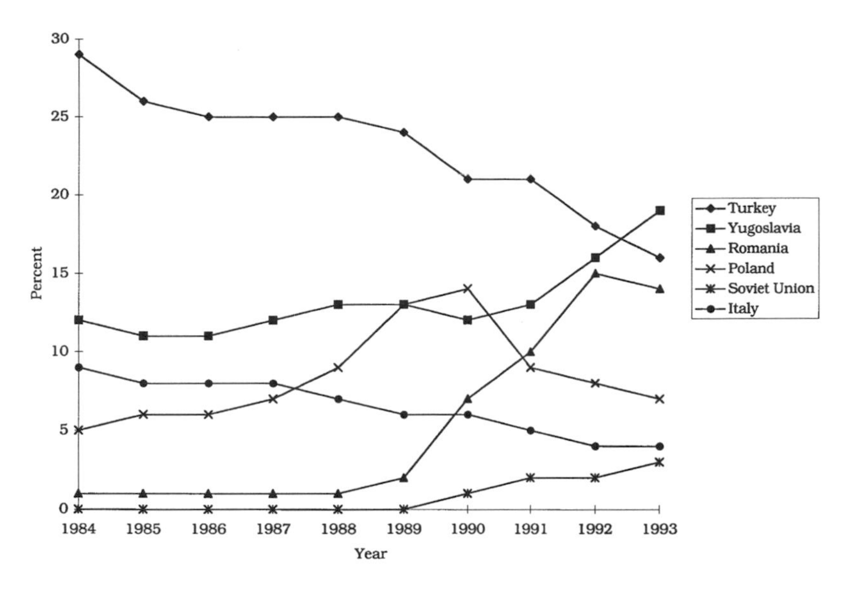

FIG. 11.—Citizenship of foreign suspects, Germany, 1984–93. Note: Not all groups are shown; totals per year equal less than 100. Source: Bundeskriminalamt (1994).

Although most crimes committed by minorities are property crimes, disproportionate crime involvement is especially marked for violent offenses such as assault, rape, robbery, and homicide. Findings from a longitudinal study on criminal offending in a birth cohort (based on police information on offenses and suspects for all those born in 1970 in the state of Baden-Württemberg; see Karger and Sutterer 1988) showed the prevalence rate for all offenses to be 29 percent in the eighteen-year-old birth cohort of foreign males; their German counterparts had a prevalence rate of 14 percent. For violent offenses, the respective prevalence rates were 7 percent and 2 percent (Karger and Sutterer 1990).

The composition of various ethnic subgroups among all foreigners has changed significantly over time. The proportions of Turkish, Italian, and Greek suspects, for example, have decreased dramatically over the last ten years, while the proportions from former Yugoslavia, Romania, Poland, the former Soviet Union, and some African countries increased considerably (see fig. 11). These shifts point to a significant shift in immigration patterns.

Considerable changes also occurred with respect to the immigration status of immigrants suspected of crimes. In the mid-1980s, one-third

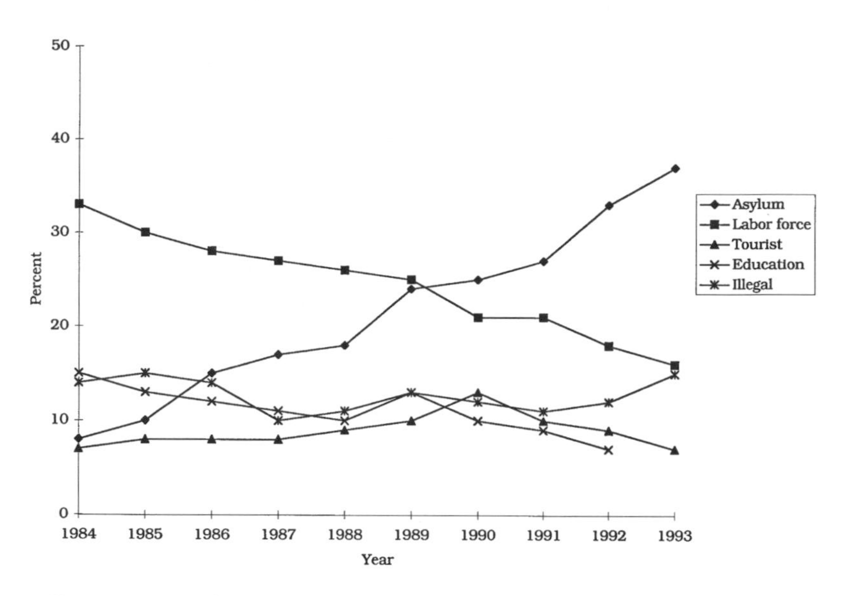

FIG. 12.—Basis of presence in Germany, foreign suspects, 1984–93. Source: Bundeskriminalamt (1994).

of foreign suspects were guest workers; this group's share dropped to 18 percent in 1992. One-third of foreign suspects in 1992 were foreigners seeking asylum (see fig. 12). Changes in the asylum provisions of the German constitution, which took effect July 1, 1993, affected the number of crimes committed by asylum seekers by drastically reducing the number of asylum seekers admitted into Germany. The number of asylum seekers suspected of crimes dropped from 225,501 to 134,348 between 1993 and 1994.

B. How Should Police Statistics Be Interpreted?

Official records are never perfect indicators of behavior. Before police records on minority overrepresentation among suspects are taken at face value, several questions warrant consideration. Does police-recorded crime among ethnic minorities result from disproportionate crime involvement or from disproportionate crime control directed at minorities? Are minorities more likely to be arrested relative to the number of criminal acts they commit than are majority citizens? Are police crime data misleading when used for analyses of crime involvement of minorities because they do not control for relevant demographic or other variables?

These questions are not easy to answer. Criminological research shows that police data cover only a small fraction of offenses committed. Victimization surveys find that only a minority of victimizing events are reported to police. So, police crime data could easily be biased against minorities. The strategy generally used to overcome such deficiencies in official data is to conduct self-report surveys on offending and victimization. But few victimization and virtually no self-report studies include ethnic or foreign minorities, mainly because of methodological problems similar to those found in intercultural and international comparative research (Albrecht 1989*b;* Junger 1989).

Attention has been devoted to whether controls of important demographic variables can account for disproportionate crime involvement by minorities in police data. Some minority populations differ sharply from the majority in distribution of age, sex, and other variables that are associated strongly with officially recorded crime.

Findings from a comparative study on foreigners' crime using police and population data in Bavaria illustrate the effects of proper controls on levels of police-recorded crime (Steffen 1992). First, the general offender rate in the immigrant population was 5.6 times higher than the offender rate in the German population. Second, when "place of residence" is controlled, and only foreigners with a permanent place of residence in Germany are included, the offender rate is reduced to the 2.8 times that of the German population. Third, if immigration offenses are excluded, the offender rate is reduced further to 2.5 times the German rate. Fourth, if age and gender are controlled, crime involvement of eighteen-to-twenty-four-year-old males drops to 2.2 times the rate of the corresponding German population (see also Kubink 1993).

Petty offending, especially shoplifting, predominates among illegal immigrants, tourists, and foreigners seeking asylum (Ahlf 1993, p. 137). Their contribution to serious crime is negligible in quantitative terms. Rates of serious crime involvement distinguish illegals, tourists, and asylum seekers from the foreign resident population.

Police statistics available in the states allow for the analyses in crime trends within foreign minorities. Data from the state of Hessen permit differentiation of at least four groups of foreign offenders who exhibit distinct offense patterns.

Figures 13 and 14 show trends among Indian and Pakistani offenders. Immigration offenses and fraud and forgery are most common; these offenses typically relate to attempts to enter the country without

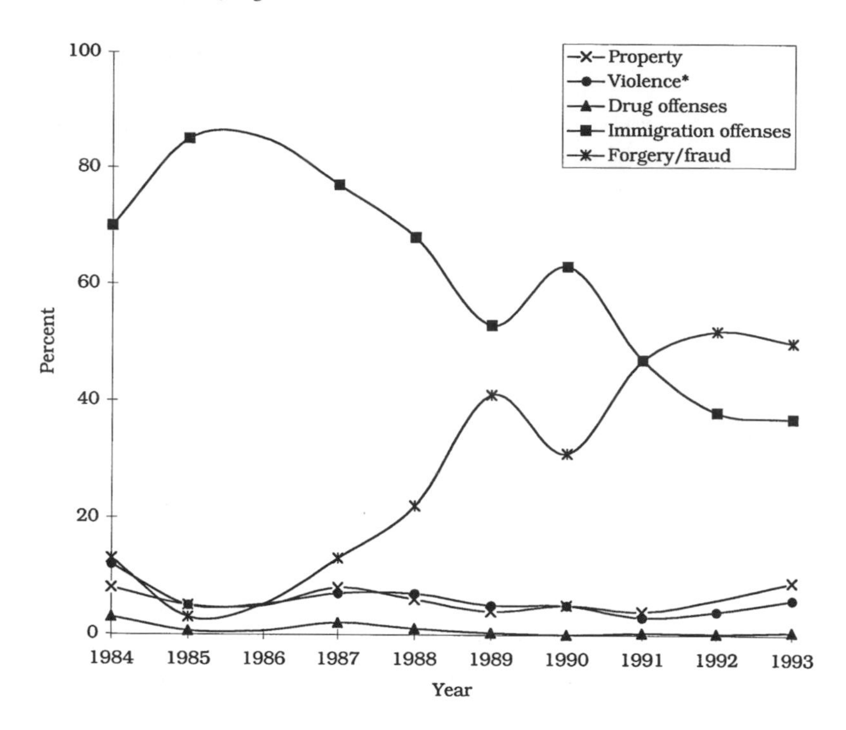

Fig. 13.—Offense types, suspects in State of Hessen from India, 1984–93. *Violence = homicide, assault, sexual offenses, robbery. Source: Landeskriminalamt Hessen (1994).

proper permission (the forgery is mainly in use of false documents or passports). Traditional crimes, especially property crimes, are rare. Afghan and Ceylonese citizens display roughly the same offense patterns.

A second group of foreign populations is characterized by extremely high proportions of property and immigration offenses (figs. 15 and 16 demonstrate the trends for Polish and Romanian suspects; similar trends can be observed for Bulgarian and Russian offenders). Other crime (especially violent crimes and drug offenses) is negligible.

A third group of foreign offenders belong to traditional guest worker populations (characterized by stable and large resident populations). This group, represented by the Turkish offender population in figure 17, exhibits more or less "ordinary" offense patterns comparable to German patterns, with a large share of property offenses and a somewhat elevated level of violent offenses. Immigration offenses are at low levels.

A fourth distinct group are nationalities with a significant share of

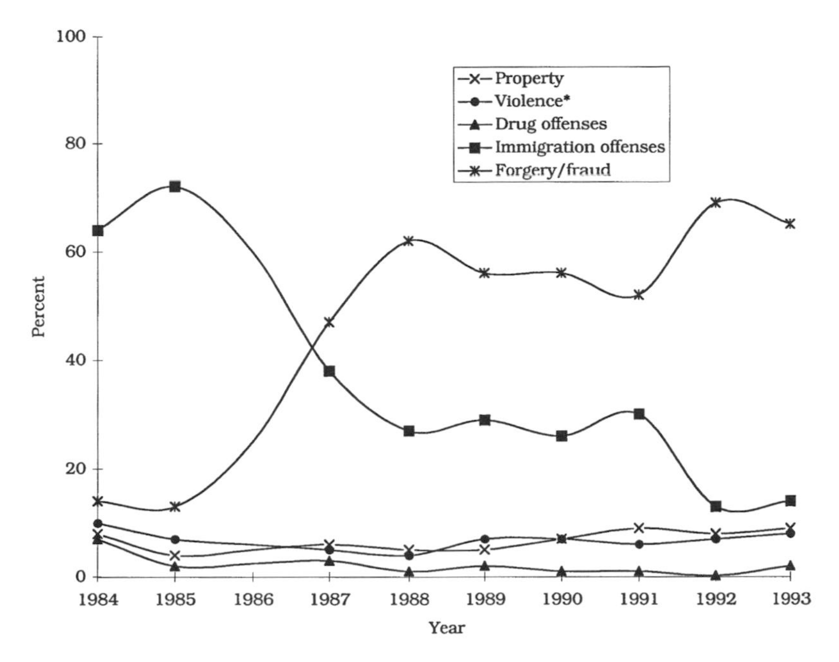

FIG. 14.— Offense types, suspects in State of Hessen from Pakistan, 1984–93. *Violence = homicide, assault, sexual offenses, robbery. Source: Landeskriminalamt Hessen (1994).

drug offenders, as shown in figure 18. Several subgroups may be differentiated, with extreme examples of Senegalese and Gambian offenders showing up in the early 1980s in several German states and being registered as suspects almost exclusively because of drug (and immigration) offenses. These groups were engaged in heroin distribution in some metropolitan areas. In the second half of the 1980s, Senegalese and Gambians faded out of police statistics as police pressure on the drug distribution schemes became too strong and resident Senegalese or Gambian populations were not significant. Colombians also seem to belong to this extreme group, as in some periods they mainly are registered because of cocaine trafficking (plus immigration offenses).

A second subgroup concerns nationalities whose share of drug offenses is high though not dominant among the general distribution of offenses. Moroccans, who are heavily involved in cannabis trafficking and distribution, are an example. There is also, however, a small resident community of Moroccans, which contributes to a more "normal distribution" of offenses.

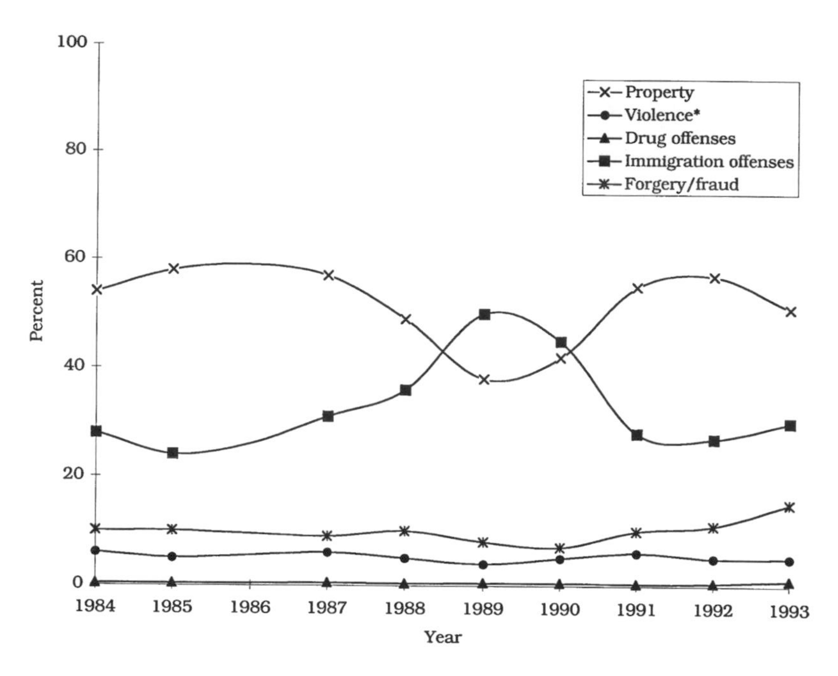

FIG. 15.— Offense types, suspects in State of Hessen from Poland, 1984–93. *Violence = homicide, assault, sexual offenses, robbery. Source: Landeskriminalamt Hessen (1994).

A third subgroup includes Spanish, Italians, and Turks, among whom drug offenses are higher than for other groups, indicating that groups of these nationalities are active in all types of drug offenses. Among Turkish drug offenders, the Kurdish minority is masked by use of the variable "Turkish nationality." Kurdish groups have a large share of the heroin market in Germany.

The data available on foreign minorities and police-recorded crime should be interpreted as displaying different trends. Opening of the borders after the breakdown of communist regimes in eastern Europe led to a sharp rise in petty property offenses mainly committed by tourists and asylum seekers (these are overlapping categories as tourists may ask for asylum during their stay). The wealth on display in department stores, for example, served and serves as a powerful enticement to shoplifting by short-term visitors from the east. Some cities in eastern Germany experienced a huge increase in shoplifting after the borders were opened. (Ahlf [1993, p. 137] suggests that a sharp increase in shoplifting after 1989 in cities near the former border between East

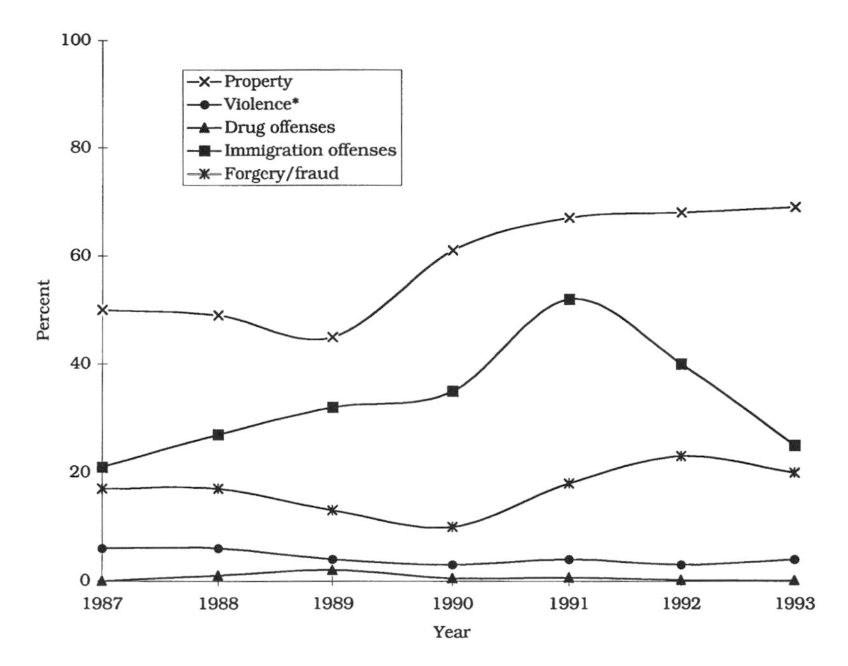

FIG. 16.— Offense types, suspects in State of Hessen from Romania, 1987–93. *Violence = homicide, assault, sexual offenses, robbery. Source: Landeskriminalamt Hessen (1994).

and West Germany reflects the sudden "cross-border" mobility of the East German population.) So, for example, the shoplifting figures in Berlin jumped between 1989 and 1990 from 36,000 cases to more than 60,000 cases (Landeskriminalamt Berlin 1995). This may be understood as something like "migration crime" associated with short-term individual migration and illegal immigration, especially in the case of asylum seekers with little property and severe restrictions on legal employment.

Huge black markets in eastern Europe have emerged with a growing demand for all types of goods not produced and available in sufficient quantities in east European countries (e.g., cars, communication technology). Foreign nationals are involved, although they do not belong to populations resident in Germany. These crimes are linked with black market economies.

Finally, black markets in Germany, especially drug markets, create demands which are met by various ethnic and foreign groups (e.g., South American groups for cocaine, North and sub-Saharan Africans,

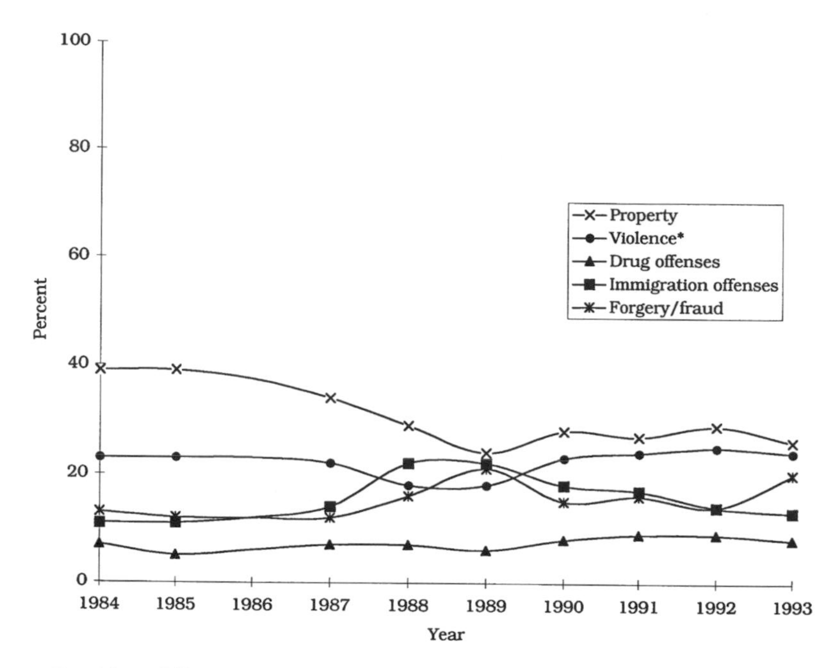

Fig. 17.— Offense types, suspects in State of Hessen from Turkey, 1984–93. *Violence = homicide, assault, sexual offenses, robbery. Source: Landeskriminalamt Hessen (1994).

Kurds, and Arab groups for heroin and cannabis). In black markets, as in legal markets, international networks require participation by residents from other countries on both supply and demand sides. Trafficking routes change because of alterations in police pressure, and with them changes the nationalities of offenders involved in drug trafficking and arrested in Germany.

Interesting examples come from case studies in Frankfurt. During the 1980s, several African nationalities were heavily involved in heroin trafficking and distribution. A special task force was created focusing on Senegalese, Gambians, and Nigerians (Arbeitsgruppe [Task Force] Lagos), which led to numerous arrests of Senegalese, Gambians, and Nigerians for drug offenses (Kriminalabteilung Frankfurt a.M. 1990, p. 3). As the number of drug suspects of these nationalities decreased, trafficking routes and distribution networks adjusted. By the early 1990s, the number of drug suspects from sub-Saharan Africa approached zero. However, by the late 1980s, Algerians and Moroccans

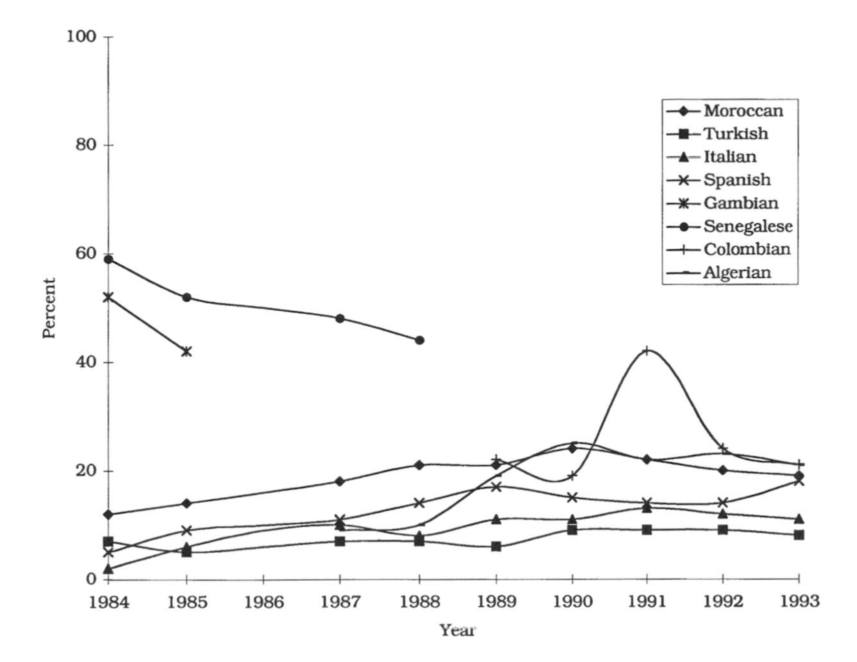

FIG. 18.—Drug offenses as a percentage of all offenses in the State of Hessen, selected foreign suspect groups, 1984–93. Source: Landeskriminalamt Hessen (1994).

gained a big share of the cannabis and heroin markets, which led law enforcement to focus on Moroccans (with a Task Force Morocco, Kriminalabteilung Frankfurt a.M. 1992, p. 10).

However, resident ethnic minorities are also involved in the demand side of drug markets. Drug-related death rates were 2.1 per 100,000 for the German population and 1.9 per 100,000 for the Turkish population, but twice as high (4.6 per 100,000) for the Italian population (Bundeskriminalamt 1993). Vietnamese were recruited as "guest workers" in the former German Democratic Republic and stayed in Germany after 1989. They were particularly affected by unemployment and became heavily involved in importation and distribution of untaxed cigarettes. Otherwise, the Vietnamese population become known to police mostly for immigration and tax offenses, except for isolated gang-related acts of violence (Landeskriminalamt Berlin 1994, p. 24).

Findings from studies based on comparative designs and on nonpolice data can be used to assess differences in crime involvement of local resident minority and majority populations. A small study in southern

Germany showed that a focus on the number of offenders rather than on the number of offenses is too narrow and probably misleading. No differences were found with respect to the annual offender rate between the minority juveniles and young adults, mostly Turkish, Italian, and Yugoslavian, aged fourteen to twenty-one and the corresponding group of German citizens. However, taking into account the number of offenses committed by each offender, minority juveniles were contributing considerably less to the annual volume of offenses than were the Germans (Oppermann 1986). City population data and data on suspects and their offenses over several years were analyzed on the level of city quarters, on the assumption that demographic, social, economic, and employment characteristics of foreign and German citizens living in the same quarters are likely to be similar.

A comprehensive study on crime involvement among minority and majority juveniles was recently completed in the Netherlands. The research relies on both self-report measures of delinquency and crime and official crime data and includes Moroccan, Surinamese, and Turkish juveniles and a matched group of Dutch juveniles (in relation to socioeconomic status etc.). The results indicate that self-report data are not superior to official crime data.

Validity of self-report measures compared with official records differed for the various ethnic groups (Junger 1989, p. 154). Validity was high for Dutch juveniles and Surinamese, but low for Moroccans and Turks. Differences in validity thus seem to be rooted in culture or religion rather than in ethnicity (also see essays by Junger-Tas and Martens, both in this volume). Thus self-reports are not necessarily a better way to estimate group differences in crime involvement. Moreover, as self-reports typically include nonserious delinquent and criminal behavior, and official crime data cover more serious and repetitive crimes, it seems justified to rely on official crime data in the attempt to control crime rates for relevant nonethnic variables. When comparing the minority and matched Dutch juveniles using statistical controls, the differences were reduced significantly although they did not vanish completely (Junger 1989, p. 154). Differences were observed among the three minority groups, consistent with data from other countries demonstrating varying degrees of crime involvement among ethnic minorities.

Most German self-report surveys do not include ethnic or foreign minorities, and those that do have generated inconsistent findings (G. Albrecht 1988). Evidence from surveys that included foreign juveniles is not conclusive. In the early 1980s, self-report research from Bremen failed to show high levels of delinquency by foreign juveniles but concluded that those foreign juveniles interviewed seemed remarkably conformist (Schumann 1987, p. 70). A small study of self-reported delinquent behavior among youth in a large city in the south of Germany (Mannheim) came to similar conclusions: rates of offending behavior reported by German youth matched those reported by foreign youth (Sutterer and Karger 1994, p. 168). However, a more recent self-report survey of a larger sample of German and foreign youth found a significantly larger proportion of foreign juveniles reporting violent behavior (Heitmeyer 1995, p. 399).

III. Explaining Crime Involvement of Ethnic Minorities

In the 1970s and 1980s, it was suggested that cultural conflict concepts do not adequately explain crime activities of immigrants (Kaiser 1974, p. 228; Sack 1974, p. 211; Schüler-Springorum 1983, p. 532; Kubink 1993, p. 69; Villmow 1993, p. 44). Among first generations of immigrant workers, neither the extent of crime involvement nor the types of crime committed were said to point to cultural conflicts. Norm conflicts do not account for large proportions of immigrants' crime because central criminal norms (theft, assault, rape, murder) do not differ among different cultures or nations to such an extent that conflicting expectations could be produced (Kubink 1993, p. 70). Norm conflicts might be useful explanations for some criminal law subjects about which large variation may be observed internationally. Environmental offenses, or what might be termed "side criminal laws" (Schöch and Gebauer 1991, p. 56), involve behaviors, for example, where there might be a difference between an external (culture) conflict and an internal (culture) conflict that might affect second- and third-generation immigrants, thus explaining increasing crime involvement. Socialization theory, control theory, and anomie theory are combined with the intent to highlight an elevated level of social strain.

But for most crimes, the theoretical focus has shifted to general theories of crime such as deprivation and control theories. Such theories emphasize social structure and problems of social integration and give ethnic variables marginal or indirect importance (serving, e.g., as amplifier of social strain or disintegration). For immigrant populations, therefore, it is not specific cultural expectations that produce conflicts resulting in criminal offending; the very same variables account for crime among immigrants that explain crime in the general population.

Theories of deprivation predict higher levels of crime among immigrants who experience unemployment, poor education, low average income, and low socioeconomic status, just as those variables predict crime involvement among similarly situated Germans.

Control theory suggests that disproportionate crime involvement of immigrant populations occurs because of reduced opportunities to develop bonds to conventional society. Control theory may even account for the increase of foreign offender rates along the generation chain. For juveniles of the second, third, or fourth generation of immigrants, the development of bonds might be at serious risks due to conflicts arising between immigrant generations (Bielefeld 1982; Kaiser 1988, p. 599; Aronowitz 1989). Informal controls thus are weakened, and the influence of delinquent peer groups may increase (Kaiser 1988, p. 599; Villmow 1993, p. 45).

However, independent of theories of crime involvement among immigrants and of the question whether differences in the crime involvement may be explained by nonethnic and nonimmigration variables, police-recorded crime data manifestly indicate a deep involvement of immigrant populations in the criminal justice system that deserves careful observation. A longitudinal study on police contacts of children and juveniles has shown that approximately 14 percent of male foreign juveniles had at least one contact with police by age fourteen (Karger and Sutterer 1988). By age eighteen, 29 percent had experienced at least one arrest. These findings demonstrate that encounters between police and immigrant populations are not exceptions but affect major parts of the young male immigrant population. At least in some metropolitan areas, contacts with the criminal justice system must be considered normal for some immigrant populations; having no contacts with police in turn must be an exception or rather abnormal. This raises questions about the effects of such overcriminalization on norm acceptance and general preventive functions of criminal law within minorities.

In some German jurisdictions, foreign suspects account for half or more of all suspects (Bundeskriminalamt 1994, p. 104). In Frankfurt in 1993, two-thirds of all suspects were foreigners. This trend is even more pronounced among juveniles and young adults. Almost 75 percent of eighteen-to-twenty-year-old suspects are members of foreign minorities in Frankfurt. This raises the question of how criminal justice agencies devised and established to handle German offenders can function under such conditions.

IV. Biased Law Enforcement and Discrimination in the Justice System

Theoretical approaches to discrimination and biased law enforcement must differentiate explanations for the emergence of ethnic minorities' crime involvement as an eminent social problem and hypotheses concerning decision making in the administrative and criminal justice systems. Explanations of the recognition of foreigners' crime as a social problem fall into several groups. Scapegoating was a commonplace explanation during the 1970s and 1980s; social competition between disadvantaged Germans was also often discussed. Administrative agencies' search for "new" social problems to conquer has been suggested as has the potential function of the social problem of foreigners' crime involvement in stabilizing political power and attracting support within majority groups (Kubink 1993, p. 143).

A. Discrimination through Reporting Behavior

It is possible that crimes by minority groups are more likely than crimes by Germans to be reported to the police. Unfortunately, little evidence is available on the influence of ethnic variables on reporting behavior by the public or by victims (Killias 1989, p. 17).

Studies that included such variables as perceptions of the nationality or race of the offender have generated ambiguous results (Donner 1986; Kubink 1993, p. 56). Some studies that claim evidence of overreporting of ethnic minorities by the public are based on misinterpretation of police data. For example, Donner (1986) and Kubink (1993) drew a sample of cases from police files of juvenile suspects in Berlin. Approximately 20 percent of minority suspects and 28 percent of German suspects were reported by the police and not by victims. From this they concluded that ethnic minorities are subject to more rigorous reporting than are Germans. However, the difference is easily explained by the much heavier involvement of young foreigners in shoplifting and fare dodging. For these types of offenses (which are reported by private police in warehouses and public transportation), the proportions of suspects brought to the attention of police by private complainants are the same for young foreigners and young Germans.

Minority victims of crime, however, seem to be slightly more reluctant to report an offense by an offender of the same national or ethnic background (Pitsela 1986, p. 340). This supports the hypotheses of underreporting of ethnic minorities' crimes, especially since substantial proportions of crimes committed by members of ethnic minorities are within-group crimes, for example, in the case of personal crimes (Sessar 1981). However, ethnic minority offenders seem to run a somewhat higher risk of being reported for shoplifting or offenses at work (Blankenburg 1973; Kaiser and Metzger-Pregizer 1986; Killias 1988).

B. Discrimination within the Justice System

Two dimensions of discrimination within the justice system must be distinguished: a subjective dimension which includes perceptions of discriminatory treatment, and an objective dimension consisting of outcomes of decisions including arrests, rates of nonprosecution, adjudication rates, sentencing, and correctional decision making.

There is some evidence that racist attitudes are present in police forces (Bielefeld 1982; Weschke 1985). Criminal justice staff and police presumably do not differ much from the public at large in terms of attitudes and perceptions (Villmow 1990, p. 242). There is little objective evidence to suggest bias in making arrests or in stop and search activities (Staudt 1983, p. 21), although complaints are quite often heard about police harassment of minority juveniles (Bielefeld 1982).

A small German study on attitudes of German, Turkish, and Italian male juveniles toward police behavior found that German juveniles (matched to minority juveniles on socioeconomic variables) felt much more than the other boys that they and their neighborhoods are intensively controlled by police (Staudt 1983). A somewhat larger proportion of German boys complained about police behavior. A smaller proportion of Turkish juveniles complained about police behavior, but their complaints were based on the view that police discriminated against Turkish juveniles because they were Turkish (Bielefeld and Kreissl 1982, p. 161). This study suggests that differences in perceptions arise from different motives imputed to police activities, rather than from differences in how police control minority and other youths. Corresponding findings are available from other European countries (Albrecht 1993, p. 92).

A recent study of attitudes toward crime and criminal justice shows that minorities are less tolerant of crime and criminal offenders than are Germans. Minority respondents were more supportive of severe penalties and deterrence as a primary aim of sentencing and corrections (Pitsela 1986). A substantial proportion of minority respondents felt that criminal courts restrict police too much in controlling criminals and investigating crime.

1. *Police and Discrimination.* German police do not make arrest decisions. When informed of a criminal event, German police investigate and bring it to the public prosecutor's staff, who decide whether to bring the case to court or whether to initiate pretrial detention. A consensus seems to exist that minority and majority offenders face the same probability of being processed as a criminal suspect, given a certain number of offenses committed. The probability of being suspected of a criminal offense is extremely low for most offenses, and police investigations seem to be guided by characteristics of the offense, especially its seriousness (Steffen 1987). It has been hypothesized that higher rates of suspects among ethnic minorities could be a product of greater hostility of ethnic minority members toward police during encounters (Smith, Visher, and Davidson 1984), but preliminary research based on an experimental design does not support this hypothesis. Ethnic minority suspects appear to be more cooperative than Germans when being questioned (Vrij and Winkel 1991). Research also does not confirm the hypothesis that minority suspects face a higher risk of being charged and indicted with a criminal offense (Kubink 1993, p. 60).

2. *Public Prosecution and Discrimination.* The decisive criteria for bringing suspects to criminal courts are prior record, offense seriousness, and a guilty plea (Blankenburg, Sessar, and Steffen 1978). There is considerable evidence that minority offenders are less often brought to court in Germany (Villmow 1993; Reichertz 1994). It has been argued that dismissals are common because of the petty nature of many criminal acts and because a large proportion of cases involve weak evidence. In effect, the public prosecutor acts as a counterweight against a trend toward overreporting of minority offenders by police. Similar findings exist for rape cases (Steinhilper 1986).

Another explanation for differences in attrition rates is that special problems of proof lead to higher rates of nonprosecution against foreign suspects (Donk 1994, p. 38). The argument starts with an assumption of the structural "dominance" of foreign suspects (Reichertz and Schröer 1993) in interactions with police and public prosecutors (Donk 1994, p. 38) because police interrogations are dependent on hints the suspect gives. This type of interaction is not possible when a translator must serve as a mediator. So far the data are inconclusive. Preliminary

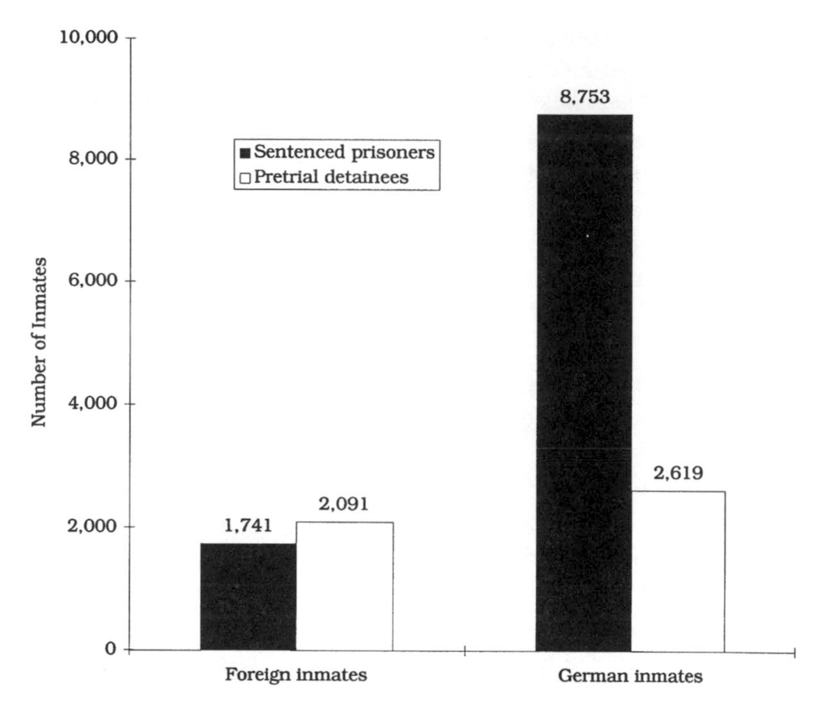

Fig. 19.—Numbers of pretrial detainees and sentenced prisoners, foreign and German, North Rhine–Westphalia (January 31, 1993). Source: Drucksache (1993).

data suggest that translators in some cases function as "deputies" to police officers. This undermines the "structural dominance" arguments because translators may tilt the balance back in favor of the police.

Recent research demonstrates that rates of adjudicated juvenile offenders are similar in the groups of foreign and German juvenile suspects when illegal immigrants, tourists, and asylum seekers are excluded from the analysis (Sutterer and Karger 1993, p. 23). These findings clearly point to consistent prosecution patterns that are not distorted by variables such as race, ethnicity, and citizenship. The finding of consistency in decision making by the public prosecutor is not undermined by a higher rate of dismissals in cases involving tourists, illegal immigrants, and asylum seekers. As these suspects are typically difficult to trace, dismissals can be expected more frequently.

3. *Discrimination and Pretrial Detention.* Foreign suspects face a higher risk of pretrial detention, as figure 19, showing North Rhine–

Westphalia data, demonstrates. While the ratio of sentenced prisoners to pretrial detainees is 3.3 to 1 for German inmates, the ratio for foreign inmates is 0.8 to 1. Elevated rates of pretrial detention for foreign suspects can be expected, however, because German law bases detention decisions on the type and intensity of incentives for absconding. The key factors are the possible severity of the sentence, the nature and intensity of bonds to society, and where the trial will be held. Because foreign suspects are likely to have fewer social bonds to their communities, the conditions of pretrial detention are more likely to be established against them.

Routine decision making in the criminal justice system may account for higher rates of pretrial detention in general. However, regional particulars may account for particularly high pretrial detention rates for certain nationalities.

A study of pretrial detainees in the Frankfurt region during 1992 found that a sharp increase in pretrial detention was due to an increasing number of foreigners being held (Gebauer 1993). Moroccans account for 0.4 percent of the population in the state of Hessen but 15 percent of detainees. The pattern these data show may exist because pretrial detention keeps foreigners in secure facilities to allow for administrative processes relating to deportation. The high proportion of Moroccans serving time in detention centers might also be explained by other processes.

When the research on pretrial detention was being done, Frankfurt police had established a special task force to crack down on Moroccan drug trafficking groups, which in the early 1990s had set up a large drug distribution network in the Frankfurt region (involving mainly cannabis) (Kriminalabteilung Frankfurt a.M. 1992, p. 10; 1993, p. 7). This task force ("Arbeitsgruppe Marokko") traced Moroccan groups over an extended period, monitoring movements and sell and buy operations, and busted the networks when enough evidence was available. The rate of pretrial detention among Moroccan drug suspects was high, resulting in detention of approximately 50 percent of all Moroccan suspects (Kriminalabteilung Frankfurt a.M. 1993, p. 9).

There is evidence that pretrial detention is used as a deterrent to discourage particular offender groups. In 1989, when Senegalese were involved heavily in heroin distribution in Frankfurt, virtually every Senegalese drug suspect was held in pretrial detention (independent of the amount of drugs found on him or her), which led to certain peaks in the number of Senegalese being detained during certain periods (up to 150; see Kriminalabteilung Frankfurt a.M. 1990, p. 41).

4. *Probation and Young Foreign Offenders.* The activities of probation services and juvenile court aides have been investigated. Juvenile court aides are assumed to influence the disposition of juvenile offenders by providing presentence reports on the offender and his or her social, educational, and familial background; different cultural, ethnic, or national backgrounds of offenders could make a difference. Social workers experience special problems when preparing presentence reports on foreign juveniles, which could have negative (or discriminatory) effects on the disposition. Among these are problems of understanding, lack of knowledge about juvenile offenders' cultural backgrounds and culturally patterned reactions by parents. This can lead to presentence reports that differ significantly from those prepared for majority youth (Savelsberg 1982). This finding is especially important because foreign youths in some metropolitan areas constitute a majority of suspects processed through the juvenile justice system. Foreign youths entering Germany illegally or as tourists create particular problems. Some of these youth are involved in criminal networks involved in professional theft (Romanian, Polish, Yugoslavian, South American youth) and drug trafficking (South American, Lebanese, Algerian, Moroccan, and Turkish youth) (Johne 1995, p. 41). Professional social work activities are limited to attempts to assure safe return to home countries (Johne 1995), as illegal foreign youth are not entitled to benefit from services provided by the law on Support for Children and Juveniles (§ 6 Kinder- und Jugendhilfegesetz; see Huber 1995, p. 45).

5. *Foreign Offenders and Sentencing.* Small effects of discrimination on sentencing have been found. Minority defendants run a somewhat higher risk to receive prison or custodial sentences and are somewhat less likely to receive suspended sentences or probation (Steinhilper 1986). In general, however, ethnic and minority variables add only very modestly to explanations of sentencing variation (Greger 1987; Albrecht 1994*b*). This is true for adult criminal sentencing and juvenile dispositions (Albrecht and Pfeiffer 1979; Oppermann 1987; Geissler and Marissen 1990, p. 683). A slight difference in juvenile imprisonment between young German offenders and young foreigners (2.4 percent vs. 3.4 percent of all offenders adjudicated and sentenced) found by Geissler and Marissen (1990) results mostly from sentences for drug trafficking. After controlling for this offense, the difference disappears.

Differences in dispositions are virtually nonexistent for violent and sexual offenses; similar results have been obtained by Oppermann (1987). As ethnicity is a diffuse status variable, its influence on sentencing can be expected to be slight or nonexistent in cases where a consistent set of offense and offender related characteristics (e.g., seriousness of the offense, prior record), well-established sentencing tariffs (petty cases), or administrative convenience indicate dispositional strategies (Unnever and Hembroff 1988). Therefore, only an uncommon set of characteristics would be expected to produce effects of ethnicity or nationality on sentencing. It has been hypothesized that the relatively small effects of ethnic variables on sentencing outcomes might be because serious personal crimes committed by minority offenders generally involve minority victims, too, and that effects might be larger for crimes involving minority offenders and majority victims. This question has not as yet been adequately addressed.

Superior courts have considered whether ethnicity and status as a foreigner may legitimately be used to justify harsher penalties for minority offenders. Criminal courts sometimes suggest that such status variables are indicators of needs for more severe punishment. The Supreme Court has stressed that these status variables cannot justify increases in sentence severity as the constitution precludes differential treatment based on citizenship or ethnicity (Bundesgerichtshof [BGH] Beschluss [Supreme Court decision], November 29, 1990, 1 Strafrecht [criminal law] 618/90). The Supreme Court regularly sets aside verdicts that seem to be influenced by the opinion that asylum seekers or other foreigners have special obligations to comply with the laws of the country providing shelter (Bundesgerichtshof 1987, p. 20; Bundesgerichtshof 1991, p. 557; BGH Beschluss, January 28, 1992, 4 Strafrecht [criminal law] 99/92; Oberlandesgericht Bremen 1994, p. 130).

The argument has been made that German sentences should match the sanctions in countries from which foreign offenders come (Schroeder 1983; Grundmann 1985). The argument is that minority offenders might consider sentencing in Germany as lenient because of harsher sentencing strategies in their home country and thereby see Germany as a less dangerous place in which to commit crimes (Nestler-Tremel 1986). Although such considerations are not supported in criminal court practice, the Supreme Court has accepted that a need for deterrence may be established in cases of sharp increases in violent acts associated with interethnic or national conflicts (BGH Beschluss, November 29, 1990, 1 Strafrecht [criminal law] 618/90) or if drug traffickers relocate their business because of milder penalties meted out in Germany (BGH 1982, p. 112; Wolfslast 1982).

Superior courts have ruled also that ethnicity or status as a foreigner may be a legitimate reason to mitigate punishment as some minority offenders might be especially vulnerable to criminal penalties (Bundesgerichtshof 1992, p. 106; other legal problems related to ethnicity involve differences in values and social norms raised in the defense of ignorance of the law as to the prohibited nature and characteristics establishing first-degree murder; see, e.g., BGH 1994, p. 430). The burden of criminal penalties on some foreign offenders may be different from Germans' because of further formal and informal consequences criminal convictions are likely to engender.

Claims of discriminatory treatment of foreign victims of crime (especially when victimized by majority members) were heard after the first criminal trials for bias-motivated violence against foreigners. For example, the question has been considered whether an intent to commit murder must be established in the case of juvenile or young adult arsonists who preyed on homes of refugees or asylum seekers (BGH 1994, p. 654; Frommel 1994) and whether an intent to commit murder was established in the case of an attack of a home for refugees by means of Molotov cocktails.

Any assessment of discrimination in prosecution and sentencing must take overall trends in sanctions into account. There has in recent decades been a considerable reduction of intensity of sanctions and especially a significant reduction in the use of imprisonment. With this general reduction in sentencing severity has come a dramatic reduction in the variation of punishment. This can be seen by looking at the distribution of criminal penalties in the Federal Republic of Germany. In Germany in the 1990s, only 2 percent of all criminal sentences exceed two year's imprisonment. Within the remaining variation, offense seriousness is decisive for the choice between tariffs that have been developed for both petty and more serious crimes (Albrecht 1994*b*). Discrimination, should it occur, may not be traceable through quantitative approaches because of the minor differences between sentences now imposed.

Another trend in criminal justice that undermines hypotheses about discriminatory treatment concerns simplification and streamlining of criminal procedures. The first important change occurred very early in the 1960s when section 153 of the German Procedural Code was introduced providing that the public prosecutor may dismiss a case if the guilt of the suspect is slight. In 1975, the discretionary powers of the public prosecutor were extended considerably. Section 153a of the German Procedural Code went into force and empowered the public prosecutor to dismiss cases of minor guilt (felonies excluded) if the offender complied with certain conditions determined by the public prosecutor. A simplified procedure may be initiated which consists only of written proceedings. If the public prosecutor concludes that the case is not complicated in terms of proving guilt and that a fine is a sufficient punishment, a penal order may be suggested to the judge in which, besides the indictment, the public prosecutor proposes a fine (according to the day-fine system). If the court agrees, a penal order is mailed to the suspect, who may appeal it within two weeks. If an appeal is filed, ordinary proceedings take place.

Thirty percent of ordinary crimes which could be brought to the court (approximately 1.3 million cases per year) are dismissed (half by way of fulfillment of conditions imposed by the public prosecutor), another 40 percent are dealt with in simplified procedures, and the final 30 percent receive a full trial. These data demonstrate that most offenders do not go through a full-blown criminal procedure but are dealt by a simplified procedure that might be called "administrative dispositions."

Reunification brought with it the need to establish the rule of law in eastern Germany. In March 1993, after a short but hot debate, new laws took effect to address economic needs associated with reunification (Gesetz zur Entlastung der Rechtspflege [Law on reducing the burden of the justice system], January 11, 1993, Bundesgesetzblatt [Federal Law Reporter] I, p. 50; Böttcher and Mayer 1993). The goal was to streamline procedures throughout the country to reduce costs. Two features are of particular interest. First, the power of public prosecutors to dismiss cases was extended dramatically. Now, the public prosecutor may dismiss a case if the offender's guilt does not require a criminal penalty. Second, the procedural option of simplified procedures was greatly expanded. The prosecutor may propose in a simplified procedure a suspended sentence of imprisonment of up to one year if the offender had counsel during the procedure. As only 6 percent of all sentences ordered by German courts involve prison sentences more than one year, in theory a full trial could be restricted to a small fraction of criminal cases.

C. *Immigration Authorities and the Foreign Offender*

A foreign offender who has been convicted and sentenced may be expelled and deported (Otte 1994). The recently amended immigration law (Ausländergesetz) differentiates among the different groups of foreigners who have been mentioned above (EC, non-EC countries, etc.). The German constitution and the European Convention on Human Rights occasion further differentiation (Otte 1994, p. 73; see also Gusy 1993). Prison sentences are among the most important legal grounds justifying or requiring deportation. Decision making within those administrative bodies implementing immigration laws is of paramount importance when an immigrant minority offender is an "alien." Deportation and expulsion statutes grant large discretionary powers; research has demonstrated large variations in the criteria adopted in administrative decision making and in decision outcomes (Otte 1994, p. 68; with a summary of the debate on whether a sentence of juvenile imprisonment can justify deportation). There has been little research on the role of immigration authorities reacting to crimes by immigrants, despite the links between criminal justice and immigration authorities in framing policies toward immigrant groups. Criminal justice objectives are relevant to immigration policies because it is widely accepted that general deterrence is a legitimate aim of deportation.

Data from Baden-Württemberg show that 2–3 percent of foreign minority offenders found guilty and sentenced in the early 1990s (see fig. 20) were deported, with an upward trend since 1992. Detailed information is available on decisions made by immigration authorities for foreign offenders released from youth correctional facilities in Baden-Württemberg. Of those released during 1993, 25 percent were deported immediately, another 25 percent were ordered to leave German territory, and one-fifth were cautioned by immigration authorities. The administrative procedure was not yet finished for 15 percent and no administrative action was taken for the last 15 percent.

D. *The Correctional System and Foreign Prisoners*

There has been little research on minority offenders in adult and juvenile corrections. Pragmatic approaches have been developed for integration of minority juvenile offenders into the correctional system. For example, multiethnic social training courses have been developed and implemented in some jurisdictions (Institut für Sozialarbeit und Sozialpädagogik 1992). The capacity, however, of the prison system to cope with the ethnic diversity of foreign prisoners seems limited.

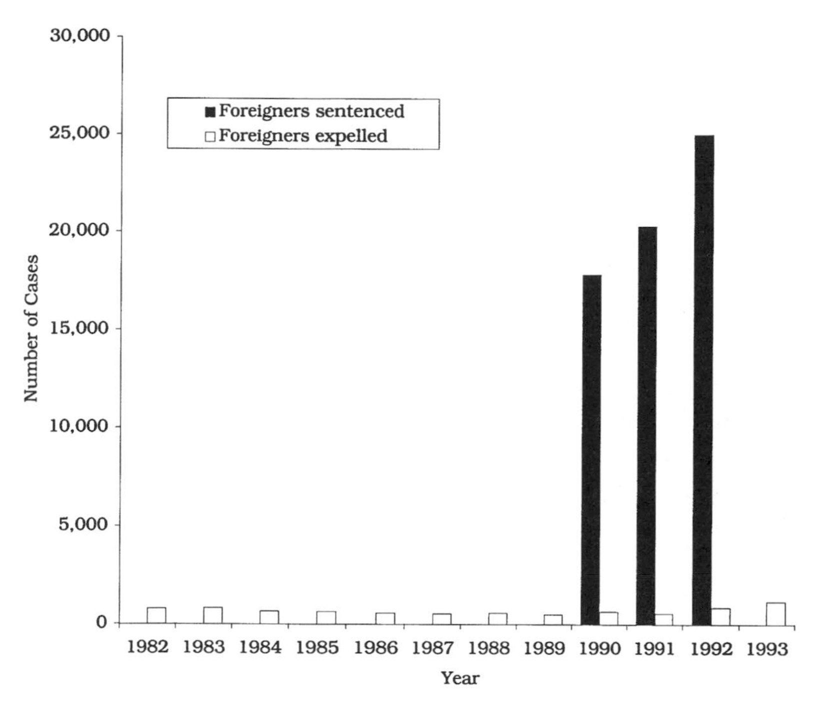

FIG. 20.—Foreign offenders sentenced and expelled, Baden-Württemberg, 1982–93. Note: Expelled because of criminal offenses. Sources: Ministry of the Interior, Baden-Württemberg, unpublished data; Statistisches Landesamt (1994).

Moreover, the character of a prison regime for foreign prisoners who are likely to be expelled after completing their sentences must be different from regimes for other prisoners. The goals of integration and provision of support and programs within the prison to foster reintegration into German society are not appropriate policies and investments for prisoners who will be deported into a foreign environment with which the prison system has no links (Müller-Dietz 1993, p. 26).

Treatment of immigrant offenders in the correctional system has received comparatively little attention. The proportion of immigrant prisoners rose considerably in the last decade and amounts to a fourth of the prison population (including pretrial detainees and sentenced prisoners, youth and adult prisoners). There are significant differences in imprisonment rates among foreign minorities. Substantial differences also exist in subcategories of imprisonment. The most striking is in pretrial detention. As figure 21 shows, the number of foreigners detained in North Rhine–Westphalia before trial constitutes nearly half

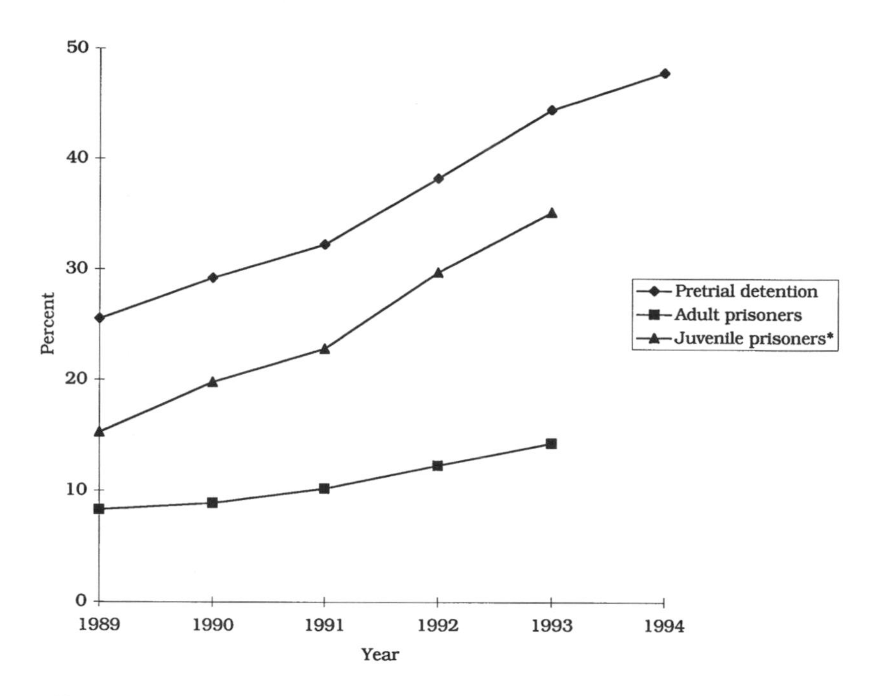

FIG. 21.—Foreign percentages, among pretrial detainees, sentenced adults, sentenced juveniles, North Rhine–Westphalia, 1989–94. *Sentenced juveniles = up to the age of 21. Source: Drucksache (1993).

of the pretrial detention population. This patterns exists in other German states; for example, in Hessen 69 percent of pretrial detainees are of foreign origin. In juvenile pretrial detention, the proportion of foreigners is even more pronounced. Foreign youth made up 57 percent in Hessian youth correctional facilities in 1994 (Hessian Ministry of Justice, unpublished prison data as of March 31, 1994). In Niedersachsen and Berlin, the proportion of foreign pretrial detainees rose to approximately two-thirds in 1992 (Schütze 1993; Abgeordnetenhaus Berlin 1993). There was also a sharp increase in the number of foreigners serving sentences of youth imprisonment, which corresponds with the rising rate of foreign juveniles and young adults in police statistics.

As figure 21 shows, the proportion of sentenced foreigners in the adult system has risen, approaching 15 percent of adult sentenced prisoners in North Rhine–Westphalia; in Hessen, 30 percent of sentenced prisoners are foreigners.

Detention of foreigners awaiting deportation has increased consid-

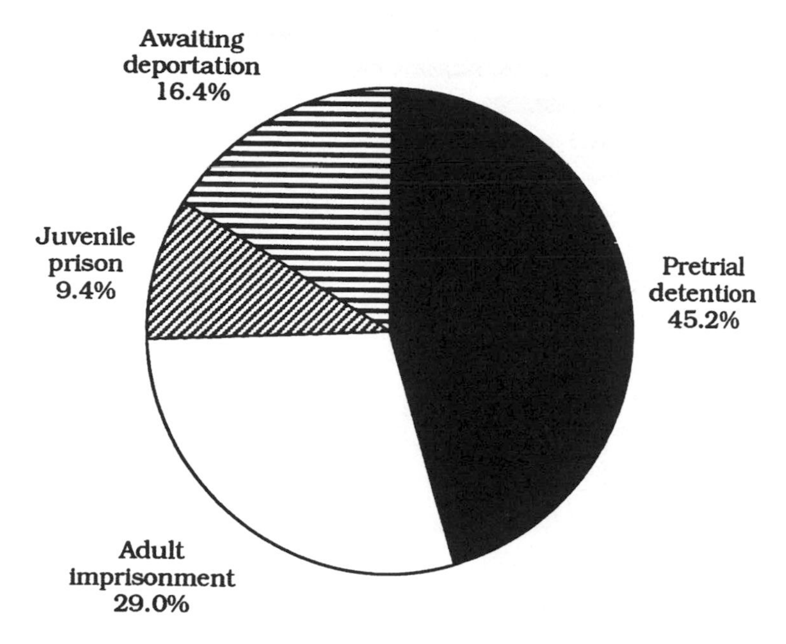

FIG. 22.—Foreign prisoners, by nature of confinement, North Rhine–Westphalia (January 31, 1994). N = 5,689. Source: Ministry of Justice, unpublished prison data.

erably. Figure 22 shows that every sixth foreigner in prisons in North Rhine–Westphalia on January 31, 1994, was awaiting deportation and was not serving time because of criminal offending.

Data from North Rhine–Westphalia and other states allow calculation of prisoner ratios for foreign minorities. Figures 23 and 24 demonstrate dramatic variation in rates of imprisonment per 100,000 same-group population that correspond with variations in participation in migration, illegal immigration, and different types of crimes. Regional particulars are evident in figure 24, with consistent imprisonment rates evident only for large resident foreign populations, for example, Greeks and Turks.

Figure 25 shows the ratio of arrests to imprisonment in 1993 for various nationality groups. For most groups, there are twelve to sixteen people arrested for each person imprisoned. Exceptions are British, Greeks, Yugoslavians, Polish, and Romanians, for whom larger numbers of trivial offenses, or in the case of Britons, diversion to another jurisdiction, explain the difference.

Imprisonment trends show that rates of imprisonment are decreas-

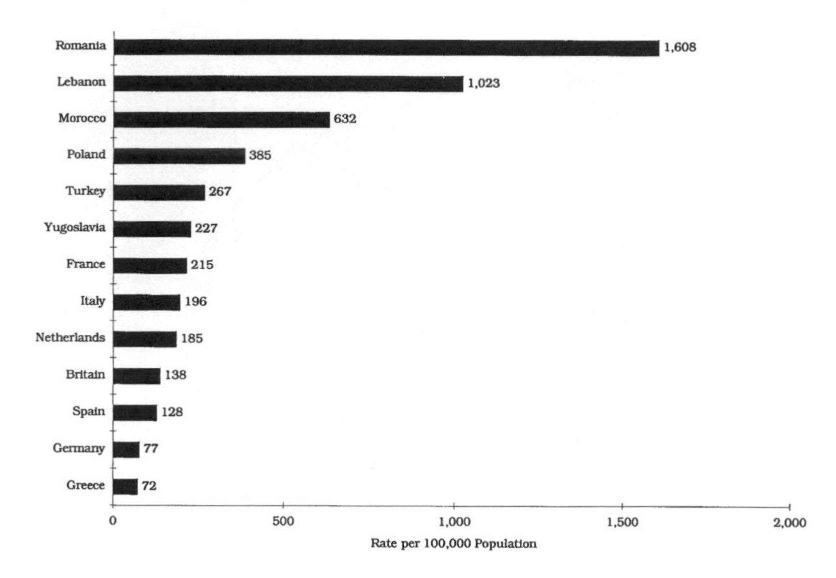

FIG. 23.—Prisoners per 100,000 population, various groups, North Rhine–Westphalia, 1993. Source: Ministry of Justice, unpublished prison data.

ing for German offenders, a well-established phenomenon that originated at the end of the sixties. The increase in the number of prisoners at large is solely due to increased numbers of foreign minorities. This can be demonstrated by Hessian prison statistics in figure 26.

Drug offenders are a major reason for the sharp increase in foreign offenders since the late 1980s. Prison data from Hamburg (fig. 27) show that drug offenses substantially account for the increase in foreign prisoners during the 1980s and 1990s. Property offenses add also considerably to imprisonment rates.

Criminological research on immigrant populations and their treatment in the correctional system is virtually nonexistent. A study of some characteristics of prison regimes revealed that some minorities experience a different kind of prison regime from that experienced by German inmates (fig. 28). Foreign prisoners participate less in furlough programs and prison leave programs (Albrecht 1989*a;* Janetzky 1993, p. 114).

Differential treatment emerges among foreign prisoners. Extreme isolation can be observed in a group of South American prisoners, who because of drug trafficking (acting as couriers) received long prison sentences. They have no substantial group of countrymen outside the prison.

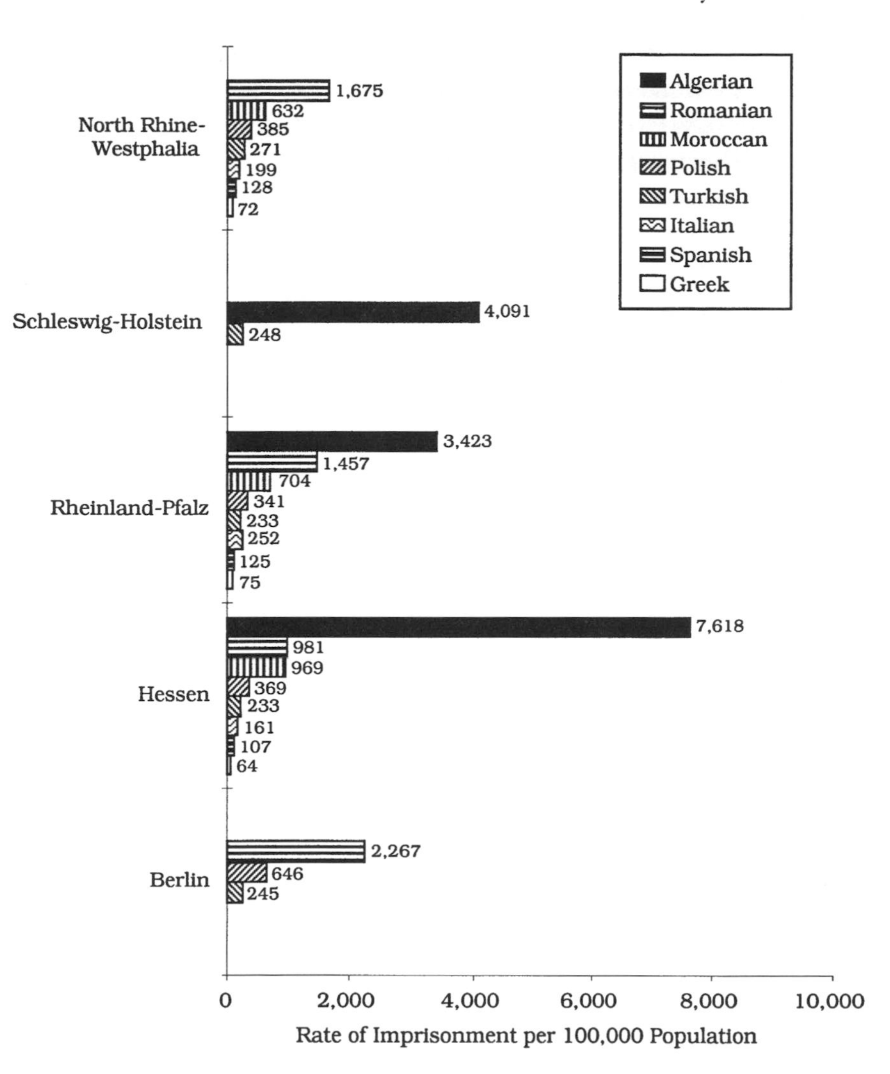

FIG. 24.—Prisoners per 100,000 population, various groups in five German jurisdictions. Source: Ministries of Justice (Hessen, North Rhine–Westphalia, Schleswig-Holstein, Berlin, Rheinland-Pfalz), unpublished data.

Foreign offenders pose particular problems within prisons, including equal treatment in terms of access to television, newspapers, and books (Janetzky 1993, p. 112; Schütze 1993). Reports on interethnic and intraethnic conflicts between various groups (e.g., from former Yugoslavia or from Turkey) expose a need for reliable information on such

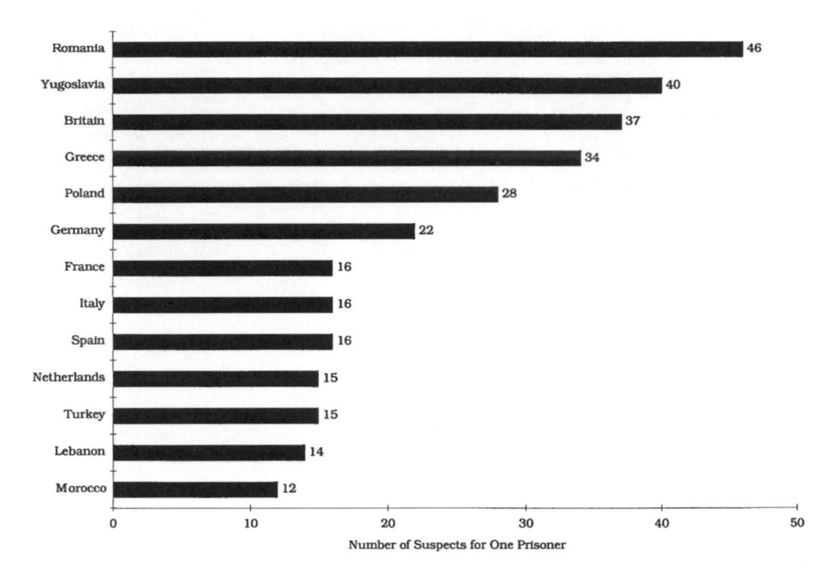

FIG. 25.—Ratios of suspects to prisoners in North Rhine–Westphalia, selected groups, 1993. Sources: Landeskriminalamt Düsseldorf (1994); Ministry of Justice, unpublished prison data.

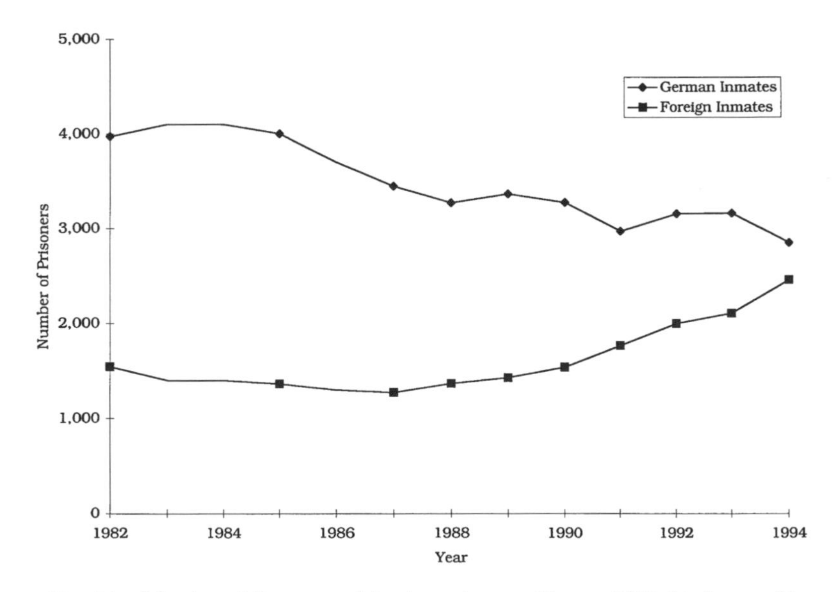

FIG. 26.—Number of German and foreign prisoners, Hessen, 1982–94. Source: Hessian Ministry of Justice (1994).

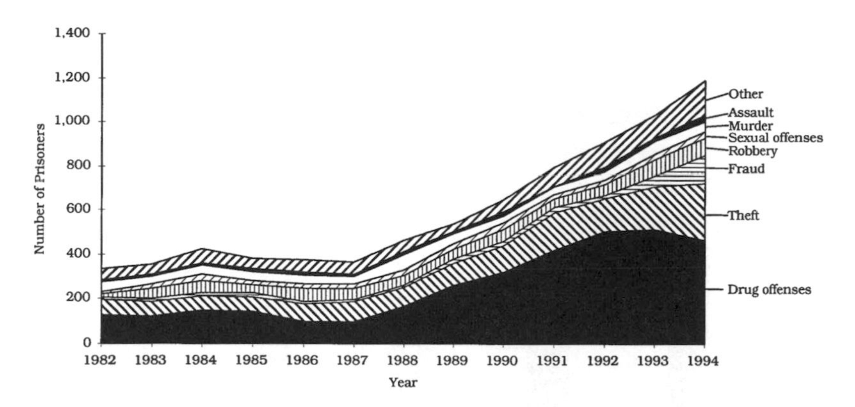

FIG. 27.—Foreign prisoners and conviction offenses, Hamburg, 1982–94 (February 15). Source: Ministry of Justice, Hamburg, unpublished prison data, July 12, 1994.

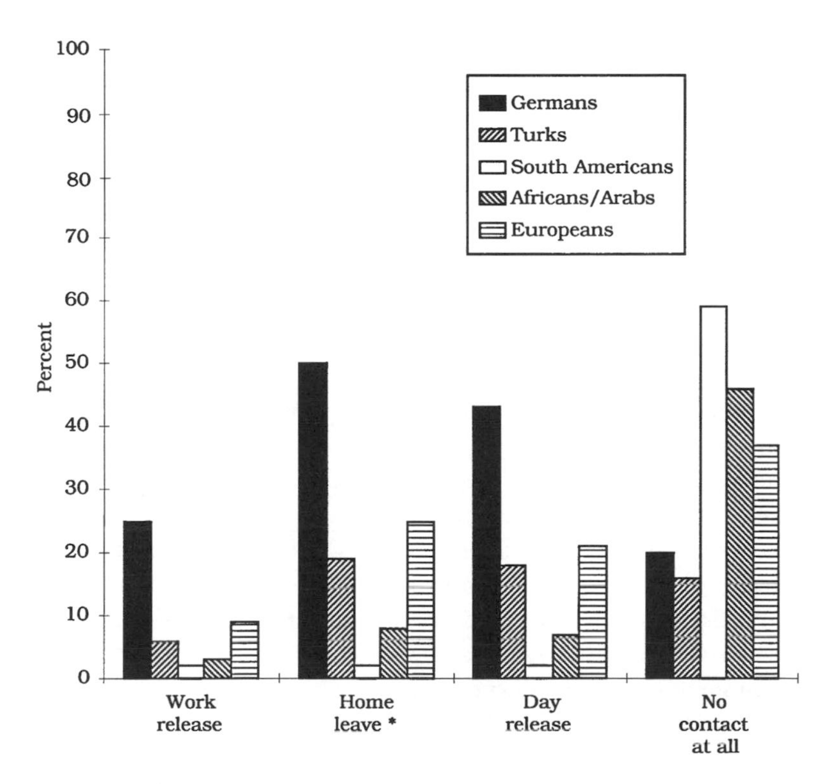

FIG. 28.—Prisoners' contact with the outside world, by group, in percent. *Home leave = furlough with overnight absence. Source: Albrecht (1989*a*).

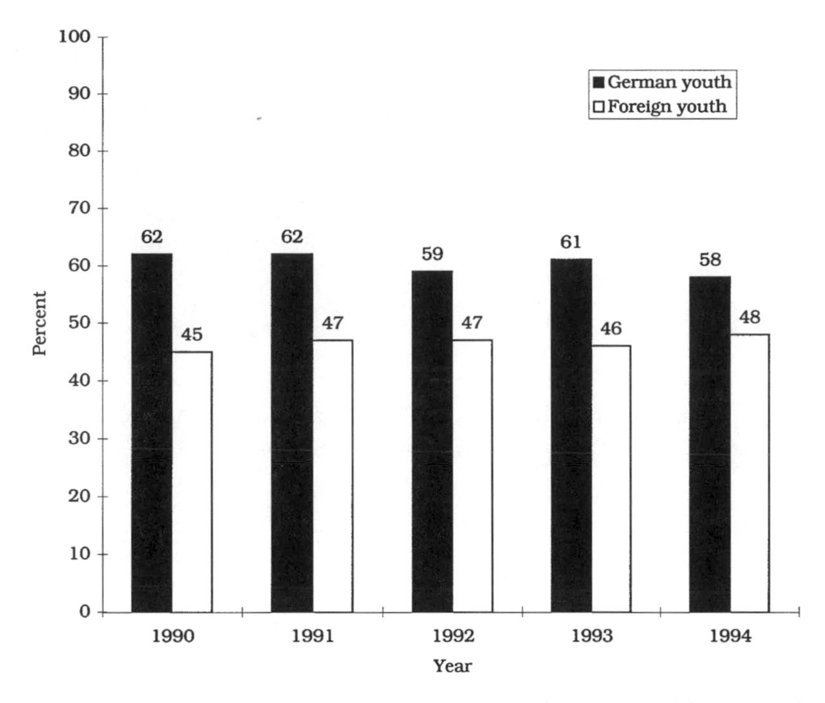

FIG. 29.—Mean percentage of original sentence served, German and foreign youth, Baden-Württemberg Youth Correctional System, 1990–94. Source: Justizvollzugsanstalt Adelsheim (1995).

conflicts if risks of violence within prison facilities are to be reduced (Janetzky 1993, p. 116).

Foreign nationals sentenced to imprisonment can be released on parole after serving half of the prison sentence under section 456a of the German Procedural Code if deportation takes place immediately after release. Otherwise, parole may be granted after two-thirds of the prison term has been served. Drug couriers are usually paroled and deported to their home countries three to four months before completing two-thirds of their prison sentences (Kraushaar 1992). There has been reluctance by parole authorities to reduce prison sentences to half, although some state governments have recently expressed interest in cutting down the time foreign offenders spend in prison to save money. This may explain why average times served by young German and young foreign offenders differ significantly. Information from Baden-Württemberg (see fig. 29) reveals that young foreign inmates serve less than half of the original prison sentence while German inmates serve approximately 60 percent.

V. Summary and Conclusions

Germany has become a more heterogeneous country, and that trend will continue. German research on ethnic disparities in crime and system processing is likely to increase in the 1990s. This section summarizes major findings of research to date, identifies major policy implications, and suggests promising steps for the future.

A. Summary of Results

1. German research on involvement of minorities in crime and criminal justice has emphasized criminology. Data for criminological research on ethnic and foreign minorities derive mostly from the police and to a lesser extent other justice information systems. Survey research has been neglected.

2. Research has also been limited conceptually. Research has been based almost exclusively on the overbroad category "foreign national," which does not accord with more useful concepts such as visible, ethnic, or national minority.

3. Research on foreign minorities, crime, and justice is affected by political and ideological potential for conflicts that are inherent to the topic.

4. When proper controls are introduced into research designs and data analyses, offending is not more widespread among resident ethnic and foreign minorities (as distinguished from nonresidents such as tourists, illegal immigrants, and asylum seekers) than it is among comparable national groups.

5. Ethnic and foreign minorities do not create exceptional crime problems or pose special dangers for safety in society. Crime among ethnic minorities reflects social and economic marginalization and structural problems in societies. In general, ethnic segmentation in German society takes place with foreign minorities predominantly placed in lower segments, that is, the working class.

6. Besides resident foreign minorities, many with a history as "guest workers," other ethnic and foreign groups have to be distinguished. Traditional migrating groups like "gypsies," which have experienced an extended history of discrimination and pogroms, are in a unique position; "deviant" lifestyles expose them to conflicts and create a setting in which petty theft and immigration offenses are relatively com-

mon. Another distinct group of minority offenders are short-term migrants involved mainly with petty theft. Black market participation in Germany creates another group of foreign or ethnic offenders who are involved in organizing importation and supply of illicit drugs or vices.

7. Explanations of crime among ethnic minorities should rely on the same kinds of variables that are used to explain crime generally. There is no evidence that—in themselves—variables referring to ethnicity or nationality are useful and meaningful in etiological research.

8. A sharp distinction must be made between resident minority populations and migrating groups or black market participants. The last two categories should not be analyzed from a minority perspective in relation to migration (and push-and-pull factors affecting migration and offending patterns) or economic considerations. Police and judicial information systems do not provide adequate data to study these phenomena.

9. There is little evidence of biased treatment at the front end of the criminal process even though differential treatment can be observed in prison regimes. A tentative explanation might be that routinized decision making and powerful trends toward simplification and streamlining of criminal justice have drastically reduced the number of variables considered in sentencing.

10. Discriminatory treatment occurs also in use of offensive language or harassing behavior that may not affect the actual outcomes but nevertheless may be destructive of relations between minorities and justice agencies.

11. Imprisonment rates among foreign minorities have increased dramatically in the last decade. Drug policies are a major explanation.

12. For many members of foreign minorities in Germany, criminal justice system encounters include a risk of expulsion and deportation. This type of reaction should be used only in cases of the most serious crimes or chronic offending.

B. Policy Implications

1. Basic remedies for problems of ethnic minorities and criminal justice can be derived from theories outlined earlier. This means that opportunities to overcome deprivation and to develop bonds to conventional society must be provided. As many Western societies have not been successful at doing that for long-term resident marginal groups, which grew considerably in size in recent years, the chances that the

structural conditions shaping minority offending will soon be remedied are perhaps not promising.

2. Better relations between minorities and police and justice agencies should be promoted by means of training and education programs. However, it should be noted that neither police nor other justice personnel can be made responsible for race relations problems or ethnic group relations in general. Training of criminal justice professionals alone cannot resolve these pervasive social problems.

3. The percentages of foreigners in groups of suspects, defendants, and prisoners in metropolitan areas are so large today that police, justice, and prison staff regularly encounter problems different from those usually presented by the traditional German clientele. The criminal justice system must adjust.

4. Proposals have been made to expand recruitment of police and other justice staff from Turkish or other minorities. Such policies are justified on the ground of providing equal employment opportunities but are unlikely to overcome deeper problems in relations between majority society and minority groups.

C. Future Research

1. Research on victimization among ethnic minorities should be expanded. Victimization rates are higher in these groups, and the effects of victimization are reinforced by marginal positions that hinder adequate access to relevant institutions. Trafficking in women and children presents special challenges.

2. Victimization research should address both intraethnic and interethnic victimization. Interethnic victimization and offending (including hate violence) should be given priority.

3. Attention should be paid to participation of ethnic minorities in black markets, traditional crime, and the vice industry. Ethnographic research is needed to study the mechanisms that link particular minorities to particular black markets or vice industries. Research should investigate integration processes that link national black markets and subcultures in eastern and western Europe.

4. Research on foreign minorities and criminal justice in Germany is limited and piecemeal. Systematic and continuing data collection is needed to identify points in the criminal justice process at which minority-related problems occur.

5. Research should be carried out on why majorities in societies are interested in the crime-proneness issue and why belief patterns associ-

ating "foreigners" and ethnic differences with danger and social unrest are so powerful.

6. Independent of issues of crime involvement by foreign minorities and discrimination against them, the finding that foreigners are involved in substantial proportions of cases on all levels of the criminal justice system reveals a need to study the general performance of justice and correctional agencies under such conditions.

REFERENCES

Abgeordnetenhaus Berlin (Parliament of the state of Berlin). 1993. Drucksache (printed matters) 11/5139. February 26.

Ahlf, Ernst-Heinrich. 1993. "Ausländerkriminalität in der Bundesrepublik Deutschland nach Öffnung der Grenzen." *Zeitschrift für Ausländerrecht*, no. 3:132–38.

Albrecht, Günther. 1988. "Neue Ergebnisse zum Dunkelfeld der Jugenddelinquenz: Selbstberichtete Delinquenz von Jugendlichen in zwei westdeutschen Grossstädten." In *Kriminologische Forschung in den 80er Jahren. Projektberichte aus der Bundesrepublik Deutschland*, edited by Günther Kaiser. Freiburg: Beck Verlag.

Albrecht, Hans-Jörg. 1987. "Foreign Minorities and the Criminal Justice System in the Federal Republic of Germany." *Howard Journal of Criminal Justice* 26:272–88.

———. 1988. "Ausländerkriminalität." In *Fälle zum Wahlfach Kriminologie, Jugendstrafrecht, Strafvollzug*, 2d ed., edited by Heike Jung. München: Beck Verlag.

———. 1989*a*. "Ethnic Minorities, Crime and Public Policy." In *Crime and Criminal Policy in Europe*, edited by Roger Hood. Oxford: Oxford University, Center for Criminological Research.

———. 1989*b*. "Comparative Research on Crime and Delinquency—the Role and Relevance of National Penal Codes and Criminal Justice Systems." In *Cross-National Research in Self-Reported Crime and Delinquency*, edited by Malcolm W. Klein. Dordrecht, Boston, and London: Kluwer.

———. 1993. "Ethnic Minorities: Crime and Criminal Justice in Europe." In *Crime in Europe*, edited by Francis Heidensohn and Michael Farrell. London and New York: Routledge.

———. 1994*a*. *Kinderhandel—Eine Untersuchung zum (gewerblichen) Handel mit Kindern*. Bonn: Bundesjustizministerium.

———. 1994*b*. *Strafzumessung bei schwerer Kriminalität*. Berlin: Duncker & Humblot.

Albrecht, Hans-Jörg, and Harald Arnold. 1991. "Research on Victimization and Related Topics in the Federal Republic of Germany." In *Victims and*

Criminal Justice, edited by Günther Kaiser. Freiburg: Max-Planck Institut für Ausländisches und Internationales Strafrecht.

Albrecht, Hans-Jörg, and Raymond Teske. 1992. "Prosecution and Sentencing Patterns in the Federal Republic of Germany." *International Criminal Justice Review* 2:76–104.

Albrecht, Peter-Alexis, and Christian Pfeiffer. 1979. *Die Kriminalisierung junger Ausländer: Befunde und Reaktionen Sozialer Kontrollinstanzen.* München: Juventa.

Arbeitsgruppe "Strafrechtliche Rechtstatsachenforschung und Empirische Kriminologie." 1995. *Opfererfahrungen, Kriminalitätsfurcht und Vorstellungen zur Prävention von Kriminalität.* Konstanz: Universität Konstanz, Institut für Rechtstatsachenforschung.

Aronowitz, Alexis A. 1989. *Assimilation, Acculturation, and Juvenile Delinqency among Second Generation Turkish Youth in Berlin, West Germany.* Albany: State University of New York Press.

Bach, Rolf P. 1986. *Gekaufte Kinder: Babyhandel mit der Dritten Welt.* Hamburg: Rowohlt Verlag.

———. 1991. "Vom Kindeswohl zum Kindermarkt: Ausmass, Methoden und Ursachen des Handelns mit Adoptivkindern aus der Dritten Welt." In *Die letzte Chance? Adoptionen aus der 3. Welt*, edited by Bernd S. Wacker. Hamburg: Rowohlt Verlag.

Bade, Klaus. 1994. *Ausländer, Aussiedler, Asyl: Eine Bestandsaufnahme.* München: Beck.

Bärtling, Thomas. 1982. "Schwangerschaftskonflikt und Schwangerschaftsabbruch in Ausländischen Arbeitnehmerfamilien." In *Die ungewollte Schwangerschaft*, edited by Herwig Poettgen. Köln: Deutscher Ärzte-Verlag.

Berbüsse, Volker. 1992. "Das Bild 'der Zigeuner' in Deutschsprachigen Lehrbüchern seit 1949." In *Jahrbuch für Antisemitismusforschung 1*, edited by Wolfgang Benz. Frankfurt and New York: Campus.

Bielefeld, Uli. 1982. *Junge Ausländer im Konflikt: Lebenssituationen und Überlebensformen.* München: Juventa.

Bielefeld, Uli, and Reinhard Kreissl. 1982. *Junge Ausländer im Konflikt: Lebenssituationen und Überlebensformen.* München: Juventa Verlag.

Blankenburg, Erhard. 1973. "Die Selektivität Strafrechtlicher Sanktionierung." In *Teilnehmende Beobachtung abweichenden Verhaltens*, edited by Jürgen Friedrichs. Stuttgart: Enke.

Blankenburg, Erhard, Klaus Sessar, and Wiebke Steffen. 1978. *Die Staatsanwaltschaft im Prozess Strafrechtlicher Sozialkontrolle.* Berlin: Duncker & Humblot.

Bliesener, Thomas. 1992. "Psychologische Hintergründe der Gewalt gegen Ausländer." In *Ausländer im Jugendstrafrecht: Neue Dimensionen*, edited by DVJJ-Regionalgruppe Nordbayern. Erlangen: Deutsche Vereinigung für Jugendgerichte und Jugendgerichtshilfen.

Boers, Klaus. 1993*a*. "Kriminalitätsfurcht." *Monatsschrift für Kriminologie und Strafrechtsreform* 76:65–82.

———, ed. 1993*b*. "Kriminalitätseinstellungen in den neuen Bundesländern."

In *Sozialer Umbruch und Kriminalität in Deutschland, Mittel- und Osteuropa.* Bonn: Forum Verlag.

Boers, Klaus, Uwe Ewald, Hans-Jürgen Kerner, Erwin Lautsch, and Klaus Sessar, eds. 1994. *Sozialer Umbruch und Kriminalität—Ergebnisse einer Kriminalitätsbefragung in den neuen Bundesländern.* Bonn: Forum Verlag.

Boers, Klaus, Hans-Juergen Kerner, and Peter Kurz. 1995. *Pressemitteilung. Rückgang der Kriminalitätsfurcht.* Tübingen: Universität Tübingen.

Boge, Heinrich. 1989. "Einflüsse nichtdeutscher Straftäter auf die organisierte Kriminalität." In *Ausländerkriminalität in der Bundesrepublik Deutschland,* edited by Bundeskriminalamt. Wiesbaden: Bundeskriminalamt.

Böttcher, Reinhard, and Elmar Mayer. 1993. "Änderungen des Strafverfahrensrechts durch das Entlastungsgesetz." *Neue Zeitschrift für Strafrecht* 13:153–58.

Bovenkerk, Frank. 1993. "Crime and the Multi-ethnic Society: A View from Europe." *Crime, Law and Social Change* 19:271–80.

Brock, Ditmar. 1993. "Wiederkehr der Klassen? Über Mechanismen der Integration und Ausgrenzung in Entwickelten Industriegesellschaften." *Soziale Welt* 44:177–98.

Brockhaus, Gudrun. 1994. "Fremdenfeindliche Gewalt und die Sentimentalität Moralischer Appelle." *Kriminologisches Journal* 26:2–10.

Buiks, Petrus E. J. 1983. *Surinaamse Jongeren op de Kruiskade, Oberleben in een Etnische Randgroep.* Deventer: van Loghum Slaterus.

Bundesgerichtshof. 1982. *Neue Zeitschrift für Strafrecht,* p. 112.

———. 1987. *Strafverteidiger,* p. 20.

———. 1991. *Strafverteidiger,* p. 557.

Bundeskriminalamt. 1991. *Lagebild Organisierte Kriminalität: Bundesrepublik Deutschland.* Wiesbaden: Bundeskriminalamt.

———. 1992. *Lagebild Organisierte Kriminalität: Bundesrepublik Deutschland.* Wiesbaden: Bundeskriminalamt.

———. 1993. *Polizeiliche Kriminalstatistik 1992.* Wiesbaden: Bundeskriminalamt.

———. 1994. *Polizeiliche Kriminalstatistik 1993.* Wiesbaden: Bundeskriminalamt.

———. 1995. *Polizeiliche Kriminalstatistik 1994.* Wiesbaden: Bundeskriminalamt.

Bundesministerium des Innern. 1993. *Informationen des Bundesministers des Innern: Innere Sicherheit.* Bonn: Bundesministerium des Innern.

Delgado, Manuel-Jesus. 1972. *Die Gastarbeiter in der Presse: Eine inhaltsanalytische Untersuchung.* Opladen: Leske Verlag.

Donk, Ute. 1994. "Der Dolmetscher als Hilfspolizist—Zwischenergebnis einer Feldstudi." *Zeitschrift für Rechtssoziologie* 15:37–57.

Donner, Olaf. 1986. "Junge Ausländer im polizeilichen Ermittlungsverfahren." *Recht der Jugend und des Bildungswesens* 34:128–36.

European Parliament. 1993. Initiative against "Racism in Europe and the Dangers of Right Wing Extremism." *Europäische Grundrechtezeitschrift* 12:322–24.

Feuerhelm, Wolfgang. 1988. "Die fortgesetzte 'Bekämpfung des Landfahrerunwesens.' " *Monatsschrift für Kriminologie und Strafrechtsreform* 71:299–314.

Fijnaut, Cyrille. 1994. *Prostitutie, Vrouwenhandel en (vermeende) Politiecorruptie in Antwerpen.* Amersfoort: Leuven.

Forbes, Ian, and Geoffrey Mead. 1992. *Measure for Measure: A Comparative Analysis of Measures to Combat Racial Discrimination in the Member States of the European Community.* Southampton: University of Southampton.

Friedrich-Naumann-Stiftung. 1993. *Dokumentation. Rechtsextremismus und Gewalt.* Sankt Augustin: COMDOK Verlag.

Frommel, Monika. 1994. "Alles nur ein Vollzugsdefizit? Warum die Strafjustiz nicht Angemessen auf die Gewaltverbrechen gegen Ausländer Reagiert." *DVJJ-Journal* 1:67–68.

Gebauer, Michael. 1993. "Untersuchungshaft—'Verlegenheitslösung' für Nichtdeutsche Straftäter?" *Kriminalpädagogische Praxis* 21:20–26.

Geissler, Rainer, and Norbert Marissen. 1990. "Kriminalität und Kriminalisierung junger Ausländer: Die Tickende Soziale Zeitbombe—ein Artefakt der Kriminalstatistik." *Kölner Zeitschrift für Soziologie und Sozialpsychologie* 42:663–87.

Gewerkschaft der Polizei. 1994. *Organisierte Kriminalität in Deutschland.* Hamburg: Gewerkschaft der Polizei.

Greger, Reinhard. 1987. "Strafzumessung bei Vergewaltigung." *Monatsschrift für Kriminologie und Strafrechtsreform* 70:261–77.

Grundmann, Stefan. 1985. "Berücksichtigung Ausländischer Rechtsvorstellungen im Strafrecht." *Neue Juristische Wochenschrift* 38:1251–55.

Gusy, Christoph. 1993. "Zur Bedeutung von Art. 3 EMRK im Ausländerrecht." *Zeitschrift für Ausländerrecht,* no. 2:63–70.

Habermas, Jürgen. 1994. *Vorstudien und Ergänzungen zur Theorie des kommunikativen Handelns.* Frankfurt: Suhrkamp.

Hagemann-White, Carol. 1981. *Hilfen für misshandelte Frauen.* Stuttgart: Enke.

Headey, Bruce, Peter Krause, and Roland Habich. 1990. *The Duration and Extent of Poverty: Is Germany a Two-Thirds-Society?* Berlin: Wissenschaftszentrum Berlin.

Heine-Wiedenmann, Dagmar. 1992. "Konstruktion und Management von Menschenhandels-Fällen." *MschrKrim* 75:121–30.

Heine-Wiedenmann, Dagmar, and Lea Ackermann. 1992. *Umfeld und Ausmass des Menschenhandels mit Ausländischen Mädchen und Frauen.* Stuttgart and Berlin: Köln.

Heitmeyer, Wilhelm. 1995. *Gewalt: Schattenseiten der Individualisierung Jugendlicher aus Unterschiedlichen Milieus.* München: Juventa, Weinheim.

Hessian Ministry of Justice. 1994. AZ 4510/4–IV/5-487/94. Unpublished prison data of March 31, 1994.

Hondrich, Karl-Otto. 1992. "Wovon wir Nichts Wissen Wollten." *Die Zeit,* 47:40.

Huber, Bertold. 1995. "Flüchtlinge, Asylbewerber, Durchreisende: Was Kann die Jugendgerichtshilfe Tun?" *DVJJ-Journal* 6:44–45.

Institut für Sozialarbeit und Sozialpädagogik. 1992. *Informationsdienst zur*

Ausländerarbeit. No. 1. Frankfurt: Institut für Sozialarbeit und Sozialpädagogik.

Jäger, Joachim. 1984. "Ethnic Minorities and Police Problems in Germany." In *Policing and Social Policy: The Cranfield-Wolfson Colloquium on Multi-Ethnic Areas in Europe*, edited by John Brown. London: Police Review Publications.

Janetzky, Klaus. 1993. "Ausländer im Strafvollzug." In *Gewalt gegen Ausländer—Gewalt von Ausländern*, edited by Der Generalstaatsanwalt von Schleswig-Holstein. Kiel: Generalstaatsanwaltschaft.

Johne, Rainer. 1995. "Flüchtlinge, Asylbewerber, Durchreisende. Was Kann die Jugendgerichtshilfe Tun?" *DVJJ-Journal* 6:41–43.

Junger, Marianne. 1989. "Ethnic Minorities, Crime and Public Policy." In *Crime and Criminal Policy in Europe*, edited by Roger Hood. Oxford: Oxford University, Centre for Criminological Research.

———. 1990. *Delinquency and Ethnicity.* Deventer: Kluwer.

Junger-Tas, Josine. In this volume. "Ethnic Minorities and Criminal Justice in the Netherlands."

Kaiser, Günther. 1974. "Gastarbeiterkriminalität und ihre Erklärung als Kulturkonflikt." In *Gastarbeiter in Gesellschaft und Recht*, edited by Tugrul Ansay and Volkmar Gessner. München: Beck.

———. 1988. *Kriminologie.* 2d ed. Karlsruhe: C. F. Müller.

Kaiser, Günther, and Jörg-Martin Jehle, eds. 1995. *Kriminologische Opferforschung.* Vol. 2. Heidelberg: Kriminalisitik Verlag.

Kaiser, Günther, and Gerhard Metzger-Pregizer. 1986. *Betriebsjustiz.* Berlin: Duncker & Humblot.

Karger, Thomas, and Peter Sutterer. 1988. "Cohort Study on the Development of Police-Recorded Criminality and Criminal Sanctioning." In *Crime and Criminal Justice*, edited by Günther Kaiser and Isolde Geissler. Freiburg: Max-Planck-Institut für Strafrecht.

———. 1990. "Polizeilich Registrierte Gewaltdelinquenz bei Jungen Ausländern." *Monatsschrift für Kriminologie und Strafrechtsreform* 73:369–83.

Kerner, Siegfried R. 1994*a*. "Kriminologische Erklärungsansätze für Fremdenfeindlichkeit, Rechtsextremismus und Gewalt." *Kriminalist* 26:147–51.

———. 1994*b*. "Nichtdeutsche Tatverdächtige in der Polizeilichen Kriminalstatistik." *Die Polizei* 85:105–9.

Killias, Martin. 1988. "Diskriminierendes Anzeigeverhalten von Opfern Gegenüber Ausländern?" *Monatsschrift für Kriminologie und Strafrechtsreform* 71:156–65.

———. 1989. "Criminality among Second-Generation Immigrants in Western Europe: A Review of the Evidence." *Criminal Justice Review* 14:13–42.

Korf, D. J. 1993. "Neue Grenzen—neue Szenen? Die Bedeutung von Entwicklungen in Mittel- und Osteuropa für den Illegalen Drogenhandel in Deutschland." *Sucht* 39:105–10.

Kraushaar, Horst. 1992. *Der Körperschmuggel von Kokain.* Giessen: University of Giessen.

Kriminalabteilung Frankfurt a.M. 1990. *Lagebericht Rauschgift 1989.* Frankfurt: Kriminalabteilung Frankfurt a.M.

———. 1992. *Lagebericht Rauschgift 1991.* Frankfurt: Kriminalabteilung Frankfurt a.M.
———. 1993. *Lagebericht Rauschgift 1992.* Frankfurt: Kriminalabteilung Frankfurt a.M.
Kube, Edwin, and Karl-Friedrich Koch. 1990. "Zur Kriminalität Jugendlicher Ausländer aus Polizeilicher Sicht." *Monatsschrift für Kriminologie und Strafrechtsreform* 73:14–24.
Kubink, Michael. 1993. *Verständnis und Bedeutung von Ausländerkriminalität: Eine Analyse der Konstitution Sozialer Probleme.* Pfaffenweiler: Centaurus.
Kühne, Hans-Heiner. 1991. *Kriminalitätsbekämpfung durch Innereuropäische Grenzkontrollen? Auswirkungen der Schengener Abkommen auf die Innere Sicherheit.* Berlin: Duncker & Humblot.
Kunz, Karl-Ludwig. 1989. "Ausländerkriminalität in der Schweiz—Umfang, Struktur und Erklärungsversuch." *Schweizerische Zeitschrift für Strafrecht* 106:373–92.
Kurz, Ursula. 1965. "Partielle Anpassung und Kulturkonflikt: Gruppenstruktur und Anpassungsdispositionen in Einem Italienischen Gastarbeiter-Lager." *Kölner Zeitschrift für Soziologie und Sozialpsychologie* 17:814–32.
Lajios, Konstantin. 1993. *Die psychosoziale Situation von Ausländern in der Bundesrepublik Deutschland: Integrationsprobleme und Seelische Folgen.* Opladen: Leske & Budrich.
Landeskriminalamt Berlin. 1994. *Polizeiliche Kriminalstatistik Berlin: Ausländerkriminalität 1993.* Berlin: Landeskriminalamt.
———. 1995. *Polizeiliche Kriminalstatististik: Langzeitvergleich Städtedaten.* Berlin: Landeskriminalamt.
Landeskriminalamt Dusseldorf. 1994. *Police Statistics of Northrhine-Westfalia.* Dusseldorf: Landeskriminalamt.
Landeskriminalamt Hessen. 1994. *Polizeiliche Kriminalstatististik: 1993.* Wiesbaden: Landeskriminalamt.
Landeskriminalamt Sachsen. 1993*a. Dokumentation: Rechtsorientierte/Fremdenfeindliche Straftaten im Freistaat Sachsen 1991/1992.* Dresden: Landeskriminalamt Sachsen.
———. 1993*b. Jugenddelinquenz und Jugendgefährdung im Freistaat Sachsen: Jahresbericht 1992.* Dresden: Landeskriminalamt Sachsen.
Landtag Nordrhein-Westfalen (Parliament of the state of North Rhine–Westphalia). 1993. Drucksache (printed matters) 11/5183. March 4.
Legge, Ingeborg. 1994. *Kriminologische Regionalanalyse Hamburg-Altona.* Hamburg: Landeskriminalamt.
Manfrass, Klaus. 1991. *Türken in der Bundesrepublik: Nordafrikaner in Frankreich.* Bonn and Berlin: Bouvier.
Mansel, Jürgen. 1986. "Die unterschiedliche Selektion von Jungen Deutschen, Türken und Italienern auf dem Weg vom Polizeilich Tatverdächtigen zum Gerichtlich Verurteilten." *Monatsschrift für Kriminologie und Strafrechtsreform* 69:309–25.
———. 1988. "Gezielte Produktion von Kriminellen? Das Ausmass der Kriminalisierung von Gastarbeiternachkommen durch Organe der Strafrechtspflege in der Bundesrepublik Deutschland." In *Kriminologische Forschung in*

den 80er Jahren, vol. 35/2, edited by Günther Kaiser, Helmut Kury, and Hans-Jörg Albrecht. Freiburg: Max-Planck-Institut.

———. 1990. *Kriminalisierung als Instrument der Ausgrenzung und Disziplinierung.* Paper presented at the twenty-fifth meeting of the German Association of Sociology. Frankfurt: German Association of Sociology.

———. 1994. "Schweigsame 'Kriminelle' Ausländer? Eine Replik auf Jo Reichertz und Norbert Schröer." *Kölner Zeitschrift für Soziologie und Sozialpsychologie* 46:299–307.

Martens, Peter. In this volume. "Immigrants, Crime, and Criminal Justice in Sweden."

Ministry of Internal Affairs. 1972–94. *Verfassungsschutzberichte, 1971–1993.* Bonn: Ministry of Internal Affairs.

Möller, Kurt. 1993. "Rechtsextremismus und Gewalt: Empirische Befunde und Individualisierungstheoretische Erklärungen." In *Lust auf Randale: Jugendliche Gewalt gegen Fremde*, edited by Wilfried Breyvogel. Dietz and Bonn: Verlag.

Müller-Dietz, Heinz. 1993. *Lagebeurteilung und Neuere Entwicklungen im Strafvollzug. Caritas Schweiz: Die Reform in Gang Bringen* (Pushing towards reform). Bericht 1/93. Luzern: Caritas Schweiz.

Münch, Richard. 1995. "Elemente Einer Theorie der Integration Moderner Gesellschaften. Eine Bestandsaufnahme." *Berliner Journal für Soziologie* 5:5–24.

Nestler-Tremel, Cornelius. 1986. "Auch für Ausländer Gilt das Deutsche Strafrecht." *Strafverteidiger*, pp. 83–87.

Noelle-Neumann, Elisabeth, and Renate Köcher. 1993. *Allensbacher Jahrbuch der Demoskopie, 1984–1992.* München: Verlag für Demoskopie.

Oberlandesgericht (High Court/High District Court) Bremen. 1994. *Strafverteidiger*, p. 130.

Oppermann, Antje. 1986. *Die Kriminalität Junger Ausländer—Selektion oder Soziale Mängellage.* Freiburg: Evangelische Fachhochschule für Sozialarbeit.

———. 1987. "Straffällige Junge Ausländer: Kriminalitätsbelastung und Soziale Bedingungen." *Bewährungshilfe* 34:83–95.

Otte, W. 1994. "Die Ausweisung nach dem Ausländergesetz." *Zeitschrift für Ausländerrecht* no. 2:67–76.

Pearson, Geoffrey. 1992. "Political Ideologies and Drug Policy." Paper presented at the Third European Colloquium on Crime and Public Policy in Europe, Noordwijkerhout.

Pfeiffer, Christian. 1995. *Kriminalität Junger Menschen im Vereinigten Deutschland: Eine Analyse auf der Basis der Polizeilichen Kriminalstatistik, 1984–1994.* Hannover: Kriminologisches Forschungsinstitut Niedersachsen.

Pichler, T. 1991. *Der unterschiedliche Umfang der Registrierten Kriminalität der Arbeitsmigranten.* Pfaffenweiler: Centaurus.

Pilgram, Arno. 1993. "Mobilität, Migration und Kriminalität—Gegen die Vordergründigkeit Kriminologischer Studien über Ausländer." In *Grenzöffnung, Migration, Kriminalität*, edited by Arno Pilgram. Baden-Baden: Nomos.

Pitsela, Angelika. 1986. *Straffälligkeit und Kriminelle Viktimisierung Ausländischer Minderheiten in der BRD.* Freiburg: Max-Planck-Institut.

Presse- und Informationsdienst der Bundesregierung. 1994. *Bulletin: Die Kriminalität in der Bundesrepublik Deutschland.* No. 50. Bonn: Presse- und Informationsdienst der Bundesregierung.

Regtmeier, Wilhelm. 1990. *Menschenhandel—Erfahrungen einer Sonderkommission in einem besonderen Deliktsbereich der Organisierten Kriminalität.* Schriftenreihe der Polizeiführungsakademie (quarterly publication of the Academy of Higher Police Education), no. 3/4:81–94.

Reichertz, Jo. 1994. "Zur Definitionsmacht der Polizei." *Kriminalistik* 48:610–16.

Reichertz, Jo, and Norbert Schröer. 1993. "Beschuldigtennationalität und Polizeiliche Ermittlungspraxis. Plädoyer für eine Qualitative Sozialforschung." *Kölner Zeitschrift für Soziologie und Sozialpsychologie* 45:755–71.

———. 1994. "Gute Gesinnung oder Prüfende Forschung? Eine Erwiderung zu Jürgen Mansels Replik." *Kölner Zeitschrift für Soziologie und Sozialpsychologie* 46:308–11.

Riek, Götz-Achim. 1995. *Die neue Ost-West-Migration. Am Beispiel der Russlanddeutschen in der Russischen Föderation.* Neuried: ars una.

Rommelspacher, Birgit. 1993. "Männliche Jugendliche als Projektionsfiguren Gesellschaftlicher Gewaltphantasien: Rassismus im Selbstverständnis der Mehrheitskultur." In *Lust auf Randale: Jugendliche Gewalt gegen Fremde,* edited by Wilfried Breyvogel. Bonn: Verlag Dietz.

Rusinek, Bernd-A. 1993. "Das Glück der Provokation. Gewalt in Historischen Jugendkulturen." In *Lust auf Randale: Jugendliche Gewalt gegen Fremde,* edited by Wilfried Breyvogel. Bonn: Dietz.

Sack, Fritz. 1974. "Kultur, Subkultur, Kulturkonflikt." In *Kleines Kriminologisches Wörterbuch,* edited by Günther Kaiser, Hans-Jürgen Kerner, Fritz Sack, and Hartmut Schellhoss. Heidelberg: C. F. Müller.

Savelsberg, Joachim J. 1982. *Ausländische Jugendliche: Assimilative Integration, Kriminalität und Kriminalisierung und die Rolle der Jugendhilfe.* München: Minerva.

Schöch, Heinz, and Michael Gebauer. 1991. *Ausländerkriminalität in der Bundesrepublik Deutschland: Kriminologische, Rechtliche und Soziale Aspekte eines Gesellschaftlichen Problems.* Baden-Baden: Nomos.

Schroeder, Friedrich Christian. 1983. "Strafen zum Heimattarif." *Frankfurter Allgemeine Zeitung* (October 13).

Schüler-Springorum, Horst. 1983. "Ausländerkriminalität. Ursachen, Umfang und Entwicklung." *Neue Zeitschrift für Strafrecht* 3:529–36.

Schumann, Karl F. 1987. *Jugendkriminalität und die Grenzen der Generalprävention.* Neuwied: Luchterhand Verlag.

Schütze, Hans. 1993. "Junge Ausländer im Vollzug der Straf- und Untersuchungshaft." In *Freiheitsentzug bei Jungen Straffälligen,* edited by Thomas Trenczek. Bonn: Forum Verlag.

Schwencken, Karl P. 1822. *Aktenmässige Nachrichten von dem Gauner- und Vagabundengesindel.* Cassel: N.p.

Seifert, Wolfgang. 1991. *Ausländer in der Bundesrepublik—Soziale und ökonomische Mobilität.* Berlin: Wissenschaftszentrum Berlin.

Sessar, Klaus. 1981. *Rechtliche und soziale Prozesse einer Definition der Tötungskriminalität.* Freiburg: Max-Planck-Institut.

———. 1993. "Ausländer als Opfer." In *Festschrift für Schüler-Springorum*, edited by Peter-Alexis Albrecht, Alexander Ehlers, Franziska Lamott, Christian Pfeiffer, Hans-Dieter Schwind, and Michael Walter. Köln, Berlin, Bonn, and München: Carl Heymanns.

Sieber, Ulrich, and Marion Bögel. 1993. *Logistik der organisierten Kriminalität.* Wiesbaden: Bundeskriminalamt.

Smith, Douglas A., Christy A. Visher, and Laura A. Davidson. 1984. "Equity and Discretionary Justice: The Influence of Race on Police Arrest Decisions." *Journal of Criminal Law and Criminology* 75:234–50.

Solon, Jochen. 1994. "Jugendgewalt in München—Ausdruck deutscher Fremdenfeindlichkeit oder unvermeidbare ethnische Konflikte." *der Kriminalist* 26:73–79.

Statistisches Bundesamt. 1993. *Statistisches Jahrbuch 1992.* Wiesbaden: Statistisches Bundesamt.

———. 1994*a*. *Bevölkerung und Erwerbstätigkeit. Fachserie 1. Reihe 2. Ausländer* (Special series no. 1. Series 2. Foreigners). Wiesbaden: Metzler-Poeschel.

———. 1994*b*. *Statistisches Jahrbuch 1993.* Wiesbaden: Statistisches Bundesamt.

———. 1995*a*. *Bevölkerung und Erwerbstätigkeit. Fachserie 1. Reihe 2. Ausländer, 1994.* Stuttgart: Metzler-Poeschel.

———. 1995*b*. *Statistisches Jahrbuch 1994.* Wiesbaden: Statistisches Bundesamt.

Statistisches Landesamt. 1994. *Strafverfolgung, 1990–1992.* Stuttgart: Statistisches Landesamt.

Staudt, Gerhard. 1983. *Kriminelles und Konformes Verhalten der Gastarbeiternachkommen.* Saarbrücken: University of Saarbrücken.

Stefanski, Valentina. 1995. "Die Polnische Minderheit." In *Ethnische Minderheiten in der Bundesrepublik Deutschland*, edited by Cornelia Schmalz-Jacobsen and Hansen Georg. München: Beck.

Steffen, Wiebke. 1987. *Die Effizienz Polizeilicher Ermittlungen aus der Sicht des Späteren Strafverfahrens.* Wiesbaden: Bundeskriminalamt.

———. 1992. *Ausländerkriminalität in Bayern: Eine Analyse der von 1983 bis 1990 Polizeilich Registrierten Kriminalität Deutscher und Ausländischer Tatverdächtiger.* München: Bayerisches Landeskriminalamt.

Steinhilper, Udo. 1986. *Definitions- und Entscheidungsprozesse bei Sexuell Motivierten Gewaltdelikten.* Konstanz: Universitätsverlag Konstanz.

Stork, Jürgen, and Lutz Klein. 1994. "Hat die Polizei ein Ausländerproblem? Überlegungen zu Konfliktpotential und Gegenstrategien." *Monatsschrift für Kriminologie und Strafrechtsreform* 77:286–96.

Strobl, Richard. 1994. *The Victimization of Turkish Migrants and the Consequences for German Society.* Hannover: Kriminologisches Forschungsinstitut Niedersachsen.

Suddeutsche Zeitung. 1995. Untitled note (December 9), p. 6.

Sutterer, Peter, and Thomas Karger. 1993. *Kohortenstudie zur Entwicklung Polizeilich Registrierter Kriminalität und Strafrechtlicher Sanktionierung: Kriminologische Projektberichte 1992.* Freiburg: Max-Planck-Institut für Ausländisches und Internationales Strafrecht.

———. 1994. "Self-Reported Juvenile Delinquency in Mannheim, Germany." In *Delinquent Behavior among Young People in the Western World*, edited by Josine Junger-Tas, Gert-Jan Terlouw, and Malcolm W. Klein. Amsterdam and New York: Kugler.

Swientek, Christine. 1988. "Gekaufte Frauen—Gekaufte Kinder: Menschen als Letzte Kolonialwaren." *Frauenforschung* 6:87–114.

Traulsen, Monika. 1988. "Die Kriminalität der jungen Ausländer nach der Polizeilichen Kriminalstatistik." *Monatsschrift für Kriminologie und Strafrechtsreform* 71:28–41.

Tübinger Projektgruppe Frauenhandel. 1989. *Frauenhandel in Deutschland.* Bonn: Tübinger Projektgruppe Frauenhandel.

Unnever, James D., and Larry A. Hembroff. 1988. "The Prediction of Racial/Ethnic Sentencing Disparities: An Expectation States Approach." *Journal of Research in Crime and Delinquency* 25:53–82.

Villmow, Bernhard. 1990. "Polizei, Justiz und Sozialarbeit im Umgang mit mehrfach auffälligen jungen Ausländern." In *Mehrfach Auffällige—Mehrfach Betroffene: Erlebnisweisen und Reaktionsformen*, edited by Deutsche Vereinigung für Jugendgerichte und Jugendgerichtshilfen. Bonn: Forum Verlag.

———. 1993. "Ausländerkriminalität." In *Kleines Kriminologisches Wörterbuch*, 3d ed., edited by Günther Kaiser. Heidelberg: C. F. Müller.

Vrij, Aldert, and Frans W. Winkel. 1991. "Encounters between the Dutch Police and Minorities: Testing the Non-cooperation Hypothesis of Differential Treatment. Police Studies." *International Review of Police Development* 14:17–21.

Walter, Michael. 1995. *Jugendkriminalität.* Stuttgart, München, Hannover, Berlin, Weimar, and Dresden: Boorberg.

Walter, Michael, and Michael Kubink. 1993. "Ausländerkriminalität—Phänomen oder Phantom der (Kriminal-) Politik?" *Monatsschrift für Kriminologie und Strafrechtsreform* 76:306–17.

Walter, Michael, and Angelika Pitsela. 1993. "Ausländerkriminalität in der statistischen (Re-)Konstruktion." *Kriminalpädagogische Praxis* 21:6–19.

Weschke, Erwin. 1985. *Innovative Möglichkeiten für polizeiliche Massnahmen zur Verbesserung des Verhältnisses zwischen Ausländern und Polizei.* Berlin: Fachhochschule.

Wiles, Paul. 1993. "Ghettoization in Europe?" *European Journal on Criminal Policy and Research* 1:52–69.

Wilkiewicz, Leszek. 1989. *Aussiedlerschicksal: Migration und Familialer Wandel.* Pfaffenweiler: Centaurus.

Willems, Helmut. 1993. *Fremdenfeindliche Gewalt: Einstellungen, Täter, Konflikteskalation.* Opladen: Leske & Budrich.

Wolfslast, Gabriele. 1982. "Anmerkung zu BGH Urteil vom 16.9.1981." *Neue Zeitschrift für Strafrecht* 2:112–13.

David J. Smith

Ethnic Origins, Crime, and Criminal Justice in England and Wales

ABSTRACT

The main ethnic minorities in Britain arise from postcolonial migrations from the West Indies and the Indian subcontinent. South Asians adopted survival strategies based on the family, religion, and ethnic community, whereas Afro-Caribbeans initially adopted more outgoing and integrative strategies. Both groups have been subject to similar levels of racial discrimination in the fields of employment and housing. The rate of imprisonment of black people is currently seven times that of whites or South Asians. The theory that this disparity is mostly caused by cumulative bias at the various stages of law enforcement and criminal process is implausible in the light of the fragmentary evidence available. There is evidence that law enforcement targets black people, that certain stages of criminal process are biased against them, and that apparently neutral criteria used by the criminal justice system work to their disadvantage; but these effects are small compared with the disparity in rates of imprisonment. Despite conflicting evidence from a major self-report study, it is likely that the actual offending rate is substantially higher among black people than among other groups.

The starting point for this volume is that in many different countries certain specific ethnic or racial groups are far more often caught in the net of criminal justice than others. It is striking that the particular ethnic groups having elevated rates of official offending can be completely different from one country to another. In England and Wales, it is black people, whose families originally came from the Caribbean from the late 1940s onward, who are particularly likely to be criminalized.

David J. Smith is professor of criminology within the Centre for Law and Society at the University of Edinburgh, Scotland.

0192-3234/97/0021-0002$01.00

Is this because the criminal justice system treats black people unfairly, or because black people are more likely than others to offend? Since there is a strong incentive for various actors to invest heavily in one or other of these explanations, the issue has become highly contentious. In seeking to address the question in a serious way, we come up against difficult conceptual issues, as well as a deficit of useful information.

The central conceptual problem is to decide what constitutes fairness in this context. It would clearly be unfair for a police officer to stop and search someone because he was black or for a court to give someone a stiffer sentence for the same reason. That would be to use race or ethnic group as a criterion for decision making, to the detriment of an ethnic minority. It would be akin to direct discrimination against a black person applying for a job or seeking to rent accommodation, which has been unlawful in Britain under the Race Relations Acts since 1968. However, the difficult problems concern decision making that is apparently blind to race or ethnicity, but in practice tends to work to the disadvantage of black people. For example, black suspects may tend to be held in custody before trial (rather than granted bail) because they are judged to have an unstable family background, and convicted black offenders may tend to be given longer sentences because they have pleaded not guilty. There is no widely agreed method for deciding which criteria, among those having an uneven effect on different ethnic groups, are nevertheless legitimate.

There should be a way of settling the question, because the law, at least in its rhetoric, seeks to impose a universal framework which, among other things, determines what behavior is lawful and what criminal. Whenever we ask the question whether crime rates vary between ethnic groups, we are appealing to a universal framework of this kind. The model works best in a homogeneous society. It tends to break down to the extent that there are diverse groups that differ in their perceptions and definitions of deviance, in the methods they use to control it, and in their readiness to appeal to the formal legal process or where decision making rules or enforcement methods have an uneven effect on these diverse groups.

Especially in the case of the postcolonial countries, a further dimension of the problem is the close connection between the law and the concept of the nation. The majority group has a unique connection with the moral, religious, and cultural tradition that shaped the legal system. At the same time, adherence to the law "symbolizes the imagined community of the nation and expresses the fundamental unity and equality of its citizens" (Gilroy 1987, p. 74). Yet neither the law nor the corresponding sense of identity grew out of a tradition that included the present ethnic minorities. It may be argued, therefore, that the rules and processes according to which they are judged to be criminal spring from a tradition which, far from being universal, belongs exclusively to the dominant group.

Against this, it may be said that the rule of law is part of the enterprise of nation building. The project, which will never be finally accomplished, is to establish the law as a universal framework that is equally the property of all citizens. One objective of this essay is to assess how far this has yet been accomplished, at least in the case of ethnic minorities.

From a review of the fragmentary evidence available, a further objective is to judge how far the elevated official offending rate of black people is a consequence of bias, impartial application of rules or criteria that work to the disadvantage of black people, or an elevated actual rate of offending. If the effects of apparently neutral criteria turn out to be an important part of the explanation, then deciding which of these criteria are justifiable becomes a central issue. Some of the problems that arise in trying to resolve this issue are discussed. Finally, the essay rehearses some possible explanations of an elevated rate of actual offending among black people. Although the evidence for England and Wales is too thin at present to rule out any of these theories, it is enough to make some of them seem more plausible than others.

The essay is organized as follows. Section I considers the conceptual issues that arise when analyzing why rates of criminalization vary between ethnic or racial groups. Section II provides a minimum of background information about ethnic minorities in Britain to support the later account of their interactions with the criminal justice system. Section III summarizes what is known about rates of victimization among different ethnic groups, and the service that ethnic minorities as victims of crime receive from the police. It also focuses on racially motivated crime and harassment, which is an important part of the context of relations between the police and ethnic minorities in Britain. Section IV, which considers ethnic minorities as suspects and offenders, first looks at their presence in the prison population, then analyses each step in the criminal justice process. Section V sets out the main conclusions, rehearses possible explanations, and identifies the main questions for future research.

I. Conceptual Issues

The central question to be addressed is how close the criminal justice system comes to constituting a universal framework within which all ethnic groups are treated equally. There is room for considerable discussion about what is meant by equal treatment in this context. It certainly cannot mean that everyone should be treated the same. Obviously, the guilty, and not the innocent, should be punished, and people should be punished more or less severely depending on the seriousness of the offense. Slightly less obviously, someone with a long record of past offending should be punished more severely than someone convicted for the first time. Possibly, although this is more controversial, a person with a stable family life and a steady job should be given a community-based sanction whereas a person without those supports should be sent to prison. In other words, treating people equally must mean that people in like circumstances and categories in relevant respects should be treated equally.

It is common ground that race or ethnic group is not a relevant or legitimate criterion here. Beyond that, however, there is wide room for discussion as to what do count as relevant and legitimate criteria. In the present context, the important question is how far, if at all, the effect on different ethnic groups should be taken into account in deciding which are the relevant and legitimate criteria. At one extreme there is the view that equal treatment means the impartial application of existing rules and principles regardless of their effect on different ethnic groups. On that view, differential effect is not relevant. If, for example, more black than white people are committed to prison because more black people are judged to lack a stable family or a steady job, that does not constitute unequal treatment. At the other extreme, there is the view put forward, for example, by Hudson (1993) that any policies, rules, or procedures that have the effect of punishing a higher proportion of one ethnic group than another are unjust and that law and policy should be adjusted so as to achieve equal outcomes (say, in terms of proportion imprisoned) for different ethnic groups and also for different social classes.

It is difficult to defend either of these extreme views. Ensuring that equal proportions of different social groups are punished has never been seen as an objective of the criminal justice system and does not seem a valid interpretation of the ideal of equality before the law. It is deeply ingrained in our tradition that the verdict in individual cases depends on the evidence, whereas the sentence depends on the seriousness of the offense and the previous record of the offender. What is meant to determine the pattern of law enforcement by the police and other official agencies is much more open to doubt, but few would accept the idea that either enforcement or the decisions of the courts should have the primary aim of achieving equality of outcome for different social groups. That would imply unequal treatment of individuals, and it would mean that an increase in the rate of offending among any social group would be accompanied by a decline in the proportion of offenders within that group who were penalized.

However, the view that equal treatment means impartial application of existing rules and criteria regardless of any uneven effect on different ethnic groups seems equally questionable. It is possible that some of these rules or criteria may work to the disadvantage of a particular ethnic group, yet could be changed without the sacrifice of any fundamental principle or objective. For example, many police forces will not caution juveniles (instead of setting in train a prosecution) if they are known to have committed two or more previous offenses. In an area where police law enforcement tends to target black youths (e.g., there are many drugs raids on Reggae clubs) a rule of this kind works to the disadvantage of black people and, arguably, amounts to treating them unequally. The rule could be relaxed without sacrificing any fundamental principle or objective: after all, police cautions are already given to juveniles who are known to have committed previous offenses, and it may be argued that the objective of crime control will be better served by diversion of juveniles than by stigmatizing them as criminals.

This analysis suggests that equality of treatment within the criminal justice system cannot be interpreted as equality of outcome (say, the same proportion of different ethnic groups committed to prison). Nor can it be interpreted as merely the neutral application of existing rules and criteria, whatever their effect. Instead, it is necessary to adopt an intermediate position. The legitimacy and suitability of existing rules and criteria must be critically reviewed in the light of their effect on different ethnic groups.

These two polar views about what constitutes equal treatment are similar to the two opposing models of justice implied in discussion of antidiscrimination law. McCrudden, Smith, and Brown (1991) describe them as the *individual justice model* and the *group justice model* of legislation against race and sex discrimination. On the *individual justice model*,

> It is argued that the aim of the legislation is to secure the reduction of discrimination by eliminating from decisional

> processes illegitimate considerations based on race which have harmful consequences for individuals. The model concentrates on cleansing the process of decision making, and is not concerned with the result except as an indicator of a flawed process. It is also heavily individualistic in its orientation: it concentrates on securing fairness for the individual. It does not appear to depend on a recognition of social classes or groups. It is also generally expressed in universal and symmetrical terms: blacks and whites are equally protected.

On the *group justice model*, by contrast,

> The basic aim is the improvement of the relative economic position of blacks, whether to redress past subordination and discrimination, or out of concern for distributive justice at the present time. . . . The model depends on the recognition of social classes or groups. It is often expressed in asymmetrical terms as focusing on the betterment of blacks in particular and is less concerned with protection for whites. (McCrudden, Smith, and Brown 1991, pp. 5–6)

The aims of these polar models of antidiscrimination legislation conflict in important ways, and the actual legislation represents a compromise between them. The main element of the group justice model incorporated within the Race Relations Act 1976 and the Sex Discrimination Act 1975 is the concept of *indirect discrimination:* the use of a condition or requirement which is such that a considerably smaller proportion of one than of another group can comply with it, which is to the other's detriment, and where the person using the condition or requirement cannot show it to be justified. The concept of indirect discrimination belongs within the group justice model to the extent that it is concerned with the outcomes for groups resulting from the application of some rule or principle. However, conflict with the individual justice model is minimized by the qualification that criteria working to the disadvantage of a particular ethnic group may always be used as long as they can be justified. The statute did not enlarge on what would constitute a justification. In many cases, the condition or requirement is presented as a test of performance or ability. For example, where job applicants are required to take an aptitude test on which members of an ethnic minority tend to score lower than whites, the point at issue is whether the test is a valid and appropriate measure of performance in the job: if it is, then its use is justifiable (and nondiscriminatory) even though it works to the disadvantage of the ethnic minority.

However, the test of justifiability is not always so clear-cut. For example, until the 1970s, some local authorities in England required that people should have lived for five or sometimes ten years in the locality before becoming eligible for tenancies in public housing (this was known as a residence qualification). This worked to the disadvantage of incomers, including members of ethnic minority groups, who at that time were mostly recent immigrants (Smith 1977). Although there was no decisive court case, it was successfully argued that this practice was indirectly discriminatory, and local authorities were persuaded to abandon it. The argument in favor of residence qualifications was that public housing was intended to benefit local people who had paid local taxes for a period. The arguments against them were that whereas public housing was intended to help the disadvantaged, incomers tended to be among the most disadvantaged, and that it was public policy to encourage rather than hinder mobility in response to labor market pressures. From the statute it was not clear how the courts would resolve the conflict between these arguments. Thus, what is meant by a justifiable condition or requirement has still not become entirely clear. Even though it has been tacitly accepted that residential qualifications are probably not justifiable, it is not clear why.

At present the decisions at certain key stages of the criminal justice process do not fall within the provisions of the antidiscrimination legislation, although there have been calls for this to be changed (Commission for Racial Equality 1991). If the scope of the legislation were to be extended to criminal justice, this would highlight the problem of deciding whether particular criteria that work to the disadvantage of an ethnic minority can be justified. On the surface, decision-making criteria within the criminal justice system are often analogous to aptitude tests. For example, a police officer might adopt the practice of stopping and searching any group of two or more young men with long hair and earrings walking on the streets after midnight. This might be justifiable in terms of results, in the sense that young men of this description are often found to be in possession of illicit drugs. Again, wherever a suspect was cheeky or uncooperative, a police officer might decide to arrest and charge him with some offense or other. This also might be justifiable in terms of results, in the sense that cheeky or uncooperative suspects usually end up being convicted of some offense. Yet these examples, of course, illustrate that decision-making criteria within the criminal justice system, unlike employee selection criteria, can seldom, if ever, be justified purely in terms of results. In the first example, it may be granted that long-haired youths with earrings out after midnight are more likely to be in possession of illicit drugs than pensioners at noon, but invasion of a person's liberty and privacy is only justified, under English law, if there is a specific reason to suspect that he has committed an offense. In the second example, the police officer's use of the criterion of cheekiness and lack of cooperation is self-validating, because he is in a position to construct the arrest and in most cases to ensure a successful prosecution. Similarly, those who plead guilty are nearly always found guilty, but that does not show that the plea is a valid test of guilt. In the context of criminal justice, there is usually no genuinely independent test of a criterion in terms of the results achieved by using it, and some other kind of justification is usually required.

This essay does not tackle the problem of how to determine whether rules or criteria that work to the disadvantage of an ethnic minority are justifiable. The more limited aim is to show whether the uneven effect of neutrally applied rules accounts in large or small part for the overrepresentation of black people in English prisons and to provide illustrations of the rules in question.

II. Ethnic Minorities in Britain

According to the 1991 census, which for the first time included a question on ethnic origin, 5.5 percent of the population of Britain belonged to an ethnic minority group at that time. Among these, three broad groups can be identified: black people, who were 1.6 percent of the population, among which 0.9 percent originated from the Caribbean; South Asians, who were 2.7 percent, among whom 1.5 percent originated from India, 0.9 percent from Pakistan, and 0.3 percent from Bangladesh; and other minorities, which accounted for 1.2 percent, among whom 0.3 percent were of Chinese origin, while 0.4 percent were other Asians.

Ethnic minorities have a distinctly younger age structure than the majority white population. For example, all ethnic minorities accounted at the census date for 6.93 percent of the population aged sixteen to twenty-four, compared with 5.5 percent of all age-groups, and 2.7 percent of those aged forty-five and over. Because most crime is committed by males up to the age of thirty, it is important to take account of the unusual age structure of the ethnic minority groups when evaluating their recorded crime rates.

The ethnic minorities counted in these statistics are those which are perceived by the majority to be physically distinct and which are visually identifiable. The vast majority of these people are either themselves migrants or descendants of people who migrated to Britain since the Second World War. The earliest wave of migration, which was from the Caribbean, got under way in the early 1950s, but most of the inflow happened more recently.

It was the Race Relations Act 1968 which first made it unlawful to discriminate on grounds of race, color, or ethnic or national origins in the provision of goods, facilities, and services. A pioneering research project carried out in 1966–67, before the Act was passed, which used a combination of field experiments and surveys, showed that racial discrimination "ranged from the massive to the substantial" (Daniel 1968). In this study, the findings from three complementary methods of research converged in a particularly powerful way. First, Daniel carried out the first major sample survey of ethnic minorities in six English towns that were already centers of immigrant settlement. A specially recruited field force was drawn from the ethnic minority groups themselves, and an innovative two-stage sampling method allowed interviewers to be ethnically matched with respondents. Where the respondent did not speak English well, the interview was conducted in one of five other languages, using a bilingual questionnaire. Respondents were asked for their general views on the extent of racial discrimination and also about any personal experience of it. Second, Daniel developed a series of controlled experiments to test the extent of racial discrimination in natural situations. For example, rented accommodation was commonly advertised in local newspapers and in the windows of estate agents and newspaper shops. At the time, many of these advertisements specified "no coloreds." Eliminating these, Daniel sent four testers belonging to different ethnic groups to apply to rent a sample of the properties on offer. In the case of recruitment to employment, the experiments were conceived as a validation of claims made by survey respondents. Where respondents had claimed personal experience of racial discrimination on applying for a job, testers belonging to various ethnic groups were sent to apply for a job currently on offer at the same firm. Third, Daniel conducted interviews with people in a position to discriminate, such as the owners or managers of firms and the staff of local authority housing departments, and in some cases confronted them with evidence from a controlled test of their own organization that showed discrimination had occurred.

Daniel used trained actors to conduct his experiments. In each test, all four actors applied for the same job or accommodation. Each actor was assigned a brief life history and set of qualifications. These had to be different enough to establish distinct personal identities, but were without significance in terms of suitability for the job or accommodation. The order in which the four testers presented themselves was rotated. In some cases they applied in person, and in others by telephone. They were coached in how to present themselves, so as to eliminate significant differences in self-presentation as far as possible. Where the tests were conducted by telephone, the researchers were able to overhear the conversation and to satisfy themselves that each of the testers presented himself in a similar way.

Neither the field experiments nor the interviews with discriminators showed any difference in the extent or nature of discrimination against specific groups, as long as these were considered to be racially distinct from the majority. The study demonstrated that perceived "color" was the important factor, by including a Turkish Cypriot actor in the experiments. Discrimination against the Turkish Cypriot was substantially lower than against the Afro-Caribbean, Indian, or Pakistani, but there was no difference in the level of discrimination against these last three groups.

The Indian and Pakistani respondents in the survey were much less likely than the Afro-Caribbeans to say they had encountered discrimination, but Daniel showed that this was because of the radically different survival strategies adopted by South Asians compared with Afro-Caribbeans in Britain. Afro-Caribbeans, expecting much more of British people, adopted a far more outgoing style of life: they were likely to apply for a job at a firm they had never heard of before, and where no other black people were working, or apply cold to rent accommodation. South Asians looked for job opportunities through their established social networks and from the beginning made extraordinary efforts to buy rather than rent accommodation. Daniel's experiments showed that the level of discrimination against members of the two groups was the same, where they put themselves in the same situation. But in real life, the Afro-Caribbeans placed themselves in situations in which they might face discrimination more often than South Asians. They were therefore more likely to encounter face-to-face the hostility and rejection that South Asians tended to avoid. Hence, levels of discrimination against South Asians and Afro-Caribbeans in comparable situations were the same, but personal experience of discrimination, and awareness of it, was substantially greater among Afro-Caribbeans. Subsequent research in the 1970s (Smith 1977) and 1980s (Brown 1984; Brown and Gay 1986) confirmed that the initial pattern continued. Jowell and Prescott-Clarke (1970) pioneered the method of correspondence testing for job discrimination in recruitment to employment, which was then used again in several subsequent studies (Smith 1977; Brown and Gay 1986). With the correspondence method, all relevant factors can be tightly controlled, because they are expressed in a written application; and life histories and qualifications can be rotated among the different ethnic groups. Correspondence tests, like personal and telephone tests, have always shown the same level of discrimination against Afro-Caribbeans and South Asians. Of course, this research has concentrated on access to jobs or housing and has not extended to the criminal justice process. However, the findings form an important background to discussion of criminal justice issues.

In the 1960s, the migrants were largely concentrated in unskilled and semiskilled manual jobs in the main conurbations and the textile towns of Lancashire and Yorkshire. Initially, a large proportion of South Asians spoke little English, and even today a substantial minority (around 20 percent) do not speak English well. The South Asian population was always diverse, with a substantial minority of highly educated people together with a larger proportion having little or no education. From 1969 onward, the migration of Asians from East Africa swelled the number who were well-educated and who had experience of managing businesses. More recently, migration from Bangladesh has introduced a group of generally poor Asians with little education. By contrast, Afro-Caribbeans were always a more homogeneous population in social, economic, and cultural terms. Very few were uneducated, but few had higher education qualifications obtained in the West Indies. From the beginning, a high proportion of the men were skilled manual workers, and that remains the case today.

The process of development for ethnic minorities from the 1960s to the present time has been one of increasing differentiation (Jones 1993). There are increasing differences between specific minority groups and also between members of each particular group. On the one hand, people of African, Asian, and Indian origin now have a profile similar to that of white people in terms of educational qualifications and job levels. On the other hand, the Muslim groups (principally those of Pakistani and Bangladeshi origin) are at a substantial disadvantage in terms of job levels, rate of unemployment, educational and job qualifications, income, and standard of living (Jones 1993). Afro-Caribbeans occupy an intermediate position. In cultural terms, the specific ethnic minorities have always been more different from each other than each group is from the white majority. What they had in common was the racial discrimination and hostility displayed by white people and institutions. The different groups adopted entirely different strategies. The outcome is that the original cultural differences, and the differences in human and financial capital, have proved far more influential than the hostility and discrimination directed impartially at all groups perceived to be racially distinct. As a result, the socioeconomic positions of the specific minority groups are drawing further apart.

The sequence of field experiments suggests that there was a substantial decline in racial discrimination following the Race Relations Act 1968 but that discrimination nevertheless continued at a fairly high level (Smith 1977). No further declines in the level have been recorded since 1974, although the latest experiments were carried out in 1986. These showed that about 40 percent of South Asian and Afro-Caribbean job applicants were refused an interview where a similarly qualified white applicant was offered one (Brown and Gay 1986).

It is clear that concern about high crime rates among Afro-Caribbeans is relatively recent. In a report published in 1972, the Home Affairs Committee of the House of Commons on Race Relations and Immigration expressed some disquiet about difficult relations between the police and young Afro-Caribbeans, but on the whole tended toward the view that Afro-Caribbeans were less criminal than whites; certainly, two chief constables put forward that view in their evidence to the Committee (House of Commons Select Committee on Race Relations and Immigration 1972). The years between 1972 and 1976 "saw the definition of blacks as a low crime group turned round 180 degrees" (Gilroy 1987, p. 92). Giving evidence to the Home Affairs Select Committee in the 1975–76 session, the Metropolitan Police made it clear that they considered crime rates were high among Afro-Caribbeans, and also complained about antipolice campaigning by black activist groups (House of Commons Select Committee on Race Relations and Immigration 1976, p. 182). As Gilroy (1987) has pointed out, this swing in official opinion was probably the result of a series of high-profile confrontations between the police and Afro-Caribbeans.

In the context of disturbances such as these, the Metropolitan Police provided statistical evidence in its 1976 submission to the Home Affairs Committee to support the proposition that there was a specific crime problem among ethnic minorities. These statistics were confined to street offenses, in which black people were most often involved, and left out other offenses, such as burglary or fraud, in which they were least often involved. From this point onward, public discussion of the threat of rising crime was linked with discussion of racial conflict and with the perceived problem of crime, especially street crime (usually labeled "mugging") among Afro-Caribbeans. It has been argued that the growing public and police perception of black people as criminal was closely connected with the conception of "mugging" and its promotion in the media as a typically black crime (Hall et al. 1978), even though a substantial proportion of these street offenses were handbag snatches without any use or threat of violence.

In the 1980s, relations between black (Afro-Caribbean) people and the police were at the forefront of public consciousness. There were a considerable number of disturbances expressing hostility by black people toward the police during the 1980s, most notably the riots in 1981 in Brixton and several other urban areas. These disturbances led to various official and unofficial reports, of which the Scarman report on the Brixton Disorders (Scarman 1981) was by far the most influential. This period also saw the publication of the Policy Studies Institute (PSI) report on *Police and People in London* (Small 1983; Smith 1983*a*, 1983*b*; Smith and Gray 1983), which attracted headline coverage for its account of racial prejudice among police officers. The finding that racist attitudes among the police were usually not expressed in their behavior toward ethnic minorities was less prominently displayed in the press. In the space of ten years, therefore, there was a swing from muted official concern about relations between Afro-Caribbeans and the police, together with an official view that crime rates among ethnic minorities were the same as among whites, or lower, to antipolice riots in which black people played the major part, and an official view (backed up by some limited statistical evidence) that rates for certain types of crime were high among Afro-Caribbeans.

Throughout the period, it was Afro-Caribbeans, and not South Asians, who were highlighted in public discussion of crime and disorder. The famous conflicts in the 1970s revolved around Afro-Caribbean clubs and cultural events such as the Notting Hill Carnival. The antipolice riots of the 1980s took place in areas of Afro-Caribbean concentration (such as St. Paul's in Bristol, Brixton in south London, and

Moss Side in Manchester); although white people as well as Afro-Caribbeans took part, there is little evidence that South Asians were involved. Many South Asian shopkeepers were victims in the 1985 riots in the Lozells and Handsworth areas of Birmingham.

Survey results and experiments on racial discrimination have consistently shown that prejudice and hostility among the public at large is just as great against South Asians as against Afro-Caribbeans (Daniel 1968; Rose et al. 1969; Jowell and Prescott-Clarke 1970; Smith 1977; Brown 1984; Brown and Gay 1986). Nevertheless, it is only Afro-Caribbeans, and not South Asians, who have become associated in public debate and in the public mind with predatory crime.

In the 1990s, the Muslim groups (originating from India as well as from Pakistan and Bangladesh) have become more active, assertive, and politically organized as a consequence of the Rushdie affair. This development has been associated with the growth of specifically anti-Muslim prejudice. There are some early indications that public debate may come to focus on Muslim involvement in crime: for example, this was one theme of a BBC Panorama program transmitted in April 1993 on "Britain's New Muslim Underclass," which used anecdotal evidence from towns in the West Midlands and Yorkshire to support an assertion that there was a rising tide of crime among unemployed young Muslims. More recently, a race relations specialist employed within government has argued that a rise in Muslim involvement in crime is to be expected (FitzGerald 1995), but no convincing evidence has yet emerged to show that this is already happening.

III. Ethnic Minorities as Victims of Crime

Racial harassment and racially motivated crime has been an issue in British public debate since the Notting Hill Race Riots of 1958. Except where racial hatred was involved, however, there has been little interest over most of this period in criminal victimization of ethnic minorities and far more interest in offending by black people and in conflicts between black people and the police. One consequence of this unbalanced debate is that little is known about the links between victimization and offending among ethnic minorities. These matters are inherently difficult to research in Britain, where specific ethnic minorities form such small proportions of the population—for example, Afro-Caribbeans were about 1 percent of the population of England and Wales in 1991. Elaborate and expensive sample designs are required to approach the subject through surveys. In general, there are no official statistics based on police records that show the race or ethnic group of the victim, or of the offender according to the victim, and none about persons arrested. The main sources of information are the 1988 British Crime Survey (BCS) and statistics for London on crimes recorded by the police. The 1988 BCS for the first time provided a national analysis of rates of victimization according to ethnic group, but it only included rudimentary data about the pattern of intraracial crime. The London statistics that have so far been published are for selected years up to the mid-1980s. They provide very limited data on intraracial offending for two kinds of offense, and they use an obviously inadequate classification of the race or ethnic group of the offender.

The following brief account of what is known about ethnicity and victimization therefore raises more questions than it answers and points to the need for further research.

A. Rates of Victimization

The BCS 1988 showed that rates of victimization were distinctly higher among both Afro-Caribbeans and South Asians than among white people both for household crimes and for personal crimes (see table 1). Among Afro-Caribbeans, the differences are particularly marked for burglary, bicycle theft, assault, and robbery or theft from the person. In the case of South Asians, the differences are most marked for household vandalism, vehicle vandalism, threats, and robbery or theft from the person.

The risk of victimization tends to be strongly associated with characteristics of the areas where respondents live, and after these area characteristics have been taken into account, the differences in risks between ethnic minorities and white people are considerably reduced. To some extent, therefore, the relatively high risks of victimization suffered by ethnic minorities are associated with the areas where they live. This was demonstrated by Mayhew, Elliott, and Dowds (1989) using logit models with the risk of victimization as the dependent variable. Three of these models included South Asians and whites only. In the two cases of threats and vandalism, the area characteristics associated with victimization were captured by a scale composed of the following highly correlated variables: neighborhood cohesion, how long the respondent has lived in the area, likelihood of moving from the area, housing conditions, and (in the case of vandalism only) level of incivilities. It can be seen that this is not a true ecological variable: it partly reflects the individual's circumstances, aspirations, and perceptions of

TABLE 1

Victimization Rates by Ethnic Group (British Crime Survey 1988)

	Percentage of Respondents Reporting Victimization		
Household Victimization	White	Afro-Caribbean	Asian
Household vandalism	4.7	3.6*	7.5**
Burglary with loss	2.7	6.4**	3.5
Vehicle crime (owners):			
Vandalism	9.4	8.7	13.7**
All thefts	17.9	26.3**	19.5**
Bicycle theft (owners)	4.2	8.4*	3.9
Other household theft	7.9	6.9	9.3*
All household	29.8	32.7*	35.5**
Personal victimization:			
Assaults	3.4	7.4**	4.4
Threats	2.5	3.9	5.3**
Assaults or threats	5.5	9.4**	10.8**
Robbery/theft from person	1.1	3.3**	3.0**
Other personal thefts	4.0	5.5	3.1
All personal	9.6	16.1**	14.8**

Source.—Mayhew, Elliott, and Dowds (1989), table 11.

* Statistically significant at the 10 percent level (two-tailed test, taking account of the sample design factor). For further explanatory details, see the original table.

** Statistically significant at the 5 percent level (two-tailed test, taking account of sample design factor). For further explanatory details, see original table.

the area. Hence it would not be accurate to say that characteristics of the area which are common to all residents partly explain the difference in victimization between whites and Asians. It would be more accurate to say that the relatively high level of victimization among Asians is bound up with the way they and white people perceive the area where they live. In the case of contact theft, the significant area characteristic was simply inner city versus the rest. Separate models were computed for Afro-Caribbean and white respondents only. In the case of burglary and assault, the significant geographical characteristics were again captured by complex scales which partly reflect individual circumstances and perceptions. In the case of contact theft, the relevant area characteristic was again inner city versus the rest (Mayhew, Elliott, and Dowds 1989, pp. 83–86, tables B1–B6).

These same models also included a number of other, rather heterogeneous, variables, such as sex, age, job level (manual vs. nonmanual), marital status, tenure, whether unemployed, and number of evenings spent outside the home. It was found that the ethnic differences were considerably reduced in the context of a model including a number of these variables (in detail the variables included varied between one model and the next). These findings seem difficult to interpret because the models were not designed to test any clearly specified hypothesis about the difference in rate of victimization between ethnic groups. Among the variables included, some would have an entirely different status from others in any explanatory model: for example, the association of victimization with youth seems quite different from its association with perceived incivilities in the area. To the extent that the difference in victimization between ethnic groups is a function of differences in age profiles, this does suggest that it is not due to ethnicity. However, the parallel argument does not apply in the case of perceived incivilities. In that case, the statistics might mean that Asians tend to be confined to areas that are actually disordered and unsafe, or that those subject to high risks of victimization tend to perceive the area to be unsafe, or both. These explanations would be consistent with the theory that being Asian is a factor leading to a high rate of victimization. In other words, the association with perceived incivilities, or with the other features included in the residential scale, does not "explain away" the ethnic differences.

In the case of Afro-Caribbeans, the relatively high level of victimization is connected with the relatively high crime rate. Most crime is committed near to where the offender lives and either on people the offender knows or on others in similar circumstances (e.g., belonging to the same social class or ethnic group). It is interesting, e.g., that victimization is particularly high among offenders (Smith 1983*a*). Hence, it is not surprising that black-on-black crime accounts for a substantial proportion of the victimization of black people (see fig. 1). A serious limitation of these findings from the BCS is that they only relate to the minority of cases (the actual proportion is not stated in the report) where the victim can describe the offender. This probably inflates the proportion of black offenders, because black people are more likely to commit offenses involving personal contact, such as robbery and theft from the person, than ones that do not, such as burglary (see below). It is nevertheless striking that 38 percent of offenses on Afro-Caribbeans were committed by black people, according to the victims, bearing

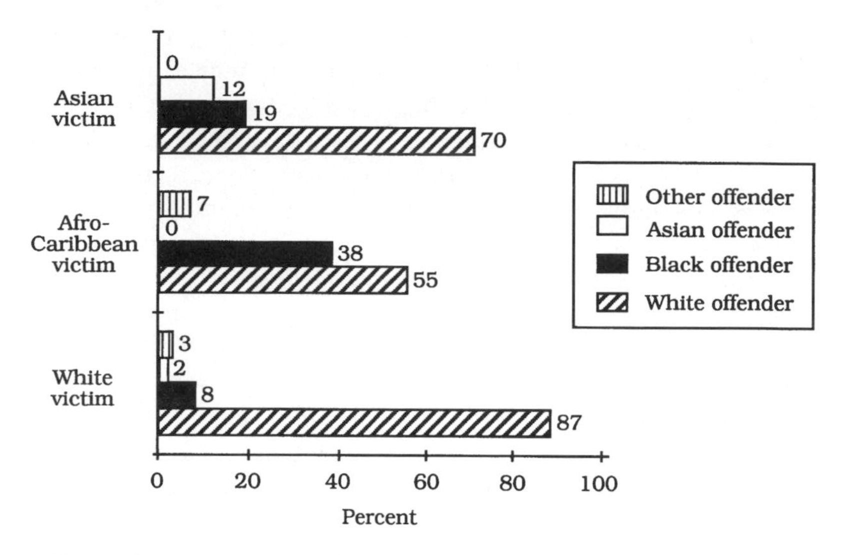

FIG. 1.—Victimization reports by race or ethnic group of victim and offender, British Crime Survey 1988. Source: Mayhew, Elliott, and Dowds 1989, table 13. Note: The figure (like the original table) is based on cases where the victim could say something about the offender.

in mind that black people account for only 1.6 percent of the population. The proportion of white victims who said the offender was black was much lower, at 8 percent.

The extent to which crime is intraracial probably varies widely according to the type of offense. The published BCS findings do not throw light on this, and small sample sizes may make it difficult or impossible to do so. Some fragmentary data are, however, available for crimes recorded by the police in London in 1984 and 1985. A reworking of some of these data for 1985 is shown in table 2. Two categories of offense are shown: assaults, and robbery and other violent theft. These two offenses may have been chosen because the personal contact they involve means that the victim often gets a look at the offender. As set out in a later section, they are offenses for which the black offending rate tends to be high. Confining the analysis to cases where the victim could describe the offender (the percent excluding "not known" data), 60 percent of black victims of assault, and 75 percent of black victims of robbery and violent theft, said their assailant had been nonwhite. In the case of assaults, there was a large difference between black and white victims in this respect: only 26 percent of

TABLE 2

Race or Ethnic Group of Assailants and Victims: London, 1985

	Victim's Appearance							
	All Victims		White European		Afro-Caribbean		Asian	
Assailant's Appearance	Percent of All	Percent Excluding "Not Known"	Percent of All	Percent Excluding "Not Known"	Percent of All	Percent Excluding "Not Known"	Percent of All	Percent Excluding "Not Known"
Assaults:								
White	37	63	40	69	17	28	27	51
Nonwhite	18	31	15	26	37	60	23	42
Mixed	3	6	3	5	7	11	4	7
Not known	41		42		39		46	
Robbery:*								
White	20	24	21	25	14	16	18	20
Nonwhite	56	67	55	66	64	75	60	69
Mixed	8	10	8	9	7	9	9	11
Not known	16		17		15		13	

Source.—Home Office (1989*a*), table 3.

Note.—Under each victim group, the first column shows percentage distributions including "not known" data; the second shows recalculated percentage distributions omitting "not known" data. Classifications used for victims and assailants do not match. For example, "nonwhite" in the assailant classification presumably includes "black-skinned" and "Asian" in the victim classification. Three categories in the victim classification ("dark European," "other," and "unrecorded") have been left out of the above table, but these cases are included in the total column above. This table is recalculated from the original, which showed rounded percentages: it therefore involves some approximation.

* Also includes "other violent theft."

white victims of assault said their assailant had been nonwhite. In the case of robbery and other violent theft, however, the proportion who said their assailant had been black was almost as high among white as among black victims (66 percent compared with 75 percent).

From these highly incomplete findings, it is clear that the high rate of victimization of black people is explained at least in part by their high rate of offending. However, it is not possible to say how important offending is in explaining victimization. Far more detailed research would be needed to pursue this matter further, but some aspects of the high rate of black victimization are unlikely to be explained by black offending. For example, burglary victimization with loss was twice as high in the 1988 BCS among Afro-Caribbean as among white households (see table 1), yet burglary is an offense that is probably not particularly high among black people (see later section). The high rate of victimization of South Asians, of course, cannot be explained by intraracial offending, since offending levels are certainly no higher among South Asians than among whites. In small part, and for certain offenses only, it may possibly be explained by black-on-Asian offending. Figure 1 shows that Asian victims were more than twice as likely as white victims to report that the offender was black. Probably black-on-Asian crime is relatively common because the two groups tend to live in the same or adjoining neighborhoods.

The pattern of victimization by ethnic group shown by the PSI survey of Londoners carried out in 1981 was different from that shown by the BCS 1988 for England and Wales. In London the rate of victimization was about the same among Afro-Caribbeans and white people, but considerably lower among Asians. However, the PSI survey like the BCS showed that Afro-Caribbeans were more likely to be victims of contact theft than white people. The low level of victimization of Asians found in London as a whole in 1981 may reflect the numerical strength in London of middle-class Asians living away from the inner-city areas. Working-class Asians are relatively more numerous outside London. The Islington Crime Survey carried out in 1985 showed about the same rate of victimization among Asian and white people within that relatively small inner-city and deprived area of London, but it showed a considerably higher rate of victimization among black people (Jones, MacLean, and Young 1986).

B. *Victims and the Police*

The 1988 BCS found little difference between ethnic groups in the proportion of victims who reported the incident to the police. A higher proportion of Asian and Afro-Caribbean than of white people reported burglaries and vandalism in the home, but this "seems largely explained by higher levels of loss and damage" (Mayhew, Elliott, and Dowds 1989, p. 28). The PSI London survey 1981 similarly found no significant differences between ethnic groups in the proportion of victims who reported incidents to the police (Smith 1983*a*, p. 76).

The 1988 BCS found that satisfaction after reporting to the police was lower among ethnic minorities than among white people: "61% of white victims said they were 'fairly' or 'very satisfied' with the way the police had dealt with the matter, as against 49% of Afro-Caribbeans and 44% of Asian victims. Both Afro-Caribbean and Asian victims were more likely than whites to feel that the police did not do enough. Afro-Caribbean victims more often perceived impoliteness or unpleasantness on the part of the police, and they were more likely to feel that the police should have apprehended the offender. Asian victims were relatively more dissatisfied because the police did not appear to be interested" (Mayhew, Elliott, and Dowds 1989, pp. 28–29). Levels of satisfaction shown by the 1981 London survey were generally higher, though again ethnic minorities, in this case especially the Asians, were less likely to be satisfied than white people. The proportion who were "very satisfied" was 45 percent among white people, 36 percent among Afro-Caribbeans, and 18 percent among South Asians. In marked contrast to the 1988 BCS, however, the 1981 London survey showed that the police appeared to have been more active and successful where the victim was Afro-Caribbean than white. "Where the victim was a West Indian, the police were more likely to take some action, to make a full investigation, to move quickly and to catch the offender than where the victim was white or Asian" (Smith 1983*a*, p. 84). Possibly this contrast arises because the PSI survey asked more concrete and factual questions than the BCS, so that the BCS findings reflect general anti-police attitudes among ethnic minorities (especially Afro-Caribbeans) rather than police actions in the particular case.

In the 1988 BCS, respondents were asked whether they had taken action about incidents they had observed in the past five years. Over 10 percent in each case had observed instances of shoplifting, vandalism, and "serious fights," while a few (3 percent) had observed theft from parked cars. The proportion who had reported such incidents to the police ranged from around one-quarter (for stealing from cars and vandalism) to around one-tenth (for shoplifting and serious fights). The proportion who had reported such incidents to the police did not vary between ethnic groups (Skogan 1990, p. 48). Both Smith (1983*a*) and Tuck and Southgate (1981) found on the basis of hypothetical questions ("*would* you call the police") that Afro-Caribbeans were less inclined to do so than others, although the differences were not large. Again, the answers to the hypothetical questions may reflect attitudes that are not expressed in behavior. Smith (1983*a*) also asked hypothetically about willingness to serve as a witness and appear in court, and here found a more marked difference between the responses of Afro-Caribbean and white respondents. The Islington Crime Survey using closely similar hypothetical questions found a lower level of willingness to help the police than the PSI survey for London as a whole and a sharper contrast between white people on the one hand and both Afro-Caribbeans and South Asians on the other (Jones, MacLean, and Young 1986, pp. 139–45).

C. Racially Motivated Crime and Harassment

The best evidence—that from the 1988 British Crime Survey—suggests that South Asians and Afro-Caribbeans are at considerably higher risk than white people of being victims of a number of kinds of crime. To some extent, this is because they fall into demographic groups (e.g., the young) which are at higher than average risk. It is also associated with the actual and perceived characteristics of the areas where ethnic minorities live, although, as argued above, this does not "explain the difference away." In addition, Afro-Caribbeans have an elevated risk of crime *victimization* because *offending* rates among Afro-Caribbeans are several times higher than among white people, and a considerable proportion of the crimes committed by Afro-Caribbeans are on Afro-Caribbean victims.

However, another reason why rates of victimization are high among ethnic minorities is that they are the objects of some racially motivated crimes. They may also be the victims of a pattern of repeated incidents motivated by racial hostility, where many of these events on their own do not constitute crimes, although some crimes may occur in the sequence, so that the cumulative effect is alarming and imposes severe constraints on a person's freedom and ability to live a full life. Racial harassment is the term that is used to describe a pattern of repeated incidents of this kind.

Genn (1988) and Bowling (1993) have pointed out that victim surveys have not been designed to describe patterns which develop over time. Instead, they have up to now aimed to categorize and count discrete incidents using parallel definitions to those applied by the courts. This is most appropriate for crimes such as car theft or burglary, where most incidents *are* discrete from the viewpoint of the victim. It is least appropriate for crimes which take place within a continuing relationship (family violence, incest) or within a restricted social setting (the school, the workplace, the street).

A further difficulty in studying racially motivated crime or racial harassment is establishing racial motivation. One approach is to accept the victim's view; another is for an observer to make a judgment based on a description of the facts. Definitions used vary in the emphasis given to these two types of criterion, and in other detailed ways, so that it is often difficult to compare the results from different studies.

Although racial attacks and harassment, on any reasonable definition, are ancient phenomena, they have "arrived relatively late on the political policy agenda and thence onto the agenda of various statutory agencies" (FitzGerald 1989). The first major report on the subject, *Blood on the Streets*, was published by Bethnal Green and Stepney Trades Council in 1978. Since then there has been an official report by the Home Office (1981) based on statistics of incidents recorded by the police; a report by the House of Commons Home Affairs Committee (1986), which has also recently initiated a further inquiry; and two reports by an Inter-Departmental Group set up to consider racial attacks (Home Office 1989*c*, 1991). National statistics on racial incidents recorded by the police have been regularly reported in *Hansard.* Very few national survey-based statistics have become available, the main sources being the third PSI survey of racial minorities carried out in 1982 (Brown 1984) and the British Crime Survey (Mayhew, Elliott, and Dowds 1989). There has been a much larger number of local studies and initiatives, but most will not be cited here because they tend to have severe limitations as sources of hard information. The same can be said of reports compiled by the Commission for Racial Equality (1985) and the Greater London Council on this subject.

As FitzGerald (1989) has pointed out, the Home Office study of 1981 is generally used as a benchmark for the national scale of the problem. However, these statistics are virtually useless as a measure of racially motivated crime and racial harassment, because they are derived from police records. Later research has shown that most of these incidents are not reported to the police (especially the low-level harassment that forms part of a cumulative pattern); also, there is likely to be a large amount of imprecision and inconsistency in the way the police record and classify these incidents. Despite their severe limitations, statistics based on police records may perhaps be of use as an indication of trends over time. The number recorded in London has risen from 1,945 in 1985 to 3,373 in 1991; in the rest of England and Wales, it rose from 3,955 to 4,509 over the same period (*Hansard* 1992).

The PSI 1982 survey of racial minorities did not attempt to capture racial harassment but asked about two types of crime victimization: physical attack or molestation, and burglary or damage to property. From detailed descriptions of the incidents (including the ethnic origin of the persons concerned) the researcher identified those where there was a probable racial motive. The classification did not, therefore, primarily depend on the victim's view as to whether there was a racial motivation. In most cases of burglary and damage to property, there were few clues as to whether there might have been a racial motivation: for example, the ethnic group of the offender was usually unknown.

The analysis therefore concentrated on assaults. Over a sixteen-to-eighteen-month-period, among the 4,833 people asked these questions of interracial assaults, there were ten cases where a racial motive or racial background was specifically mentioned; there were a further twenty-eight unprovoked interracial assaults with no stated motive, many of which were probably motivated by racial hostility; and eighteen other incidents involving interracial assault (Brown 1984, p. 260, table 134). Even on the most restrictive definition (counting only the ten assaults where the motive was plainly racist) the survey showed an incidence of racial attacks around ten times that revealed by the statistics derived from police records and published in the 1981 Home Office report.

The PSI survey also tapped views of members of ethnic minorities on racial attacks. Among both Afro-Caribbeans and South Asians, the balance of opinion was clearly that racist attacks and insults had gotten worse over the previous five years. A majority of Afro-Caribbeans, and a substantial minority of South Asians, believed they could not rely on the police to protect them (Brown 1984, pp. 261–62, tables 135–36).

In the 1988 British Crime Survey, 24 percent of offenses reported by South Asians, and 15 percent of those reported by Afro-Caribbeans, were racially motivated in the respondent's view. Types of incident most often seen as racially motivated were vandalism, physical and sexual assaults, and threats (Mayhew, Elliott, and Dowds 1989, pp. 47–48).

Local surveys have adopted various definitions, but have generally been more inclusive, and have tried to cover low-level harassment as well as criminal offenses. They tend to suggest that racial harassment, on a broad definition, is a problem affecting a high proportion of South Asians and Afro-Caribbeans. For example, a survey in the London borough of Newham in 1986 suggested that one in four of Newham's black residents had experienced some form of racial harassment in the previous twelve months (London Borough of Newham 1987). A survey carried out in Plaistow, East London, in 1989 found that between one in five and one in six Afro-Caribbean and Asian men and women suffered a racial incident in an eighteen-month period. About one in twelve of white people said they had experienced a racial incident (Saulsbury and Bowling 1991). These incidents covered a wide range of seriousness; some were one-off events, while others were part of a pattern. "Some of those interviewed mentioned the effect that persistent door-knocking, egg-throwing, damage to property, verbal abuse, threats and intimidation had on victims, even though the events may not look serious as individual 'incidents'" (Saulsbury and Bowling 1991, p. 118). A much higher level of racial victimization was found in a study of an East London local authority housing estate where there was a history of racial abuse (Sampson and Phillips 1992). Over a period of six months, there was an average of four and a half attacks against each of thirty Bengali families, although seven families were not attacked, while six families were attacked twelve or more times. A sequence of incidents recorded for one family was stones thrown and chased, threatened and prevented from entering flat, punched and verbal abuse, attempted robbery, chased by gang of youths, stones thrown and chased, common assault.

The problems of definition and of evidence in this field are severe, and no ready solutions are in sight. However, from available evidence it is likely that racially motivated crimes form an important although fairly small proportion of offenses committed against members of ethnic minority groups. In addition, racial harassment (a pattern of criminal and noncriminal attacks, threats, and insults) probably affects a substantial proportion (but well under half) of the ethnic minority population, but a much higher proportion in certain areas.

IV. Ethnic Minorities as Suspects and Offenders

The criminal justice process can be regarded as a sequence of decisions starting with behavior that someone considers to be deviant or offensive and ending with the punishment of an offender. A number of choices are available at every stage. Most of these result in the matter being dropped or resolved or in action being taken by methods other than the criminal justice process. Hence the number of remaining cases successively diminishes from one stage to the next. One reason why the process takes this form is that people and organizations have a number of resources and sanctions to deploy against deviant and offensive behavior, of which criminal justice is only one. Many matters which could be treated as crimes are never referred to the criminal justice system at all. Many others are initially referred, but are later dealt with in some other way instead.

The decisions made at each stage determine which incidents and individuals remain within the system to be processed at the next stage. In that way the various stages are linked. For example, the acquittal rate partly depends on the selection of cases that get to court, and the acquittal rate could vary between ethnic groups because weak cases are more likely to reach trial where the defendant belongs to one ethnic group rather than another. Because the system takes this form, a longitudinal study following individuals through several stages would offer substantial benefits, but no research of that kind has yet been attempted. However, by studying each stage separately, much progress can be made toward showing whether there is equal treatment at that stage and how much contribution any unequal treatment makes to overrepresentation of ethnic minorities at the end of the whole process.

In summarizing the research results, it would be neat to start at the beginning of the sequence and move toward the end. However, the ethnic composition of the prison population must be examined first, because it provides striking evidence of something that needs to be explained.

A. The Prison Population

Statistics of the prison population by ethnic group were first published for 1985 and have been published annually since. These are a count of the population on a reference date: no statistics on the flow of people into prisons ("receptions") by ethnic group have yet been published. The prison population on a reference day of course reflects both the number admitted into prison, and the length of their sentences.

Figure 2 compares the prison population in 1993 with the general population aged sixteen to thirty-nine.[1] The most striking feature is the strong overrepresentation of the black groups (people of West Indian, Guyanese, and African origin) among the prison population. These groups were 11 percent of the male prison population, compared with 1.8 percent of the general population aged sixteen to thirty-nine. Females were only a small proportion of the prison population: they accounted for a mere 3.4 percent in 1991. However, the black groups formed an astonishing 20.4 percent of this small female prison population, compared with 2 percent of the general population aged sixteen to thirty-nine. A substantial proportion of these black female prisoners are known to be foreign "mules" caught bringing drugs into

[1] The National Prison Survey showed that 84 percent of the prison population in 1991 consisted of people aged seventeen to thirty-nine (Walmsley, Howard, and White 1992, p. 9, table 1), making it appropriate to compare the prison population with the general population within this age band. The main reference year is 1991, so that comparisons can be made with the general population data from the decennial census of that year.

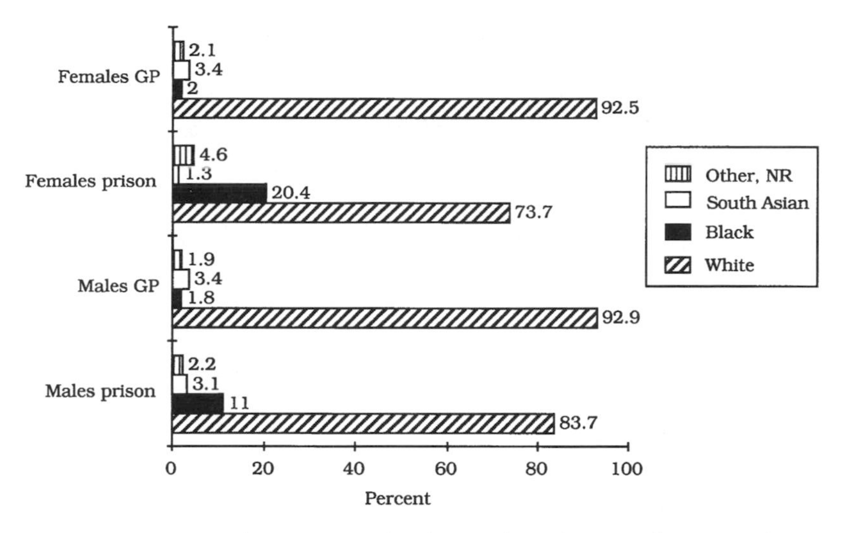

Fig. 2.—Prison population compared with general population aged sixteen to thirty-nine, by race and ethnic group, England and Wales, 1993. Sources: Office of Population Censuses and Surveys 1994; Home Office 1995.

Britain (Green 1991). Among sentenced female black prisoners, nearly half were sentenced for drugs offenses, compared with 15 percent of white female prisoners.

The statistics lump together people of Indian, Pakistani, and Bangladeshi origin. This group forms a slightly smaller proportion of the prison than of the general population in the case of males and a distinctly smaller proportion in the case of females. The other groups (including those of Chinese, Arab, and mixed origin) seem to be overrepresented among the prison population, but this is hard to interpret since the category is so heterogeneous, and it is not possible to make an exact comparison with the 1991 census of the general population.

Figure 3 compares the prison population in 1985 (when these statistics first became available) and 1993. There was some increase over this period in the proportion of prisoners belonging to the black groups. This increase was particularly marked in the case of females, possibly reflecting an increase in the number of drugs "mules" arrested.

The black groups accounted for about the same proportion of prisoners on remand as of those under sentence (see fig. 4). However, in 1993 they accounted for a considerably smaller proportion of sen-

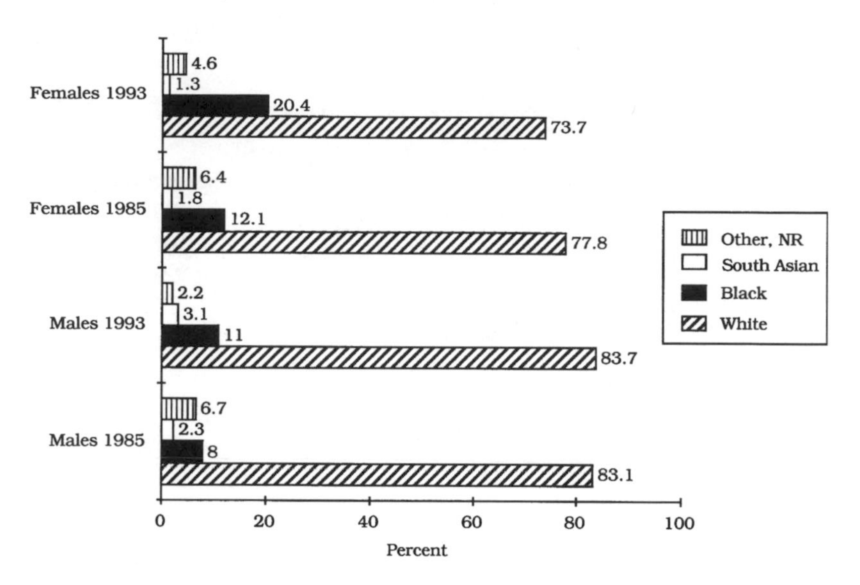

FIG. 3.—Prison population by race and ethnic group, and sex, England and Wales, 1985 and 1993. Source: Home Office 1995.

tenced young offenders than of sentenced adults; this contrast had become more marked between 1985 and 1993.

These comparisons between the prison population and the general population show that the black groups have been heavily overrepresented in prison since records began in 1985. This can be demonstrated more clearly by calculating the rate of imprisonment per head of population in the relevant age-groups. Among sentenced adult males, for example, the rate of imprisonment in 1993 was about the same for South Asians and whites but nearly seven times as high among blacks (see fig. 5). This contrast was slightly stronger among remand prisoners than among sentenced prisoners.

The great majority of prisoners (78 percent in 1991) were under sentence, whereas the remainder were on remand or had been convicted but not yet sentenced. For those under sentence, the published statistics show the type of offense they committed according to ethnic group. For each group of offenses, these counts for 1991 have been used to calculate rates of imprisonment per head of population in the relevant age band (see Figs. 6 and 7).[2] The rate of imprisonment for

[2] Figures 6 and 7 use the statistics from 1991 in preference to those from 1993. The reason is that in 1991 young and adult prisoners under sentence were shown separately according to the offense, whereas in 1993 young and adult prisoners were combined in

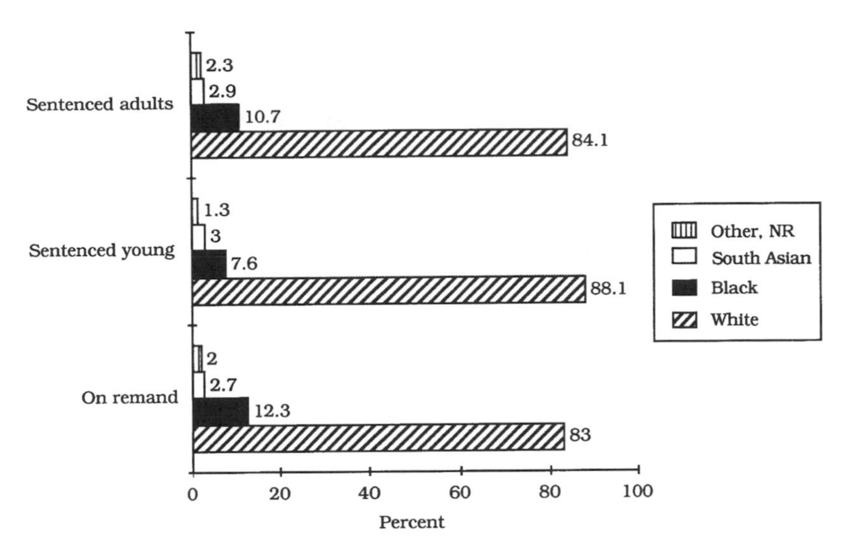

FIG. 4.—Prison population by type of male prisoner, England and Wales, 1993. Source: Home Office 1995.

black males was much higher than for white males for every group of offenses, but there were wide variations between offense groups. About twenty-seven times as many black as white adult males per head of population were in prison for drugs offenses, and eight to nine times as many for rape and for robbery (see fig. 6). This ratio was comparatively low for burglary (about three) and for sexual offenses other than rape (1.5). Among South Asian adult males, the rate of imprisonment for drugs offenses was also very high—about four times as high as among white men. However, the rate of imprisonment of South Asian men for burglary was particularly low at around one-fifth the rate for white men.

In broad terms, the pattern for young offenders was similar (see fig. 7). Young black males had exceptionally high rates of imprisonment for rape, robbery, and drugs offenses—eleven to twelve times the rate for young white males in each case. Again, the contrast was least marked in the case of burglary.

Whereas the prison statistics lump together people of Indian, Pakistani, and Bangladeshi origin, the National Prison Survey provides more detailed information for 1991. These show that the proportions

---

the comparable table. Differences between young and adult offenders here are far more significant than those between 1991 and 1993.

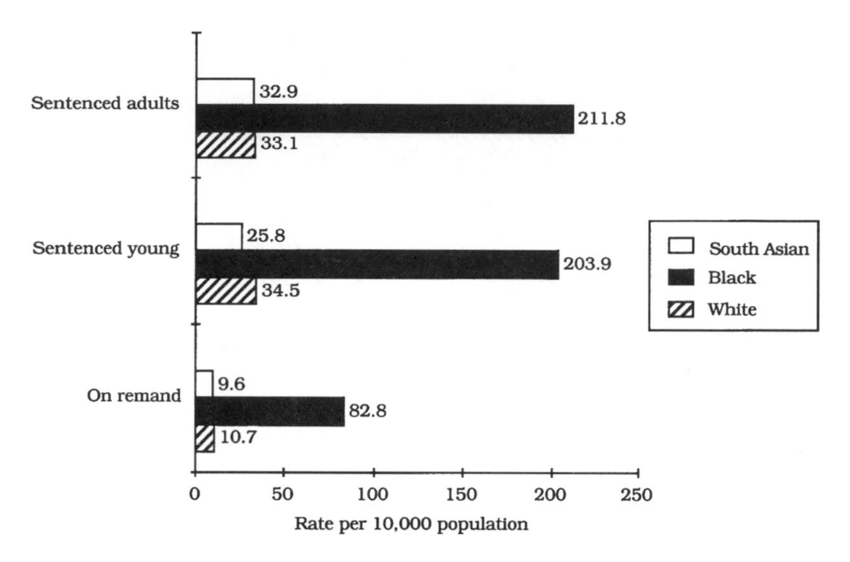

Fig. 5.—Rates of imprisonment, by type of male prisoner, England and Wales, 1993. Sources: Office of Population Censuses and Surveys 1994; Home Office 1995. Note: For prisoners on remand: rate per 10,000 population aged sixteen to thirty-nine. For sentenced young offenders: rate per 10,000 population aged sixteen to nineteen. For sentenced adults: rate per 10,000 population aged twenty to thirty-nine.

of Indians and Bangladeshis in the prison population were about the same as in the general population, but that Pakistanis were overrepresented in the prison population to some extent (Walmsley, Howard, and White 1992, p. 11). Sampling error prevents an exact estimate of this overrepresentation, but it cannot be very marked, particularly if the age structure of the Pakistani population is taken into account. It is important to note that this slight tendency to overrepresentation among the prison population did not apply to all Muslim groups: Bangladeshis were a clear exception.

The prison statistics show that by the end of the criminal justice process, black people (Afro-Caribbeans and black Africans) were far more likely to be undergoing the most severe penalty available—a prison sentence—than white people. Equally striking, they show that South Asians were no more likely to be in prison than white people. Finally, they show that the contrast in rates of imprisonment between black and white people varied dramatically according to the type of offense. The evidence about the outcome of the criminal justice process at the final stage therefore strongly raises the question whether black people are equally treated. Answering that question is much more dif-

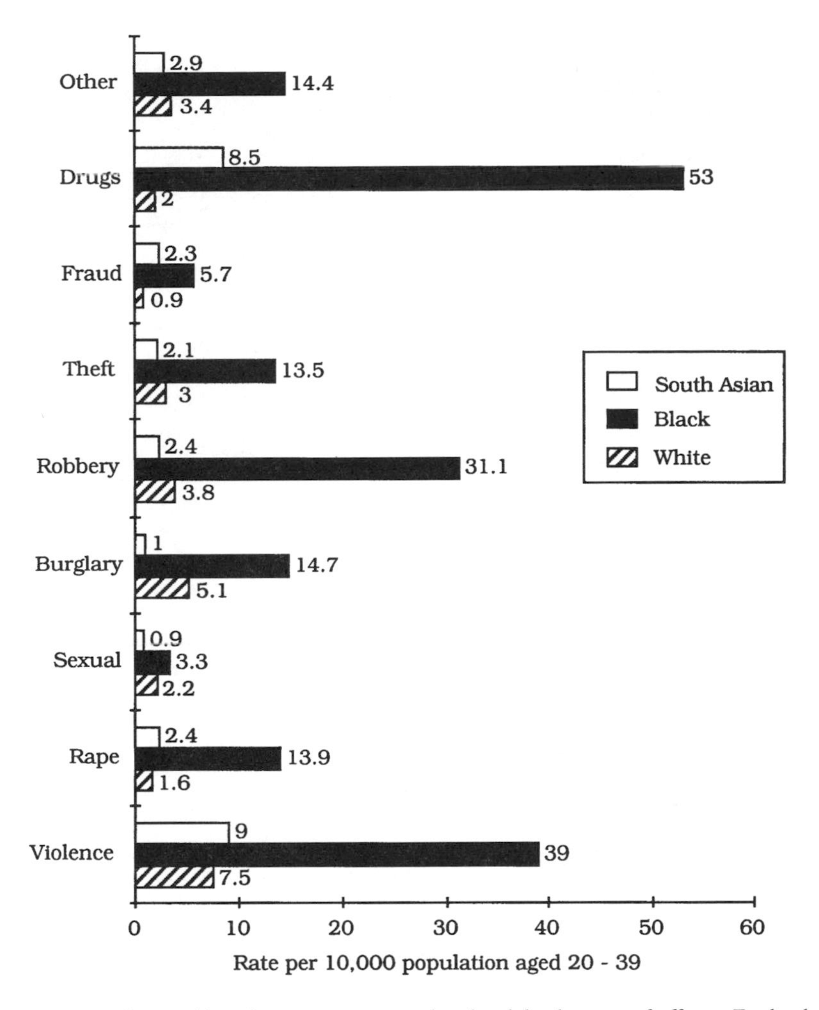

Fig. 6.—Rates of imprisonment, sentenced male adults, by type of offense, England and Wales, 1991. Sources: Office of Population Censuses and Surveys 1994; Home Office 1993.

ficult, but the pattern of results within the prison statistics themselves already gives some purchase.

First, it is highly significant—but has generally been ignored by most commentators—that rates of imprisonment are no higher among South Asians than among white people. As set out earlier, racial discrimination against South Asians, for example, in employment and housing, is just as prevalent as against Afro-Caribbeans (Daniel 1968;

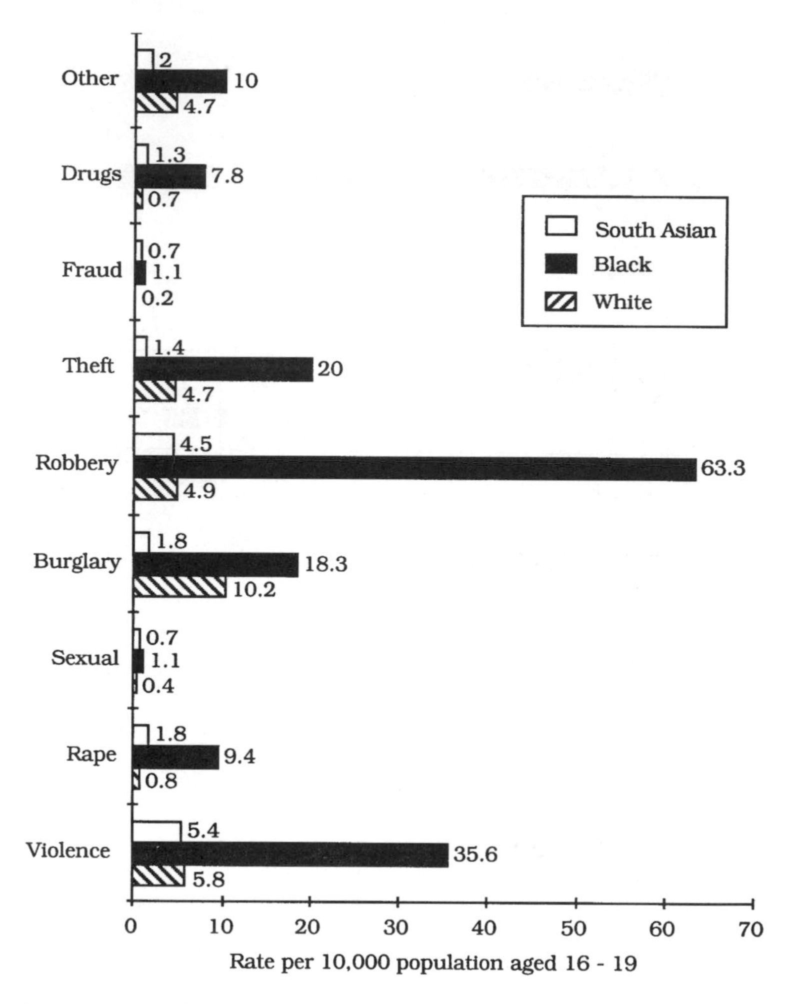

FIG. 7.— Rates of imprisonment, young male sentenced offenders, by type of offense, England and Wales, 1991. Sources: Office of Population Censuses and Surveys 1994; Home Office 1993.

Smith 1977; Brown and Gay 1986). Other manifestations of hostility, such as racial attacks, are also at least as common against South Asians as against Afro-Caribbeans (Home Office 1981; Brown 1984; Mayhew, Elliott, and Dowds 1989). It follows that any generalized notion of "racism" is incapable of explaining the high rate of imprisonment of Afro-Caribbeans. Some commentators, such as Reiner (1989, 1993) and Hudson (1993), have simply ignored this fundamental point. Others, such as Jefferson (1993), have recognized its importance but have sought to preserve the theory that "racism" explains the criminality of ethnic minority groups by postulating that the forms of racism directed against South Asians and Afro-Caribbeans are different. The problem with this approach is that if "racism" takes such extremely different forms it loses its coherence as a concept. Instead of a generalized "racism," what is then being postulated is differentiated forms of hostility toward specific groups. If this differentiated hostility is thought to be the cause of the criminalization of a specific group, it is then necessary to explain why that particular group should have been criminalized rather than other minorities, when those other minorities are equally subject to hostility of other kinds.

Second, it is also potentially important that the contrast in rates of imprisonment between black and white people varies so starkly according to the type of offense. If the overrepresentation of black people among prisoners is the result of bias at various stages of the criminal justice process, then the contrast in rates of imprisonment between black and white people should be greatest for offenses whose detection depends on proactive investigation and the use of discretion; the contrast should be least for offenses where victims generally do not know the ethnic group of the offender, and where the authorities have to decide whether to investigate before they know the ethnic group of the offender. This analytic point is similar to one made by Wilbanks (1987, p. 65) about the pattern of arrests according to offense. In fact, some of the main features of the observed pattern do fit the theory that black people end up in prison because of selective reporting of offenses and discretionary law enforcement. The high rate of imprisonment of black people for drugs offenses is particularly telling. Arrests for drugs offenses notoriously arise from the exercise of police discretion, and it is easy for police and customs officers to target law enforcement in this field at a particular ethnic group. The relatively low rate of imprisonment of black people for burglary may also fit the theory. Householders do not know the ethnic group of the burglar when they decide to report a burglary to the police, and police action against burglary tends to be untargeted and ineffective. However, prosecutions for burglary sometimes arise out of stop-and-search activity, which is known to target black people (as set out in a later section), and from "rounding up the usual suspects," which could in principle be targeted on black people. Thus interpretation of the pattern is based on rather vague assumptions at present, and more detailed information is needed before firm conclusions can be drawn.

B. *Self-Reported Offending*

As part of an international research project, the Home Office carried out a national survey of young people aged fourteen to twenty-five between November 1992 and January 1993. The sampling strategy allowed for overrepresentation of ethnic minorities (before reweighting) and produced subsamples of about 200 black people and 500 South Asians within a total sample of around 2,500. The core of the study was a battery of (normally self-completed) questions about the respondent's own offending and use of illicit drugs. The questioning covered two expressive property offenses, fifteen acquisitive property offenses, and five violent offenses, together with use of thirteen mostly illicit drugs. There were no significant differences in patterns of self-reported offending between black and white respondents, either in terms of lifetime participation in the three types of offense, or in terms of frequency over the past twelve months. Self-reported offending was considerably lower among each of the three South Asian groups (those of Indian, Pakistani, and Bangladeshi origin) than among white or black respondents. Self-reported use of drugs was considerably lower among all four ethnic minority groups than among white respondents. For individual drugs, these differences were statistically significant in the case of cannabis, LSD, amphetamines, magic mushrooms, and glue or gas (Graham and Bowling 1996).

The findings for young black people contradict evidence from other sources, such as victims' reports, which suggest that the rate of offending is considerably higher among black than among white people. Although the self-report method has been widely used by psychologists and criminologists to study patterns of offending and conduct disorders in young people, there has never been good evidence to show that it is an adequate basis for making quantitative estimates. Farrington (1973) demonstrated that self-reports had some validity, in the sense that extent of self-reported offending is related to the acquisition of an official criminal record. He was also able to show in the context of a longitudinal study that self-reported offending to some extent predicts the later acquisition of a criminal record (so the correlation does not arise merely because those who are caught thereby become more likely to admit to their offending). However, he also showed that self-report measures, although having some validity, are rather unreliable. For example, many respondents denied having committed offenses which they claimed to have committed at an earlier interview.

There is evidence from American studies of systematic differences between ethnic groups in the extent to which people conceal or exaggerate their offending (see Sampson and Lauritsen in this volume). Junger (1989) found large systematic biases of this kind in a study of young people in the Netherlands, although her conclusions were contested by Bowling (1990). More generally, differences between all groups (e.g., between males and females) tend to be much smaller in self-report studies than indicated by any other method.

There are obviously serious sampling problems in carrying out self-report studies. Individuals leading unconventional lives, particularly those who carry out a large number of offenses, are unlikely to be included in these surveys for a variety of reasons. A substantial proportion of frequent offenders will be living in some kind of institution at any given time and will therefore be excluded from a survey.

On the balance of the evidence, it seems unlikely that Graham and Bowling's self-report study provides a useful indication of differences in rates of offending among young people according to ethnic group.

C. *Victims' Reports*

So far the analysis has established that the final outcome of the criminal justice process is a very high rate of imprisonment of black people (but *not* South Asians). The next step is to return to the beginning of the process and to consider the limited evidence on how the disparity arises at each successive stage.

Some offenses, such as obstructing a police officer in the execution of his duty, are generated by the decisions of officials; others, such as possession of drugs, only come to notice as a result of action by officials. However, apart from drugs and traffic offenses, the great bulk of offenses processed by the police and the courts first come to notice as a result of victims' reports. The great majority of crime victims (well over 90 percent) are, of course, white; and although there is a considerable tendency for offending to be intraracial, because black people are such a small proportion of the population, most of the offenses they commit are on white people. Indeed, according to BCS data, it is likely that more than 85 percent of offenses committed by black people are on white victims (calculated from Mayhew, Elliott, and Dowds 1989,

p. 47, table 1.3).[3] A possible theory, therefore, is that because of racial hostility or fear, white victims are more strongly motivated to report an incident to the police if they think the offender was black. A grave problem for such a theory, of course, is that racial hostility among the general public is directed just as much against South Asians as against black people. Nevertheless, it is important to consider whether there is specific evidence to support it.

Victim survey data show that in only about one-third of cases can the victim say something about the offender. (See, e.g., Smith 1983*a*, p. 71. In this survey of Londoners carried out in 1981, 36 percent of victims could say something about the offender.) The remaining two-thirds of cases are not relevant to the hypothesis that victims are more likely to report an offense to the police if the offender was black, since the victim did not know the ethnic group of the offender in these cases. This substantially reduces the scope for the victim's reporting behavior to have an influence.

Among offenders that *are* described by victims, there is a substantial overrepresentation of black people.[4] The PSI survey of Londoners carried out in 1981 found that people described as "black" were represented among offenders about four times as strongly as among the general population (Smith 1983*a*, p. 73). The proportion of offenders described as black was highest for theft from the person (about eight times the proportion of black people in the general population). It was not particularly high for assault (lower than for all offenses taken together). Asians were substantially underrepresented among offenders described by victims at that time. The findings of the BCS are broadly in agreement (see fig. 1). For example, the 1988 BCS showed that 8 percent of offenders described by white victims were "black," while 2

[3] The true proportion is probably considerably higher than 85 percent, because the BCS data are confined to cases where the victim could say something about the offender. The proportion of black-on-black crimes tends to be higher for personal contact offenses where the victim is likely to be able to describe the offender.

[4] According to the PSI survey (Smith 1983, table III.3), cases where the victim could say something about the offender varied from a high of 83 percent in the case of assault to a low of 17 percent in the case of damage to a motor vehicle. Just 39 percent of victims of theft from the person could describe the offender, and of these 46 percent said the offender was black. The proportion who could describe the offender was well under half for every type of offense except assault. This suggests that victims' descriptions provide only limited information. It is possible, in principle, that the proportion of offenders who were black was lower among those that victims could not than among those they could describe, but it is hard to think of any reason why this should be so. It is reasonable to suppose, therefore, that victims' reports are a useful indicator of the ethnic composition of offenders, even though they are highly incomplete.

percent were Asian (Mayhew, Elliott, and Dowds 1989, p. 47, table 1.3). At that time, all the "black" groups accounted for around 1.6 percent of the population of Britain, so offenders described by white people as "black" were overrepresented by a factor of 5:1. Asians were, again, somewhat underrepresented among the offenders described by victims.

Police data are available for London in 1984 and 1985 for two kinds of offense (assaults, and robbery or other violent theft; see table 2). Confining the analysis to cases where the victim could describe the offender, 31 percent of assailants were nonwhite in the case of assaults, and 67 percent in the case of robbery and other violent thefts. These statistics are difficult to interpret because of the vagueness of the term "nonwhite." The proportion of offenders described by victims as "nonwhite" was extraordinarily high in the case of robbery and other violent theft.[5]

A combined analysis of the 1982, 1984, and 1988 BCS data shows little difference in the proportion of incidents reported to the police according to whether the offender was described as white or nonwhite (Shah and Pease 1992). This analysis was confined to offenses of personal violence (including sexual assaults and robbery). In detail, the probability of an incident being reported to the police was related to its seriousness in combination with the described race of the offender, but none of these differences was large, and they tended to cancel out. Shah and Pease (1992, pp. 198–99, table 6) also showed that recalled incidents involving a white offender were no more recent than those involving a black offender, which argues against differential recall according to the ethnic group of the offender.

Three points emerge from this analysis of evidence about the first stage of the criminal justice process. First, if victims are more likely to report incidents to the police where the offender is perceived to be black, this can only have an influence in about one-third of cases involving individual victims, for in the remaining two-thirds of cases the victim cannot describe the offender. Second, black people are heavily overrepresented among offenders described by victims before the criminal justice process begins, that is, among the descriptions in victim surveys which include incidents that were and were not reported

[5] These miscellaneous findings are very hard to compare with one another. For example, the PSI findings for "theft from the person" cannot be compared with the police data for "robbery and other violent theft" because the former category is largely nonviolent.

to the police. Third, there is little or no difference in the proportion of incidents reported to the police according to whether the offender is perceived to be black. These findings suggest that differential reporting to the police is not a significant factor leading to the criminalization of black people and that much of the difference in rate of criminalization between black and white people arises at the earliest possible stage: when the offense is observed, and before it is reported.

Against this, there is one piece of indirect evidence on reporting rates (Stevens and Willis 1979). From analysis of statistics on recorded crimes of violence in 1975 produced by the London police, Stevens and Willis showed that a much smaller proportion of black-on-white crimes than of other types caused injury. One possible explanation of this pattern is that victims report to the police assaults on nonwhites which would be too trivial to report when committed by whites. However, this conflicts with the BCS evidence summarized above, and as Shah and Pease (1992) point out, because these statistics relate to recorded crime, the observed pattern could be a reflection of police recording behavior. The likely explanation is that "some offenses are recorded by the police as having been committed by non-whites or as involving assaultive behavior when the event was not reported to them in these terms" (Shah and Pease 1992, p. 193).

D. *Police Stops*

Among those offenders who are processed by the criminal justice system, a considerable proportion are drawn into the net through the exercise of discretionary powers by the police, particularly stop and search. Thus, a survey of London police officers carried out in 1982 showed that 23 percent of arrests arose from a stop (Smith 1983*b*, p. 81, table V.3). The proportion of arrests arising from a stop was particularly high for driving offenses (64 percent), taking and driving away a vehicle or vehicle theft (47 percent), and drugs offenses (39 percent) (Smith 1983*b*, p. 87, table V.6). At that time, most of the stop and search powers were not consolidated within national legislation, although a variety of local powers existed. Consequently, police practice on stops may have varied widely between different parts of the country, and the use of stop and search was probably greater in London than in most other places. Since the Police and Criminal Evidence Act 1984 (PACE) came into force, police throughout England and Wales have had authority to stop persons or vehicles on the reasonable suspicion that they would find stolen goods or prohibited articles and to carry out searches of vehicles and persons stopped. Other legislation also gives police authority to stop and search for other reasons, for example, to look for controlled drugs. Although up-to-date statistics are not available, it seems likely that a substantial proportion of arrests now result from stops throughout the country. Clearly the overrepresentation of black people at later stages in the process could in principle arise partly because the police use their discretion to stop a larger proportion of black people than of other ethnic groups.

1. *Pattern.* A survey carried out in three parts of Manchester in 1980 found no significant difference between Afro-Caribbeans and whites in terms of the proportion who had been "stopped, searched or arrested" within the last year or in the number of times this had happened (Tuck and Southgate 1981). These data do not distinguish between stops and arrests, and because of the rather small sample sizes, the 1.43:1 ratio between the 10 percent of Afro-Caribbeans and the 7 percent of white people who were "stopped, searched, or arrested" does not reach statistical significance. This survey covered a single police division which extended over parts of five wards and had a population of 33,000.

Other studies, which have all covered larger and more heterogeneous areas, have found differences in stop rates between black and white people. Willis (1983), who analyzed stops recorded at four police stations, found that these were two to three times as high for black people as for the general population.[6] The PSI survey of Londoners carried out in 1981 found that the proportion stopped in the previous twelve months was 24 percent for Afro-Caribbeans, 17 percent for whites, and 7 percent for South Asians. Also, among those who had been stopped at all, Afro-Caribbeans had on average been stopped twice as often as white people. The stop rate among young males aged fifteen to twenty-four was found to be very high. Within this group, 66 percent of the Afro-Caribbeans had been stopped an average number of 4.1 times in twelve months, while 44 percent of the whites had been stopped an average number of 2.6 times (Smith 1983*a*, pp. 96–100). In an observational study carried out in 1986–87 in three police divisions (two in London and one in Surrey), Norris et al. (1992) found that black people accounted for 28 percent of persons stopped by the police, compared with 10 percent of the local population. Among males aged up to thirty-five, they calculated that the stop rate per 100

[6] Willis estimated that about half of the stops actually carried out were recorded.

population was about thirty-three for blacks, compared with about ten for whites.[7]

National data are available from the 1988 British Crime Survey, which was carried out well after national stop powers were consolidated in the Police and Criminal Evidence Act. Within the fourteen-month reference period, 15 percent of white people, 20 percent of Afro-Caribbeans, and 14 percent of South Asians said they had been stopped by the police. The difference in stop rates between Afro-Caribbeans and white people or South Asians remained significant within a multivariate model including the following variables: age, income, sex, vehicle access, occupation, tenure, urban versus rural area (five types), length of education, marital status, and whether unemployed (Skogan 1990, p. 28). An analysis of the 1992 BCS used a wider definition of "stops," including, as well as traffic and pedestrian stops, orders to show documents or give a statement, and other police-initiated contacts in which respondents were under suspicion. On this basis, 36 percent of Afro-Caribbean respondents had been "stopped" during the reference period, compared with 22 percent of whites and the same proportion of Asians (Skogan 1994).

Jefferson (1988) and Walker (1987) have suggested that the study of parts of Manchester (Tuck and Southgate 1981) failed to find a difference between Afro-Caribbean and white people in stop rates because it was carried out in a relatively small and homogeneous area. They believe that what is being observed in the BCS and the PSI London survey is differences in policing practice between types of area: for example, higher stop rates in disadvantaged urban settings where concentrations of Afro-Caribbeans tend to be high. Jefferson (1993) has suggested in particular that the style of policing is more a response to the social and housing composition of the area than to the ethnic group of potential suspects. Whatever the merits of this argument in general terms, it is not needed to explain the Tuck and Southgate findings. These do not relate to stops alone, and as Skogan has pointed out (1990, p. 53), they do not necessarily indicate a different ratio between the rate of police-initiated encounters among Afro-Caribbean and white people from that shown by the BCS: the sample size in the Tuck and Southgate study was simply too small to demonstrate a contrast of the order shown by the BCS.

[7] Because the same individuals are often stopped repeatedly, this does not equate with the proportion of the population who were stopped.

In a later article, Jefferson, Walker, and Seneviratne (1992) used police records of stops and searches to compare parts of Leeds where ethnic minorities account for more versus less than 10 percent of the population.[8] They found that in areas of *low* ethnic concentration, the stop rate was *higher* for black than for white or South Asian people, whereas in areas of *high* ethnic concentration, the stop rate was *lower* for black than for white or South Asian people. However, the 1981 PSI survey of Londoners showed no difference in stop rates (all stops, regardless of whether there was a search) among either Afro-Caribbeans or South Asians according to the concentration of ethnic minorities in the local area, defined as a census enumeration district, which contains 150 households on average. Also, the survey showed no difference in stop rates among white people according to the concentration of ethnic minorities in the ward where they lived (unpublished data available from the author on request).

From a survey carried out as part of the Leeds study within census enumeration districts having a high concentration (10 percent or more) of ethnic minorities, Jefferson and Walker (1992, 1993) found that the stop rate (in 1987) was *lower* among black and South Asian people than among white people living nearby. They interpreted this result as showing that the stop rate is determined by the social characteristics of the areas rather than the ethnic group of the individual. It is more likely, however, that the finding reflects the unusual characteristics of those white people who live in areas of high ethnic concentration. For example, Jefferson and Walker's own results show that a high proportion of this particular white population lives in rented accommodation and is transient, characteristics associated with police targeting.

On balance, there is a consistent body of evidence to show that Afro-Caribbeans are more likely to be stopped than white people or South Asians. There is some conflict of evidence about how marked these differences are, but they are much smaller than the differences in rates of imprisonment. They probably do make some contribution to explaining the high rate of imprisonment of Afro-Caribbeans, but they can only explain a small part of it. That is not only because the ethnic

[8] The Police and Criminal Evidence Act 1984 requires the police to make a record where a member of the public is stopped and searched, and these are the records used by Jefferson, Walker, and Seneviratne. The earlier survey findings referred to stops as a whole, a far more inclusive category.

differences in stop rates are relatively small but also because this kind of policing generates less than one-quarter of arrests.

2. *Decision.* Given that black people (but not South Asians) are more likely to be stopped by police than white people, the question that arises is how police officers take these decisions and whether they amount to unequal treatment of black people. As Skogan (1990, p. 32) has pointed out, the most important factor here is that the vast majority of stops do not produce an arrest or prosecution.[9] The implication of the low "strike rate" is that the exercise of this kind of police power is highly discretionary. The law requires in principle that the police officer should have "reasonable suspicion" to justify stopping or searching someone, but in practice this criterion is extremely weak and largely unenforceable. The BCS 1988 showed that of those stopped on foot, only 4 percent reported being arrested and 3 percent were prosecuted. The comparable figures for those involved in traffic stops were 1 percent arrested and 10 percent prosecuted—the prosecutions being mainly fixed penalty and vehicle defect notices (Skogan 1990, p. 32). The low "strike rate" is confirmed by local surveys in Merseyside (Kinsey 1985) and London (Smith 1983*a*) and by earlier national estimates from police records (Willis 1983).

Because the criteria that determine whether a stop is justified are weak, vague, and unenforceable, the question whether the relatively high stop rate for black people amounts to unequal treatment is very hard to answer. The PSI survey of Londoners found that the proportion of stops leading to an arrest or to an offense being reported was the same for Afro-Caribbeans and white people (Smith 1983*a*, p. 116). In their observational study, Norris et al. (1992) found that the police took "formal action" in 40 percent of cases following a stop of a black person, compared with 31 percent of cases where the person was white, a difference that was not statistically significant. "Formal action" included issuing a fixed penalty notice, requiring documents to be produced at a police station at a later date, filling in a crime report, officially recording the person's name and address, and arrest. At one level these findings show that the higher stop rate of Afro-Caribbeans is "justified by results," which may suggest that it does not amount to unequal treatment. As pointed out in Section I above, however, decisions made within the criminal justice system tend to be self-validating.

[9] However, because such a vast number of stops are carried out, a considerable proportion of arrests arise from stops.

Decisions at later stages may be influenced by a need to justify a decision earlier on. In the present case, it remains possible that the police, given that they stop a higher proportion of black than of white people, then work harder to find an offense with which to charge a black than a white person they have stopped and to put together the evidence to support the charge.

Observational research casts some further light on the factors that influence the police in deciding to make a stop. In the course of extensive observational research on policing in London, Smith and Gray (1983) observed a total of 129 stops. In 18 percent of cases the person was seen to commit a traffic offense, in half of cases the researchers judged there was some other specific reason for "reasonable suspicion," while they judged that there was no reason at all to make the stop in one-third of cases. On a number of occasions, stops made for no reason did produce a "result." Smith and Gray concluded that "it is clear from the way that police officers talk about stops that the question of what their legal powers may be does not enter into their decision-making except in the case of rarc individuals." Specific reasons for making a stop, apart from traffic offenses, were that a person was running, hurrying, or loitering, was rowdy or drunk, or was driving in an erratic manner. Where there was no specific reason, the criteria that police officers used were ones they associated with the chance of getting a "result." They tended to choose young males, especially young black males; people who looked scruffy or poor, people who had long hair or unconventional dress, and homosexuals. They also tended to choose cars with several young males in them, old cars, and certain specific car models (believed to be often stolen). The researchers gained the impression that whether the person was Afro-Caribbean was a criterion, but that other criteria were more important.

The observational study by Norris et al. (1992) is the only one to cast light on the question whether police decisions are influenced by the demeanor of black and white people. In all, Norris and colleagues, working in two police divisions in London and one in Surrey, observed 213 police stops which involved 319 people, although the number of cases is often reduced for specific analyses because of incomplete information. The bulk of the stops were related to traffic matters or to order maintenance; only 7 percent were crime-related. There was no significant difference between stops of black and white people in this respect. A higher proportion of blacks than of whites (56 compared with 42 percent) were stopped on general suspicion rather than tangible evidence.[10] Turning to the person's demeanor, there was no difference between white and black persons with regard to whether they were calm versus agitated, or civil versus antagonistic, either at the time of the stop or at the time of processing. A significantly higher proportion of white than of black persons stopped appeared to be under the influence of alcohol (20 percent compared with 8 percent at the time of the stop). Police demeanor toward the person stopped was rated as "negative" in a higher proportion of cases where the person was white than where he or she was black (27 percent compared with 10 percent at the time of the stop). These findings speak strongly against the theory that the high stop rate of black people is caused by their hostile behavior toward the police. They suggest, instead, that stops of black people are rather more likely to be speculative than stops of white people.

This last conclusion is confirmed by the 1981 survey of Londoners (Smith 1983*a*, p. 112), which found that people who had been stopped thought the police had good reasons for stopping them in 59 percent of cases. A lower proportion of Afro-Caribbeans (38 percent) than of white people (59 percent) or South Asians (62 percent) thought there was a good reason for the stop. The PSI study (Smith and Gray 1983) also agreed with Norris et al. (1992) in finding that encounters between the police and black people were no more strained than those between the police and other ethnic groups.

The 1988 BCS found that once stopped, Afro-Caribbeans were substantially more likely to be searched than white people or South Asians (Skogan 1990, p. 34). In the case of traffic stops, this difference remained significant after controlling for the effects of a number of factors including past arrests within a multivariate model.

3. *Police Behavior.* The 1988 BCS found that about one quarter of those stopped by the police while on foot, and about one in five of those involved in a traffic stop, thought the police behavior had been impolite. Afro-Caribbeans were much more likely than white people or South Asians to think the police had been impolite, and this difference remained after controlling for a range of other factors (Skogan 1990, p. 36). In particular, people were more critical of police behavior if the stop led to some sanction (such as arrest or a reported offense), but this did not explain the difference between Afro-Caribbeans and white

[10] This difference is significant at better than the 5 percent level of confidence (calculated by the present author from Norris et al.'s published results).

people. Respondents were more likely to think the police had been polite where a reason was given for the stop, a finding which replicates the 1981 London survey (Smith 1983*a*). Again, this did not explain the difference between Afro-Caribbean and white people.

The 1981 London survey found little or no difference between ethnic groups in the proportion who said the police explained the reason for the stop (Smith 1983*a*, pp. 107–9). A smaller proportion of Afro-Caribbeans than of white people or South Asians thought the police were polite and that they behaved in a fair and reasonable manner, but these differences were not striking (Smith 1983*a*, p. 112). From their observational work as part of the same study, Smith and Gray (1983) concluded that where people were stopped the encounter was fairly relaxed and friendly in the great majority of cases. While the survey showed that for 19 percent of stops people thought the police had not behaved in a fair and reasonable manner, the researchers judged from their observations that the police behaved aggressively in a smaller proportion of cases than that, but a failure to give an explanation might underlie people's responses in some cases. Norris et al. (1992) in their observational study found that police were more likely to behave in a "negative" way toward white than toward black suspects.

Smith (1983*a*) conducted an intensive analysis of the relationship between critical views of the police (the belief that they fabricate evidence, use unnecessary violence, etc.) and patterns of contact with them. This showed a strong correlation between the amount of contact (of any kind) and critical views, although a later analysis (unpublished) showed that service contacts, primarily as a victim of crime, were only associated with negative views if those specific contacts were negatively evaluated. Within this general framework, stops tended to dominate the picture as (mildly) adversarial contacts that were very large in quantity and associated with critical views of the police. In a survey of parts of Leeds, Jefferson and Walker (1993) also found a relationship between the number of times stopped and critical views. From these findings it is likely that the large-scale practice of stop and search, and the disproportionate stopping of Afro-Caribbeans, has been among the causes of hostility between Afro-Caribbeans and the police. However, both the Leeds and London studies show that the relatively high level of criticism of the police among Afro-Caribbeans compared with white people cannot be wholly explained by their personal encounters with the police (see Smith [1991] for further discussion of this point on the basis of the London findings).

E. Arrests

No national statistics are available on the ethnic group of persons arrested, but data are available for London (the Metropolitan Police District) starting in 1975.[11] Figure 8 summarizes the results for 1987. Black people formed a much higher proportion of those arrested than of the general population, whereas South Asians formed exactly the same proportion of the two groups; this pattern had been broadly the same from 1975 onward. Figure 8 shows that the proportion of those arrested who were black varied little according to the offense, except that it was extraordinarily high for robbery (54 percent in 1987).

For certain offenses between 1975 and 1985, the Metropolitan Police also recorded the ethnic origin of the offender from the victim's description. For these offenses, there is a fairly close correspondence between the proportion of offenders described as nonwhite by victims and the proportion of people arrested who were nonwhite (see fig. 9). It is notable that both for persons arrested and for offenders as described by victims, the proportion who were nonwhite was much lower in the case of assaults than in the case of robberies and snatches. The statistics cover only a few specific offenses, and they may well be influenced by police recording practices. Nonetheless, they suggest that there was little or no tendency for the arrest rate *per offender* to be higher for black than for white suspects.

Disregarding the victims' descriptions of offenders, the London statistics show such a large difference in arrest rates *per head of population* between black and white people that an explanation substantially in terms of biased policing is implausible. Walker (1987) hinted at this conclusion, but added that "this must be a subjective judgement." That considerably understates the strength of the evidence. Using the 1983 statistics, Walker calculated that if the actual rate of burglary by black and white offenders were the same, then the arrest statistics would imply that black burglars had four and a half times the chance of being arrested compared with white burglars. That is an implausible hypothesis, because police action against burglars is so ineffective. The police are incapable of increasing the arrest rate for burglary by more than a small amount. Even if they could substantially increase the burglary arrest rate, it is unlikely that they could target such an increase on black people with any degree of accuracy. The relatively high rate of

[11] These statistics cover arrests for notifiable offenses (that excludes minor including most traffic offenses) that were followed by further action (caution, referral to juvenile bureau, or charge).

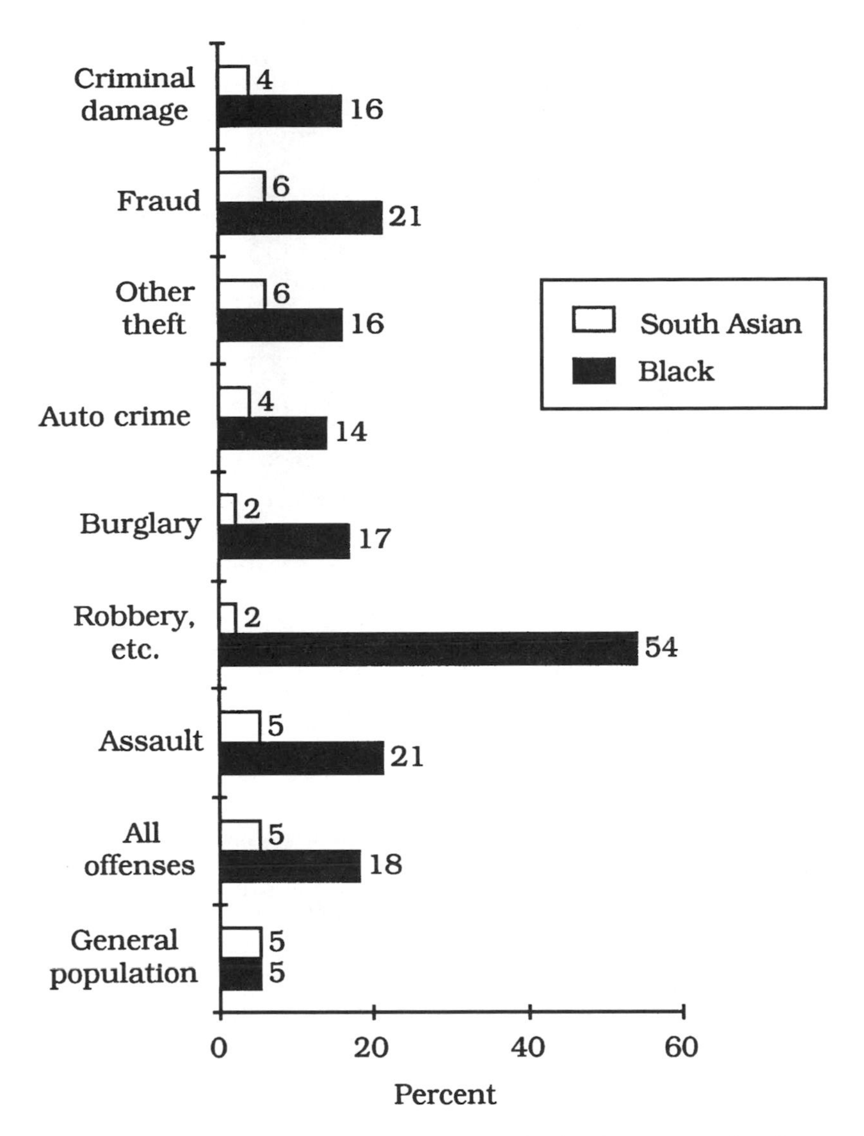

FIG. 8.—Percentages of persons arrested who were black and South Asian, by offense, London, 1987. Source: Home Office 1989*a*, table 4. Note: The figure includes persons arrested in London for notifiable offenses that were followed by further action (caution, referral to juvenile bureau, charge). The general population figures are estimates for 1984–86 of the black and South Asian population of London aged ten and over as a percentage of the total population aged ten and over. "Robbery, etc." includes "theft from the person" except for pickpocketing, which is included under "other theft."

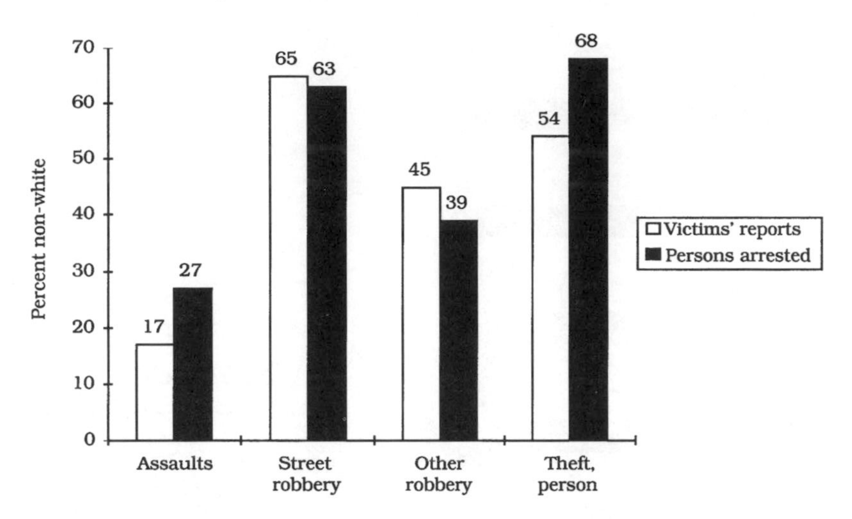

Fig. 9.—Victim's descriptions of offenders compared with police records of persons arrested, London, 1985. Source: Home Office (1989*a*). Note: For victims' reports, the figure shows the percentage who were "nonwhite," whereas for arrests it shows the percentage who were "black or Asian." For victims' reports, the percentages are based on cases where the victim could describe the offender. They otherwise cover all recorded offenses in the categories shown.

stops of black people (see the previous section) would produce a few extra arrests of burglars, but the effect would be trivial in the context of a 4.5:1 ratio in arrest rates. Targeting previous black offenders would be a possible strategy, but there is evidence that not many burglary arrests are made in this way (Smith 1983*b*, p. 87, table V.6). In the case of robbery, Walker calculated that if actual rates of offending were the same for black and white people, the statistics imply that the rate of arrest was fourteen times higher for black than for white robbers in 1983. There is more that the police could do in the case of robbery to target an increase in detections on black people, but the scope for this is nevertheless limited, and the hypothesis of a fourteen times increase seems absurd.

On any reasonable assessment, therefore, the London statistics reflect a much higher rate of offending among black than white people. Unfortunately, they do not resolve the issue as to whether there is bias in policing practice. The comparison between victims' reports and arrest statistics (fig. 9) tends to suggest that the overall effect of any such bias is fairly small, but this evidence is fragmentary.

Walker (1992) analyzed the arrest rates of males aged eleven to thirty-five in six police subdivisions within Leeds during a six-month period in 1987, when police recorded whether people arrested were white, black, or Asian. Like other elements within this research program, this analysis compares white and black people living in the same very small areas (census enumeration districts [EDs], containing 150 households on average). In the high ethnic concentration EDs (those with more than 10 percent "nonwhite households"), the arrest rate for black people was lower than for white people, while in the lower-concentration EDs the arrest rate was higher for black than for white people. This mirrors the pattern shown for stops (see earlier section). As before, the likely explanation is that white people in areas of high ethnic concentration are an unusual and high-crime group. In the city as a whole, the arrest rate was more than twice as high for black as for white people.

In the PSI London survey respondents were asked whether they had ever been arrested and whether they had been arrested in the past five years. Because respondents have strong motives for concealment, and for other reasons, these questions were not expected to produce good estimates of arrest rates, but where respondents said they had been arrested in the past five years, they were asked detailed questions about each of the last three occasions.[12] The sample size is rather small (137 people gave accounts of a total of 169 arrests) but large enough to form a reasonable basis for generalization.

[12] It is stated in the report that "there are strong motives for concealment" and that "it is fair to assume that there are people in the survey who have been arrested but deny it" (Smith 1983*a*, p. 118). Walker (1987) argues that the survey data show much lower arrest rates than the official statistics. In fact, estimated arrest rates cannot be derived from the data shown in the report (Smith 1983*a*, pp. 118 ff.) so it is unclear where Walker's "PSI-based" arrest rates come from. Estimates were not attempted because it was assumed that a small proportion of people are arrested a large number of times, and that these people will (*a*) tend not to be included in surveys, (*b*) tend not to tell the truth, and (*c*) find it hard to remember about all their arrests over a five-year period. A further, serious, problem is that at any given time a substantial proportion of this often-arrested group will be in prison, and therefore ineligible for inclusion in a survey of people in private households. In spite of these problems, it was judged that the survey could provide reasonably accurate estimates of the proportion of stops leading to an arrest, because these questions used a twelve-month recall period (instead of the five years for arrests generally) and because the population of people stopped is large and unlikely to have highly unusual characteristics. Because not all respondents admitted to arrests that had actually occurred, there is clearly the possibility of bias when comparing experience of arrest between ethnic groups. All that can be said about this is that the comparisons will have some validity unless the tendency to deny experience of arrest is stronger among members of one ethnic group than another. Also, the problem will not be serious unless a substantial proportion of those who have been arrested deny all experience of arrest, rather than simply failing to report some of the arrests that have occurred.

> A statistical analysis of the pre-coded questions shows that in 47 percent of cases people thought the police were behaving unreasonably in arresting them; in 59 percent of cases, people had criticisms to make of the way the police behaved toward them; in 26 percent of cases they thought a police officer said something rude or insulting to them; in 22 percent of cases they said that police officers used force or hit them, in 18 percent of cases unjustifiably in the person's opinion; in 20 percent of cases people thought the police threatened them or put unfair pressure on them in some other way; and in 47 percent of cases people thought they were treated unfairly overall in connection with the arrest. (Smith 1983*a*, p. 312)

Thus, a substantial proportion of people who said they had been arrested had serious criticisms to make of the way they were treated. From the accounts that respondents also gave in their own words, a substantial proportion made very specific allegations against the police, ones involving gross misconduct in many cases. However, Afro-Caribbeans were no more likely than white people to think they had been badly treated or to make serious allegations of this kind: in fact, if anything, the answers given by Afro-Caribbeans were more favorable to the police. The number of South Asians who said they had been arrested was too small for any conclusion to be drawn in their case.

F. Decision to Prosecute

A majority of arrests overall lead to the arrested person answering in court to a criminal charge or charges, but a substantial minority of arrested persons do not end up in court.[13] In the case of juveniles (aged up to seventeen) official policy over the past twenty years has increasingly encouraged alternatives to prosecution, chiefly formal cautions. Currently, only about one-third of arrests of juveniles lead to a prosecution. Under the Home Office *Guidelines on Cautioning*, it is an absolute requirement that the accused person should admit the offense if a caution is to be granted. The guidelines also say that both the offense and the offender's past record should be taken into account. Within these rather wide constraints, different police forces have adopted dif-

[13] A large number of prosecutions—nearly all for minor, especially traffic, offenses—originate from the police reporting an offense, followed by a summons, without the suspect ever being arrested. However, in the vast majority of cases involving more serious (notifiable) offenses, the criminal process is started by an arrest, so the analysis here concentrates on the path from arrest to prosecution.

ferent criteria for deciding whether to caution or charge juveniles and there is wide scope for the exercise of discretion by individual officers in applying forcewide criteria, since the decision to charge rather than caution cannot be challenged by the accused or by any independent person or authority.

In a proportion of cases (probably around 5 percent) the police decide to take no further action following an arrest: that is, they release the person without issuing a charge or caution.

Not everyone charged with an offense ultimately stands trial. The most important factor here is that following the establishment through the Prosecution of Offenses Act 1985 of a Crown Prosecution Service independent of the police, the prosecuting authority may decide that the evidence is insufficient to justify a prosecution.

Unfortunately, evidence on the flow of cases from arrest to prosecution is fragmentary. It is here that longitudinal studies are particularly needed, but they have not yet been carried out. In principle it is entirely possible that following an arrest ethnic minorities are more likely than white people to be prosecuted. This is a large potential source of inequality in the case of juveniles, since most juvenile offenses do not result in a charge. Because a relatively high proportion of arrested adults are prosecuted, the scope for bias in their case is not as great, but it must still be substantial.[14] In the United States, the evidence that black people are at a disadvantage within the criminal justice process is much stronger for juveniles than for adults (see Sampson and Lauritsen, in this volume).

The very limited data available about the treatment of ethnic minorities in England and Wales at this important stage of the process relate mainly to juveniles. The Commission for Racial Equality (1992) summarized the early results of ethnic monitoring in seven police forces of the processing of juvenile suspects, although so far useful data were available for only five of these forces. In four of the five areas, a considerably higher proportion of Afro-Caribbean than of white juvenile suspects were prosecuted. The data from these monitoring exercises were not consolidated nor subjected to intensive analysis. However, from certain limited analyses reported, it seems likely that the difference in treatment between ethnic groups may be explained by the proportion denying the offense (there is evidence that this is higher for Afro-

[14] I have not been able to find good data on the proportion of arrested adults who are prosecuted, but this is likely to be well over half.

Caribbeans than for whites), the proportion having previous convictions (higher among Afro-Caribbeans than whites in some areas), and the proportion already on bail or warrant or still subject to conditional discharge (apparently higher among Afro-Caribbeans than whites in the West Midlands). However, because the analyses reported are rudimentary, no firm conclusions can be drawn.

A few more detailed studies have been reported of the police processing of juvenile suspects, but even the most recent of these (Landau and Nathan 1983) uses data that are now fifteen years old. The processing of juvenile offenders has changed substantially over the last fifteen years, so there is no knowledge, based on systematic research, of the operation of current policies and practices. Landau (1981) and Landau and Nathan (1983) examined police decisions on juvenile suspects made during the last quarter of 1978 in five police divisions in London. At that time there was a two-stage procedure. At stage A, the police either charged immediately (19.6 percent of cases) or referred the case to the juvenile bureau (80.4 percent). At stage B, the bureau decided either to charge after all (37.9 percent), to caution (36.3 percent) or to take "no further action" (6.2 percent). The first paper considered stage A, while the second considered stage B. The analyses compared black (Afro-Caribbean and black African) juveniles with whites; South Asians and other ethnic groups were excluded. At the first stage, a substantially higher proportion of black than of white juveniles were immediately charged, and this applied to every type of offense except auto crime. In the context of a multivariate model including age, sex, offense, area (two boroughs included in each of three areas), and previous offenses, there remained a substantial difference in the probability of immediate charge between black and white juveniles. As Walker (1987) has pointed out, the analysis did not take account of social class. At the second stage, the minority (6.2 percent) for whom no further action was taken were unaccountably excluded. Among the remainder, 53.7 percent of the whites, compared with 39.7 percent of the blacks, were cautioned. A substantial difference remained between black and white juveniles in the probability of being cautioned in the context of a logistic regression model including the following independent variables: previous criminal record; offense; ethnic group; whether a "latchkey child," that is, according to the official record, left on their own without parental control on a regular basis; age; and area (three groups of two boroughs). Sex and tenure of accommodation (a proxy for social class) were also investigated but were only weakly related to whether the juvenile was cautioned or charged, and were not included in the final model. The probability of a caution was higher for white than for black juveniles for all six types of offense except "traffic and other." Although white were more likely than black juveniles to be charged immediately with car crimes at stage A, this was compensated by stage B, where they were much more likely to be cautioned.

In the second of the two articles, Landau and Nathan (1983) included an interesting discussion of the principles underlying juvenile justice and considered the implications of their findings in the light of those principles. If the police decisions on the processing of juvenile suspects are to be made on the basis of formal rationality, as interpreted by Weber (1954), then only "legal variables" should be taken into account (previous criminal record, the nature and seriousness of the offense, whether the offense is admitted). However, it can be argued that the principle guiding the juvenile justice system is substantive justice (on the model of Weber's substantive rationality) rather than formal justice. In that case, it is important to distinguish between variables that reflect legitimate criteria of substantive justice, such as the character and social circumstances of the suspect, and other nonlegal variables that cannot be legitimate criteria, such as sex, ethnic group, and social class.

Against that background, the variables included in Landau and Nathan's analysis can be sorted into three groups: criteria of formal justice (the offense, previous criminal record), criteria of substantive justice (age, whether a latchkey child), and illegitimate criteria (sex, ethnic group, tenure, area). The analysis shows that variables of all three types have an important influence on the outcome, but previous criminal record (a criterion of formal justice) has the strongest effect.

Landau and Nathan described the illegitimate criteria as discriminatory, by which they meant directly discriminatory. They recognized that the use of "substantive criteria" could work to the disadvantage of black juveniles: for example, a higher proportion of the black juveniles were charged partly because a higher proportion were classified as "latchkey children." This is a clear example of the use of a criterion that works to the disadvantage of black people; it also clearly illustrates the difficulty of deciding whether the use of such criteria can be justified, as discussed in Section I. Landau and Nathan apparently thought that the use of what they called "substantive criteria" could not be justified, although they did not explain why. They concluded that the system should revert to emphasizing criteria of formal justice, so that "a more balanced representation of blacks among juveniles sent to court may be achieved" (Landau and Nathan 1983, p. 147).

Landau and Nathan made an interesting contribution, but the discussion needs to be taken further. From their results it looks as though direct discrimination is considerably more important than the use of apparently neutral criteria as a cause of the difference in cautioning rate between black and white juveniles. For example, their model suggests that among latchkey children aged ten to fourteen in area 2 who were accused of crimes of violence, the probability of being cautioned was 0.663 for white children compared with 0.271 for black children (Landau and Nathan 1983, table 4). It follows that a reversion to formal criteria (e.g., abandoning the criterion of parental control) would not make much difference. In any case, what is most distinctive about police decisions on juveniles is that they lie outside the system of formal justice, since they cannot be challenged or reviewed by a court. In those circumstances, the distinction between formal and substantive criteria may not have much importance, since even the application of the formal criteria cannot be formally challenged. The problem for policy is to find a way of changing the way the police use their wide discretion in this matter; Landau and Nathan's analysis does not demonstrate that the best way to do this is to revert to legalistic principles of decision making.

A study of juveniles from one London police division referred to the juvenile bureau in 1973 showed no significant difference in the proportion cautioned between whites and nonwhites (Farrington and Bennett 1981). This result is not enlightening, since the nonwhite group included South Asians (who probably had a high rate of cautioning) and Afro-Caribbeans (who probably had a low rate). A study of juveniles in Bradford (Mawby, McCulloch, and Batta 1979) showed a higher rate of cautioning for Pakistanis than for Indians or non-Asians, but this result is hard to interpret, as there was no analysis by offense type.

In broad terms, there is clear evidence from studies now at least fifteen years old that a higher proportion of Afro-Caribbean than of white juvenile suspects were prosecuted but no evidence about current practice. This seems to have occurred mainly because of direct discrimination but also because of the application of intelligible criteria which may or may not be justifiable but which work to the disadvantage of Afro-Caribbeans. Of course, the few studies that have been carried out were inevitably subject to limitations. It is possible that studies including more detailed information about the social background of juvenile suspects, or about the legal variables in the case, would be able to attribute more of the difference in cautioning rates to the application of apparently neutral criteria and less therefore to direct discrimination. In the case of adults, there is less scope for discrimination at this stage, because a much higher proportion of adult suspects is prosecuted. For adults, there is no detailed evidence about the extent of discrimination at this stage.

Although the available statistics are not detailed, there is clear evidence that in London the overall proportion of persons arrested who are subsequently prosecuted is only slightly higher for ethnic minorities than for white people. This can be shown by comparing persons arrested in London in 1985 with persons proceeded against for indictable offenses at magistrates' courts in 1984 and 1985. As can be seen from figure 10, this comparison shows no appreciable difference between the ethnic composition of these two groups, which suggests that ethnic group was not a factor in determining whether arrested persons would be prosecuted. However, these overall results may conceal differences for persons charged with specific offenses. The previous discussion has concentrated on cautioning rates for juveniles, but juveniles account for only about 10 percent of the cases that come to court. The general picture is dominated by adults, and the overall London statistics indicate that bias in decisions about prosecution has little significance as an explanation of the overrepresentation of Afro-Caribbeans in the prison population. However, the results for juveniles may have wider significance, if interactions with the police and courts during youth are an important influence on the development of an adult criminal career.

G. *The Courts*

All persons prosecuted should initially appear in the magistrates' courts. Summary offenses (the least serious) can be dealt with only in the magistrates' courts. Indictable-only offenses (the most serious) have to be tried in the Crown Court, and the task of the magistrates is to decide whether the case should be committed for trial there, or dropped. Triable-either-way offenses can be dealt with either in the

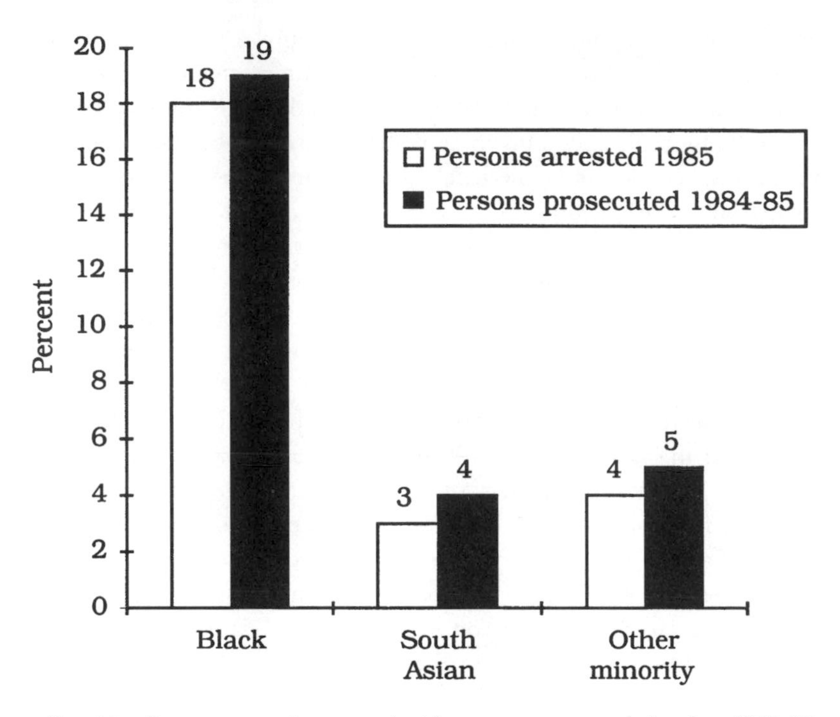

FIG. 10.—Persons arrested compared with persons prosecuted, London, 1984–85. Sources: Home Office (1989*a*, table 4; 1989*b*, table 1).

magistrates' courts or in the Crown Courts. At the hearing in the magistrates' court, the defendant may elect to be tried in the Crown Court. Also, the magistrates may commit the case for trial in the Crown Court if they feel that their own court is not able to deal with it adequately.

1. *The Process prior to Sentencing.* Which court the defendant is tried in has important implications for the outcome of the case. A high proportion of defendants in the magistrates' courts plead guilty, and a high proportion are found guilty, whereas a higher proportion in the Crown Courts plead not guilty, and a higher proportion are acquitted. However, the penalties imposed by the Crown Courts tend to be more severe. Hence, any tendency for ethnic minorities to be tried in Crown Courts rather than in magistrates' courts could lead to a relatively high rate of imprisonment for those groups.

A small proportion of cases never get started in the magistrates' courts either because the defendant fails to appear or because the case is withdrawn for lack of evidence. Walker (1988) found for London in 1983 that a slightly higher proportion of cases against young black than white men (aged fourteen to sixteen) were withdrawn for lack of evidence (9 percent compared with 6 percent). She found no difference for men aged seventeen to twenty-five (Walker 1989).

It is fairly well established that a higher proportion of cases against black people (Afro-Caribbeans and black Africans) than against whites are dealt with by the Crown Courts. Statistics have been published for London in 1984 and 1985 covering prosecutions for indictable offenses: that includes indictable-only offenses (which have to be tried in the Crown Court) and triable-either-way offenses, but excludes summary offenses. Among males, the proportion committed for trial at the Crown Court was 27 percent for whites, 36 percent for blacks, 35 percent for South Asians, and 27 percent for other ethnic groups (see fig. 11). Also, a higher proportion of black females than of white females was committed for trial at the Crown Court, although the proportion of South Asian females and of females belonging to other ethnic groups committed for trial was lower than for whites (Home Office 1989*b*, table 4). This general pattern is confirmed by an analysis of prosecutions of boys aged fourteen to sixteen and another of men aged seventeen to twenty-five, in London in 1983 (Walker 1988, 1989) and by a survey of defendants in Leeds magistrates' courts in 1988 (Brown and Hullin 1992).

The tendency for black defendants to be tried at Crown Courts may arise partly because of the distribution of offenses: for example, a relatively high proportion of black defendants are charged with robbery, and a high proportion of robbery cases (over 80 percent) are tried at Crown Courts. However, this is not the main explanation, since the difference remains within broad offense types, with the exception of robbery, where it is reversed (see fig. 11). The proportion of black defendants committed for trial at the Crown Court was particularly high in the case of sexual offenses. That may be because a relatively high proportion of the alleged sexual offenses are rapes in the case of black defendants.

The anomalous finding for robbery is significant, since it has been argued (Blom-Cooper and Drabble 1982) that black people tend to be charged with robbery in circumstances where a white person would be charged with theft. That would mean that robbery offenses tend to be less serious in the case of black than white defendants, which would explain why a smaller proportion of these cases against black people go to the Crown Court.

It is well established that among cases going to the Crown Court,

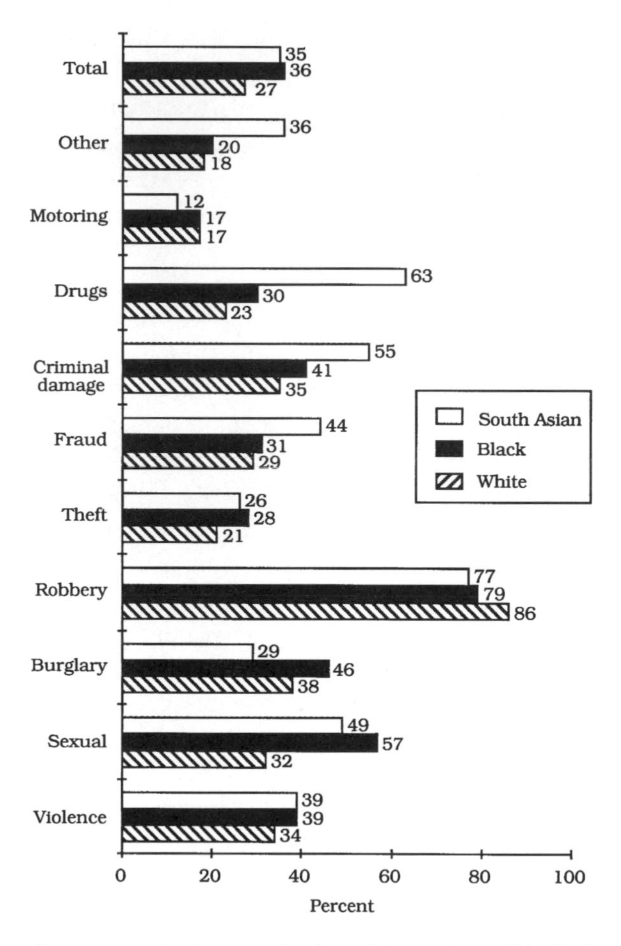

FIG. 11.—Proportion of males committed to trial, London, 1984–85. Source: Home Office (1989*b*, table 3). Note: Violence = violence against the person. Sexual = sexual offenses. Theft = theft and handling. Fraud = fraud and forgery. The figure shows the percentage of those proceeded against at magistrates courts for indictable offenses who were committed for trial.

the proportion that *have* to be tried there (because the offense is indictable only) is higher for black male than for white male defendants (Walker 1989, p. 359, table 8; Hood 1992, p. 51, table 5). Hood's study of cases heard at five Crown Courts in the West Midlands in 1989 also showed that the proportion of defendants *electing* for trial at the Crown Court was no higher for black males (8 percent) than for whites (11 percent). Citing some other as yet unpublished findings, Hood suggested that there may be considerable regional variation in committal of triable-either-way offenses (Hood 1992, p. 52n.). However, a study of cases heard by magistrates' courts in Leeds in 1989 confirmed the West Midlands pattern; it showed that a higher proportion of Afro-Caribbean than of white defendants were committed for trial at the Crown Court, but this reflected the pattern of committals by magistrates, and not the choices of defendants. The same study also showed that in deciding to commit to trial at the Crown Court, magistrates were following the recommendation of the Crown Prosecution Service in the vast majority of cases (Brown and Hullin 1992, p. 51).

From Hood's findings, a considerably higher proportion of the black (23 percent) than of the white male defendants (11 percent) pleaded not guilty at trial. This confirms earlier indications from Walker's (1989) data for London.

Persons to be prosecuted can be summoned to the magistrates' court and tried immediately, and this is what happens with many summary offenses. However, for more serious offenses (triable-either-way or indictable only) the usual sequence is as follows: first, arrest; second, remand by the police either on bail or in custody; third, hearing at the magistrates' court: either remand by magistrates either on bail or in custody pending a full hearing in the magistrates' court or committal for trial at Crown Court either on bail or in custody. *If more than one hearing at the Crown Court:* fourth, remand either on bail or in custody by the Crown Court pending the subsequent hearing there.

Whether ethnic minority defendants are more likely than white defendants to be remanded in custody at any stage is important for two reasons. First, imprisonment before trial is serious in itself, so that a higher likelihood of imprisonment before trial, if not shown to be justifiable, would be unequal treatment of a particularly serious kind. Second, defendants in prison find it more difficult to prepare a defense than those at liberty, and there is evidence (Hood 1992) that they receive stiffer sentences.

The London statistics for 1984 and 1985 (Home Office 1989*b*, table 3) showed that a higher proportion of black (9 percent) and South Asian (8 percent) than of white men (5 percent) accused of indictable offenses were committed in custody by magistrates for trial at the Crown Court. The difference remains for each group of offenses considered separately, except for robbery.

Walker (1989) has conducted a detailed analysis of remands at every stage for her database of London cases in 1983 involving males aged seventeen to twenty-five. In the case of both police remands and remands by magistrates at some stage, a higher proportion of black than of white defendants were remanded in custody. For example, of those remanded by magistrates before trial for indictable-only offenses, 53 percent of the black men aged seventeen to twenty were remanded in custody at some point, compared with 41 percent of the whites; in the case of those aged twenty-one to twenty-five, the comparable figures were 61 percent for black men and 48 percent for white men (Walker 1989, p. 363, table 14). In the case of police remands, these differences were smaller. There is no information from Walker's study about how decisions were made by police and magistrates on whether to bail or remand in custody. These officials may have been using apparently neutral criteria that work to the disadvantage of black suspects, but nothing is known about the criteria used in practice, or about their precise effects.

Walker did investigate the extent to which bail decisions by magistrates were consistent with those earlier taken by police. The police were much more likely to remand in custody than magistrates, but allowing for that difference of policy, there was a high degree of consistency between police and magistrates: for example, very few defendants bailed by police were later remanded in custody or given a custodial sentence by magistrates. Walker argued that police decisions about black and white defendants could be justified in the sense that they tended to predict later decisions by magistrates. Similarly, magistrates' decisions about remands tended to predict the final outcome of cases in the magistrates' courts.

> The conclusion is that more blacks than whites were kept in custody by the police and by the magistrate before conviction or sentence, but there was no difference between blacks and whites with regard to whether this was justified in terms of the later outcome. The final custodial decision (sentence or remand for Crown Court trial or sentence) had the same relationship to earlier custody for the two race groups.
>
> However, the combination of remand and final decision leads to a higher proportion of blacks in custody. (Walker 1989, p. 364)

As discussed in Section I, however, decisions within criminal process cannot be convincingly validated in this way. An equally plausible interpretation is that when deciding whether or not to grant bail, magistrates are strongly influenced by the prior decision taken by the police;

and that the outcome of the case, and the sentence, are strongly influenced by whether the suspect was remanded in custody. On that alternative interpretation, an early police decision not to grant bail could have repercussions right through the process; and that early decision might be influenced by racial prejudice, or by social background factors (e.g., whether the suspect is thought to have a stable family life). The consistency of later decisions and outcomes with the early decision would indicate that the early decision had a powerful effect, and not necessarily that it was justified.

Walker's data showed no difference between black and white men aged seventeen to twenty in the proportion remanded in custody by the Crown Court (rather than by magistrates), although there was a difference (12 percent compared with 8 percent) for those aged twenty-one to twenty-five.

The London statistics showed little or no difference for all age-groups combined in the rate of acquittal between ethnic groups either at the magistrates' courts or at the Crown Courts (Home Office 1989*b*, tables 5 and 6). There were, however, some differences in acquittal rates for certain indictable offenses. The most striking of these was that among males tried at the Crown Court for criminal damage, 44 percent of blacks, 38 percent of South Asians, but only 27 percent of whites were acquitted. Similarly, Walker's findings for males aged seventeen to twenty-five prosecuted in London in 1983 showed little or no difference overall in acquittal rates between ethnic groups (Walker 1989). However, her findings for boys aged fourteen to sixteen showed a higher rate of acquittal for blacks than for whites both at the magistrates' courts and at the Crown Courts (Walker 1988, p. 448, table 6). For both courts combined, 15.3 percent of young black defendants were acquitted completely, compared with 9.5 percent of whites, and 10.9 percent of South Asians.

Hood's study of cases at five West Midlands Crown Courts in 1989 concentrated on sentencing but provided some information about acquittal rates. Among male defendants at the five courts combined, the acquittal rates were 9.1 percent for whites, 11.1 percent for blacks, and 16.7 percent for South Asians and others (Hood 1992; calculated from table 1, page 32). However, there was considerable variation between the five courts. At one of them (Dudley) the acquittal rate was higher among whites than among blacks, whereas at three courts acquittal rates were considerably higher among blacks than among whites: for male defendants at these three courts combined, the acquittal rates were 9.1 percent for whites, 21.3 percent for blacks, and 26.9 percent for South Asians and others.

Although these data about acquittal rates are not national, they do cover the two largest areas of ethnic minority settlement (London and the West Midlands). They indicate that there is, if anything, a tendency for acquittal rates to be higher among ethnic minorities than whites, with considerable variation between individual courts. However, this tendency is overall rather weak. On one interpretation, this suggests an absence of massive bias at earlier stages. For if a much higher proportion of black than of white people had been drawn into the net through bias, then the cases against black defendants should tend to be considerably weaker, so that the acquittal rate should be substantially lower for black than for white defendants. The fact that it is only slightly lower argues against the hypothesis of massive bias earlier.

However, this argument is by no means conclusive. What the findings do demonstrate is a considerable degree of consistency between the various stages of the criminal justice process as it impinges on black people. There could, in principle, be a degree of bias by the courts in reaching their verdicts that mirrors a massive bias at earlier stages. In that case, acquittal rates would be much the same for black and white defendants even though the evidence against black defendants was much weaker. Unfortunately, this idea cannot be tested at present, since there has been no study that tried to evaluate verdicts by ethnic group according to the state of the evidence or other characteristics of the case or the defendant. It is also possible, in principle, that greater efforts are made to construct cogent cases against black than against white defendants, so that in spite of massive bias against black people at earlier stages, roughly the same proportion of black as of white defendants are convicted.

For reasons such as these, the pattern of acquittals does not provide conclusive evidence on its own, but it fits most easily with the hypothesis that there is no massive bias at earlier stages.

2. *Sentencing.* London statistics on prosecutions for indictable offenses in 1984 and 1985 (Home Office 1989*b*) show that there was no significant difference between sentences imposed in magistrates courts on white and black offenders but that South Asians and members of other ethnic minority groups were much more likely than whites or blacks to be fined and less likely to be given a custodial sentence. At

the Crown Court, however, 57 percent of black offenders were given immediate custody, compared with 51 percent of whites, 50 percent of South Asians, and 49 percent of other ethnic groups. The high figure for blacks was due to the higher proportion given youth custody (19 percent of blacks compared with 11 percent of whites). Analysis by age of the offender and offense group (the only other information available in these official statistics) explains a part of these differences, but considerable variation between ethnic groups in the use of custody remains within offense groups for each age-group considered separately.

One feature of the results was that black men were far more likely than white men to be given custodial sentences for sexual offenses. This is partly because a higher proportion of these sexual offenses were rapes where the offender was black (24 percent) than where he was white (3 percent). However, as already observed, the converse pattern exists in the case of robbery (robberies committed by white men are more serious [Blom-Cooper and Drabble 1982]), yet black men were still more likely than white men to receive immediate custody for robbery. For the most part, the difference in sentences imposed on black and white men cannot be explained by the offense, as far as that is known from the official statistics.

Among those receiving sentences of immediate custody at the magistrates' courts, there was no difference in average sentence length between ethnic groups. At the Crown Court, South Asians received considerably longer custodial sentences, on average, than whites. Also, young black males (aged seventeen to twenty) received longer custodial sentences than young white males, although there was no similar difference among those aged twenty-one or more. The Home Office suggested that "the longer sentence length for Asians reflect[s] the high proportion of drug trafficking offenders" (1989*b*, para. 24). A separate table showed that among those convicted of drugs offenses, the specific offense was drug trafficking for 64 percent of Asians compared with 17 percent of whites and 27 percent of blacks (1989*b*, table 18). However, it has not been demonstrated that this accounts for the longer custodial sentences imposed on Asians.

From the limited information available in these statistics, it is not possible to tell whether the sentences imposed reflect equal or unequal treatment of different ethnic groups. A number of studies have pursued this question (McConville and Baldwin 1982; Crow and Cove 1984; Mair 1986; Moxon 1988; Hudson 1989; Voakes and Fowler 1989;

Brown and Hullin 1992; Hood 1992). However, as Hood (1992) has convincingly argued, the earlier studies had serious limitations which for the most part prevent any definite conclusions being drawn from them on the central question under consideration. Among the problems with these earlier studies were inadequate information about variables that might explain sentencing decisions, small samples, failure to quantify the effects of different variables, aggregation of data from magistrates' and Crown courts, failure to distinguish different ethnic minority groups, and confounding of differences between courts with those between groups (Hood 1992, pp. 11–18). Hood's study of sentencing in five Crown Courts in the West Midlands collected far more extensive information than the others about the cases and offenders and used far more powerful analytic methods, so it is at present the best available source. Its main limitation (but also a strength in analytic terms) is that it did not cover sentencing by the magistrates' courts. Some up-to-date information about that is, however, available from Brown and Hullin's study in Leeds.

There were 2,884 sentenced male offenders in Hood's sample. Over the five Crown Courts covered by the study, 56.6 percent of the blacks were sentenced to custody, compared with 48.4 percent of the whites, and 39.6 percent of the Asians, although there were substantial variations between the individual courts. There were also substantial differences between individual judges in the relative sentences they imposed on blacks and whites. At the same time, there were considerable differences between the three ethnic groups in terms of the three types of variables that could justifiably have influenced the sentencing decision: how the case had been processed to date, the type of offense, and the prior history of offending. Also, there were some differences between ethnic groups in their personal and social characteristics, some of which might be considered relevant, especially if sentencing is meant to be influenced by considerations of substantive (as well as formal) justice.

A tabular analysis suggested "that differences in the use of custody were not evident when the case characteristics were generally regarded as the most serious and where there was consequently little room to exercise discretion in choosing between custody and an alternative sentence. They do suggest, however, that where there was room to exercise greater discretion, the racial factor was associated with a pattern in the use of custody which was disadvantageous to blacks and that the degree of this disadvantage was much more evident at the Dudley courts than at Birmingham" (Hood 1992, p. 65).

More detailed and precise results were obtained by carrying out several types of multivariate analysis. One method, for example, was a logistic regression analysis in which the dependent variable was whether or not the offender had been sentenced to custody. The independent (or predictor) variables described the legal process, the characteristics of the offense, and the prior history of offending. In more detail, they included the most serious offense of which convicted, the mode of trial (main offense triable only on indictment, either way), whether remanded in custody when appeared for sentence, plea, number of charges of which convicted, outstanding court orders, violence in the offense, degree of injury, motive for violence, effect of violence, amount of financial loss involved, vulnerability of victim, number of previous convictions, previous custodial history for similar type of offense, and previous breach of community service order. Each of these items was found to be significantly related to the probability of custody, and the logistic regression model reflected the best possible method of predicting whether there would be a custodial sentence from this combination of variables. In the context of this model, it was found that the probability of custody remained 5 percent higher for black than for white men, while it remained 5 percent lower for South Asian men. The raw difference in use of custody between ethnic groups was reduced after taking account of the process, offense, and prior record variables, but it did not disappear. The difference between black and white men was significant at the 93 percent level of confidence.

Differences in the use of custody between ethnic groups were found to be greatest where the judges' discretion was greatest, that is, for offenses at a middling level of seriousness. In fact, for each type of offense examined, there was no such difference for the most serious offenses or for the least serious ones. This finding parallels the results of American studies which show that differences between white and black people in rates of imprisonment for rape, robbery, and homicide are largely explained by differences in actual rates of offending, whereas unaccountable differences in rates of imprisonment are greater for less serious offenses (see Sampson and Lauritsen, in this volume).

All of the difference between ethnic groups occurred among those aged twenty-one or over: there was no difference for young offenders. Also, there was no difference in custody rate between black and white offenders in employment: the differences were confined to those who were unemployed. This happened because "being unemployed was a factor significantly correlated with receiving a custodial sentence if the defendant was black but not if he was white or Asian" (Hood 1992, p. 86). A higher proportion of the black male defendants pleaded not guilty than of the whites (23 compared with 11 percent), and a not guilty plea was associated overall with an increased probability of custody. However, because of the detailed pattern of the relationships, the difference in pleas between ethnic groups did not help to explain the difference in the use of custody.

In the context of the multivariate model, there was a large difference between sentencing practice at Dudley and Birmingham, the two largest of the five court areas, which between them accounted for 89 percent of the cases. At Dudley, black defendants were considerably more likely than white defendants to receive custody, and this applied fairly consistently to all of the individual judges. At Birmingham, overall black and white defendants were equally likely to receive custody, but there was variation between individual judges, such that some tended to favor whites, while others tended to favor blacks, and these biases canceled each other out.

Among adult males given custodial sentences, these sentences tended to be considerably longer for South Asians and blacks than for whites. This was partly because South Asians and blacks were more likely to plead not guilty than whites, and because of the detailed characteristics of their case and prior record, summed up as the seriousness of the offense. Those pleading not guilty were given considerably longer sentences on average. Among those who pleaded guilty, there was little difference in length of sentence between ethnic groups after controlling for the seriousness of the offense. Among those who pleaded not guilty, however, sentences were considerably longer for blacks and Asians than for whites after allowing for the seriousness of the offense.

The plea as a criterion influencing the sentence is an important example of an apparently neutral criterion that works to the disadvantage of black people. It is important because it raises difficult conceptual issues in a particularly acute form. On the one hand, it is argued that the discount for a not guilty plea is what makes a fair system of criminal justice a practical possibility. Without it, the number of full trials would grow to unmanageable proportions. This would lead to underfunding, a decline in the quality of decision making, and increased inequality between defendants according to their resources. On the other side, it is argued that black people are hostile to mainstream institutions in part because they believe the conditions of their lives are shaped by racial bias. Refusal to plead guilty is therefore a consequence of past experience of racial bias. So if the tariff is higher for those pleading not guilty, the effect is that black people are being punished more severely than others because they have been subject to racial bias and hostility in the past. Without explaining just how he would evaluate the balance between these conflicting arguments, Hood concluded that "[t]here is clearly a need to consider the implications of the policy which favours so strongly those who plead guilty, when ethnic minorities are less willing to let the prosecution go unchallenged" (1992, p. 191).

Hood estimated that in the West Midlands, 24.4 percent of the male prison population was black, compared with 3.8 percent of the resident population, a ratio of 6.4:1.[15] He estimated that 70 percent of this difference was accounted for by the number appearing for sentence, taking account of all stages prior to sentence, but not the profile of offenses; 10 percent "by the more serious nature of the offenses and other legally relevant characteristics of the charges on which black defendants were convicted" (1992, p. 130); 7 percent by greater use of custody than expected (after taking account of legally relevant variables); and 13 percent "by lengthier sentences, which appears to be entirely due to a greater propensity to plead not guilty, and to the lengthier sentences for those who did so" (1992, p. 130). These findings imply that 80 percent of the difference can be explained by the number from different ethnic groups appearing at the Crown Court, the nature of the offenses, and other legally relevant characteristics of the charges. These numbers and patterns emerge from stages prior to the Crown Court, although "decisions at all these stages . . . might be affected by racial factors" (Hood 1992, p. 130). The 13 percent of the difference that relates to lengthier sentences for black males arose in its entirety from the higher tariffs attaching to not guilty pleas. The remaining 7 percent of the difference related to greater than expected use of custodial sentences and cannot, therefore, be explained by legally rel-

[15] The comparison is a rough one, because not all persons in prison in the West Midlands are drawn from the resident population of the region.

evant variables. It might be attributable to direct discrimination or, alternatively, to legally relevant variables not captured by the study.

Hood's data show that a higher proportion of offenses committed by black and South Asian men than by white men came to light as a result of proactive policing, for example, stop and search, or discovery at the scene of the crime. Although this cannot be quantified, the findings suggest that some of the overrepresentation of blacks does occur because policing is targeted on them. More of the South Asians and blacks than of the whites had legal advice at the police station, which may help to explain why more pleaded not guilty and consequently tended to receive lengthier sentences. An important factor associated with the greater use of custody for blacks was that they were more likely to be remanded in custody when they were sentenced. This higher probability of being remanded in custody could not be wholly explained by variables known to be legally relevant to the bail/custody decision. The proportion who had no social inquiry report prepared on them varied significantly between South Asian men (43 percent) and blacks (42 percent), on the one hand, and whites (28 percent), on the other. Most of this variation occurred because a higher proportion of the ethnic minorities had signaled their intention to plead guilty. Most of the difference in use of custody between black and white men arose among those for whom no social inquiry report was prepared, but it is not clear that a failure to prepare a report is the causal factor.

No study comparable to Hood's (which covered only Crown Courts) has been carried out of race and sentencing in magistrates' courts. As mentioned above, London statistics for 1984 and 1985 (Home Office 1989*b*) showed no difference in sentences imposed on black and white offenders, although those imposed on South Asians were less severe. A recent study by Brown and Hullin (1992) of sentencing in magistrates' courts in Leeds found no significant difference overall in sentences imposed according to ethnic group. Although differences between ethnic groups did appear within certain subgroups (e.g., Afro-Caribbean females were more likely to receive custodial sentences than white females), these could probably be explained by the use of legally relevant criteria (offenses committed by Afro-Caribbean females tended to be more serious than those committed by white females). The information collected by this study was relatively limited, and the analysis was not sufficient to address the question whether discrimination had occurred. However, together with the London statistics, these findings do suggest that the extent of any racial discrimination in sentencing is considerably less in the magistrates' than in the Crown Courts.

V. Discussion

In the light of the findings set out in the last three sections, fragmentary as they often are, I now return to the central questions raised at the beginning of this essay. It is important to establish whether rates of crime victimization vary between ethnic groups, not only because of the importance of victimization in itself, but also because elevated rates of victimization may be related, through black-on-black crime, with elevated rates of offending. For whatever reason, black people (but not South Asians) are more likely to become entangled with the web of criminal justice than white people. The central task of this essay is to consider how far this has happened because of bias, impartial application of criteria that work to the disadvantage of black people, or an elevated rate of offending.

If there is evidence of racial or ethnic bias in criminal justice, we need to consider why this bias is against black people but not South Asians, who have been equally subject to discrimination in other spheres. Where black people are placed at a disadvantage through the application of apparently neutral criteria, there is a need to review these criteria in the light of their consequences for ethnic minorities, and to consider whether it is justifiable to go on using them. If there is evidence of higher actual rates of offending among black people than among other ethnic groups, then the next step is to explain why this is so and, in particular, to consider the links between any bias in law enforcement and criminal process and the criminalization of the black minority.

A. Main Findings

First, ethnic minorities—both black people and South Asians—are found to be at higher risk of crime victimization than white people. This difference arises partly because the sociodemographic profile of ethnic minorities tends to increase their risk of victimization, but a considerable difference remains after controlling for the effect of these variables. The elevated risk of victimization is also connected with characteristics of the neighborhoods where ethnic minorities live. A third factor is that a substantial minority of offenses on black people (and to a lesser extent on South Asians) are committed by black people, who probably have an elevated level of offending (see below). However, black-on-black crime is only a small part of the explanation of high black victimization. It is far less significant than in the United States, for the simple reason that black people are such a small proportion of the population of England and Wales (1.6 percent in 1991).

Second, at the end of the criminal justice process, black people (Afro-Caribbeans and black Africans) are about seven times as likely to be in prison as white people or South Asians.

Third, the pattern of offenses for which black people were arrested and imprisoned is consistent with the theory that they tend to be the targets of proactive law enforcement. Also, there is some evidence of bias against black people at various stages: in the targeting of police enforcement, the decision to prosecute juveniles, and sentencing by the Crown Courts. None of this evidence, however, is entirely clear-cut. It can be argued, for example, that the high police stop rate of black people is "justified" by results (reported offenses, arrests, and prosecutions). With regard to decisions to prosecute juveniles, the relevant studies are out of date and probably did not include all of the relevant variables. With regard to sentencing, the leading study (Hood 1992) did suggest some racial bias, but its measured effects were rather small, especially when compared with the effects of other variables.

Fourth, at various points, black people are placed at a disadvantage by the application of apparently neutral criteria. The clearest examples are the influence of social background factors on the decision to prosecute rather than caution a juvenile (black children are less likely to have the stable family background that makes cautioning more likely), the influence of social background factors on sentencing, and the lower sentencing tariff for suspects who plead not guilty. The relationship between guilty plea and sentence accounts for a substantial part (perhaps around 15 percent) of the difference in rate of imprisonment between black and white people.

Fifth, although some bias against black people has been demonstrated at several stages, and although some apparently neutral criteria have been shown to work to the disadvantage of black people, the magnitude of these effects seems small compared with the stark contrast in rates of arrest and imprisonment between black and white people. A possible theory is that the stark contrast is mainly or entirely caused by cumulative bias and the use of criteria that work to the disadvantage of black people at each different stage of the criminal justice process.

That theory has recently received support from the results of a study of young people aged fourteen to twenty-five (Graham and Bowling 1996) which showed no difference in rates of self-reported offending between black and white youths. However, those findings do not seem convincing in the light of sampling problems, the inherent limitations of the self-report method in terms of validity and reliability, and the evidence that the truthfulness of self-reports may be systematically related to ethnic group (Junger 1989, but see also Bowling 1990). There is a considerable weight of evidence that contradicts the findings of the self-report study and suggests instead that the stark contrast in rates of imprisonment cannot be mainly the cumulative result of the operations of criminal justice process at each stage.

• The cumulative effects theory would predict a steady increase in the proportion of black people among suspects and offenders from the earliest to the latest stage of the process. In fact, the proportion of black people is about the same among suspects as described by victims, persons arrested, and the prison population.

• Arising directly from the first point, it is impossible to account for the high representation of black people at early stages (e.g., according to victims' reports) in terms of bias.

• Even at stages where bias has been demonstrated, its potential effect is fairly limited. For example, proactive law enforcement does target black people to some extent: but most clear-ups do not result from proactive law enforcement, and most proactive law enforcement cannot be targeted on black people. Hence the total effect of this bias must be modest, especially in relation to the stark differences in rates of arrest and imprisonment between black and white people. To take another example, black juveniles are considerably more likely to be prosecuted rather than cautioned compared with comparable white juveniles, but there is no evidence of a similar difference in the case of adult offenders, who account for 90 percent of the cases coming before the courts. Hence, the bias in cautioning of juveniles, though important, has only a small significance as an explanation of the difference in rates of imprisonment between black and white people.

• Although proactive law enforcement targeted on black people can help to explain the arrest rates for certain offenses (notably, robbery), it cannot for others (such as burglary) for which proactive law enforcement cannot for the most part be targeted on black people and is in any case singularly ineffective.

- Contrary to what has been stated by some commentators (e.g., Reiner 1989, p. 1993), it is not the case that bias has been demonstrated at every stage of the process. Most notably, black people are, if anything, more likely to be acquitted than white people. There is not a steady accumulation of bias from one stage to the next.
- The acquittal rate is only slightly higher among black than white defendants. This is difficult to reconcile with the hypothesis of massive bias against black people at earlier stages, which should lead to the cases against them being relatively weak. Although not conclusive in itself, this argument carries some weight in the context of the rest of the evidence.

A fair assessment of the limited evidence is that although some bias against black people has been demonstrated at several stages of the process, and although some decision making criteria clearly work to the disadvantage of black people, in large part the difference in rate of arrest and imprisonment between black and white people arises from a difference in the rate of offending.

Sixth, South Asians—collectively the largest part of the ethnic minority population—are not overrepresented among offenders described by victims, persons arrested, or the prison population. No bias has been demonstrated against them at any stage, and at various points they tend to be favored compared to white or black people. In other contexts, South Asians are just as much subject to racial hostility and discrimination as black people. The bias against black people that has been demonstrated within the criminal justice system is therefore different from that existing in other contexts such as employment. It is not adequately described as part of a generalized "racism." More plausibly it springs from a perception of black people specifically, as distinct from other ethnic minorities, as a threat to law and order. Those perceptions both are justified by reality, since crime rates are in fact relatively high among black people, and help to shape that reality, since racial hostility and discrimination will through a sequence of interactions cause black crime rates to rise still further.

Returning to the broad perspective established at the beginning of this essay, the process of gaining acceptance for a single, universal standard of law applicable equally to all ethnic groups seems in some ways to be well advanced. Ethnic group is by no means the most important characteristic influencing rates of offending or victimization, or the way people interact with the police, the probation service, or the courts. Sex and age are far more important predictors, and social class is probably more important, too. Although Afro-Caribbeans are considerably more hostile to the police than white people or Asians, the contrast between age-groups is much starker. The ethnic minorities do not reject the criminal justice system or deny its legitimacy. As victims of crime, or as bystanders, they are just as likely as white people to report matters to the police.

However, it cannot be claimed that law enforcement and criminal process have the same effect on black and white people. In the past, claims of unequal treatment have tended to be exaggerated and, hence, to lack credibility. There is evidence that law enforcement targets black people, and there is some evidence of bias at various stages of criminal process. Probably more important than bias is the effect of apparently neutral criteria which nevertheless work to the disadvantage of black people. Yet these effects seem much too small to account for the stark difference in rates of imprisonment between black and white people. In large part, this difference probably reflects a difference in rates of offending.

B. Explaining Bias

To the extent that there is bias in law enforcement and criminal process, there is a need to explain why this is directed against black people and not against South Asians. A part of the background to any explanation is that criminalization is the result of a sequence of interactions between black people and the authorities. Thus, high crime rates among black people may possibly be explained partly in terms of labeling and deviance amplification, and racial prejudice among the authorities may have had a role in initiating and maintaining such a system of interaction. It may be impossible to answer the question "Which came first?" A widely shared official view of the early 1970s that people originating from the West Indies were a law-abiding community changed within three or four years to an equally widespread official view that black crime was a particular threat. It has been argued that this was a cultural shift (Hall et al. 1978), yet it could alternatively have been caused by rising crime rates among the second generation of young people whose parents had migrated from the West Indies.

Bias against black people specifically in law enforcement and criminal justice process seems like the counterpart to a growing tendency from the late 1970s onward for young black people to define their identity in opposition to the central structures of authority in British society, most notably, the police. From the Notting Hill Carnival of 1978 onward, there has been a succession of antipolice riots or uprisings, in which black people have always played a central role. Survey research shows that young black people are generally very hostile to the police, and considerably more so than young white people (Smith 1983*a;* Skogan 1990). Yet, surprisingly, the evidence from observational studies of police-black encounters does not support this kind of explanation (Smith and Gray 1983; Norris et al. 1992). The collective hostility of the police and black people toward each other does not seem to be expressed at the micro level of individual encounters.

The outgoing survival strategy adopted by black people in Britain contrasts with the culturally enclosed strategy of South Asians (Daniel 1968; Smith 1977). White people were just as much inclined to discriminate against South Asians as against black people, but black people were far more likely to encounter discrimination because they were more likely, for example, to apply for a job cold, whereas the South Asian would be more likely to seek out opportunities through relatives and friends. One consequence of these different approaches to surviving in Britain may be that white people have formed very different notions of the black and South Asian communities. They are more likely to feel the need to control the behavior of black than that of South Asian people, because the behavior of South Asians tends to be hidden from them.

C. Reviewing Decision-Making Criteria

Black people are placed at a substantial disadvantage because guilty pleas attract a lower sentencing tariff. They also suffer from the use of factors such as stable family background in making decisions for example about cautioning versus prosecution, especially of juveniles. As set out in Section I, the question of which decision-making criteria are justifiable or legitimate raises deep and difficult problems in the philosophy of law, which are outside the scope of this essay. Nevertheless, three simple conclusions do emerge from the present analysis.

First, it seems important that decision-making criteria should be reviewed in the light of their consequences for different groups, including racial or ethnic ones. However particular criteria are to be justified in detail, at a minimum their effects on racial or ethnic groups should be taken into consideration. The reason for taking this view is that membership of an ethnic group is an important source of personal identity. The use of a criterion that has an adverse effect on a whole ethnic group will be seen as an attack on that group, unless the reasons for adopting it are extremely compelling.

Second, these decision-making criteria cannot be validated internally by the results they produce within criminal process. For example, the criteria used by the police when deciding whom to stop and search cannot be validated by pointing to the results (such as offenses reported, arrests, or prosecutions); police decisions to refuse bail cannot be validated by the later decisions of magistrates to refuse bail to the same suspects; and the system of offering inducements to plead guilty cannot be validated by showing that nearly all of those who plead guilty are convicted. The reason is that the later outcomes are not independent of the earlier decisions but flow from them and are partly shaped by them; hence they cannot alone justify them. The most that can be said is that outcomes need to be taken into consideration when evaluating decision-making procedures.

Third, it is, unfortunately, not likely that disadvantage to ethnic minorities from the application of apparently neutral criteria can be altogether avoided by changing the criteria. The reason is that the unavoidable element of discretion in the application of the criteria will remain. The best example here is the decision about whether to caution or charge juvenile suspects. A system for diverting juvenile offenders from the courts is likely to be advantageous to a relatively high-offending group, such as black people. On the face of it, such a system (particularly if operated by the police) is bound to involve a large amount of discretion, subject to minimal oversight and review. This allows scope for direct racial discrimination. The obvious response is to require greater use of formal criteria. Any criteria that fit with the underlying principles of cautioning are, however, likely to work to the disadvantage of a high offending group, such as black people. That means either adopting inappropriate criteria that have an equal effect on different ethnic groups, which would undermine support for cautioning, or reverting to a more discretionary approach. This illustrates the substantial practical problems that arise in seeking to improve decision-making procedures.

D. Explaining Black Offending

It seems likely that the two main findings of this review are linked: that is, discrimination against black minorities interacts with high rates of offending by those same groups. Crime arises from a sequence of interactions. It seems likely that in certain sequences racial hostility on one side and antagonism to authority on the other become mutually reinforcing. Within this sequence of interactions, actual rates of offending among black people begin to rise; this rise in turn causes an increase in racial hostility and discrimination. It can well be imagined that the interaction between racial stereotypes, discrimination, antagonism to authority, and actual rates of offending among black people produces a cycle of deviance amplification. These effects would be magnified by the large-scale conflicts between black people and the police that became so salient over the past fifteen years and acquired intense significance for young black people (Small 1983).

Despite the claims that some have made, researchers have not demonstrated that there is a steady cumulation of discrimination through each stage of the criminal justice process. However, a more relevant perspective would be the life cycle of the individual. For the young black male, there may be a cumulation of interactions which greatly increase the likelihood of entanglement with criminal process and subsequent criminality.

It will also be important to consider broader causes of crime. Black people tend to live in areas of social stress, where crime rates among all ethnic groups are high; they have a much higher rate of unemployment overall than white people, and a lower standard of living, and a higher proportion are in poverty (Jones 1993). However, certain other racial minority groups—South Asian Muslims, in particular—are more disadvantaged in these respects than black people, yet have much lower crime rates. It would be fruitful to focus on this striking difference in future research.

It would be wrong to assume that these contrasts are a permanent feature of the social scene. Concern about crime among black people did not appear until the mid-1970s, although it is difficult to say whether there was an actual increase in the black crime rate around that time. Recent research (Jones 1993) has shown some improvement in the conditions of life of black people in Britain over the ten years up to 1990. There is currently a striking increase in the number of black people going into higher education. Along with such changes, it is entirely possible that the proportion of young black people who are criminalized will decrease. It is also, unfortunately, possible that the crime rate will rise among South Asian Muslims who arrived in Britain more recently than migrants from the West Indies and who currently suffer greater social and economic disadvantages (FitzGerald 1995).

Nevertheless, the difference in rate of imprisonment between black and South Asian people is so striking that it can hardly be explained by differences in economic hardship or in the timing of the migration. What the difference may possibly indicate is that the outgoing and integrative strategy initially adopted by migrants from the Caribbean was met by rejection leading to conflict, which the more separatist and inward-looking strategy of South Asians tended to avoid. Of course these broad generalizations greatly oversimplify the great range of adaptations made by different groups over more than one generation, but they may contain a kernel of truth.

E. Questions for Future Research

If the main structure of the foregoing analysis is accepted, then the central project for future research is to understand the processes of interaction between black people and the criminal justice agencies that have led to an elevated rate of crime among that group. This implies the need for more longitudinal studies in the developmental tradition. However, these should not just be more of the same. They would differ from previous British studies in a number of crucial ways.

1. These studies would give equal weight to the concerns of psychologists and sociologists. Information would be collected from and about criminal justice agencies as well as individuals. Use would also be made of information about the social and economic structure of the areas where individuals live. Interactions between individuals and criminal justice agencies would be intensively studied.

2. The studies would be designed to support detailed comparisons between ethnic groups.

3. Both normal samples and samples of "heavy end" offenders would be studied.

Some will consider the main conclusions drawn above to be premature and will wish to test them more intensively than is possible from existing evidence. Perhaps the most promising line of inquiry would be to take a particular type of offense (such as burglary, robbery, or theft from the person) and collect detailed information about the flow of cases through the system. The main objective would be to show how the decision is taken as to whether to proceed at each stage, where the evidence comes from, and how it is assembled. In this way it would be possible to test the hypothesis that equally good cases are constructed against black as compared with white defendants even though more black people are accused because of bias in the system. A closely connected point is the need for longitudinal studies tracing the flow of cases from arrest to prosecution.

A major conclusion of this review is that bias against black people has been demonstrated at several stages. An important objective of future research should be to establish how this can be prevented. The most controversial issue in this large area of study is whether discrimination can best be prevented by limiting discretion through further rules or by changing the structure or management of organizations and the objectives they set themselves. This contest between the legalistic and managerial approaches to limiting discrimination should be a central theme of future research.

REFERENCES

Bethnal Green and Stepney Trades Council. 1978. *Blood on the Streets.* London: Bethnal Green and Stepney Trades Council.

Blom-Cooper, L., and R. Drabble. 1982. "Police Perception of Crime: Brixton and the Operational Response." *British Journal of Criminology* 22:184–87.

Bowling, B. 1990. "Conceptual and Methodological Problems in Measuring 'Race' Differences in Delinquency: A Reply to Marianne Junger." *British Journal of Criminology* 30:483–92.

———. 1993. "Racist Harassment and the Process of Victimization: Conceptual and Methodological Implications for the Local Crime Survey." In *Realist Criminology: Crime and Policing in the 1990s,* edited by J. Lowman and B. D. MacLean. Vancouver: Collective Press.

Brown, C. 1984. *Black and White Britain: The Third PSI Survey.* London: Heinemann.

Brown, C., and P. Gay. 1986. *Racial Discrimination: 17 Years after the Act.* London: Policy Studies Institute.

Brown, I., and R. Hullin. 1992. "A Study of Sentencing in the Leeds Magistrates' Courts: The Treatment of Ethnic Minority and White Offenders." *British Journal of Criminology* 32:41–53.

Commission for Racial Equality. 1985. *Review of the Race Relations Act 1976: Proposals for Change.* London: Commission for Racial Equality.

———. 1991. *Review of the Race Relations Act.* London: Commission for Racial Equality.

———. 1992. *Cautions v. Prosecutions: Ethnic Monitoring of Juveniles by Seven Police Forces.* London: Commission for Racial Equality.

Crow, I., and J. Cove. 1984. "Ethnic Minorities and the Courts." *Criminal Law Review* 413–17.

Daniel, W. W. 1968. *Racial Discrimination in England.* Harmondsworth: Penguin.

Farrington, D. P. 1973. "Self-Reports of Deviant Behaviour: Predictive and Stable?" *Journal of Criminal Law and Criminology* 64:99–110.

Farrington, D. P., and T. Bennett. 1981. "Police Cautioning of Juveniles in London." *British Journal of Criminology* 21:123–35.

FitzGerald, M. 1989. "Legal Approaches to Racial Harassment in Council Housing: The Case for Reassessment." *New Community* 16(1):93–105.

———. 1995. " 'Race' and Crime: The Facts?" Paper presented at the British Society of Criminology biennial conference, Loughborough, July.

Genn, H. 1988. "Multiple Victimization." In *Victims of Crime: A New Deal?* edited by M. Maguire and J. Pointing. Milton Keynes: Open University Press.

Gilroy, P. 1987. *There Ain't No Black in the Union Jack: The Cultural Politics of Race and Nation.* London: Hutchinson.

Graham, J., and B. Bowling. 1996. *Young People and Crime.* Research Study 145. London: Home Office Research and Statistics Department.

Green, P. 1991. *Drug Couriers.* London: Howard League for Penal Reform.

Hall, S., C. Critcher, J. Clarke, T. Jefferson, and B. Roberts. 1978. *Policing the Crisis.* London: Macmillan.

Hansard. 1992. *Parliamentary Debates,* H.C., 5th ser., 216, no. 79 (December 17), col. 443.

Home Office. 1981. *Racial Attacks: Report of a Home Office Study.* London: Home Office.

———. 1989*a*. *Crime Statistics for the Metropolitan Police District by Ethnic Group, 1987: Victims, Suspects and Those Arrested.* Home Office Statistical Bulletin 5/89. London: Home Office.

———. 1989*b*. *The Ethnic Group of Those Proceeded Against or Sentenced by the Courts in the Metropolitan Police District in 1984 and 1985.* Home Office Statistical Bulletin 6/89. London: Home Office.

———. 1989*c*. *The Response to Racial Attacks and Harassment: Guidance for the Statutory Agencies: Report of the Inter-departmental Racial Attacks Group.* London: Home Office.

———. 1991. *The Response to Racial Attacks: Sustaining the Momentum: The Second Report of the Inter-departmental Racial Attacks Group.* London: Home Office.

———. 1993. *Prison Statistics England and Wales 1991.* Cm. 2157. London: H.M. Stationery Office.

———. 1995. *Prison Statistics England and Wales 1993.* Cm. 2893. London: H.M. Stationery Office.

Hood, R. 1992. *Race and Sentencing.* Oxford: Clarendon Press.

House of Commons Home Affairs Committee. 1986. *Racial Attacks and Harassment.* Session 1985-86, HC 409. London: H.M. Stationery Office.

House of Commons Select Committee on Race Relations and Immigration. 1972. *Police/Immigrant Relations.* HC 71. London: H.M. Stationery Office.

———. 1976. *The West Indian Community.* HC 180. London: H.M. Stationery Office.

Hudson, B. A. 1989. "Discrimination and Disparity: The Influence of Race on Sentencing." *New Community* 16(1):23–34.

———. 1993. "Penal Policy and Racial Justice." In *Minority Ethnic Groups and the Criminal Justice System,* edited by L. Gelsthorpe and W. McWilliam. Cambridge: University of Cambridge, Institute of Criminology.

Jefferson, T. 1988. "Race, Crime and Policing: Empirical, Theoretical and Methodological Issues." *International Journal of the Sociology of Law* 16:521–39.

———. 1993. "The Racism of Criminalization: Policing and the Reproduction of the Criminal Other." In *Minority Ethnic Groups and the Criminal Justice System,* edited by L. Gelsthorpe and W. McWilliam. Cambridge: University of Cambridge, Institute of Criminology.

Jefferson, T., and M. A. Walker. 1992. "Ethnic Minorities in the Criminal Justice System." *Criminal Law Review,* pp. 83–95.

———. 1993. "Attitudes to the Police of the Ethnic Minorities in a Provincial City." *British Journal of Criminology* 33:251–66.

Jefferson, T., M. Walker, and M. Seneviratne. 1992. "Ethnic Minorities, Crime and Criminal Justice: A Study in a Provincial City." In *Unravelling Criminal Justice,* edited by D. Downes. London: Macmillan.

Jones, T. 1993. *Britain's Ethnic Minorities.* London: Policy Studies Institute.

Jones, T., B. MacLean, and J. Young. 1986. *The Islington Crime Survey: Crime, Victimization and Policing in Inner-City London.* Aldershot: Gower.

Jowell, R., and P. Prescott-Clarke. 1970. "Racial Discrimination and White-Collar Workers in Britain." *Race* 11:397–417.

Junger, M. 1989. "Discrepancies between Police and Self-Report Data for Dutch Racial Minorities." *British Journal of Criminology* 29:273–84.

Kinsey, R. 1985. *Final Report of the Merseyside Crime and Police Surveys.* Liverpool: Merseyside County Council.

Landau, S. 1981. "Juveniles and the Police." *British Journal of Criminology* 21:27–46.

Landau, S. F., and G. Nathan. 1983. "Selecting Delinquents for Cautioning in the London Metropolitan Area." *British Journal of Criminology* 23:128–49.

London Borough of Newham. 1987. *Report of a Survey of Crime and Racial Harassment in Newham.* London: L. B. Newham.

Mair, G. 1986. "Ethnic Minorities, Probation and the Magistrates' Courts." *British Journal of Criminology* 26:147–55.

Mawby, R. I., J. W. McCulloch, and I. D. Batta. 1979. "Crime among Asian Juveniles in Bradford." *International Journal of the Sociology of Law* 7:297–306.

Mayhew, P., D. Elliott, and L. Dowds. 1989. *The 1988 British Crime Survey.* Home Office Research Study 111. London: H.M. Stationery Office.

McConville, M., and J. Baldwin. 1982. "The Influence of Race on Sentencing in England." *Criminal Law Review* 652–58.

McCrudden, C., D. J. Smith, and C. Brown. 1991. *Racial Justice at Work: The Enforcement of the 1976 Race Relations Act in Employment.* London: Policy Studies Institute.

Moxon, D. 1988. *Sentencing Practice in the Crown Court.* Home Office Research Study no. 103. London: H.M. Stationery Office.

Norris, C., N. Fielding, C. Kemp, and J. Fielding. 1992. "Black and Blue: An Analysis of the Influence of Race on Being Stopped by the Police." *British Journal of Sociology* 43:207–24.

Office of Population Censuses and Surveys. 1994. *1991 Census: Ethnic Group and Country of Birth Tables: Great Britain.* London: H.M. Stationery Office.

Reiner, R. 1989. "Race and Criminal Justice." *New Community* 16:5–22.

———. 1993. "Race, Crime and Justice: Models of Interpretation." In *Minority Ethnic Groups and the Criminal Justice System*, edited by L. Gelsthorpe and W. McWilliam. Cambridge: University of Cambridge, Institute of Criminology.

Rose, E. J. B., N. Deakin, M. Abrams, V. Jackson, M. Peston, A. H. Vanags, B. Cohen, J. Gaitskell, and P. Ward. 1969. *Colour and Citizenship.* London: Oxford University Press.

Sampson, A., and C. Phillips. 1992. *Multiple Victimisation: Racial Attacks on an East London Estate.* Police Research Group, Crime Prevention Unit Series, Paper 36. London: H.M. Stationery Office.

Sampson, R. J., and J. L. Lauritsen. In this volume. "Racial and Ethnic Disparities in Crime and Criminal Justice in the United States."

Saulsbury, W., and B. Bowling. 1991. *The Multi-agency Approach in Practice: The North Plaistow Racial Harassment Project.* Research and Planning Unit Paper 64. London: H.M. Stationery Office.

Scarman, Lord. 1981. *The Brixton Disorders 10-12 April 1981: Report of an Inquiry by the Rt. Hon. the Lord Scarman, OBE.* Cmnd. 8427. London: H.M. Stationery Office.

Shah, R., and K. Pease. 1992. "Crime, Race and Reporting to the Police." *Howard Journal* 31:192–99.

Skogan, W. 1990. *The Police and Public in England and Wales: A British Crime Survey Report.* Home Office Research Study 117. London: H.M. Stationery Office.

———. 1994. *Contacts between Police and Public: Findings from the 1992 British Crime Survey.* Home Office Research Study 134. London: H.M. Stationery Office.

Small, S. 1983. *Police and People in London: II. A Group of Young Black People.* London: Policy Studies Institute.

Smith D. J. 1977. *Racial Disadvantage in Britain.* Harmondsworth: Penguin.

———. 1983*a*. *Police and People in London: I. A Survey of Londoners.* London: Policy Studies Institute.

———. 1983*b*. *Police and People in London: III. A Survey of Police Officers.* London: Policy Studies Institute.

———. 1991. "Police and Racial Minorities." *Policing and Society* 2:1–15.

Smith, D. J., and J. Gray. 1983. *Police and People in London: IV. The Police in Action.* London: Policy Studies Institute.

Stevens, P., and C. Willis. 1979. *Race, Crime and Arrests.* Home Office Research Study no. 58. London: H.M. Stationery Office.

Tuck, M., and P. Southgate. 1981. *Ethnic Minorities, Crime and Policing: A Survey of the Experiences of West Indians and Whites.* Home Office Research Study no. 70. London: H.M. Stationery Office.

Voakes, R., and Q. Fowler. 1989. *Sentencing Race and Social Inquiry Reports.* Bradford: West Yorkshire Probation Service.

Walker, M. A. 1987. "Interpreting Race and Crime Statistics." *Journal of the Royal Statistical Society,* ser. A, 150, part 1:39–56.

———. 1988. "The Court Disposal of Young Males, by Race, in London in 1983." *British Journal of Criminology* 28:441–59.

———. 1989. "The Court Disposal and Remands of White, Afro-Caribbean, and Asian Men London, 1983." *British Journal of Criminology* 29:353–67.

———. 1992. "Arrest Rates and Ethnic Minorities: A Study in a Provincial City." *Journal of the Royal Statistical Society,* ser. A, 155, pt. 2:259–72.

Walmsley, R., L. Howard, and S. White. 1992. *The National Prison Survey 1991: Main Findings.* Home Office Research Study no. 128. London: H.M. Stationery Office.

Weber, M. 1954. *Max Weber on Law in Economy and Society,* edited by M. Rheinstein. Cambridge, Mass.: Harvard University Press.

Wilbanks, W. 1987. *The Myth of a Racist Criminal Justice System.* Monterey, Calif.: Brooks/Cole.

Willis, C. F. 1983. *The Use, Effectiveness and Impact of Police Stop and Search Powers.* Home Office Research and Planning Unit Paper 15. London: Home Office.

Peter L. Martens

Immigrants, Crime, and Criminal Justice in Sweden

ABSTRACT

Immigrants generally have higher crime rates than do indigenous Swedes, particularly for violence and theft, and are likelier to be victims of violence. Both first- and second-generation immigrants have higher crime rates than indigenous Swedes, but second-generation immigrants have lower rates than first-generation immigrants—a finding contradicting results in other countries. These lower rates may be a consequence of Swedish social welfare policy. The offending pattern of second-generation immigrants is similar to the pattern of native Swedes. Groups with a high total crime rate in the first generation tend to have a relatively high total crime rate in the second generation and vice versa.

It is not fitting in Sweden to describe immigrants in terms of race or ethnic minority groups. Even if there is a terminology for race (e.g., black or white skin color) and ethnic minority groups (e.g., Gypsies, Jews, Sami, etc.) in everyday language, no official concepts have been developed to register persons in such terms. It would widely be considered as discriminatory to ask a person about his or her "race" in a survey or an official questionnaire. The basic concepts used when officially classifying immigrants' ethnic background are citizenship and country of birth.

Moreover, Sweden never accepted the arrangement of temporary "guest workers" as did several other Western European countries in the 1960s and 1970s. The "labor market immigrants" in Sweden were welcome to settle permanently (Hammar 1992).

Peter L. Martens is associate professor in sociology at Stockholm University and head of division at the National Council for Crime Prevention in Sweden.

0192-3234/97/0021-0003$01.00

Quite a lot of research has been carried out in Sweden to illuminate various aspects of the immigrants' social situation (Martens 1995; National Board of Health and Welfare 1995; Persson and Roselius 1995). Several studies have shown that immigrants, or rather some immigrant groups, by comparison with indigenous Swedes more often have weak economic resources and a low standard of housing, live in housing areas with social problems, have health problems, and so forth (Biterman 1989; Ginsburg 1995; Kindlund 1995; Leiniö 1995). It may be symptomatic of a social welfare state like Sweden to have a special predilection for conducting research on the social conditions of various groups within the population. At the same time it has been taboo to discuss negative behaviors among immigrants such as law breaking. This is due to a general fear of giving grist to the mills of xenophobic elements within the community.

The general debate on immigrants and crime has occurred in two waves (Eriksson and Tham 1983; von Hofer 1990). The first occurred during the late 1970s and the early 1980s. The official crime statistics had year after year shown that foreign citizens were overrepresented among persons suspected and convicted of offenses. A more detailed study by Sveri (1973, 1980) confirmed higher conviction rates among the foreign citizens. However, the topic was sensitive, and the patterns shown in crime statistics were denied by some administrators. The debate faded.

The second wave started in 1989 and is still in progress. When it started, Sweden had shortly before established the office of the Ombudsman against Ethnic Discrimination, whose task is "to work so that ethnic discrimination does not occur in working life or in other areas of social life" (Official Yearbook of Sweden 1995, p. 470 [in Swedish; throughout, all translations are mine unless otherwise noted]). Peter Nobel, who held the office when the debate started, argued that it was time to learn the facts about immigrant criminality. His attitude was that nobody will profit from remaining silent and that the best thing for all involved was to face the facts. In consequence, in spring 1990 the Swedish government proposed that priority should be given to research on offending among immigrants and Swedes (Governmental Proposition 1989/90:90, p. 105). A few research projects were started, and some of their results and conclusions are discussed later in this essay.

Swedish criminal policy is widely known for its humane treatment of offenders and prisoners. However, the arguments in the criminal policy debate changed during the 1980s and have become more punitive. This has probably contributed to drawing greater attention to the issue of criminal behavior among immigrants (Tham 1995).

The years since 1989 have been highly dramatic in the history of Europe. The breakdown of communism in eastern Europe generated many refugees—not least to Sweden. The confusion and reorientation in the political and economic life of the former Soviet states have formed a basis for organized crime. The St. Petersburg area in Russia and the Baltic States have become a strategic geographical position for smuggling drugs, goods, and illegal refugees to Finland and Sweden. There is, therefore, a general fear in Sweden that crime will enter from the countries across the Baltic Sea. Sweden's joining the European Union in 1995 has also led to worries that uncontrolled criminality might soon enter the country from continental Europe.

The civil war in the former Yugoslavia also resulted in a stream of refugees to neighboring countries. Sweden received more than 80,000 refugees in 1992, the majority (almost 70,000 persons) coming from the former Yugoslavia. Refugees from Kosovo-Albania were accused of extensive thefts in the shops and houses adjacent to one of their refugee camps in Sweden. These accusations were widely debated in the mass media, especially after the minister of immigration unhappily declared that stealing is a part of the culture among the people of Kosovo. In 1993, a visa became necessary for persons from the former Yugoslavia to enter Sweden; refugee numbers have declined tremendously.

Between 1991 and 1994 a new political party (New Democracy) was active in the Swedish Parliament, pleading for, among other things, law and order and a more restrictive immigration policy. One theme that recurred again and again was the higher crime rate for immigrants shown by the crime statistics.

In 1994, a law was passed that has made it easier to expel foreign citizens convicted of an offense even when a foreigner has committed a relatively minor offense. The committee that proposed this law had cited official crime statistics showing that the crime rate among foreign citizens had increased markedly (Official Reports of the Swedish Government 1993).

Several Swedish studies touching on the topic of immigrants' deviant behavior exist, but the results are scattered throughout the domestic criminological research literature. Most studies on immigrants' offending are based on registered offenses (Sveri 1973, 1980, 1987;

Wikström 1985, forthcoming; Martens 1990, 1994; von Hofer 1990, 1994; Ahlberg 1996). Self-report studies on offending (Martens 1992*b*, forthcoming) and victimization (Statistics Sweden 1995*a;* Martens, forthcoming) have been carried out, but they are few in number. No research has investigated whether there are ethnic biases in, for example, police stops and arrests. This essay seeks to report on the more important studies carried out in Sweden in this field and to present some of their results. It begins with a description of the immigrant population in Sweden and how Sweden developed into a country of immigration after the Second World War (Section I). In Section II, the social situation of immigrants living in Sweden is briefly described. Section III gives a general overview of research on offending among immigrants in Sweden. Section IV discusses offending among Swedish and foreign citizens as reflected in the official crime statistics. Because it is based on citizenship of the persons suspected of an offense, the definition of immigrants is a narrow one. In Section V, a special study is discussed that used a wider definition of immigrants and allows a discussion of offending among native Swedes and first- and second-generation immigrants. Both the first- and the second-generation immigrants are more often involved in offending than are native Swedes. Contrary to expectations, first-generation immigrants tend to be more often involved in criminal activities than second-generation immigrants. In Section VI, results from self-report surveys on offending and victimization are summarized and discussed. Immigrants report their own violent behavior and being victims of violence and threats of violence more often than Swedes. Section VII summarizes and critically discusses the results of Swedish research on offending among immigrants. Ideas for future research are offered.

I. Immigrants in Sweden

Sweden is surrounded by its Scandinavian neighbors: Denmark in the south, Norway in the west, and Finland in the east. Across the Baltic are the Baltic States (Estonia, Latvia, and Lithuania), Poland, and Germany. Some parts of Russia also border the Baltic. Immigration to Sweden is to some extent influenced by its geographical position.

A. Composition of the Immigrant Population

At the end of 1994, the population of Sweden was approximately 8.8 million. About 922,000 persons were born abroad. Inhabitants born abroad are first-generation immigrants. Thus nearly 10.5 percent of the Swedish population consists of first-generation immigrants. About 537,500 persons were foreign nationals, slightly more than 6 percent of the population. Foreign nationals with a residence permit can apply for Swedish citizenship after five years in the country. Slightly more than one-half of the first-generation immigrants had become Swedish citizens by the end of 1994.

Second-generation immigrants are persons who were born in Sweden and have at least one parent born abroad. About 676,500 persons were second-generation immigrants at the end of 1994 (8.5 percent of the population). Second-generation immigrants are usually Swedish citizens. Only 15 percent are foreign citizens.

All in all, 1.6 million people in Sweden at the end of 1994 were immigrants or had an immigrant background, slightly more than 18 percent of the Swedish population. Most, 72 percent, were Swedish citizens, and 28 percent were foreign nationals.

The statistics of the immigrants' country of birth reveal that at the end of 1994 (table 1), first-generation immigrants were to a considerable extent persons born in a European country. One-third of immigrants were from a Scandinavian country and one-third from another European country (Turkey not included). The Finns were by far the largest group, comprising almost 23 percent of the total. Persons born in the former Yugoslavia come next, comprising 12 percent of first-generation immigrants, followed by Iran and Norway (5 percent each); Denmark, Poland, and Germany (4 percent each); and finally Turkey and Chile (3 percent each).

Second-generation immigrants are predominantly persons of Nordic background. Fifty percent have parents from a Nordic country. By far the largest group has Finnish forebears (one-third of all second-generation immigrants). Persons whose parents came from Norway, Denmark, and (West) Germany are also relatively common, with percentages ranging from 7 to 10 percent. The national backgrounds of second-generation immigrants are influenced by labor force immigrants who settled in Sweden in the 1970s and earlier. The composition of second-generation immigrants by the end of 1994 is quite similar to the composition of first-generation immigrants at the end of 1983.

The proportion of persons born abroad is largest in the big cities. At the end of 1992, 16 percent of persons in Greater Stockholm were born abroad, just over 13 percent in Greater Malmö, and just over 12 percent in Greater Göteborg. (The proportions of persons of foreign

TABLE 1

Persons with Immigrant Backgrounds, December 31, 1994

	Born Abroad, First Generation		Born in Sweden, Second Generation		
Country of Birth	Swedish Nationals	Foreign Nationals	Swedish Nationals	Foreign Nationals	Total
Nordic countries:	173,023	125,821	305,283	43,857	647,984
Denmark	21,765	19,142	45,787	6,956	93,650
Finland	129,618	78,178	206,759	28,283	442,838
Iceland	380	3,905	1,152	921	6,358
Norway	21,260	24,591	54,787	7,697	108,340
Other European countries:	151,921	154,582	161,358	21,638	489,499
Greece	8,890	3,551	10,078	1,153	23,671
Yugoslavia	28,642	83,678	28,289	8,396	149,005
Poland	24,461	14,548	21,838	1,686	62,533
Romania	6,258	4,627	2,781	355	14,021
Great Britain	3,733	8,836	10,362	1,657	24,588
Germany	26,153	10,347	47,272	3,122	86,894
Hungary	11,783	3,016	12,524	323	27,646
Africa	18,037	26,924	19,544	3,196	67,501
Ethiopia	4,449	6,935	3,189	867	17,440
North America	7,245	8,353	15,872	1,498	32,968
United States	6,362	7,384	14,239	1,347	29,332
Latin America	29,396	24,075	20,462	800	74,733
Chile	13,241	13,954	10,350	184	37,729
Asia:	97,555	102,767	59,414	14,737	274,473
India	8,299	1,654	3,513	141	13,607
Iraq	6,712	16,677	4,349	1,716	29,454
Iran	19,146	29,547	7,617	2,936	59,246
Republic of Korea	7,981	466	1,421	27	9,895
Lebanon	10,414	11,179	8,591	1,064	31,248
Socialist Republic of Vietnam	5,872	3,347	2,964	443	12,626
Syria	5,157	3,915	5,538	435	15,045
Thailand	3,206	4,116	2,429	319	10,070
Turkey	13,450	15,792	14,237	6,706	50,185
Oceania	638	1,594	1,101	142	3,475
Unknown	44	80	389	7,377	7,890
Total	477,859	444,196	583,223*	93,245	1,598,523

Source.—Swedish Immigration Board (1995), p. 15.

Note.—Totals are for geographic regions. “Swedish Nationals” includes about 10,000 children of Swedes living abroad; foreign-born “Swedish Nationals” includes former foreign nationals.

* The grand total of 583,223 is the number of people with Swedish citizenship who have at least one parent born in another country. The subtotals show the number who have at least one parent from the indicated region. A person with one parent born in one region and the other parent born in another will be counted twice in the subtotals but only once in the total.

nationality in these cities were 10.2 percent, 8.0 percent, and 7.8 percent, respectively.) There are large variations within the big cities, with a tendency for immigrant density to be greatest in the neighborhoods with social problems (low-status neighborhoods) and least in high-status neighborhoods (neighborhoods with private housing). If immigrant density in different municipalities in Sweden is compared, the municipalities that border Finland, Denmark, and Norway have relatively high proportions of immigrants born abroad. There is also relatively high immigrant density in the mining district, Bergslagen, resulting from an influx of immigrant labor around 1970 (Statistics Sweden and Swedish Immigration Board 1993, pp. 30–31).

B. Immigration to Sweden

Compared with other Western European countries, Sweden has a high percentage of immigrants. Six percent of the population is of foreign nationality. This is a larger proportion than for all the countries of the European Union together (Statistics Sweden and Swedish Immigration Board 1993). Countries of the European Union with a higher proportion of foreign nationals are Luxembourg (29.4 percent), Belgium (9.2 percent), Germany (6.9 percent), and France (6.3 percent). Switzerland (a non–European Union country) had 17.4 percent foreign nationals. However, Sweden has a generous policy on the naturalization of foreign nationals. Among the 922,000 persons born elsewhere but living in Sweden at the end of 1994, about 478,000 persons were Swedish citizens. Thus over half of the persons born abroad have Swedish nationality.

Sweden became an immigrant country after the Second World War. Lundh and Olsson (1994) have presented an in-depth analysis of the immigration to Sweden since the Second World War. The Swedish Immigration Board has a yearly publication in which recent statistics are presented and discussed. The population flows described in this section are to a great extent based on the information from these sources (both in Swedish).

Sweden has not always been an immigrant country. Before 1930 Sweden was more an emigrant country. By 1920, about 1.2 million people emigrated to North America, which equals 23 percent of the population in 1900.

During World War II, Sweden accepted around 130,000 refugees from occupied Nordic countries and 30,000 from the Baltic States. After World War II, Sweden adopted a generous policy on refugees and immigrants, and immigration exceeded emigration. Since then immigration has changed in character and may be described as having two main phases: immigrant labor through the end of the 1960s and refugees from the beginning of the 1970s.

Swedish industry expanded rapidly after the war, and there was a shortage of indigenous labor. Labor had to be recruited in other countries. From the postwar years up to the beginning of the 1970s, immigration consisted mainly of immigrant labor. Most came from the Nordic countries. During the 1950s, there was also an influx of labor from Germany, Austria, and Italy and in the 1960s from Yugoslavia and Greece. Throughout these years immigration was relatively unrestricted, and virtually anyone resident abroad could come to Sweden and arrange a work permit on the spot. Active recruitment also took place.

However, at the end of the 1960s, the rules controlling immigrant labor from non-Nordic countries were tightened and recruitment was brought into line with labor market requirements. In 1972, recruitment of foreign labor ceased entirely. Persons from the other Nordic countries were exempted from these rules as the Nordic countries have had an open labor market since 1954. Since the mid-1970s, the volume of Nordic labor has also dwindled, owing to a reduced demand for labor.

Since the early 1970s, immigration of refugees has gradually increased, mainly from eastern Europe and the Third World. Another category of immigrants arise from family reunification. This means relatives of former labor immigrants, mainly Yugoslavs and Greeks, but above all members of the families of refugees. Refugees produced a radical change in the composition of the immigrant population. Increasingly, immigrants come from non-European countries such as Chile, Iran, and Turkey. But in recent years there has been an increase of immigrants from eastern Europe as a consequence of the fall of communism and, above all, the war in the former Yugoslavia.

During the 1950s and 1960s more than half of immigrants came from the Nordic countries. After a peak in 1970, the proportion gradually fell to one-third during the 1980s and decreased further during the 1990s. In 1994 slightly less than 10 percent of immigrants came from the other Nordic countries. Immigration from other European countries has, on the whole, been relatively stable. However, if we look at immigration from the various countries during various periods the picture becomes less stable. During the 1940s, immigration from eastern Europe was relatively high, while immigration from countries in Western Europe was more common during the 1950s. During the years 1960–75, immigration from southern Europe dominated, mainly because of immigration from Greece. After 1965, immigration from the eastern European countries increased again. Events in eastern Europe have influenced immigration to Sweden. The Soviet Union's military invasion of Czechoslovakia in 1968, the persecution of Jews in Poland in the early 1970s, the military state of emergency in Poland at the beginning of the 1980s, and the fall of communism in the eastern bloc at the end of the 1980s are all events that led to increased immigration from the eastern European countries. The major emigrant countries in eastern Europe have been Poland and the former Yugoslavia. Immigration from Poland has been an immigration of refugees. Immigration from the former Yugoslavia has been both an influx of immigrant labor (during the initial phase) and then an immigration of refugees as a result of war in recent years. At the end of 1991, 64,500 persons with a Yugoslavian background resided in Sweden; three years later there were 149,000 (Swedish Immigration Board 1992, 1995).

Up to the beginning of the 1970s, roughly 10 percent of immigrants came from a non-European country. Since then, this percentage has gradually increased. From the mid-1980s up to the early 1990s, around half of immigrants came from a country outside Europe. Immigration from non-European countries has, with few exceptions, been immigration of refugees and has been strongly linked with political developments in the countries concerned, such as the military coup in Chile in 1973, the civil war in Eritrea (1985–91), and the civil wars in the Middle East (Iran, Iraq, Lebanon, etc.)

In 1994, there was a drastic change in the immigration pattern. The number of immigrants from European countries other than the Nordic exceeded the number of immigrants from countries outside Europe. Nine percent of the immigrants came from a Nordic country, 26 percent from a non-European country, and 65 percent from a European country outside Scandinavia. The increase of European immigrants is, of course, a consequence of the political development in the former Yugoslavia.

C. *Persons Seeking Asylum*

Apart from immigrants, refugees and persons seeking asylum also affect the composition of modern Sweden. At the end of 1992, 80,000 persons were registered with the Swedish Immigration Board.

The number of persons seeking asylum has gradually increased. The figure was 3,000–4,000 persons a year at the beginning of the 1980s. In 1984, a marked increase took place and reached 12,000 persons. This continued until 1989 when 30,300 persons sought asylum. Numbers remained relatively constant over the next two years (29,400 persons in 1990 and 27,500 in 1991). In 1992 there was, however, a sharp increase to about 84,000 persons seeking asylum, of whom 69,000 were from the former Yugoslavia. The other major groups came from Iraq (3,200 persons) and Somalia (2,700 persons) (Statistics Sweden 1994*a*, table 66). In 1993, the number of asylum applicants dropped to 38,000, the two largest groups of applicants being 29,000 from the former Yugoslavia and 2,500 from Iraq. In 1994, the number returned to approximately the same level as in 1987, namely, 18,600 persons, because of a new rule that required persons from Bosnia-Herzegovina to have a visa to enter the country (Swedish Immigration Board 1995). During 1995, the expected number of applicants was about 800 per month, that is, not quite 10,000 persons for the whole year (personal communication with the Swedish Immigration Board, August 1995).

In recent years, by no means have all persons seeking asylum been granted a residence permit. In 1992, 65 percent of all first-time applications for asylum were rejected (Statistics Sweden and Swedish Immigration Board 1993). In 1993, about 36,000 persons were given a residence permit, 20,500 on humanitarian grounds. The majority of these asylum applicants came from the former Yugoslavia (Statistics Sweden 1994*a*, table 69). In 1994, however, the number granted increased to 45,000, vastly more than for applicants. This is partly a consequence of a lag in handling cases from the previous years (mostly applicants from Bosnia-Herzegovina) and partly a result of the government's decision to make temporary exceptions from the practice of asylum.

D. *Motives to Emigrate to Sweden*

What makes Sweden an attractive country to emigrate to? Sweden is one of the most advanced welfare states in the world with a high living standard. Until quite recently unemployment was low. The income level is relatively high. The country has a long tradition of democracy and political stability. It is a peaceful country that has managed to stay outside the conflicts between the great powers during the two world wars thanks to a resolute neutrality policy. The educational level is high and education is free. There is a political effort to reach equality between the sexes and between inhabitants with different ethnic backgrounds. There is on the whole a generous attitude toward immigration (in particular toward political refugees and family reunion). The social welfare system more or less guarantees the asylum seekers a minimum financial standard while the authorities examine their cases. A minimum financial standard is guaranteed as long as the refugee (a person with a residence permit) is outside the labor market and cannot earn a living.

Immigrants living in Sweden supply their compatriots in the home country with information about the living conditions and future possibilities for immigrants in Sweden by personal communication (letters, telephone calls, visits during vacations, etc.). Once an ethnic group has been accepted as refugees this often brings with it a continued immigration from this group, partly family reunion and partly immigration of friends. It is sometimes stated that the main cause of immigration to Sweden is earlier immigration (Lundh and Olsson 1994, p. 18).

Emigrating to a distant country (say from Bolivia to Sweden) involves high direct costs. People from the lower social strata cannot usually afford to emigrate to a country in another part of the world. It is usually people from the middle or the upper social strata who can afford it. The greater the distance to the country of destination, the higher the emigrant's socioeconomic status in the home country tends to be (Lundh and Olsson 1994, p. 17). Other resources for a potential emigrant are the relatives and friends who have already settled in the country of destination and can help to finance the travel costs.

The indirect costs are emotional. Persons place differing value on leaving close relatives and friends and the place of residence. Persons also value differently the reduced possibilities to engage in cultural, political, and religious activities in a new country. The higher the indirect costs of emigration, probably the stronger is resistance to integration into the new society.

Principal motives to emigrate to Sweden are to escape from political pursuit, family reunion, or just to start a better life in a country with a high standard of living (pure financial reasons sometimes combined with "excitement seeking"). Even if there are pure political reasons for a person to flee his or her country, there might be financial motives behind the choice of Sweden as a destination. "Adventurers," whose foremost dream is to start a better life in a country with a high standard of living, can take advantage of a political crisis in their country. Being well informed about the refugee policy and the living conditions in Sweden, they travel to Sweden and seek asylum there, arguing the likelihood of being politically persecuted in their home country. They have everything to win and nothing to lose. In reality it is sometimes difficult to distinguish between a political and an economic refugee.

Immigration from the Nordic countries to Sweden is based on quite different considerations. There is an open labor market among the

Nordic countries, and Sweden used to have a lower unemployment rate than its neighbors. Motives to emigrate to Sweden from another Nordic country have been unemployment, threats of unemployment, or just dissatisfaction with low wages in the home country. Other motives have been more achievement-oriented, for example, to attend professional training not available at home, take university courses, or learn Swedish. The open borders within the Nordic countries and the open labor market are inviting for young "adventurers" and "excitement seekers." The distance between the countries is small, but they differ enough culturally to give the feeling of moving from one country to another when one is traveling around. For many young people in the neighboring countries, the driving force to move to Sweden has been the pure excitement that goes with living in a foreign country.

II. Immigrants' Social Situation

Having a job is most important for immigrants to adapt into the new society. Regular work implies economic independence. It also gives a basis for developing social contacts and a personal identity in the new country.

A. Immigrants in the Labor Force

During the 1950s and 1960s, immigrants had, on average, a higher level of employment than indigenous Swedes. This was because immigrants at that time were mainly labor immigrants. During the 1980s, the employment rates for immigrants became lower than for Swedes. This applied in particular to recently arrived refugee immigrants.

The general conditions of the Swedish labor market have undergone a tremendous change since the beginning of the 1990s. The unemployment rate was about 3 percent in 1984 and fell below 2 percent in 1989. After 1991, however, the rate gradually increased and reached about 10 percent in 1994. The change has been more dramatic for foreign nationals than for Swedish citizens. Until the beginning of the 1990s, the unemployment rate was between 4 percent and 6 percent among the foreign citizens but then started to increase. The rate was about 8 percent in 1991, 15 percent in 1992, and 21 percent in the two following years. Among Swedish citizens the rate used to be between 1 percent and 3 percent until 1991 but then increased to 5 percent in 1992 and to almost 8 percent in 1993 and 1994 (Swedish Immigration Board 1995, p. 11). The gap between foreign and Swedish citizens' unemployment rate used to be about 3 percent until 1990. It then grew to 13 percent in 1993 and 1994. Naturalized foreign-born persons have a lower unemployment rate than foreign citizens. In 1994 immigrants from the Nordic countries, other European countries, and non-European countries had unemployment rates of 12 percent, 17 percent, and 36 percent, respectively, if they were foreign nationals and 11 percent, 11 percent, and 22 percent, respectively, if they were Swedish citizens. The unemployment rate among young people is high in general, but it is higher among foreign citizens than among Swedes. In 1994, 16 percent of the Swedish citizens aged 16–24 years were unemployed compared with 30 percent among the corresponding age-group of foreign nationals.

B. Establishment in Swedish Society

The rapid changes in the Swedish labor market undoubtedly affect the social conditions of the population. Not having a job implies depending on the supplementary benefits of the social welfare system and hence limited economic resources. A limited household economy also means limitations in daily social life combined with a lot of spare time. Being outside the workforce can thus be very frustrating. Psychologically, extended unemployment leads to lowered self-esteem and can also cause various kinds of psychosomatic problems (Arnetz 1988). The most vulnerable are recently arrived immigrants. The consequences of recent high unemployment rates on social conditions for immigrants have not, as yet, been fully investigated.

Previous research shows that the social situation of immigrants may be difficult at first, but conditions generally change for the better the longer they stay. The process of establishment may sometimes take as much as ten years (Bernow and Boalt 1989). It is not sufficient to characterize the social situation of immigrants merely in terms of socioeconomic status. Assessment should indicate how well the immigrants have found their bearings psychologically and socially within the new society (on the labor market, financially, in terms of housing and of health). Psychological and social adaptation take place in parallel and each influences the other. Good social adaptation within the new society is dependent on good psychological adaptation. Good psychological adaptation means that the immigrant is open to accept the norms and values of the new society and learns to deal with differences between the old and new culture constructively (see further Martens 1995). What needs further illumination in the near future is how unemployment increases have influenced immigrants' psychological and social adaptation.

C. Previous Research on Social Adaptation

Research on the social adaptation of immigrants in Sweden paints an optimistic picture, at least seen in a long-range perspective.

1. The distribution of occupations of immigrants shows a change with length of stay. The occupational structure among immigrants becomes increasingly similar over time to that of the indigenous Swedish population (Bernow and Boalt 1989, p. 35).

2. The initial occupations of immigrants on arrival are often different from the occupations with which they end up. Introductory occupations are usually ones that do not require a knowledge of Swedish, often within the manufacturing and service sectors. When the immigrant has learned the language, for example, this occupation is abandoned, and a job more commensurate with his or her qualifications is found.

3. The upward socioeconomic and occupational mobility among immigrants is, generally speaking, slower than among equivalent groups of native-born Swedes. However, the difference is not great (Ekberg 1989). The differences among different groups of immigrants are more striking. Finnish, Greek, and Yugoslavian immigrants show much less mobility than do Swedes. Immigrants from Poland, the former Czechoslovakia, and western Europe show much more upward mobility than do Swedes.

4. The longer immigrants stay in Sweden, the less dependent they are on supplementary benefits. Thus the economic resources of immigrants improve the more established they become on the labor market. Only after ten years in the country do financial troubles decrease significantly (Bernow and Boalt 1989, p. 43). Some groups of immigrants disproportionately remain dependent on supplementary benefits even after a long stay in Sweden. These are mainly Turkish immigrant groups and part of the Finnish group (Bernow and Boalt 1989, p. 44).

5. Overcrowding among immigrants is also a function of their length of stay. "The longer people live in the Stockholm region the fewer of them live in overcrowded conditions" (Bernow and Boalt 1989, p. 46). Overcrowding generally decreases to the same levels as for native-born Swedes after about ten years in Stockholm. However, there are differences between different groups of immigrants. The highest levels of overcrowding, even after ten years in Sweden, are to be found among typical labor immigrants.

6. In a survey of immigrants in the Stockholm region carried out by the regional planning and traffic office, it was found that "the longer a person born abroad stayed in the Stockholm region the lower the probability of his living in a neighbourhood with a high immigrant density" (Bernow and Boalt 1989, p. 50). This tendency was similar for all immigrant groups studied even though it might be heightened to different degrees for different groups. Immigrants who live in neighborhoods with a high immigrant density are primarily those who arrived in Sweden relatively recently. The neighborhoods with very high immigrant density are the least attractive neighborhoods in the city, and a large proportion of native-born Swedes who live there belong to the socioeconomically weak groups that have difficulty asserting themselves on the housing market. Bernow and Boalt (1989, p. 51) conclude that "it appears as though many of the neighborhoods with a high immigrant density act as transit areas for newly arrived immigrants and that they move from these neighborhoods after having stayed there for a certain time."

7. The proportion of persons registered as sick for long periods is higher among immigrants (persons born abroad) than among native-born Swedes in all age-groups between twenty and sixty-four years. The level of illness is higher among women than among men. Immigrants from a country outside northwest Europe are registered as long-term sick cases to a greater extent than are western European immigrants and Swedes. Among men between twenty-five and thirty-four years and women between twenty and twenty-nine years, born outside western Europe, the level of registration as long-term sick cases is particularly high. Immigrants born outside western Europe are also more likely to take early retirement. Early retirement is becoming more common within these groups as early as forty-five and at that age is about 10 percent higher than for western European immigrants and native-born Swedes. Persons born in Greece, former Yugoslavia, and Turkey have extremely high levels of early retirement. It is very common for younger people (twenty-three to thirty-nine years) who are immigrants born in, for example, Ethiopia, Iraq, and Syria to be registered as sick for long periods (Bernow and Boalt 1989, p. 59).

D. Harder Times for Immigrants

During the last few years Sweden has experienced an economic recession. Budgetary constraints have led to cutbacks in the social welfare system. These have been extensive in the child-care sector and have affected the personal and material resources of child day-care centers, preschools, schools, and recreation centers. The reduced resources have most affected municipalities in the big-city areas (National Board of Health and Welfare 1994).

From 1985 to 1993, receipt of social assistance increased in almost all types of household and age categories. The number of households on assistance increased by just over 25 percent, and costs (fixed prices, calculated on the basis of the 1994 cost level) by about 65 percent. There is a tremendous difference in cost increase between Swedish and foreign households. Payments to Swedish households increased by almost 35 percent and to foreign households by almost 140 percent. Nearly two-thirds of the cost increase is due to increased disbursements to foreign households. The latter receive more social assistance, among other factors because of their larger households. Assistance to the foreign households also covers a longer average time period than for the Swedish households (National Board of Health and Welfare 1995, p. 10).

The recent increase in unemployment rates has particularly affected foreign citizens and was highest among youth with an immigrant background. An economic recession coupled with increasing unemployment means that more and more families with children live under trying economic and social conditions. The budget cuts within the systems of child care, school, and recreation also affect the need for the individual and family care services of the social welfare agencies. The possibilities for "individual and family care" to compensate for deficiencies in the child's home environment or other areas of the child's life are, however, reduced if there are fewer well-functioning day-care activities (kindergartens, schools, recreation centers) (National Board of Health and Welfare 1994, p. 11).

The immigrants who arrived in Sweden during the last few years will have a harder time finding regular work than those who arrived in the 1980s or earlier. To the extent they find a job, it will quite likely be temporary. It is also likely that they will have small chance, even in a long-time perspective, of finding a job corresponding to their qualifications. The most recently arrived immigrants may remain dependent on social assistance and supplementary benefits even in the future.

Limited economic resources set limits on these immigrants' housing conditions. They have to continue to live in the neighborhood area and the dwelling to which they were first assigned by the authorities. These neighborhood areas are usually areas with a high density of immigrants and of persons with economic and social problems. Persons and families living in these less attractive areas and possessing sufficient economic resources might leave the area and move to an area with fewer social problems, thus making room for new immigrants. In the future this can lead to a greater ethnic segregation than is the case today, particularly in the big cities in Sweden (Wikström 1994; Persson and Roselius 1995).

The deteriorated social conditions among immigrants in particular will probably lead to more health problems. Those who arrived in recent years are the most vulnerable. "One can predict that the refugee immigrants' health in the long run will become worse than was the case for the 'old' immigrants. Many of the newly arrived immigrants come from a culturally different society. They more often have traumatic experiences behind them. They are less prepared for living in Sweden. They often do not know if it will ever be possible to return to their home or when it will be possible. The (constant) dream of a return home can make the integration into the new society more difficult" (Ginsburg 1995, p. 68 [in Swedish]).

Hence, the prospects are quite pessimistic for newly arrived immigrants. They will more often than the previous immigrant groups have difficulties in getting work, be more dependent on supplementary benefits, more often be settled in a less attractive neighborhood, more often have social and psychological problems, and thus be less willing (or even able) to integrate into Swedish society. This in turn affects the living conditions of the immigrants' children growing up in Sweden (i.e., the second-generation immigrants). Probably the children of those immigrants who came to Sweden before the mid-1980s were better off than the children of the immigrants who arrived during the most recent ten-year period.

III. Research into Criminal Behavior of Immigrants

Relatively little empirical research has been carried out on immigrant crime in Sweden. Most studies based on official crime statistics are published by Statistics Sweden.

A. Police-Recorded Offenses

Having learned of an offense, the police have to make a preliminary investigation, unless the offense is a minor offense such as a petty traffic violation or a less serious case of smuggling, in which case the police can issue a summary fine at the scene of the crime. The clearance of a case implies that one or more persons are suspected of the offense.

Suspected persons under age fifteen (the age of criminal responsibility) are turned over to the social welfare system and do not appear in the crime statistics. The prosecutor must decide whether a suspected person will be prosecuted. Where prosecution is initiated, the court chooses a sanction: conditional sentence, probation, fine, or imprisonment. Some persons are acquitted.

The official crime statistics present relatively detailed information about the persons suspected of an offense and even more detailed information on those found guilty.

A distinction is made between persons (suspected and convicted) with a Swedish and those with a foreign citizenship. Furthermore, the foreign nationals are categorized into those from a Nordic country and those from a non-Nordic country. Unlike some other European countries, Swedish crime statistics distinguish between foreign nationals who reside in Sweden and those who do not reside in Sweden. The nonresidents are persons seeking asylum, engaged in business, tourists, illegal entrants, and so forth.

From 1987 on, the official crime statistics also present the number of suspects and convicted persons in different national groups: Nordic citizens, citizens from the other European countries including Russia and Turkey, citizens from an African country, North American citizens, Central and South American (here referred to as Latin American) citizens, citizens from an Asian country, citizens of Australia and Oceania, and stateless citizens.

One shortcoming of the official crime statistics is that they have adopted a narrow definition of immigrants. Statistics are produced with respect to nationality (citizenship) of the persons suspected of an offense. This means that persons with Swedish nationality but who were born abroad (first-generation immigrants) are registered not as immigrants but as native Swedes. Immigrants can apply for naturalization after five years of living in Sweden, and more than one-half of the foreign-born inhabitants have acquired Swedish citizenship. Naturalization authorities check whether applicants have been registered for criminal behavior, and if they have, their applications are generally turned down. The longer immigrants have lived in Sweden, the less their propensity for criminal behavior, even after holding age constant (Ahlberg 1996). Thus there is reason to believe that naturalized Swedes are less criminal than foreign citizens.

For these reasons, the National Council for Crime Prevention initiated a project to study registered criminality among immigrants, using a broader definition than in the official record and referring to the immigrants' countries of birth. This makes possible a distinction between first-generation immigrants, defined as inhabitants born abroad, and second-generation immigrants, defined as inhabitants with at least one parent born abroad. Ahlberg (1996) has made special analyses of inhabitants born between 1945 and 1974 who lived in Sweden in 1985, concerning their registered offenses during the five-year period 1985–89. The number of inhabitants falling within this definition is about 3.5 million. Ahlberg studied suspected offenses among native Swedes, immigrants (first-generation), and children of the immigrants born in Sweden (second-generation). He also examined the countries of origin of the suspected persons in much greater detail than is possible on the basis of the official crime statistics.

Wikström (1985) also has made special studies of police-recorded violent crimes and deadly violence, recording, among other background variables, the suspected persons' countries of birth.

B. Crime Surveys

Victim surveys in Sweden are very rare. Sweden participated in the International Crime Survey (Alvazzi del Frate, Zvekic, and van Dijk 1993), but this study did not collect information about the respondents' immigrant backgrounds. Statistics Sweden has carried out continuous surveys on the living conditions of the population since 1974 (Statistics Sweden 1995*a*). The purpose of these surveys is to study various welfare indicators such as health, economy, employment, education, housing, and social life. Since 1978 "social safety" was included as an area of social welfare. Under this heading the surveys have included some questions about respondents' exposure to crime and fear of crime. The focus has been on crimes of violence and property crimes. In these surveys the respondents' ethnic background was registered in terms of born in Sweden, born abroad, and parents born abroad.

In the 1990s, some smaller local crime surveys were carried out and included both adults and schoolchildren. The Stockholm Project is an example (Wikström 1990*a*). This project focused on eight neighborhood areas in Stockholm. In the adult survey of 1990, about 1,600 persons living in the areas were sampled and interviewed by telephone, and among other things, asked whether they had ever been suspected of crime and interviewed by the police and whether they ever had been found guilty of a crime in court. They were also asked about being victims of violence and theft. The survey was replicated in 1992. The study of juveniles was carried out among ninth-grade pupils in the classrooms of the schools located in the eight neighborhood areas. A questionnaire was administered containing, among other things, questions on victimization and self-reported crime. The study was carried out in 1990 and then replicated with a few changes in the questionnaire in 1992.

In 1993, the Swedish Center for Immigration Research (CEIFO) at Stockholm University carried out an extensive survey of attitudes toward immigrants in the Swedish population (Lange and Westin 1993; Westin and Lange 1993; Lange 1995). A special survey of the attitudes of immigrants from Finland, Poland, Chile, and Iran toward Swedes was also carried out. In cooperation with the Swedish National Council for Crime Prevention, questions on fear of crime and being victims of violence and theft were included. The respondents were also asked if they had been suspected of crime and interviewed by the police and if they had been found guilty of a crime in court in Sweden.

The following sections focus on offending among Swedish and foreign citizens as reflected in the official crime statistics, Ahlberg's special study of registered offenses among first- and second-generation immigrants, and results from victim and self-report studies.

IV. Offending among Swedish and Foreign Citizens

Of all the offenses reported to the police during a year, only a fraction can reasonably be ascribed to a particular person by the police. These persons are identified as suspects. In 1994, 1,112,500 offenses were reported to the police. Of these, 285,600 were attributed to almost 102,000 suspected persons.

A. Persons Suspected of an Offense, 1984–94

Statistics Sweden distinguishes between suspected offenders registered as residents in Sweden and suspected persons not registered as residents, as do I in this section. The nonresidents include asylum seekers, tourists, persons in business, and illegal entrants.

1. *Nonresidents.* There were about 3,500 nonresident suspects a year until 1988. This increased to about 9,300 persons in 1993 but fell to 5,600 persons one year later. Where do nonresident suspects come from? Table 2 shows that they usually come from other Nordic or European countries. The number of Nordic citizens suspected of an offense has gradually decreased from 1,700 to 1,200. However, the num-

TABLE 2

Number of Suspected Persons by Nationality Group, for Foreign Nationals Not Residing in Sweden, 1987–94

Year	Other Nordic Country	Other European Country	African Country	Latin American Country	Asian Country	Other Country	Total
1987:							
N	1,729	976	233	218	154	69	3,379
Percent	51.2	28.9	6.9	6.4	4.5	2.0	100.0
1988:							
N	1,552	1,095	315	292	244	82	3,580
Percent	43.3	30.6	8.8	8.2	6.8	2.3	100.0
1989:							
N	1,708	1,597	340	218	144	72	4,079
Percent	41.9	39.1	8.3	5.3	3.5	1.8	100.0
1990:							
N	1,681	2,301	433	147	358	123	5,043
Percent	33.3	45.6	8.6	2.9	7.1	2.4	100.0
1991:							
N	1,589	2,952	826	214	599	131	6,311
Percent	25.2	46.8	13.1	3.4	9.5	2.1	100.0
1992:							
N	1,275	5,353	581	241	364	146	7,960
Percent	16.0	67.2	7.2	3.0	4.6	1.8	100.0
1993:							
N	1,248	6,781	471	268	385	179	9,332
Percent	13.4	72.7	5.0	2.9	4.1	1.9	100.0
1994:							
N	1,173	3,390	356	313	278	125	5,635
Percent	20.8	60.1	6.3	5.5	4.9	2.2	100.0

SOURCE.—Statistics Sweden (1988*a*–1993*b*), table 3.2.9; National Council for Crime Prevention Sweden (1994), table 2.6; Statistics Sweden (1995*b*), table 410A.

ber of other European citizens has changed strikingly during the period 1987–94. There were 1,000 suspects in 1987, 3,000 in 1991, and 7,000 in 1993. In 1994, the number suddenly went down to about 3,500 suspects.

These changes can be explained by the political changes in eastern Europe since the end of the 1980s. The breakdown of communism and the former Soviet Union made it possible for eastern Europeans to travel to western Europe, including Sweden. The war in the former Yugoslavia resulted in a stream of refugees and asylum seekers to Sweden. The sudden increase of nonresident suspects in 1991 can also be

TABLE 3

Number of Suspected Persons with Foreign Citizenship Residing in Sweden by Nationality Group, 1987–94

Year	Other Nordic Country	Other European Country	African Country	Latin American Country	Asian Country	Other Country	Total
1987:							
N	5,378	3,487	458	836	1,375	255	11,789
Percent	45.6	29.6	3.9	7.1	11.7	2.2	100.0
1988:							
N	5,118	3,398	461	1,016	1,624	317	11,934
Percent	42.9	28.5	3.9	8.5	13.6	2.6	100.0
1989:							
N	5,501	3,644	620	1,293	2,092	381	13,531
Percent	40.6	26.9	4.6	9.5	15.5	2.8	100.0
1990:							
N	5,661	4,078	724	1,487	2,509	483	14,942
Percent	37.9	27.3	4.8	9.9	16.8	3.2	100.0
1991:							
N	5,641	4,450	993	1,551	2,873	605	16,113
Percent	35.0	27.6	6.2	9.6	17.8	3.7	100.0
1992:							
N	5,210	4,469	1,279	1,586	2,894	599	16,037
Percent	32.5	27.8	8.0	9.9	18.0	3.7	100.0
1993:							
N	4,787	4,488	1,288	1,404	2,787	619	15,373
Percent	31.1	29.2	8.4	9.1	18.1	4.0	100.0
1994:							
N	4,349	4,570	1,216	1,225	2,444	523	14,327
Percent	30.3	31.9	8.5	8.5	17.0	3.9	100.0

SOURCE.—Statistics Sweden (1988*a*–1993*b*), table 3.2.9; National Council for Crime Prevention Sweden (1994), table 2.6; Statistics Sweden (1995*b*), table 410A.

ascribed to more suspects with African and Asian citizenship. The sudden decrease in the number of European suspects in 1994 can probably be ascribed to the decreasing number of asylum applicants that year.

2. *Residents.* Before 1989, the number of suspects with foreign nationality residing in Sweden was below 12,000 persons a year. It gradually increased to 16,000 persons in 1991 and 1992 and decreased the next two years to 14,500 suspects in 1994.

About 12 percent of suspects who resided in Sweden in 1984 were foreign citizens. After 1990, the level went up to almost 16 percent and in 1994 went down slightly to less than 15 percent. Looking at the different nationality groups among the suspects in table 3 reveals that the Nordic and other European citizens have dominated, even if the number of the former decreased (from 5,500 to 4,500 suspects during the ten-year period) and the number of the latter increased (from 3,500 to 4,600 suspects). Asian citizens have comprised about 20 percent of the foreign suspects since the beginning of the 1990s and have almost doubled their proportion since 1984. African citizens have increased sharply from about 500 suspects in 1984 to nearly 1,300 after 1991. Seen as a whole, then, the percentage of Nordic citizens among suspects has gradually decreased during the past ten years along with slight increases for other European citizens and marked increases for non-European citizens.

B. Crime Structure

Of what kinds of crimes are foreign and Swedish citizens suspected? Figure 1*a–e* presents an overview of the patterns of offenses against the Penal Code and other laws and regulations of which persons with Swedish and non-Swedish citizenship were suspected in 1994.

1. *Residents.* On the whole, Swedish, other Nordic, and non-Nordic nationals residing in Sweden are suspected of about the same patterns of offenses. Of these, offenses of theft (theft, petty theft, robbery, unlawful taking of a vehicle) are the most common, followed by road traffic offenses, offenses against the person, fraud, and offenses against the Narcotic Drugs (Punishment) Act.

Some small differences between the groups warrant mention. The citizens from other Nordic countries more often than Swedes and non-Nordic citizens were suspected of road traffic offenses, whereas non-Nordic citizens more often were suspected of offenses against the person and theft. Crimes against the person are offenses of assault and sexual offenses.

2. *Nonresidents.* A striking but not unexpected finding is that foreign citizens not residing in Sweden are more often suspected of smuggling offenses than are their counterparts living in Sweden. Moreover, they were to a less extent suspected of offenses against the person. Nordic citizens not living in Sweden have relatively often been suspected of fraud, whereas non-Nordic citizens (mainly other European citizens) have a strikingly high proportion of thefts, with shoplifting dominating.

C. Overrepresentation of Foreign Citizens

Six percent of the Swedish population in 1994 were foreign citizens. Of the 96,257 suspected persons living in Sweden, 85 percent were

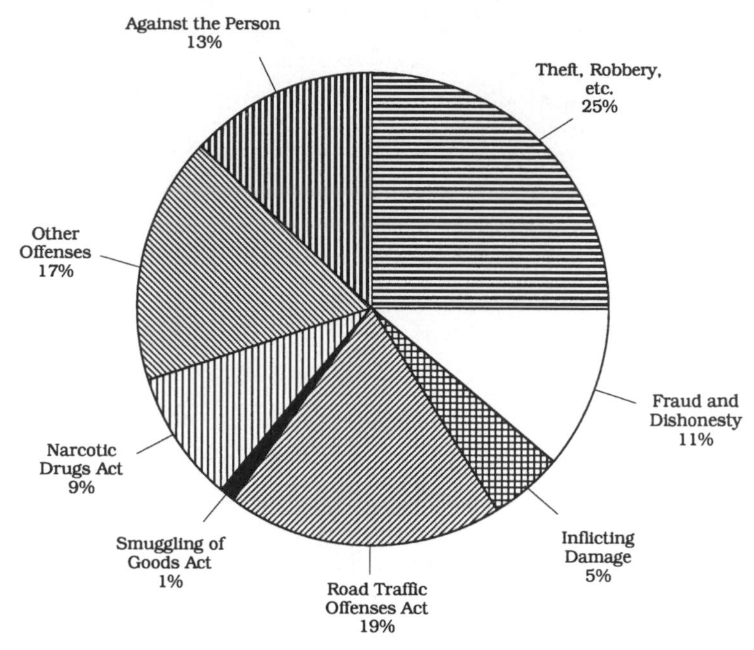

a, Swedish citizens

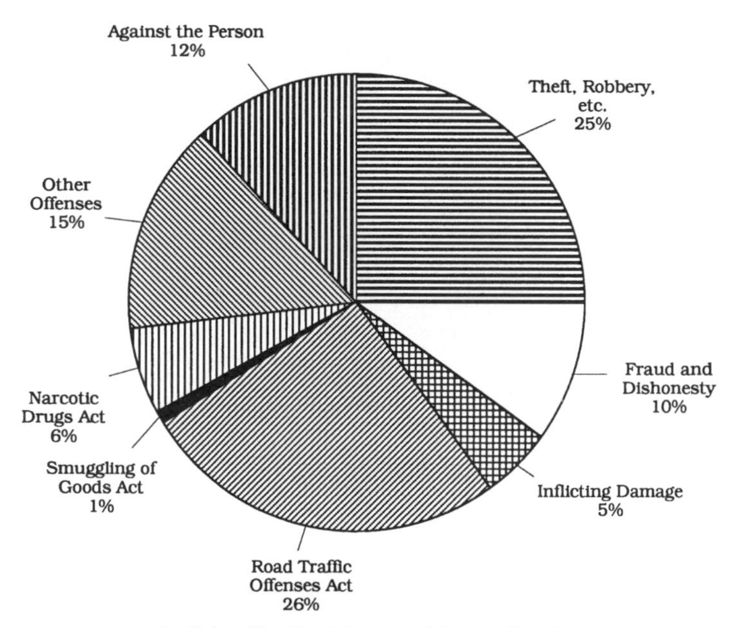

b, Other Nordic citizens, resident in Sweden

FIG. 1.—Crime structure among suspects, 1994. *a*, Swedish citizens. *b*, other Nordic citizens, residents of Sweden. *c*, non-Nordic citizens, residents of Sweden. *d*, other Nordic citizens, nonresidents. *e*, non-Nordic citizens, nonresidents. Source: Statistics Sweden 1995*b*, table 403.

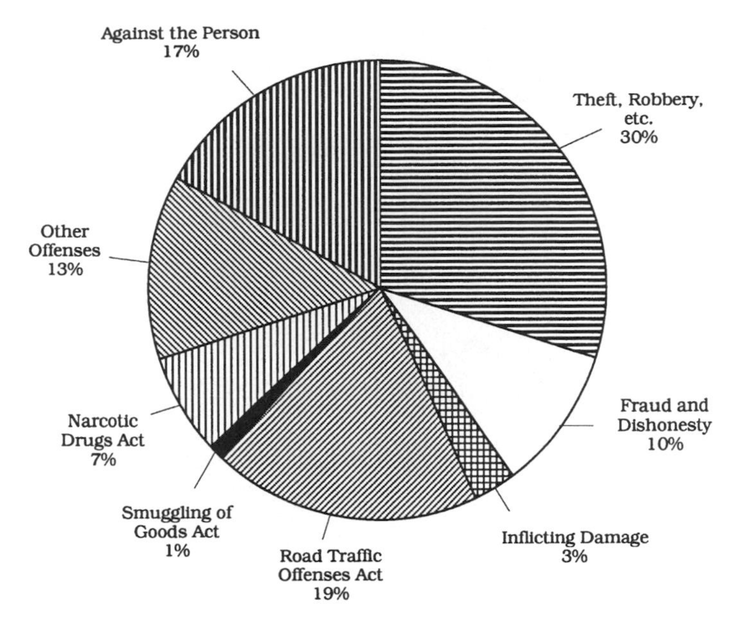

c, Non-Nordic citizens, resident in Sweden

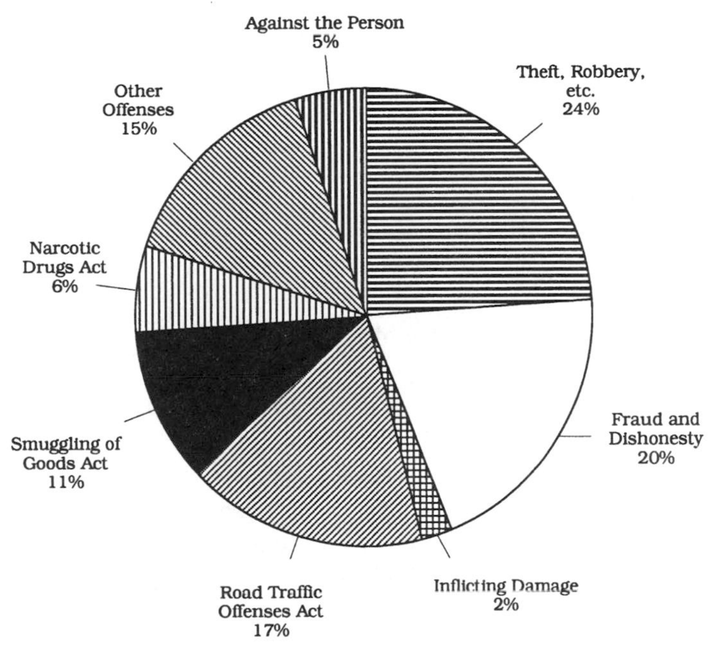

d, Other Nordic citizens, not resident in Sweden

FIG. 1.—(*Continued*)

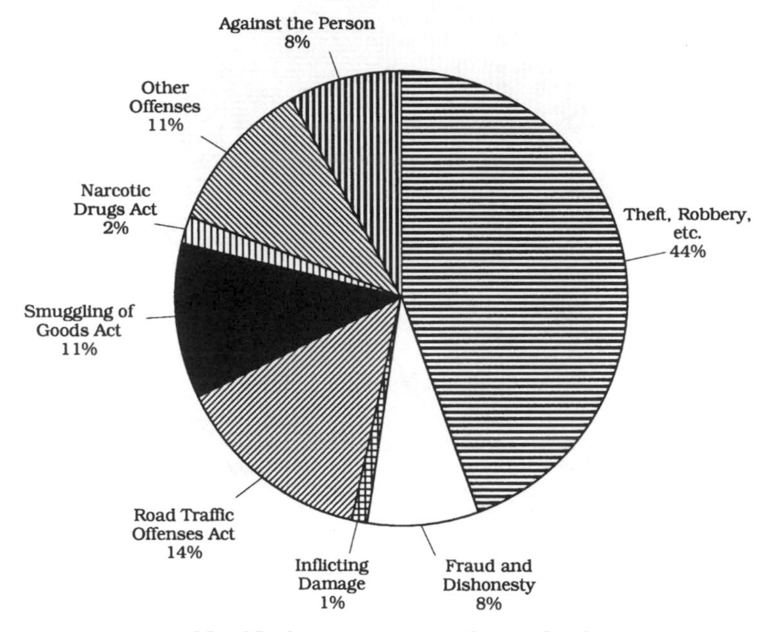

e, Non-Nordic citizens, not resident in Sweden

FIG. 1.—(*Continued*)

Swedish citizens, and 15 percent foreign nationals. Among the 7.2 million persons over fourteen years, about 416,000 were foreign citizens (5.8 percent). The proportion of foreign nationals among persons suspected of offenses is 2.5 times higher than one can expect from the population structure.

The overrepresentation of foreign citizens varies for different types of offenses, with the highest overrepresentation under two main headings: violent offenses and theft offenses (table 4). Rape, assault of children, and attempted murder or manslaughter show proportions of foreign citizens that are at least four times higher than might be expected relative to their proportion of the national population. Aggravated robbery, pickpocketing, and thefts and petty thefts in shops and department stores also show proportions of foreign citizens among the suspects which are about four times higher than expected. Not surprisingly, smuggling offenses are also relatively more common for foreign citizens.

TABLE 4

Percentage of Foreign Citizens among Persons Suspected of Different Types of Offenses, Residents, 1994

Type of Offense	Foreign Citizens	Overrepresentation
Violent Offenses:		
Rape, aggravated rape	27.1	4.7
Assault of children:		
7–14 years	27.6	4.7
0–6 years	25.2	4.3
Attempt to murder/manslaughter	23.4	4.0
Murder/manslaughter	21.7	3.7
Aggravated assault:		
Against women	22.2	3.8
Against men	18.6	3.2
Unlawful threat	19.4	3.3
Violence to public servant	17.7	3.0
Violent resistance	17.8	3.0
Offenses of stealing:		
Theft, petty theft in shop or department store	21.2	3.6
Pickpocketing	28.1	4.8
Aggravated robbery	18.0	3.1
Goods Smuggling Act	23.2	4.0

Source.—Statistics Sweden (1995*b*), table 403.

D. Crime Participation Rates

The number of suspects in different groups who live in Sweden is related to the number of persons at the age of criminal responsibility (fifteen years and above) per 100,000 inhabitants in that group. This rate gives information about the relative frequency of suspects in each nationality group and shows rates per 100,000 persons in each group who have been suspected of at least one offense per year on average for the years 1987–93 (see fig. 2). It is thus a measure of the suspect rate in each nationality group. But it can also be seen as a measure of a yearly rate of crime participation. It is in this sense that the rate is referred to here. The yearly crime participation rate is also calculated for persons in the different age-groups.

1. *Nationality Group.* The yearly participation rate among the Swedish citizens is 1,200 suspects per 100,000 citizens. Thus 1.2 percent of Swedish citizens aged fifteen years and above on average were suspected of an offense per year during 1987–93.

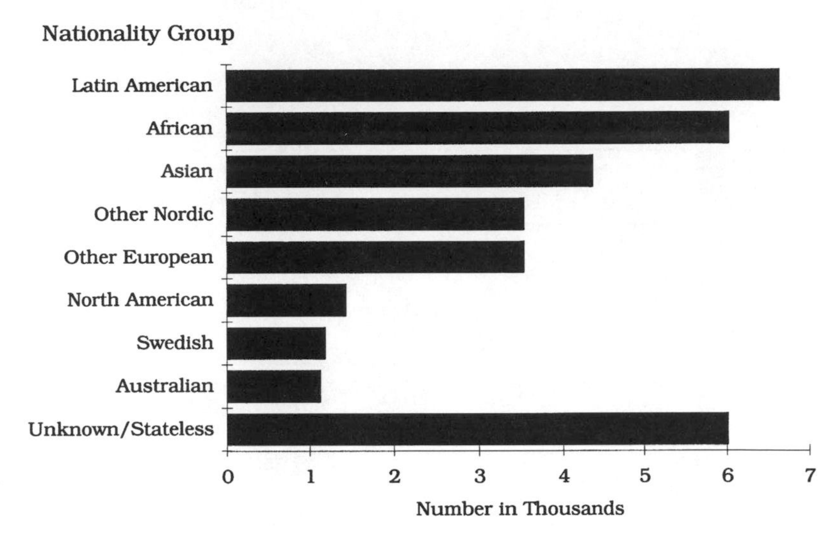

FIG. 2.—Number of suspects per 100,000 inhabitants over 14 years old, by nationality group; mean values are for 1987–93. "Asian" excludes Turkey; "Other European" includes Turkey and the former Soviet Union. Sources: Statistics Sweden (1988*a*–93*a*), table 3.2.9; National Council for Crime Prevention Sweden (1994), table 2.6; Statistics Sweden (1988*b*–92*b*), table 2.3; Statistics Sweden (1993*b*, 1994*b*), table 2.2.

Latin Americans, Africans, and stateless persons have the highest yearly participation rates. Between 6 percent and 7 percent of the persons in these nationality groups living in Sweden have been suspected yearly of at least one offense. These rates are more than five times higher than for the Swedish citizens.

Citizens of the other Nordic and European countries have a yearly participation rate of 3.5 percent, which is three times higher than for the citizens of Sweden. This is slightly lower than for citizens of Asian countries who have a rate slightly less than 4.5 percent. Citizens of the United States, Canada, and Australia living in Sweden have a yearly crime participation rate close to that of Swedish citizens.

2. *Age and Nationality Group.* Swedish criminological research has repeatedly shown that young people aged fifteen to seventeen years have the highest crime participation rates and that the rate gradually decreases with age (Stattin, Magnusson, and Reichel 1989; Wikström 1990*b;* Farrington and Wikström 1994).

Figure 3*a* shows the crime participation rates in different age-groups among Swedish citizens fifteen years and older. As expected, the youngest group has the highest rate, with 3,100 suspects per 100,000 inhab-

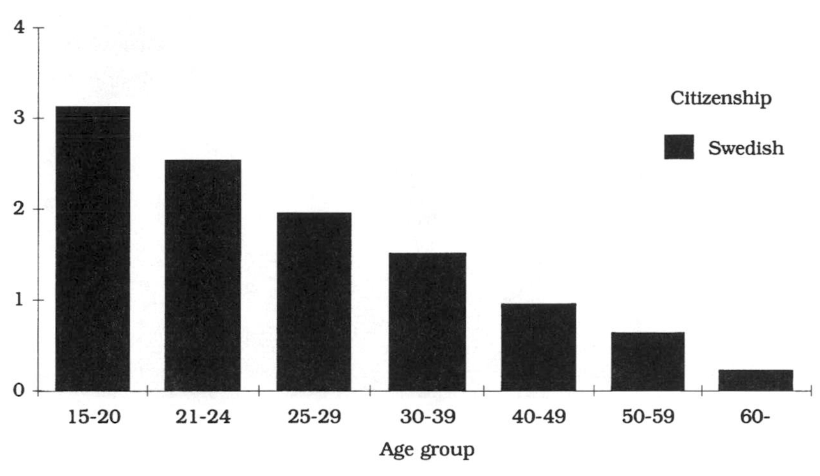

a, Swedish citizens

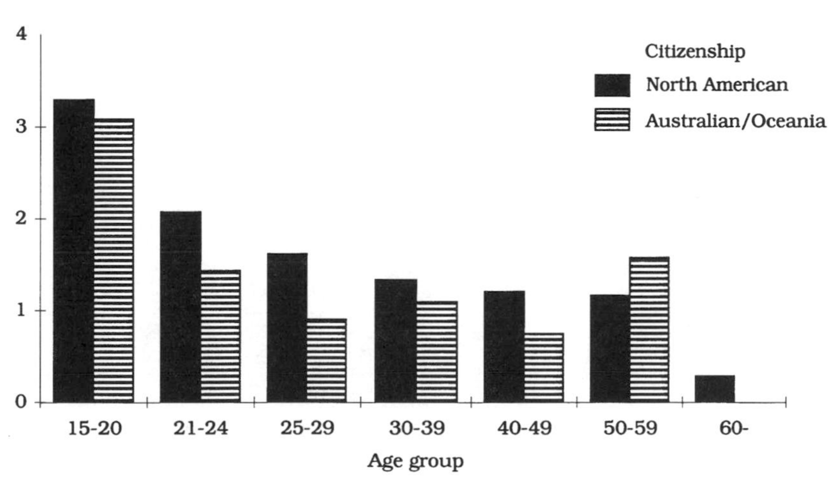

b, North American and Australian/Oceanian citizens

Fig. 3.—Number of suspects per 100,000 inhabitants of Sweden, by age-group and nationality, 1987–93. *a*, Swedish citizens. *b*, North American and Australian/Oceanian citizens. *c*, Nordic and Other European citizens. "Other European" includes Turkey and the former Soviet Union. *d*, Latin American citizens and stateless persons or persons with unknown citizenship. *e*, Asian citizens. *f*, African citizens. Sources: Statistics Sweden (1988*a*–93*a*), table 3.2.9; National Council for Crime Prevention Sweden (1994), table 2.6; Statistics Sweden (1988*b*–92*b*), table 2.3; Statistics Sweden (1993*b*, 1994*b*), table 2.2.

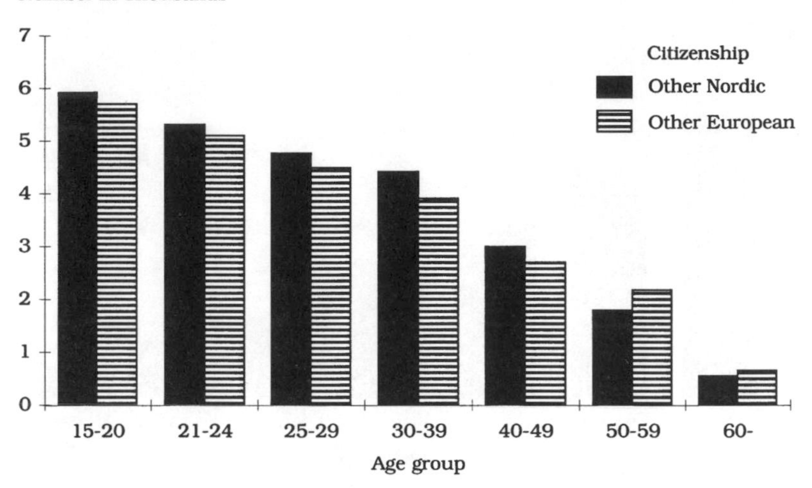

c, Nordic and other European citizens

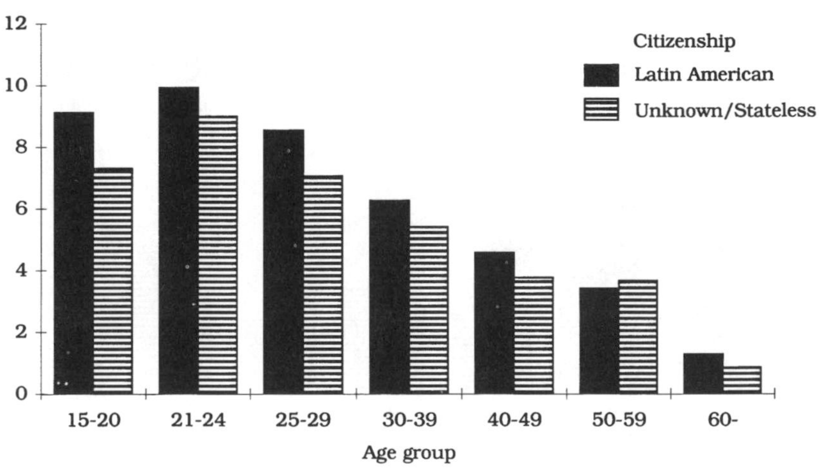

d, Latin American citizens, stateless, and citizenship unknowns

Fig. 3.—(*Continued*)

itants of that age in the population. Hence, about 3.1 percent among the young Swedish citizens aged fifteen to twenty years have been suspected of at least one offense a year during the seven-year period. The annual participation rate decreases gradually with higher age, and at sixty and above, the rate is 220 suspects per 100,000.

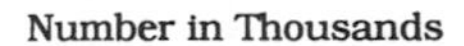

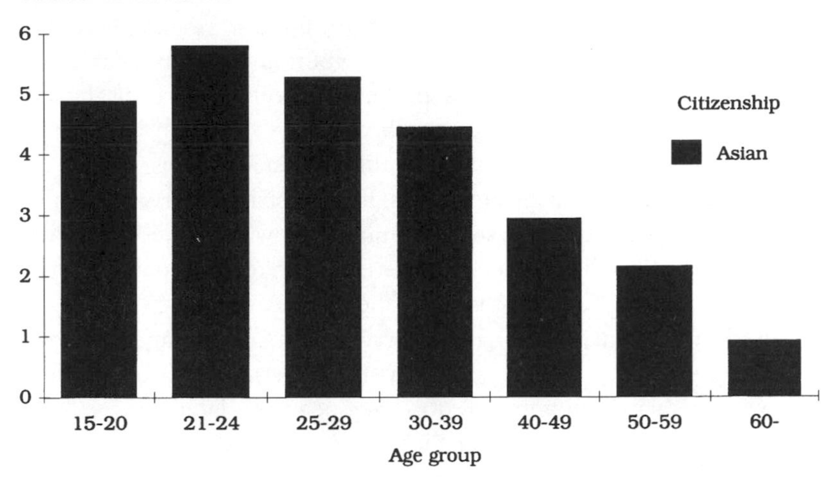

e, Asian citizens

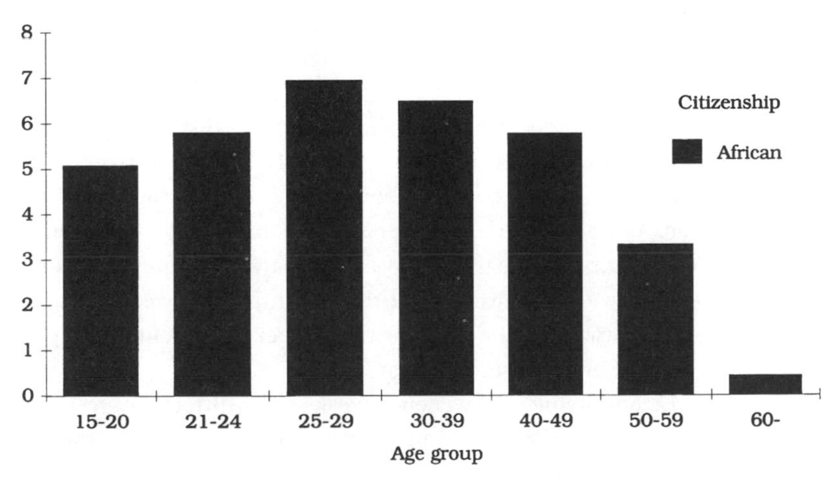

f, African citizens

FIG. 3.—(*Continued*)

This age-crime distribution can be assumed to illustrate the prevalence of registered criminality in different age-groups in the Swedish population and can serve as a frame of reference for discussing the registered criminality of foreign citizens.

North American and Australian citizens who live in Sweden have about the same annual crime participation rate as the Swedish citizens. As figure 3*b* shows, these two nationality groups also resemble Swedish citizens regarding the age-crime rate distribution. The irregular distribution for Australian citizens is probably a consequence of the low number of persons in each age category.

The annual participation rates in different age-groups among the Nordic and other European citizens form distributions with similar shapes. They have the same diminishing trend with higher age as was found for the Swedish citizens. However, the rates are constantly two or three times higher than those for the Swedes.

Swedish residents from Latin America, Asia, Africa, and unknown countries show a different pattern in the age-crime distribution than the previous nationality groups do. They peak at a later age.

Latin American citizens and the stateless have the highest annual crime participation rate at the age of twenty-one to twenty-four years. The youngest age-group has indeed a high rate but not quite as high as the subsequent age-group. More than 9 percent of Latin American citizens aged fifteen to twenty years have been suspected of an offense compared with almost 10 percent in the age-group of twenty-one to twenty-four years.

Asian citizens residing in Sweden show a similar distribution of the annual participation rates as the two nationality groups just discussed with, however, rates being considerably lower. The distribution of the Asian citizens deviates from the others in that the age-group twenty-five to twenty-nine years has a higher rate than the youngest group. Hence, Asian citizens in Sweden are most criminal between the ages of twenty-one to twenty-nine years, with between 5 percent and 6 percent suspected of an offense each year.

African citizens living in Sweden have a quite different age-crime distribution showing a rather even distribution for the age range of fifteen to forty-nine years, with a peak at the age of twenty-five to twenty-nine years. The rate increases gradually up to the age of twenty-five to twenty-nine years and then gradually declines to the age of forty to forty-nine years. After the age of forty-nine there is a marked decline of the crime participation rate. Another striking observation among the Africans is that those aged forty to forty-nine years have the same participation rate as have those between twenty-one and twenty-four years of age.

3. *Overrisks by Age and Nationality Group.* The higher likelihood (the "overrisk") that a member of an immigrant group will be sus-

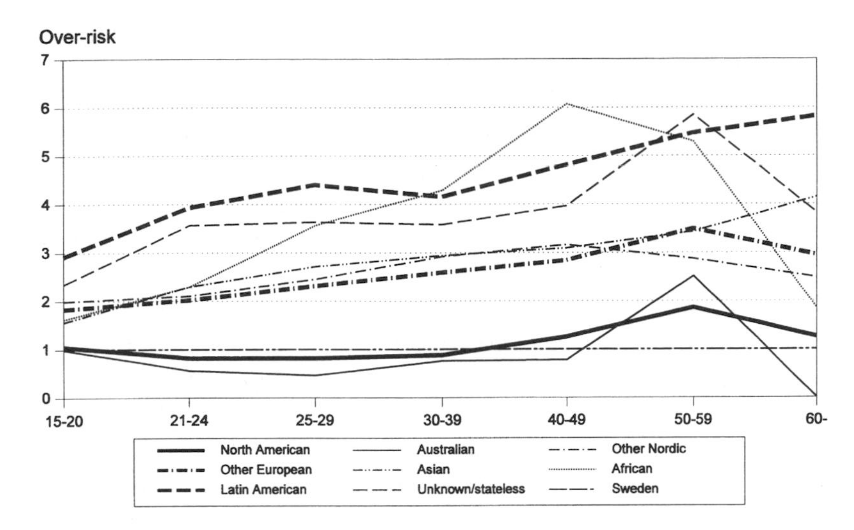

FIG. 4.—Overrisk of being suspected of an offense, by age-group and nationality, 1987–93. Sources: Statistics Sweden (1988*a*–93*a*), table 3.2.9; National Council for Crime Prevention Sweden (1994), table 2.6; Statistics Sweden (1988*b*–92*b*), table 2.3; Statistics Sweden (1993*b*, 1994*b*), table 2.2.

pected of a criminal offense vis-à-vis Swedish citizens is obtained by relating the immigrant groups' crime participation rate to the rate for the Swedish citizens. The ratio tells us how much higher the crime participation rate is for the immigrant group as compared with the Swedish nationals. The ratio can also be interpreted as an overrepresentation of suspects in a nationality group in relation to the Swedish citizens. The overrisk is calculated for each age category. Figure 4 shows the trends of the overrisks by age and nationality. The figure reveals that the immigrant groups cluster on three levels. For one group, namely, the African citizens, the trend differs remarkably.

The North American and Australian citizens have the lowest overrisk in all age categories. The values of the overrisks fluctuate around one, which implies that these two immigrant groups have the same risk for being suspected of an offense as the Swedes. On the next level are the Scandinavian and other European citizens as well as citizens of Asian countries, with an overrisk of between two and four. The Latin Americans have the highest overrisk, with between three and six times higher risk of being suspected of an offense than Swedes. The stateless persons and those whose citizenship is unknown also have a high overrisk, but on a slightly lower level than the Latin Americans.

For all the immigrant groups mentioned, the overrisk of being suspected of a criminal offense tends to be greater with increasing age. This means that young immigrants are generally more similar to their Swedish companions concerning participation in criminal activities than are the older immigrants. Older immigrants tend to be less similar to older Swedes. African citizens, however, show a quite different pattern from the other groups. The youngest age-group among the Africans has an overrisk on the same level as the young European and Asian citizens, but the overrisk then gradually increases with age and reaches the ratio of 6:1 at the age of forty to forty-nine years. This ratio exceeds even the overrisk of the Latin-Americans of that age. The overrisk for the oldest age-group among the Africans is, however, even lower than for their European counterparts.

The lower overrisks among the younger immigrants as compared with the older immigrants might indirectly suggest that second-generation immigrants tend to be less overrepresented in offending than are first-generation immigrants. This is contrary to what has been pointed out in the international research literature (Killias 1989) and in the general debate in Sweden. This question is taken up again in greater detail in Section V.

4. *On the Age-Crime Distribution.* Research on criminal careers has found that the older a person is when suspected for an offense, the more likely it is that he or she has been involved in criminal activities earlier in life (for an analysis of Swedish longitudinal data, see Wikström [1990*b*]). After the age of twenty, the probability that a person who commits a crime is a first-time offender decreases rapidly. Correspondingly, if a person commits a crime after the age of twenty, the probability that he or she is a recidivist increases with age.

Against this background, the groups of citizens with their highest crime participation rates occurring after the age of twenty years become particularly noteworthy. The later the crime participation peak of a given group occurs, the more remarkable the finding. Most extreme are the African citizens, with a peak as late as from twenty-five to twenty-nine years. Citizens from Asia and Latin America as well as the stateless persons living in Sweden have the highest participation rate at twenty-one and twenty-four years.

Nordic and other European citizens seem to show a "normal" pattern of relationship between age and crime participation, even if the level of the rates is higher in all age-groups than for the Swedish citizens. The levels of the participation rates are generally higher for all groups of citizens than for the Swedes, except for the North American and Australian citizens who seem to resemble the Swedish in their crime participation rates.

How can the higher crime participation rates among the foreign citizens living in Sweden be explained? A number of possible explanations can be identified.

1. Being an immigrant may involve day-to-day incidents generating psychological and emotional stress. For example, they may feel insecure and threatened, especially when manifestations of xenophobia are widespread. In social interactions both inside and outside the family this stress can generate frictions (Wikström 1995) resulting in violence and the threat of violence.

2. Immigrants who have come from circumstances in which it was extremely difficult to obtain the essential means of survival to a society that lives in material affluence, that is, with a wide range of attractive goods apparently displayed with minimum surveillance, may easily become tempted to steal.

3. Emigration may in itself be based on a selection process. Persons who are dissatisfied with their social and material conditions, who are adventure-loving and looking for excitement, and who moreover have weak bonds to conventional others in their home country may be more prone to emigrate than steady and loyal (or even patriotic) persons. In addition, a relatively high proportion of the persons who emigrate may already have started on a criminal career in their country of origin (and even have a bad reputation there) and just continue it in the new country. Studies of offenders from Finland have shown that some come to Sweden in order to commit crimes and have crime records in Finland (Olsson 1986). Lenke (1983) has, however, characterized some of the Finnish immigrants in Sweden as sociopolitical refugees.

4. Some immigrants may start their criminal careers relatively late ("late bloomers") as a consequence of the combination of their culture of origin, their personality, and the stress and strain that goes with the situation of being an immigrant (see DiLalla and Gottesman [1989], referred to in Hämäläinen and Pulkinen [1995]).

5. The higher level of offending among the immigrants may be a consequence of the combination of all the factors mentioned. But the factors may have different weights for different groups of immigrants.

The differences between the nationality groups can probably also be explained to some extent by differences in the types of crime they have been suspected of. Unfortunately, there is no detailed information in the official crime statistics about offending within the various nationality groups. It was shown earlier in this essay that the crime structure of Swedish citizens, other Nordic citizens, and non-Nordic citizens living in Sweden was fairly similar, with offenses against the person, however, being slightly more common among non-Nordics. Offenses such as domestic violence and physical assault (occurring, e.g., when socializing with countrymen) are slightly more prevalent among non-Nordic citizens than among Swedish and other Nordic citizens. Such offenses are committed by adults. This can partly explain why some of the nationalities have such high suspect rates at a relatively high age.

The immigrants have a higher overrepresentation in the more serious offenses, and these offenses also tend to have a relatively high clearance rate. These serious crimes are often more frequent later in the individual's criminal career. This can contribute to the higher overrepresentation among the foreign-born suspects in general and the higher overrisks at the higher age-groups among some of the nationality groups.

During the last fifteen years, between 10,000 and 20,000 persons per year, predominantly foreign citizens, have emigrated from Sweden. There is a continuous in- and outflow of people in the immigrant population. Are the emigrants more serious people who return to their home country because of political changes for the better there? Nothing is known about the criminal behavior of those who emigrate from Sweden. Are they less criminal than those who stay in Sweden? If so, there is a selection process going on, with a growing proportion of lawbreakers among those remaining in Sweden. Aggregated over the years, this process would mean that lawbreakers are overrepresented among the immigrants, at least among the foreign citizens living in Sweden.

E. Discrimination

Another important factor that may contribute to higher observed participation rates among foreign citizens is the possible discrimination against foreigners in the criminal justice system.

It is difficult to draw conclusions about discrimination on the basis of the official crime statistics. Table 5 shows the percentages of foreign citizens among persons suspected of an offense, convicted of an offense, and registered in the Swedish prisons during the period

TABLE 5

Annual Percentage of Foreign Citizens among Persons Suspected of an Offense, Convicted of an Offense, and Registered in the Prisons, 1983–94 (Residents and Nonresidents Included)

	Suspected of a Crime	Found Guilty of a Criminal Offense	Registered in Prison
1984	15	13	17
1985	16	14	17
1986	15	14	16
1987	16	14	16
1988	17	15	17
1989	18	16	17
1990	20	17	18
1991	21	18	20
1992	22	19	21
1993	22	20	21
1994	20	19	20

Source.—For suspects: Statistics Sweden (1985–1993*b*), table 3.2.8; National Council for Crime Prevention Sweden (1994), table 2.1; Statistics Sweden (1995*b*), table 411. For the convicted: Statistics Sweden (1985–1993*b*), table 3.4.6; National Council for Crime Prevention Sweden (1994), table 3.6; Statistics Sweden (1995*b*), table 940. For persons registered in the prisons: statistics are from the Information Unit of the National Prison and Probation Administration in Sweden.

1984–94. The percentages include all foreign citizens, both residents and nonresidents.

The percentages are fairly consistent among the three levels. There is also consistency over time. When the percentage of foreigners among suspected persons increases, there are corresponding increases among persons convicted and in the prisons. When the foreign percentage of suspects decreases, corresponding changes are also found among convicted persons and persons in prison. This suggests that Swedish and foreign citizens are treated in much the same way within the criminal justice system.

Another approach is to compare decisions made by the courts con-

TABLE 6

Percentage of Persons Convicted of an Offense, by Principle Sanction and National Background, 1994

Sanction	Foreign Nationals, Residents and Nonresidents	Foreign Nationals, Residents Only	Swedish Nationals	Percent Foreign Nationality
Imprisonment	14.9	14.4	12.5	20.8
Forensic psychiatric treatment	.6	.8	.5	20.6
Probation	4.5	5.6	7.4	11.7
Conditional sentence	14.3	13.3	14.5	17.8
Special care/treatment	2.2	2.8	2.4	16.7
Fines	50.2	48.3	44.2	20.0
Waivers of prosecution	10.9	12.0	14.8	12.9
Other	2.4	2.8	3.7	
Total	100.0	100.0	100.0	18.0
N	11,895	9,180	54,094	

SOURCE.—Statistics Sweden (1995*b*), table 531.

NOTE.—Offenses are against the penal code. Percentage of foreign citizens within each type of sanction is also shown.

cerning Swedish and foreign citizens convicted of similar offenses. Table 6 shows the distribution of sanctions for all foreign citizens, foreign citizens living in Sweden, and Swedish citizens for 1994. The table also shows the percentage of foreign citizens (both residents and nonresidents included) within each type of sanction.

Sanctions imposed on foreign and Swedish citizens are on the whole similar. There are, however, small differences concerning the imposition of a fine, imprisonment, and waivers of prosecution. The imposition of both fines and imprisonment is slightly more common among foreign citizens, whereas the use of waivers of prosecution is slightly more common among Swedish citizens. Smuggling of narcotics was a relatively common offense among foreign citizens not living in Sweden, and this could partly explain the higher proportion of imprisonment imposed on them. Violent crimes were slightly more common among resident foreign citizens. Thefts and petty thefts were the most common offenses among nonresident foreign citizens, and this could explain the high proportion of fines among the foreigners. The differences between the foreign and Swedish citizens concerning the imposition of sanctions are small and can most probably be explained by the types of offenses for which the various groups have been suspected and convicted.

On the basis of these data, it is not possible to identify any systematic discrimination against foreign citizens in the criminal justice system. However, the information available in the crime statistics is too superficial to permit close examination of the question of discrimination. And there is certainly something in von Hofer's concluding remarks on the discrimination hypothesis. Although there are no obvious signs of discrimination against the foreign citizens within the Swedish criminal justice system, he notes that "the fact that almost half (44 percent) of all the persons who have been sentenced to life imprisonment for murder since 1966 are foreign nationals makes one reflect" (von Hofer 1994, p. 18 [in Swedish]).

Even if there is equal treatment of Swedish and foreign citizens within the criminal justice system, there may be differences in the reporting of offenses to the police. It is possible that there could be a greater tendency to report a detected offense to the police when the offender is a foreigner, which may in part be a result of prejudice. Moreover, the police may be more likely to stop and check persons who are foreign in appearance. However, studies in some other European countries (the Netherlands and the former West Germany) have not been able to document such tendencies among the police (Junger 1989). There may also be a greater risk that a foreigner will be discovered when committing an offense, especially if he or she attracts attention owing to an unusual appearance. However, no Swedish research illuminates the question of possible differences in reporting or police checks for different groups.

V. Offending among First- and Second-Generation Immigrants

The previous section focused on foreign citizens suspected of an offense as reflected in the official crime statistics. The analysis concerns only a limited part of the Swedish immigrant population, namely, those over the age of fourteen who have not obtained Swedish citizenship, because records are maintained in terms of nationality. Since naturalization was readily available, naturalized immigrants are reported as "Swedes." Ahlberg (1996) has compared suspected offending among first- and second-generation immigrants and among native Swedes during the five-year period 1985–89. Concerning the immigrants, the study comprises both foreign nationals and naturalized Swedish citizens. A focus on first- and second-generation immigrants implies that the concept of immigrant is based on the individual's country of birth or the country of birth of the individual's parents. All immigrants and the children of the immigrants born in Sweden are included, however, with the reservation that they must have been born between 1945 and 1974 and were living in Sweden in 1985. There were 3.5 million inhabitants in Sweden within this age range in 1985. Appendices A and B provide an overview of the national backgrounds of the population studied. Ahlberg's study has necessitated special computer runs on various registers performed by Statistics Sweden. These have provided relevant information about each individual in the population concerning social and national background and suspected offending. Information from the different registers (to which only Statistics Sweden has access) was merged. This procedure for gathering information about private persons is of course a delicate issue and can only be carried out with special authorization from the Data Inspection Board.

This section focuses first on different types of crime and discusses how first-generation immigrants, second-generation immigrants, and native Swedes differ in their offending behavior. Immigrants and Swedes are then compared with respect to their crime participation on the basis of national background.

A. Types of Offenses

Table 7 is based on the number of offenses registered during the five-year period studied in the various crime categories and presents the proportions of offenses of a specific crime category which can be ascribed to native Swedes and first- and second-generation immigrants.

Table 8 shows the percentage of persons among first- and second-generation immigrants and among native Swedes who have been suspected of at least one offense within a specific crime category during the study period. This percentage is equivalent to the crime participation rate. The rates are standardized, which means that the rates for the immigrants have been calculated on the basis of the distribution of sex, age, and region of residence (categorized as living in a big city or not) among native Swedes. Thus the background variables mentioned, which are of some importance for criminal behavior, have been held constant to make the crime participation rates between the groups more comparable. The table also presents the overrisk or overrepresentation among the first- and second-generation immigrants, respec-

TABLE 7

Offending among First and Second Generation Immigrants and Native Swedes by Type of Offense, 1985–89

	First Generation	Second Generation	Native Swedes
N	308,581	315,423	2,920,700
Percent in population	8.9	8.7	82.4
Assault, aggravated assault (in percent):			
Against unknown women	19	14	67
Against acquainted women	19	11	70
Against unknown men	18	14	68
Against acquainted men	18	12	69
Rape, aggravated rape	38	15	47
Other sexual offenses	10	8	82
Unauthorized takings and thefts of motorcars	12	17	71
Thefts from a motorcar	10	16	74
Robbery, aggravated robbery	22	17	60
Theft, petty theft in shop or department store	24	12	64
Fraud	17	11	72
Offenses inflicting damage	6	7	87
Road Traffic Offenses Act	15	12	72
Driving under the influence of alcohol	16	11	74
Narcotics Drug Law	11	11	78
Murder, manslaughter	28	10	61
Offenses against liberty and peace	20	12	69
Burglary, aggravated burglary in apartment or house	14	16	70

Source.—Ahlberg (1996), table 22.

Note.—Numbers are percentages calculated on the number of offenses within each type of offense.

tively. The overrisk value tells us how many times higher the participation rate is for an immigrant category as compared with the rate for native Swedes. The higher the ratio, the higher the overrisk or overrepresentation.

1. *First-Generation Immigrants.* Of all the suspected offenses involving the population members in Ahlberg's study, 15.4 percent can be ascribed to first-generation immigrants.

Table 7 shows that foreign-born suspects are a low proportion of those suspected of offenses of inflicting damage (6 percent) but quite a large proportion concerning violent crimes such as rape (38 percent)

TABLE 8

Crime Participation Rates in Different Types of Offenses for First- and Second-Generation Immigrants and Native Swedes, 1985–89

	First Generation	Second Generation	Native Swedes	Overrepresentation	
				First Generation	Second Generation
N	308,581	315,423	2,920,700	. . .	. . .
All kinds of offenses	12.50	7.90	5.80	2.2	1.4
Offenses against the penal code	9.80	5.90	4.20	2.3	1.4
Violent crimes	3.10	1.80	1.20	2.7	1.5
Offenses of stealing	5.20	3.30	2.20	2.5	1.5
Assault, aggravated assault:					
Against unknown women	.19	.10	.05	3.8	2.0
Against acquainted women	.76	.32	. . .	. . .	. . .
Against acquainted men	.61	.38	.24	2.9	1.6
Against unknown men	.94	.54	.20	4.7	2.7
Rape, aggravated rape	.08	.03	.02	4.0	1.5
Unauthorized takings and thefts of motorcar	.84	.68	.41	2.0	1.6
Thefts from a motorcar	.66	.57	.35	1.9	1.6
Robbery, aggravated robbery	.23	.12	.07	3.3	1.7
Theft, petty theft in shop, department store	3.54	1.50	1.00	3.4	1.5
Fraud	1.46	.91	.69	2.1	1.3
Offenses inflicting damage	1.65	1.30	.82	2.0	1.5
Road Traffic Offenses Act	2.83	1.80	1.30	2.2	1.3
Driving under the influence of alcohol	2.32	1.60	1.20	1.9	1.3
Narcotics Drug Law	.75	.77	.47	1.6	1.6
Murder, manslaughter	.07	.03	.02	3.5	1.3
Offenses against liberty and peace	1.30	.80	1.00	1.3	.8
Burglary, aggravated burglary in apartment or house	.27	.21	.12	2.3	1.8

SOURCE.—Ahlberg (1996), tables 9 and 28.

NOTE.—Overrepresentation among first- and second-generation immigrants for the different types of offenses is also shown.

and murder or manslaughter (28 percent). They constitute a relatively large proportion of those suspected of robbery (22 percent), offenses against liberty and peace (20 percent), and assault (slightly below 19 percent). There is a tendency for the proportion of offenses committed by foreign-born persons to increase with the seriousness of the offense. Thus the more serious the offense, the higher the probability that the suspected person is foreign-born. Theft in shops and department stores is an exception. Almost 25 percent of the thefts in stores and department stores with an identified suspected person were ascribed to foreign-born suspects.

The crime-participation rates confirm these observations. Table 8 shows that foreign-born persons generally have a higher participation rate than native Swedes. The participation rates are on the whole more than twice as high for the foreign-born as for native Swedes. The overrepresentation is most pronounced for the violent crimes. Physical assault of a person unknown to the offender is about four times higher among the foreign-born than among native Swedes. The rates for murder and manslaughter and for robbery are about 3.5 times higher among the foreign-born. The rates for the most serious offenses such as rape and murder or manslaughter are very low, less than .1 percent.

Thefts in shops and department stores also have a high overrepresentation among the foreign-born. Foreign-born persons were suspected of thefts in shops and department stores almost 3.5 times more often than the native Swedes.

2. *Second-Generation Immigrants.* According to Ahlberg (1996), about 12 percent of the suspected offenses among the population members in the study can be ascribed to second-generation immigrants.

Table 7 shows that second-generation immigrants are on the whole less involved in the suspected offenses than are first-generation immigrants, and the variation in percentages between the different types of offenses is smaller. The second-generation immigrants are involved to a greater extent than the first generation in car thefts and thefts from a car. The second generation is slightly more often involved in suspected offenses of burglary.

Table 8 shows that second-generation immigrants generally have lower crime participation rates than first-generation immigrants. The rates for the second-generation immigrants are about 1.5 times higher than the rates for native Swedes. For first-generation immigrants, the rates are more than twice as high. The participation rates for second-generation immigrants also show a more limited variation. Their highest overrepresentation occurs with offenses of physical assault against persons not known to the offender. Their overrepresentation in burglary is also relatively high.

To sum up, first-generation immigrants were more often involved in criminal activities during the study period of five years than the second generation. This finding is contrary to the observations made in some other European countries where it has been found that second-generation immigrants tend to be more engaged in criminal activities than the first-generation immigrants (Loll and Friedrichs 1983; Killias 1989). It is also contrary to the conventional wisdom in the general debate in Sweden.

First- and second-generation immigrants show different profiles in their offending. First-generation immigrants appear relatively more often in relation to violent offenses such as rape, murder or manslaughter, physical assault, and robbery. They also appear relatively often as offenders for theft in shops and department stores.

The offending of second-generation immigrants is more often directed to cars and items related to cars. But burglary in apartments and houses is also slightly related to the offending of the offspring of the foreign-born. Second-generation immigrants are relatively often involved in situations where they have physically attacked (both males and females) persons with whom they are not acquainted. The pattern of offending among the second-generation immigrants is closer to the pattern of native Swedes than that of first-generation immigrants.

B. National Background

Ahlberg (1996) also focused on the crime participation rates among the first- and second-generation immigrants with different national backgrounds. Table 9 shows the crime participation rates of first-generation immigrants with different nationality backgrounds. The rates in the table are standardized, which means that they have been calculated on the basis of the distribution of sex, age, and region of living among native Swedes.

1. *First-Generation Immigrants.* Table 9 ranks countries from which first-generation immigrants come according to their crime participation rates. Native Swedes have the lowest participation rate (5.8 percent). Foreign-born persons, irrespective of country of origin, have higher crime participation rates than native Swedes. Immigrants from Taiwan, China, Japan, Vietnam, United States, and Great Britain have

TABLE 9

Total Crime Participation Rates in Percentages by Country of Birth, 1985–89

Country of Birth	Participation	Overrisk
Algeria, Libya, Tunisia, Morocco	20.6	3.6
Chile	20.0	3.4
Iraq	18.2	3.1
Jordan, Palestine, Syria	17.4	3.0
Iran	17.2	3.0
Soviet Union	17.0	2.9
Poland	16.8	2.9
Lebanon	15.7	2.7
Bolivia, Peru, Equador	15.4	2.7
Romania	15.1	2.6
Ethiopia	14.7	2.5
Turkey	14.2	2.4
Yugoslavia	14.1	2.4
Colombia	14.0	2.4
Czechoslovakia	13.6	2.3
Italy	13.5	2.3
Finland	13.2	2.3
Hungary	12.4	2.1
Argentina, Uruguay	12.2	2.1
Portugal, Spain	10.9	1.9
Thailand	10.6	1.8
Denmark	10.5	1.8
Norway	10.5	1.8
Austria	10.3	1.8
Bangladesh/Pakistan	10.1	1.7
Germany (West)	9.1	1.6
Greece	9.1	1.6
Korea	8.7	1.5
India	8.2	1.4
Great Britain	6.9	1.2
Vietnam	6.6	1.1
United States	6.5	1.1
Taiwan, China, Japan	6.4	1.1
Sweden	5.8	1.0
Remaining countries in:		
Africa excluding Uganda	13.7	2.4
North America	11.2	1.9
Asia	9.4	1.6
Europe	8.0	1.4
Unspecified	9.5	1.6

Source.—Ahlberg (1996), table 15.

Note.—Rates are standardized. The overrisks in relation to native Swedes (second-generation immigrants not included) are also shown.

rates close to that of Swedes. At the top of the list are the immigrants from North Africa and Chile.

Generally speaking, immigrants from the Arab countries have the highest rates. Those born in Algeria, Libya, Morocco, Tunisia, Iraq, Jordan, Palestine, Syria, and Lebanon all have standardized participation rates of between 15 percent and 20 percent. Relatively high rates (between 13.5 percent and 17 percent) are also found among immigrants born in eastern European countries such as Yugoslavia, Poland, Romania, Bulgaria, Czechoslovakia, and the Soviet Union. Latin Americans from Argentina, Uruguay, Bolivia, Peru, Ecuador, and Colombia come next, with a standardized rate ranging from 12 percent to 15 percent. The Chileans are outliers among the Latin Americans with a rate of 20 percent. Africans other than from Arab countries in North Africa have also standardized rates of 12–15 percent. Immigrants from Nordic countries have rates of 10–13 percent. Rates below 10 percent are found among immigrants from western European countries (except Italy, Spain, and Portugal), the United States, and Southeast Asia.

Further observations can be made concerning Chilean immigrants. They have arrived in Sweden in two waves. The first to arrive were pure refugees since they were escaping from the military coup in 1973. Then came Chileans who had emigrated for economic rather than political reasons. Ahlberg (1996) has compared the Chilean immigrants who came between 1975 and 1978 with those who arrived between 1979 and 1985. Among the former, 16.4 percent were suspected of at least one offense during 1985–89 compared with 22.5 percent of the latter. This difference remains when sex, age, and region of living have been held constant. On the basis of this finding, Ahlberg has hypothesized that immigrants who come to Sweden in connection with a political event in their home country ought to have a lower rate of offending than those who emigrate during other periods. However, this hypothesis was not confirmed in general when applied to other countries with similar political changes.

2. *Second-Generation Immigrants.* Ahlberg (1996) has compared the crime participation rates for second-generation immigrants with only one parent born abroad with their counterparts with both parents born abroad. He found that the latter tend to have a higher participation in criminal activities than the former (table 10).

In table 11, the crime participation rates for the second-generation immigrants with both parents born in the same foreign country are

TABLE 10

Crime Participation Rates in Percentages for Some Types of Offenses for Second-Generation Immigrants by the Parents' Immigrant Background, Standardized Rates, 1985–89

	Parent(s) Born Abroad		
	Father	Mother	Both
All kinds of offenses	7.2	7.0	8.9
Offenses against the penal code	5.3	5.1	6.9
Violent crimes	1.6	1.5	2.2
Offenses of stealing	2.9	2.7	3.8

Source.—Ahlberg (1996), table 31.

displayed. The different national backgrounds are ranked from those with the highest participation rates to the lowest. The rates are unstandardized. The corresponding unstandardized rates for the first-generation immigrants are shown in the column to the right of the table.

Consistent with earlier observations, second-generation immigrants tend to have lower crime participation rates than first-generation immigrants, with the exception of some of the Nordic countries. Ahlberg (1996) reports a high correlation between the participation rates of the first- and second-generation immigrants ($r = .80$). This implies that first-generation immigrants from countries with high crime participation rates (Algeria, Libya, Tunisia, and Morocco) tend to have offspring with high rates as well. Correspondingly, first-generation immigrants from a country with low crime participation rates (Taiwan, China, Japan, Vietnam, and the United States) also have offspring with low rates.

C. *Violent Crimes*

Ahlberg's study showed that first-generation immigrants are overrepresented for violent offenses, which Wikström (1985) posits can be attributed to two principal sources: violence among immigrants living in neighborhoods with social problems and violence between Swedes and immigrants that takes place in the city area, often in the context of public entertainment. Violence between immigrants consists of family

TABLE 11

Total Crime Participation Rates in Percentages for Second Generation Immigrants by the Parents' Country of Birth, 1985–89

Second Generation—Both Parents Born In:	Crime Participation Rates for	
	Second Generation	First Generation
Algeria, Libya, Morocco, Tunisia	18.7	26.9
Turkey	12.2	14.4
Jordan, Palestine, Syria	11.6	16.9
Yugoslavia	11.6	14.7
Finland	11.5	11.5
Portugal, Spain	10.6	10.8
Denmark	10.0	9.6
Greece	9.6	10.2
Hungary	9.5	11.6
Norway	9.0	8.6
Italy	8.6	11.8
Romania, Bulgaria	8.2	15.3
Soviet Union	8.1	13.7
Czechoslovakia	7.1	13.6
Poland	6.8	15.0
Germany	6.7	8.0
United States	6.3	5.7
Austria	6.1	8.4
Great Britain	4.3	6.4
Estonia	3.8	...
Korea	2.9	6.4
Taiwan, China, Japan	2.4	4.9
Remaining countries in:		
Africa	8.3	15.7
Europe	5.2	7.5

Source.—Ahlberg (1996), table 32.

Note.—Only persons with both parents born abroad are included. Total crime participation rates for first-generation immigrants born in the stated country are also shown. Rates are unstandardized crime participation rates.

conflicts and conflicts emerging in daily social intercourse among acquaintances. Violence between Swedes and immigrants is concentrated to the pubs and restaurants and other places of public entertainment in the city area.

In a study of the violence resulting in death in Stockholm between

TABLE 12

Offenders Involved in Violence Causing Death, 1980–91, by Ethnic Background

Country of Birth	Per 100,000
Sweden	1.1
Born abroad—total	5.5
Finland	11.1
Other Nordic countries	1.4
Northern Europe	1.9
Southern Europe	1.9
Eastern Europe	1.7
Asia	3.9
Africa	12.7
North America	3.0
South and Central America	5.4

Source.—Wikström (forthcoming).

Note.—Rates are per 100,000 of the mean number in the respective group of countries in the population.

1951 and 1991, Wikström (forthcoming) found (table 12) that in the 1980s, Africans (mainly from Ethiopia and Morocco) had the highest involvement in violence leading to death, followed by Finns. The involvement of Africans and Finns was more than twice that of any other ethnic background.

Wikström also found that the percentage of male offenders with an immigrant background increased from 13.6 percent in the 1950s to 40.7 percent in the 1980s. This is because offenders among first-generation immigrants increased from 10.6 percent of the total in the 1950s to 33.9 percent in the 1980s.

VI. Crime Surveys

Not all offending is detected, and even when a crime is known it is not always reported to the police. To obtain a better picture, crime surveys have been conducted. Crime surveys are based on statistical samples drawn from the population which ask respondents if they have committed certain crimes (self-report studies) or if they have been victims of certain crimes (victim studies).

A. Self-Reported Crime

International studies show that crime differences between the indigenous population and immigrants are less pronounced for self-reported crime than for recorded crime. The reliability of the respondents' answers to questions touching on such a sensitive topic as deviant and criminal behavior can be questioned. An assumption among Swedish criminologists is that young people give more reliable answers to such questions than do adults. There are detailed Swedish self-report studies of criminal behavior among Swedes and immigrants. Results from some of the studies made in this country are presented here. Results from the Stockholm Project and the CEIFO survey mentioned below will be published in Martens (forthcoming).

As mentioned earlier in the essay (Section III*B*), the Stockholm Project carried out two waves of surveys among adults as well as among ninth-grade pupils living in eight neighborhood areas in Stockholm. Questions were asked about victimization and their own offending, among other things (Wikström 1990*a;* Martens 1992*b*, and forthcoming). The CEIFO survey was an extensive study of attitudes toward immigrants in the Swedish population between eighteen and seventy-one years of age. The study was further completed with a special survey of immigrants from Finland, Poland, Chile, and Iran focusing on their attitudes toward Swedes. The CEIFO survey also included questions asking about the respondents' victimization and own offenses (Lange and Westin 1993; Westin and Lange 1993; Martens, forthcoming).

1. *Adult Respondents.* Two groups of telephone interviews of the adults in the Stockholm Project do not reveal great differences between respondents born in Sweden and respondents born abroad who admit being suspected of crimes. In the 1990 study, the proportion in both groups was between 10 percent and 11 percent (Martens 1992*b*). In the 1992 study there was, however, only a small difference showing that 10.6 percent of the respondents born in Sweden had been suspected of crime as compared to 6.7 percent among those born abroad (Martens, forthcoming).

The two studies also asked the respondents if they had been found guilty by a court. The 1990 study shows a slightly larger percentage found guilty by a court among those born abroad (4.8 percent) than among those born in Sweden (3.6 percent). In the second study the pattern reversed. Of respondents born in Sweden, 3.9 percent had been found guilty by a court, compared with 2.7 percent of those born abroad. However, these differences are not statistically significant.

The CEIFO survey, which used the same questions as in the Stockholm Project but also involved face-to-face interviews and permitted respondents to answer the self-report questions anonymously, arrived at higher prevalence rates. Among native Swedes, almost 20 percent reported that they had been suspected of crimes, compared with 25 percent of Finns, 20 percent of Chileans, 15 percent of Poles, and 14 percent of Iranians. The difference between the groups is statistically significant ($p < 0.01$). Of native Swedes, 9 percent reported that they had been found guilty by a court, compared with 12 percent of the Finns, 8 percent of the Iranians, 9 percent of the Chileans, and 7 percent of the Poles. These differences are not statistically significant (Martens, forthcoming).

In the CEIFO survey, respondents were also asked if they themselves had threatened somebody, stolen something, or damaged something during 1992. Native Swedes had the highest participation rate, followed by Chileans and Finns. The Iranians and Poles had the lowest rates. For males, the participation rates were 15 percent for the Swedes, 8 percent for the Chileans, 6 percent for the Finns, and 3 percent for the Poles and Iranians (Martens, forthcoming).

2. *Young Respondents.* Self-report studies have been carried out several times in Swedish research on youth crime. Studies carried out in the 1960s (the 1956 Clientele Study and the Individual Development and Adaptation [IDA] Project) did not focus on criminal behavior among young people with an immigrant background (e.g., Olofsson 1971; Carlsson 1972; Humble and Zettergren-Carlsson 1974).

Suikkila (1983) was the first to focus on ethnic background. He carried out a study on the children of Finnish immigrants and compared youngsters with a Finnish background living in Sweden with native Swedish counterparts and Finnish counterparts living in Finland. He found that young immigrant Finns admitted committing more crimes than did either young Swedish people or young Finns in Finland. Young Finns in Finland had committed the least crimes. Unfortunately, this study has not been reported in completed form.

The Stockholm Project school survey of 1990 was the first Swedish study of delinquent behavior among youth using immigrant background as a social background variable. When young people with an immigrant background were compared with young Swedes regarding criminal behavior, different results were found for girls and boys (Martens 1992*b*).

The school study of the Stockholm Project was carried out in two waves in 1990 and 1992. The first school survey (Martens 1992*b*) revealed that boys with one or two parents born abroad (second-generation immigrants) did not differ appreciably with regard to their total criminality. However, when the focus was on specific types of crimes, boys with an immigrant background more often reported an act of violence than boys with a Swedish background. When boys born abroad were compared with boys born in Sweden, those born abroad more often reported a criminal act. The differences were particularly pronounced for violence and the more serious theft crimes.

In this first survey immigrant girls appeared to be more conformist in their behavior than Swedish girls. The Swedish girls generally had a higher crime participation rate than the girls with an immigrant background.

The 1992 school survey in part produced contrary results (Martens, forthcoming). Boys with a Swedish background were found to have a significantly higher total participation rate than boys with an immigrant background (56 percent vs. 44 percent), whereas girls with an immigrant background were found to have a higher rate of total crime participation than Swedish girls (43 percent vs. 33 percent—an almost significant difference). However, both immigrant boys and girls reported more often than their Swedish counterparts that they had committed a violent act. In the second school survey, some other offenses were added to the questionnaire, and it was found that boys and girls with an immigrant background more often than their Swedish counterparts had bought goods they knew were stolen (i.e., receiving stolen goods).

A comparison of the response pattern on the self-report items for the young people with an immigrant background between the two school surveys reveals an inconsistency for those born abroad in particular, but also for those whose parents were born in a foreign country. Boys born abroad more often reported that they had committed a crime in the first study than they did in the second study. For the girls born abroad the tendency was the reverse: the girls more often reported that they had committed a crime in the second study than in the first one. This observation might indicate that special attention needs to be paid to foreign-born respondents when asking questions on sensitive topics like criminal and antisocial behavior. Junger (1990) has noticed that some immigrant groups in the Netherlands gave less reliable answers to self-report items on crime than others. "The data show that rather large differences exist in the tendency to admit delinquent activities among boys with recorded police contacts. Youth coming from Morocco and Turkey were much more reluctant to admit delinquent activities than Dutch and Surinamese youths. This means that the answers of Moroccan and Turkish respondents are more strongly influenced by a social desirability bias than the answers of Surinamese and Dutch respondents" (Junger 1990, p. 13).

3. *Comments.* The self-report studies have produced inconsistent results, which probably reflect methodological weaknesses in gathering information on offending. Asking detailed questions about an individual's antisocial acts is to intrude into private matters. The more value-laden the behavior, the more reluctant the respondents may be to give an honest answer. For example, the data generated would be meaningless if people were asked whether they had raped or committed some other sexual offense against a child (Martens 1992*a*).

Moreover, as Junger (1990) suggests, persons from different cultures have different frames of reference about what is a sensitive topic, and they have higher or lower thresholds concerning the disclosure of criminal and other antisocial acts. An interesting contrast emerges when the data from the CEIFO survey are compared with Ahlberg's study of Iranian female offenses of theft in shops and department stores. In Ahlberg's study, nearly 10 percent of Iranian women had been suspected of such an offense during the period studied. Not one Iranian woman in the CEIFO survey self-reported committing such an offense. Police records show Iranian women to have the highest participation rate for thefts in shops and department stores of any group, but they had the lowest rate according to the self-report study. In a society like Sweden where the immigrants come from many cultural backgrounds, it is necessary to be sensitive to the cultural differences among immigrant groups and to develop a better understanding of their different ways of reacting to questions about criminal and other antisocial acts. It is particularly necessary to avoid treating immigrants as if they are a homogenous group, as has been done in a majority of Swedish self-report studies.

Swedish self-report studies of adults suggest that telephone interviews produce lower crime participation rates than do personal interviews in which the sensitive questions are answered anonymously. Different methods of gathering information on criminal acts produce different results, and even the techniques might work differently depending on the respondents' cultural background. Hence, more research is needed in the future about the effectiveness of different self-report techniques.

B. Victims of Crime

Swedish victim studies have focused on violence, the threat of violence, and property offenses (in particular theft and property damage).

1. *Violence and Threat of Violence.* According to investigations of living conditions of the Swedish population by Statistics Sweden during the period 1978–93, immigrants and people with an immigrant background are more exposed to some forms of violence and threats of violence than are native Swedes (Statistics Sweden 1995*a*, table 2.6). Second-generation immigrants are most exposed to violence. Only 6 percent (in a year) of indigenous Swedes had been victims of violence or threats compared with 11 percent of second-generation immigrants. The most serious violence—with physical injury—is more than twice as common among second-generation immigrants than among indigenous Swedes (4.4 percent vs. 2 percent). This immigrant group is, however, quite young: 37 percent are between sixteen and twenty-four years old compared with 16 percent in the whole population (Statistics Sweden 1995*a*, p. 75). If age is controlled, the differences become less pronounced. Young people (sixteen to twenty-four years) are most exposed to crimes of violence: throughout the population, 16 percent experienced violence and violent threats during 1992–93. Among second-generation immigrants of that age, the proportion is 19 percent. In the other age categories there is no difference worth mentioning (Statistics Sweden 1995*a*, p. 76).

Logistic regression analyses based on the respondents' sex, age, region of residence, family conditions, and national background reveal that second-generation immigrants are 30 percent more likely to experience violence than are indigenous Swedes. This relatively small difference can be attributed to a greater risk of being a victim of violence in the streets and other public places (Statistics Sweden 1995*a*, p. 116). Women with a foreign background have an 80 percent greater likelihood of being "victims of violence indoors" (an indirect measure of domestic violence) than native Swedish females (Statistics Sweden 1995*a*, p. 116).

The adult interviews in the Stockholm Project in 1990 also showed some differences between persons born in Sweden and persons born abroad concerning exposure to violence. In 1989, 3.7 percent of persons born abroad experienced violence during the preceding year that required medical attention compared to .6 percent of indigenous Swedes (Martens, forthcoming).

However, the CEIFO survey showed no significant differences. Of the native Swedes, 2.3 percent reported that they had been exposed to violence causing injuries in 1992 compared with 1.8 percent for Finns, 2.2 percent for Chileans, and 2.1 percent for Poles and Iranians (Martens, forthcoming).

In the two school surveys of the Stockholm Project, the ninth-grade pupils were asked if they had been a victim of violence, theft, and bullying during the preceding year. In the 1990 survey, no significant differences were found between Swedish youth and youth with an immigrant background, except for exposure to violence. Boys with an immigrant background reported slightly more often that they had been exposed to violence than Swedish boys. For the girls the tendency was the reverse (Martens, forthcoming).

In the CEIFO survey the respondents were also asked if they had been victims of a threat of violence during 1992. The differences between ethnic groups in the study are statistically significant ($p < .001$). Immigrants from non-European countries (Chile and Iran) most frequently reported being threatened. The prevalence rates were 19 percent for Iranians, 16 percent for Chileans, 14 percent for Swedes, 10 percent for Finns, and 9 percent for Poles. Among native Swedes a threat of violence was more often reported by the men than by the women (16 percent vs. 11 percent). Among the immigrant groups the tendency was the reverse; females reported slightly more often than males that they had been victims of threat (Martens, forthcoming).

2. *Victims of Violence Causing Death.* The ethnic structure of the victims of deadly violence in Stockholm during 1951–91 has changed over four decades according to Wikström (forthcoming). In the 1950s, 4 percent of male victims were born in a foreign country, while in the 1980s, 28 percent were. For female victims the increase was from 5 percent in the 1950s to 24 percent in the 1980s. The victimization risk of violence leading to death (during the period 1980–91) is most pronounced for immigrants with a Finnish background (9.4 per 100,000), followed by those with African and Latin American backgrounds (5.4 and 2.7 per 100,000, respectively). For the Swedes the risk is 1.6 per 100,000, and for the foreign born in total 4.7 per 100,000.

3. *Victims of Theft and Damage of Property.* The CEIFO survey shows some differences between ethnic groups concerning theft (Mar-

tens, forthcoming). Thirty-two percent of Poles and Iranians, 7 percent of native Swedes, 25 percent of Chileans, and 24 percent of Finns reported that they or someone in their household had been victims of theft during 1992. The same question was asked in the two adult interviews of the Stockholm Project (Martens, forthcoming). No significant differences were found between respondents born in Sweden and those born abroad. Twenty-six percent of the Swedish-born and 28 percent of the foreign-born were victims of theft in 1989. In 1991 the prevalences were 21 percent and 23 percent, respectively.

In the CEIFO survey and the 1990 adult survey of the Stockholm Project, respondents were also asked if they or someone in their household had been victims of property damage during the preceding year. No statistically significant differences were found. However, the percentages of victims were higher in the Stockholm survey than in the CEIFO survey. In the Stockholm study the prevalence was about 20 percent, and in the nationwide survey the prevalence was between 10 and 15 percent.

In the Statistics Sweden study it was found that 24 percent of native Swedes lived in a household where someone had been a victim of theft or property damage during a one-year period. The corresponding percentages for foreign citizens and for second-generation immigrants were 33 percent (Statistics Sweden 1995*a*, p. 139). However, when sex, age, region of residence, family conditions, and national background were statistically controlled, the differences between national groups for exposure to thefts and property damages disappeared. The originally observed differences between Swedes and immigrants can be attributed to various demographic factors (Statistics Sweden 1995*a*, p. 158).

4. *Comments.* Generally speaking, there is only a small risk of becoming a victim of serious violence in Swedish society. However, various Swedish victim studies show that the risk is slightly higher among immigrants than among native Swedes. Even if the extra risk is small in different categories of immigrants, that among second-generation immigrants is worth mentioning. For violence causing death, Finns and North Africans have the greatest victimization risk. Immigrants have also experienced threats of violence more often than the native Swedes. It appears that immigrants from non-European countries experience more threats than immigrants from Europe.

Response biases similar to those that affect self-report surveys that ask about particularly notorious crimes may also affect victimization surveys, for example, when a criminal act has caused a psychological trauma for the victim. The more traumatizing the incident, the greater the victim's likely resistance to recall and report the experience—in particular in a face-to-face interview with a stranger. A person who has been a victim of serious violent acts often represses the traumatic experience from the conscious level and thus avoids being reminded of it. The victim may, therefore, have difficulty recalling an experience of a serious violent act. It may even be difficult to answer questions about the incident in a questionnaire even though anonymity is guaranteed. To obtain reliable information on experience repressed from immediate consciousness requires very special investigation techniques. But this raises ethical problems and also raises questions about the researcher's responsibility for the respondents' psychological health (Martens 1989, chap. 9).

Self-report studies often have large nonresponse rates (sometimes more than 50 percent; Martens 1989, chap. 10), and they seldom include the most active offenders. Nor do they include the most victimized persons in society. Special studies are needed that focus on the nonresponding persons in self-report surveys.

VII. Conclusions and Research Needs

Several issues treated in this essay deserve further comment: immigrants' overrepresentation as offenders, differences between immigrants and Swedes concerning their criminal acts, the higher prevalence of both violence and theft among immigrants, differences in offending between groups of immigrants, and differences in offending between first- and second-generation immigrants. In addition, proposals for and problems of future research on immigrants and crime are discussed.

A. Overrepresentation in Offending

Immigrants are clearly overrepresented among persons who have been suspected of an offense, irrespective of whether "immigrant" is defined in terms of foreign citizenship or country of birth. However, as shown by Ahlberg (1996), when the narrower definition is used—foreign citizenship—as in the official crime statistics, the overrepresentation is slightly exaggerated.

In both the general and the academic discussions, it is often argued that the overrepresentation may occur because immigrants differ markedly from native Swedes on background factors such as sex, age, place of residence, and socioeconomic status. Ahlberg (1996) has shown that the overrepresentation of immigrants remains when these background variables have been held constant, although crime rates among the foreign-born are comparatively lower after the control procedure has been used.

The overrepresentation exists for both first- and second-generation immigrants. Contrary to expectation, the first generation has a higher overrepresentation than the second generation. The crime rate is more than twice as high for first-generation immigrants as for native Swedes. For second-generation immigrants, the rate is about 1.5 times higher than for Swedes.

B. Differences in Offending

Official crime statistics reveal that foreign citizens living in Sweden on the whole have crime patterns fairly similar to those of Swedish citizens.

Swedish residents who are citizens of a country outside Scandinavia are slightly more often suspected of an offense against the person and an offense of theft. The highest overrepresentation was for rape, murder, or manslaughter; assault against children; and robbery. Ahlberg's results (1996) accord with the official crime statistics. Foreign-born persons (first-generation immigrants) are most overrepresented as suspects of violent offenses—in particular of rape, homicide, robbery, and physical assault. The foreign-born also have a relatively high overrepresentation for theft—in particular theft in shops and department stores. Women contribute particularly to the higher overrepresentation in theft.

The offspring of the foreign-born who were born in Sweden (second-generation immigrants) were found to have a pattern of offending that was similar to that of native Swedes. They have a higher participation rate than first-generation immigrants for car-related offenses, specifically, car thefts and thefts from a car and burglary of an apartment or a house. Compared to the native Swedes, second-generation immigrants have a higher overrepresentation for physical assaults.

1. *Violent Offenses.* Official crime statistics reveal that foreign citizens are overrepresented in violent offenses. Ahlberg's (1996) analyses also show that foreign-born persons are overrepresented for violent crimes. Self-report studies on offending among young persons have shown that violent acts are more often reported among pupils with an immigrant background. Victim studies have found that immigrants have a slightly higher risk of being victims of violence—particularly

women and second-generation immigrants. The Swedish studies on immigrants and crime done so far seem to agree that immigrants and their Swedish-born children tend to be involved to a greater extent than native Swedes in violence both as offenders and as victims.

The reasons for overrepresentation of the immigrants in violent offenses can partly be explained by a higher degree of in-group violence among immigrants (family and acquaintances) taking place in neighborhoods with social problems and violence between immigrants and Swedes taking place in public places (pubs and restaurants and other places of public entertainment) (Wikström 1985).

Does this mean that immigrants are more aggressive or violent than native Swedes? It is not possible completely to exclude the likelihood that persons who have emigrated are more violence-prone than the rest of the population in their home country. Furthermore, persons who come from countries at war have been found to be relatively prone to react violently in conflict situations, particularly when these persons themselves have taken an active part in the war as soldiers. Immigrants who have been victims of war and torture show signs of post-traumatic stress disorder (see American Psychiatric Association 1987; Friedman and Jaranson 1994). However, this is not the only explanation for immigrant overrepresentation in violent offenses.

Being an immigrant is frustrating in many ways (Martens 1995). It takes time for a newly arrived immigrant to become integrated into the new society and get established. He or she cannot change personal appearance, and only a few persons coming as adults manage to learn Swedish perfectly and to speak without an accent. The immigrant will always be reminded that he or she is an alien. This becomes more frustrating in a society with a high unemployment rate and a growing xenophobia (Lange 1995). There is no prospect of change for the better in the future. Having difficulties entering the labor market makes immigrants dependent on welfare benefits. A highly limited private economy sets the limits to freedom of movement concerning housing choices and personal consumption. This dependency on the social welfare system in turn reduces the immigrant's self-esteem. A low self-esteem makes the immigrant more vulnerable to the growing xenophobia.

There is reason to believe that immigrants perceive their situation as threatening to a greater extent than do native Swedes. Immigrants may be more inclined to interpret differences in opinion or a reproof as a conflict situation and a personal threat. This increases the risk for violent acts. When it comes to physical and sexual violence among immigrants, it may in part occur because they perceive existence and self-esteem as being threatened to a greater extent than do the native Swedes. In addition, there may also be cultural differences in ways of handling and solving interpersonal conflicts.

2. *Theft.* Different studies agree that immigrants are overrepresented among theft suspects. Among the foreign-born, shoplifting has the highest overrepresentation, primarily because women tend to have a high overrepresentation. Shoplifting is the most common offense among young people according to some self-report studies. There is no pronounced difference for shoplifting as between native Swedes and those with an immigrant background. However, self-report studies on youngsters show that those with an immigrant background tend more often to buy goods they know are stolen. Second-generation immigrants have been suspected of car thefts, thefts from a car, and burglary more often than native Swedes.

Higher rates of shoplifting and thefts may occur because immigrants succumb more easily than native Swedes to the temptation to acquire the luxuries of an affluent society (Martens 1995). Adult immigrants, in particular those newly arrived, may be fascinated and tempted by an affluent society's display of goods, the more so because a customer can personally pick through goods and try them without a shop assistant providing personal service. The limited economic circumstances of many immigrants may provide a motive for shoplifting. Young people growing up in Sweden can easily see cars and various kinds of technical and electronic equipment as especially attractive since they symbolize success and high social status. This may motivate youth with an immigrant background to steal such items or buy them cheaply from sellers of stolen goods to a greater extent than Swedish youth.

C. Nationality and Offending

Only Ahlberg's study (1996) distinguishes the original nationalities of suspected offenders. The countries involved can be ranked from the highest to the lowest crime participation rates: Arab countries in North Africa and Chile, eastern European countries, Latin American countries except Chile, African countries except the Arab countries in North Africa, Nordic countries other than Sweden, western European countries, the United States, Southeast Asian countries, and native Swedes.

The tendency for criminal behavior seems to be transmitted from one generation to another, even if the rates for the second generation are at a lower level than for the first. For example, when the first generation has a high crime participation rate, the second generation also tends to have a high rate. Correspondingly, when the first generation has a low rate the second generation also tends to have a low rate. However, second-generation immigrants suspected of offenses seem to have offending patterns similar to that of native Swedes.

It is sometimes stated that the greater the cultural distance between an immigrant group and a host country, the more difficult will be the group's integration into the new society and the greater the risks for maladjustment and criminal activities. The North African countries and the Southeast Asian countries differ considerably from Sweden culturally, but nevertheless North African immigrants have much higher crime participation rates than do Southeast Asian immigrants, who have crime participation rates at the same level as native Swedes. The global statement about the relation between cultural difference and crime does not hold true.

An interesting question for future research would be to investigate further why immigrants from some countries are more crime-prone than immigrants from other countries. It would also be interesting to study how the criminality of the first-generation immigrants influences the criminality of second-generation immigrants for different national backgrounds.

D. *First- and Second-Generation Immigrants*

Ahlberg (1996) concluded that both first- and second-generation immigrants are overrepresented as suspects of crime. Contrary to expectation, first-generation immigrants were found to have a higher overrepresentation than the second generation, regardless of whether the immigrant group belongs to the early arrivers (labor market immigrants in the 1960s) or the late arrivers (refugees in the 1980s).

It is tempting to interpret these observations of a relatively lower level of offending among the children of the immigrants who were born and raised in Sweden compared with the parent-generation as a favorable effect of the Swedish social welfare system. The social welfare system has many regular compensatory measures for less well-to-do persons, their families, and their children. The welfare system provides services on a nationwide basis that are often considered social crime prevention programs (on a pilot project basis) in other countries.

There are, for example, in Sweden continuous general health checks of pregnant mothers and of children from birth through infancy and during compulsory school. Mothers and their infants regularly meet a nurse with whom they can discuss health problems. Children with "special needs" (i.e., disadvantaged children) get additional educational support to catch up in their intellectual and social development with more advantaged children. Immigrant children are given special training in their mother tongue (home language) to keep them in touch with their culture of origin. Many of the pedagogical ideas behind the concept of compensatory education for disadvantaged children put forward by the creators of Project Head Start in the United States in the 1960s influenced the Swedish child welfare system of the early 1970s (Official Reports of the Swedish Government SOU 1972:26). The idea of compensatory education for disadvantaged children was further developed and attuned to the prevailing Swedish sociopolitical ideology of that time. The preschool and school systems were reorganized and the teaching instructions rewritten to meet these new pedagogical ideas, but there have never been any serious attempts to evaluate the effects of these changes on the children's intellectual and social skills. However, recent evaluations of Project Head Start have found some evidence that the programs in which the children (at that time) were involved might have had some impact on the pattern of their offending as adults (Yoshikawa 1994). Those who were involved in the educational programs had lower offending rates as adults than those in a matched comparison group.

It would, therefore, be theoretically quite plausible that the Swedish social welfare system with all its compensatory measures for disadvantaged children has managed to keep offending among second-generation immigrants at a relatively low level—even if their crime rate is still on a higher level than that of the native Swedes. But before singing the praises of the Swedish welfare system, questions must be answered regarding the conclusions about second-generation immigrants' experience in Sweden. The pattern found for Sweden might be a consequence of using an operational definition of the concept of "second-generation" immigrant, which differs from that used by other European researchers.

Killias (1989), when reviewing research on "criminality among second-generation immigrants in Western Europe," defined the concept of second-generation immigrants differently from the definition used in the present essay. Killias says that "by second-generation immigrant we understand a person whose father and mother were of foreign origin, and who lived during his childhood and adolescence in the host country, either completely or predominantly. Under this definition, a person who came to the host country after the age of 15 is not considered a second-generation immigrant" (Killias 1989, p. 3).

Note first that Killias's definition includes children whose parents were both born in another country but excludes the children of mixed marriages. Ahlberg's study showed that persons whose parents were both born abroad have a higher crime participation rate than persons with only one parent born abroad.

Second, Killias's definition also includes foreign-born children who emigrated with their parents and arrived in the new country before the age of fifteen. As discussed in greater detail elsewhere in Martens (1995), young people who were born abroad and emigrated together with their parents are probably at greater risk for maladjustment than are the children of the immigrants born in the new country. Self-report studies on offending among ninth-grade pupils in Stockholm also suggest that boys born abroad participate in criminal acts more often than boys with an immigrant background born in Sweden (Martens, forthcoming).

Killias's definition probably generates higher crime rates among the second-generation immigrants than the definition used by Statistics Sweden and Ahlberg (1996). Before drawing any further theoretical conclusions about the deviation of Swedish results on offending among first- and second-generation immigrants, supplementary research needs to be performed. An in-depth discussion among European researchers on different aspects of the immigrants' integration into the new society is needed. This discussion must try to arrive at a common framework to describe or conceptualize immigrants and their children. In this context, the general criticism that traditional immigration research tends to lump together all groups of immigrants as one homogeneous category of immigrants has to be taken into account.

Account must also be taken of the finding that the longer a foreign-born person lives in a new country, the less likely that he or she will commit a crime. This tendency holds true even after holding constant immigrants' ages at arrival (Ahlberg 1996). However, the immigrants' crime rates do not drop to the level of that of native Swedes. But it is theoretically possible that the crime rates could continue to drop for a further generation. From this perspective, the lower crime rates among second-generation immigrants compared with the first generation makes sense (Martens 1990).

E. Future Research

The topic "immigrants and crime" has been neglected in Swedish criminological research. This essay has brought to notice at least four broad problems warranting further attention. These questions touch on discrimination against immigrants within the criminal justice system, the reasons for the differences in offending between nationality groups, the different offending patterns among first- and second-generation immigrants in Sweden as compared to some other European countries, and the influence of ongoing social changes in present Swedish society on the immigrants' offending behavior.

1. *Discrimination within the Criminal Justice System.* The purpose of the crime statistics is, among other things, to provide an annual overview of the number of crimes reported to the police and of decisions made at different levels of the criminal justice system. A superficial examination of information from the different levels of the system does not reveal any noticeable discrimination against immigrants in Sweden. However, the information provided by the official crime statistics is not sufficiently exhaustive for a final answer to the question. A systematic study on a broad basis covering all steps in the total criminal justice process is needed.

A major question is: are there biases to the disadvantage of immigrants, or some immigrant groups, concerning reporting to the police, police checks and arrests, police investigations, prosecutors' handling of cases and decisions, legal assistance, court proceedings, court decisions (choice of sanction), implementation of the sentence, appealing against the sentence, and bringing the case to a higher court?

Another question that is relevant for all levels in the justice system is how the language problem is handled and how a poor knowledge of Swedish might influence the interaction between the various components in the system. To what extent do immigrants receive assistance from an interpreter during the various phases of the criminal justice process? And how competent are the interpreters to assist a suspected or convicted immigrant in these matters?

A further question is how immigrants and nonresident foreign citizens sentenced to imprisonment are treated in the prisons. What social and sociopsychological processes are generated within the prison when the number of foreigners increases? Are inmates with a Swedish and a foreign background treated differently by the staff? If so, in what ways? What does the language problem imply for the interaction between the inmates with a foreign background and the staff?

2. *Differences in Offending between Immigrant Groups.* Why do some immigrant groups have a higher rate of offending than other groups?

This is an interesting question from a criminological viewpoint because the answer could give insights into the factors that offer protection against the development of criminal behavior and the risk factors involved in moving from one country or culture to another. An answer could also suggest approaches for preventing crime among newly arrived immigrants.

Are the less criminal immigrant groups better psychologically and socially integrated into the Swedish society than the groups with a higher crime rate? Or is it possible that the groups with a low crime rate commit crimes with a low detection risk and thus appear in the crime statistics to a lesser extent? If true, a lower level of criminality among some immigrant groups could be an illusion.

More in-depth research on the mechanisms behind observed differences in offending among immigrant groups is needed. This research would contribute to further testing and developing criminological theory and finding new paths in crime prevention work.

3. *First- and Second-Generation Immigrants.* The question of offending patterns among the first and second generation is important not only in Sweden but in all European countries.

Prevailing theoretical explanations of differences in offending between generations are hypothetical rather than empirically founded. Hence, more empirical research is needed to illuminate the relations between immigrants' and their children's integration into the new society and their antisocial and criminal behavior.

Much research in this field has been based on prevalence rates of offending among different immigrant groups. In the future more attention should be paid to the sociological and social psychological mechanisms behind the process of social integration and the development of adjustment problems among different immigrant groups. This research should seek to explain why some immigrant groups adapt more easily to the new society than other groups. In this connection, the children of immigrants who were born in Sweden and those who were born abroad should be studied separately. As discussed in greater detail in Martens (1995), there are three groups of immigrants who need further attention and research. These are immigrants who have been victims of war and torture, young immigrants who marry and have children, and children and youth who immigrate to the host country with their parents. These groups are all at risk for maladjustment in the new society, especially when unemployment has increased greatly over a short period of time and the indigenous population has become more skeptical about the country's immigration policy.

4. *Immigrants and Crime in a Changing Society.* Both unemployment and economic dependence on supplementary benefits have increased markedly among immigrants during the last few years. These changes in Swedish society are a consequence of an economic recession since the beginning of the 1990s and most affect immigrants who have arrived since the mid-1980s.

Young families with financial and social problems currently do not receive the help and support they would have previously. Instead they run the risk of entering a vicious circle that can break down their self-esteem and their belief in the future. One of the most vulnerable groups are immigrants and their families. When the resources for compensatory arrangements to counteract a less stimulating home environment among disadvantaged children are reduced, it is quite possible that the prevalence of criminal and other antisocial behavior increases among these children. When recreation centers are closed down and access to other organized leisure time activities is limited, the risk of being pushed into the streets and to the shopping centers increases. Youngsters who hang out on the streets and in other public places easily get away or even hide from the social control of parents and other socialization agents. The opportunity to commit crime may also be increased in this environment, as is the risk of socializing with crime-prone companions. These risks are most pronounced in the big cities, in particular in housing areas that already have many social problems and much criminality.

More sociological research monitoring the social and psychological consequences of development in a changing society is needed. So is research on the segregation and marginalization effects of current social changes (National Board of Health and Welfare 1994). The more vulnerable groups in society, including immigrants, should be of particular interest. Such a broad approach could very well be ordered by criminal-sociological studies focusing on how changes in immigrants' social conditions influence their offending patterns. Specific questions such as "How do the changes in society influence young immigrants born abroad, young immigrants born in Sweden, young immigrant families with small children, immigrant families with adolescent children?" could be convenient points of departure for in-depth studies on antisocial and criminal behavior among various groups of immigrants and their children.

APPENDIX A

TABLE A1

Description of the Immigrant Background of the Population Members in Ahlberg's (1996) Study

		Second-Generation Immigrants		
	First-Generation Immigrants (Born Abroad)	Father Swedish, Mother Born Abroad	Mother Swedish, Father Born Abroad	Both Parents Born Abroad in the Same Country
Denmark	14,065	10,886	13,427	4,630
Finland	114,356	53,679	20,508	34,925
Norway	13,026	21,368	12,378	2,388
Estonia	0	4,118	4,636	2,744
Greece	7,848	143	807	1,786
Italy	2,095	491	2,308	602
Yugoslavia	20,532	581	2,343	5,892
Poland	15,976	2,122	1,663	1,357
Portugal/Spain	3,779	587	1,077	97
Great Britain	5,787	1,546	1,619	69
Czechoslovakia	2,943	860	1,011	619
West Germany	8,200	15,010	11,137	4,186
Hungary	4,778	848	2,572	1,945
Austria	2,091	1,336	2,414	427
Soviet Union	1,233	1,109	1,315	777
Algeria/Libya/Morocco/ Tunisia	3,023	38	389	123
Ethiopia	2,601	34	78	6
United States	4,751	3,456	3,827	32
Argentina/Uruguay	3,139	153	153	12
Bolivia/Peru/Equador	1,992	77	79	6
Chile	8,169	43	72	8
Colombia	947	28	61	1
Bangladesh/Pakistan	1,881	0	54	10
India	2,923	209	317	40
Iraq	3,234	13	19	7
Iran	7,075	57	147	12
Jordan/Palestine/Syria	2,612	12	146	69
Taiwan/China/Japan	2,032	390	397	42
Korea	4,281	55	17	35
Lebanon	3,277	16	46	28
Thailand	1,887	15	9	1
Turkey	13,348	47	347	649
Vietnam	2,753	28	17	1
Remaining countries in:				
Africa (excluding Uganda)	3,892	279	582	36
Europe	7,167	2,989	4,242	974
North America	2,080	576	575	4
Asia	4,094	158	278	15
Other countries	2,801	271	222	13

SOURCE.—Ahlberg (1996), table 1.

APPENDIX B

TABLE B1

Crime Participation Rates among Second-Generation Immigrants with Only One Parent Born Abroad, by National Background of the Immigrant Parent, 1985–89

One of the Parents Born in Sweden and One Born In:	Offspring's Crime Participation Rate
Algeria, Libya, Morocco, Tunisia	12.2
Turkey	10.9
Yugoslavia	10.4
Portugal, Spain	10.4
Greece	10.4
Iran	10.3
Iraq	9.4
Pakistan, Bangladesh	9.3
Italy	9.2
Hungary	9.0
Bolivia, Peru, Ecuador	8.3
Austria	8.3
Jordan, Palestine, Syria	8.2
Finland	8.2
Colombia	7.9
Norway	7.4
Argentina, Uruguay	7.2
Great Britain	7.2
Ethiopia	7.1
Romania, Bulgaria	7.1
Chile	7.0
Germany (West)	7.0
Poland	6.8
Czechoslovakia	6.5
Lebanon	6.5
Soviet Union	6.0
India	5.9
Estonia	5.7
Taiwan, China, Japan	4.2
United States	4.0
Denmark	3.9
Vietnam	2.2
Korea	1.4
Remaining countries in:	
Asia	7.3
Africa	7.0
Europe	7.0
North America	6.4
Unspecified	9.5

SOURCE.—Ahlberg (1996), table 32.

NOTE.—Participation rates are unstandardized.

REFERENCES

Ahlberg, Jan. 1996. *Criminality among Immigrants and Their Children: A Statistical Analysis.* (In Swedish.) Brottsförebyggande rådet BRÅ-Report. Stockholm: Fritzes. Forthcoming.

Alvazzi del Frate, Anna, Ugljesa Zvekic, and Jan J. M. van Dijk, eds. 1993. *Understanding Crime: Experiences of Crime and Crime Control.* Acts of the International Conference, Rome, November 18–20, 1992. UN Interregional Crime and Justice Research Institute, Ministry of Justice the Netherlands and Ministry of the Interior Italy. Publication no. 49. Rome: UN Interregional Crime and Justice Research Institute.

American Psychiatric Association. 1987. *Diagnostic and Statistical Manual of Mental Disorders.* Rev. 3d ed. (DSM-III-R). Washington, D.C.: American Psychiatric Association.

Arnetz, Bengt B. 1988. *Stress Reactions in Relation to Threat of Job Loss and Actual Unemployment: Physiological, Psychological and Economic Effects of Job Loss and Unemployment.* Stockholm: National Institute for Psychosocial Factors and Health.

Bernow, Roger, and Åke Boalt. 1989. *Immigrants in the Big City.* (In Swedish.) Official Reports of the Swedish Government (Statens offentliga utredningar [SOU]) 1989:111. Stockholm: Allmänna Förlaget.

Biterman, Danuta. 1989. *The Segregation of Living in the County of Stockholm.* (In Swedish.) Official Reports of the Swedish Government SOU 1989:111. Stockholm: Allmänna Förlaget.

Carlsson, Gösta. 1972. *Young Law-Breakers II. Family, School and Society as Reflected in Official Data.* (In Swedish.) Official Reports of the Swedish Government SOU 1972:76. Justice Department. Stockholm: Allmänna Förlaget.

DiLalla, L. F., and I. I. Gottesman. 1989. "Heterogeneity of Causes for Delinquency and Criminality: Lifespan Perspectives." *Development and Psychopathology* 1:339–49.

Ekberg, Jan. 1989. *Socioeconomic Career among Immigrants.* (In Swedish.) Official Reports of the Swedish Government SOU 1989:111. Stockholm: Allmänna Förlaget.

Eriksson, Ulla-Britt, and Henrik Tham, eds. 1983. The Foreigners and Criminality. (In Swedish.) BRÅ-Report 1983:4. Stockholm: Allmänna Förlaget.

Farrington, David P., and Per-Olof H. Wikström. 1994. "Criminal Careers in London and Stockholm: A Cross-National Comparative Study." In *Cross-National Longitudinal Research on Human Development and Criminal Behavior,* edited by Elmar G. M. Weitekamp and Hans-Jürgen Kerner. Dordrecht: Kluwer.

Friedman, J., and J. Jaranson. 1994. "The Applicability of the Posttraumatic Stress Disorder to Refugees." In *Amidst Peril and Pain: The Mental Health and Well-Being of the World's Refugees,* edited by A. J. Marsella, T. Bornemann, S. Ekblad, and J. Orley. Washington, D.C.: American Psychological Association.

Ginsburg, Bengt-Erik. 1995. "Refugees and Asylum Seekers—Health Problems at the Arrival." (In Swedish.) In *Health and Social Conditions among the Immigrants,* edited by Gudrun Persson and Maria Roselius. Stockholm: National Board of Health and Welfare.

Governmental Proposition 1989/90:90. *On Research. Section 11. Field of Activities of the Justice Department.* (In Swedish.) Stockholm: Administrative Office of the Riksdag.

Hämäläinen, Minna, and Lea Pulkinen. 1995. "Aggressive and Non-Prosocial Behaviour as Precursors of Criminality." *Studies on Crime and Crime Prevention* 4(1):6–21.

Hammar, Tomas. 1992. "Immigration Policies." (In Swedish.) *National Encyclopedia*, 9:533. Höganäs: Bra Böcker.

Humble, Kristina, and Gitte Zettergren-Carlsson. 1974. *Young Law-Breakers V: Personality and Relations as Illuminated by Projective Methods.* (In Swedish.) Official Reports of the Swedish Government SOU 1974:31. Stockholm: Allmänna Förlaget.

Junger, Marianne. 1989. "Ethnic Minorities, Crime and Public Policy." In *Crime and Criminal Policy in Europe*, edited by Roger Hood. Proceedings of a European Colloquium, July 3–6, 1988, pp. 142–73. Oxford: Oxford University, Centre for Criminological Research.

———. 1990. *Delinquency and Ethnicity: An Investigation on Social Factors Relating to Delinquency among Moroccan, Turkish, Surinamese, and Dutch Boys.* Deventer-Boston: Kluwer Law and Taxation Publishers.

Killias, Martin. 1989. "Criminality among Second Generation Immigrants in Western Europe: A Review of the Evidence." Paper presented at the seventh International Workshop on Juvenile Criminology on "The Future of the Juvenile Justice System," Leeuwenhorst, May 29–31.

Kindlund, Hannelotte. 1995. "Early Retirement and Absence due to Illness in 1990 among Immigrants and Swedes." (In Swedish.) In *Health and Social Conditions among Immigrants*, edited by Gudrun Persson and Maria Roselius. Stockholm: National Board of Health and Welfare.

Lange, Anders. 1995. *Immigrants about Discrimination: A Study on Ethnic Discrimination by Order of the Ombudsman against Ethnic Discrimination Based on a Questionnaire and Personal Interviews.* (In Swedish.) Stockholm: University of Stockholm, Swedish Center for Immigration Research CEIFO and Statistics Sweden.

Lange, Anders, and Charles Westin. 1993. *Youth about the Immigration II: Ways of Relating to Immigration and Immigrants 1993.* (In Swedish.) Stockholm: Stockholm University, Swedish Center for Immigration Research CEIFO.

Leiniö, Tarja-Liisa. 1995. "The Immigrants' Health." (In Swedish.) In *Health and Social Conditions among the Immigrants*, edited by Gudrun Persson and Maria Roselius. Stockholm: National Board of Health and Welfare.

Lenke, Leif. 1983. "The 'Socio-Political Refugees'—a Case of Selective Migration." (In Swedish.) In *The Foreigners and Criminality*, edited by Ulla-Britt Eriksson and Henrik Tham. BRÅ-Report 1983:4. Stockholm: Allmänna Förlaget.

Loll, Bernd-Uwe, and J. Friedrichs. 1983. *Juvenile Delinquency among Foreigners of the Second and Third Generation.* (In German.) Study ordered by the Federal Criminal Police Office. Final Report. University of Hamburg, Institute of Comparative City Research. Wiesbaden: Federal Criminal Police Office.

Lundh, C., and R. Olsson. 1994. *From Import of Labour Force to Immigration of Refugees.* (In Swedish.) Stockholm: Studieförbundet näringsliv och samhälle (SNS) Förlag.

Martens, Peter L. 1989. *Sexual Offences against Children: Presentation and Discussion of Some Central Themes in the Current Research of the Area.* (In Swedish.) BRÅ-Report 1989:1. Stockholm: Allmänna Förlaget.

———. 1990. "Criminal Behaviour among Young People with Immigrant Background." In *Crime and Measures against Crime in the City*, edited by Per-Olof H. Wikström. BRÅ-Report 1990:5. (In Swedish.) Stockholm: Allmänna Förlaget.

———. 1992*a*. "Sexual Offences against Children: Some Results from a Swedish Study." *Studies on Crime and Crime Prevention.* 1:167–75.

———. 1992*b*. *Family Environment and Delinquency.* (In Swedish.) BRÅ-Report 1992:1. Stockholm: Allmänna Förlaget.

———. 1994. "Criminal and Other Antisocial Behaviour among Persons with Immigrant and Swedish Background—a Research Note." In *Studies of a Stockholm Cohort.* Project Metropolitan Research Report no. 39. Stockholm: University of Stockholm, Department of Sociology.

———. 1995. "Immigrants and Crime Prevention." In *Integrating Crime Prevention Strategies: Propensity and Opportunity*, edited by Per-Olof H. Wikström, Ron V. Clarke, and Joan McCord. Stockholm: Fritzes.

———. Forthcoming. *Self-Reported Crime and Victimization among Persons with Swedish and Immigrant Background.* (In Swedish.) National Council for Crime Prevention. BRÅ-Report.

National Board of Health and Welfare. 1994. *Life Conditions for Children in Changing Times.* Final Report. (In Swedish.) Report 1994:4. Stockholm: National Board of Health and Welfare.

———. 1995. *Social Assistance—Its Recipients and Development.* (In Swedish.) Stockholm: National Board of Health and Welfare.

National Council for Crime Prevention Sweden. 1994. *Criminal Statistics: Official Statistics of Sweden 1993.* BRÅ-Report 1994:4. Stockholm: Fritzes.

Office of Economic Opportunities. 1968. *Head Start: A Community Action Program.* Washington, D.C.: U.S. Government Printing Office.

Official Reports of the Swedish Government. 1972. *The Pre-school.* Report from the Day Nursery Investigation of 1968. Part 1. (In Swedish.) SOU 1972:26. Stockholm: Allmänna Förlaget.

———. 1993. *Deportation Because of Criminality.* (In Swedish.) SOU 1993:54. Stockholm: Department of Culture.

Official Yearbook of Sweden. 1995. *Sveriges statskalender, 1995.* Stockholm: Fritzes.

Olofsson, Birgitta. 1971. *What Did We Say! About Criminal and Conformist Behaviour among School Boys.* (In Swedish.) Stockholm: Utbildningsförlaget.

Olsson, Monika. 1986. *Finland Both Ways.* (In Swedish.) BRÅ-Report 1986:1. Stockholm: Allmänna Förlaget.

Persson, Gudrun, and Maria Roselius, eds. 1995. *Health and Social Conditions among the Immigrants.* (In Swedish.) Stockholm: National Board of Health and Welfare.

Statistics Sweden. 1984. *Yearbook of Judicial Statistics, 1984.* Stockholm: Statistics Sweden.

———. 1985. *Yearbook of Judicial Statistics, 1985.* Stockholm: Statistics Sweden.

———. 1986. *Yearbook of Judicial Statistics, 1986.* Stockholm: Statistics Sweden.

———. 1987. *Yearbook of Judicial Statistics, 1987.* Stockholm: Statistics Sweden.

———. 1988*a*. *Yearbook of Judicial Statistics, 1988.* Stockholm: Statistics Sweden.

———. 1988*b*. *Population Dec. 31, 1987.* Part 3. Distribution by Sex, Age, Marital Status, Citizenship, etc. Stockholm: Statistics Sweden.

———. 1989*a*. *Yearbook of Judicial Statistics, 1989.* Stockholm: Statistics Sweden.

———. 1989*b*. *Population Dec. 31, 1988.* Part 3. Distribution by Sex, Age, Marital Status, Citizenship, etc. Stockholm: Statistics Sweden.

———. 1990*a*. *Yearbook of Judicial Statistics, 1990.* Stockholm: Statistics Sweden.

———. 1990*b*. *Population Dec. 31, 1989.* Part 3. Distribution by Sex, Age, Marital Status, Citizenship, etc. Stockholm: Statistics Sweden.

———. 1991*a*. *Yearbook of Judicial Statistics, 1991.* Stockholm: Statistics Sweden.

———. 1991*b*. *Population Dec. 31, 1990.* Part 3. Distribution by Sex, Age, Marital Status, Citizenship, etc. Stockholm: Statistics Sweden.

———. 1992*a*. *Yearbook of Judicial Statistics, 1992.* Stockholm: Statistics Sweden.

———. 1992*b*. *Population Statistics, 1991.* Part 3. Distribution by Sex, Age, Citizenship, etc. Stockholm: Statistics Sweden.

———. 1993*a*. *Yearbook of Judicial Statistics 1993.* Stockholm: Statistics Sweden.

———. 1993*b*. *Population Statistics, 1992.* Part 3. Distribution by Sex, Age, Citizenship, etc. Stockholm: Statistics Sweden.

———. 1994*a*. *Statistical Yearbook of Sweden, 1994.* Stockholm: Statistics Sweden.

———. 1994*b*. *Population Statistics, 1993.* Part 3. Distribution by Sex, Age, Citizenship, etc. Stockholm: Statistics Sweden.

———. 1995*a*. *Victims of Violence and Property Crimes, 1978–93.* (In Swedish.) Statistics Sweden Report no. 88. Stockholm: Statistics Sweden.

———. 1995*b*. Printout tables with information about persons suspected of an offense and convicted of an offense. Stockholm: Statistics Sweden.

Statistics Sweden and Swedish Immigration Board. 1993. *Statistical Notes about Immigrants.* (In Swedish.) Stockholm: Statistics Sweden and Swedish Immigration Board.

Stattin, Håkan, David Magnusson, and Howard Reichel. 1989. "Criminal Activity at Different Ages: A Study Based on a Swedish Longitudinal Research Population." *British Journal of Criminology* 29:368–85.

Suikkila, Juhanni. 1983. "Some Viewpoints on Use of Alcohol and Crime among Youth in Sweden and Finland." (In Swedish.) In *The Foreigners and Criminality*, edited by Ulla-Britt Eriksson and Henrik Tham. BRÅ-Report 1983:4. Stockholm: Liber/Allmänna Förlaget.

Sveri, Britt. 1973. "Criminality among Foreigners: A Comparison between Swedish and Foreign Citizens Based on the Criminal Statistics." (In Swedish.) *Svensk Juristtidning* 1973:279–310.

———. 1980. *Criminality among Foreigners: A Comparison between Persons Convicted for More Serious Crimes in 1967 and 1977.* (In Swedish.) Stockholm: Stockholm University.

———. 1987. *Recidivism in Crime among Foreign Citizens.* (In Swedish.) Stockholm: Stockholm University.

Swedish Immigration Board. 1992. *Statistics 1991.* Norrköping: Swedish Immigration Board.

———. 1995. *Statistics 1994.* (In Swedish.) Norrköping: Swedish Immigration Board.

Tham, Henrik. 1995. "From Treatment to Just Deserts in a Changing Welfare State." *Scandinavian Studies in Criminology* 14:89–122.

von Hofer, Hanns. 1990. *Foreign Citizens in the Criminal Statistics.* (In Swedish.) Statistics Sweden Promemoria 1990:2. Stockholm: Statistics Sweden.

———. 1994. *Foreign Citizens in the Criminal Statistics, 1993.* (In Swedish.) Statistics Sweden Promemoria 1994:1. Stockholm: Statistics Sweden.

Westin, Charles, and Anders Lange. 1993. *The Ambiguous Tolerance: Ways of Relating to Immigration and Immigrants, 1993.* (In Swedish.) Stockholm: University of Stockholm, Swedish Center for Immigration Research CEIFO.

Wikström, Per-Olof H. 1985. *Everyday Violence in Contemporary Sweden: Ecological and Situational Aspects.* BRÅ-Report 1985:15. Stockholm: Liber/Allmänna Förlaget.

———. 1990*a*. "The Stockholm Project: An Introduction." In *Crime and Measures against Crime in the City*, edited by Per-Olof H. Wikström. BRÅ-Report 1990:5. Stockholm: Allmänna Förlaget.

———. 1990*b*. "Age and Crime in a Stockholm Cohort." *Journal of Quantitative Criminology* 6:61–84.

———. 1994. "Crime, Crime Prevention and Criminal Policy." In *Crime, Crime Prevention and Criminal Policy*, edited by Per-Olof H. Wikström, Jan Ahlberg, and Lars Dolmén. BRÅ-Report 1994:1. Stockholm: Fritzes.

———. 1995. "Self-Control, Temptations, Frictions and Punishment: An Integrated Approach to Crime Prevention." In *Integrating Crime Prevention Strategies: Propensity and Opportunity*, edited by Per-Olof H. Wikström, Ron V. Clarke, and Joan McCord. BRÅ-Report 1995:5. Stockholm: Fritzes.

———. 1996. *Deadly Violence—Social Contexts and Trends.* (In Swedish.) Research report from the Swedish Police College. Forthcoming.

Yoshikawa, H. 1994. "Prevention as Cumulative Protection: Effects of Early Family Support and Education on Chronic Delinquency and Its Risk." *Psychological Bulletin* 115(1):28–54.

Josine Junger-Tas

Ethnic Minorities and Criminal Justice in the Netherlands

ABSTRACT

Several ethnic minorities in the Netherlands, relative to population, commit more crimes and more serious crimes than do Dutch offenders. There are indications that minority offenders who commit less serious or nonserious offenses seem to be punished more harshly than similar Dutch offenders. Relatively more ethnic minority members are placed in pretrial detention and sentenced to prison—partly because of different crime patterns, partly because many have no fixed residence, and partly because many are less likely than Dutch defendants to turn up at the trial and to plead guilty. Even taking account of these variables, minority membership continues to be a factor in explaining sentencing. Although ethnic stereotyping may play a role, disparities appear to result largely from the unfavorable economic, social, and legal position of ethnic minorities.

The Netherlands, which has about 15 million inhabitants, long had a homogeneous population, with the exceptions of residents of mixed Dutch-Indonesian descent, who now number 250,000 to 300,000, and a small group of Moluccans who emigrated in 1951 after Indonesia's independence. Both groups have Dutch nationality.

Compared to other European countries, the Netherlands became an immigration country only recently. The large influx of guest workers from Mediterranean countries—essentially Turkey and Morocco—began in the seventies, while the bulk of Surinamese and Antillean mi-

Josine Junger-Tas is visiting professor of criminology at the University of Lausanne and visiting research fellow at the University of Leyden. I would like to thank Frits Huls of the Dutch Central Bureau of Statistics for his assistance in gathering additional statistical information on the situation of ethnic minorities in the Netherlands.

0192-3234/97/0021-0004$01.00

grants of Dutch nationality entered between 1969 and 1975, when Surinam became independent.[1]

The influx of immigrants abruptly ended in 1981 (Penninx 1982). In 1980, the bilateral agreement between the Netherlands and Surinam, providing for free migration of Surinamese residents to the Netherlands, was reviewed, and stricter rules for migration were established. With respect to the Mediterranean countries, a restricted admittance policy was introduced in 1973. Stricter requirements were imposed for family sustenance, and housing and visa obligations were introduced, first for Turkish immigrants and then also for Moroccan and Surinamese citizens.

The nature of immigration also changed. Starting in 1981, few guest workers were admitted, and from then on most immigration was for family reunification. Seventy percent of persons admitted in 1988–89 came into the country under family reunification policies (Naborn 1992). By the late eighties, this process was nearly complete for Turks, but it was much slower for Moroccans. One consequence is that Moroccan children have been separated from their fathers for much longer than Turkish children. Some attribute the higher involvement of Moroccan boys in the criminal justice system to this experience. Family reunification remains a basis for immigration, but it is gradually being succeeded by family formation (in which a marriage partner is sought from the country of origin). Family formation immigration is still increasing.

At the same time, as labor immigration has virtually stopped, there has been a growing influx of asylum seekers from trouble spots such as Somalia, Iran, Iraq, Ethiopia, Sri Lanka, and the former Yugoslavia. Asylum seekers increased from about 8,000 in 1988 to 20,000 in 1992. A restrictive German law (enacted July 1, 1993) caused a temporary increase in these numbers, but the Netherlands has followed the German example, and new policies have restricted further increases. The largest number of asylum seekers in 1992 came from the former Yugoslavia (5,000), Somalia (4,000), Iran (1,300), Sri Lanka (1,000), Iraq (770), and Afghanistan (350). The number of asylum seekers in 1992 from Eastern Europe was 3,600 and has been decreasing. Between

[1] Unskilled laborers were recruited in nine countries (the so-called recruitment countries): Turkey, Morocco, Spain, Italy, Portugal, Yugoslavia, Greece, Tunisia, and the Cape Verdian Isles. However, recruitment was unequal. Most workers who came from Spain, Portugal, and Italy later returned home. Large numbers came from Turkey and Morocco. The majority became permanent residents.

1985 and 1993, about 10,500 persons were admitted as refugees (according to UN standards), about 4,700 persons were not considered refugees but were given "green cards" (permits for residence) on humanitarian grounds, and 15,800 persons were denied admission (Huls 1995).

Members of minority groups are overrepresented among victims, offenders, and persons processed by the justice system. Available evidence suggests that disparities result in part from differential involvement in crime and differences in the nature of the crimes committed, in part from background factors and specific legal dispositions, and in part from behavioral differences that result when minority offenders find themselves in the criminal justice system. Although there is no evidence of conscious discrimination in the system, unconscious stereotyping could play a role. For example, such stereotyping has been found in the labor market and among the police.

Section I describes the demographic and socioeconomic situation of different groups compared to the Dutch population. Section II examines differences in criminal involvement and draws on police data, victimization surveys, and self-report surveys. Section III considers decision making by the police, prosecutors, and judges and examines legal and extralegal factors that could account for disparities in disposition. Section IV summarizes the preceding discussions and their implications.

I. Ethnic Minorities in the Netherlands

The Dutch people may be divided into "autochtones" and "allochtones." Autochtones have Dutch nationality, but, as this measure includes naturalized persons, this category is overstated. Allochtones are persons who were born abroad or whose parents were born abroad. However, this includes the children of Dutch parents born in a foreign country, so the number of allochtones is also overestimated (Huls 1995). The term "ethnic minorities" refers to target groups of official and specific Dutch minorities policies, operative since 1983 (Muus 1991). As an official term, "ethnic minorities" was introduced by the Research Council for Government Policy, an advisory body of the government, in its 1979 report (Research Council for Government Policy 1979). Groups are not defined as "ethnic minorities" solely because of their ethnic or racial background and their size. Crucial to the definition is low social and economic position and transmission of this status from generation to generation (van Amersfoort 1974). According to this definition—based on official counts (of foreigners) and estimates (of allochtones having Dutch nationality)—the Dutch population of ethnic minorities consists of 380,000 Mediterranean nationals and their families; 250,000 immigrants from Surinam and 82,000 from the Netherlands Antilles, most of whom have Dutch nationality; 40,000 Moluccans and their descendants, who also have Dutch nationality; 39,000 officially recognized refugees (excluding asylum seekers); 3,500 Gypsies; and 30,000 (Dutch) caravan (trailer park) dwellers.[2]

Of course, this definition has an element of arbitrariness. For example, the nearly 40,000 Chinese—of whom only 8,000 have Chinese nationality—are not included (Central Bureau of Statistics 1992–93). There were substantial numbers of Chinese in the country before World War II, but they have never given the government any cause for concern. They constitute a closed, hard-working group with a strong family tradition and little crime. Recently their socioeconomic situation has become more vulnerable, and they have sought governmental support.

The last four groups on the list, including the Moluccans, are relatively small and have not been the subject of much systematic research. Thus, the "ethnic minorities" considered in this essay are Turkish residents, Moroccan residents, Surinamese residents, of whom more than 90 percent have Dutch nationality, and migrants from the Netherlands Antilles, who also have Dutch nationality.

Enumerating these groups is difficult (Muus 1991). Any objective count of ethnic minorities should indicate a person's nationality, country of birth, and country of birth of at least one parent. Otherwise, increasing numbers of second-generation immigrants who have acquired Dutch nationality will not be registered as members of ethnic minorities in official population statistics or in other official surveys, such as the regular Labor Force Survey.[3] Relying on self-identification reports becomes problematic as many in the second and third generations think of themselves as Dutch.

[2] Counts are based on several sources: official (state) bodies such as the Central Bureau of Statistics; the municipal registry offices, which register births, marriages, and deaths; and the Institute of Socioeconomic Studies. Registration is based on country of origin of the first and second generation, rather than nationality, and on self-identification by later generations.

[3] The Dutch Central Bureau of Statistics registers only foreigners as a distinctive population category. Once persons have Dutch nationality, they are registered as nationals without mention of ethnic origin.

TABLE 1

Ethnic Minorities in the Four Largest Cities in the Netherlands, January 1, 1993

	Total Inhabitants	Ethnic Minorities	Percent
Amsterdam	719,923	189,231	26.3
Rotterdam	596,116	132,424	22.2
The Hague	444,598	93,127	20.9
Utrecht	234,465	36,629	15.6
Total	1,995,102	451,411	22.6

Sources.—Central Bureau of Statistics, Municipal Registry Offices, and Muus (1993).

A. Population Data

In 1993, under a restrictive definition that required both parents to be born abroad, all target groups of ethnic minorities policy were estimated to total about 900,000, which is 6 percent of the total population (Muus 1993). When the definition is broadened to include people with one parent born abroad, 1,165,000 citizens in 1994, 7.6 percent of the population could be considered members of ethnic minorities.

However, ethnic minorities are concentrated in large cities. Aliens and ethnic groups make up 22.6 percent of the population in the four largest cities, although there are some differences in their distribution (see table 1).

The proportion born abroad is diminishing, while the proportion born in the Netherlands with at least one foreign-born parent is increasing. This is shown in figures 1*a* and 1*b* both for the whole country and for the four largest cities. The category "foreign-born" includes both nationals and nonnationals.

As figure 1*a* shows, for the country as a whole on January 1, 1992, most older minority group members had been born abroad, but a growing percentage of those under sixty-five were born in the Netherlands, in particular those from birth to age fifteen. In 1993, for example, 91 percent of Turkish children under ten were born in the Netherlands (Huls 1995). This shows several things. First, immigration has slowed, although there are still a considerable number of newcomers from fifteen to forty. Second, the proportion of ethnic minority members is growing, particularly in the large cities. The main reason is a

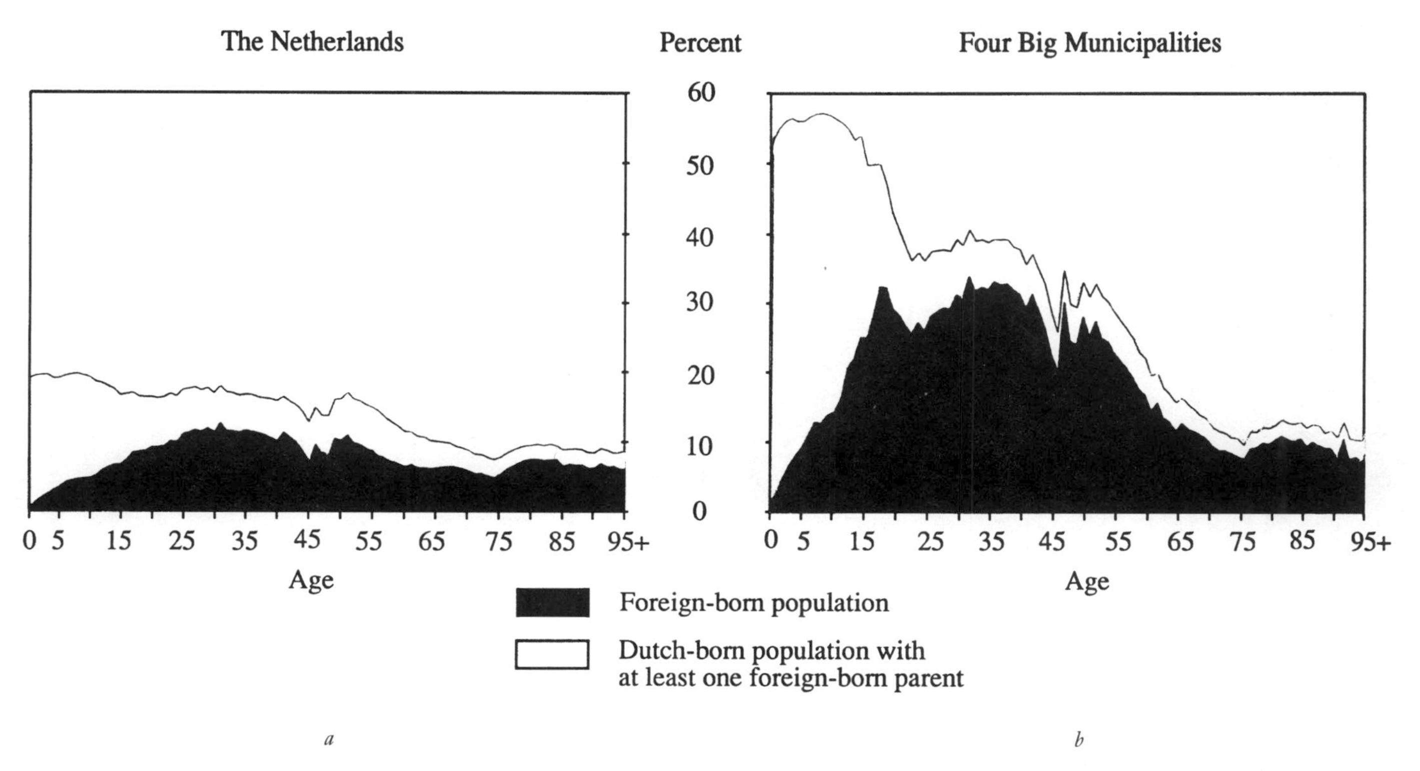

Fig. 1.—Foreign-born and Dutch-born population in the Netherlands with at least one foreign-born parent per 100 of the total population, by age, January 1, 1992. *a*, For the entire country. *b*, For the four largest cities. Source: Muus (1993), p. 29.

TABLE 2

Total Fertility Rates in the Netherlands per 1,000 Women by Country of Nationality, 1978–92

	Dutch Nationals	Turkish	Moroccan	Surinamese*	Total
1978	1.54	4.97	7.37	2.33	1.58
1980	1.54	4.76	6.96	1.74	1.60
1982	1.43	3.73	6.28	1.73	1.50
1984	1.44	3.31	5.85	1.90	1.49
1986	1.53	2.92	5.21	1.95	1.55
1988	1.52	3.22	5.13	1.91	1.55
1990	1.59	3.09	4.71	1.89	1.60
1992	1.58	2.73	4.14	1.66	1.59

SOURCE.–Muus (1991).
* Live births to women born in Surinam.

high birthrate among minority groups compared to the Dutch population. By the year 2000, half of the large city population is expected to be composed of members of ethnic minorities.

Table 2 shows that birth rates of all groups, except Dutch nationals, have been decreasing gradually over the years. However, Moroccans still have the highest rate, followed by the Turks. The rate for the Surinamese closely approximates that of the Dutch population.

B. Education

Education levels for minority groups in 1991 for people aged fifteen to sixty-five are low: about half of the Moroccan men and one-third of the Turkish men have had only some years of primary education. The situation among the Surinamese and Antilleans is better, although their education levels remain considerably below that of the indigenous population. Even among those aged fifteen to twenty-four, a sizable proportion has not completed primary education. Among Moroccan girls, this is more than a quarter.

Among younger people, the situation is changing. This is especially true of those who attend Dutch schools. Members of ethnic minorities who receive secondary education in Holland are more likely to complete their education with a diploma: this is the case for 60 percent of the Turkish and Moroccans and 80 percent of Surinamese and Antilleans, compared to 87 percent of the indigenous population. Based on these figures and on participation in secondary education, estimates can be made of the proportion of minority members aged fifteen to sixty-five who will obtain a diploma (see fig. 2).

Successful completion of secondary education decreases with age. Practically none of the older Moroccan and Turkish men have obtained a diploma. Of those aged fifteen to twenty-four, the percentage with diplomas is between 35 percent and 53 percent. A cohort study from the Dutch Central Bureau of Statistics (CBS) based on a sample of 20,000 students (Diederen 1995) compared the proportions of those leaving school in September 1994 after five years of secondary education by ethnic group. One-third of all pupils had left school since 1989. Thirty percent of the autochtone pupils and 46 percent of the allochtone pupils left school after five years of some form of secondary education, ranging from lower vocational training to grammar school: Moroccans—55 percent, Turks—47 percent, Surinamese—45 percent, Antilleans—47 percent, other—40 percent. Because the Surinamese group is the largest, its experience largely determined the school-leaving average. Ethnic minorities are more likely to participate in the lower forms of secondary education, and one in four leaves school without a diploma versus one in ten among the indigenous school population.

The participation of ethnic minorities in higher education is extremely limited. Counts of the Higher Education Inspectorate indicate that 0.6 percent of all registered students in higher vocational training institutions were Turkish or Moroccan and 1.3 percent were Surinamese or Antillean.[4] Only 0.4 percent of all enrolled university students in 1989–90 were Turks or Moroccans. According to a CBS survey on Social Position and Use of Services (Central Bureau of Statistics 1991), 35 percent of Dutch males and females aged fifteen to twenty-four participate in higher education, compared to 22 percent of Antillean, 16 percent of Surinamese, 9 percent of Turkish, and 6 percent of Moroccan males of that age group. Participation of minority females in that age group is considerably lower than that of males, with the exception of Turkish females (8 percent).

Limited enrollment in higher education is, of course, related to limited participation in secondary education. The difference is largest for the Moroccans and smallest for the Antilleans. When members of these groups continue their education after primary school, they

[4] These institutions provide training for professions such as teaching, social work, nursing, and various technical professions.

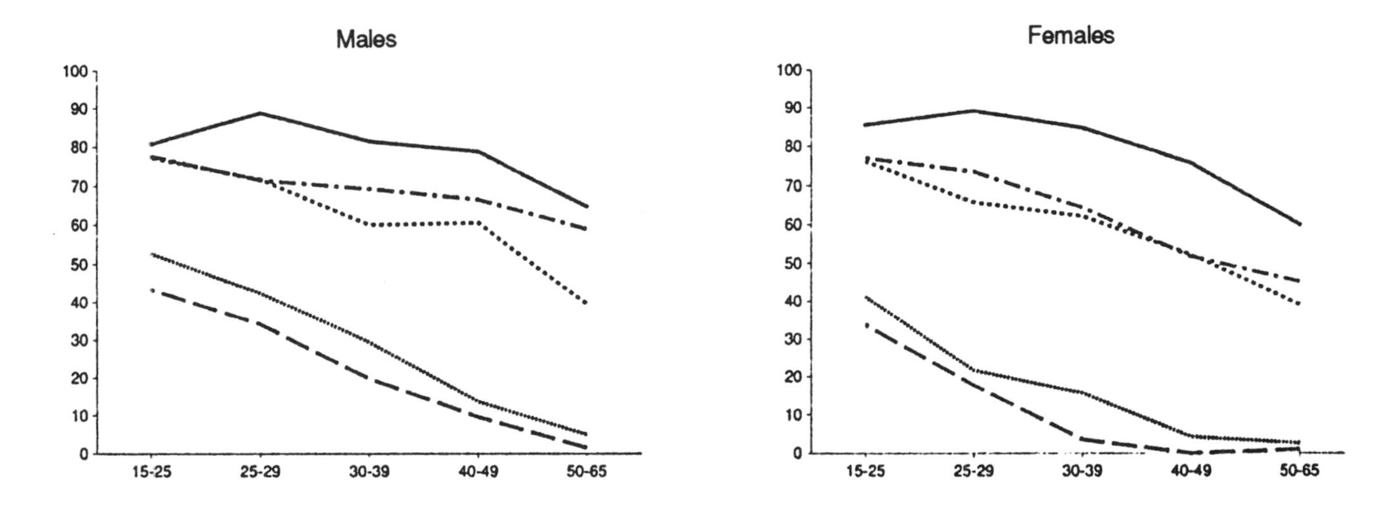

Fig. 2.—The number of diplomas obtained by males and females according to age and ethnic origin, in 1992, in percent. Sources: Erasmus University, Institute for Socio-Economic Studies (1991); Tesser (1993).

mostly select vocational training. More than half of the Moroccan and Turkish students opt for vocational training, against only a quarter of Dutch students. Moreover, whatever the level of education, minority students' results in school achievement and examination success are much worse than those of Dutch students. Differences in language abilities and other skills are evident from the time minority children enter primary school. It is as if the education system perpetuates disadvantaged starting positions demonstrated at age six.

The most important disadvantage is lack of mastery of Dutch. In some cases, 60 percent of total instruction time is completely lost on these students because they do not understand the explanations (Appel 1992). The average school achievement of Surinamese and Antilleans lies one standard deviation below that of Dutch students, while for Moroccan students the disadvantage is one and a half standard deviations, and for Turkish students, two. A second disadvantage is the low education level of minority students' parents. This is important because verbal interaction between parents and children functions as informal instruction: parents answer questions, explain problems, suggest solutions, give examples (Leseman 1989; Tesser 1993). If parent-child interactions are inadequate in this respect, the child is badly prepared for school. There are indications that the education level of parents is more important for the school achievement than is children's socioeconomic position or ethnic background (Meesters, Dronkers, and Schijf 1983), although this is a controversial issue because of contradictory research findings (Tesser 1993).

The schools do little to help minority students overcome learning difficulties, for example, by giving extra training to individual students or to small groups. Experiments have shown that much can be gained by such extra instruction and practice (Slavin and Madden 1989).

C. Employment

Dutch industry in the late 1950s experienced an acute shortage of unskilled labor, caused by an expansion of the service sector, which offered improved working conditions for Dutch workers. Unskilled laborers were recruited from the Mediterranean countries, which faced massive unemployment in agriculture because of mechanization. This was the origin of the influx of Turkish and Moroccan laborers.

The influx of the Surinamese was related to other factors. The first wave, in the sixties, was composed of skilled workers who feared deteriorating economic conditions in their country. The second wave, between 1975 and 1980, left from fear of cultural, social, and economic conditions after independence and included many persons of little or no schooling.

The oil crisis in 1973 put an end to recruitment of foreign workers, and labor immigration stopped. Furthermore, forced restructuring of many industries led to growing unemployment among labor migrants. Although most migrants planned to return to their homelands with some capital as soon as possible, and to stay in Holland only for a limited period, many were not able to realize their plans. The economic situation in their countries was not much better than in the host country. Many stayed on and arranged for their families to join them.

Although employment increased from 1984 on, the new jobs were for skilled workers. Unemployment among minorities remained high and even increased. This is illustrated in figure 3, which shows registered unemployment between 1988 and 1994 for all target groups of government policy, including Moroccans, Turks, and Surinamese.

Since 1989 there has been a slow improvement in the labor market position of ethnic minorities, but in 1992 the situation deteriorated again for all categories of minorities. The highest unemployment rate is to be found among the Moroccans. In 1991, the unemployment rate for Moroccans was six times as high as for the indigenous population. Among Turks it was five times as high, and among Surinamese and Antilleans four times as high. In 1992, one-third of the Turkish and Moroccan and one-quarter of the Surinamese population was unemployed.

As Tesser (1993, p. 73) shows in his report on the situation of ethnic minorities in the Netherlands in 1993, a number of interacting factors produce the high unemployment figures of minorities. It is difficult to evaluate each factor's contribution.

One factor is the changing economic and market situation. The demand for unskilled workers continues to decrease, and there is a change toward a more flexible organization of labor. This requires from workers more collaboration, more consultation, frequent adaptation to changes in the organization, more communication, and language skills. These changes have been accompanied by a general displacement of lower-skilled workers by higher skilled ones, which has been to the detriment of minorities. This probably explains why unemployment among Dutch workers declined between 1983 and 1989 but increased among minority workers. Employment possibilities for un-

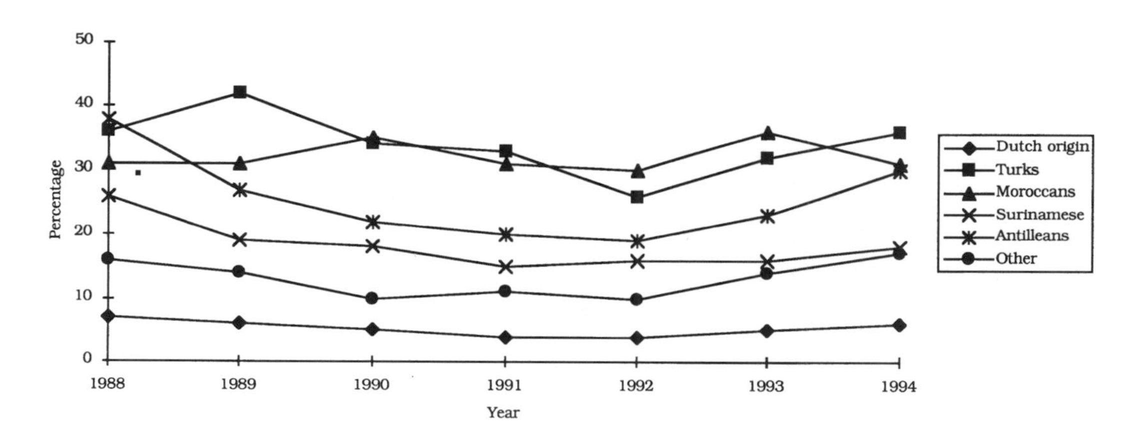

Fig. 3.—Registered unemployment by nationality and country of origin, 1988–94. Sources: Muus (1993), p. 34; Central Bureau of Statistics (1995), p. 70.

skilled workers in industry have never again regained the level of those in the sixties. In 1972, 80 percent of ethnic minority workers worked in industrial enterprises; in 1987, the figure was barely 50 percent. In addition, because of high Dutch payroll taxes, the relation between productivity and labor costs is unfavorable: unskilled labor is expensive. This, too, has contributed to a decrease in the types of jobs available for minorities.

An additional factor is that the minority population is growing about as fast as their labor participation is increasing. This is due both to continuing immigration and to relatively high birth rates.

Finally, low professional and language skills and direct and indirect discrimination are believed to cause unemployment. For example, there are twice as many nonworking among those who have only had primary education than at any other education level. Seventy-two percent of the Moroccans and 66 percent of the Turks aged fifteen to sixty-five in 1991 had achieved only primary education, against 1 percent of the Dutch, a difference likely to be strongly related to unemployment among minorities. However, according to the Labor Survey of 1990, unemployment of minority residents is higher than that of the Dutch at every education level. If minorities had the same distribution of education levels as the indigenous population, their unemployment rate in 1990 would have been 19 percent; it was in fact 23 percent (Kloek 1992; reported by Tesser 1993). The unemployment rate of the indigenous population at that time was 8 percent. Thus, only a quarter of the difference in unemployment rates between the two groups was explained by education differences. Other researchers (Niesing and Veenman 1990) have taken into account education, professional level, age, sex, local unemployment levels, and discrimination in personnel recruitment and selection. Logistic regression was used to calculate the effect of the first five factors on indigenous unemployment in 1988. Using those estimates, they calculated the expected unemployment of minority members. Table 3 shows the difference between the expected and observed unemployment rates of minority members and the Dutch workforce.

These five variables explain only a small part of high unemployment among minority members. Recruitment and selection of personnel appear to be very important factors. Minorities frequently search for jobs either through family and relatives or through agencies for temporary work. The employment agencies look for unskilled jobs to present to them. They seldom suggest higher skilled jobs, in response to prefer-

TABLE 3

Observed and Expected Unemployment in the Minority and Dutch Workforce, Based on Five Variables, 1988, in Percent

	Observed Unemployment	Expected Unemployment
Turks	38	17
Moroccans	38	16
Surinamese	33	15
Antilleans	35	14
Indigenous	12	12

SOURCE.—Niesing and Veenman (1990); Tesser (1993), p. 77.

NOTE.—See text for list of variables.

ences expressed by personnel officers charged to recruit workers. Widely publicized research on this subject (Meloen 1990) seems somewhat to have improved agencies' willingness to find jobs for minority workers. Questions on personnel managers' preferences showed that, when considering applicants with equal qualifications, 80 percent preferred indigenous to minority applicants; 20 percent would not accept minority members under any circumstances (van Beek and van Praag 1992). These findings, however, refer basically to low-skilled jobs. It is not improbable that minority members with higher qualifications speak better Dutch and might be perceived as more adaptable to organizational culture, more flexible, and better motivated. These and other social and normative criteria operate to the detriment of minorities because they form the basis of negative stereotypes about the productivity of minority workers. However, judgments and perceptions of the younger generations born in the Netherlands and who speak the language well are more positive.

To what extent similar stereotypes play a role in the operation of the criminal justice system is unclear. One obvious difference is that employers' attitudes concern anticipated future behavior, while the criminal justice system is generally reacting to concrete past criminal events.

D. Public Opinion and Ethnic Minorities

Since 1973 the European Commission has conducted public opinion surveys, called Eurobarometers, covering a number of different sub-

TABLE 4

Opinions on the Presence of Ethnic Minorities in Some Selected European Countries in 1988, in Percent

	The Netherlands	West Germany	Belgium	France	Great Britain	Italy
Quality of education suffers	48	50	54	49	55	23
Unemployment among own people rises	41	58	73	58	66	67
Abuse of social security by ethnic minorities	37	41	74	65	56	29
Cause of crime and insecurity	24	35	63	51	40	38

Source.—Dekker and van Praag (1990).

jects. A common questionnaire is administered to representative samples of the population of about 1,000 respondents, aged fifteen and over, in each country of the European Union. In the autumn of 1988 a great part of the Eurobarometer was devoted to questions on ethnic minorities (Eurobarometer 1989). It should be observed that opinion surveys have limited value (Dekker and van Praag 1990). Opinions and prejudice have probably little predictive value with respect to behavior: prejudiced people do not inevitably discriminate, while discrimination is not necessarily the result of prejudice. Discriminating behavior, treating someone unfairly according to irrelevant criteria, is based on power—the power of an employer, a landlord, a teacher, or a police officer. However, despite these limitations, the survey's findings give us some idea about how the general public perceives the presence of ethnic minorities in its country.

The questions in the survey referred to persons of different nationality, different race, different culture, different religion, and different social class. The following questions are of special relevance: "What are the consequences of the presence of large numbers of persons of different nationality and/or race in your country? Does the quality of education suffer? Does unemployment among your own people increase? Do they abuse social security provisions? Are they causing crime and insecurity?" (Dekker and van Praag 1990).

Table 4 shows that, compared to their immediate neighbors, the Dutch do not appear to be particularly xenophobic. The differences are especially marked when opinions are expressed on the rise of unemployment of "one's own people" and on the increase of crime and insecurity. Trying to establish some relationships, Dekker and van

Praag found that the explained variance resulting from standard sociodemographic variables (sex, age, social class, education, and urbanization) was not very high, ranging from 2.3 percent in Portugal to 13.2 percent in Great Britain, with the Netherlands 8.7 percent.[5] However, the relationships were similar in all participating countries, the strongest correlations being for education and age: the lower the education level and the older the respondent, the more xenophobic attitudes are found.

Six years of rising unemployment and crime rates have occurred since then. Had the survey been conducted in 1995, the Dutch results would likely have been considerably less favorable. Ethnic minorities, including the growing influx of asylum seekers, have become an important political issue and media issue since 1988. Some Dutch papers pay disproportionate attention to crime by ethnic minorities, without it being clear whether they merely reflect popular attitudes or contribute to shaping those attitudes.

For example, the Dutch Demographic Institute conducted three surveys in 1983, 1986, and 1990 on "Attitudes and Opinions on Aspects of Population Issues," including migration, minorities policies, integration, and xenophobia (van den Brekel and Moors 1993). As table 5 shows, 42 percent of respondents believed that the presence of so many foreigners in the country led to more terrorism and criminality, a considerably higher percentage than was found in the Eurobarometer. Age and education of respondents again showed a strong relationship with xenophobia.

The available evidence suggests that intolerance toward persons of different nationality or race has increased over the years. In an effort to explain this phenomenon, Halman (1994) examined value orientations in modern European society. His observations are based on a comparative European Values Study (EVS), coordinated by the Universities of Louvain, Belgium, and Tilburg, the Netherlands, which took place in 1981 and 1990. The EVS examined individualization and modernization in the fields of religion, morality, society, politics, family, marriage, and sexuality (Halman and Vloet 1992). It found that tolerance is a characteristic of modern and individualized persons: "Tolerant people express modern values, they are less religious, less traditional, more progressive, more inclined to protest and more inter-

[5] Explained variance in the Dutch study: age, 3.1 percent; education, 6.3 percent; and social class, 3.1 percent; all together, 8.7 percent.

TABLE 5

Respondents Agreeing with the Proposition "The Large Number of Foreigners Leads to More Terrorism and Criminality," in Percent (N = 1,500)

Demographic Categories	Percent Agreeing
All respondents	42
Sex:	
Men	44
Women	40
Age:	
20–39	34
40–64	47
65–74	54
Education:	
High	23
Medium	40
Low	52
Urbanization:	
Four largest cities	36
50,000–100,000 population	43
Under 50,000 population	43

SOURCE.—van den Brekel and Moors (1993).

ested in politics" (Halman 1994, p. 33). These findings are confirmed by Dekker and Ester who concluded that xenophobia is inversely correlated with support for democracy and political interest (Dekker and Ester 1993).

How can one explain the decline in tolerance in Europe since the eighties? One hypothesis is that many people in European society feel threatened in what they perceive as their rightful interests: good jobs, quality education, and comfortable and affordable houses (Halman 1994). These groups are afraid of growing competition for jobs, houses, and social security benefits by foreigners. Moreover, low levels of confidence in politics and in the ability of existing institutions to cope with the problems of contemporary society go together with feelings of threat and insecurity (Halman 1994). From this perspective, the mixture of generalized feelings of insecurity and fear are projected on foreigners and minorities who are blamed for all of society's problems.

II. Crime and Victimization among Ethnic Minorities

Much debate has taken place in political circles and the civil service as to whether ethnicity should be recorded in official statistics, such as in the police and the judiciary records of the Central Bureau of Statistics, or in other regular government surveys. The arguments against focus on the need to preserve individuals' privacy and the wish to avoid stigmatization of ethnic groups. The Ministry of Justice, in particular, has strongly opposed recording of ethnicity data for these reasons. This is now official policy, and Dutch police and judicial statistics do not maintain data on ethnicity. The only exception is prison statistics, which give information on inmates' nationality or country of origin. As a result of these policies, I am unable to offer any national police, prosecutorial, or judicial statistics specifying the distributions of members of different ethnic categories. Similar policies exist in other countries such as Canada (Gabor 1994).[6] Fortunately, there is some good research material providing information on police figures, self-report data, and victimization data.

A. Police Figures according to Ethnicity

At the request of the Ministry of Internal Affairs, research has been conducted on recorded crime of juvenile members of minority groups in the four largest Dutch cities (Etman, Mutsaers, and Werdmölder 1993). A majority of the Surinamese, half of the Moroccans, and more than one-third of the Turks and the Antilleans live in these cities.

The researchers consulted records maintained by the juvenile police. Ethnicity was routinely recorded by noting the country of birth of the juvenile and of one of his parents. Girls constitute only 14 percent of all arrested juveniles, and were omitted from the analysis. Although twelve years is the lower limit of criminal responsibility, which means that children under age twelve cannot (as a legal matter) commit offenses, the juvenile police gather information on children aged nine to twelve who commit delinquent acts.[7] Thirteen thousand police con-

[6] Gabor argues that statistics based on race and ethnicity should be collected. His arguments are that the public is entitled to this information, which will help to combat stereotyping minorities and prejudice, and that policy makers need the information to develop effective policy measures. I think the latter argument is valid but the former is not. There is no evidence that disclosing the facts has ever changed stereotypes and prejudice. The facts are simply not believed unless they confirm the stereotypes already held.

[7] Status offenses in Holland—noncriminal acts related to juvenile status, such as truancy, incorrigibility, lack of supervision—are not defined as delinquent behavior. These behaviors may eventually lead to a civil order of youth protection, but they are *not* included in statistical data on delinquent behavior.

TABLE 6

Proportions of Four Ethnic Groups among Apprehended Male Suspects, Aged 9–17, and in the Same Age Male Juvenile Population in the Four Largest Cities, 1988 and 1990, in Percent

	1988		1990	
Nationality	Suspects	Population	Suspects	Population
Dutch	32.0	66.0	28.0	58.0
Surinamese	23.0	11.0	18.0	12.0
Turkish	7.5	7.0	8.5	8.5
Moroccan	24.5	8.5	32.0	10.5
Other*	13.0	7.5	13.5	11.0

SOURCE.—Etman, Mutsaers, and Werdmölder (1993), p. 83.
NOTE.—All percentages sum to 100.0.
* Antilleans are included in "other."

tacts were recorded in police files in 1988 and 1990. Not all of these records deal with serious offenses. About half of reported cases resulted in an unofficial reprimand by the police and have no judicial consequences, while in somewhat less than half, an official report was sent to the prosecutor for examination.

Table 6 shows that in 1988 ethnic minorities made up one-third of the youth population in the four cities but were responsible for two-thirds of offenses known by the juvenile police. In 1990, they represented 40 percent of the population and were responsible for 70 percent of known offenses. However, there are large differences among the groups. Calculations (not shown in table 6) per 100 boys, aged nine to seventeen in the same age population, revealed that in 1990 the Turkish boys were not overrepresented among the apprehended boys (8 percent), nor were the Surinamese (11 percent), but the Moroccans were heavily overrepresented with 22.5 percent in the nine to seventeen age group and 30.5 percent in the twelve to seventeen age group. Recidivism rates are high (about 60 percent) but do not differ significantly among groups.

Since the mid-1980s, there has been growing concern in police circles and the judiciary about serious and violent crime among Antillean juveniles and young adults. That is why the Ministry of Justice asked for a study of this specific ethnic group, concerning both involvement in crime and possible causal factors. The study covers three large po-

TABLE 7

Number of Recorded Minority Juveniles (12–24 Years Old) in Three Police Regions (Amsterdam, Rotterdam, and Tilburg) Related to the Same Age Population in 1990, in Percent

Ethnic Group	Population (*N* = 550,716)	Report to Prosecutor (*N* = 16,090)
Antillean*	1.0	11.5
Moroccan	3.0	9.5
Dutch	75.0	2.5
Surinamese	3.5	5.5
Turkish	3.5	3.5
Other	14.0	2.5
Total	100.0	2.9

Source.—Van Hulst and Bos (1993), p. 62.

* Eighty-three percent of the Antillean group came from the island of Curaçao; 12 percent came from Aruba, the rest from the other four islands (Bonaire, Sint Maarten, Saba, and Sint Eustatius).

lice regions—including the cities of Amsterdam, Rotterdam, and Tilburg—and is based on official police reports that are sent to the prosecutor (van Hulst and Bos 1993). The age group involved is twelve to twenty-four, and the offenses covered are on the whole of a more serious nature than those in the earlier study. Moreover, the Antillean young people, including girls, are systematically compared to other ethnic groups.

Of all youths aged twelve to twenty-four in these three police regions, only 3 percent had a report sent to the prosecutor. However, as table 7 shows, two groups—the Antilleans and the Moroccans—are heavily overrepresented in recorded crime. The Surinamese are somewhat overrepresented. The Turks are not. All groups, with the exception of the Turks, have considerably higher proportions of recorded crime than the Dutch group.

Another recorded crime measure is the number of police reports and the number of offenses mentioned in the reports per individual offender (see table 8). Moroccan offenders have the highest number of reports to the prosecutor and the highest number of recorded offenses

TABLE 8

Number of Police Reports and Number of Recorded Offenses per Individual Offender in the Three Police Regions (Amsterdam, Rotterdam, and Tilberg), 1989–91

Ethnic Group	Number of Police Reports	Average Number of Offenses
Curaçao	1.91	2.38
Other Antillean	1.69	2.10
Moroccan	2.16	2.71
Dutch	1.60	1.95
Surinamese	1.66	2.09
Turkish	1.79	2.11
Other	1.53	1.77
Total	1.67	2.03

SOURCE.—Van Hulst and Bos (1993), p. 63.

per person, followed by offenders from Curaçao, the largest Antillean island. The latter have higher recorded crime figures than the other Antillean offenders. The lowest numbers of reports and offenses are found in the Dutch group, followed by the Turks, and the other Antillean offenders. These figures confirm the patterns shown in the first study, pointing to a difference in criminal involvement between the Moroccans and Antilleans and the remainder of the youth population.

The third major study combines information from the police with self-report data and victimization data. It is based on national representative samples of boys of three different ethnic groups—Surinamese, Turks, and Moroccans—aged twelve to seventeen and a control group of Dutch boys living in the same neighborhoods as members of ethnic minorities (Junger and Zeilstra 1989). The Turkish and Moroccan samples are drawn from police records, and the Surinamese sample is a subsample of a larger one drawn by the Central Bureau of Statistics.

Table 9 shows registered police information both on (unofficial) police contacts "ever" and "last year" and on recorded police contacts leading to an official report sent to the public prosecutor. Many police contacts of juveniles are dealt with informally, comparable to the English "no further action." The police may send the juvenile home, rep-

TABLE 9

Police Contacts and Official Reports of Four Ethnic Groups, in Percent

	Moroccan	Turks (Dutch)	Surinamese	Dutch Controls	*p*
Police contacts "ever"	33	23	23	15	
Police contacts "last year"	20	11	10	6	<.05
Official reports	15	8	6	6	<.05

Source.—Junger and Zeilstra (1989), p. 40.

rimand him, or send him to a diversion project, all actions followed by dismissal of the case. When the offense is considered serious, an official report is made and sent to the prosecutor, who also has a number of sanctioning options other than adjudication.[8] Sending a report to the prosecutor might be regarded as equivalent to the American definition of "arrest."

About twice as many Moroccans as the other ethnic groups had police contacts and more than twice as many had at least one official report. The Dutch boys had considerably fewer police contacts, whether "ever" or "last year," but there is little or no difference in the number of Dutch, Surinamese, and Turkish boys who have received an official report. This suggests that, although boys in all three ethnic groups have far more police contacts, especially at younger ages, than Dutch boys, this does not mean that they will all be officially recorded.[9] In this respect there is little difference among Dutch, Surinamese, and Turkish boys.

However, a number of observations should be made. First, it is at ages twelve to thirteen and fourteen to fifteen that more minority boys than Dutch boys have police contacts. Dutch boys seem to start committing delinquent acts somewhat later. Second, ethnic groups are not homogeneous. For example, the Surinamese group consists of Surinamese Creoles, Hindustani, Javanese, and other Asian people. The

[8] The prosecutor may reprimand a youngster in his office, send him a warning, impose mediation, impose restitution, or impose community service up to forty hours. All these "sanctions," if performed well, will be followed by dropping the charges.

[9] Both Junger (1990) and Etman, Mutsaers, and Werdmölder (1993) found this. In the latter study, more than a quarter of the children coming into contact with the police were aged nine to thirteen, with the Turkish (36 percent) and Moroccans (28 percent) overrepresented and the Dutch (21 percent) underrepresented.

TABLE 10

Delinquency Profile by Ethnic Group Aged 12–24 in Three Police Regions (Amsterdam, Rotterdam, and Tilburg), in Percent

Ethnic Group	Antillean	Moroccan	Surinamese	Turkish	Dutch
Public order and vandalism	6.6	7.3	8.2	11.8	17.7
Offenses:					
Property	61.0	61.3	53.0	47.9	48.5
Violent	16.3	15.8	19.6	14.0	10.4
Sexual	1.4	.3	1.7	1.5	1.1
Drug	2.3	3.7	2.8	3.8	1.2
Traffic	3.4	3.4	4.3	11.1	12.0
Other	9.0	8.2	10.4	9.9	9.1

Source.—Van Hulst and Bos (1993), p. 68.
Note.—Percentages sum to 100.0.

study found large differences in police involvement between Creoles and the other groups, with the Creoles having many more contacts. Third, the number of boys getting an official report does not vary very much among most ethnic groups (except for the Moroccans), and Turkish and Surinamese boys have more police contacts than the Dutch boys. This could indicate two things: first, that because these children spend more time on the streets and at younger ages than Dutch children (Junger and Steehouwer 1990), they are more likely to have contact with the police; second, that the police pay more attention to ethnic minority kids, thus discovering more petty offenses, many of which are not serious enough to prosecute. Both these surmises might be correct.

1. *The Nature of Criminality.* There are group differences in the nature of offenses committed. Taking account of the nine to thirteen age group, and considering contacts including police disposals and official reports, minorities are overrepresented for petty property offenses. For a more accurate picture, different groups are compared in relation to reports transferred to the prosecutor, using the latest data available in three police regions, Amsterdam, Rotterdam, and Tilburg (van Hulst and Bos 1993).

The age composition of groups differs. Half of the Moroccans and 40 percent of the Turks are under eighteen, versus about one-third of the other groups. This may influence both offense patterns and offense seriousness. Unfortunately, table 10 cannot be disaggregated according to age so that it is difficult to tell whether the high proportion of property offenses committed by the Moroccan group is related to their age composition. According to the police data in table 10, the major difference is that both Moroccans and Antilleans commit more property offenses than the other groups. Moreover, all ethnic offenders are more often recorded for violent offenses and drug offenses than are Dutch offenders, while the Dutch and the Turkish seem to have committed more traffic offenses than the others. Acquisitive crime appears to characterize Antillean, Moroccan, and Surinamese offenders, and in committing these offenses they more frequently use violence: compared to the Dutch group, three times as many Antilleans and twice as many from the other groups commit theft with violence. They also tend to commit these offenses in groups, which adds to the fear and insecurity of victims.

Earlier research on drug addiction in a group of young adult Moroccans showed that, compared to other addicted groups, the Moroccans committed more serious thefts, such as group thefts, theft with damage, or with burglary. Moreover, they were likelier to use violence while committing their offenses (Kaufman and Verbraeck 1986).

2. *A Special Offense—Street Robbery.* Two researchers in 1989 called attention to the increase and seriousness of street robbery in Amsterdam (Loef and Holla 1989). Research in the red-light district of the city showed that street robbery is a characteristic offense of recent, poor, and deprived migrants. Street robbery is an unsophisticated crime, easy to commit, requiring few skills or knowledge of the local criminal structure, and gives immediate returns.

Street robbery is a typical urban offense. Three-quarters of all street robberies reported to the police occur in cities of over 100,000 population, two-thirds in the four largest cities, and nearly half in Amsterdam. It is an offense that provokes much fear. In view of the increase in reported cases of street robbery, a large-scale study was undertaken of all cases reported to the police in Amsterdam and Utrecht in 1991. Ninety percent of all reports to the police have been analyzed, and half of all records of arrested suspects. Interviews were held with forty-four offenders and thirty-two victims (de Haan 1993).

Four thousand, five hundred street robberies were reported to the Amsterdam police in 1991. The most common offense was theft of money under the threat of violence; one-third was purse snatching from older women. In 40 percent of the cases no violence was used and in about one-third the robber was armed, generally with a knife. One-third of the victims were foreign tourists and two-thirds were

Dutch. Both offenders and victims were mainly men. Most robberies occurred in three places: the city center, the red-light district, and Amsterdam southeast, an agglomeration of public housing estates, populated in large majority by ethnic minorities. In 17 percent of all cases the victim was physically hurt, and in one-quarter of those cases (4.5 percent of all cases), he was seriously hurt. Street robbery is considered by offenders to be a low-status offense that gives little profit. For most of them it is a second-choice offense, mainly committed when one needs money badly and because it is easy to commit.

According to victims' reports, 85 percent of the offenders were nonwhite: about half were said to be "colored," one-third were classified as "North African," 3.5 percent as South European, 2 percent as Asian, and only 13.5 percent as "white." Comparison of these figures with the ethnic background of arrested suspects showed reasonable concordance: among the nonwhites most of the North Africans were of Moroccan origin, more than one-quarter were born in Surinam or the Antilles or had Surinamese parents, and the others came from fifty different countries. This does suggest that street robbery in the Netherlands is an offense committed mainly by foreigners and minorities.

De Haan distinguishes different motives for the offense: acquisitive crime serves to finance drug use, survival crime serves those who are illegal residents and have no regular income, recreational robbery is committed "just for the kick of it" mainly by offenders under eighteen, and property crime is committed purely for gains with an explicit element of planning.

This produces the following offender profiles based on more extensive records of those who had been taken to court in Amsterdam: acquisitive crime (35 percent), survival crime (25 percent), recreational robbery (20 percent), property crime (5 percent), and unclear motive (15 percent).

De Haan concludes that street robbery is mainly committed for survival (90 percent of the arrested suspects who were illegal migrants) or to sustain a drug habit (half of the legal-resident suspects). The general increase in street robberies is strongly related to migration and segregation of foreigners, unemployment, illegal residence in the country, and heroin consumption.

B. Self-Report Data

The self-report method is generally used successfully with juveniles and appears to have quite acceptable validity (Antilla and Jaakkola 1966; Gold 1970; Junger-Tas 1977; Hindelang, Hirschi, and Weiss

1981; Huizinga and Elliott 1986; Junger 1990; Junger-Tas, Klein, and Zhang 1992). There is some evidence that the method is less valid when used on adults, as was shown by comparing self-report data of a large adult sample with their recorded criminality (Veendrick 1976).

Self-report studies have been used to investigate the behavior of minority juveniles. Outcomes in a number of such studies suggest that minority juveniles are considerably less delinquent than the indigenous juvenile population (Junger-Tas 1977; Junger 1990; Terlouw and Susanne 1991; Terlouw and Bruinsma 1994). For example, Terlouw and Bruinsma (1994), in a Dutch survey of a national random sample of youth aged fourteen to twenty-one, found that 70.5 percent of Surinamese and 62.5 percent of Dutch youth reported having "ever" committed a delinquent act, against 37.5 percent of the Moroccans and 47 percent of the Turkish. Reported (soft) drug use was also much lower among Surinamese (7.8 percent), Moroccan (3.1 percent), and Turkish (2.1 percent) respondents than among Dutch young people (17.2 percent). Comparable outcomes have been found in an English survey (Bowling, Graham, and Ross 1994), suggesting lower delinquency rates among minorities than among the national youth population.[10]

Junger (1990) compared her respondents' self-reports with their police records. A police record meant that the boy was believed to have committed at least one offense and had been in contact with the police. Junger found—as might be expected on the basis of the research literature—reasonable validity for the Dutch and the Surinamese boys, but quite unexpectedly, low validity for the Moroccan and Turkish respondents. As a result, she did not analyze self-report data of the latter two groups but only those of the Dutch and Surinamese boys. Interestingly, she found little difference in property offenses between the Dutch and the Creoles, but the Hindustani and Asians had much lower rates ($p < 0.001$). Similar differences were found for vandalism, while violence rates differed little among the groups. With respect to the "ever" prevalence of all self-reports taken together, the largest group of delinquents was to be found among Surinamese Creole boys (80 percent), followed by Dutch (68 percent), Hindustani (58 percent), and Asian boys (50 percent). A similar distribution was found with respect to the prevalence "last year."

[10] These three studies are part of the International Self-Report Delinquency Study, which is coordinated by the Scientific Research and Documentation Center, Dutch Ministry of Justice. Thirteen Western countries participate in the study, which is based on a common research instrument.

What are the reasons for these disparities in validity, which seem to be more widespread than one would expect? Junger (1990) showed that the stronger the bond with the original ethnic community, the more disparities. Boys who share values and norms condemning delinquency more often tend to conceal offenses and police contacts than do less prosocial boys. There is also a relation between disparities and insufficient mastery of the language of the host country; this may mean that some respondents have difficulties in understanding the meaning of the questions. Disparities are also related to the number of judicial contacts: the more official contacts with the system, the better the correspondence between self-report data and police records.

However, there may be additional explanations. Surveys in Belgium and Switzerland involving mostly southern European juveniles who were long-term residents and who were well integrated into the host country showed no difference in self-reported delinquency compared with indigenous youths (Junger-Tas 1976; Killias, Villetaz, and Rabasa 1994). Perhaps factors such as long-term residence in the host country, socioeconomic and cultural integration, and the absence of external visible differences between indigenous juveniles and immigrant juveniles influence the willingness of the latter to report offenses. In other words, the fewer the differences between indigenous youths and immigrant youths, the more alike they will be in their actual and reported behaviors. Surinamese juveniles in the Netherlands may be a case in point. Although visibly different from indigenous youths, the majority have Dutch citizenship, had Dutch education in their country of origin, speak the language, and are familiar with Dutch culture. In these respects, their situation is very different from that of Moroccans and Turks. Junger tested the hypothesis that fear of expulsion might cause immigrant juveniles to hide information on offending but found no evidence of such fears.

It is also possible that the disparities between self-reported and officially recorded offenses and police contacts result from discriminatory practices by the police. For example, police patrols pay more attention to members of minority groups, thereby increasing the number of contacts and inflating the number and seriousness of delinquent acts committed by them. This is not a plausible explanation of disparities in the Netherlands. It is not likely that the police would discriminate against Turkish and Moroccan juveniles but not Surinamese youth. Finally, the disparities might relate to such factors as different cultural values or to fear of the authorities.

C. Victimization of Ethnic Minorities

Between 1980–92 the CBS conducted biannual victimization surveys, including sixteen offenses, on a representative sample of 4,500–5,000 individual respondents aged fifteen and over and living in a household. The sample is stratified according to province and urbanization, with automatic selection of the largest cities. Respondents are randomly selected from postal system and telephone service registrations. A weighing procedure is used to adjust for household size and over- and underrepresentation of specific groups. This procedure does not correct for the nonrepresentation of institutionalized and homeless people, groups that have high victimization risks.

The CBS victimization surveys, which distinguish between Dutch citizens and foreigners, show that foreigners have considerably higher victimization rates than does the indigenous population.

A number of qualifications, however, must be made. First, the category "Dutch" includes all who have Dutch citizenship through naturalization and thus includes most Surinamese. Second, although the category "foreigners" does include some members of ethnic minority groups, such as the Turks and Moroccans, European Community citizens form the largest group of foreigners. Third, most foreigners live in the large cities where crime rates are higher than in the rest of the country. Moreover, members of ethnic minorities are generally of lower socioeconomic status and live in poor, relatively crime-ridden urban neighborhoods.

For all those reasons, some disparities in victimization rates may be expected when comparing the rates of the foreign population with those of the average Dutch population. Table 11 must therefore be viewed with some caution, and one must be tentative in drawing conclusions from these data. The overall pattern is for higher victimization rates for members of ethnic minorities.

Other research on victimization among ethnic minorities gives more details (Junger 1990; van Dijk and van Soomeren 1993). A small victimization survey was conducted in 1992 among 297 adult Surinamese, Turks, and Moroccans in Amsterdam and Rotterdam. The results are not necessarily representative for these groups because respondents were selected and interviewed on the streets. The study was meant to provide a "first impression" of minority victimization. About 75 percent of respondents were long-term residents (ten years or more). Two-thirds were men. Education and employment were somewhat above average for those groups. Results were compared with the stan-

TABLE 11

Victimization Rates of Dutch and Non-Dutch Residents in 1992, in Percent

	Dutch (*N* = 4,341)	Non-Dutch (*N* = 107)*
Bicycle theft	5.9	12.0
Car theft	.4	2.0†
Theft from car	3.7	5.7
Theft out of car	3.7	8.1
Vandalism	6.7	7.6
Theft of purse	2.5	4.4
Burglary	2.8	7.2
Other thefts	5.0	6.9
Harassment in own home	1.4	2.0
Harassment on the street	.7	.7
Threatened in own home	2.4	3.0
Threatened on the street	3.4	1.7
Hit and run offense	1.5	2.5
Total rate	34.8	47.4

Source.—Central Bureau of Statistics (1992, 1993).

* The low number of non-Dutch respondents is related to a high level of nonresponse among minority members.

† Car theft Non-Dutch rate is from 1988.

dardized population survey on victimization, fear of crime, and police services—the "Politiemonitor"—which is regularly held in most Dutch cities (Geerlof and Schouten 1991; Geerlof et al. 1993). Comparisons were made with the police monitor's results in Amsterdam and Rotterdam.

Table 12 shows considerable differences: the risk of becoming a victim of a property crime or a violent offense is much higher for members of minority groups than the average risk in Amsterdam and Rotterdam. The risk of becoming a victim of violence and vandalism is particularly high. Victimization of Moroccans has an especially violent character: this group suffers more from assault and violent purse snatching than from property offenses; among Surinamese and Turks, the pattern is reversed. This may be because much offending is intra-

TABLE 12

Victimization of Three Ethnic Groups of Respondents in Amsterdam and Rotterdam in 1992, in Percent, Compared with General Population Rates

	Surinamese (N = 100)	Turkish (N = 98)	Moroccan (N = 99)	Standardized General Population Rate
Property Offenses:				
Bicycle Theft	22	28	20	17
Auto theft	3	5	2	1
Theft from car	16	21	13	7
Vandalism of car	22	25	12	9
Theft of purse	19	14	9	5
Burglary	7	1	4	2
Other thefts	13	20	5	4
Total property	66	68	47	43
Violent Offenses:				
Purse snatching	3	6	9	2
Physical threats	13	12	11	7
Assault	2	7	29	2
Total violent	14	12	34	9

SOURCE.—Van Dijk and Soomeren (1993).

group: groups that have high offending rates usually have high victimization rates. From other victimization surveys, such as the biannual surveys conducted by the Central Bureau of Statistics from 1980 on, as well as the international survey (van Dijk and Mayhew 1992), we know that men and young people are more often victimized than are women and older persons. The survey found higher risks for those with more education (68 percent) than for those with lower education (55 percent). The latter are more frequently victims of violence than of property offenses.[11] Moreover, 60 percent of the respondents had been victimized more than once (by two to four offenses). However, it bears reiteration that these results are biased by comparison of victimization of mainly lower socioeconomic-status persons living in high-crime neighborhoods with that of a random sample of inhabitants of Amsterdam and Rotterdam. An average risk group is being compared to a high-risk group and this does not give an accurate picture.

[11] This group overlaps partly with the Moroccans, of whom 81 percent have only lower education, against 44 percent of the Turks and 26 percent of the Surinamese.

To remedy this, additional research was undertaken. A telephone victimization survey of Turks and Moroccans in four large and four medium-sized cities was complemented with face-to-face interviews. The three groups—including the Surinamese—were then compared with a matched group of Dutch citizens living in the same neighborhoods (van Dijk and van Soomeren 1994).

The first comparison showed that minority group members interviewed by telephone were better educated and had higher incomes than those who were interviewed face-to-face; thus the phone sample was not representative of ethnic groups in Holland. Moreover, they lived throughout the country while the face-to-face interviews were concentrated in the larger cities.

The second comparison showed no difference in victimization risk between the three ethnic groups and the Dutch group living in the same neighborhoods. The conclusion is that victimization risk and fear of crime are more strongly related to degree of urbanization and to neighborhood quality rather than to ethnic origin.

Research in England and Wales (Tuck and Southgate 1981) also shows that the degree of urbanization and type of home were more strongly related to victimization risk than ethnicity and that environmental factors were more important than ethnicity.

Junger's findings, although limited to juveniles, confirmed these conclusions for the Netherlands. The control group was composed of boys living in the same neighborhood or street as the minority groups. Dutch juveniles had most often been victims of property offenses (75 percent); Moroccan (60 percent) and Hindustani boys (59 percent), least often. The same is true for violent offenses: more Dutch boys (31 percent) than Turkish (21 percent), Creoles (22 percent), and Moroccans (15 percent) had been a victim of physical threats or assault. On the whole, however, differences are slight.

Factors related to victimization of ethnic minorities are length of residence in the country and age: the longer in the country and the higher the age, the higher the risk of becoming a victim both of property and violent offenses. Other factors are similar to all ethnic groups (see also van Dijk and Mayhew 1992). For example, how young people spend their leisure time is related to victimization risk. To the extent that they often spend their free evenings in discos and bars, the risk of becoming a victim of a property offense is tripled, and that of becoming a victim of violence is doubled. In other words, lifestyle is an important determinant factor of victimization probabilities.

With respect to fear of crime, ethnic minorities do not seem to be more fearful of becoming a victim than is the average Dutch citizen (van Dijk and van Soomeren 1993). Women and recent victims of violence have higher than average feelings of fear.

Do ethnic minorities feel discriminated against? They undoubtedly do. Fifty-five percent report having experienced discrimination by Dutch citizens or agencies. More Turks (87 percent) and Moroccans (45 percent) than Surinamese (32 percent) report such events. The most common perceptions of discrimination involve anonymous situations, such as in the street by young people, in bars or discos, and formal interactions between public officials, such as civil servants in their public function or police officers. Direct discrimination in the work or home environment seems to be rare. This may be because employees get to know each other at the workplace, and personal characteristics in the work situation are more important than ethnic stereotypes. One in three respondents reports avoiding going to certain places, such as specific bars and discos, shops and markets, in particular when these are outside their own neighborhood (van Dijk and van Soomeren 1993).

D. *Summary*

With respect to recorded crime, Moroccans and Antilleans are considerably overrepresented in the crime statistics. Moreover, they have the highest number of official records and of offenses per individual offender. Comparing the juveniles in these groups shows that they accrue official police records for having committed delinquent acts at an earlier age than Dutch juveniles.

Official records show more violence and group thefts among Moroccans and Antilleans than among the other groups. Finally, street robbery appears to be a typical offense of recently arrived, marginalized, and deprived migrants and of drug addicts.

Self-report data, on the contrary, show less involvement in crime among ethnic minorities than among Dutch juveniles. This is not the case for the Surinamese, who are better integrated into Dutch society and speak the language well, but it is true for Turks and Moroccans. There is some evidence that this possible underreporting is related to traditionalism, lack of knowledge of the Dutch language, and degree of involvement in offending. However, there is a need for more conclusive evidence.

Victimization rates of minorities are considerably higher than those of the average citizen. This is true for all types of offenses but particularly so for violent offenses. However, controlling for neighborhood makes most of the differences disappear. Victimization of minority members seems to be related to age and length of residence in Holland. Lifestyle and leisure behavior are also related to victimization risk, but this is similar for Dutch persons.

III. Ethnic Minorities in the Criminal Justice System

> All those who reside in The Netherlands are treated alike in like cases. Any distinction on the basis of religion, race, political conviction, sex, or sexual inclination is prohibited. (Article 1 of the Dutch Constitution)

The Netherlands constitution expresses the principle of equality before the law. Neither the police nor other officials should treat members of ethnic minorities, including foreigners, any different than Dutch citizens.

Two arguments can be raised to qualify this principle. First, Article 2 of the constitution states that the law—in particular the Aliens Act—regulates the admission and expulsion of foreigners; and second, the claim may always be made that cases are not alike (Kruyt 1986).

There is patently no legal basis for treating the Surinamese, most of whom have Dutch nationality, any differently than other Dutch citizens. However, foreigners may be expelled and returned to their home countries. This does not happen very often, but that this possibility exists means that foreigners may find themselves at a disadvantage compared to Dutch suspects with respect to pretrial detention, activities of the probation service, sentencing, and prison regime.

A. Expulsion

Three categories of foreigners can be expelled. First, illegal residents, who have by far the weakest legal position. Second, asylum seekers who lose their petitions for legal residence and as a consequence must leave. Third, criminal foreigners who have legal residence but lose it because of a criminal conviction (Aalberts and Dijkhoff 1992). When awaiting expulsion, foreigners are routinely held in "aliens custody." They are detained either in police cells for a short time or in jail. Jail records for 1989–92 show that criminal foreigners formed about 40 percent of all foreign detainees and illegals about 50 percent (Aalberts and Dijkhoff 1992).

Expulsion is a much harsher punishment than prison. There has been much debate among lawyers as to whether expulsion means that an offender is punished twice. This would violate the values underlying double jeopardy principles. However, the Council of State ruled (in 1978) that expulsion is not a criminal penalty but an administrative measure on the basis of the Aliens Act and in the interest of public order (Kruyt 1986). A foreigner can also be declared "undesirable." The consequence is that he is not allowed to visit relatives in the Netherlands and, if apprehended, can receive a prison sentence of six months maximum. A foreigner may be declared "undesirable" when convicted of a crime incurring a prison sentence of three years or more.

Expulsion has serious consequences: the expellee may be completely uprooted and may lack skills to build a new existence in the country of origin; the same is true for family members, especially the children; expulsion leads to disparate processing in most phases of the justice process, but especially in the execution of a prison sentence; and the possibility of expulsion may lead to feelings of insecurity among legal residents (Swart 1978).

Expulsion is dependent on a number of factors, such as seriousness of the crime, length of the prison sentence, length of legal residence, bonds with the Netherlands, whether first or second generation, and risk of recidivism. The longer the residence, the smaller the risk of expulsion. Drug dealing practically always leads to expulsion. The probation service tends not to produce presentence reports for foreign suspects on the ground that "they will be expelled anyhow." Absence of a presentence report may, however, lead to a higher sentence, which may later influence an expulsion decision.

The Aliens Act provides that minors cannot be expelled as long as they live with their legally resident families. Minors aged sixteen to eighteen who have committed a very serious crime may be transferred to adult court and sentenced to prison. They then run the risk of expulsion, although this can be enforced only after they become eighteen or if the offender does not return to live with his family after serving the sentence. This happens rarely.

Research has examined expulsion of foreigners who were residents for at least five years and what crimes they committed (Groenendijk 1987). There were seventy-four cases of expulsion in 1982 and 1984,

TABLE 13

Nature of Committed Offenses followed by Expulsion, 1982 and 1984

	No. of Offenses
Drug offenses (sometimes combined with firearms offenses)	38
Manslaughter (attempted)	14
Murder	2
Serious assault	2
Theft with violence	5
Rape	3
Arson	3

SOURCE.—Groenendijk (1987), p. 134.

of which sixty-seven could be studied. With the exception of one woman, all were men aged between forty and fifty. More than half had been convicted for a drug offense, the others for offenses of violence (see table 13).

Half were sentenced to unconditional terms of two years or less and one-seventh to more than five years. In only one-third of cases did the records mention reconvictions. Two of three expelled offenders had not been convicted earlier for a similar serious offense. In two-thirds of cases the offender was also declared "undesirable" as an additional measure. This was related to the length of the prison sentence. However, one-third of these declarations were later withdrawn, in particular when offenders had families in Holland. Assistance by a lawyer was quite effective: in 28 percent of cases, assistance led to suspension of the expulsion procedure, and the foreigner could retain residence.

The research looked only at those cases where the decision was to expel the offender. It did not consider cases where the Ministry did *not* suspend legal residence. There is some information on such cases. They appear to be related to length of the prison sentence (under three years) and length of legal residence (over ten years). Offenders married to a Dutch woman were never expelled. In only half the cases was there a presentence report. This is unfortunate because offenders were more often successful in cases where such a report existed than when there was no such report. However, expelled offenders make up only 1 or 2 percent of offenders convicted of serious offenses. Nonetheless, the mere possibility of expulsion results in unequal treatment in the justice system of legally resident foreigners compared with offenders with Dutch nationality.

B. *The Police*

A number of studies have explored the interactions between the police and ethnic minorities. Aalberts and Kamminga (1983) observed that interactions were often strained and that police officers tend to be rude to blacks. An older observation study found that in situations defined by the patrol officers as suspicious, blacks are stopped twice as often as whites (Junger-Tas and van der Zee-Nefkens 1977; Junger-Tas 1978). Other studies explored potential misconceptions due to miscommunication between members of ethnic minorities and police officers. For example, in a social-psychological experiment with 55 percent Dutch and 45 percent Surinamese persons, speech and gaze behaviors during questioning by the police were studied (Vrij and Winkel 1990; Vrij, Winkel, and Koppelaar 1991). Surinamese avoid eye contact more than Dutch men and are less "matter of fact" in expressing themselves. Both can lead to unfavorable reactions by the police. External validity questions can be raised about such experiments in which a property offense is faked, but the real question is not whether the police misinterpreted the speech or behavior of minorities or are prejudiced against minorities. The real question is whether police reports reflect the reality of committed offenses or merely reflect police preconceptions and prejudices.

In my own observation study, I found that differential stop-and-search procedures did not result in greater arrests of minority members compared with Dutch citizens. Other studies reached similar conclusions. An experimental study of a real life situation observed police reactions to an attempt of car theft (Willemse and Meyboom 1978). Sex, race, and tidiness were the independent variables. Although the police were less polite and respectful of minority suspects, arrests were triggered by concrete offending behavior (or attempts), and not by race or looks. A large-scale study in thirteen cities and towns on internal immigration control by the police confirmed these results (Aalberts 1990). Aliens have to carry identity documents, which must be produced when requested by the police. Although there have been complaints by ethnic minorities about these controls, the study concludes that the police mostly exercise their supervising and controlling function evenhandedly when they suspect that a crime has been committed by a minority member.

There is no active internal immigration control, and there are no raids on aliens. The main reason is that Dutch values and norms condemn prejudice and discrimination. Police need to establish good relationships with local communities, and chief constables use their discretion to give internal immigration control little priority. They have put limits on police powers and on coercion that may be used by officers.

Once an offender is detected, the police have several options. In the case of minors, the police may send them home, send them to diversion programs and dismiss the case, or send reports to the prosecutor. There is no evidence that police decisions at this stage of the procedure are influenced by suspects' ethnicity. Van der Hoeven, who found some selectivity in police contacts with minority members, concluded that there was no difference among ethnic groups in police decisions on dismissal or official arrest (van der Hoeven 1986). Veendrick and Jongman (1976) and Junger-Tas (1981) confirmed these findings.

Dutch research illustrates the discrepancy between attitudes and behavior or between verbal and overt behavior. Junger (1990) observes that a police officer on duty is confronted with powerful constraints derived from the police organization, the specific situation in which he finds himself, and the norms of the larger community, all of which oppose racial discrimination. International research also shows that police officers are trained to follow rules and procedures that do not take into account a person's personal characteristics (Reiss and Black 1965; Petersilia 1985).

C. Prosecution

Much research has analyzed sentencing patterns, but first the role of the public prosecutor should be considered. The public prosecutor has three decisions to make: whether the suspect will be held in custody; whether the case will be taken to court; and what sentence to demand. Controlling for the nature of the offense, even foreigners with fixed abode are more often remanded in custody than Dutch suspects, although less often than foreigners without fixed abode.

1. *Pretrial Detention.* Foreign suspects run a higher risk than Dutch offenders of being remanded in custody: in 1977, the risk was twice as great for foreign suspects (27 percent) as for Dutch suspects (13.5 percent) (Berghuis and Tigges 1981). This is often attributed to the higher number of foreigners without a fixed address and the related

risk that they will not appear at trial. A 1978 study showed that 34 percent of foreigner suspects had no fixed address (van der Werff and van der Zee-Nefkens 1978). There are likely two reasons for the pretrial confinement pattern: either foreigners commit more serious offenses than Dutch offenders, or nationality differentially affects the probability of detention. Comparison of offense patterns for Dutch and foreign suspects shows only slight differences, mostly concerning infractions of the opium law. Proportionately more foreign arrestees are charged with drug offenses (12 percent) than are Dutch men (3 percent). They also tend to be somewhat more likely to be involved in violence. However, as these differences cannot explain the high number of pretrial detentions, it must be a question of differential policy.

The more serious the crime, the less the disparity in pretrial detention. The higher the maximum possible penalty, the less the disproportions. Four times as many foreigners as Dutch suspects are held pretrial when the maximum penalty is less than four years; when the maximum is four to six years, this proportion is three times as many, and with a maximum of six to nine years, it is two times as many.

It is in cases that are *not* very serious that the prosecutor decides more frequently on pretrial detention for foreigners than for Dutch offenders. However, there are large differences between courts (see Hood [1992] for England and Wales): in one district the prosecutor imposed pretrial detention in one of twenty-five cases of foreigners, in another, in three of five. This variation may partly be explained by the high numbers of nonresident foreigners in some court districts, such as Amsterdam. In 1977 pretrial detention was imposed on 59 percent of foreign suspects in Amsterdam.

The length of pretrial detention did not differ according to nationality, but, of course, if foreigners are detained for less serious cases than are Dutch suspects, this outcome adds to the inequality in treatment of the two groups.

2. *Dismissal Policy.* Although patterns differ somewhat for different offenses, charges are more likely to be dismissed against Dutch suspects than against minority suspects. Through 1985, charges against minority suspects were more likely to be dismissed, but that pattern reversed after 1985. One old but carefully executed study (van der Werff and van der Zee-Nefkens 1978) looked separately at dismissals and sentences demanded. Comparing judicial records of Dutch men and foreigners in 1974, the authors found higher dismissal rates for foreigners (53 percent vs. 44 percent). The crimes committed by

foreigners had higher maximum penalties, were more often committed with accomplices, more often involved property offenses, and were on average more serious than crimes of Dutch defendants. Moreover, foreign defendants were younger, less often married, more often unemployed, and more often first offenders.

The difference in charges dropped was especially marked among foreigners without fixed addresses (including tourists). Among these a certain number of dismissals were followed by expulsion.

These data must be placed in the context of a general increase in dismissals during the period 1970–85. This was due to a deliberate policy to relieve burdens on the judicial authorities who faced a sudden increase in petty crime. Later research (1976–81) confirmed van der Werff's findings of higher proportions of dismissals among foreigners than among Dutchmen (Frid, Maas, and Stuyling de Lange 1986). However, from 1985 on official policy was to reduce drastically the proportion of dismissals and this led to several changes.

A more recent study using 1985 data examined dismissals for Surinamese/Antilleans and Turkish/Moroccan suspects with fixed addresses (Maas and Stuyling de Lange 1989).[12] For property offenses, differences in the percentage of dismissals are slight, with the exception of simple theft and for public-order offenses, crimes against life, and simple assault. For vandalism, sex offenses, simple theft, hard drugs, and firearms offenses, Dutch suspects are more likely than Surinamese/Antilleans or Turkish/Moroccan suspects to receive dismissals. Controlling for reconvictions did not change this conclusion. Dutch suspects are more often dealt with by use of a "transaction," a fine imposed by the prosecutor, which, if paid, is followed by dropping the charges. This may be related to a higher number of persons pleading not guilty among ethnic minorities: pleading guilty is a precondition to a transaction.

3. *Sentences Demanded by the Prosecution.* Most studies do not examine this part of the process but pass on to the sentencing stage. This may be because the judge tends generally to follow the prosecutor's demand. In the Netherlands, the prosecutor plays a key role in penal proceedings and has a very powerful position. That is why it is of some interest to look at the penalties demanded by prosecutors.

The only relevant study is by van der Werff and van der Zee-

[12] It was impossible to disaggregate the data on Surinamese/Antilleans and Turkish/Moroccans, which is unfortunate because of differences in criminal involvement within these groups.

Nefkens (1978). They found that prosecutors more often demand an unconditional prison sentence for foreigners (58 percent) than in Dutch cases (38 percent), and they demand longer terms.

A stepwise regression analysis was performed including as independent variables *offense variables* (nature and seriousness of the offense, maximum penalty, attempted or completed act, criminal history, circumstances of the act, alcohol or drug use), *person-related variables* (age, nationality, social class, employment), and *process variables* (judicial investigation, pretrial detention, length of remand period, presence of presentence report, time lag between offense and case completion, court district). The nature of the penalty was the dependent variable.

Prosecutors tend more often to demand a prison sentence for defendants who are put on remand, are unemployed, and have committed an offense with a high maximum penalty. Explained variance was 40 percent. Much the greatest variance was explained by the occurrence of pretrial detention, followed by employment situation, and the maximum possible penalty for the offense. Including nationality adds little to the explained variance.

Pretrial detention thus appears to be the strongest predictor. There is some question why this is so. One reason may be that, according to Dutch Penal Law (Article 67a), pretrial detention is not to be ordered if the defendant is *not* likely to be sentenced to prison (i.e., if the offense is not serious enough). Thus prison sentences are likely to be demanded for those already in detention. A second reason may be that prosecutors both request pretrial detention and demand the sentence at trial; they are likely to stick to their original positions with respect to custody. A last explanation concerns prison sentences for young or first offenders. Pretrial detention is sometimes used as a "short sharp shock" punishment. The offender can be locked up immediately and, at trial, time served is transformed into a prison sentence of equal length.

Because most variance in the nature of the sentence is explained by pretrial detention, a second stepwise regression analysis was then conducted, excluding the process variables. This analysis indicated that *nationality* explained most of the variance in the nature of the penalty (total variance = 30 percent). Other factors were the *maximum possible penalty* (the longer the possible prison term, the higher the risk of a prison sentence), the *employment situation* (unemployed defendants face a higher risk of getting a prison sentence), the *value of stolen property* (the higher the value or damage, the higher the risk of prison), the *criminal history* (the longer that history, the higher the risk of prison), and the *age* (the younger the defendant, the more often a prison sentence is demanded). When the analysis is repeated for those who were not remanded in custody, nationality continued to have some effect on the nature of the sentence demanded.

D. Sentencing

Judges tend to accept prosecutors' sentencing demands. In 80 percent of cases, the nature of the sentence is as proposed by the prosecutor (Slotboom et al. 1992). However, the length of the prison sentence corresponds only in half of cases. In general the sentence imposed by the judge is somewhat lighter than the prosecutor demands.

A stepwise regression analysis showed again that pretrial detention explained most (37 percent) of the total variance (47 percent). Eliminating the process variables, *nationality and unemployment* explained most of the variance in the nature of the sentence. And again, if those not remanded are considered separately, nationality plays a reduced role (16 percent of total explained variance).

The length of the unconditional part of the prison sentence does not depend on nationality. This is determined by the maximum authorized penalty, the nature of any violence used, the value of stolen goods, and whether the offense was completed or was an attempt. Thus in this study nationality affects the nature of the sentence but not its length. One explanation for the higher number of prison sentences meted out to foreigners, even to those not remanded in custody, is that more foreigners than Dutch defendants do not appear at the trial. This was the case for 41 percent of the foreigners versus 16 percent of the Dutch in van der Werff's and van der Zee-Nefkens's (1978) study. The apprehension that foreigners will not appear at the trial is also an explanation for the higher number of pretrial detentions imposed on them. A related negative consequence is that once in prison foreigners, compared with Dutch prisoners, are less likely to be placed in (semi-)open penal institutions or given weekend furloughs (Kruyt 1986). Among juveniles, minority juveniles are more often placed in an institution and are less often sentenced to alternative sanctions than Dutch juveniles, controlling for offense type (van der Laan 1988). The proportion of Dutch juveniles to Surinamese was 3:2, while the number of Turkish and Moroccan juveniles so punished was extremely small.

A later study, drawing samples from the years 1971–79 of Dutch,

Surinamese/Antillean, and guest workers,[13] confirmed earlier findings (Timmerman, Bosma, and Jongman 1986). To simplify the analysis, only one offense, simple theft, was selected for comparison, and those who had been remanded in custody were eliminated. Controlling for recidivism, Surinamese first offenders were about four times as often sentenced to prison as Dutch first offenders. For Surinamese reconvicted offenders, this was twice as often. However, with respect to length of sentence or the amount of the fine, Dutch offenders were punished more severely. This was especially true for recidivists; in the case of first offenders there was no difference. Similar outcomes were found in the case of guest workers: first offenders run a higher risk of being sentenced to prison and for longer periods, but in the case of recidivists the Dutch are more severely punished, both in terms of sentence length and in the amount of the fine. Although the study controlled for recidivism, employment, civil status, court district, and nature of sentence, there was no control for appearance at the trial. This is unfortunate because many more Surinamese and guest workers than Dutch offenders do not appear at the trial, and we know that nonappearance leads to more severe sentences.

A more recent secondary analysis of national data examined sentencing patterns of Dutch, Surinamese/Antillean, and Turkish/Moroccan offenders sentenced in 1985 (Maas and Stuyling de Lange 1989). There was a greater proportion of first offenders among ethnic minorities than among Dutch offenders. This might be because minorities have not been residents in Holland for a very long time. Some might have committed crimes in their country of origin, but in most cases that would not be known. A second possibility is that reporting behavior by the public and selective attention by the police might also lead to more first offenders appearing in court.

Differences among ethnic groups in prison sentences are shown in figure 4. Among property offenses, differences are slight. Dutch and Turkish/Moroccan offenders are sentenced equally often to prison; Surinamese offenders somewhat more often. The largest differences involve crimes against life, simple assault, sexual offenses, hard drugs offenses, and firearms offenses. Similar outcomes are found for first offenders, but the differences are more pronounced and are apparent also for theft with violence. Confirming earlier findings, minority first of-

[13] These are persons coming from the nine authorized "recruitment" countries, including Turkey, Morocco, Spain, Italy, Portugal, Yugoslavia, Greece, Tunisia, and the Cape Verdian Isles.

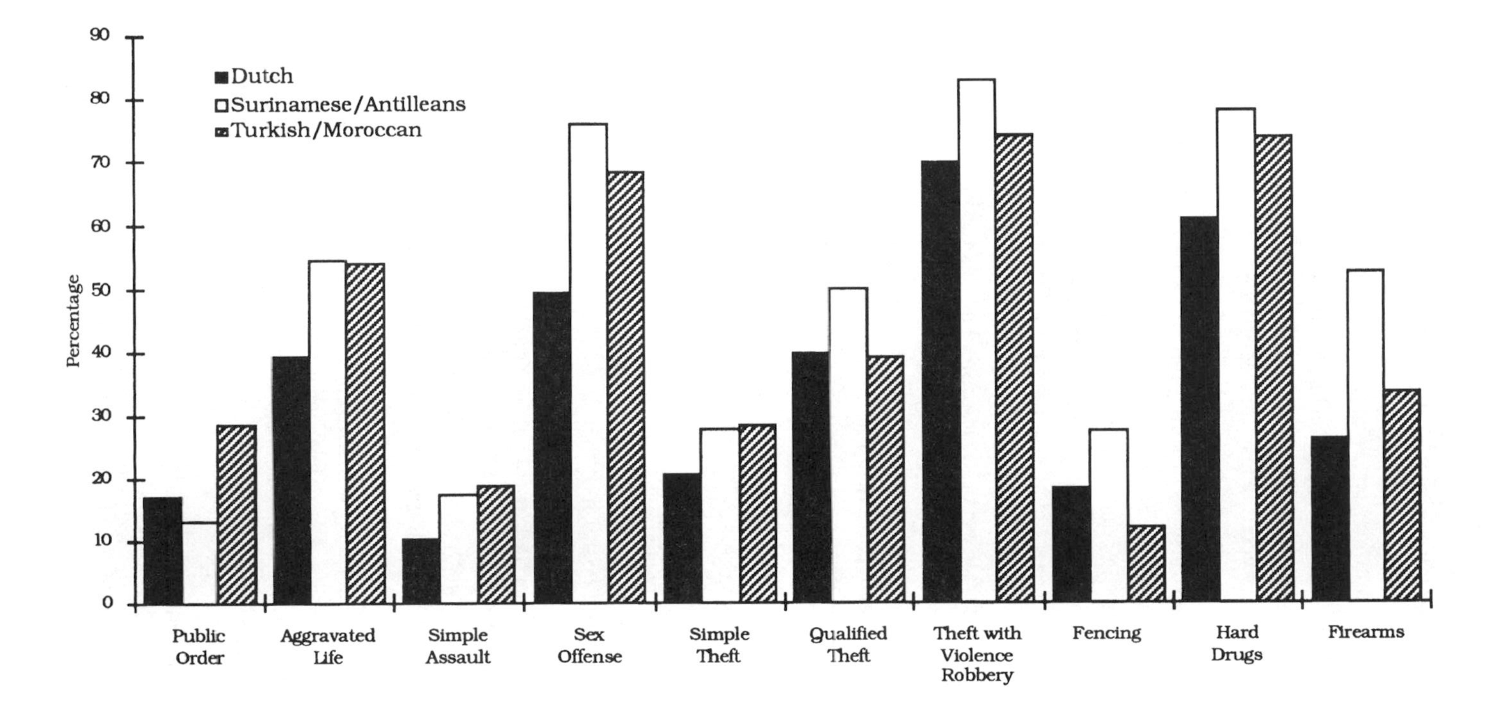

Fig. 4.—Unconditional prison sentences for first offenders according to offense and ethnic origin, 1985, in percent. Source: Maas and Stuyling de Lange (1989).

fenders were more often sentenced to unconditional prison than were Dutch first offenders.

The study just discussed has some shortcomings, most of which the authors acknowledge. First, the ethnic categories are very large, and important differences in criminal involvement may exist between groups, such as between Turkish and Moroccan offenders, that are included in the same category. Second, there may be considerable variation in offense seriousness within offense categories, which has not been taken into account. Third, employment situation, civil status, and nonappearance at the trial, which all affect sentencing, have not been analyzed. Another important missing variable is whether the defendant pled guilty. This variable has an effect on the way cases are dealt with by both prosecutor and judge, a feature also found in the United Kingdom (Hood 1992). However, despite weaknesses in the design of some of the studies and the age of some material, all studies point to more severe punishment—in terms of prison sentences—for members of ethnic minority groups than for Dutch offenders. This appears to result from many factors related to the specific situations of minorities. Minority status in itself seems to be related only weakly to sentencing, although an independent effect remains even when other variables have been controlled for.

IV. Discussion and Conclusions

This essay has two aims: first, to examine the question whether, and to what extent, the position of members of ethnic minorities in the justice system in the Netherlands is any different from that of the indigenous population; second, if this appears to be so, to try to offer some explanations for this situation. In order to investigate those two subjects, other questions had to be looked at, such as differences in criminal involvement, in demographic circumstances, and in socioeconomic participation.

The Netherlands has two main types of immigrants: those from ex-colonies of whom a large majority are Dutch citizens, and foreigners, recruited as unskilled workers, many of whom have become permanent residents. These groups differ in legal status, but their situations are in many respects similar.

The socioeconomic position of ethnic minorities is generally very weak. Most groups had a considerable "culture lag" with respect to the host country: some came from rural or mountainous regions and had very little education when arriving. When guest worker groups arrived, there was full employment and a large market for unskilled labor. Most of the families had no "schooling" tradition, unlike, for example, Jewish and Asian immigrants in the United States and Europe. School achievement is low, although slowly improving, and frequently limited to vocational training. Major drawbacks are language problems and lack of learning skills, which are related to a general lack of verbal interactions and informal instruction by parents in the preschool period, as well as to insufficient additional instruction and support in the school system.

The employment situation is dramatic. This is to a great extent the consequence of the changing labor market. Unskilled work is rapidly disappearing: because of rapid social changes, such jobs have become expensive for employers who replace them with growing computerization. Available jobs require more education as well as adaptability, flexibility, and communication skills, qualities that, according to many employers, many members of minority groups do not possess. Although Dutch unskilled workers also suffer from relatively high unemployment rates, the economic situation hits ethnic minorities much harder, and unemployment among these groups is disproportionately higher.

Related to this are discriminatory attitudes and practices. Public opinion surveys indicate that large sections of the population consider that the presence of minority groups—be it resident migrants or asylum seekers—causes an increase in unemployment, terrorism, and crime. These attitudes were not so common in the 1960s and 1970s but have since spread. Moreover, they have practical consequences as is shown by the unfavorable employment situation of minorities. Research evidence documents both direct and indirect discrimination practices. Jobs are hard to get, but in the case of minorities agencies tend to look only for unskilled jobs, while employers express a preference for Dutch workers on the basis of stereotypes about the productivity of minority workers.

Similar tendencies are found in police behavior. Police officers tend to be less respectful of ethnic minority members. Some groups are susceptible to being stereotyped as potential offenders, which shows in the number of police stops in "suspect" situations. Moreover, the behavior of minority members when interrogated by the police, which is often different from that of indigenous persons in similar situations, is sometimes interpreted as negative and suspect. An important caveat is, however, that official police action is taken on the basis of objective criteria, when there is concrete evidence of a committed or an attempted crime. There is little evidence that stops based on stereotypes often translate into arrests without valid bases. When there is no crime but only vague suspicions based on prejudice, the system cannot, and will not, handle the case. Prejudice and discriminatory attitudes may be more widespread than is expected or desirable, but they are not automatically translated into discriminatory acts.

Police figures and victimization data suggest that some minority groups do commit more and more serious crimes than Dutch offenders. In the case of the Moroccans, Antilleans, and some Surinamese subgroups, this seems to be related to their marginal socioeconomic position in Dutch society. This is shown by a typical minority and immigrant crime, street robbery, a crime typically committed for survival or to sustain a drug habit by persons who do not speak the language and have no marketable skills. More generally, members of some minority groups tend to commit more serious crimes, such as violent crimes and drug offenses.

However, the marginal position of minorities cannot be the only explanation for their higher criminal involvement. Criminal involvement among ethnic groups is strikingly different. Among Surinamese juveniles, for example, Hindustani and Asians have much lower involvement in delinquency than do others. The same seems to be true when Moroccan juveniles are compared with Turkish juveniles. One possible explanation may be found in differential family integration. Tight and supportive families tend to protect against delinquency (Hirschi 1969; Junger-Tas 1988). A second might be differential parental interest and support in making their children pursue secondary and higher education. A third might be group values that emphasize support for group members in social and economic life. For example, there are indications that some groups, such as the Turkish and the Chinese, give considerable (financial) support to group members in their efforts to improve their social and economic position (Werdmölder and Meel 1993).

Members of ethnic minorities are more often victims of crime than the average Dutch population, although it is not clear how much more often. This is related to the cities and the neighborhoods minorities disproportionately live in: poor, high-crime neighborhoods with few resources to combat crime. Moreover, as much offending is intragroup and as there is a relationship between offending and victimization, it is no surprise that high criminal involvement in specific groups goes together with high victimization rates in those same groups.

Finally, the available evidence shows that there is unequal treatment in the criminal justice system. In the case of foreigners this is self-evidently related to the fact of the possibility of expulsion. This possibility has an unfavorable prejudicial effect on pretrial detention, sentencing, and prison regime.

All studies show that minority members are far more often remanded in custody than are Dutch suspects. This does not automatically indicate discrimination but may also be seen as a measure of prevention by the prosecution. Indeed, a greater number of minority than Dutch offenders have no fixed address and a larger percentage do not appear at trial. The result is that minority suspects are detained more frequently and for less serious offenses than are Dutch suspects. When minority offenders commit serious crimes, however, differences in treatment with Dutch serious offenders are considerably smaller.

Minority offenders are also sent more often to prison. This is partly because more of them have been remanded in custody and partly because more plead not guilty; both factors are related to more severe punishment.

The available evidence makes it clear that ethnic minorities and indigenous offenders are treated differently in the criminal justice system. However, the causes are not immediately evident. I think that it is the result of the interplay of different factors. One factor is the special laws and policies to which only minorities are subjected. A second is the higher involvement in crime of some minority groups and that they commit more serious offenses. A third is the counterproductive behavior of many minority members, once they find themselves in the system, which is partly based on ignorance of the Dutch criminal justice system and partly on different cultural values. A fourth is unfavorable generalizing stereotypes held by prosecutors and judges about minorities and their behavior and negative behavior evaluations and expectations. Exactly how these factors are interrelated and how much each contributes is difficult to say and may be disentangled by further research.

My hypothesis is that many of the inequalities noted in this essay are not primarily the result of any conscious discrimination—although this is not to be denied—but are largely the outcome of major drawbacks linked to the position of ethnic minorities as disadvantaged citizens and to specific policies and legislation, such as the Aliens Law.

What can be done? With respect to the socioeconomic situation, the government fears the rise of a growing underclass consisting mainly of ethnic minorities and living in separated ghettos in the large cities. In an effort to improve their position, different measures have been taken.

The legal position of minorities is reinforced by allowing legal residents to vote in local elections. Moreover, in order to encourage integration, the law allows double nationality, which has resulted in an increase in naturalizations of Moroccan and Turkish citizens. In an effort to make employers hire more minorities, parliament has adopted the Act "Stimulation Equal Employment Allochtones," requiring registration of the ethnic origins of employees and the presentation of plans to increase minority employment in organizations. There are pressures to introduce a system of contract compliance. Special budgets are allocated to schools with a large number of minority pupils and programs inspired by the American Head Start programs have been introduced. A considerable budget has been voted by parliament for what is called an "integral security policy" in the large cities, with special attention to minority juveniles and to the drug situation. These are all useful efforts, which ideally should reduce marginalization, improve integration in mainstream society, and reduce criminal involvement. However, to what extent these policies will have the effects sought is uncertain. Much will depend on their implementation.

I am less optimistic about efforts to alter preconceptions and stereotypes. Stereotypes are hard to fight and very resistant to empirical findings that refute them. The media could play a constructive role, and some do, for example, by regularly publishing success stories of minority members who succeed in business, local politics, or parliament. But, of course, this is not the rule. Considering the close parallel between the economic situation and discriminatory attitudes, the best way to end discrimination is economic growth, improved employment possibilities, cultural tolerance from the Dutch population, and educational achievement and cultural emancipation from the side of minorities. This will take considerable time.

Several measures should be taken with respect to the situation of minority offenders in the justice system. First, it remains necessary to educate police officers not only to stick to the facts and not let their personal feelings interfere but also to teach them the clues of social behavior of various groups so they can interpret behavior correctly. Second, even though some laws are effectively prejudicial to minorities, lawyers should be more alert in assisting their minority clients, who should be better informed about the operation of the Dutch criminal justice system so that their behaviors conform to the requirements of the system and the expectations of the judiciary. This might significantly improve their position and positively influence sentencing. Third, to the extent that the discretionary power of the judiciary is great in the Netherlands and the probation service considerably more "control-minded" than it used to be, it should be possible for judges to sentence more minority members than hitherto to community service or intensive probation instead of prison.

Much of what has been suggested above is speculative. A number of fundamental questions remain unanswered. Many policy measures are based on hypotheses or incomplete knowledge. Although evaluation of these measures is imperative, more fundamental research also seems necessary because, without it, real understanding of the causes of success or failure of policy interventions remains difficult.

There is a need for research into the large differences among ethnic groups concerning their involvement in crime and in the criminal justice system. Compared to the indigenous population, some groups commit more crimes and are more frequently involved in criminal justice than might be expected on the basis of their proportion in the population, while other groups have lower involvement and still others show no distinctive pattern. It is an important question to learn both from theoretical and policy perspectives why this is so and what may cause these differences.

Basic questions need answers. What factors can be found in any country that might explain differences in participation in crime and in crime patterns among the ethnic groups living in that country? What factors might explain differential involvement in the criminal justice system? Is it just the crime pattern that explains differential involvement, or do other factors play a role? What factors account for the disparity in treatment at different levels of the criminal justice system of these groups? Finding the answers to these questions will help us a great deal in understanding what measures should be taken to combat crime and to combat decision making that impedes fair and equal justice and perpetuates social inequality.

REFERENCES

Aalberts, M. M. J. 1990. *Politie tussen Discretie en Discriminatie: Operationeel vreemdelingentoezicht in Nederland.* Antwerpen: Kluwer Rechtswetenschappen.

Aalberts, M. M. J., and N. Dijkhoff. 1992. "Illegale vreemdelingen, vreemdelingen bewaring en uitzetting." *Justitiële Verkeningen* 18(9):8–30.

Aalberts, M. M. J., and E. M. Kamminga. 1983. *Politie en Allochtonen.* The Hague: Staatsuitgeverij.

Antilla, I., and R. Jaakkola. 1966. *Unrecorded Criminality in Finland.* Helsinki: Kriminologiness Tutkimuslaitos.

Appel, R. 1992. "Allochtonen hebben beter basisonderwijs nodig." *Samenwijs* 13(3):56–57.

Berghuis, A. C., and L. C. M. Tigges. 1981. "Voorlopige hechtenis bij buitenlanders." *Delikten Delinkwent* 11(4):24–30.

Bowling, B., J. Graham, and A. Ross. 1994. "Self-Reported Offending among Young People in England and Wales." In *Delinquent Behavior among Young People in the Western World,* edited by J. Junger-Tas, G.-J. Terlouw, and Malcolm W. Klein. Amsterdam and New York: Kugler.

Central Bureau of Statistics. 1991. Survey on Social Position and Use of Services. Voorburg: Municipal Registry Office.

———. 1992–93. *Minderheden in Nederland—Statistisch Vademecum.* Voorburg: Centraal Bureau voor de Statistiek.

———. 1995. *Allochtonen in Nederland, 1995.* The Hague: Staatsuitgeverij.

de Haan, W. 1993. *Beroving van voorbijgangers: Rapport van een onderzoek naar straatroof in 1991 in Amsterdam en Utrecht.* The Hague: Ministry of Internal Affairs.

Dekker, P., and P. Ester. 1993. *Social and Political Attitudes in Dutch Society.* Rijswijk: Social and Cultural Planning Office.

Dekker, P., and C. S. van Praag. 1990. *Opvattingen over allochtonen in landen van de Europese Gemeenschap.* Document no. 8. Rijswijk: Sociaal Cultureel Planbureau.

Diederen, H. M. N. 1995. "Onderwijsprestaties van allochtone leerlingen in het Voortgezet Onderwijs." In *Allochtonen in Nederland* by the Central Bureau of Statistics. Voorburg: Central Bureau of Statistics.

Erasmus University, Institute for Socio-Economic Studies. 1991. *Social Position and Use of Services of Autochtones and Allochtones.* Rotterdam: Erasmus University, Institute for Socio-Economic Studies.

Etman, O., P. Mutsaers, and H. Werdmölder. 1993. "Onveiligheid en Allochtonen." In *Integrale Veiligheidsrapportage—Achtergrondstudies.* Report to the Minister of Internal Affairs. The Hague: Ministry of Internal Affairs.

Eurobarometer. 1989. *Racism and Xenophobia.* Brussels: Commission of the European Community.

Frid, A., C. Maas, and J. Stuyling de Lange. 1986. *Allochtonen in ons Strafproces.* Amsterdam: Stichting Onderzoek Recht en Beleid.

Gabor, Th. 1994. "The Suppression of Crime Statistics on Race and Ethnicity: The Price of Political Correctness." *Canadian Journal of Criminology* 36 (April): 153–64.

Geerlof, J., O. Heuneken, M. Samsa, T. Spakens, and M. de Vries. 1993. *Politiemonitor Bevolking—Meting, 1993.* The Hague: Staatsuitgeverij.

Geerlof, J., and R. Schouten. 1991. *Politiemonitor: Landelijke uitkomsten en gestandaardiseerd Bevolkingsonderzoek.* The Hague: Nederlandse Stichting voor de Statistiek.

Gold, M. 1970. *Delinquent Behavior in an American City.* Belmont, Calif.: Brooks-Cole.

Groenendijk, C. A. 1987. "Uitzetting na zeer lang legaal verblijf: Angst, traditie of onwetendheid?" *Nederlands Juristenblad*, no. 42:1341–48.

Halman, L. 1994. "Varieties in Tolerance in Europe: Evidence from the Eurobarometers and European Values Study." *European Journal on Criminal Policy and Research* 2(3):15–39.

Halman, L., and A. Vloet. 1992. *Measuring and Comparing Values in 16 Countries of the Western World in 1990 and 1981.* Tilburg: University of Tilburg.

Hindelang, M., T. Hirschi, and J. Weiss. 1981. *Measuring Delinquency.* Beverly Hills, Calif.: Sage.

Hirschi, Travis. 1969. *Causes of Delinquency.* Berkeley: University of California Press.

Hood, R. 1992. *Race and Sentencing: A Study in the Crown Court.* Oxford: Clarendon Press.

Huizinga, David, and Delbert S. Elliott. 1986. "Reassessing the Reliability and Validity of Self-Report Delinquency Measures." *Journal of Quantitative Criminology* 2:293–327.

Huls, F. W. M. 1995. *Minderheden in Nederland, 1987–1993.* Voorburg: Centraal Bureau voor de Statistiek.

Junger, M. 1990. *Delinquency and Ethnicity: An Investigation on Social Factors relating to Delinquency among Moroccan, Turkish, Surinamese and Dutch Boys.* Deventer and Boston: Kluwer Law & Taxation.

Junger, M., and L. C. Steehouwer. 1990. *Verkeersongevallen bij Kinderen uit Etnische Minderheden.* The Hague: Ministry of Justice, Scientific Research and Documentation Center.

Junger, M., and M. Zeilstra. 1989. *Deviant gedrag en Slachtofferschap onder Jongens uit Etnische Minderheden I.* The Hague: Gouda Quint—Scientific Research and Documentation Center.

Junger-Tas, J. 1976. *Verborgen jeugddelinquentie en gerechtelijke selectie.* Publication no. 38. Brussels: Studiecentrum voor Jeugdmisdadigheid.

———. 1977. "Hidden Delinquency and Judicial Selection in Belgium." In *Youth Crime and Juvenile Justice*, edited by P. C. Friday and V. Lorne Stewart. New York: Praeger.

———. 1978. "Discretie bij het politieoptreden." In *Beslissingsmomenten in het Strafrechtelijk systeem*, edited by Lodewijk Gunther Moor and Ed Leuw. Utrecht: Are Aequi Libri.

———. 1981. *Politiecontacten van minderjarigen en justitiële afdoening.* The Hague: Ministry of Justice, Scientific Research and Documentation Center.

———. 1988. "Causal Factors: Social Control Theory." In *Juvenile Delinquency in the Netherlands*, edited by J. Junger-Tas and Richard L. Block. Amstelveen: Kugler.

Junger-Tas, J., M. W. Klein, and Xiaodong Zhang. 1992. "Problems and Dilemmas in Comparative Self-Report Delinquency Research." In *Offenders and Victims: Theory and Policy*, edited by D. P. Farrington and S. Walklate. London: British Society of Criminology.

Junger-Tas, J., and A. van der Zee-Nefkens. 1977. *Een Observatieonderzoek naar het werk van de Politiesurveillance.* The Hague: Ministry of Justice, Scientific Research and Documentation Center.

Kaufman, W. J., and H. T. Verbraeck. 1986. *Marokkaan en Verslaafd, een studie naar randgroepvorming, heroïnegebruik en criminalisering.* Utrecht: Gemeentelijke diensten, afdeling Onderzoek.

Killias, M., P. Villetaz, and J. Rabasa. 1994. "Self-Reported Juvenile Delinquency in Switzerland." In *Delinquent Behavior among Young People in the Western World,* edited by J. Junger-Tas, G.-J. Terlouw, and Malcolm W. Klein. Amsterdam and New York: Kugler.

Kloek, W. G. 1992. *De positie van Allochtonen op de arbeidmarkt.* Supplement bij de Sociaal-Economische Maandstatistiek. Voorburg: Centraal Bureau voor de Statistiek.

Kruyt, A. 1986. "De vreemdeling in het Strafrecht." *Proces, Maandblad voor Berechting en Reclassering* 65(11):299–306.

Leseman, P. P. M. 1989. *Structurele en Pedagogische determinanten van schoolloopbanen.* Rotterdam: Schooladviesdienst.

Loef, C. J., and P. J. H. M. Holla. 1989. "Straatroof in Amsterdam." *Justitiële Verkenningen* 15(8):92–102.

Maas, C. J., and J. Stuyling de Lange. 1989. "Selectiviteit in de Rechtsgang van buitenlandse verdachten en verdachten behorende tot etnische groepen." *Tijdschrift voor Criminologie,* no. 1:1–14.

Meesters, M., J. Dronkers, and J. Schijf. 1983. "Veranderde onderwijskansen? Een derde voorbeeld en afrondende conclusies." *Mens en Maatschappij* 58(1):5–27.

Meloen, J. D. 1990. "Makkelijker gezegd . . . een onderzoek naar de werking van een gedragscode voor uitzendbureaus ter voorkoming van discriminatie." The Hague: VUGA Publications.

Muus, Ph. J. 1991. *Migration, Minorities and Policy in the Netherlands—Recent Trends and Developments.* Report to the Organization for Economic Cooperation and Development. Amsterdam: University of Amsterdam, Center for Migration Research.

———. 1993. *Migration, Minorities and Policy in the Netherlands—Recent Trends and Developments.* Report to the Organization for Economic Cooperation and Development. Amsterdam: University of Amsterdam, Center for Migration Research.

Naborn, E. M. 1992. *Gezinshereniging—de overkomst van gezinsleden van migranten en Nederlanders.* The Hague: Ministry of Justice, Scientific Research and Documentation Center.

Niesing, W., and J. Veenman. 1990. "Achterstand en Achterstelling op de Arbeidsmarkt." In *Achterstand en Achterstelling bij Allochtonen,* edited by J. Veenman. Rotterdam: Erasmus University, Institute for Sociological and Economic Research.

Penninx, R. 1982. *Migration, Minorities and Policy in the Netherlands: Recent Trends and Developments.* Report to the Organization for Economic Cooperation and Development. The Hague: Ministry of Welfare, Health and Culture.

Petersilia, J. 1985. "Racial Disparities in the Criminal Justice System: A Summary." *Crime and Delinquency* 31:15–34.

Reiss, A. J., and D. J. Black. 1965. *Studies in Crime and Law Enforcement in Major Metropolitan Areas.* Vol. 2. Report for the Presidential Commission on

Law Enforcement and Administration of Justice. Washington, D.C.: World Health Organization.

Research Council for Government Policy. 1979. *Etnische Minderheden: Rapport aan de Regering, 1979.* No. 17. The Hague: Staatsuitgeverij.

Slavin, R. E., and N. E. Madden. 1989. "Effective Classroom Programs for Students at Risk." In *Effective Programs for Students at Risk,* edited by R. E. Slavin, N. L. Karweit, and N. A. Madden. Boston and London: Allyn & Bacon.

Slotboom, A., H. Koppe, I. Passchier, L. de Jonge, and R. Meijer. 1992. "De relatie tussen eis en vonnis: Strafvordering en en straftoemeting in vier arrondissementen" (The relationship between demand and sentence in four court districts). *Justitiële Verkenningen* 8:59–72.

Swart, A. H. J. 1978. *De toelating en uitzetting van vreemdelingen.* Deventer: Kluwer.

Terlouw, G.-J., and G. Bruinsma. 1994. "Self-Reported Delinquency in The Netherlands." In *Delinquent Behavior of Young people in the Western World,* edited by J. Junger-Tas, G.-J. Terlouw, and Malcolm W. Klein. Amsterdam and New York: Kugler.

Terlouw, G.-J, and G. Susanne. 1991. *Criminaliteitspreventie onder Allochtonen: Evaluatie van een project voor Marokkaanse jongeren.* The Hague: Ministry of Justice, Scientific Research and Documentation Center.

Tesser, P. T. M. 1993. *Rapportage Minderheden, 1993.* Rijswijk: Sociaal Cultureel Planbureau.

Timmerman, H., J. Bosma, and R. Jongman. 1986. "Minderheden voor de Rechter." *Tijdschrift voor Criminologie* 2:57–73.

Tuck, M., and P. Southgate. 1981. *Ethnic Minorities, Crime and Policing: A Survey of the Experiences of West-Indians and Whites.* Home Office Research Study no. 70. London: H. M. Stationery Office.

van Amersfoort, J. J. M. 1974. *Immigratie en Minderheidsvorming: Een analyse van de Nederlandse situatie, 1945–1973.* Alphen aan den Rijn: Samson.

van Beek, K. W. H., and B. M. S. van Praag. 1992. *Kiezen uit sollicitanten: Concurrentie tussen werkzoekenden zonder baan.* Wetenschappelijke Raad voor het Regeringsbeleid. The Hague: Staatsuitgeverij.

van den Brekel, H., and H. Moors. 1993. "Opvattingen over Buitenlanders en over Migratiebeleid." *Bevolking en Gezin* 1:1–24.

van der Hoeven, E. 1986. *De Jeugdpolitie: Een observatieonderzoek.* The Hague: Coördinatiecommissie Wetenschappelijk Onderzoek Kinderbescherming.

van der Laan, P. H. 1988. "Innovations in the Dutch Juvenile Justice System." In *Juvenile Delinquency in the Netherlands,* edited by J. Junger-Tas and Richard L. Block. Amsterdam: Kugler.

van der Werff, C., and A. A. van der Zee-Nefkens. 1978. *Strafrechtelijke Vervolging en Bestraffing van Nederlanders en Buitenlanders.* The Hague: Ministry of Justice, Scientific Research and Documentation Center.

van Dijk, J. J. M., and P. Mayhew. 1992. *Criminal Victimization in the Industrialized World: Key Findings of the 1989 and the 1992 International Crime Surveys.* The Hague: Ministry of Justice.

van Dijk, and van Soomeren. 1993. "Slachtofferenquête allochtonen." In *Inte-*

grale Veiligheidsrapportage. Report to the Minister of Internal Affairs. The Hague: Ministry of Internal Affairs.

———. 1994. "Onveiligheid en Allochtonen." In *Integrale Veiligheidsrapportage.* Report to the Minister of Internal Affairs. The Hague: Ministry of Internal Affairs.

van Hulst, H., and J. Bos. 1993. *Criminaliteit van Geïmmigreerde Curaçaose Jongeren.* Utrecht: Onderzoek Kollektief Utrecht.

Veendrick, L. 1976. *Verborgen en geregistreerde criminaliteit in Groningen.* Groningen: Rijksuniversiteit Groningen, Criminologisch Instituut.

Veendrick, L., and R. Jongman. 1976. *Met de Politie op Pad.* Groningen: Rijksuniversiteit Groningen, Criminologisch Instituut.

Vrij, A., and F. W. Winkel. 1990. "Culturele verschillen in spreekstijl van Surinamers en Nederlanders." *Recht der Werkelijkheid* 11(1):3–14.

Vrij, A., F. W. Winkel, and L. Koppelaar. 1991. "Interactie tussen Politiefunctionarissen en Allochtone burgers." *Nederlands Tijdschrift voor de Psychologie* 46(1):8–19.

Werdmölder, H., and Peter Meel. 1993. "Jeugdige Allochtonen en Criminaliteit: Een vergelijkend onderzoek onder Marokkaanse, Turkse, Surinaamse en Antilliaanse jongens." *Tijdschrift voor Criminologie* 35(3):252–77.

Willemse, H. M., and M. L. Meyboom. 1978. "Personal Characteristics of Suspects and Treatment by the Police: A Street Experiment." *Abstracts on Police Science* 6:275–301.

Robert J. Sampson and Janet L. Lauritsen

Racial and Ethnic Disparities in Crime and Criminal Justice in the United States

ABSTRACT

Although racial discrimination emerges some of the time at some stages of criminal justice processing—such as juvenile justice—there is little evidence that racial disparities result from systematic, overt bias. Discrimination appears to be indirect, stemming from the amplification of initial disadvantages over time, along with the social construction of "moral panics" and associated political responses. The "drug war" of the 1980s and 1990s exacerbated the disproportionate representation of blacks in state and federal prisons. Race and ethnic disparities in violent offending and victimization are pronounced and long-standing. Blacks, and to a lesser extent Hispanics, suffer much higher rates of robbery and homicide victimization than do whites. Homicide is the leading cause of death among young black males and females. These differences result in part from social forces that ecologically concentrate race with poverty and other social dislocations. Useful research would emphasize multilevel (contextual) designs, the idea of "cumulative disadvantage" over the life course, the need for multiracial conceptualizations, and comparative, cross-national designs.

Research on race and crime has become a growth industry in the United States. For much of this century, studies have poured forth on racial differences in delinquency, crime, victimization, and, most of all, criminal justice processing. To take but one example, racial differences in sentencing have captured the attention of numerous journal articles,

Robert J. Sampson is professor of sociology at the University of Chicago and research fellow at the American Bar Foundation. Janet L. Lauritsen is associate professor of criminology and criminal justice at the University of Missouri at St. Louis. We thank John Laub, Michael Tonry, and participants in the 1994 Race, Ethnicity, and Criminal Justice conference in Oxford for helpful comments on an earlier draft.

0192-3234/97/0021-0005$01.00

books, meta-analyses, and a panel of the National Academy of Sciences (among others, see reviews in Kleck 1981; Hagan and Bumiller 1983; Petersilia 1985).

The volume of research has not gone hand in hand with dispassionate scholarly debate. The topic of race and crime still rankles, fueling ideologically charged discussions over competing schools of thought such as discrimination versus differential involvement, cultures of violence versus structural inequality, and empiricism versus critical theory. Some argue that bringing empirical data to bear on the race and crime question is itself evidence of racism (MacLean and Milovanovic 1990). It is thus not surprising that, despite the abundance of empirical data, many criminologists are loathe to speak openly on race and crime for fear of being misunderstood or labeled a racist. This situation is not unique, for until recently scholars of urban poverty also consciously avoided forthright discussion of race and social problems in the inner city lest they be accused of blaming the victim (see Wilson 1987, pp. 3–19; Sampson and Wilson 1995).

What, then, does one make of the charge to assess the current state of knowledge on racial-ethnic disparities and discrimination in the justice systems of the United States and of the sources of knowledge from which such conclusions can be drawn? The sheer volume of research makes a review of empirical studies impossible in one essay, and the political climate suggests a no-win substantive outcome as well. In addition, many important questions remain unanswered either because we lack the necessary data or because results are conflicting across alternative forms of measurement. Recognizing these perils, we nonetheless tackle the topic of race, ethnicity, and crime in the United States by focusing on four general questions: What are the key empirical findings on race, ethnicity, and crime? What are the most promising theoretical explanations? What are the major limitations of both research and theory? and Where do we go from here?

Rather than try to review all individual studies, we close in on the "big picture"—that is, the one painted by robust findings that hold up across disparate investigators, forms of data collection, and analytical methods. But empirical generalizations only take us so far (we have yet to hear data speak), so the second question becomes crucial—what theoretical and substantive interpretations can we place on the empirical data? Of course, both the answers to this question and the empirical backdrop of data are subject to numerous pitfalls, and hence question three prompts an inquiry into the limitations of extant knowledge.

Consideration of limitations leads naturally to the final question of future research designs. In probing this issue, we focus on how knowledge might be advanced by using a comparative, international perspective with collaborative research designs.

Our essay addresses these questions in the following way. We start with a discussion of general contextual issues relevant to the United States. For background purposes, Section I describes the racial and ethnic makeup of the U.S. population and the American criminal justice system. Sections II–VI subdivide the empirical morass of U.S. data into several interrelated domains. Section II discusses race, ethnicity, and criminal *victimization* (who becomes victimized by crime?), whereas Section III overviews the literature on race, ethnicity, and criminal *offending* (who commits criminal acts?). The findings presented in these two sections represent the dominant tradition in criminology, which seeks to distinguish individual offenders from nonoffenders and victims from nonvictims. Section IV discusses the community structure of race, ethnicity, and crime in the United States, namely, what are the characteristics of communities that contribute to rates of crime for different race and ethnic groups? The findings from the community literature are compared with evidence on individual differences in criminal involvement, and critical problems in interpretation are discussed.[1] Section V summarizes the findings on racial disparities in the U.S. criminal justice system (e.g., who gets convicted and imprisoned?), and Section VI reviews the various approaches for understanding differential treatment. Finally, Section VII presents our interpretations of the literature on race, crime, and criminal justice and discusses what we believe are the important implications for future research.

Before we begin, it is important to qualify our use of the terms "race" and "ethnicity." In the United States, the term "race" traditionally refers to skin pigmentation or color, whereas ethnicity refers to the countries from which a person's ancestors can be traced. For various historical and social reasons, definitions of race in the United States have referred mainly to categories that are allegedly mutually exclusive—(*a*) white, (*b*) black, (*c*) American Indian, Eskimo, or Aleut, and (*d*) Asian or Pacific Islander. The American conception of eth-

[1] Our review of the empirical evidence on racial differences in victimization and offending, and our theoretical arguments regarding communities, race, and crime, are drawn in large part from two previous papers—Sampson and Lauritsen (1994) and Sampson and Wilson (1995).

nicity differs from that of race in that it is usually reported by subjects themselves (as opposed to visual identification), and it may consist of as many categories as one believes necessary to indicate his or her heritage. Clearly, however, there are ongoing scholarly and political debates that challenge the definitions and usefulness of these terms in U.S. society. For example, it has been argued that the American conception of race is arbitrary insofar as there is no single set of traits that satisfactorily distinguish one group from another. Biological research reminds us that race definitions are socially constructed and reflect the concerns and preoccupations of a particular society (e.g., Hawkins 1995; Marks 1995). Simple classification attempts rooted in biological analogies are also invalidated because many individuals are of mixed races. Furthermore, we sympathize with those who argue that by highlighting race differences in crime and criminal justice sanctioning, such work has the potential to exacerbate problems of institutional racism and stereotyping in the United States.

Yet to acknowledge these points does not undermine the salience of race or ethnicity, however socially constructed, in a given society. There are profound race and ethnic differences in the representation of citizens in the U.S. criminal justice system. It seems to us that knowledge about the origins and consequences of these discrepancies is preferable to ignorance—even as we acknowledge that observed differences between groups are not due to inherent differences in physical traits. We would add that while definitions and records of race and ethnicity differ across countries, the social conception of race has validity and reliability *within* the United States. We are less certain of the validity of the term "ethnicity" since social agreement as to whether someone is, for example, Hispanic or of some other ethnic heritage is likely to be much lower. For our purposes, then, the definition of race imposed by administrative and political structures is an important subject of study in its own right, but it should not be a significant source of error when making cross-group comparisons. The interpretation of ethnic differences (much less available in the data) requires more caution. Other data limitations, not relevant to definitional issues, are discussed when appropriate.

I. The U.S. Context

The Census Bureau currently defines race in five broad categories—"white," "black," "American Indian, Eskimo, or Aleut," "Asian or

Pacific Islander" (further subdivided into ten groups), and "other."[2] Recent data on ethnicity usually focus on whether persons are of "Hispanic" origin. The term Hispanic is meant to define persons of Spanish-speaking origin who may identify themselves as any one of the racial groups. There is great diversity in how Hispanics define themselves racially, and there are perhaps even greater cultural differences between, say, Puerto Ricans and Cubans, as there are between racial groups. Not sharing a common culture, the myriad groups classified as Hispanic thus fail to meet the criteria we typically think of as constituting an ethnic group. For these and other reasons, the construct of Hispanic has been criticized as a political definition that has little meaning (e.g., Mann 1993, pp. 8–12), with many preferring the label "Latino" instead. Similar arguments have been made about the meaning of race categories, namely, that there is more within-group variation (in terms of traditional cultural experiences) than there are differences between race groups.

Though few still hold to the notion of the United States as a "melting pot" of racial and ethnic cultures, there is little doubt that the pot is becoming increasingly diverse. Table 1 presents census data on the resident population of the United States and changes from 1980 to 1990 by race and Hispanic origin. Whites made up 80 percent of the approximately 250,000,000 residents of the U.S. population in 1990. This represents a decline from 83 percent in 1980. Blacks represent 12 percent of the 1990 population, up modestly from 1980. Native American Indians comprise a very small portion of the population—less than 1 percent. However, each of the Chinese, Asian Indian, Korean, and Vietnamese populations increased more than 100 percent over the decade.

The other striking feature of table 1 is the sharp growth in the number of Hispanic Americans—53 percent—to the point where they now make up almost 10 percent of the U.S. population. If the growth rate of more than 50 percent continues into the next century as demographic predictions suggest, Hispanic Americans will represent the

[2] The U.S. Bureau of the Census is likely to change how it measures "race" and "ethnicity" before implementation of the next decennial census. Race and ethnicity are self-identified in the census questionnaires, and many have argued that existing categories do not capture many persons' sense of identity. The most pressing issues involve the classification of multiracial persons and individuals who consider themselves neither "white" nor "black." Whatever the decision of the Bureau of the Census, it will affect the kinds of questions researchers ask and the politics of race in America (e.g., eligibility for federal aid to minorities, minority redistricting for elections).

TABLE 1

Resident Population, by Race and Hispanic Origin: 1980 and 1990 (as of April 1)

Race and Hispanic Origin	*N* (in Thousands)		Change, 1980–90	
	1980	1990	*N* (in Thousands)	Percent
All persons	226,546	248,710	22,164	9.8
Race:				
White	188,372	199,686	11,314	6.0
Black	26,495	29,986	3,491	13.2
American Indian, Eskimo, or Aleut:	1,420	1,959	539	37.9
American Indian	1,364	1,878	514	37.7
Eskimo	42	57	15	35.6
Aleut	14	24	10	67.5
Asian or Pacific Islander:	3,500	7,274	3,773	107.8
Chinese	806	1,645	839	104.1
Filipino	775	1,407	632	81.6
Japanese	701	848	147	20.9
Asian Indian	362	815	454	125.6
Korean	355	799	444	125.3
Vietnamese	262	615	353	134.8
Hawaiian	167	211	44	26.5
Samoan	42	63	21	50.1
Guamanian	32	49	17	53.4
Other Asian or Pacific Islander	N.A.	822	N.A.	N.A.
Other race	6,758	9,805	3,047	45.1
Hispanic origin:				
Of Hispanic origin:	14,609	22,354	7,745	53.0
Mexican	8,740	13,496	4,755	54.4
Puerto Rican	2,014	2,728	714	35.4
Cuban	803	1,044	241	30.0
Other Hispanic	3,051	5,086	2,035	68.7
Not of Hispanic origin	211,937	228,356	14,419	6.8

Source.—U.S. Bureau of the Census (1993), p. 18.
Note.—N.A. = not available. $Z < 0.05\%$.

largest "minority" group. Overall, if the data are reclassified to take account of both race and ethnic identification, the United States is dominated by three race and ethnic groups—non-Hispanic whites (75 percent), non-Hispanic blacks (12 percent), and Hispanics (9 percent). In urban areas where crime rates tend to be highest, non-Hispanic whites no longer represent the majority population in many of the nation's largest cities (e.g., Los Angeles, Chicago, Detroit).

Despite the changing racial and ethnic diversity of U.S. society, in this essay we focus mainly on "black" and "white" comparisons. The reason stems primarily from a lack of data on crime that consistently classifies information for Hispanic and non-Hispanics, and for groups such as Asians and Native Americans. Where available and appropriate, data reflecting these latter classifications is presented (e.g., arrest statistics). Moreover, most analytical work on disparity and discrimination in crime and sanctioning has focused on comparisons between whites and blacks.

Unfortunately, the types of crime covered in this essay's explication of race and ethnic disparities are not fully representative of the landscape of criminal behavior in the United States. For many "white-collar" and "organized" crimes, sound data are hard to come by.[3] Perhaps more crucially, the data that do exist are rarely presented to permit systematic study of race and ethnic variations. Although there is excellent reason to believe that whites are overrepresented in "crimes of the suite," an analysis of this phenomenon is beyond the scope of current efforts. However, a large body of research in the United States on racial and ethnic disparities focuses on "street" or "index" crimes—especially *violence* (e.g., murder, rape, robbery, assault) and *property crime* (e.g., larceny, motor vehicle theft, burglary). Race and ethnic comparisons are usually possible for these offenses, and hence we focus disproportionately on crimes against persons and property.

Of these two general crime types, we give more coverage to violence. As seen below, race and ethnic disparities in both criminal offending and criminal victimization tend to be greatest among violent crimes. With homicide mortality rates now at least eight times higher among young black males than young white males (National Center for Health Statistics 1995, table 6), a sense of public urgency has also emerged regarding a crisis of violence in the black community (DiIulio 1994; Sampson and Wilson 1995). Understanding racial disparities in urban violence is thus a major priority for criminal justice in the United States, and our review reflects this concern. We recognize that by focusing our attention on violence, we are in danger of overemphasizing the importance of race or ethnicity in offending and victimization and underemphasizing its influence on criminal justice decision making. We attempt to compensate for this possible bias by includ-

[3] Corporate crimes are excluded because the "offender" is an institution rather than an individual. In theory, however, one could characterize the race and ethnic composition of corporate decision makers.

ing relevant information on other crime types—particularly drug offending and drug sanctioning, which have attracted much recent concern in the United States (see Blumstein 1993*a;* Tonry 1995).

A further complication is that the justice system in the United States is decidedly complex, making the task of tracking racial disparities even more difficult. It is probably a misnomer to speak of a "system" of criminal justice because some 90 percent of all crimes are prosecuted at state and local levels. With fifty states and separate procedures for juveniles and adults, the United States is characterized by wide variation in local practices, laws, and criminal justice operations. Still, there is a common thread that ties together the way that most criminal cases are processed (see U.S. Department of Justice 1988, p. 56). The bulk of previous research has centered on key decision points in the processing of adults, especially arrest, bail (pretrial release), charging, plea bargaining, conviction, sentencing (e.g., to probation, imprisonment), and postcorrectional release (e.g., parole). Like the social organization of the criminal justice system, data reflecting this process are similarly complex. They run the gamut from local records (e.g., arrest statistics for a city precinct) to national figures published by the U.S. government. Because of this variation, data sources are described below in tandem with the phenomenon under consideration.

II. Race-Ethnicity and Criminal Victimization

What are the risks of victimization to individuals of different racial and ethnic groups? Are these differences stable over recent time periods? Answers to these types of questions have been obtained largely through analyses of National Crime Victimization Survey (NCVS) data. The NCVS (previously known as the National Crime Survey [NCS]) is an ongoing survey conducted by the Bureau of Justice Statistics, designed to measure the extent of personal and household victimization in the United States. Interviews are conducted at six-month intervals with all persons twelve years of age or older living in a sampled household. As many as 150,000 persons in 80,000 households are interviewed on a biannual basis. The major advantage of the NCVS is the ability to estimate victimizations that may be incorrectly reflected in official police data (e.g., because of nonreporting of incidents or arrest bias). The NCVS therefore constitutes the best available data source on the risk of victimization for various population subgroups living in the United States. The exception, naturally, is for homicide, where most estimates are based on vital statistics (e.g., Fingerhut and Kleinman 1990) and the FBI's supplemental homicide reports which provide a racial classification of homicide victims.

Victimization research over the past twenty years has consistently shown that the overall risk of experiencing personal violence (i.e., homicide, rape, robbery, or assault) is much lower than the risk of household victimization (U.S. Department of Justice 1994*a*). For example, the combined risk of suffering a violent victimization by either rape, robbery, *or* assault in 1992 was estimated at approximately 1 in 31, while the risk of household burglary was nearly 1 in 6. However, the major finding for our purposes is that the distribution of victimization varies systematically across different subgroups. In terms of race, both the NCVS and official statistics confirm that blacks are disproportionately the victims of violent crimes (U.S. Department of Justice 1993*a*, 1994*b*). Differences in homicide risk are the most pronounced. According to the U.S. Department of Justice, in 1992 blacks were nearly seven times more likely than whites to become victims of homicide (1993*a*). Similarly, data derived from death certificates (rather than crime reports) and that adjust for differences in the age composition of the two populations show that the 1992 rate of homicide for the black population was 6.5 times that for the white population (National Center for Health Statistics 1995).

Estimates of homicide risk over the life span further underscore racial disparities. By 1990, black women and black men were, respectively, four and six times more likely than white women and white men to be murdered in their lifetime (Reiss and Roth 1993, p. 63). The leading cause of death among black males and black females ages fifteen to twenty-four is homicide (National Center for Health Statistics 1995). These differentials help explain estimates that a resident of rural Bangladesh has a greater chance of surviving to age forty than does a black male in Harlem (McCord and Freeman 1990).

Estimates of lifetime homicide risk for American Indians, blacks, and whites are presented in Reiss and Roth (1993, pp. 62–63). The lifetime risk for black males is 4.16 per 100, followed by Native Indian males (1.75), black females (1.02), white males (.62), Native Indian females (.46), and white females (.26). Thus Native Indian males' risk falls approximately halfway between that of black and white males. Reiss and Roth also note that less than one-fourth of Americans' lifetime risk for homicide is incurred before the twenty-fifth birthday. Consequently,

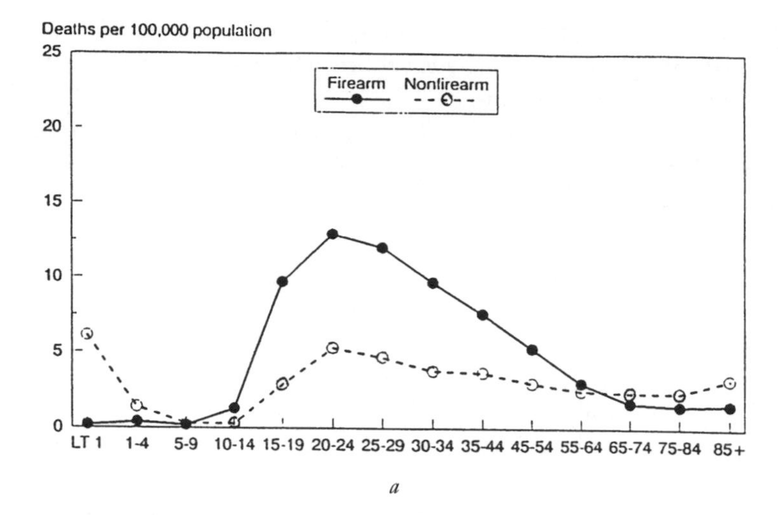

a

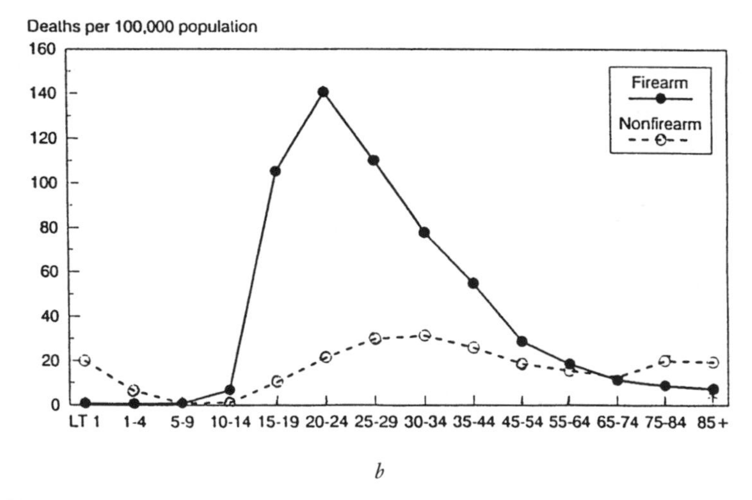

b

Fig. 1.—Homicide among males by firearm status in the United States. *a*, Among white males. *b*, Among black males. Source: Fingerhut (1993), pp. 16–17.

the very high homicide rates among young black males in particular must be considered in conjunction with the higher homicide rates of black males at all ages.

Racial disparities for gun-related homicide victimization are particularly striking. Figure 1 displays the age-specific 1990 U.S. death rate by firearms for white males and black males according to mortality reports from vital statistics (Fingerhut 1993). Note that the peak death rate for young black males (140 per 100,000) is more than ten times greater than the peak death rate for young white males (twelve per 100,000). Given the nature of death reports, these differentials in victimization cannot reasonably be attributed to bias in official reaction by the criminal justice system.

As with homicide, blacks report greater levels of robbery victimization than do whites (U.S. Department of Justice 1994*a*). Over the past twenty years, blacks' risk of robbery has been between two and three times greater than that of whites. While the risk of robbery among whites has slightly declined over the last two decades, the risk among blacks fluctuates more from year to year and shows no clear evidence of decline.

Unlike homicide and robbery, rates of assault victimization for blacks and whites have not differed consistently over the last twenty years, although the majority of assault victimizations reported by blacks tend to be incidents of aggravated assault, whereas simple assaults predominate among whites (U.S. Department of Justice 1994*a*). The lack of race differences in assaults overall may be the result of differences in reporting. Specifically, it has been hypothesized that blacks may underreport less serious forms of assault and that whites may overreport minor assaults (Skogan 1981; Gottfredson 1986).

Race differentials in victimization risk decline significantly for personal theft (larceny with or without contact) and crimes against property. The personal theft victimization rate is very similar, at fifty-nine per 1,000 for blacks and sixty per 1,000 for whites (U.S. Department of Justice 1994*b*). However, rates of household victimization (burglary, larceny, and motor vehicle theft) are consistently higher for blacks than for whites. For example, the burglary victimization rate per 1,000 households is sixty-eight for blacks and forty-six for whites (U.S. Department of Justice 1994*b*). Compared over time, *trends* in property victimization reveal similar patterns by race. Since about 1980, both whites and blacks have experienced general declines in personal theft and household victimization.

For violence, however, both rate and trend differences by race are substantial. Beginning about 1990, reported rates of violence among blacks increased to their highest level ever recorded in the NCVS. This trend parallels the trajectory of homicides measured by death records—increases in homicide rates since the mid- to late 1980s in the United States have been racially selective. For example, while white rates remained relatively stable, the firearms death rate among young black males more than doubled from 1984 to 1988 alone (see Fingerhut et al. 1991).[4]

In short, the available race-specific data on victimization suggest a fairly straightforward pattern. Blacks suffer much higher rates of personal violence and homicide victimization than do whites. Racial differences are reduced considerably in magnitude when it comes to household crimes and especially personal theft victimizations. And while overall victimization trends are similar for blacks and whites, robbery and homicide are the two notable exceptions. Recent trends for these two violent crimes show greater increases for blacks than whites.

The NCVS provides only limited information on ethnic differences in victimization risk, restricted mainly to Hispanic versus non-Hispanic comparisons. According to the NCVS, Hispanics experience higher rates of violent and household victimization than non-Hispanics (39.6 vs. 35.3, and 265.6 vs. 204.5, respectively). Conversely, non-Hispanics report higher rates of personal theft (80.3) than Hispanics (74.9) (U.S. Department of Justice 1990). Government vital statistics on mortality provide another source of comparison, as they report the cause of death for Hispanics and non-Hispanic whites. As is true for blacks, the leading cause of death among Hispanics aged 15–24 is homicide (National Center for Health Statistics 1995).

Recall that in the United States race and ethnicity are not mutually exclusive categories. Because Hispanics may be designated as either black or white (or "other"), compositional effects may account for the higher NCVS victimization rates of Hispanics than of non-Hispanics. Since NCVS summary reports do not present differences between non-Hispanic whites, non-Hispanic blacks, and Hispanics, it is difficult to know precisely to what degree these subgroups differ in their risks of victimization. Similarly, vital statistics do not provide homicide rates for Hispanics because population estimates by race-ethnicity remain uncertain.

The primary explanation of the race-victimization connection in violence stems from "lifestyle" (Hindelang, Gottfredson, and Garofalo 1978; Garofalo 1987) and "routine activity" (Cohen and Felson 1979) theories of victimization. The essential proposition of lifestyle-routine activity theories is that the convergence in time and space of suitable targets and the absence of capable guardians leads to increases in crime independent of the structural and cultural conditions that may moti-

[4] The most recent data indicate that the overall age-adjusted firearm death rates declined slightly between 1991 and 1992 (National Center for Health Statistics 1995, table 19).

vate individuals to engage in crime (e.g., poverty, unemployment, subcultural values). Derived from this general proposition, the "principle of homogamy" in lifestyle theory states that persons are more likely to be victimized when they disproportionately associate with, or come into contact with, members of demographic groups that contain a disproportionate share of offenders (Hindelang, Gottfredson, and Garofalo 1978, pp. 256–57).

According to this explanation, blacks suffer a higher risk of violent victimization than do whites because they are more likely to associate with other blacks who are themselves disproportionately involved in violence. In other words, race-shaped lifestyle factors such as friendship patterns and leisure activities account for higher levels of risk. Similarly, the "proximity" hypothesis posits that ecological propinquity to the residences of high-rate offender groups will increase one's risk of victimization. The theoretical implication here is that blacks are segregated from whites and live in closer proximity to other blacks who commit crimes at higher rates than whites. As discussed below, the veracity of the differential offending claim has been challenged; however, the key point is that homogamy of personal associations and proximity to offender groups are the leading hypotheses for the race differentials in victimization risk.

The limitations of lifestyle-routine activities theory and research have been discussed at length elsewhere (for overviews, see Gottfredson 1986; Garofalo 1987; Meier and Miethe 1993; Sampson and Lauritsen 1994). The most common criticism of empirical research has been the inadequate measurement of explanatory variables—direct measures of lifestyle activities and proximity to offender populations are not usually included in models containing social and demographic characteristics. In particular, most research on race differences in risk has not been able to distinguish between individual-level interpretations (such as lifestyle and friendship choices) and contextual explanations (such as proximity to offender groups resulting from housing segregation patterns). Clearly, this is an important issue to resolve.

Subcultural explanations have also been used to explain higher rates of victimization, especially violence, among various subgroups (e.g., Wolfgang 1958; Wolfgang and Ferracuti 1967; Singer 1981). The subculture of violence thesis argues that certain subgroups share norms conducive to the use of violence for resolving disputes, thereby generating subgroup differences in victimization. However, this hypothesis has not been empirically validated with respect to race. As discussed more below, key methodological difficulties need to be resolved before it can be determined whether differences in normative contexts account for racial differences in violent victimization (see e.g., Kornhauser 1978; Hawley and Messner 1989).

III. Race-Ethnicity and Criminal Offending

Prior research on the correlates of criminal offending has extensively reviewed the methodological issues that limit the validity of findings (see e.g., Hindelang 1978; Hindelang, Hirschi, and Weis 1979; Elliott and Ageton 1980), and therefore we mention only a few of these qualifications here. A primary concern is the source of data on offending—whether the findings are based on official, self-report, or victimization data. Findings based on official data such as arrest statistics published by the FBI's Uniform Crime Reports (UCR) are limited to the extent that apprehended offenders differ in some way from nonapprehended offenders (e.g., because of racial bias). They are also limited in that persons who are arrested more than once in any year are overrepresented in arrest statistics. Findings based on self-report surveys may be limited by either the respondents' intentional or unintentional errors in reporting or by sampling restrictions (e.g., an almost exclusive focus on juveniles or males, or on minor offenses).

Although NCVS victimization data provide information on the *perceived* race of offenders, estimates are available only for those incidents involving a single or lone offender, and where there is face-to-face contact between the offender and victim.[5] Thus this restriction excludes race-specific data on crimes committed by two or more offenders, or by groups (such as gangs). It is also the case that victims of personal crimes have been found to underreport certain types of incidents, especially those involving victimizations by family members and acquaintances (Hindelang 1978). These sources of error are all relevant to inferences about race and crime. Consequently, we emphasize convergent findings across various data sources.

A. Arrest Data

Because nationwide arrest reports are available by race but not by ethnicity, we focus on the most recent race-specific arrest data by of-

[5] The NCVS distinguishes between "lone"-offender and "multiple"-offender incidents. Multiple-offender incidents are crimes involving more than one offender per incident. Approximately three-fourths of violent crimes in the United States are committed by lone offenders (see Reiss and Roth 1993, p. 75).

fense type. Presented in table 2, these 1993 data suggest that race is related to criminal offending (see also Maguire and Pastore 1995, table 4.11). Although whites are arrested for the majority of all crimes (approximately 67 percent), blacks and American Indians are most likely to be overrepresented in arrests reported in the UCR. For example, in 1993 blacks comprised 31 percent of total arrests yet constituted 12 percent of the population, and American Indians comprised 1.1 percent of total arrests while constituting .8 percent of the population. Asians, however, appear to be underrepresented in arrest statistics. Note that Asians account for 1.0 percent of all arrests, yet make up 2.9 percent of the population.

The relationship between race and offending is not the same for all crime types; there are certain offenses for which each is overrepresented. For instance, whites are disproportionately arrested for driving while intoxicated, and Asians are over-represented in arrests for illegal gambling. Blacks are consistently more likely to be arrested for crimes of violence (Hindelang 1978; Elliott and Ageton 1980; Bridges and Weis 1989; U.S. Department of Justice 1993*b*). In 1993, blacks accounted for 45 percent and 50 percent of adult and youth arrestees, respectively, for murder, rape, robbery, and aggravated assault (Maguire and Pastore 1995, pp. 389–90). The crime in which blacks are most overrepresented is robbery (for a fascinating albeit controversial discussion, see Katz 1988), comprising 62 percent of arrestees in 1993. In general, blacks are approximately six times more likely to be arrested for violent crimes than are whites (U.S. Department of Justice 1993*b*).

Overall trends in index-crime arrest rates for the last twenty-five years show a fluctuating pattern, peaking in the early 1990s for adults and in the mid-1970s and early 1990s for juveniles (U.S. Department of Justice 1993*b*).[6] When race-specific trends in these crimes are compared, black and white differences in rates of offending have decreased somewhat over time. For example, in 1965, black juveniles' and adults' arrest rates were 3.1 and 5.7 times that of white juveniles and adults. By 1992, black-white differences in index crime arrest rates had dropped to 2.3 and 4.9 (U.S. Department of Justice 1993*b*). With respect to violence, murder arrest rates for juveniles also increased in a

[6] Index offenses include murder, rape, robbery, aggravated assault, burglary, larceny theft, motor vehicle theft, and arson. However, arson has only recently been added to the classification.

TABLE 2

Breakdown by Offense Charged, Age Group, and Race, United States, 1993 (10,509 Agencies; 1993 Estimated Population = 213,093,000)

Offense Charged	Percent			
	White	Black	American Indian or Alaskan Native	Asian or Pacific Islander
Total	66.9	31.1	1.1	1.0
Murder and nonnegligent manslaughter	40.7	57.6	.6	1.1
Forcible rape	56.9	41.3	1.0	.8
Robbery	36.5	62.1	.4	1.0
Aggravated assault	58.4	39.8	.9	1.0
Burglary	67.2	30.9	.9	1.0
Larceny theft	64.6	33.0	1.0	1.4
Motor vehicle theft	57.1	40.3	.9	1.7
Arson	74.6	23.5	.9	.9
Violent crime	52.6	45.7	.8	1.0
Property crime	64.4	33.2	1.0	1.4
Total crime index	61.3	36.5	.9	1.3
Other assaults	62.9	34.9	1.2	1.0
Forgery and counterfeiting	63.0	35.4	.6	1.0
Fraud	62.3	36.6	.5	.7
Embezzlement	67.4	31.0	.4	1.2
Stolen property; buying, receiving, possessing	56.1	42.3	.6	1.1
Vandalism	74.8	22.9	1.1	1.2
Weapons; carrying, possessing, etc.	55.4	43.0	.5	1.1
Prostitution and commercialized vice	62.0	35.9	.6	1.5
Sex offenses (except forcible rape and prostitution)	77.0	20.9	1.0	1.1
Drug abuse violations	59.8	39.3	.4	.5
Gambling	48.2	46.9	.4	4.6
Offenses against family and children	65.6	31.2	1.3	2.0
Driving under the influence	87.2	10.6	1.3	.9
Liquor laws	84.5	12.6	2.3	.6
Drunkenness	79.7	17.8	2.1	.3
Disorderly conduct	64.6	33.6	1.3	.5
Vagrancy	56.6	41.2	1.9	.4
All other offenses (except traffic)	62.6	35.5	1.0	.9
Suspicion	46.9	52.0	.6	.5
Curfew and loitering law violations	78.8	18.1	1.1	2.0
Runaways	78.1	17.2	1.3	3.4

Source.—Maguire and Pastore (1995), p. 388.

Note.—Percents sum to 100.0 for each row.

similar pattern for both blacks and whites in the period 1985–90 (Blumstein 1995, p. 8).

An important exception to these time trends is drug-related arrests. From 1965 through the early 1980s, blacks were approximately twice as likely as whites to be arrested for drug-related offenses (Blumstein 1993*a;* Tonry 1995). Following the federal government's initiation of the "war on drugs," black arrest rates skyrocketed, while white arrest rates increased only slightly. By the end of the 1980s, blacks were more than five times more likely than whites to be arrested for drug-related offenses. It is highly unlikely that these race differences represent general substance use patterns since drug arrests grew at a time when national self-report data showed that drug use was declining among both blacks and whites. Rather, these differences reflect the government's targeting and enforcement of specific types of drug use and trafficking (Blumstein 1993*a;* Tonry 1995).

B. Victimization-Based Estimates

The data presented thus far focus on "offending" as measured by official statistics on arrests. The obvious critique, long voiced in U.S. criminology, is that police decisions to arrest are biased. According to conflict theory, the police believe that blacks—especially low-income blacks—commit more crimes and therefore more often take action to arrest them. The general stereotype of blacks as "disreputable" and "dangerous" (Irwin 1985) thus leads the police to watch and arrest minorities more frequently than warranted based on actual criminal behavior (for further elaboration, see Sampson 1986).

In an important investigation, Hindelang (1978) disentangled the extent to which black overrepresentation in official violent crime data was explained by differential involvement or by differential selection into the criminal justice system via arrests by police. In comparing the distribution of arrestees by race from the 1974 UCR to the distribution of perceived race of offenders derived from the 1974 NCS,[7] he found some evidence for the differential selection hypothesis with respect to assault and rape. Overall, however, reports by victims suggest that most of the race difference found in arrest rates for violence is explained by greater black involvement in personal crimes, especially robbery. In 1974, both the NCS and UCR estimated that 62 percent of offenders committing robbery were black.

[7] Recall that the NCS data are restricted to those victim-reported incidents consisting of a lone-offender and face-to-face contact between the victim and the offender.

Data for violent crimes as reported in the 1992 NCVS and 1992 UCR arrest data show much the same pattern as reported earlier by Hindelang (1978). However, there is a slightly larger discrepancy between the two estimates of racial involvement (see table 2 and U.S. Department of Justice 1994*b*, table 45). For instance, the NCVS estimate of black involvement in robbery in 1992 is 56 percent, whereas the UCR data report that 61 percent of robbery arrestees were black. These differences between UCR and NCVS data do not necessarily indicate increasing selection bias in robbery arrests over time. If black robbery offending is more likely to involve two or more offenders now compared to twenty years ago, such changes would differentially influence the estimates of the percentage black involvement in UCR and NCVS data.

The limitations of using NCVS victim reports to validate UCR arrest data have been discussed elsewhere (e.g., Hindelang 1981; Reiss and Roth 1993; Sampson and Lauritsen 1994), including the concern that race estimates are based solely on NCVS victim reports of lone-offender crimes and that the NCVS data produce incidence rates instead of prevalence rates. The problem of relying on NCVS incidence rates is important to the extent that each racial subgroup contains different proportions of repeat offenders. The UCR data share a similar limitation in that they use arrest incidents as the unit of analysis (and not offenders). The potential inaccuracy of victims' reports of an offender's race in the NCVS data is also a concern, but it is not considered to be a serious limitation. Hindelang (1981), for example, compared NCS rape victims' reports of their offender's age and race to police reports of the offender's demographic characteristics and found substantial agreement. Victims' reports of race agreed with police reports in over 96 percent of the cases. These findings are not definitive, however, because arrests are usually made on the basis of victims' descriptions of offenders.

Since blacks are at greater risk for violent victimization and are disproportionately involved in violent offending, it may not be surprising that the majority of violent crimes are disproportionately *intraracial* (see Sampson and Lauritsen 1994 for reviews). For example, whites tend to assault other whites and blacks tend to assault other blacks more so than expected, based on chance encounters (Sampson 1984; O'Brien 1987). Racial cross-over is especially rare in nonfelony homicides—that is, killings that occur without an accompanying felony such as a robbery or rape (Cook 1987). Because nonfelony homicides tend to be nonstranger homicides, and the routine activities and residences of blacks and whites are in large part segregated, these findings are to be expected. However, felony homicides (e.g., robbery-murders) are more likely to be interracial than are nonfelony homicides because they typically involve strangers (Block 1985; Cook 1987). In felony homicides, as in robberies, black offenders are more likely to victimize whites than white offenders are to victimize blacks (Wilbanks 1985). Yet this is still what we should expect because blacks are the smaller group and have more chances to interact with whites. Variations in the relative sizes of the black and white populations thus explain the patterning of interracial violence (see Sampson 1984; O'Brien 1987; Reiss and Roth 1993).

As noted earlier, it is impossible to validate race differences in certain kinds of crimes reported in UCR arrest data with NCVS victim reports. Common crimes such as burglaries and larcenies do not often result in victim-offender interaction, and therefore validation with NCVS data is not feasible. For these types of crimes, then, we must be less certain of race and ethnic differentials.

C. *Self-Reported Offending*

In an attempt to overcome the limitations of both official statistics and victimization surveys, self-reported delinquency data have been brought to bear on the race question. Many studies, especially those in the 1960s and 1970s, found little or no differences in self-reported offending among juveniles of different racial and ethnic groups (see Hindelang, Hirschi, and Weis 1979, 1981). One reaction to these findings was to attribute racial bias to official statistics. Others posited methodological explanations. In particular, Hindelang, Hirschi, and Weis (1979) argued that self-report studies typically measure less serious forms of common delinquency, whereas official arrest statistics showing race differentials refer primarily to serious index crimes. Nationally representative self-report data on serious offense involvement for adults are rare, and cross-method validation has not been completed (Elliott 1994). Consequently, the evidence to date suggests that the domains of behavior are not isomorphic across data sources.

Another critique, in many ways more powerful, is that the self-report method itself is differentially valid by race, with blacks underreporting certain offenses at higher rates than whites. In a reverse record check analysis, Hindelang, Hirschi, and Weis found that black males were least likely to self-report offenses recorded by the police (e.g., 33 percent of total offenses known and 57 percent of serious offenses known to police were not self-reported by black males; Hindelang, Hirschi, and Weis 1981, p. 172). Hence the issue of differential validity according to race is of concern even when the behavior elicited by the self-report method is a serious offense such as burglary, robbery, or weapons violation.[8]

Advances in self-report methodology have resolved some of these issues. For example, Elliott and Ageton (1980) have shown that police and self-report differences in the relationships between race and offense involvement are to a large extent a function of delinquency instrument construction, especially item content and response set range. Using nationally representative data, they found self-reported race (and class) differences in delinquency at the high end of the frequency continuum and for serious offenses like robbery where police contacts are more likely (see also Elliott 1994). Consequently, the magnitude of the race-crime correlation is higher in official statistics than in self-reported data. While limitations exist for both official and self-report data, it thus appears that race differences in offending as recorded in arrest reports and victimization surveys "reflect real differences in the frequency and seriousness of delinquent acts" (Elliott and Ageton 1980, p. 107).

D. *Explaining Racial Disparities in Offending*

Few criminological theories have been designed "a priori" to explain racial differences in official, victimization, or self-report data. Rather, most theories have been applied "post hoc" to race-related differences, not just for offending but victimization as well. In this regard, it is of theoretical relevance that offenders and victims share a similar demographic profile—especially for violence. Both violent offenders and victims of violent crime tend to be young, male, black, and live in urban areas (see Hindelang, Gottfredson, and Garofalo 1978; Gottfredson 1986). Subcultural perspectives even suggest that victims and offenders are often the same people (Wolfgang 1958; Singer 1981). Lifestyle-routine activity theory also tries to explain the overlap among victims and offenders. For example, in analyses of panel data, Laurit-

[8] Interestingly, differential validity of self-reported delinquency has also been found in other countries, with some national minorities underreporting known offenses (Junger 1989).

sen, Sampson, and Laub (1991) found that delinquency involvement made independent contributions to victimization risk among adolescents and that increases in victimization, in turn, increased subsequent offending. This pattern, often neglected by criminological theory, suggests that an explanation of offending may go a long way toward explaining racial differences in victimization as well. Nevertheless, most thinking on race and crime focuses on the causes of offending differentials.

There are numerous ways to categorize the many theories devoted to explaining variations in crime. Some of the most common hypotheses used in attempts to explain individual-level race differences in offending are based on constitutional, family socialization, the subculture of violence, and economic inequality/deprivation theories (Wilson and Herrnstein 1985). As most criminologists are aware, constitutional theories are least popular. The idea that IQ, temperament, and other individual characteristics explain the race-crime connection is anathema to many on political and policy grounds. But there are better reasons to reject the constitutional argument—empirical invalidity. Even Wilson and Herrnstein, sympathetic in general to constitutional explanations, largely dismiss them as providing little insight on racial disparities. The reason is simple; there are more variations *within* any race or ethnic group than *between* them. As noted earlier, "race" is socially constructed, and the explanation of apparent differences is linked to the fact that race is serving as a proxy for some other set of variables.

A second explanation of race differences in crime is that the family socialization of black children is somehow inadequate. Culture of poverty and lower-class culture theories assert that inadequate socialization can be traced to the female-headed family structure more commonly found among blacks than whites (e.g., Miller 1958), while structurally oriented theories assert that differences in child socialization practices are the consequence of economic deprivation (Kornhauser 1978). Although there is good evidence that family socialization influences children's delinquency and aggressive behavior patterns (e.g., Loeber and Stouthamer-Loeber 1986), there is no consistent evidence that factors such as lack of supervision and erratic or harsh discipline account for race differences in crime net of socioeconomic conditions.

Deviant subcultures have also been proposed to account for group differences in crime. These perspectives vary in details but in general claim that blacks are more likely to commit offenses because they are socialized into a culture in which crime, aggressive behaviors, and illegitimate activities are not strongly condemned. The most influential of these perspectives is the subculture of violence thesis (Wolfgang and Ferracuti 1967) which argues that in certain areas and for certain subgroups (i.e., blacks), there is a subcultural value system that supports the use of violence and other behaviors (e.g., sexual machismo) not emphasized in the dominant culture (Curtis 1975). In addition to the methodological difficulties noted earlier, one of the primary weaknesses in the subculture of violence literature has been the problem of tautology—that is, violent behaviors are used to infer the existence of a subcultural system, which in turn is used to explain behavior. There is little evidence from social surveys that black and white Americans differ significantly in their attitudes and values toward crime (Kornhauser 1978; DiIulio 1995).[9] In addition, empirical support for subcultural explanations requires finding that the normative context of different groups has an influence on behavior independent of structural differences (Kornhauser 1978). Consequently, the role of subcultural value systems in producing race differences in crime remains to be demonstrated.

Finally, racial differences in offending have been attributed to group differences in economic opportunities and success. For example, strain theories argue that individuals who aspire to cultural goals such as wealth, but lack access to the legitimate means for achieving those goals, are most strongly motivated to use illegitimate means for success (see Merton 1938; Blau and Blau 1982). In such theories, race is expected to be related to offending differences insofar as it serves as a proxy variable for access to legitimate means of success. Yet at the individual level, economic strain theories have not fared well empirically—race differences persist even after controlling for socioeconomic status (Kornhauser 1978). Relatedly, other race, ethnic, and immigrant groups, such as Chinese, Japanese, and Hispanic, have also experienced economic exclusion but exhibit offending rates much lower than those of African Americans. It is unknown to what extent structural or cultural differences account for lower offending rates among other ethnic

[9] Attitudes toward criminal justice issues, however, do differ between blacks and whites. For example, data from the National Opinion Research Center's General Social Surveys show that blacks have been less likely than whites to support the use of capital punishment and are more likely to favor handgun restrictions. Racial divisions in attitudes about criminal justice have become even sharper in the wake of the Rodney King beating and the O. J. Simpson trial.

groups, but clearly socioeconomic status and deprivation alone are inadequate explanations (Wilson and Herrnstein 1985).

Unfortunately then, traditional theories do not seem to have gotten us very far in unraveling race differences. For this reason, recent scholars have begun to look at the macro- and community-level underpinnings of the race-crime connection. Because of its potential importance and the surge in recent research, we discuss the community context of crime in some detail.

IV. The Community Structure of Race and Crime

Unlike the dominant tradition in criminology that seeks to distinguish offenders from nonoffenders, the macrosocial or community level of explanation asks what it is about community structures and cultures that produce differential *rates* of crime. As such, the goal of macrolevel research is not to explain individual involvement in criminal behavior but to isolate characteristics of communities, cities, or even societies that lead to high rates of criminality. From this viewpoint the "ecological fallacy"—inferring individual-level relations based on aggregate data—is not at issue because the unit of explanation and analysis is the community.

The Chicago-school research of Shaw and McKay spearheaded the community-level approach of American studies of ecology and crime. In their classic work, *Juvenile Delinquency and Urban Areas*, Shaw and McKay (1969 [1942]) argued that three structural factors—low economic status, racial or ethnic heterogeneity, and residential mobility—led to the disruption of local community social organization, which in turn accounted for variations in crime and delinquency rates. Subsequent research has generally supported these findings, although most research on violence has examined racial composition—usually percent black—rather than racial heterogeneity per se. Also, while descriptive data show that percentage black is positively and strongly correlated with rates of violence, multivariate research has yielded conflicting findings. Namely, some studies report a sharply attenuated effect of race once other factors are controlled, whereas others report that the percent black effect remains strong (Sampson and Lauritsen 1994, pp. 53–54).

Whether or not race has a direct effect on crime rates, Sampson and Wilson (1995) argue that a major key to solving the race-crime conundrum is traceable to Shaw and McKay (1969 [1942]). Arguably, the most significant aspect of Shaw and McKay's research was their demonstration that high rates of delinquency persisted in certain areas over many years, regardless of population turnover (but see Bursik and Webb 1982). This finding, more than any other, led them to reject individual-level explanations of delinquency and focus instead on the processes by which delinquent patterns of behavior were transmitted across generations in areas of social disorganization and weak social controls (Shaw and McKay 1969 [1942], p. 174). This community-level orientation led Shaw and McKay to an explicit contextual interpretation of correlations between race or ethnicity and rates of delinquency. Their logic was set forth in a rejoinder to a critique in 1949 by Jonassen, who had argued that ethnicity had direct effects on delinquency. Shaw and McKay countered (1949, p. 614): "The important fact about rates of delinquents for Negro boys is that they too vary by type of area. They are higher than the rates for white boys, but it cannot be said that they are higher than rates for white boys in comparable areas, since it is impossible to reproduce in white communities the circumstances under which Negro children live. Even if it were possible to parallel the low economic status and the inadequacy of institutions in the white community, it would not be possible to reproduce the effects of segregation and the barriers to upward mobility."

Sampson and Wilson (1995) argue that Shaw and McKay's insight almost a half century ago raises interesting questions still relevant today. First, to what extent do rates of black crime vary by type of ecological area? Second, is it possible to reproduce in white communities the structural circumstances under which many blacks live? The first question is crucial, for it signals that blacks are not a homogeneous group any more than are whites. It is racial stereotyping that assigns to blacks a distinct or homogeneous character, allowing simplistic comparisons of black-white group differences in crime. As Shaw and McKay thus recognized, the key point is that there is *heterogeneity* among black neighborhoods that corresponds to variations in crime rates. To the extent that the structural sources of variation in black crime are not unique, rates of crime by blacks should also vary with social-ecological conditions in a manner similar to whites.

A. Structural Variations in Black Violence

To disentangle the contextual basis for race and crime requires racial disaggregation of both the crime rate and the explanatory variables of theoretical interest. This approach was used in research that examined racially disaggregated rates of homicide and robbery by juveniles and adults in over 150 U.S. cities in 1980 (Sampson 1987). Substantively, this study focused on the role of joblessness among black males in predicting violent crime rates through the mediating influence of black family disruption. The results showed that the scarcity of employed black males relative to black women was directly related to the prevalence of families headed by females in black communities (see also Wilson 1987). Black family disruption was in turn significantly related to rates of black murder and robbery—especially by juveniles—independently of income, region, density, city size, and welfare benefits. The finding that family disruption had a stronger relationship with juvenile violence than adult violence, in conjunction with the inconsistent findings of previous research on individual-level delinquency and broken homes, supports the idea that family structure is related to macrolevel patterns of social control and guardianship, especially regarding youth and their peers (Sampson and Groves 1989). Moreover, the results offer a clue as to why unemployment and economic deprivation have had weak or inconsistent direct effects on violence rates in past research—joblessness and poverty appear to exert much of their influence indirectly through family disruption.

Despite a large difference in mean levels of family disruption between black and white communities, the percentage of *white* families headed by a female also had a significant effect on white juvenile and white adult violence. The relationships for white robbery were in large part identical in sign and magnitude to those for blacks. As a result, the influence of black family disruption on black crime was independent of alternative explanations (e.g., region, income, density, age composition) and could not be attributed to unique factors within the black community because of the similar effect of white family disruption on white crime.[10]

Black communities are thus not homogeneous in either their crime rates or levels of social organization. Moreover, that the considerable variations in black violence are explained by generic features of urban social structure goes some way toward dispelling the idea of a unique "black" subculture. As Sampson and Wilson (1995) argue, how else can we make sense of the systematic variations *within* race—for exam-

[10] There is some recent evidence that black crime rates are related to some structural features differently than white crime rates (see especially LaFree et al. 1992; Harer and Steffensmeier 1992). However, these studies have been based either on national trends over time or large macrolevel units (standard metropolitan statistical areas). More important, the point is not so much whether all the predictors of white and black crime rates match exactly, but the systematic variation in rates of black violence according to basic features of structural context.

ple, if a uniform subculture of violence explains black crime, are we to assume that this subculture is three times as potent in, say, New York as Chicago (where black homicide differed by a factor of three in 1980)? These distinct variations exist at the state level as well. For example, rates of black homicide in California were triple those in Maryland in 1980 (see Hawkins 1986; Wilbanks 1986). As Sampson and Wilson (1995) ask, must whites then be part of the black subculture of violence in California, given that white homicide rates were also more than triple the homicide rates for whites in Maryland? It does not seem likely. The sources of violent crime appear to be remarkably similar across race and rooted instead in the structural differences among communities, cities, and regions in economic and family organization. It is important to note, however, that a structural perspective need not dismiss wholesale the relevance of culture. Rather, cultural influences may be triggered by structural features of the urban environment (for further elaboration, see Sampson and Wilson 1995).

B. The Ecological Concentration of Race and Social Dislocations

Bearing in mind the general similarity of black-white variations by social-ecological context, consider the next logical question. To what extent are blacks as a group differentially exposed to criminogenic structural conditions (Sampson and Wilson 1995)? More than forty years after Shaw and McKay's assessment of race and urban ecology, we still cannot say that blacks and whites share a similar environment—especially with regard to concentrated urban poverty. Although approximately 70 percent of all poor non-Hispanic whites lived in nonpoverty areas in the ten largest U.S. central cities in 1980, only 16 percent of poor blacks did. Moreover, whereas less than 7 percent of poor whites lived in extreme poverty or ghetto areas, 38 percent of poor blacks lived in such areas (Wilson et al. 1988, p. 130). Quite simply, race and poverty are confounded in the United States (Land, McCall, and Cohen 1990).

The combination of urban poverty and family disruption concentrated by race is particularly severe. Whereas the majority of poor blacks live in communities characterized by high rates of family disruption, most poor whites, even those from "broken homes," live in areas of relative family stability (Sampson 1987; Sullivan 1989). As an example, consider Sampson and Wilson's (1995) examination of race-specific census data on the 171 largest cities in the United States as of 1980. To get some idea of concentrated social dislocations by race, they searched for cities where the proportion of blacks living in poverty was equal to or less than whites *and* where the proportion of black families with children headed by a single parent was equal to or less than white families. Although the national rate of family disruption and poverty among blacks is two to four times higher than among whites, the number of distinct ecological contexts in which blacks achieve equality to whites is striking. In not one city over 100,000 in the United States do blacks live in ecological equality to whites when it comes to these basic features of economic and family organization. Accordingly, racial differences in poverty and family disruption are so strong that the "worst" urban contexts in which whites reside are considerably better off than the average context of black communities (see also Sampson 1987, p. 354).

Taken as a whole, these patterns underscore what Wilson (1987) has labeled "concentration effects"—the effects of living in a neighborhood that is overwhelmingly impoverished. These concentration effects, reflected in a range of outcomes from degree of labor force attachment to social dispositions, are created by the constraints and opportunities that the residents of inner-city neighborhoods face in terms of access to jobs and job networks, involvement in quality schools, availability of marriageable partners, and exposure to conventional role models. Moreover, the social transformation of inner cities in recent decades has resulted in an increased concentration of the most disadvantaged segments of the urban black population—especially poor, female-headed families with children. Whereas one of every five poor blacks resided in ghetto or extreme poverty areas in 1970, by 1980 nearly two out of every five did so (Wilson et al. 1988, p. 131).

This process of social transformation has been fueled by macrostructural economic changes related to the deindustrialization of central cities where disadvantaged minorities are concentrated (e.g., shifts from goods-producing to service-producing industries; increasing polarization of the labor market into low-wage and high-wage sectors; and relocation of manufacturing out of the inner city). The exodus of middle- and upper-income black families from the inner city has also removed an important social buffer that could potentially deflect the full impact of prolonged joblessness and industrial transformation (Wilson 1987). At the same time, inner-city neighborhoods have suffered disproportionately from severe population and housing loss of the sort identified by Shaw and McKay (1969 [1942]) as disruptive of the social and institutional order. For example, Skogan (1986, p. 206) has noted how urban renewal and forced migration contributed to the wholesale uprooting of many urban black communities, especially the extent to which freeway networks driven through the hearts of many cities in the 1950s destroyed viable, low-income communities. Nationwide, fully 20 percent of all central city housing units occupied by blacks were lost in the period 1960–70 alone. As Logan and Molotch (1987, p. 114) observe, this displacement does not even include that brought about by routine market forces (e.g., evictions, rent increases).

An understanding of concentration effects is not complete without recognizing the negative consequences of deliberate policy decisions to concentrate minorities and the poor in public housing. Opposition from organized community groups to the building of public housing in "their" neighborhoods, de facto federal policy to tolerate extensive segregation against blacks in urban housing markets, and the decision by local governments to neglect the rehabilitation of existing residential units (many of them single family homes) have led to massive, segregated housing projects which have become ghettos for minorities and the disadvantaged. The cumulative result is that even given the same objective socioeconomic status, blacks and whites face vastly different environments in which to live, work, and raise their children. As Bickford and Massey (1991, p. 1035) have argued, public housing represents a federally funded, physically permanent institution for the isolation of black families by class and must therefore be considered an important structural constraint on ecological area of residence (see also Massey and Denton 1993). When segregation and concentrated poverty represent structural constraints embodied in public policy and historical patterns of racial subjugation, concerns that individual differences (or self-selection) explain community-level effects on violence are considerably diminished (see also Tienda 1991; Sampson and Lauritsen 1994).

C. *Implications for Explaining Race and Crime*

These differential ecological distributions by race lead to the systematic confounding of correlations between community contexts and crime with correlations between race and crime. Analogous to research on urban poverty, simple comparisons between poor whites and poor blacks are confounded with the finding that poor whites reside in areas which are ecologically and economically very different from those of poor blacks. For example, regardless of whether a black juvenile is raised in an intact or single-parent family, or a rich or poor home, he or she is not likely to grow up in a community context similar to whites with regard to family structure and the concentration of poverty (Sampson 1987). Hence, observed relationships involving race and crime are likely to reflect unmeasured advantages in the ecological niches that poor whites occupy (Wilson 1987, pp. 58–60).

Partial evidence supporting this interpretation is found in Peeples and Loeber's (1994) contextual analysis of ethnic difference in delinquency using data from a longitudinal study of male juveniles in Pittsburgh. Consistent with past research, African-American youth exhibited much higher rates of delinquency, especially serious crime, than did whites. However, when the "underclass" status of the subject's residential neighborhood was controlled, race/ethnic differences in delinquency disappeared. Similar to Wilson's (1987) concentration thesis, the "underclass" index was composed of variables that clustered significantly on one factor—joblessness, female-headed families, nonmarital births, poverty, welfare, and percent black. Perhaps most striking, the delinquency rates of African-American youth living in *non*underclass neighborhoods were largely equivalent to those of whites living in nonunderclass areas. Although unable to study whites in disadvantaged areas, Peeples and Loeber's findings support the idea that community context helps us interpret the race-crime association.

With respect to theories on race and crime, community-level inquiry also exposes what Sampson and Wilson (1995) call the "individualistic fallacy"—the often-invoked assumption that individual-level causal relations necessarily generate individual-level correlations. In particular, research conducted using individuals as units of analysis—especially in national probability samples—rarely questions whether obtained results might be spurious and confounded with community-level context. As noted earlier, the most common strategies in criminology search for individual-level (e.g., constitutional), social-psychological (e.g., relative deprivation), or group-level (e.g., social class) explanations for race and crime. That these efforts have largely failed to explain the race-violence linkage is, we believe, a direct result of the decontextualization that attends reductionist explanations.

Boiled down to its essentials, then, linking theories of community social organization with research on political economy and urban poverty suggests that both historical and contemporary macrosocial forces (e.g., segregation, migration, housing discrimination, structural transformation of the economy) interact with local community-level factors (e.g., residential turnover, concentrated poverty, family disruption) to impede the social organization of inner cities. This viewpoint focuses attention on the proximate structural characteristics and mediating processes of community social organization that help explain crime and its connection to race in contemporary American cities, while at the same time recognizing the larger historical, social, and political forces shaping local communities (Sampson and Wilson 1995).

Perhaps most important, the logic of this theoretical strategy suggests that the profound changes in the structure of urban minority communities in the 1970s may hold a key to understanding recent increases in violence. Research has consistently demonstrated the early onset of delinquency and its relative long-term stability (Sampson and Laub 1992). These differences among individuals that are highly stable over time imply that to understand the present high crime rates among youth we must come to grips with their experiences in early adolescence. Much longitudinal research shows that delinquent tendencies are fairly well established at early ages—at eight or so, and certainly by the early teens. Socialization and learning begin even earlier, prompting us to consider the social context of childhood as well.

Considered from this perspective, the roots of urban violence among today's fifteen- to twenty-one-year-old cohorts may in part be attributable to childhood socialization that took place in the late 1970s. Indeed, recent large increases in crime among youth—but not adults—may be a harbinger of things to come as the massive secular changes that transformed the context of childhood socialization in the 1970s and 1980s are now beginning to exert their influence on those entering the peak years of offending. Cohorts born in 1970–76 spent their childhood in the context of a rapidly changing urban environment unlike that of previous points in recent U.S. history. As documented in more detail by Wilson (1987), the concentration of urban poverty and other social dislocations began increasing sharply at about 1970 and continued throughout the decade and into the early 1980s. For example, the proportion of black families headed by women increased over 50 percent from 1970 to 1984 alone (Wilson 1987, p. 26). Large increases were also seen for the ecological concentration of poverty, racial segregation, and joblessness. By comparison, these social dislocations were relatively stable in earlier decades.

In short, massive social change in the inner cities of the United States during the 1970s and continuing into the 1980s may be the clue to unraveling recent race-related increases in urban violence. This thesis has import for the comparative study of social change in international context, especially considering the economic and racial/ethnic upheavals now emerging globally. Before explicating this idea further, we complete the picture of race and crime by turning to the U.S. system of criminal justice.

V. Criminal Justice Processing

Criminologists have produced a voluminous body of research on racial differences in criminal justice processing. This research, conducted over the course of several decades, has covered the major decision points in the justice systems of the United States. Rather than trying to make sense of each and every study, we consult state-of-the-art reviews of research to provide an overview of major findings. In some cases we consider seminal or recent studies in detail, but for the most part we highlight general patterns and trends established in multiple works. We focus on critical decision points in the criminal justice "system" (see U.S. Department of Justice 1988, p. 56)—especially racial disparities in arrest, sentencing, and imprisonment. Although a focus on the criminal justice system leads primarily to research on adult processing, it is important first to consider the literature on race differences in juvenile justice.

A. Juvenile Justice

As Pope and Feyerherm (1990) have argued, minority discrimination in the juvenile and adult systems should be considered separately for two reasons. First, the greater level of discretion allowed in the juvenile justice system may mean that race discrimination is more evident compared to the adult system. Second, because most adult offenders begin their criminal contact with the state through the juvenile justice system, disadvantages incurred as juveniles may influence criminal justice outcomes as adults through characteristics such as prior record, which is typically considered in key decision points throughout life (Pope and Feyerherm 1990, p. 328).[11]

[11] It should be noted that in the United States, the age at which the state treats an adolescent as a "juvenile" or an "adult" varies across both jurisdictions and crime types. The age at which an adolescent is considered an adult varies from sixteen to eighteen years of age, although many jurisdictions allow juveniles to be waived to the adult system as young as age thirteen or fourteen if the charge is a serious violent crime. In general, the juvenile justice system is characterized by greater discretion and less formality than the adult system. However, in some larger urban jurisdictions, juvenile justice systems operate with a considerable degree of procedural formality. The juvenile justice system is constituted by many organizational units which vary in caseloads, resources, procedures and practices, structures, and institutional norms.

A recent overview of the literature on minority status and juvenile justice processing summarizes the findings on the relationships between race and postarrest decision making (see Pope and Feyerherm [1990] for more details and an extended bibliography). Pope and Feyerherm (1990) draw three major conclusions about minority status and juvenile-justice decision making. First, two-thirds of the studies reviewed showed evidence of either direct or indirect discrimination against minorities, or a mixed pattern of bias. *Direct* evidence of disproportionate treatment was inferred when significant race differences in processing (e.g., detention) persisted after controlling for relevant case characteristics (for a recent example, see Wordes, Bynum, and Corley 1994). *Indirect* evidence of race discrimination was said to exist when a significant race effect operated through some other case characteristic closely associated with race. A mixed pattern of effects was established when an investigator analyzed several decision points and race was found to be significant at some stages but not others, or when race differences existed for specific subgroups of offenders or offenses.

Second, Pope and Feyerherm (1990) argue that studies reporting evidence of differential minority treatment were no less sophisticated in their methodology or statistical techniques than studies reporting otherwise. Inadequacies of research design and execution thus do not appear responsible for evident patterns of discrimination. Third, they report evidence that race differences in outcome may appear minor for any particular decision-making stage, but become more pronounced as earlier decisions accumulate toward a final disposition.

These findings underscore important methodological issues relevant to the study of minority differences in criminal justice processing. As Pope and Feyerherm (1990) note, most research asserts no evidence of discrimination for a processing decision if the statistical significance of the race coefficient is eliminated by controlling for some other individual-level variable (e.g., family structure, prior record). However, as they correctly argue, "logically, what has occurred in these studies is the identification of the mechanism by which differences between white and minority youths are created. Whether these types of variables ought to be used in justice system decision making, and whether they ought to produce the degree of differences between white and minority youths that they appear to produce, are issues that must be addressed" (Pope and Feyerherm 1990, pp. 334–35; see also Kempf-Leonard, Pope, and Feyerherm 1995).

The importance of understanding the consequences of data aggregation is noted as well. Where racially discriminatory practices operate in relatively few jurisdictions in a region, the process of aggregating data across jurisdictions is likely to mask evidence of differential treatment (see also Crutchfield, Bridges, and Pritchford 1994). For example, Pope and Feyerherm found no overall minority discrimination in juvenile justice processing in California and Florida, despite the fact that racially discriminatory practices were evident in several of the counties in each state. Alternatively, they also describe data from a different state in which there appeared to be no racial discrimination *within* each court or jurisdiction, yet the race composition of the jurisdiction (i.e., county) was associated with *between*-court differences in the use of incarceration. Specifically, counties with greater proportions of blacks and Hispanics were found to rely more heavily on out-of-home placement (Pope and Feyerherm 1990, p. 335). An independent analysis of juvenile processing across a representative sample of jurisdictions supports this "macrolevel" pattern. Sampson and Laub (1993*a*) report that counties with greater poverty and race inequality are more apt to use predispositional detention and adjudicated out-of-home placement.

In short, the relationship between race and juvenile justice decision making is complex and requires careful methodological consideration. The use of data from multiple levels of analyses is undoubtedly important as both macro- and individual-level factors (including community race composition and inequality, and suspect's race) have been shown to predict the severity of dispositions among juveniles. Furthermore, several multilevel analyses suggest that macro- and individual-level factors *interact* to produce racial differences in juvenile justice outcomes. In a later section we elaborate on the implications of a contextual perspective for understanding racial differences in justice processing.

B. Police-Citizen Encounters and Arrest

We now turn to a consideration of research on the sequential nature of processing in the criminal justice system. We begin with the institution that suspects (whether juvenile or adult) are likely to first encounter—the police. In evaluating rival hypotheses on racial differences in criminal offending, research on arrest disparities was covered in Section III (e.g., NCVS victimization reports vs. the UCR). There we saw that, for the most part, racial differences in arrests for "street" crimes are attributable to the differential involvement of blacks in criminal offending irrespective of age (Hindelang 1978, 1981). However, there are two other dimensions to policing that bear on race disparities: police-citizen encounters that may or may not result in arrest, and police shootings of civilians.

The literature in the area of police discretion to arrest originated with research on juvenile encounters. In general, the data have shown that when offenses are minor in nature, officers typically rely on the juvenile's demeanor or attitude to determine how they will handle the case (Piliavin and Briar 1964; Black and Reiss 1970). The suspect's race is relevant insofar as it serves as a proxy for police perceptions of disrespectful attitudes, which increase the likelihood of an official write-up or arrest.

Extending the scope of analysis to adults, Smith (1986) found that neighborhood context influenced the willingness of police to arrest and use coercive authority. Smith reports that the police are more likely to arrest, or use or threaten to use force, against suspects in racially mixed or minority neighborhoods. Within these areas, however, suspect's race did not serve as an additional predictor of police behavior. Smith (1986) also reports that black suspects in white neighborhoods are treated less coercively than black suspects in minority neighborhoods and that white suspects are treated similarly regardless of neighborhood. In other words, neighborhood characteristics such as racial composition and socioeconomic status interact with suspect characteristics to predict arrest and use of coercive authority.

Another line of inquiry into police-citizen encounters involves the overrepresentation of blacks in police shootings of criminal suspects. In analyses of data from New York City, Fyfe (1982) reports that blacks were more likely than whites to be shot by police because they were disproportionately involved in armed incidents at the time of the encounter. By contrast, a similar analysis based on data from the city of Memphis showed that blacks were no more likely than whites to be involved in armed incidents, and yet disproportionately more blacks were shot by police while retreating. Fyfe (1982) concludes that in Memphis, police use of deadly force varies significantly according to suspect's race. Similar to the interaction effects noted above, the importance of a suspect's race for predicting police use of deadly force appears to vary across context (e.g., neighborhoods, cities).

C. *Bail*

Following an arrest, the next major point of contact within the criminal justice system centers on whether an accused will be held in detention pending case disposition or released on bond (i.e., bail). Research on pretrial release practices by the criminal justice system shows that defendants who are detained prior to prosecution tend to receive more serious penalties on conviction (Goldkamp 1979). For this reason, and because pretrial detention constitutes "punishment" before conviction, discriminatory processes in pretrial release are an important concern. For the overwhelming majority of offenses charged, prosecutors and judges have considerable discretion whether defendants are "released on their own recognizance" or as to the dollar amount of bail requested to secure a pretrial release. United States courts are legally allowed to use dangerousness to the community and flight risk in pretrial decision making. Typically, the court relies on the defendant's employment status, marital status, and length of residence to indicate "community ties" which, in turn, are used to predict whether a defendant is likely to flee the area or fail to appear at trial (Albonetti et al. 1989).

Although few in number, prior studies tend to show that the direct influence of race on pretrial release is insignificant once a defendant's dangerousness to the community (e.g., offense charged, prior record, weapons use) and prior history of failing to appear at trial are controlled. Nonetheless, as Albonetti et al. (1989) show, race is related to bail decision making in complex, interactive ways. In a study of more than 5,000 male defendants across ten federal court districts, Albonetti et al. report that defendants with lower levels of education and income receive significantly more serious pretrial release decisions, controlling for community ties and dangerousness. Moreover, they report that white defendants benefited more from the (nonlegal) effects of education and income than did black defendants with equal resources. Prior record also had a stronger negative effect on pretrial release decisions among blacks than it did for whites. However, dangerousness and offense severity had stronger influences on bail decisions for whites. While these results reveal that under certain conditions whites are treated more severely at pretrial release, in the main they suggest that white defendants "receive better returns on their resources" (Albonetti et al. 1989, p. 80).

D. Conviction

The consensus of prior research goes against a simplistic discrimination thesis—in the aggregate, blacks tend to be convicted less than whites (Burke and Turk 1975; Petersilia 1983; Wilbanks 1987, appendix). Several researchers, however, have argued that this finding stems from a confounding of case mix (i.e., type of crime charged) with race. Once type of charge against the defendant is controlled in multivariate analysis, the direct influence of race tends to disappear in studies of conviction. As Burke and Turk (1975, pp. 328–29) conclude, "race has no independent effect upon case dispositions" (see also Petersilia 1983, p. 19). With or without control of type of crime, then, there is no consistent evidence that minorities are disadvantaged at the stage of criminal conviction. The caveat here, as elsewhere, concerns race or ethnic comparisons other than black versus white. We have no empirical basis from which to draw conclusions about convictions among Hispanic, Asian, and Native Americans.

It is thus clear that more research is needed on this subject that includes the full array of ethnic groups that make up an increasingly diverse society.

E. Sentencing

Research on the sentencing of criminal defendants has generated the greatest interest among those studying racial disparities. As Zatz (1987, p. 69) argues, research on whether the legal system discriminates on the basis of racial or ethnic group membership was *the* question for studies of sentencing in the 1970s and early 1980s. The topic has an even earlier history, however, as Zatz (1987) demonstrates in her review of four "waves" of research on racial disparities. The first wave of research conducted through the mid-1960s tended to suggest that bias against minority defendants was significant. These studies included the research of Thorsten Sellin, in particular his well-known assertion that equality before the law is a social fiction (Sellin 1935).

Wave 2 followed in the wake of civil unrest in the United States and began to address the assertion that race was a determinative factor in sentencing in a more sophisticated way. Wave 1 studies were crude methodologically, and almost none controlled for legally relevant variables in assessing race effects. In an effort to ameliorate these limitations, wave 2 inspired a large number of studies that have been the subject of widely cited and influential reviews by Hagan (1974), Kleck (1981), and Hagan and Bumiller (1983). Kleck (1981) assessed fifty-seven studies, while Hagan and Bumiller (1983) reviewed more than sixty for the National Academy of Sciences. These assessments converged in their conclusion that the effect of race in prior studies was in large part a proxy for the legally relevant factor of *prior criminal record*—once the latter was controlled the direct effect of race on sentencing was for the most part eliminated. That is, the racial disparities in sentencing (e.g., to prison) arose from the greater proportional involvement of minorities in criminal behavior, which was in turn reflected in longer or more serious prior records.

Hagan's and Kleck's exhaustive reviews, covering dozens of empirical studies, were largely responsible for creating what has been labeled by Wilbanks (1987) as the "no discrimination thesis" (NDT). However, as Zatz (1987, p. 73) argues, many criminologists quoting the NDT glossed over two of the caveats that these reviews emphasized. Similar to the concerns raised in research on juvenile justice processing, one caveat was that race might have a cumulative effect on sentencing outcomes by operating *indirectly* through other variables that disadvantage minority group members. The second is that race may *interact* with other factors to influence decision making. We return to these arguments below, but for now, it is important to clarify that the NDT refers specifically to the insignificant *direct* effects of race on sentencing.

Conducted mainly in the late 1970s and 1980s, wave 3 of research witnessed yet another round of methodological refinements, including corrections for "selection bias" (the nonrandom selection of defendants into the system) and "specification error" (the omission of explanatory variables; see Zatz 1987, p. 75). Researchers also investigated historical changes in sentencing practices and expanded the focus to types of crime not previously emphasized (e.g., drug processing). For example, Peterson and Hagan (1984) found that the sentencing of black drug offenders in New York depended on shifting symbolic contexts—minor black dealers were treated more leniently than their white counterparts, but major black dealers ("kingpins") were treated more harshly than white dealers because they were perceived as inflicting further harm on an already victimized nonwhite population (Peterson and Hagan 1984, p. 67). Other research began to examine racial bias in terms of the *victim's* status rather than that of the offender. This line of inquiry suggests that defendants are more harshly sentenced by the criminal justice system when the victim is white rather than black (Myers 1979).

Research from wave 3 is thus not easily summarized, for many studies began to uncover contradictory findings or began to explore hypotheses tangential to the NDT. For example, some researchers found expected patterns of discrimination while others did not, and a fair number of studies showed that whites received harsher sentences than blacks in certain cases (Zatz 1987, pp. 74–78). Overall, though, the thrust of research during this era seemed to shift away from the NDT to the idea that there is *some* discrimination, *some* of the time, in *some* places. These contingencies undermine the broad reach of the NDT, but the damage is not fatal to the basic argument that race discrimination is not pervasive (or systemic) in criminal justice processing.

What Zatz (1987) calls wave 4 of research is still in progress. Based on data from the late 1970s and 1980s and conducted from the 1980s to the present, this era of research continues to use advanced statistical techniques. But perhaps the main distinguishing feature is the research exploitation of policy changes that introduced determinate sentencing. First enacted in the United States in the mid-1970s, the fixed sentencing mandate has grown even stronger, with the latest manifestation found in the politically popular "three strikes and you're out" laws.[12] In one of the larger studies, Klein, Petersilia, and Turner (1990) analyzed over 11,000 cases in California and found slight racial disparities in sentencing one year after that state had implemented a determinate sentencing act. However, once prior record and other legally relevant variables were controlled, Klein, Petersilia, and Turner (1990, p. 815) found that "racial disparity in sentencing does not reflect racial discrimination." Also analyzing data from California after determinate sentencing, Zatz (1984) found no overt or direct bias against Hispanic-Americans compared to Anglos (i.e., non-Hispanic whites).

The research in wave 4 on determinate sentencing is interesting because it shifts attention to prior stages of the system where discretion by prosecutors may potentially disadvantage minorities. In other words, if sentences are (relatively) fixed, then charging and plea bargaining become more crucial in the criminal justice process. Accordingly, some studies have turned to the study of the relatively hidden dimension of prosecutorial discretion. Although little research has accumulated, especially on racial differences in charging (see Wilbanks 1987), Spohn, Gruhl, and Welch (1987) found a pattern of discrimination in favor of female defendants and against blacks and Hispanics. More specifically, their analysis of more than 30,000 cases from Los Angeles County showed that, after adjusting for age, prior record, seriousness of charge, and weapon use, cases against blacks and Hispanics

[12] "Three strikes and you're out" laws refer to legislation first enacted in Washington State in 1993 and subsequently replicated elsewhere making the consequence of a third conviction for a violent crime an automatic life sentence without the possibility of parole. The phrase itself is popularly known from its use in the American sport of baseball.

were significantly more likely to be prosecuted than cases against whites. Spohn, Gruhl, and Welch (1987) did not control for bail status, a factor predictive of prosecution, but the findings are nonetheless provocative in suggesting that blacks and Hispanics in Los Angeles are more likely to be formally prosecuted than whites.

The research on race and plea bargaining is also sparse, but the studies of Miethe and Moore (1986) and Albonetti (1990) both find an insignificant main effect of race on plea negotiations net of control variables. Albonetti (1990) pursues interaction effects and finds that legal factors (e.g., weapon use, prior record, type of counsel) work differently for whites than blacks in a complex fashion. But the reason why blacks are less likely to plead guilty in her data remain unclear, and the fact remains that the main effect of race is insignificant. Hence the NDT fails to be rejected in this case.

The other distinguishing feature of recent research on sentencing is a deeper appreciation for the salience of macrosocial contexts. Primed by the research in wave 3 suggesting interaction and contextual effects, scholars began to design research that could disentangle the role of macrolevel contexts (e.g., county poverty, urbanism) on sentencing. One of the best studies to date of race and sentencing emerges from this concern—Myers and Talarico's *The Social Contexts of Criminal Sentencing* (1987). Analyzing more than 26,000 felons convicted between 1976 and 1985 in the forty-five judicial courts of Georgia, Myers and Talarico employ state-of-the-art statistical methods to counter the limitations of previous research outlined by Zatz (1987). With the southern state of Georgia as its focus, it is hard to imagine a better test case for discrimination in the modern era. The findings are complex, and as the title would indicate, Myers and Talarico report that sentencing outcomes vary significantly as a function of social context (e.g., urbanization of the county). This pattern supports the contingency model of criminal sentencing and rejects the idea that invariant laws or modes of behavior characterize the "system" as a whole.

In terms of race, however, the data analyzed by Myers and Talarico (1987) clearly failed to support the thesis of systemic race discrimination—even in a contingent manner. As they summarize the book's key findings:

> The analyses reported in previous chapters indicate that there is little system-wide discrimination against blacks in criminal sentencing. This is an important finding, because general charges

> of discrimination are common not only in some interpretations of conflict theory, but also in some sectors of the popular and academic press. To be sure, the absence of evidence of system-wide discrimination does not mean that all courts and judges are [color] blind in the administration of criminal law. Interactive analysis revealed context-specific patterns of discrimination. Importantly, however, there were many instances in which blacks received disproportionately lenient punishment. Although this pattern may reflect a paternalism that is just as discriminatory as disproportionate punitiveness, it nonetheless indicates that the courts in Georgia do not have a heavy hand with black defendants in the general systemic sense or in every context where differential treatment is observed. (Myers and Talarico 1987, pp. 170–71)

This conclusion matches that of the U.S. Justice Department's recent survey of felony cases in the seventy-five most populous urban areas in the United States (Smith 1993; Langan 1994). These areas represent the jurisdictions in which most black defendants come into contact with the criminal justice system, and thus the data are useful for describing overall differences in prosecution, conviction, and sentencing of felony cases. The survey findings showed that following a felony charge, blacks were prosecuted at a slightly lower rate than whites (e.g., 66 percent of black defendants were prosecuted compared to 69 percent of whites). Once prosecuted, black defendants were also slightly less likely to be found guilty than were whites (75 percent vs. 78 percent). However, of those convicted, blacks were more likely to be sentenced to prison (51 percent vs. 38 percent). Among those sentenced to prison, there were no significant race differences in length of sentence.

Langan (1994) reports that the observed race differences in imprisonment were the result of type of crime, prior record, and aggregation effects. Black defendants were more likely to be charged with robbery or another violent offense than were whites. Also, a greater percentage of the black defendants had prior felony convictions. Examination of aggregation effects revealed that black defendants were more likely to be adjudicated in jurisdictions that were more likely to hand out prison sentences. Yet, within these harsher jurisdictions, blacks were treated no differently than whites. Based on these findings, Langan (1994, p. 51) concludes that the "Justice Department survey provides no evidence that, in the places where blacks in the United States have most of their contacts with the justice system, the system treats them more harshly than whites." It could have been argued, however, that what the survey revealed was a potential contextual relationship between race and the decision to imprison.

A recent review of thirty-eight studies on race and sentencing by Chiricos and Crawford (1995) suggests that this latter interpretation is plausible. By separating the evidence on the decision to imprison and the length of sentence once imprisoned, these authors confirm the Justice Department's report; most studies showed that blacks were more likely to be sentenced to prison than were whites, but there was no pattern of race differences in sentence length. However, Chiricos and Crawford also investigated the contextual conditions of the samples used in each of the studies and found that, controlling for crime type and prior record, black defendants were more likely to receive imprisonment in high unemployment areas, in places where blacks constitute a larger percentage of the population, and in the South. This meta-analysis strongly suggests the plausibility of contextual influences on the decision to imprison. As they argue, "these specific structural contexts lend support to the premise that criminal punishment not only responds to crime, but responds as well to specific community conditions" (Chiricos and Crawford 1995, p. 301). Thus unlike Langan's dismissal of the race differences in the decision to imprison, Chiricos and Crawford focus explicitly on the context in which these decisions are most likely to occur.[13]

Langan's interpretation, however, matches those of other scholars such as Petersilia (1985) and Wilbanks (1987) in suggesting that systemic discrimination does not exist. Zatz (1987) is more sympathetic to the thesis of discrimination in the form of indirect effects and subtle racism. But the proponents of this line of reasoning face a considerable burden. If the effects of race are so contingent, interactive, and indirect in a way that has to date not proved replicable, how can one allege that the "system" is discriminatory? At least some part of the differences in the interpretation of existing findings is semantic. For some, *any* evidence of differential treatment, whether anecdotal or empirical, direct or indirect, or at the individual or jurisdictional level, is indicative of a discriminatory system. For those at the other end of the continuum (e.g., Wilbanks 1987), the term is reserved for widespread and consistent differentials in processing unaccounted for by relevant legal factors. Recognizing these differences in the use of terms implies that the

[13] The findings of the Justice Department may be a function of the urban sampling frame. Chiricos and Crawford (1995) note that black defendants were least disadvantaged in non-Southern urban areas where minority concentration was highest.

assessment of racial discrimination is not simply a matter of empirical debate.

Perhaps more importantly, "the inconsistency in findings offers clues to the contextual character of possible race effects" (Chiricos and Crawford 1995, p. 284). This assessment suggests that multilevel research designs are necessary to assess the impact of race on within- and between-jurisdiction differences in the decision to imprison. We return to this issue below.

F. Imprisonment Disparities

The sentencing studies considered to this point are for the most part drawn from one jurisdiction or state. Attempting to make broader contributions to the race-sentencing debate, a series of recent efforts has engaged national-level data to account for the racial disproportionality of U.S. prison populations. Generating considerable attention, the seminal article in this area was published by Blumstein in 1982. To study the racial distribution of state prison populations in 1974 and 1979, Blumstein used UCR arrest statistics from the same years to estimate the racial composition of offenders committing offenses punishable by imprisonment. Although blacks represented 11 percent of the U.S. population, they comprised approximately 49 percent of the prison population in both 1974 and 1979. However, blacks also represented 43 percent of the arrestees in these years, leading Blumstein to conclude that racial disproportionality in offending explained 80 percent of the racial disproportionality in prison populations.

Using arrest data as a simple indicator of offending is controversial for reasons discussed earlier. Langan (1985) counteracted this problem by replicating Blumstein's analysis with estimates for black offending derived from victims' reports in the NCVS. Essentially, Langan's strategy followed that of Hindelang's (1978) in estimating offenders rather than arrestees. By estimating the expected number of black offenders admitted to prison for the years 1973, 1979, and 1982 using the probability of *whites* going to prison, Langan was able directly to assess the racial disparity argument by comparing these estimates to the observed number of black offenders admitted to prison. For 1973, there is almost exact agreement between the two estimates—19,344 expected to 19,953 admitted black prisoners. The differences are greater in 1979 and 1982, leading to speculation whether a trend of increasing discrimination was set in motion around 1980 (see below). However, Langan (1985) emphasized the overall agreement of the figures and concluded that approximately 85 percent of the disproportionality in prison admissions by race is explained by differential offending.

Crutchfield, Bridges, and Pritchford (1994) extend the Blumstein-Langan strategy by disaggregating racial disproportionality estimates across the fifty states. As did Pope and Feyerherm (1990), they argue that if there is variation across states in the degree to which levels of criminal involvement among blacks explain observed imprisonment rates, studies that aggregate to the national level are likely to mask this variation (Crutchfield, Bridges, and Pritchford 1994, p. 179). Similar to Blumstein and Langan, Crutchfield and colleagues find that for the United States as a whole, the lion's share of variation in the observed racial disproportionality of prisons—90 percent—is explained by arrest differentials (NCVS estimates of offending are unavailable by state). However, they uncover striking variations in this ratio across the fifty states. In some states such as New York, Pennsylvania, Delaware, and Kentucky, the percentage of imprisonment disparity explained by arrest is virtually 100—suggesting little to no discrimination. By contrast, in many other states the percent dips well below 100, and in some cases below fifty. States with extreme racial differentials in arrests compared to imprisonment include Massachusetts (40 percent), Idaho (53 percent), Colorado (62 percent), Alabama (54 percent), and Maine (58 percent).

The common denominator in these patterns is hard to discern, although most of the states indicating large racial imbalances in imprisonment decisions are smaller in population, with a relatively low percentage of blacks. It may simply be that the estimates are unreliable due to the small number of cases on which the state-specific disparity ratios are calculated. Crutchfield, Bridges, and Pritchford (1994) interpret them substantively, however, arguing that contextual differences have heretofore been hidden by the tendency of researchers to aggregate data across jurisdictions. Similar to the context-specific arguments of Myers and Talarico (1987) and Zatz (1987), the implication is that multiple-jurisdiction or comparative studies are essential to disentangling racial disproportionality. Put differently, understanding racial disparity requires disaggregation of variations by social structural context. We address this concern further when discussing contextual theories and future research from a comparative perspective.

An update of the 1982 Blumstein study suggests several reasons why disaggregation by crime type might be necessary as well (Blumstein 1993*b*). First, Blumstein notes the enormous growth in imprisonment over the 1979–91 time period. Following decades of relative stability, the 1990 U.S. incarceration rate was nearly triple that of 1975. Moreover, the total number of drug offenders in prison increased nearly tenfold. Second, the 1991 level of racial disproportionality in incarceration rates remained similar to what it had been in 1979 (seven to one), and overall differences in offending (i.e., arrests) explained slightly less of disproportionality in the 1991 prison rates (76 percent). Third, the importance of the war on drugs becomes particularly pronounced for race differences in incarceration by 1991. For drug offending, differences in drug arrests accounted for only 50 percent of the race disproportionality in drug incarceration. The government's "war on drugs" was concentrated on an offense that involved high levels of discretion and hence was vulnerable to charges of racist practices. The proportion of drug offenders in U.S. prisons went from 5.7 percent in 1979 to 21.5 percent in 1991. As the distribution of offense types changes in prison populations, it thus becomes crucial to examine the issue of disparity by crime type.

G. Death Penalty

The ultimate criminal sanction—death—has been the subject of much empirical research and philosophical debate. The United States is the only Western industrialized democracy that permits states to impose capital punishment. In 1972 (*Furman v. Georgia*), the Supreme Court ordered a halt to executions because it found the application of the death penalty to be arbitrary and racially discriminatory. By 1976 (*Gregg v. Georgia*) the Supreme Court had reinstated the death penalty as long as states could show that the risk of arbitrariness had been removed through the development of explicit sentencing criteria, separate sentencing hearings, consideration of mitigating circumstances, and automatic appellate review. Nonetheless, research covering the period since the 1976 *Gregg* decision shows that, controlling for type of homicide, race is related to the prosecutor's decision to seek the death penalty and to imposition of the death penalty (Bowers and Pierce 1980; Radelet 1981; Paternoster 1984; Keil and Vito 1989; Aguirre and Baker 1990; Baldus, Woodward, and Pulaski 1990).

These studies converge in showing that it is the race of the victim interacting with the race of the offender that significantly influences prosecutors' willingness to seek the death penalty, and judges' and juries' willingness to impose a sentence of death. Paralleling the data on convictions, black offenders found guilty of murdering white victims are at the highest risk for the death penalty. Offenders (of either race) found guilty of murdering black victims are least likely to receive the death penalty. These differential patterns of risk for the death penalty were found to persist despite stringent controls for the seriousness of the incident (e.g., defendant's deliberation, heinousness of the murder) and other legally relevant factors (see Keil and Vito 1989).[14]

H. Summary

Recognizing that research on criminal justice processing in the United States is complex and fraught with methodological problems, the weight of the evidence reviewed suggests the following. When restricted to index crimes, dozens of individual-level studies have shown that a simple *direct* influence of race on pretrial release, plea bargaining, conviction, sentence length, and the death penalty among adults is small to nonexistent once legally relevant variables (e.g., prior record) are controlled. For these crimes, racial differentials in sanctioning appear to match the large racial differences in criminal offending. Findings on the processing of adult index crimes therefore generally support the NDT.

However, research on the decision to imprison suggests that race matters in certain contexts. Controlling for crime type and prior record, black defendants in some jurisdictions are more likely to receive a prison sentence than are white defendants. Research on the juvenile justice system also offers evidence of racial influences on detention and placement, although this disparity is more widespread than context-specific. Perhaps because the juvenile justice system is more informal, discrimination operates more freely. Moreover, in both the adult and juvenile systems, *indirect* racial discrimination is plausible. For example, prior record is the major control variable in processing studies and is usually interpreted as a "legally relevant" variable. But to the extent that prior record is contaminated by racial discrimination, indirect race effects may be at work. Although this argument is difficult to assess definitively, it remains a productive hypothesis to be explored. Also tentative but plausible is the idea that race *interacts* with other individ-

[14] While it has been argued that this is evidence of discrimination warranting a moratorium on capital punishment, there are those who argue that such differential treatment warrants increased use of the death penalty. For example, DiIulio (1994) calls attention to the evidence of discrimination against black victims and suggests that justice requires increased use of the death penalty for murderers of all victims. Ironically, calls for increased equity in the application of the death penalty may lead to increased executions of blacks.

ual-level variables (e.g., income, family status) to predict processing. What this means for the NDT hypothesis has yet to be fully determined.

As suggested earlier, one of the most promising lines of inquiry for uncovering discrimination patterns involves the *contextual* analyses of criminal justice outcomes. As many have argued (Hagan 1987; Myers and Talarico 1987; Sampson and Laub 1993*a;* Chiricos and Crawford 1995), the key to resolving racial differences in processing may turn in large part on contextual or macrolevel differences. This parallels the arguments made in favor of a community-level interpretation of racial differences in criminal offending. As the next section explores, recent moves in theories of official social control and processing have also adapted this contextual theme.

VI. Explaining Race-Ethnic Disparities in Criminal Justice

Most criminal justice research has drawn on consensus and conflict perspectives of society (Hagan 1989). According to the consensus view, there is an assumption of shared values, where the state is organized to protect the common interests of society at large. Criminal law is seen as an instrument to protect the interests of all, and punishment is based on legally relevant variables (e.g., seriousness of the offense, prior record).

In contrast, conflict theorists view society as consisting of groups with conflicting and differing values and posit that the state is organized to represent the interests of the powerful, ruling class. Criminal law is thus viewed as an instrument to protect the interests of the powerful and the elite, and punishment is based to a large extent on extralegal variables (e.g., race, social class). A major proposition drawn from conflict theory is that groups which threaten the hegemony of middle- and upper-class rule are more likely to be subjected to intensified social control—more criminalization, more formal processing by the criminal justice system, and increased incarceration compared with groups that are perceived as less threatening to the status quo (see also Brown and Warner 1992). Furthermore, conflict theorists have argued that minorities (especially blacks), the unemployed, and the poor represent such threatening groups (see also Turk 1969; Chambliss and Seidman 1971; Jackson and Carroll 1981; Liska and Chamlin 1984; Brown and Warner 1995).[15]

[15] There is some evidence to suggest that the relationship between percent black and increased social control is curvilinear (see e.g., Jackson and Carroll 1981). Liska and

The criticisms of conflict theory are well known. Elites do not form a unitary whole, monopolize decision making, or appear particularly vulnerable to the objective threats of subordinates (Liska 1987; Tittle 1994). Perhaps more damaging, the evidence on personal and property crimes points to legal variables as the prime determinants of criminal justice processing.

Attempting to transcend the limitations of traditional conflict theory, a recent school of thought has forged a more contextually nuanced appreciation of minority group threat. While there may indeed be a general consensus in society on core values, it is not the objective level of threat but rather the *symbolic* aspect of social conflict that may be the salient feature driving crime control (Myers 1989). For instance, Tittle and Curran (1988) emphasize perceptions of threat that "provoke jealousy, envy, or personal fear among elites" rather than the actual threat these groups represent to reigning political positions. Supporting this notion, they found differential sanctioning of juveniles in Florida counties depending on the size of the nonwhite population. Moreover, Tittle and Curran found the largest discriminatory effects in juvenile justice dispositions for drug and sexual offenses which they argue "represent overt behavioral manifestations of the very qualities [that] frighten white adults or generate resentment and envy" (Tittle and Curran 1988, p. 52). Tittle (1994, pp. 39–46) elaborates this finding with reference to the "emotional significance" of crime, especially stereotypical attributions of threat associated with the conflation of race, aggression, and sexual promiscuity.

These ideas are consistent with a study in Washington State, where nonwhites were sentenced to imprisonment at higher rates in counties with large minority populations (Bridges, Crutchfield, and Simpson 1987). Follow-up interviews with justice officials and community leaders revealed a consistent public concern with minority threat and "dangerousness." With crime conceptualized as a minority problem, leaders openly admitted using race as a code for certain patterns of dress and styles of life (e.g., being "in the hustle") thought to signify criminality. It was decision makers' perceptions of minority problems as concentrated ecologically that seemed to reinforce the use of race as a screen for criminal attribution (Bridges, Crutchfield, and Simpson 1987, p. 356). Similarly, Irwin (1985) notes the importance of subjective perceptions of "offensiveness," which are determined by social sta-

Chamlin (1984) suggest that when minorities become so large as to represent a majority, the criminal justice system takes on the stance of "benign neglect."

tus and ethnic group context. Groups deemed as threatening (often when reaching a threshold size) and offensive to the dominant majority are seen as the "rabble class—detached and disreputable persons." Irwin (1985, p. xiii) argues that the primary purpose of jails in the United States is to manage society's rabble class.

Attributions of criminality to subordinate ethnic populations have been found in other stratified societies as well. In Israel, for example, Fishman, Rattner, and Weiman (1987) found that public assignment of criminal intent was directly related to ethnic divisions. Arab Israelis, followed by Sephardic Jews, were most likely to be perceived by respondents as criminal. With recent unrest in the occupied territories, charges have also flared anew that Israeli Arabs are being targeted for increased social control by Israeli police, especially in impoverished towns where Arab concentrations are high (Hedges 1994).

In short, recent theory has turned to a macrosociological orientation by focusing on the symbolic and contextual aspects of minority group threat. In this viewpoint, "the poor," "the underclass," and "the rabble" (i.e., poor minorities) are perceived as threatening not only to political elites, but to "mainstream America"—middle-class and working-class citizens who represent the dominant majority in American society. This perspective suggests that we need to take into account the joint effects of race and poverty. Interestingly, it is here that the pejorative connotations of the term "underclass" become quite relevant. Although criticized by some social scientists (e.g., Gans 1991), the term has nonetheless been appropriated by the media and public at large as a code for dangerous, offensive, and undesirable populations that threaten social stability and a sense of order. As the social historian Michael Katz (1993, p. 4) has noted, "underclass" has become a public metaphor for social transformation in the United States, conjuring up images of group alienation and danger—a collectivity "outside of politics and social structure," a "terrain of violence and despair." Embodying its controversial nature, then, the term "underclass" captures the stereotype of pathological danger relevant to a theoretical concern with how race-class divisions bear on official social control and the "crisis in penality" (see Feeley and Simon 1992, p. 467; McGarrell 1993*a*, p. 11; Simon 1993, p. 5).

A. Structural Changes in Underclass Inequality

Debates on the underclass are linked, of course, to demographic evidence on the increasing size and concentration of the urban poverty population. A great deal of sociological attention has centered on the growing entanglement in urban areas of neighborhood poverty with other social dislocations such as joblessness, family disruption, high rates of infant mortality, and a host of factors that are detrimental to social development (e.g., school dropout). As noted earlier, the changing neighborhood context of poverty was highlighted by William Julius Wilson in *The Truly Disadvantaged* (1987), where he argued that the social transformation of the inner city has resulted in an increased geographical concentration of race, poverty, and urban social dislocations.

Recent evidence suggests that the clustering of economic and social indicators appears not only in 1990 and in neighborhoods of large cities, but also for the two previous decennial periods and at the level of macrosocial units as a whole. For example, Land, McCall, and Cohen (1990) present evidence that concentration effects grew more severe from 1970 to 1980 in U.S. cities and metropolitan areas, while Coulton et al. (1995) document an increasing clustering of indicators of social disadvantage (e.g., poverty, family disruption, welfare) in neighborhoods of Cleveland during the 1980s.

Recent data point to the existence of a large "underclass" population in *rural* areas, especially in the South. Using 1990 data, O'Hare and Curry-White (1992, p. 8) conclude that there is a large rural underclass of both whites and blacks that has not been recognized by researchers in the past and that blacks in the rural South actually have a higher prevalence of underclass characteristics than do blacks in the large cities of the urban North. Adding to this picture, the term "underclass" has recently been applied to poor whites (Murray 1993) in a call for immediate public action to stem a host of social ills usually associated in the American mind with blacks (e.g., out-of-wedlock births, welfare, crime). In a fascinating revision of the once-common stereotype of "white trash," the idea of an emerging "white underclass" that threatens to drag down a society already weakened by the black underclass is now being fostered in contemporary debate. Thus while race and poverty are strongly connected in ecological space, the wide reporting of Murray's (1993) alarm on the white underclass suggests that inequality and class tensions have extended beyond the confines of the African-American community (one might note also the general increases in hate speech and ethnic intolerance).

B. Drugs and Minorities

The symbolic nature of the "underclass" threat seems to have been operative in the recent "war on drugs" in the United States. Peterson and Hagan's (1984) analysis of drug enforcement activity during the 1960s and 1970s documents the beginning of a shifting concern with drugs and crime in society and illustrates the need to consider historical context in understanding criminal justice operations related to race. More recently, Myers (1989) found increased punitiveness for nonwhite drug dealers, underscoring the need to examine race in conjunction with drug use and drug trafficking in a particular historical context.

Two trends emerged during the 1980s that reinforce these claims. The first was the increasing number of black males under correctional supervision (Mauer 1990), and the second saw increasing punitiveness toward drug offenders, especially blacks and users of cocaine (Belenko, Fagan, and Chin 1991; Blumstein 1993*a;* McGarrell 1993*b*). By the 1990s, race, class, and drugs became intertwined; it is difficult if not impossible to disentangle the various elements of the problem. Moreover, the war on drugs in the 1980s embodied a different personae than earlier wars, leading many to charge racially discriminatory practices by the criminal justice system in the processing of drug offenders (Feeley and Simon 1992, pp. 461–70; Jackson 1992; Tonry 1995). Particularly relevant to this thesis, recall Tittle and Curran's (1988) finding that the largest discriminatory effects on juvenile dispositions concerned drug offenses.

Data from the 1980s support concerns about the changing dynamics of race and drugs. For instance, while the number of arrests for drug abuse violations by white juveniles declined 28 percent in 1985 compared with 1980, the number of arrests for drug abuse violations by black juveniles increased 25 percent over the same time period (Uniform Crime Reports 1980, 1985). Furthermore, data on arrest rate trends by race show that in 1980 the rate of drug law violations was nearly equal for whites and blacks; however, during the decade of the 1980s, white rates declined while black rates increased markedly (Snyder 1992). Juvenile court data show that the number of white youth referred to court for drug law violations declined by 6 percent between 1985 and 1986; the number of referrals for black youth increased by 42 percent (Snyder 1990). The disproportionate increase in the number of black youth detained also seemed linked to the increased number of black drug law violators referred to court. More generally, Blumstein (1993*a*) has shown that the dramatic growth in state prison populations during the 1980s was driven in large part by increasing admissions of blacks on drug convictions.

These trends suggest a recent and increasing punitiveness toward drug offenders—especially those perceived to be gang members from a growing underclass population (Feeley and Simon 1992, pp. 467–69; Jackson 1992, pp. 98–100). Drawing on a revised conflict theory, Sampson and Laub (1993*a*) argue that the rising concentration of socioeconomic disadvantage corresponds precisely with that population perceived as threatening, and the population at which the war on drugs has been aimed. The dual image of "underclass" offenders and the evils of "crack cocaine" thus appears to have triggered a "moral panic" (Goode and Ben-Yehuda 1994; Chiricos and Crawford 1995) in the middle class as well, further reinforcing a drug war by law enforcement.

At the macro level, Sampson and Laub (1993*a*) specifically hypothesized that counties characterized by racial inequality and a large concentration of the "underclass" (i.e., minorities, poverty, female-headed families, welfare) were more likely than other counties to be perceived as containing offensive and threatening populations and as a result experience increased punitiveness and hence social control by the juvenile justice system (see also Feeley and Simon 1992, pp. 467–69; Jackson 1992, pp. 98–100). A static version of this hypothesis found preliminary support in Sampson and Laub's (1993*a*) cross-sectional analysis of approximately 200 counties in 1985. Aggregating court records to the county level, they found that underclass poverty and racial income inequality were associated with higher levels of juvenile confinement (secure detention and out-of-home placement), especially for drug offenses. The effects of underclass poverty also tended to be larger for black juveniles than for white juveniles. In sum, while overt racial discrimination at the individual level appears to be weak, a body of recent contextual evidence suggests that a different scenario may be at work for macrolevel variations in juvenile and adult court processing.

VII. Implications for the Future

In his review essay on studies of criminal sentencing, John Hagan (1987, p. 426) asks: "Why has race so preoccupied us in the study of the criminal justice system?" Indeed, research in the U.S. has embarked on a seemingly unending search for racial influences on criminal justice processing. Hagan's answer is that race and sentencing are symbolically linked considerations in the criminal justice system, "giving the most visible expression to the value we place on equity in this system" (Hagan 1987, p. 426). In other words, the United States prides itself on the symbolism of equality before the law, and any threat of racial bias serves to undermine a major linchpin of the system. It is thus understandable that racial biases, even if seemingly infrequent, have been the subject of much recent concern in the United States.

Strong predictions from conflict theory and ideological beliefs notwithstanding (e.g., MacLean and Milovanovic 1990; Mann 1993), the results of this search have not been kind to a simplistic "discrimination thesis." As shown in this essay, racial discrimination emerges some of the time at some stages of the system in some locations, but there is little evidence that racial disparities reflect systematic, overt bias on the part of criminal justice decision makers. Rather, the most compelling evidence concerning racial discrimination in the administration of justice involves community and national constructions of "moral panics" and political responses to those contexts. For example, Tonry (1995) points out that the war on drugs was initiated at a time when national drug use patterns had already exhibited a considerable decline. Tonry further argues that the politically charged war on drugs, with its legislative and budgetary emphasis on the type of drug most likely to be used and detected in black disadvantaged urban areas (i.e., "crack" cocaine), could be viewed as racially discriminatory in intent and consequences.[16]

In addition, even though overt race discrimination in criminal justice processing appears to be a problem restricted to specific spatial and temporal contexts, the fact remains that racial disparities in crimes other than drugs have reached a critical stage in the United States. Not only is homicide the leading cause of death among young black males and females, it is now the case that the majority of persons in state and federal prisons are black (U.S. Department of Justice 1995). As indicated earlier, the incarceration rate of black males is currently seven times the rate for white males (2,678 vs. 372 per 100,000). Even more striking, approximately 6.3 percent of all black males ages twenty-five to twenty-nine are serving time in state prisons (U.S. Department of Justice 1994*c*), and Mauer (1990, pp. 3, 9) estimates that one of every four black men are processed by the criminal justice system *each year*. With such enormous disproportionality in sanctioning, it should be of

[16] The U.S. federal drug control budget increased from approximately 2.4 billion dollars in 1984 to more than 12.1 billion dollars in 1994 (Executive Office of the President 1994).

little comfort that most of the disparity is a result of differential involvement in nondrug criminal offending.

A. Four Crucial Questions

We believe that to more fully understand racial disparities in crime and justice, at least four areas are in need of further research. First, it is clear that racial differences in criminal victimization and offending, especially for violence, must be studied from a more complex, multilevel perspective (see Sampson and Lauritsen 1994). A lesson learned from our review is that prior theory on criminal offending is usually couched at the level of analysis least likely to yield racial differences—the individual. Posing the problem in a contextual framework, however, suggests that the relationship between race and criminal offending varies substantially across ecological contexts. With few exceptions, criminologists have only recently realized the extent to which correlations between community contexts and crime are confounded with associations between race and crime. *Macrolevel* analysis thus offers an alternative mode of inquiry into the social bases of race and crime (Sampson and Wilson 1995).

Second, the role that formal sanctioning plays in producing *cumulative disadvantage* across the life course of individuals requires a new agenda of research. As suggested throughout our synthesis, the voluminous research on the direct effects of race on conviction, sentencing, and other later stages of adult processing (e.g., imprisonment) appears to have reached a dead end. We know that by the time adults penetrate the justice system to the later stages of sentencing and imprisonment, decision makers rely primarily on prior record and seriousness to dispose of cases. But it is in the juvenile justice system that race discrimination appears most widespread—minorities (and youth in predominantly minority jurisdictions) are more likely to be detained and receive out-of-home placements than whites regardless of "legal" considerations. Because processing in the juvenile justice system is deeply implicated in the construction of a criminal (or "prior") record, experiences as a juvenile serve as a major predictor of future processing. Yet surprisingly little is known about how experiences in the juvenile justice system influence relationships with the police and criminal justice system as youth age into adulthood (Pope and Feyerherm 1990). Rather than more studies of adults in the legal versus extralegal mold, research is thus needed to track offenders backward and forward in time to understand the dynamics of criminal careers. This implies a *life-course* perspective that attempts to bridge the gap between adolescent and adult experiences and to unravel the dynamics of cumulative disadvantage associated with race or ethnicity. In particular, attention to the consequences of disproportionate detention and imprisonment must be a priority (see Sampson and Laub 1993*b*).

Third, despite the volume of previous research on race and ethnic comparisons, we know very little about criminal justice processing other than for blacks and whites. Quite simply, there is little empirical basis from which to draw firm conclusions for Hispanic, Asian, and Native Americans. As seen at the outset, the United States is becoming increasingly diverse largely because of the growing Asian- and Hispanic-American populations. Recent immigration from Mexico and Cuba in particular is reshaping the landscape of many American cities. Hence, the future picture of criminal justice processing may be closely tied to the experiences of race or ethnic groups that have heretofore been neglected by mainstream criminological research. As noted earlier, such analyses will also benefit greatly from work on the changing social constructions of race and ethnic identities in the United States.

Fourth, the extent to which crime wars are waged disproportionately against minorities needs to be examined from a contextual, social constructionist perspective (Best 1990; Goode and Ben-Yehuda 1994; Hawkins 1995). As discussed earlier, the recent drug war in the United States has had its greatest effect on the lives of minorities. While drug arrests have declined among whites, they have skyrocketed among blacks. And while "crack" cocaine has generated an intense law enforcement campaign in our nation's black ghettos, "powder" cocaine use among whites is quietly neglected (perhaps even portrayed as fashionable). These differences cannot be attributed solely to objective levels of criminal danger, but rather to the way in which minority behaviors are symbolically constructed and subjected to official social control (Chambliss 1995; Tonry 1995). As conflict theorists argue, the study of race discrimination in sentencing, controlling for crime type, is irrelevant insofar as "moral panics," legislation, and enforcement activities are designed to target the kinds of lifestyles or areas associated with racial minorities. Hence, close attention to how crime is defined and the social construction of social "problems" is necessary to the study of racial disparity in criminal justice (Goode and Ben-Yehuda 1994).

B. The Global Picture

Because of the nearly overwhelming complexity of these proposed areas of research, it is with an international, comparative approach that we feel the greatest gains will be made. As Ruback and Weiner (1993, p. 195) note, comparative analyses "take advantage of the fact that influences that are causally confounded in their relationships to [crime] within one society or culture are often unconfounded when many societies or cultures are examined." The objective of a comparative approach is to understand how complex causal influences are moderated or mediated by individual and contextual factors. Comparative research also permits the uncovering of etiological universals, and the discovery that variables assumed to be universal have effects only under unique social and cultural circumstances (Munroe, Munroe, and Whiting 1981). Furthermore, comparative analyses provide insights into the assumptions underlying a given society's definitions of race and ethnicity.

Applying a comparative framework to racial disparities in crime and justice raises a host of salient questions. Among many others, a cross-national perspective needs to address variations in how race and ethnicity are related to patterns of offending and victimization across societies. For example, are race and ethnicity effects "explained" in other societies as they are in the United States? What are the relevant theoretical constructs (e.g., community context, cultural heterogeneity, concentration of economic deprivation), and how are they manifested? What do minority groups disproportionately involved in offending have in common across societies? How are historical patterns of racial and ethnic subjugation similar or different? What role does skin color play as opposed to cultural differentiation among groups (Mann 1993)? How do ethnic conflicts over immigration influence crime and social control?

Racial disparities in criminal justice sanctioning are also ripe for comparative study across time and place. At a fundamental level, research has yet to explicate in a systematic way the nature of macrocomparative variations in race and ethnic disparities across societies and epochs of different political, economic, and social structures. For example, we need to be reminded that moral panics have long existed—from the Renaissance witch craze from the fourteenth to the seventeenth century to the "reefer madness" of the 1930s in America to present-day outcries over satanic ritual abuse on a mass scale (Goode and Ben-Yehuda 1994). Under what cultural, structural, and temporal conditions do such moral panics typically arise? Why are accompanying wars waged disproportionately against minorities (e.g., females and blacks)? At the macrocomparative level, a contextual constructionist approach may also shed light on how the structures and cultures of criminal justice organizations contribute to racial or ethnic discrimination.

To be sure, these are only a sampling of the questions that a comparative approach to race and ethnicity might address. But addressing them is a necessary first step toward eliminating racial disparities at all levels of the criminal process, not just in the United States but globally as well. As the 1992 riots in Los Angeles suggest, until racial disparities in crime and justice are reduced, the social stability of the criminal justice system—and perhaps the social structure of the United States—will remain in doubt. Unfortunately, as ethnic and racial conflicts continue to escalate around the globe (Williams 1994), the United States may be a signpost for future trends.

REFERENCES

Aguirre, Adalberto, and David Baker. 1990. "Empirical Research on Racial Discrimination in the Imposition of the Death Penalty." *Criminal Justice Abstracts* 22:135–53.

Albonetti, Celesta. 1990. "Race and the Probability of Pleading Guilty." *Journal of Quantitative Criminology* 6:315–34.

Albonetti, Celesta, Robert Hauser, John Hagan, and Ilene Nagel. 1989. "Criminal Justice Decision Making as a Stratification Process: The Role of Race and Stratification Resources in Pretrial Release." *Journal of Quantitative Criminology* 5:57–82.

Baldus, David, George Woodward, and Charles Pulaski. 1990. *Equal Justice and the Death Penalty: A Legal and Empirical Analysis.* Boston: Northeastern University Press.

Belenko, Steven, Jeffrey Fagan, and Ko-Lin Chin. 1991. "Criminal Justice Responses to Crack." *Journal of Research in Crime and Delinquency* 28:55–74.

Best, Joel. 1990. *Threatened Children.* Chicago: University of Chicago Press.

Bickford, Adam, and Douglas Massey. 1991. "Segregation in the Second Ghetto: Racial and Ethnic Segregation in American Public Housing, 1977." *Social Forces* 69:1011–36.

Black, Donald, and Albert J. Reiss, Jr. 1970. "Police Control of Juveniles." *American Sociological Review* 35:63–77.

Blau, Judith, and Peter M. Blau. 1982. "The Cost of Inequality: Metropolitan Structure and Violent Crime." *American Sociological Review* 47:114–29.

Block, Carolyn R. 1985. "Race/Ethnicity and Patterns of Chicago Homicide, 1965 to 1981." *Crime and Delinquency* 31:104–16.

Blumstein, Alfred. 1982. "On the Racial Disproportionality of the U.S. States' Prison Population." *Journal of Criminal Law and Criminology* 73:1259–81.

———. 1993*a*. "Making Rationality Relevant." *Criminology* 31:1–16.
———. 1993*b*. "Racial Disproportionality of U.S. Prison Populations Revisited." *Colorado Law Review* 64:743–60.
———. 1995. "Violence by Young People: Why the Deadly Nexus?" *National Institute of Justice Journal* 229:2–9.
Bowers, William, and Glenn Pierce. 1980. "Arbitrariness and Discrimination under Post-Furman Capital Statutes." *Crime and Delinquency* 74:1067–1100.
Bridges, George, Robert Crutchfield, and Edith Simpson. 1987. "Crime, Social Structure and Criminal Punishment: White and Nonwhite Rates of Imprisonment." *Social Problems* 34:345–61.
Bridges, George, and Joseph Weis. 1989. "Measuring Violent Behavior: Effects of Study Design on Reported Correlates of Violence." In *Violent Crime, Violent Criminals*, edited by Neil Weiner and Marvin Wolfgang. Beverly Hills, Calif.: Sage.
Brown, M. Craig, and Barbara D. Warner. 1992. "Immigrants, Urban Politics, and Policing in 1900." *American Sociological Review* 57:293–305.
———. 1995. "The Political Threat of Immigrant Groups and Police Aggressiveness in 1900." In *Ethnicity, Race, and Crime: Perspectives across Time and Place*, edited by Darnell Hawkins. Albany: State University of New York Press.
Burke, Peter, and Austin Turk. 1975. "Factors Affecting Post Arrest Decisions: A Model for Analysis." *Social Problems* 22:313–32.
Bursik, Robert J., Jr., and Jim Webb. 1982. "Community Change and Patterns of Delinquency." *American Journal of Sociology* 88:24–42.
Chambliss, William J. 1995. "Crime Control and Ethnic Minorities: Legitimizing Racial Oppression by Creating Moral Panics." In *Ethnicity, Race, and Crime: Perspectives across Time and Place*, edited by Darnell Hawkins. Albany: State University of New York Press.
Chambliss, William J., and Robert B. Seidman. 1971. *Law, Order, and Power.* Reading, Mass.: Addison-Wesley.
Chiricos, Theodore G., and Charles Crawford. 1995. "Race and Imprisonment: A Contextual Assessment of the Evidence." In *Ethnicity, Race, and Crime: Perspectives across Time and Place*, edited by Darnell Hawkins. Albany: State University of New York Press.
Cohen, Lawrence, and Marcus Felson. 1979. "Social Change and Crime Rate Trends: A Routine Activities Approach." *American Sociological Review* 44:588–607.
Cook, Philip. 1987. "Robbery Violence." *Journal of Criminal Law and Criminology* 78:357–76.
Coulton, C., J. Korbin, M. Su, and J. Chow. 1995. "Community Level Factors and Child Maltreatment Rates." *Child Development* 66:1262–76.
Crutchfield, Robert, George Bridges, and Susan Pritchford. 1994. "Analytical and Aggregation Biases in Analyses of Imprisonment: Reconciling Discrepancies in Studies of Racial Disparity." *Journal of Research in Crime and Delinquency* 31:166–82.
Curtis, Lynn. 1975. *Violence, Race, and Culture.* Lexington, Mass.: Heath.

DiIulio, John, Jr. 1994. "The Question of Black Crime." *Public Interest* 117:3–32.

———. 1995. "White Lies about Black Crime." *Public Interest* 118:30–44.

Elliott, Delbert. 1994. "Serious Violent Offenders: Onset, Developmental Course, and Termination—the American Society of Criminology 1993 Presidential Address." *Criminology* 32:1–21.

Elliott, Delbert, and Suzanne Ageton. 1980. "Reconciling Race and Class Differences in Self-Reported and Official Estimates of Delinquency." *American Sociological Review* 45:95–110.

Executive Office of the President. 1994. "National Drug Control Strategy: Budget Summary." Washington, D.C.: Office of National Drug Control Policy.

Feeley, Malcolm, and Jonathan Simon. 1992. "The New Penology: Notes on the Emerging Strategy of Corrections and Its Implications." *Criminology* 30:449–74.

Fingerhut, Lois. 1993. "The Impact of Homicide on Life Chances: International, Intranational and Demographic Comparison." In *Proceedings of the Second Annual Workshop of the Homicide Research Working Group.* Washington, D.C.: U.S. Department of Justice.

Fingerhut, Lois, and J. Kleinman. 1990. "International and Interstate Comparisons of Homicide among Young Males." *Journal of the American Medical Association* 263:3292–95.

Fingerhut, Lois, J. Kleinman, E. Godfrey, and H. Rosenberg. 1991. "Firearms Mortality among Children, Youth, and Young Adults 1–34 Years of Age, Trends and Current Status: United States, 1979–88. *Monthly Vital Statistics Report* 39(11):1–16.

Fishman, Gideon, Arye Rattner, and Gabriel Weiman. 1987. "The Effect of Ethnicity on Crime Attribution." *Criminology* 25:507–24.

Fyfe, James. 1982. "Blind Justice: Police Shootings in Memphis." *Journal of Criminal Law and Criminology* 73:707–22.

Gans, Herbert. 1991. "The Dangers of the Underclass: Its Harmfulness as a Planning Concept." In *People, Plans, and Places,* edited by H. Gans. New York: Columbia University Press.

Garofalo, James. 1987. "Reassessing the Lifestyle Model of Criminal Victimization." In *Positive Criminology,* edited by M. Gottfredson and T. Hirschi. Newbury Park, Calif.: Sage.

Goldkamp, John. 1979. *Two Classes of Accused: A Study of Bail and Detention in American Justice.* Cambridge, Mass.: Ballinger.

Goode, Erich, and Nachman Ben-Yehuda. 1994. "Moral Panics: Culture, Politics, and Social Construction." *Annual Review of Sociology* 20:149–71.

Gottfredson, Michael. 1986. "Substantive Contributions of Victimization Surveys." In *Crime and Justice: An Annual Review of Research,* vol. 7, edited by Michael Tonry and Norval Morris. Chicago: University of Chicago Press.

Hagan, John. 1974. "Extra-legal Attributes and Criminal Sentencing: An Assessment of a Sociological Viewpoint." *Law and Society Review* 8:357–84.

———. 1987. "Review Essay: A Great Truth in the Study of Crime." *Criminology* 25:421–28.

———. 1989. "Why Is There So Little Criminal Justice Theory? Neglected Macro- and Micro-Level Links between Organization and Power." *Journal of Research in Crime and Delinquency* 26:116–35.

Hagan, John, and Kristen Bumiller. 1983. "Making Sense of Sentencing: A Review and Critique of Sentencing Research." In *Research on Sentencing: The Search for Reform*, edited by Alfred Blumstein, Jacqueline Cohen, Susan Martin, and Michael Tonry. Washington, D.C.: National Academy Press.

Harer, Miles, and Darrell Steffensmeier. 1992. "The Differing Effects of Economic Inequality on Black and White Rates of Violence." *Social Forces* 70:1035–54.

Hawkins, Darnell, ed. 1986. *Homicide among Black Americans.* Lanham, Md.: University Press of America.

———. 1995. "Ethnicity, Race, and Crime: A Review of Selected Studies." In *Ethnicity, Race, and Crime*, edited by Darnell Hawkins. Albany: State University of New York Press.

Hawley, F. Frederick, and Steven F. Messner. 1989. "The Southern Violence Construct: A Review of Arguments, Evidence, and the Normative Context." *Justice Quarterly* 6:481–511.

Hedges, Chris. 1994. "Among Israeli Arabs, Latent Anger Explodes." *New York Times* (March 1), p. A7.

Hindelang, Michael. 1978. "Race and Involvement in Common-Law Personal Crimes." *American Sociological Review* 43:93–109.

———. 1981. "Variations in Sex-Race-Age-Specific Incidence Rates of Offending." *American Sociological Review* 46:461–74.

Hindelang, Michael, Michael Gottfredson, and James Garofalo. 1978. *Victims of Personal Crime: An Empirical Foundation for a Theory of Personal Victimization.* Cambridge, Mass.: Ballinger.

Hindelang, Michael, Travis Hirschi, and Joseph Weis. 1979. "Correlates of Delinquency: The Illusion of Discrepancy between Self-Report and Official Measures." *American Sociological Review* 44:995–1014.

———. 1981. *Measuring Delinquency.* Beverly Hills, Calif.: Sage.

Irwin, John. 1985. *The Jail: Managing the Underclass in American Society.* Berkeley and Los Angeles: University of California Press.

Jackson, Pamela Irving. 1992. "Minority Group Threat, Social Context, and Policing." In *Social Threat and Social Control*, edited by Allen E. Liska. Albany: State University of New York Press.

Jackson, Pamela Irving, and Leo Carroll. 1981. "Race and the War on Crime: The Sociopolitical Determinants of Municipal Police Expenditures in 90 Non-Southern Cities." *American Sociological Review* 46:290–305.

Jonassen, Christen. 1949. "A Reevaluation and Critique of the Logic and Some Methods of Shaw and McKay." *American Sociological Review* 14:608–14.

Junger, Marianne. 1989. "Discrepancies between Police and Self-Report Data for Dutch Racial Minorities." *British Journal of Criminology* 29:273–84.

Katz, Jack. 1988. *Seductions of Crime: The Sensual and Moral Attractions of Doing Evil.* New York: Basic.

Katz, Michael. 1993. "The Urban 'Underclass' as a Metaphor of Social Transformation." In *The "Underclass" Debate: Views from History*, edited by Michael Katz. Princeton, N.J.: Princeton University Press.

Keil, Thomas, and Gennaro Vito. 1989. "Race, Homicide Severity, and Application of the Death Penalty." *Criminology* 27:511–31.

Kempf-Leonard, Kimberly, Carl Pope, and William Feyerherm, eds. 1995. *Minorities in Juvenile Justice*. Thousand Oaks, Calif.: Sage.

Kleck, Gary. 1981. "Racial Discrimination in Criminal Sentencing: A Critical Evaluation of the Evidence with Additional Evidence on the Death Penalty." *American Sociological Review* 46:783–805.

Klein, Stephen, Joan Petersilia, and Susan Turner. 1990. "Race and Imprisonment Decisions in California." *Science* 247:812–16.

Kornhauser, Ruth. 1978. *Social Sources of Delinquency: An Appraisal of Analytic Models*. Chicago: University of Chicago Press.

LaFree, Gary, Kriss Day, and Patrick O'Day. 1992. "Race and Crime in Postwar America: Determinants of African American and White Rates." *Criminology* 30:157–88.

Land, Kenneth, Patricia McCall, and Lawrence Cohen. 1990. "Structural Covariates of Homicide Rates: Are There Any Invariances across Time and Space?" *American Journal of Sociology* 95:922–63.

Langan, Patrick. 1985. "Racism on Trial: New Evidence to Explain the Racial Composition of Prisons in the United States." *Journal of Criminal Law and Criminology* 76:666–83.

———. 1994. "No Racism in the Justice System." *Public Interest* 117:48–51.

Lauritsen, Janet L., Robert J. Sampson, and John H. Laub. 1991. "The Link between Offending and Victimization among Adolescents." *Criminology* 29:265–92.

Liska, Allen E. 1987. "A Critical Examination of Macro Perspectives on Crime Control." *Annual Review of Sociology* 13:67–88.

Liska, Allen E., and Mitchell Chamlin. 1984. "Social Structure and Crime Control among Macrosocial Units." *American Journal of Sociology* 90:383–95.

Loeber, Rolf, and Magda Stouthamer-Loeber. 1986. "Family Factors as Correlates and Predictors of Juvenile Conduct Problems." In *Crime and Justice: An Annual Review of Research*, vol. 7, edited by Michael Tonry and Norval Morris. Chicago: University of Chicago Press.

Logan, John, and Harvey Molotch. 1987. *Urban Fortunes: The Political Economy of Place*. Berkeley and Los Angeles: University of California Press.

MacLean, Brian, and Dragan Milovanovic, eds. 1990. *Racism, Empiricism, and Criminal Justice*. Vancouver: Collective Press.

Maguire, Kathleen, and Ann Pastore, eds. 1995. *Sourcebook of Criminal Justice Statistics, 1994*. Washington, D.C.: U.S. Government Printing Office, Bureau of Justice Statistics.

Mann, Coramae Richey. 1993. *Unequal Justice: A Question of Color*. Bloomington: Indiana University Press.

Marks, Jonathan. 1995. *Human Biodiversity: Genes, Race, and History*. Hawthorne, N.Y.: Aldine de Gruyter.

Massey, Douglas S., and Nancy Denton. 1993. *American Apartheid: Segregation and the Making of the Underclass.* Cambridge, Mass.: Harvard University Press.

Mauer, Marc. 1990. "Young Black Men and the Criminal Justice System: A Growing National Problem." Washington, D.C.: Sentencing Project.

McCord, Colin, and Harold Freeman. 1990. "Excess Mortality in Harlem." *New England Journal of Medicine* 322:173–75.

McGarrell, Edmund. 1993*a*. "Institutional Theory and the Stability of a Conflict Model of the Incarceration Rate." *Justice Quarterly* 10:7–28.

———. 1993*b*. "Trends in Racial Disproportionality in Juvenile Court Processing: 1985–1989." *Crime and Delinquency* 39:29–48.

Meier, Robert, and Terance Miethe. 1993. "Understanding Theories of Criminal Victimization." In *Crime and Justice: A Review of Research*, vol. 17, edited by Michael Tonry. Chicago: University of Chicago Press.

Merton, Robert. 1938. "Social Structure and Anomie." *American Sociological Review* 3:672–82.

Miethe, Terance, and C. Moore. 1986. "Racial Differences in Criminal Processing: The Consequences of Model Selection on Conclusions about Differential Treatment." *Sociological Quarterly* 27:217–37.

Miller, Walter. 1958. "Lower Class Culture as a Generating Milieu of Gang Delinquency." *Journal of Social Issues* 14:5–19.

Munroe, Ruth H., Robert L. Munroe, and Beatrice B. Whiting, eds. 1981. *Handbook of Cross-Cultural Human Development.* New York: Garland Press.

Murray, Charles. 1993. "The Coming White Underclass." *Wall Street Journal* (October 29), p. A14.

Myers, Martha. 1979. "Offended Parties and Official Reactions: Victims and the Sentencing of Criminal Defendants." *Sociological Quarterly* 20:529–40.

———. 1989. "Symbolic Policy and the Sentencing of Drug Offenders." *Law and Society Review* 23:295–315.

Myers, Martha, and Susette Talarico. 1987. *The Social Contexts of Criminal Sentencing.* New York: Springer-Verlag.

National Center for Health Statistics. 1995. "Advance Report of Final Mortality Statistics, 1992." Monthly Vital Statistics Report, vol. 43, no. 6, suppl. Washington, D.C.: U.S. Department of Health and Human Services.

O'Brien, Robert. 1987. "The Interracial Nature of Violent Crimes: A Reexamination." *American Journal of Sociology* 92:817–35.

O'Hare, William, and Brenda Curry-White. 1992. "Is There a Rural Underclass?" *Population Today* 20:6–8.

Paternoster, Raymond. 1984. "Prosecutorial Discretion in Requesting the Death Penalty: A Case of Victim-Based Racial Discrimination." *Law and Society Review* 18:437–78.

Peeples, Faith, and Rolf Loeber. 1994. "Do Individual Factors and Neighborhood Context Explain Ethnic Differences in Juvenile Delinquency?" *Journal of Quantitative Criminology* 10:141–58.

Petersilia, Joan. 1983. *Racial Disparities in the Criminal Justice System.* Santa Monica, Calif.: RAND.

———. 1985. "Racial Disparities in the Criminal Justice System: A Summary." *Crime and Delinquency* 31:15–34.

Peterson, Ruth D., and John Hagan. 1984. "Changing Conceptions of Race: Towards An Account of Anomalous Findings of Sentencing Research." *American Sociological Review* 49:56–70.
Piliavin, Irving, and S. Briar. 1964. "Police Encounters with Juveniles." *American Journal of Sociology* 69:206–14.
Pope, Carl, and William Feyerherm. 1990. "Minority Status and Juvenile Justice Processing: An Assessment of the Research Literature" (pts. 1, 2). *Criminal Justice Abstracts* (June):327–35, and (September):527–42.
Radelet, Michael. 1981. "Racial Characteristics and the Imposition of the Death Penalty." *American Sociological Review* 46:918–27.
Reiss, Albert J., Jr., and Jeffrey Roth, eds. 1993. *Understanding and Preventing Violence: Panel of the Understanding and Control of Violent Behavior*, vol. 1. Washington D.C.: National Academy Press.
Ruback, Barry, and Neil Weiner. 1993. "Introduction to Social and Cultural Aspects of Interpersonal Violent Behaviors." *Violence and Victims* 8:193–98.
Sampson, Robert J. 1984. "Group Size, Heterogeneity, and Intergroup Conflict: A Test of Blau's *Inequality and Heterogeneity*." *Social Forces* 62:618–39.
———. 1986. "Effects of Socioeconomic Context on Official Reaction to Juvenile Delinquency." *American Sociological Review* 51:876–85.
———. 1987. "Urban Black Violence: The Effect of Male Joblessness and Family Disruption." *American Journal of Sociology* 93:348–82.
Sampson, Robert J., and W. Byron Groves. 1989. "Community Structure and Crime: Testing Social-Disorganization Theory." *American Journal of Sociology* 94:774–802.
Sampson, Robert J., and John H. Laub. 1992. "Crime and Deviance in the Life Course." *Annual Review of Sociology* 18:63–84.
———. 1993*a*. "Structural Variations in Juvenile Court Processing: Inequality, the Underclass, and Social Control." *Law and Society Review* 27:285–311.
———. 1993*b*. *Crime in the Making: Pathways and Turning Points through Life.* Cambridge, Mass.: Harvard University Press.
Sampson, Robert J., and Janet L. Lauritsen. 1994. "Violent Victimization and Offending: Individual, Situational, and Community-Level Risk Factors." In *Understanding and Preventing Violence: Social Influences*, vol. 3, edited by Albert J. Reiss, Jr., and Jeffrey Roth. Washington, D.C.: National Academy Press.
Sampson, Robert J., and William Julius Wilson. 1995. "Toward a Theory of Race, Crime, and Urban Inequality." In *Crime and Inequality*, edited by John Hagan and Ruth Peterson. Stanford, Calif.: Stanford University Press.
Sellin, Thorsten. 1935. "Race Prejudice in the Administration of Justice." *American Journal of Sociology* 41:212–17.
Shaw, Clifford, and Henry McKay. 1969. *Juvenile Delinquency and Urban Areas.* Rev. ed. Chicago: University of Chicago Press. (Originally published 1942.)
———. 1949. "Rejoinder." *American Sociological Review* 14:614–17.
Simon, Jonathan. 1993. *Poor Discipline: Parole and the Social Control of the Underclass, 1890–1990.* Chicago: University of Chicago Press.

Singer, Simon. 1981. "Homogeneous Victim-Offender Populations: A Review and Some Research Implications." *Journal of Criminal Law and Criminology* 72:779–88.

Skogan, Wesley. 1981. "Assessing the Behavioral Context of Victimization." *Journal of Criminal Law and Criminology* 72:727–42.

———. 1986. "Fear of Crime and Neighborhood Change." In *Communities and Crime*, edited by Albert J. Reiss, Jr., and Michael Tonry. Vol. 8 of *Crime and Justice: A Review of Research*, edited by Michael Tonry and Norval Morris. Chicago: University of Chicago Press.

Smith, Douglas A. 1986. "The Neighborhood Context of Police Behavior." In *Communities and Crime*, edited by Albert J. Reiss, Jr., and Michael Tonry. Vol. 8 of *Crime and Justice: A Review of Research*, edited by Michael Tonry and Norval Morris. Chicago: University of Chicago Press.

Smith, Pheny. 1993. "Felony Defendants in Large Urban Counties, 1990." Washington, D.C.: Bureau of Justice Statistics.

Snyder, Howard. 1990. "Growth in Minority Detentions Attributed to Drug Law Violators." Washington, D.C.: Office of Juvenile Justice and Delinquency Prevention.

———. 1992. "Arrests of Youth 1990." Washington, D.C.: Office of Juvenile Justice and Delinquency Prevention.

Spohn, Cassia, John Gruhl, and Susan Welch. 1987. "The Impact of the Ethnicity and Gender of Defendants on the Decision to Reject or Dismiss Felony Charges." *Criminology* 25:175–92.

Sullivan, Mercer. 1989. *Getting Paid: Youth Crime and Work in the Inner City*. Ithaca, N.Y.: Cornell University Press.

Tienda, Marta. 1991. "Poor People and Poor Places: Deciphering Neighborhood Effects on Poverty Outcomes." In *Macro-Micro Linkages in Sociology*, edited by Joan Huber. Newbury, Calif.: Sage.

Tittle, Charles R. 1994. "The Theoretical Bases for Inequality in Formal Social Control." In *Inequality, Crime, and Social Control*, edited by George Bridges and Martha Myers. Boulder, Colo.: Westview.

Tittle, Charles R., and Debra A. Curran. 1988. "Contingencies for Dispositional Disparities in Juvenile Justice." *Social Forces* 67:23–58.

Tonry, Michael. 1995. *Malign Neglect: Race, Crime, and Punishment in America*. New York: Oxford University Press.

Turk, Austin T. 1969. *Criminality and the Legal Order*. Chicago: Rand McNally.

Uniform Crime Reports. 1980. *Crime in the United States*. Washington, D.C.: U.S. Government Printing Office.

———. 1985. *Crime in the United States*. Washington, D.C.: U.S. Government Printing Office.

U.S. Bureau of Census. 1993. *Statistical Abstract of the United States: 1993*. 113th ed. Washington, D.C.: U.S. Government Printing Office.

U. S. Department of Justice. 1988. *Report to the Nation on Crime and Justice*, 2d ed. Washington, D.C.: U.S. Government Printing Office, March.

———. 1990. *Hispanic Victims, Special Report*. Washington, D.C.: U.S. Government Printing Office.

———. 1993*a*. *Crime in the United States, 1992*. Washington, D.C.: U.S. Government Printing Office.

———. 1993*b*. *Age-Specific Arrest Rates and Race-Specific Arrest Rates for Selected Offenses, 1965–1992*. Washington, D.C.: U.S. Government Printing Office.

———. 1994*a*. *Criminal Victimization in the United States, 1973–1992 Trends*. A National Crime Victimization Survey Report. Washington, D.C.: U.S. Government Printing Office, June.

———. 1994*b*. *Criminal Victimization in the United States, 1992*. Washington, D.C.: U.S. Government Printing Office.

———. 1994*c*. *Prisoners in 1993*. Bureau of Justice Statistics Bulletin. Washington, D.C.: U.S. Government Printing Office.

———. 1995. *Correctional Populations in the United States, 1993*. Executive Summary. Washington, D.C.: U.S. Government Printing Office.

Wilbanks, William. 1985. "Is Violent Crime Intraracial?" *Crime and Delinquency* 31:117–28.

———. 1986. "Criminal Homicide Offenders in the U.S.: Black vs. White." In *Homicide among Black Americans*, edited by Darnell Hawkins. Lanham, Md.: University Press of America.

———. 1987. *The Myth of a Racist Criminal Justice System*. Monterey, Calif.: Brooks/Cole.

Williams, Robin, Jr. 1994. "The Sociology of Ethnic Conflicts: Comparative International Perspectives." *Annual Review of Sociology* 20:49–79.

Wilson, James Q., and Richard Herrnstein. 1985. *Crime and Human Nature*. New York: Simon & Schuster.

Wilson, William Julius. 1987. *The Truly Disadvantaged: The Inner City, the Underclass, and Public Policy*. Chicago: University of Chicago Press.

Wilson, William Julius, R. Aponte, J. Kirschenman, and Loic Wacquant. 1988. "The Ghetto Underclass and the Changing Structure of American Poverty." In *Quiet Riots: Race and Poverty in the United States*, edited by F. Harris and R. W. Wilkins. New York: Pantheon.

Wolfgang, Marvin. 1958. *Patterns in Criminal Homicide*. New York: Wiley.

Wolfgang, Marvin, and Franco Ferracuti. 1967. *The Subculture of Violence*. London: Tavistock.

Wordes, Madeline, Timothy Bynum, and Charles Corley. 1994. "Locking up Youth: The Impact of Race on Detention Decisions." *Journal of Research in Crime and Delinquency* 31:149–65.

Zatz, Marjorie. 1984. "Race, Ethnicity and Determinate Sentencing: A New Dimension to an Old Controversy." *Criminology* 22:147–71.

———. 1987. "The Changing Forms of Racial/Ethnic Biases in Sentencing." *Journal of Research in Crime and Delinquency* 24:69–92.

Martin Killias

Immigrants, Crime, and Criminal Justice in Switzerland

ABSTRACT

Switzerland is among the European countries with the largest foreign population and the longest immigration tradition. Over many decades, immigrants were not overrepresented in official crime data. More recently, the proportion of non-Swiss offenders increased substantially, but more for nonresident (often illegal) aliens than for legal residents. Victims' accounts of offenders' characteristics confirm the disproportionate crime involvement of immigrants, particularly in violent crime. However, disparity in reporting decisions by victims has not been observed, nor have major disparities in prosecution, sentencing, or time served. Immigrants are not disproportionately victimized, and their attitudes toward police and criminal justice are more positive than those of Swiss respondents. Nonetheless, certain groups have higher offending and victimization rates. Cultural factors, socioeconomic status, and social integration may account for these differences.

Within continental Europe, Switzerland's history of migration differed somewhat from that of other countries. During many centuries and until the end of the nineteenth century, Switzerland experienced steady and significant emigration that exceeded by far the modest number of immigrants. Shortly before 1900, the balance shifted, however, in favor of immigrants. By the beginning of World War I, immigrants, mostly from Italy and other neighboring countries, made up about 14 percent of the total population.

Martin Killias is professor of criminology at the School of Forensic Science and Criminology, University of Lausanne.

0192-3234/97/0021-0006$01.00

During the war and the following decades of depression, because of persistent unemployment, the proportion of foreign citizens in the total population fell, reaching a historic low of about 5.2 percent in 1941. But before the end of World War II, and during the following decades of prosperity, the foreign population increased rapidly (Hoffmann-Nowotny and Killias 1979). This movement has not halted.

By the end of 1994, according to the Swiss Federal Office of Statistics, Switzerland's foreign population reached 19 percent. This official figure (*Annuaire statistique de la Suisse* 1995, p. 53) does not include the personnel of foreign organizations (such as the UN headquarters in Geneva) and their families (25,000 persons), asylum seekers (around 40,000 awaiting a decision), tourists (more than 200,000 on an average day; Gilomen 1993), and illegal residents (according to estimates, 100,000–200,000). All in all, more than 20 percent of the total population are foreign nationals.

Given this background, Switzerland's situation differs in two important respects from other European countries. First, the number of foreign residents is substantially higher than in any other country, except in small states like Luxemburg, Monaco, or Liechtenstein. Second, large-scale immigration began nearly fifty years earlier than in most other European countries. Unlike countries that are experiencing only first and second generations of immigrants, Switzerland has had substantial second and even third generations for some time. Despite this long tradition, immigration in Switzerland still provokes tensions and difficulties. Switzerland, like other European countries, has so far been unable to design a consistent immigration policy (Krane 1979). Over the last twenty-five years, there have been many political initiatives to curb immigration, mostly from right-wing grass-roots movements. They all failed, but made it harder for authorities to pursue consistent efforts at promoting integration of immigrants into the Swiss economy and society (Gilomen 1993).

Recent shifts in the origins and composition of the immigrant population further complicate the issue. In 1984, three in five foreigners living in Switzerland originated from Italy (42 percent), Germany (9 percent), France (5 percent), and Austria (3 percent). By the end of 1993, the neighboring countries' share decreased to two in five—29 percent Italians, 7 percent Germans, 4 percent French, and 2 percent Austrians. During the same period, the proportion of immigrants from (former) Yugoslavia increased from 7 to 19 percent. Minor increases occurred for Turks (from 5 to 6 percent), Africans (from 1 to 2 percent),

TABLE 1

Drug Traffic Arrests in the Canton of Zurich during 1992, by Foreign and Residence Status (in Percent)

	All Suspects of Drug Trafficking	Swiss Offenders	Resident Foreign Offenders	Nonresident Foreign Offenders	Asylum Seekers
Drug trafficking	100 (1,844)	37	22	14	28
Importation of drugs	100 (198)	14	7	77	2

Source.—Unpublished data from Canton of Zurich Police Statistics (KRISTA), 1992. Sample sizes are in parentheses.

and Asians (from 3 to 4 percent). The combined share of immigrants from Spain and Portugal rose from 14 to 18 percent (*Annuaire statistique de la Suisse* 1995, p. 53).

Over many years, crimes of and among immigrants received little attention, whether in scholarly publications or public debate. The massive and sudden waves of immigrants from southern Italy during the 1950s and 1960s fueled, however, some public concern. Studies based on conviction statistics, however, did not confirm fears concerning higher conviction (or crime) rates among immigrants (Hacker 1939; Neumann 1963; Pradervand and Cardia 1966; Gillioz 1967). It seemed that first-generation immigrants had lower conviction rates than native Swiss males of comparable age. Given the low interest in crime and criminology in Switzerland at that time, even the substantial foreign population did not stimulate more than occasional research on the subject.

This peaceful picture has recently changed. In connection with the debate on Zurich's "needle park" (open drug scene), the public was shocked by press reports on the predominance of foreigners (and particularly asylum seekers) among arrested drug dealers (see table 1) and the inability of the police to deal with this problem. Current laws do not allow deportation of asylum seekers, nor is it possible to deport illegal aliens whose identity has not been ascertained. Before 1995, there was no lawful basis for detaining illegal aliens for longer than thirty days in order to prepare deportation proceedings, or to obtain a new passport from foreign embassies or consulates which are not always willing to cooperate (Conseil Fédéral 1994). Under these circumstances, many illegal aliens whom the police suspect of dealing in drugs or other criminal activities but who, because of lack of probable cause, could not be arrested destroyed their documents and made every effort to conceal their origin and identity. After thirty days, they had to be released and many returned to the drug scene immediately afterward.

This unexpected and new problem led to a public order crisis in Zurich and other cities, of proportions that overwhelmed police and prison capacity. Often police officers released foreign drug dealers a few hours after arrest because of a lack of prison cells and because immediate deportation was impossible. At times, police departments announced publicly that no arrests would be made during the next five or ten days due to lack of prison capacity. To curb these developments, the federal parliament enacted new laws ("Loi fédérale sur les mesures de contraine en matière de droit des étranges du 18 mars" 1994) to facilitate deportation of illegal aliens; these were approved by a majority of 73 percent in a referendum late in 1994 ("Résultats de la votation du 4 décembre 1994" 1995). In the meantime, the open drug scenes were closed, and large-scale heroin prescription programs were initiated. This led to a normalization of the situation, and the issue of crime is no longer as commonly perceived as being directly related to immigration (Killias 1995).

These developments suggest that crime by foreign citizens may be less a matter of immigrants in the sense of a foreign resident population and increasingly related to nonresident gangs and individuals. It may well be that recent Swiss experience provides a model for what other countries will experience in coming years. In other words, "crime and minorities" may become less related to residents from foreign countries or with distinctive racial or cultural identities, and more to groups of transient people who lack stable links to countries in whose justice systems they become entangled.

This essay first discusses the crime involvement of foreign nationals as indicated by official data and documents changes that have occurred during the last twenty years. Official statistics show high and increasing proportions of foreign nationals among suspects in recent years but not twenty years ago and show that proportions are rising more for nonresident than for resident foreigners.

Next, I look at data on self-reported delinquency among juveniles of Swiss and immigrant background, giving special attention to the so-called second generation. The second generation seems to be increasingly delinquent according to official data, although the picture is less consistent for survey data.

Third, I examine victimization studies to assess the extent of victimization among immigrants, their involvement in such events as suspects (according to victims' accounts, which seem to match police data), and the (negligible) impact of ethnicity on reporting decisions by victims. In sum, those migrants who came in the 1960s and 1970s are no more victimized than the Swiss, whereas those who came over the last ten years or so are. "Traditional" immigrants also have surprisingly positive views on the Swiss police and the criminal justice system.

Fourth, I explore possible reasons for the disproportionate numbers of foreign nationals among prison inmates and discuss the available evidence on the extent of differential treatment of Swiss and foreign nationals within the criminal justice system. Overall, although differential treatment may exist at several levels of the criminal justice process, it is unlikely to account for the wide disparities found in recent prison populations.

Finally, I consider policy implications and suggest future research priorities. Important shifts in immigration patterns and policies have occurred over the last ten years, which seem to be responsible for recent developments. However, Swiss experience in earlier periods supports a more optimistic view insofar as high levels of immigration were not, until the mid-1980s, associated with high offending and victimization among immigrants, nor with widespread discrimination by the criminal justice system and resulting hostile attitudes among minorities toward the police.

I. Foreign Offenders in Official Statistics

Official data on crime are usually collected at police, court, and correctional levels. This section looks first at how foreign nationality is registered in official statistics and then turns to conviction and police statistics and what they show about criminal involvement of foreigners in Switzerland. The final section is devoted to the so-called second generation and moves beyond official data to survey data on self-reported delinquency.

A. Measurement Problems

Comparisons made on the basis of criminal justice statistics necessarily imply the computation of rates. In this respect, criminology has always been very much concerned with the validity of the numerator, that is, the number of persons charged, prosecuted, convicted, or incarcerated, as a measure of criminal involvement by the demographic subgroup under consideration. Much less attention has been devoted to the validity of the denominator, the population by reference to which rates are calculated, although it is no less crucial to the validity of the rate on which comparisons between groups are based.

The numerator in Swiss statistics can be assumed to be reasonably reliable as far as the suspect's foreign citizenship is concerned. Nationality is routinely registered whenever a person needs to be identified, along with his name, sex, date of birth, and address, although race and ethnicity are not. Nationalized persons and Swiss with a second nationality are counted as Swiss. This way of identifying a person is deeply rooted in bureaucratic traditions and is considered unexceptionable in Switzerland and in other European countries. It means that the numerator of Swiss suspects will include a few subjects who originally immigrated from a different country. But in view of the low number of nationalizations—less than 10,000 in any of the five years from 1989 to 1993, and a foreign population of roughly 1.3 million (*Annuaire statistique de la Suisse* 1995, p. 52)—this source of error is negligible in the following analyses.

More problems with reliability arise concerning the distinction between resident and nonresident foreign suspects: in some cases, nonresident (including illegal) aliens may be counted as "residents" if they have a permanent address in Switzerland, although their status would not allow them to live officially in the country (Bauhofer 1993). Such problems in reliability may have increased in recent years given the higher numbers of asylum seekers and other nonpermanent and illegal residents.

These problems increase the difficulties with the denominator. It is relatively easy to locate data on the demographic composition of the resident foreign population by sex, age, and nationality. But no precise data are available on the composition of the nonresident population. Given the huge number of persons who cross the borders of Switzerland every year—according to estimates, around 234 million people in 1993—in a country whose legal residents now total 7 million, it is impossible to relate the total number of foreign offenders to an appropriate denominator. All we can do is relate the number of resident foreign suspects to the official resident population, taking gender and age into account. We have, however, to keep in mind that this numerator may include an unknown number of nonresident offenders and that this measurement problem may have increased in recent years. According to a recently published report (Storz, Rônez, and Baumgartner 1996, p. 12), 43 percent of those convicted as "foreign nationals with residence in Switzerland" in fact do not have legal residence status within the country.

Conviction and police statistics have always given rates for Swiss and "foreign" nationals. During the last century, statistics contained a category concerning "immigrant" offenders from other Swiss cantons (Zürcher and Sträuli 1895). The tradition of publishing separate rates for Swiss and foreign suspects has only recently been challenged as a way of "labeling" immigrants (Kunz 1989). So far, no detailed figures have been published for certain foreign nationalities. However, when the increasing involvement in crime of nonresident aliens became apparent during the 1960s (Gillioz 1967) and with the aim of deemphasizing crime by immigrants, the rates increasingly were broken down into "resident" and "nonresident" foreigners. This brought the numerator into line with the denominator and thus avoided inflating immigrant crime rates.

B. Conviction Statistics

I begin the statistical overview with conviction statistics. They are the most detailed concerning types of crime, gender, and age, and they contain details for resident and nonresident foreign convicts for a relatively long period (1974–88).

Figure 1 shows that, controlling for age, conviction rates relative to population were higher for Swiss than for foreign men in 1974 but lower in 1988. Conviction rates per 100,000 for every age-group were calculated for foreign and Swiss male citizens. For every age-group, the rate of convictions for the foreign male population has been divided by the corresponding rate for the Swiss male population. Whenever this quotient is 1.0, the Swiss and foreign conviction rates are the same relative to population; when it is above 1.0, the conviction rate is higher for the foreign male than for the Swiss male population of a given age bracket, and it is higher for the Swiss whenever the quotient is below 1.0. This form of presentation allows visualization of the shift that has occurred between 1974 and 1988. In the youngest age-group (eighteen to twenty-four), for example, the conviction rate for immigrants was about the same as for the Swiss in 1974, but was more than twice as high in 1988. Overall, the conviction rate for male resident

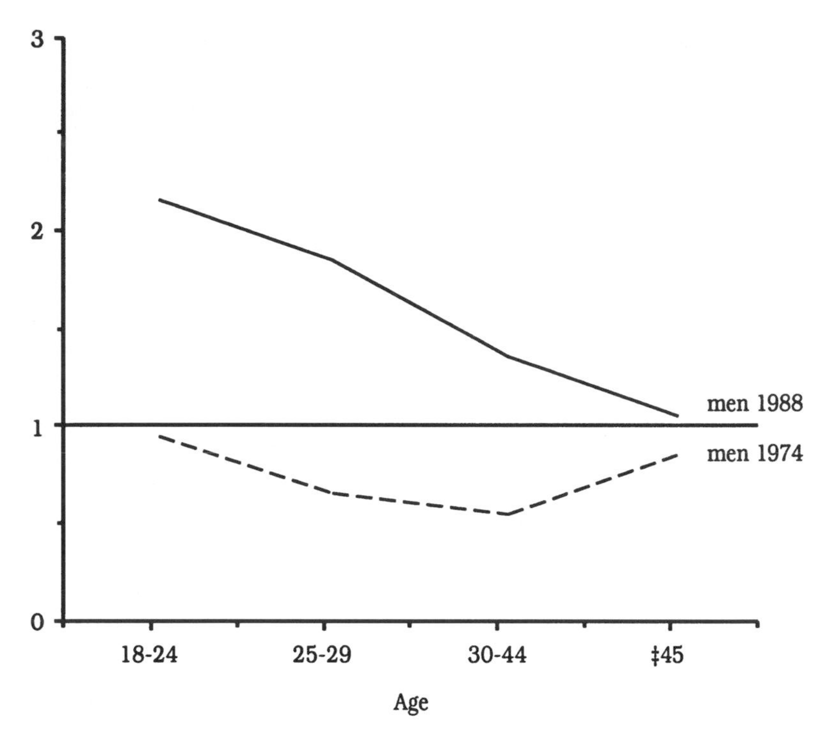

Fig. 1.—Quotient comparing conviction rates for Swiss and resident foreign males for several age-groups. Convictions are according to the Swiss criminal code, 1974 and 1988. Source: Killias (1991), p. 169 (on the base of data provided by the Office Fédéral de la Statistique).

foreigners in 1974 did not in any age bracket exceed the Swiss rate, a finding consistent with those writers who examined local conviction data at that time (Neumann 1963; Pradervand and Cardia 1966). In 1988, however, conviction rates for foreign men exceeded those for the Swiss in all but the highest age-group (forty-five years and over).

Thus there is little doubt that immigrants had a comparatively low crime rate in the early 1970s. This observation is interesting and to some extent challenging, given the contemporary European context in which immigrants seem everywhere to be overrepresented in crime statistics. There seems to be no fatal and inevitable "law" of higher crime rates among immigrants. Moreover, discrimination does not seem to be inevitable in the sense that it "automatically" and under all circumstances produces higher conviction rates for immigrants.

Several explanations may be offered for this finding. First, immigrants did not suffer from unemployment in the 1960s. They were heavily motivated to improve their position—often in view of a plan later to return to their native countries and regions, and they saw their personal situation, despite obvious and perceived disadvantages on the Swiss labor market, as favorable compared to what they had left behind (Hoffmann-Nowotny 1973). Second, they did not differ too much from the Swiss in cultural and religious background, given the prevalence of Italians and other nationals from Mediterranean European countries among immigrants to Switzerland at that time.

The picture has gradually changed since 1974 to the disadvantage of the foreign population. In 1988, young male foreign residents were more than twice as often convicted as the Swiss of the same age and sex. Several explanations are possible. First, it might be that, compared to 1974, the 1988 numerator included more nonresidents among the resident foreign convicts and that the difference between the Swiss and the foreign nationals might be spurious or, at least, much smaller than what figure 1 may suggest. (According to recently published data about two in five "resident" foreign convicts were wrongly reported as such; see Storz, Rônez, and Baumgartner 1996, p. 12.) However, it is hard to believe that this problem may have increased so dramatically that all the shift between 1974 and 1988 could be explained away by this factor alone. Second, shifts in the points of origin of the foreign population, with more immigrants coming from more remote countries, might be reflected in these figures, due either to higher criminal involvement by them or to heavier discrimination against them. Third, consistent with the decreasing overrepresentation of foreigners in the older age brackets, one might also hypothesize over an increasing demographic influence of the so-called second generation among the foreign population. In any case, the markedly deteriorated labor market of the 1990s cannot have affected conviction rates in 1988.

It is, of course, not unlikely that the disparity in conviction rates has widened since 1988. However, it is interesting to note the change between 1974 and 1988 because it occurred before and independently of the most recent shifts in immigration—following the opening of the borders in Eastern Europe in 1989—and new developments in certain illegal markets (such as drugs).

C. Police Statistics

Switzerland has only since 1982 published data on offenses recorded by the police. These statistics are a mere compilation of local (mostly cantonal) statistics, with many inconsistencies in counting (Killias

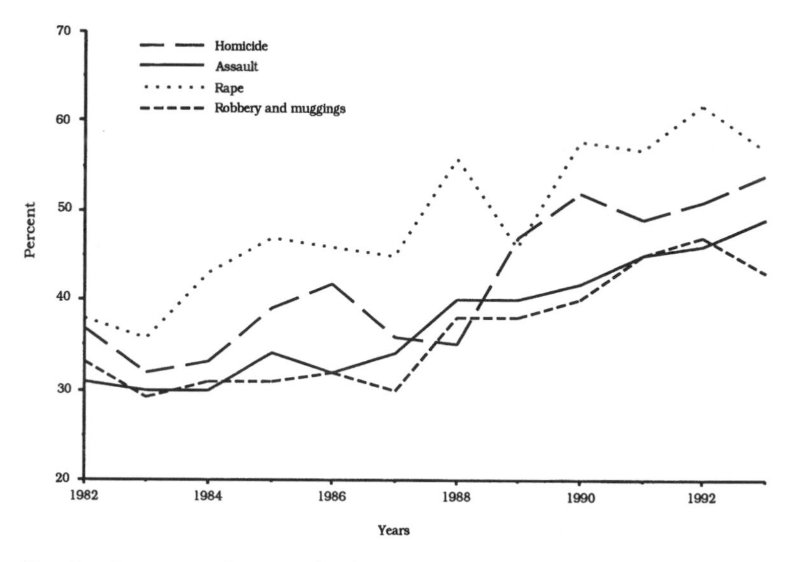

FIG. 2.—Percentage foreign offenders (residents and nonresidents combined) for selected offenses recorded by the police, 1982–93. Source: Ministère Public de la Confédération (1982–93).

1991, p. 68). Since these problems may not have changed too much over the period covered (1982–93), the federal police statistics' indications of the percentages of foreign offenders probably reasonably accurately capture the trends.

As figure 2 reveals, the proportions of foreign offenders among suspects of violent offenses recorded by the police have increased more or less steadily since 1982, and particularly since 1988–89. The increase has recently been particularly marked for drug offenses. In 1994, foreign offenders made up 88 percent of drug-trafficking suspects; if suspects who are drug addicts and who deal in drugs to sustain their consumption are included, the proportion of foreign suspects is still 55 percent. Even without drug and violent offenses, Switzerland in 1990 had, compared with other countries, a top position regarding the proportion of offenses that are committed by foreign nationals. Table 2, presenting the percentages of foreign suspects among persons arrested for thirteen crimes in France, Germany, Hungary, Sweden, and Switzerland, shows that for every crime foreigners (in Switzerland) made up the largest percentage of suspects in any of the five countries.

The most recent figures indicate that the problem has continued to grow. Table 3 gives the percentage of suspects for major crimes who

TABLE 2

Percentage of Foreign Suspects, according to Police Statistics of Five European Countries, for Selected Offenses Recorded by the Police (1990)

	France	Germany	Hungary	Sweden	Switzerland
Homicide (including attempts)	15	28	2	26	52
Homicide completed	13	...	...	29	...
Assault	17	22	1	19	42
Rape	17	33	3	40	58
Robbery (including muggings)	19	36	2	26	40
Armed robbery	11	...	...	30	...
Theft	14	27	1	23	39
Theft of a motor vehicle	11	17	...	...	26
Theft of a bicycle	...	26	...	12	...
Burglary	10	22	1	13	33
Domestic burglary	10	21	...	16	...
Drug offenses	22	23	30	20	36
Drug trafficking offenses	38	33	...	25	43

Source.—Council of Europe (1995), tables 1b/ia–vib.

TABLE 3

Percentage of Swiss, Foreign Resident, and Nonresident Suspects, for More Serious Offenses in Switzerland, in 1994

	Swiss Suspects	Foreign Resident Suspects	Foreign Nonresident Suspects
Homicide (including attempts)	53.8	37.1	9.1
Bodily injury	48.9	45.7	5.4
Robbery (including muggings)	55.3	33.2	11.5
Rape	38.4	55.8	5.8
Burglary	58.3	29.1	12.6
Drug trafficking*	44.9	33.0	11.9
Drug smuggling*	58.2	27.0	10.3

Source.—Ministère Public de la Confédération (1994); Office Fédéral de la Police (1994).

* The total of these rows is less than 100 percent because of aliens with unknown residence.

are Swiss, foreign residents, and foreign nonresidents in 1994. Swiss nationals constitute 80 percent of the population, but only 38–58 percent of suspects for various crimes.

The particular importance of nonresidents among suspects of drug trafficking is illustrated by table 1, giving detailed rates for suspects of drug trafficking according to residence status. In 1992, in Zurich Canton, Swiss nationals were only 37 percent of suspected drug traffickers and 14 percent of suspected drug importers.

There have been several shifts in nationality among the dominant drug dealers. After a period of domination by Turks, the local drug market became the "*chasse gardée*" of Albanians from the Yugoslavian province of Kosovo, followed later in 1993 and in 1994 by North Africans and Lebanese. Many of the drug dealers from Lebanon had fought in the civil war for Hesbollah and other similar organizations, a background that may explain a sharp increase in brutal violence (including homicides) in Zurich's needle park from 1992 to 1994.

Although the domination of the drug market by succeeding gangs from different countries may have economic explanations, newcomers being usually able to provide drugs at lower costs, just how and why these shifts occur is not entirely clear. According to unpublished police sources, in 1995 the price of heroin had fallen to approximately 10–20 percent of what it had been three years earlier.

The proportion of foreign suspects in various European countries should be related to the foreign population in each country, and its gender and age structure should be given due consideration. Given the unavailability of data on the nonresident population, in Switzerland as well as in other countries, the computation of valid rates is simply impossible. However, it is not feasible to exclude nonresident suspects from the numerator, because police data files do not identify the resident status of foreign suspects in all countries.

But even with these limitations, the data in figure 2 and in tables 2 and 3 illustrate the increasing importance of immigration in connection with crime in Switzerland, and particularly in relation to violent crime (including rape and homicide) and drug trafficking. It is hard to see this trend merely as the result of increasing discrimination and intolerance, although such attitudes may play a role. Especially the sharp increase after 1989 seems to suggest that the open borders across Europe (and, to some extent, the world) have increased population mobility to unprecedented levels, including mobility of those who move in search of criminal opportunities. Given its wealth and concomitantly the excellent opportunity structure for offenders, including the highly attractive open drug scenes (Eisner 1993*a;* Hug 1993), Switzerland may be an attractive place for people who seek illegitimate gains.

Even if those who move are no more motivated to commit offenses than anybody else including the resident population, small countries with huge transient populations will necessarily see their crime rate affected by the size of their nonresident population. The number of crimes committed in any given geographic space will increase with the number of offenders who operate in it, whether they live there or not.

Studies on crime and urban structure show that crime levels in city centers tend to be fairly independent of the size of the local population, but to depend mainly on the number of commuters. In a similar sense, crime rates in Switzerland, given its resident population of 7 million and perhaps 100 million individuals entering in any given year, will be affected very substantially by international migration. In countries with fewer transient nonresidents relative to the resident population, migration may affect the overall crime rate to a much lesser degree.

D. *"Second-Generation" Immigrants*

One interesting feature of Switzerland in the present context is its long tradition of immigration. Many among the younger foreigners living in Switzerland were born there or spent most of their childhood and adolescence in the country, although they may not have taken on Swiss nationality.

Following early American studies, German and French research of the last twenty years (for a review see Killias 1989*a*) tried to assess, largely on the basis of police and court statistics, whether immigrant children had higher offending rates than did first-generation immigrants or juveniles of German or French descent. In general, researchers found much higher rates for the so-called second generation and particularly for violent offenses. In a similar study (with comparable results), Killias (1977) analyzed police data from Zurich and Geneva. Queloz (1986), in a study on cases handled by juvenile courts in the canton of Neuchâtel, found a higher conviction rate for young immigrants below age fifteen, but not for those between fifteen and eighteen.

According to police statistics of the Zurich canton (which provides the best data in this regard), the rate of suspects of foreign nationality is comparable to the rate of young Swiss below age fourteen, but is generally much higher among juveniles aged fifteen to twenty. The exception is drug use where the rates were comparable until 1988, but with significantly higher rates for foreigners ever since. For violent offenses, burglary, and drug trafficking, the disparities—which were moderate before 1990, except for violent offenses—have increased significantly since that time. Thus young foreigners over fifteen seem to offend at significantly higher rates than do young Swiss of the same

TABLE 4

Last-Year Prevalence Rates of Self-Reported Delinquency among Swiss and Foreign Respondents Aged Fourteen to Twenty-One (for 1992)

	Swiss		Foreign	
Type	*N*	Percent	*N*	Percent
Property offenses	303	35.2	22	20.0
Violent offenses	255	29.7	27	24.5
Drug offenses	190	22.1	14	12.7
Other youth-related offenses	479	55.7	51	46.4
Overall delinquency prevalence (without alcohol and "problem" behavior)	635	73.8	65	59.1
"Problem" behavior (without alcohol)	190	22.1	17	15.5

SOURCE.—Killias, Villettaz, and Rabasa (1994), table 14.

age. Although Zurich is not necessarily comparable to the rest of the country, it may be particularly significant given its large immigrant population.

These observations, based on police statistics, seem to be in line with what has been found in recent years to be the general trend in research on this subject throughout Western and Northern Europe (Killias 1989*a*), namely, a relatively higher rate of offenders among juvenile immigrants compared to the first generation of immigrants and to native juveniles of the same age. It is not possible to know at what ages these juveniles came to Switzerland, whether they were born in the country, and what their status might be. However, given the predominance of economic migration after World War II and until the late 1980s, only very few are likely to have come to Switzerland as refugees.

Interestingly and despite substantial controversy and speculation, only very recently have self-report studies been undertaken on this topic. The picture that emerges is somewhat contradictory, as table 4, which presents some of the findings, shows. In the Swiss national self-report study, foreign respondents (aged fourteen to twenty-one) generally had lower rates of self-reported offending than the young Swiss.

This study, which is part of an international self-report project (Junger-Tas, Terlouw, and Klein 1994), is based on a national random sample of 970 juveniles and included 110 foreign respondents (11.3 percent). The response rate was somewhat lower among the foreign-born. More important, however, might be underreporting among minority respondents in self-report interviews, a bias noticed by Junger (1990) in the Netherlands and regarded as a robust finding in American research by Sampson and Lauritsen (in this volume). In the present context, there is, unfortunately, no way to ascertain whether and to what extent underreporting is responsible for the absence of any disparity between immigrant and Swiss juveniles. Nor is there a convincing explanation for discrepancies between trends in police data and in these self-report data.

It may be that underreporting among minorities is more important in face-to-face interview situations than with written questionnaires. Two recent studies that have used the latter technique in the classroom found results that are more in line with police statistics. Eisner, Branger, and Liechti (1994), in a survey of 594 ninth-grade students (about fifteen years old) in the city of Zurich, found a comparable or slightly lower rate for foreign youths of self-reported minor property and violent offenses, but a higher rate of more serious behaviors including gang fights (table 5). The latter finding may reflect higher involvement among minority youths in street gangs (Klein 1995, p. 225).

Interestingly, among the minority youths, those who were born abroad differed the most from the Swiss, whereas those with a foreign-born father had rates that fell between those of Swiss and the foreign born. (Similar findings occur in Sweden; see Martens, in this volume.)

Similar results were found in a recent self-report study on drug use and selected delinquency items conducted through written questionnaires filled out in the classroom. Based on a sample of classes, 9,268 students aged fifteen to twenty were interviewed throughout the entire country, including a sample of juveniles of the same ages who no longer attend school (Michaud, Narring, and Paccaud 1993). As table 6 shows, the study found equal rates among foreign and Swiss juveniles of use of soft drugs; however, foreign boys (but not girls) much more often admitted taking hard drugs (heroin and cocaine).

Thus it seems that written questionnaires produce results more in line with police statistics, whereas face-to-face interviews yield lower and presumably too low rates of offending among immigrant juveniles.

II. Victimization Studies

Victimization surveys can be helpful in more than one respect. They allow comparison of victimization rates according to ethnic subgroups within the population, as well as fear of crime and attitudes toward the

TABLE 5

Lifetime Prevalence Rates of Self-Reported Property and Violent Offenses among Swiss and Foreign Students (Aged about Fifteen) in the City of Zurich

	Respondent Born Abroad	Respondent Born in Switzerland, Father Born Abroad	Respondent Born in Switzerland
Fare dodging	81.9	89.5	94.1
Driving without a license	54.8	62.2	64.0
Spraying graffiti	18.3	17.5	21.0
Vandalism	23.4	27.9	30.8
Stealing from a vending machine	11.2	16.8	18.1
Shoplifting below 50 francs	45.2	51.6	56.0
Shoplifting above 50 francs	20.0	23.3	20.2
Stealing at home from acquaintances	20.5	25.8	36.5
Stealing from an unknown person	22.8	22.6	22.1
Stealing bike/scooter	15.7	19.2	17.5
Stealing car/motorbike	4.8	4.2	3.1
Stealing from a car	6.3	5.9	3.5
Burglary	7.1	6.6	4.4
Assault/threatening with a weapon	4.0	3.9	3.3
Hurting with a weapon	4.0	4.2	3.3
Hitting someone alone	32.0	30.4	30.7
Hitting someone in collaboration with others	9.7	11.7	9.4
Fighting with another group	22.8	22.2	14.9

Source.—Eisner, Branger, and Liechti (1994).

TABLE 6

Prevalence ("Ever") of Self-Reported Substance Use among Juveniles in Switzerland

	Swiss Boys	Foreign Boys	Swiss Girls	Foreign Girls
Cannabis	40	40	25	24
Cocaine	2.5	5.5	1.5	1.5
Heroin	2.1	3.9	1.1	.7

Source.—Unpublished data from Michaud, Narring, and Paccaud (1993).

criminal justice system in general and especially the police. But they also allow matching of the number of foreign offenders according to police statistics with the accounts by victims of their assailant's identity and characteristics and provide evidence on whether victims tend to consider the offender's origin in deciding whether to report an offense to the police.

A. Discriminatory Reporting by Victims

Victim surveys sometimes include questions concerning demographic characteristics of the offender, including his origin or appearance. This has been done in the 1987 Swiss Crime Victimization Survey (Killias 1989*b*), Switzerland's first and, so far, only national victim survey. In that survey, 6,500 household respondents were interviewed by telephone (using computer-assisted telephone interviews) on household and personal victimization. Among over 600 variables, victims of personal crimes (in German- and Italian-speaking areas) that involved some contact with the offender were asked questions about the offender's sex, approximate age, and ethnicity.

American research on the validity of victims' accounts of offender characteristics (and race in particular) has shown these indications to be fairly valid if the "unknown" or "uncertain" categories are excluded (Schneider 1981). In the case of the Swiss crime survey of 1987, no such validity check could be undertaken. Given the great awareness of the Swiss (and other central Europeans) of accents and local dialects in everyday life, however, one might assume that victims' accounts of the offender's ethnicity would be no less accurate and reliable than has been observed in this respect in America concerning race. But ultimately, we do not know.

If we assume acceptable validity of this information, the rate of offenders whom victims describe as immigrant (foreign by language or accent, appearance, or both) corresponds to patterns in police statistics (for the corresponding years) concerning rape, but is much higher for robbery and mugging, and considerably lower for assault, as table 7 shows. Overall, there is little support for the proposition that police statistics exaggerate the involvement of immigrants in these offenses.

The higher percentage of foreigners among police suspects of assault, compared with victims' accounts, may result from police recording practices. Some offenses, such as assault, are prosecuted only on the victim's formal request, and the police usually wait for a formal complaint before recording the offense. If the offense is not very seri-

TABLE 7

Percentage of Foreign Suspects of Personal Crimes, according to Police Statistics and Victims' Accounts

	Victimization Survey (German and Italian Parts of Switzerland)	Police Statistics (Switzerland, 1984–86)
Robbery (including attempts and muggings)	50	32
Rape (including attempts)	53	45
Assault	20	32

Source.—Ministère Public de la Confédération, Statistique policière suisse (1988); Killias (1991), p. 175.

ous, the victim often never files such a complaint. Foreign offenders tend to commit more assaults with weapons (35 percent), thus increasing the chance that the incident will be reported to and recorded by the police. In the case of robbery and muggings, the rate of foreigners in police statistics may be diminished by their greater ability to abscond abroad.

The offender's origin seems to play no role in the reporting decision by the victim. When only Swiss victims who did not know their assailant are considered, 41 percent of personal victimizations were reported to the police, both for presumably Swiss and for foreign offenders (Killias 1988). The questions on reporting and offender characteristics were asked at different stages in the interview; thus there was little risk of contamination.

In sum, the results of the Swiss crime survey do not support hypotheses of discrimination against foreign suspects in victims' reporting decisions. This accords with research showing that characteristics of the offense are far more important in this respect than are characteristics of victims or offenders (Skogan 1984). It also matches Hindelang's findings (1978) in relation to race and involvement in personal crimes in the United States and Shah and Pease's (1992) findings based on data from the British Crime Surveys. Unfortunately, no comparable analyses are known to me from other European countries. The necessary data seem to have been collected in the Netherlands but have not been analyzed because of concerns about misinterpretations by the public. Similar concerns seem to have prevented the collection of such data in Germany and in the several international crime surveys. It is as if the possibility of differential reporting patterns by victims was the last bastion of the discrimination thesis, and researchers were reluctant to jeopardize it by any empirical tests.

B. *Foreigners as Crime Victims*

The Swiss crime survey of 1987 showed generally comparable victimization rates for foreigners and the Swiss (Kuhn, Killias, and Berry 1993). Because the survey was conducted over the telephone, it may, however, be more valid for those immigrants who have successfully established roots in Switzerland, and its results may less accurately reflect the situation of more recent and more marginal immigrants. Given the sample size, it may also be less appropriate to draw conclusions for less numerous immigrant groups, such as those from former Yugoslavia and Turkey.

In this respect, a study based on detailed analyses of police files in Basle offers valuable insights (Eisner 1993*b*, 1996). It found considerably higher offending and victimization rates among immigrants from former Yugoslavia and Turkey but offending and victimization rates for immigrants from neighboring European countries that are comparable to those for the Swiss. Given that immigrants from neighboring European countries typically moved earlier to Switzerland, the findings are consistent with the results from the 1987 Swiss crime survey. Eisner also found that much victimization of foreigners is intraethnic, usually by offenders from the same country or local area. For Turks, for example, the odds ratio of being victimized by another Turk is 30.9, whereas it is 5.9 for Italians, 5.0 for Germans, and 0.8 for the Swiss. Thus for immigrants from Turkey, the likelihood of being victimized by another Turk is roughly thirty times higher than if offenders and victims meet randomly, given the population composition of Basle.

One reason for the absence of significantly and consistently higher victimization rates among foreign residents in Switzerland may be that, compared with immigrants in American and British cities, immigrants in Swiss cities are less concentrated in poor neighborhoods. In addition, crime in Switzerland is less concentrated in such areas than in many other countries. More recently, this perhaps slightly idyllic picture seems to be changing. Eisner (1993*b*, 1996) found sharply increasing rates of geographic segregation in Basle from 1960 to 1990 and particularly after 1980. It remains to be seen whether the increasing

TABLE 8

Attacks (Especially Arson) against Shelters for Asylum Seekers in Switzerland, 1990–93

	1990	1991	1992	1993
Bombings	2	3	2	. . .
Arsons	6	39	16	3
Firearm attacks	4	8	2	. . .
Threats	4	15	1	4
Destruction of property	11	12	21	2
Total	27	77	42	9

Source.—Unpublished data provided by the Ministère Public de la Confédération.

concentration of immigrants in poor neighborhoods will be reflected in higher victimization rates in future crime surveys.

Recent immigrant groups who are geographically concentrated may also be particularly vulnerable to racist (hate) crimes. Such offenses were not common in 1987 when the Swiss crime survey was conducted. Police data on the frequency of arson and similar attacks against asylum seekers and their shelters are shown in table 8. The frequency of racist attacks seems to have leveled off and perhaps to have declined after 1992. One possible explanation is that political elites stopped ignoring illegal immigration as an issue in 1992 as they largely had before, and this may have reduced tensions and frustrations in certain parts of the public.

C. Foreigners' Attitudes toward the Justice System

The 1987 Swiss crime survey found that foreign residents of Switzerland are less fearful when walking alone at night in their neighborhood and less concerned about crime than are Swiss nationals, but they are also more punitive and especially more supportive of capital punishment (Kuhn, Killias, and Berry 1993). The latter finding may reflect the often more punitive practices and public climates in their countries of origin.

Interestingly, foreign residents held a slightly more positive view of the Swiss police than did Swiss nationals; they gave police significantly better grades for their performance in the local area. The same is true (but to a lesser extent) for the courts. Some of my foreign students suggest that this surprising finding may reflect many immigrants' nega-

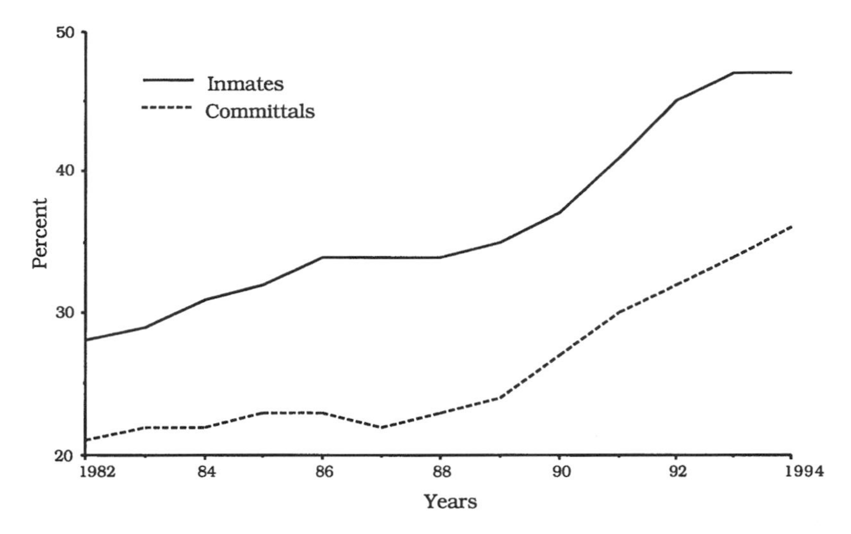

Fig. 3.—Percentage of foreign nationals among sentenced offenders entering prison, and among sentenced inmates, 1982–94. Source: Office Fédéral de la Statistique, Statistique pénitentiaire (1992, 1994), tables 2c, 3b.

tive experiences with police brutality and perhaps corruption in their native countries. Compared to what they have experienced or seen in their home countries, the behavior of the Swiss police may rise above expectations. Given this finding, at least from a community relations perspective, hiring immigrants of foreign nationality as police officers may not be necessary or a high priority. Unlike in Berlin and a few other places in Western Europe, such policies have not been seriously considered in Switzerland.

Thus it seems that the experience of immigration has not had dramatic consequences for fear of crime or hostilities toward the justice system among foreign residents in Switzerland.

III. Discrimination against Minorities

Immigrants are substantially overrepresented among prison inmates in Switzerland. In 1994, 47 percent of all sentenced inmates were of foreign nationality, residents and nonresidents combined. As figure 3 reveals, this proportion is considerably higher than the proportion of foreign nationals among sentenced offenders entering prison. Both proportions have increased consistently since 1982 when data collection started. Note that figure 3 does not include prisoners on remand (among whom the proportion of foreign nationals is probably higher).

TABLE 9

Average Sentences Imposed and Time Served for Serious Offenses, for Swiss, Foreign Resident and Foreign Nonresident Offenders, 1988–92 (in Years)

	Swiss		Resident Foreigners		Nonresident Foreigners	
	Sentence Length	Time Served	Sentence Length	Time Served	Sentence Length	Time Served
Homicide (including attempts)	8.5	6.0	7.6	4.0	9.4	5.2
Robbery	3.2	2.2	3.1	1.8	3.8	2.2
Rape	3.7	3.1	3.0	2.2	3.1	2.5
Drug trafficking (serious)	2.3	N.A.	3.0	N.A.	3.5	N.A.

SOURCE.—Unpublished data from the Swiss Federal Office of Statistics (no data available on time served by convicts of serious drug trafficking). N.A. = not available.

The higher proportion of foreigners among the inmate population indicates that they receive on average longer sentences. This trend seems to have increased over the last decade, since the proportion of foreigners among inmates increased more than the proportion among committals. The question then is whether foreign nationals receive longer sentences for similar crimes or whether they commit more serious offenses. Table 9, showing average prison sentences imposed and time served for selected serious offenses from 1988–92, provides data that are relevant to answering that question.

When average lengths of imposed sentences are compared, resident foreign and Swiss offenders tend to be treated about the same way, whereas nonresident foreigners tend to receive somewhat longer sentences for homicide, robbery, and drug trafficking. To some extent, this could be due to differences in seriousness of the average offense. For example, sentences for drug trafficking heavily reflect the quantities involved. Because foreign (and particularly nonresident foreign) offenders tend more often to be involved in large-scale operations, whereas Swiss defendants are more often drug addicts who deal in drugs to sustain their dependency, some disparity in sentences may be in line with informal judicial sentencing guidelines. However, Swiss defendants receive longer average sentences for rape than do resident or nonresident foreigners. The reason may be that criminal records are more completely available for Swiss nationals and that judges tend to pay particular attention to the defendant's record in such instances.

When times served are compared, both resident and nonresident foreign prisoners seem to be released earlier than the Swiss. The reason may be that foreigners convicted of serious crimes often lose their residence permits and are liable to deportation on release. For nonresident foreign offenders, deportation is almost inevitable. Unfortunately, no data are available on time served for serious drug trafficking.

In sum, the increasing proportion of foreign inmates from the "flow" (intake) to the "stock" of prisoners (fig. 3) mainly reflects different types of offenses, and there is little indication of sentencing disparities on grounds of nationality. The great similarity of sentences imposed on Swiss nationals and resident foreigners further illustrates the low significance of "nationality" in this regard. Of course, these comparisons are crude, and some discrimination may exist at the sentencing stage. However, even if it existed to an extent similar to that described by Hood (1992) in English courts, it would not account for the bulk of the disparity observed.

Data on time served have recently been challenged on grounds of their demographic inaccuracy (Biderman 1995). Although survival analyses, based on cohort data, would be preferable, the distortions that result from the violation of these rules may be less important in the Swiss context. Indeed, the data in table 9 are averages for a five-year period and include length of sentences imposed to complement the picture.

Disparities at the final stage of a multistage process may reinforce similar disparities at earlier stages or offset opposite disparities (Walker 1987). Unfortunately, no process data are available in Switzerland that allow assessment of such effects at the police or the prosecutorial stages. However, comparing the proportion of suspects who are Swiss nationals among offenders known to the police, among convicted defendants, among those sent to prison to serve a sentence, and among sentenced prison inmates does not reveal a decreasing trend over the several stages once the type of offense is taken into account. If discrimination operated throughout the system, the proportion of Swiss offenders should decrease from one stage to the next.

A number of factors may lower the proportion of foreign defendants. First, foreign offenders seem disproportionately to be involved in crimes against acquaintances (Eisner 1996), a finding that reduces chances of prosecution because victims are notoriously more reluctant to report crimes committed by persons they know (Skogan 1984). Second, foreign offenders—and particularly those who do not live in Switzerland—are more likely than a Swiss defendant to disappear before going to trial. Third, it may be that foreign offenders will be deported rather than prosecuted, although no data are available on the frequency of such practices (which are questionable under Swiss law, given the compulsory character of prosecution under the so-called legality maxim). Such "alternatives" may be increasingly popular because investigations directed at foreign defendants are unusually time-consuming. Indeed, they often require the use of translators and the need to contact foreign authorities.

At the trial and sentencing stages (which occur in one court hearing: see Killias, Kuhn, and Rônez 1995), the odds that foreign and Swiss defendants will receive an immediate prison sentence rather than a noncustodial sanction are hard to assess comparatively. Among convicted nonresident foreign defendants, 39 percent were subject to pretrial detention compared with 13 percent among foreign residents and 8 percent among Swiss defendants (Office Fédéral de la Statistique 1994). This disparity may be justifiable given the risks that foreign (especially nonresident) defendants may fail to appear for trial but undoubtedly increases the risk of an immediate custodial sentence because judges tend to attach some importance to whether the defendant was held in pretrial detention in deciding between unsuspended and suspended sentences. However, foreign (and particularly nonresident) offenders may fare better because their full criminal record may be unavailable or incomplete. In a sentencing system aimed at special deterrence, this difference may offset some of the advantage of Swiss defendants in relation to pretrial detention. Recently published data seem to confirm that, overall, Swiss defendants face a higher risk of conviction, that they more often receive an immediate custodial sentence, and that much of this difference may be due to the higher proportion of Swiss defendants who have a known criminal record (Storz, Rônez, and Baumgartner 1996, pp. 37–41).

A final disparity occurs during the execution of sentences. Nonresidents tend to be incarcerated in the larger, older, and less attractive high-security institutions, and certain privileges such as furloughs, "overnight detention," and community service are almost unavailable to them (Office Fédéral de la Statistique 1994). These disparities may be attributable to perceived higher risks of absconding. Although these disparities may not reflect open discrimination, they add to what has been called institutional discrimination.

IV. Explanations of Differential Criminal Involvement

Wilbanks (1987) argued that a general focus on racist and discriminatory tendencies within the criminal justice system may not only be empirically unfounded but, worse, might contribute to general ignorance of deeper-rooted and more significant discriminations in everyday life. In other words, differential rates of official offending and victimization should not be explained away with exaggerated claims of differential treatment of offenders by ethnic or racial background but accepted as the outcome of differences in involvement in crime which, in turn, result from inequalities in everyday life and concomitant hardships experienced by members of minority groups.

This approach is consistent with anomie and other strain theories. Such theories remain influential in Europe, although empirical tests of them have seldom been undertaken, partly because of the dominance of the discrimination thesis. Eisner (forthcoming) in his study based on police files from Basle tried to classify offenders and the corresponding foreign population (by national origin) in relation to socioeconomic status (SES) and to assess offending rates simultaneously by nationality and SES. The results show, overall, not only a stronger effect of SES than of nationality for all national groups and for all violent offenses combined but also a very substantial effect of nationality for some groups; Yugoslavs and Turks had far higher rates than the Swiss or the remaining nationalities, whose rates did not differ much from the Swiss.

The available evidence thus suggests that both deprivation or lack of integration and cultural variables—especially the conflict potential resulting from rigid honor codes—may increase the likelihood of offending. There is little research against which this conclusion can be tested (reviewed in Killias 1989*a;* Killias 1991, pp. 187–93), but Aronowitz (1988), studying Turkish juveniles in Berlin with different degrees of acculturation, and Junger (1990)—who compared juveniles of different ethnic background but similar SES in the Netherlands—both found substantial effects of cultural variables. But cultural orientation and acculturation may not be independent of SES and perceived structural opportunities. Thus, school achievement and access to higher education may be key variables in shaping cultural orientation, life chances, and behavior.

These explanations may also account for the unusually low criminal involvement of immigrants in the 1960s and 1970s (fig. 1). Immigrants were aware of discrimination in everyday life in Switzerland but they nonetheless expressed satisfaction about their circumstances in comparison with living conditions in their (mostly Mediterranean) home regions (Hoffmann-Nowotny 1973). From these strain models, it seemed plausible that they rarely engaged in crime, although other explanations might also have been possible. Since the decision to migrate may in itself be a sign of a higher problem-solving faculty, one might also suppose that migrants may be more stable personalities, an idea that finds some support in research on the epidemiology of psychiatric symptoms among Portuguese migrants and nonmigrants (Binder and Simoes 1980). On the basis of strain models it is plausible, however, that second-generation youths may no longer regard Southern European living conditions as their point of reference, but aspire instead to a way of life comparable to the Swiss middle-class despite being disadvantaged in education and professional achievement in competing with Swiss juveniles (Killias 1977).

Despite widespread pessimism, the Swiss educational system seems to have contributed successfully to the integration of the so-called second generation. According to statistics on educational achievement (Office Fédéral de la Statistique 1989), no less than 11 percent of immigrants from Southern Europe leave school with a degree that makes them eligible for university studies, which is not much lower than for the Swiss overall (16 percent) and is much higher than for Swiss working-class children (about 5 percent). (American readers should note that access to university studies is extremely selective throughout the Swiss school system.) In professional training programs, children from immigrant families succeed at about the same rates as Swiss juveniles. For all these reasons (Killias 1991, p. 190), young immigrants of the second generation have remarkably little trouble finding adequate jobs when they finish their educations.

In sum, there may be little basis for concern for the future of the second generation as long as Switzerland's public schools are able successfully to integrate immigrant children, that is, to equip them adequately for the Swiss labor market and as long as jobs will be available in sufficient number and quality. Areas of concern may stem from the increasing concentration of immigrants in poor city neighborhoods and the increasing segregation of children from immigrant families in schools where only a few pupils speak the local language.

Ultimately, however, the levels of crime committed by non-Swiss offenders will depend only partly on successful integration through the educational system and the labor market. Given the high proportion of foreign offenders who do not officially live in Switzerland, crime control will mainly depend on border control or successful initiatives at controlling migrants without ties to Switzerland. Most of the increasing overrepresentation of foreigners in official data over the last twenty years comes from the increasing proportion of nonresident foreigners among the offenders known to the police, convicted, or in prisons. Of course, merely relying on increased checks at the borders may not be enough. A coordinated migration policy at the European level will be needed. Within Switzerland (and other European countries), priority should be given to the reduction of drug and other illegal markets that offer illegal aliens attractive opportunities for rapid and easy gains (Killias 1995). Switzerland's medical heroin prescription program (Uchtenhagen et al. 1995) may be just one important step in that direction.

V. Conclusions

Several conclusions may be drawn from the preceding observations. First, overrepresentation of immigrants in crime statistics is neither automatic nor inevitable. During many decades, Switzerland experienced lower crime rates among immigrants than among its native population.

Second, the proportion of foreigners in police, conviction, and correctional statistics has increased over the last twenty years. This trend is explained mainly by the sharply increasing percentage of nonresident foreign offenders, but it holds true to a lesser extent for resident foreign citizens as well. The proportion of juvenile foreign offenders has considerably increased according to Zurich police statistics.

Third, the proportions of foreign offenders in official statistics are consistent with data from victimization studies. There is no indication that Swiss suspects face a lower chance of prosecution and conviction or that they receive more lenient sentences. Several structural factors may account for this such as language barriers, unavailability of criminal records of foreign defendants, and deportation as an alternative to formal prosecution. Comparable structural (or institutional) factors may also account for less favorable treatment of (nonresident) foreign offenders at the pretrial stage and in corrections.

Fourth, the proportion of foreign offenders has reached considerable dimensions, especially for drug and violent offenses. Nonresidents account for the bulk of this overrepresentation. Thus in the future the maintenance of public order will depend not only on the success of policies aimed at promoting integration of immigrants but also on successful control of migration. No clear strategies have as yet emerged by which this could be achieved.

Fifth, there is also reason for optimism. Immigrants do not seem to be disproportionately victimized or plagued by fear of crime, nor do they have especially negative attitudes toward the police and the justice system. Thus even in a country where immigration has reached considerable proportions, it does not necessarily cause serious antagonisms of these kinds.

Sixth, more attention should be paid to the increasing concentration of immigrant populations in poor city neighborhoods and resulting worsening schooling conditions. In classes without a minimum number of children from Swiss families (or who speak the local language), educational achievement, integration into the local community, and later success on the labor market may become highly uncertain, if not impossible. Perhaps exchanges of pupils from different neighborhoods ("busing") between public schools offers a possible way out of this dilemma.

Seventh, priority should be given in future research to the improvement of measures of differential treatment of offenders by ethnic or national background through the various stages of the justice system. An integrated data file is needed that allows follow-up of cohorts from the police to the correctional system. Of comparable importance would be more detailed studies on victimization by different minority groups; the way they experience crime, the police, and criminal justice; and the influence of ethnicity (of both offenders and victims) on reporting patterns. Finally, large-scale self-report studies might be helpful in assessing the effects of acculturation, educational achievement, and social integration. Such studies might be helpful in designing more successful policies aimed at promoting integration, even if the validity problems of self-reported delinquency measures may render comparisons across ethnic groups impossible.

REFERENCES

Annuaire statistique de la Suisse 1995. Zurich: Verlag der Neuen Zürcher Zeitung, 1994.

Aronowitz, A. 1988. "Assimilation, Acculturation and Juvenile Delinquency among Second-Generation Turkish Youths in Berlin West (Germany)." Ph.D. dissertation, State University of New York at Albany, School of Criminal Justice.

Bauhofer, S. 1993. "Kriminalität von Ausländern in der Schweiz: Ein kriminalstatistischer Ueberblick." In *Etrangers, criminalité et système pénal*, edited by S. Bauhofer and N. Queloz. Chur and Zurich: Rüegger.

Biderman, A. D. 1995. "Statistics of Average Time Served in Prison Are Fallacious Indicators of Severity of Punishment." Paper presented at the forty-seventh annual meeting of the American Society of Criminology, Boston, November.

Binder, J., and M. Simoes. 1980. "Psychische Beschwerden bei ausländischen Arbeitern: Eine Untersuchung bei portugiesischen Arbeitsemigranten." *Zeitschrift für Soziologie* 9(3):262–74.

Conseil Fédéral. 1994. "Messsage à l'appui d'une loi fédérale sur les mesures de contrainte en matière de droit des étrangers du 22 décembre 1993." *Feuille Fédérale*, no. 1:301–34.

Council of Europe. 1995. "Draft Model for the European Sourcebook of Crime and Criminal Justice Statistics." Strasbourg: Council of Europe, May.

Eisner, M. 1993*a*. "Policies towards Open Drug Scenes and Street Crime: The Case of the City of Zurich." *European Journal on Criminal Policy and Research* 1(2):61–75.

———. 1993*b*. "Immigration, Integration und Assimilation: Strukturen der Gewaltkriminalität von Immigrierten und Schweizern." In *Etrangers, criminalité et système pénal*, edited by S. Bauhofer and N. Queloz. Chur and Zurich: Rüegger.

———. 1996. *Gewaltdelinquenz in der Stadt: Das Beispiel Schweiz* (forthcoming).

Eisner, M., K. Branger, and F. Liechti. 1994. "Delinquenz, Gewalt und Opfererfahrungen von Jugendlichen in der Stadt Zürich." Unpublished manuscript. Zurich: Swiss Polytechnic Institute, Department of Sociology.

Gillioz, E. 1967. "La criminalité des étrangers en Suisse." *Revue Pénale Suisse* 83(2):178–91.

Gilomen, H. 1993. "Die Situation der Ausländer in der Schweiz." In *Etrangers, criminalité et système pénal*, edited by S. Bauhofer and N. Queloz. Chur and Zurich: Rüegger.

Hacker, E. 1939. *Die Kriminalität des Kanton Zürich: Versuch einer Kriminalätiologie des Kanton Zürich*. Law faculty doctoral dissertation. Zurich: Zurich University.

Hindelang, M. G. 1978. "Race and Involvement in Common Law Personal Crimes." *American Sociological Review* 43(1):93–109.

Hoffmann-Nowotny, H.-J. 1973. *Soziologie des Fremarbeiterproblems*. Stuttgart: Enke.

Hoffmann-Nowotny, H.-J., and M. Killias. 1979. "Switzerland." In *International Labor Migration in Europe*, edited by R. E. Krane. New York and London: Praeger.

Hood, R. 1992. *A Question of Judgement: Race and Sentencing*. London: Commission for Racial Equality.

Hug, T. 1993. "Ausländer als Drogenhändler am Beispiel der Stadt Zürich."

In *Etrangers, criminalité et système pénal,* edited by S. Bauhofer and N. Queloz. Chur and Zurich: Rüegger.

Junger, M. 1990. *Delinquency and Ethnicity.* Deventer and Boston: Kluwer.

Junger-Tas, J., G. J. Terlouw, and M. W. Klein, eds. 1994. *Delinquent Behavior among Young People in the Western World.* Amsterdam and New York: Kugler.

Killias, M. 1977. "Kriminelle Fremdarbeiter-Kinder? Strukturelle Determinanten der Delinquenz bei Fremdarbeitern unter besonderer Berücksichtigung der zweiten Generation." *Revue Suisse de Sociologie* 3(2):3–33.

———. 1988. "Diskriminierendes Anzeigeverhalten von Opfern gegenüber Ausländern? Neue Aspekte der Ausländerkriminalität aufgrund von Daten der Schweizerischen Opferbefragung." *Monatsschrift für Kriminologie und Strafrechtsreform* 71(3):156–65.

———. 1989*a.* "Criminality among Second-Generation Immigrants in Western Europe: A Review of the Evidence." *Criminal Justice Review* 14:13–42.

———. 1989*b. Les suisses face au crime.* Grüsch: Rüegger.

———. 1991. *Précis de criminologie.* Berne: Staempfi.

———. 1995. "Crime Policy in the Face of the Development of Crime in the New European Landscape." Report to the fifth conference on Crime Policy of the Council of Europe, Strasbourg, November.

Killias, M., A. Kuhn, and S. Rônez. 1995. "Sentencing in Switzerland." *Overcrowded Times* 6(3):1, 13–17.

Killias, M., P. Villettaz, and J. Rabasa. 1994. "Self-Reported Juvenile Delinquency in Switzerland." In *Delinquent Behavior among Young People in the Western World,* edited by J. Junger-Tas, G. J. Terlouw, and M. W. Klein. Amsterdam and New York: Kugler.

Klein, M. 1995. *The American Street Gang: Its Nature, Prevalence, and Control.* New York and Oxford: Oxford University Press.

Krane, R. E. 1979. *International Labor Migration in Europe.* New York and London: Praeger.

Kuhn, A., M. Killias, and C. Berry. 1993. "Les étrangers victimes et auteurs d'infractions selon le sondage suisse de victimisation." In *Etrangers, criminalité et système pénal,* edited by S. Bauhofer and N. Queloz. Chur and Zurich: Rüegger.

Kunz, K.-L. 1989. "Ausländerkriminalität in der Schweiz—Umfang, Struktur und Erklärungsversuch." *Revue Pénale Suisse* 106(4):373–92.

"Loi fédérale sur les mesures de contrainte en matière de droit des étrangers du 18 mars 1994." 1994. *Feuille Fédérale* 2:283–89.

Martens, Peter L. In this volume. "Immigrants, Crime, and Criminal Justice in Sweden."

Michaud, P.-A., F. Narring, and F. Paccaud. 1993. "Recherche sur la santé et les styles de vie des adolsecents romands de 15 à 20 ans." Unpublished report. Lausanne: University of Lausanne, Department of Social and Preventive Medicine.

Ministère Public de la Confédération. 1982–94. *Statistique policière de la criminalité.* Annual. Berne: Ministère Public de la Confédération.

Neumann, J. 1963. *Die Kriminalität der italienischen Arbeitskräfte im Kanton Zürich.* Law faculty doctoral dissertation. Zurich: University of Zurich.

Office Fédéral de la Police. 1994. *Statistique Suisse des stupéfiants.* Berne: Office Fédéral de la Police.

Office Fédéral de la Statistique. 1989. *Statistiques de la formation no. 8.* Berne: Office Fédéral de la Statistique.

———. 1992–94. "Strafvollzugsstatistik." Unpublished statistics. Berne: Office Fédéral de la Statistique.

———. 1994. *De la nationalité des détenus.* Berne: Office Fédéral de la Statistique.

Pradervand, P., and L. Cardia. 1966. "Quelques aspects de la délinquance italienne à Genève: Une enquête sociologique." *Revue international de Criminologie et de Police Technique* 20:43–58.

Queloz, N. 1986. *La réaction institutionnelle à la délinquance juvénile.* Neuchâtel: EDES.

"Résultats de la votation du 4 décembre 1994." 1995. *Feuille Fédérale* 1:290.

Sampson, R. J., and J. L. Lauritsen. In this volume. "Racial and Ethnic Disparities in Crime and Criminal Justice in the United States."

Schneider, A. L. 1981. "Differences between Survey and Police Information about Crime." In *The National Crime Survey: Working Papers.* Vol. 1: *Current and Historical Perspectives.* Washington, D.C.: U.S. Government Printing Office.

Shah, R., and K. Pease. 1992. "Crime, Race and Reporting to the Police." *Howard Journal* 31(3):192–99.

Skogan, W. G. 1984. "Reporting Crime to the Police: The Status of World Research." *Journal of Research in Crime and Delinquency* 21(2):113–37.

Storz, R., S. Rônez, and S. Baumgartner. 1996. *De la nationalité des condamnés.* Berne: Office fédéral de la statistique.

Uchtenhagen, A., F. Gutzwiller, A. Dobler-Mikola, and R. Blättler. 1995. "Versuche für eine ärztliche Verschreibung von Betäubungsmitteln." First intermediate report to the Swiss Federal Office of Public Health, University of Zurich, Department of Social Psychiatry and Department of Social and Preventive Medicine.

Walker, M. 1987. "Interpreting Race and Crime Statistics." *Journal of Research and Statistics in Sociology* 150, pt. 1:39–56.

Wilbanks, W. 1987. *The Myth of a Racist Criminal Justice System.* Monterey, Calif.: Cole.

Zürcher, E., and H. Sträuli. 1895. *Grundlagen und Ergebnisse der Statistik der Rechtspflege im Kanton Zürich.* Zurich: Friedrich Schulthess.

Roderic Broadhurst

Aborigines and Crime in Australia

ABSTRACT

Aborigines are 16 times more likely in Western Australia to be victims of homicide and 6.5 times more likely to report crimes against the person to police than are non-Aborigines. Aborigines are 9.2 times more likely to be arrested, 6.2 times more likely to be imprisoned by lower courts, 23.7 times more likely to be imprisoned as an adult, and 48 times more likely to be imprisoned as juveniles than non-Aborigines. The increased overrepresentation from arrest to imprisonment appears largely a function of the very high levels of recidivism found among Aborigines: 88 percent of male Aborigines are rearrested compared with 52 percent of non-Aborigines, and 75 percent of Aborigines return to prison at least once compared with 43 percent of non-Aboriginal males. States with a high Aboriginal "cultural strength" and socioeconomic "stress" index are the most punitive. "Cultural strength," "stress," and imprisonment are highly correlated and associated with those states with the most "frontier" characteristics.

This essay provides an overview of the current state of crime and imprisonment in Australia as it relates to the different experiences of the descendants of the indigenous and settler/migrant populations. Although Australia is a "multicultural" society with about one-fifth of the population born overseas (mostly from Europe and an increasing proportion arriving from Asia), the dominant focus of research has been on differences between the indigenous minority Aboriginals and Torres Strait Islanders and the predominantly European non-Aboriginals.

Roderic Broadhurst, honorary research fellow at the Crime Research Centre, Law School, University of Western Australia and lecturer, Department of Sociology, University of Hong Kong, gratefully acknowledges the assistance of Anna Ferrante, Richard Harding, and Nini Loh.

0192-3234/97/0021-0007$01.00

Statistical sources on the ethnicity of the Australian population are usually limited to "country of birth" data, and the analysis of ethnicity and crime has largely been confined to comparisons with the Aboriginal and non-Aboriginal populations.[1]

The focus on Aborigines is partly historical but also a function of their well-documented overrepresentation in the criminal justice system. The surviving descendants of the indigenous population, or Aborigines, represent only 1.6 percent of the total Australian population and are significantly overrepresented (by 12:1) in the penal system.

Aboriginal incarceration became the focus of national and international attention with the establishment in 1987 of the Royal Commission into Aboriginal Deaths in Custody (RCIADIC) following intensive lobbying by Aboriginal groups. The fundamental allegation was that Aborigines had been maltreated by police and prison officers (including accusations of murder) and as a result had a higher risk of death in custody. The RCIADIC was to determine the extent to which racial discrimination was a cause of the high rate of Aboriginal imprisonment and death in custody. Higher rates of Aboriginal custodial deaths were not found once their much higher levels of incarceration were taken into account. The frequency of Aboriginal incarceration suggested that their "lifetime" risks of a custodial death were probably greater than those of non-Aborigines (see Broadhurst and Maller 1990*a;* Biles and McDonald 1992).

The RCIADIC reported in 1991 and made sweeping recommendations aimed at reducing Aboriginal involvement in the criminal justice system and addressed the "underlying issues" related to the historical and political dispossession of the Aboriginal people and their subsequent impoverishment and disenfranchisement. Ongoing monitoring of Aboriginal deaths in custody and rates of imprisonment continues with the establishment of a special unit of the Australian Institute of Criminology. The detailed research of the RCIADIC is summarized by Biles and McDonald (1992).

In the post-RCIADIC climate, attention has shifted from deaths in custody and imprisonment to concern with juvenile offending. Aboriginal juveniles are even more overrepresented in juvenile corrections facilities. Some jurisdictions, notably Western Australia (WA), have introduced "three strikes" or repeat offender legislation to curb persistent juvenile and adult offenders, of whom the bulk are Aborigines (see Broadhurst and Loh 1993).

[1] On migrant crime in Australia, see Geis and Jesilow (1988).

In the Australian debate about racial bias in the criminal justice system, the focus of research has been dominated by Aborigines' gross overrepresentation in the prison system. Most research has focused on differences in imprisonment. This is because until recently prison data were the only ready source distinguished by race. Prison data remain the only national source, and the WA police the only provider of detailed arrest and victimization data. However, WA police data have only been available since 1992 for arrest (1993 for victim reports).

Another underused source is the 1994 National Aboriginal and Torres Strait Islander (NATSI) survey that provided self-report arrest and assault victimization data for all jurisdictions. It offers considerable scope for the analysis of the influence of sociodemographic variables (including health, housing, education, and cultural factors) on crime. The survey, however, is confined to Aborigines, is not comparative, and its findings are yet to be exploited.

There has been a remarkable absence of special purpose quantitative studies on the problem of race bias in the Australian criminal justice system along the lines pursued, for example, by Junger and Polder (1992) in the Netherlands or Hood (1992) in England. Juvenile arrest studies in South Australia (SA) by Duguid (1992) and Gale, Bailey-Harris, and Wundersitz (1990) and sentencing studies by Walker (1987) and Broadhurst (1993) provide only limited and contradictory insights and do not always fully exploit multivariate methods of analysis. Adequate racially disaggregated data, which include prior conviction information, are potentially available from SA court records, and WA's integrated crime statistics would enable rigorous analysis of race effects.

Australian research, in both the absence of ready data and a preoccupation with imprisonment, has tended to examine the issue of race bias via deduction from historical and secondary sources or via qualitative and observational methods often motivated by advocacy (see Foley 1984; Cunneen 1992). Despite these serious data limitations, the two principle assumptions have been, first, that the police are more likely to arrest and charge Aborigines than non-Aborigines and, second, that the courts are more likely to be punitive in their treatment of them. Counter to these assumptions is the proposition that Aborigines commit relatively more crime and of a more serious kind, thus accounting for their overrepresentation (Brunton 1993).

In support of the first assumption, arrest patterns show that Aborigines are arrested more often than non-Aborigines, especially for crimes against the person, and lend support to the view that Aboriginal crime is more serious than non-Aboriginal crime. Nevertheless, it is also observed that Aborigines are seldom arrested for serious fraud and drug offenses but are frequently arrested for minor public order offenses. The data also show that Aboriginal victimization, in respect to crimes against the person reported to police, is perhaps seven times greater than for non-Aborigines (and is mostly intraracial). Given these differences, higher risks of arrest and incarceration for Aborigines might be expected, especially in light of the greater frequency of arrest for public order offenses. Thus there is support for the counterview that high rates of Aboriginal arrest and incarceration are due, in part at least, to the higher incidence and severity of crime among Aborigines.

The first assumption is supported by analysis of WA arrest data, which shows that Aborigines are 9:1 times more likely to be apprehended when compared with non-Aborigines. Duguid (1992) has argued that the greater risk, however, cannot solely be attributed to extralegal factors. If Aborigines were to be incarcerated at approximately the same rate at which they were arrested, we would expect the risk of incarceration to be about the same at 9:1. However, the actual risk of Aboriginal incarceration in WA is about 23:1 or more than twice the proportion expected given arrest risk differentials. Accordingly, the second assumption, that courts are more punitive, appears relevant because, once convicted, Aborigines are estimated to be *about* five times more likely to receive a sentence of imprisonment than non-Aborigines.

The logic that apparently increasing differential risks of victimization, arrest, and incarceration imply disparity between the races is amplified the deeper the Aborigines enter the criminal justice system, and it appears as if system bias may be the inevitable cause. Despite the compelling nature of this evidence, it is not proof of bias because it critically fails to control for prior offending, which is especially relevant considering that Aborigines have significantly higher probabilities of rearrest and longer criminal careers. In any event, the logic breaks down when the expected amplification by the courts is not reflected in the differential risk of incarceration. Given an arrest differential of 9:1 and a five-times-greater chance of a custodial disposition, the logic of increasing risks would anticipate a differential risk of incarceration of approximately 45:1. Differential risks of incarceration at 23:1 fall well short of the predicted disparity and suggest contraction, not amplification, of risks. Interestingly, differential risks are much lower for noncustodial sanctions (12:1) than imprisonment, and relative to their risks of imprisonment non-Aborigines are only twice as likely to receive these sanctions than Aborigines. Thus despite the imprecision of such gross system estimates, it is difficult to sustain the proposition that overrepresentation of Aborigines in prison is the product of bias amplified by the criminal justice process.

Here is how this essay is organized. Section I defines Aboriginality and discusses common explanations of Aboriginal involvement in criminal justice, including the limited research on racial bias. In Section II, police offense reports are used to explore differences in the prevalence of personal crime victimization including the frequency of cross-race offending. Recent findings of a national self-report survey of Aborigines are compared to findings of national and state crime victim surveys. Section III summarizes trends in arrest patterns from 1990 to 1994 including interstate police custody rates and describes longitudinal estimates of the probability of rearrest. All levels of court activity are described in Section IV, as are attempts to measure differences in dispositions and penalties. Court data are inadequate to examine the issue of bias, and only very approximate measures of Aboriginal overrepresentation can be calculated. Correctional data are the most comprehensive, enabling interstate and international comparisons to be made in Section V. Section VI examines theories to explain the scale of punishment and the causes of Aboriginal overrepresentation.

I. Aboriginality and Biased Decision Making

Aboriginality has three elements as defined for official purposes by the Australian government.[2] These are that a person is of Aboriginal descent, identifies himself or herself as an Aboriginal, and is accepted by the Aboriginal community with which the person is associated. Australian Bureau of Statistics (ABS) census and statistical collections usually rely on the first two defining characteristics. Police tend to rely on physical identification, and prisons and other criminal justice agencies rely on self-reports. The third criterion is a difficult (and statistically redundant) means of defining Aboriginality, although germane in matters such as land title and religious activities. No precise definition of non-Aboriginality is applied except that it includes all persons who do not identify themselves as Aborigines.

[2] Throughout the text I use Aboriginality or Aborigine as synonymous with Aboriginal and Torres Strait Islander peoples. Names of states are abbreviated as follows: Western Australia (WA), Northern Territory (NT), New South Wales (NSW), and South Australia (SA).

A. Definitions and Population

The problem of definition is relevant to the rates that characterize Aboriginals' contacts with the justice system. Rates depend on estimation of denominator populations, and arguments have been advanced that changing levels of identification (willingness to identify as Aboriginal and the scope of the ABS census) have affected estimates of the size of the Aboriginal population. The demographic history of the descendant Aboriginal population is a source of controversy and dispute, and there is considerable difficulty in estimating age-specific and intercensus populations for Aborigines. Examining historical trends in Aboriginal crime or imprisonment is especially fraught.

Significant variations arise in estimates of Aboriginal involvement in the justice system, particularly "overrepresentation" or disparity measures, because of the variety of population denominators employed. These variations in population estimates are further complicated by differences in whether census or other measures are employed. To standardize my approach I use estimates of the resident Aboriginal population provided by the ABS for census 1991 and the NATSI survey for 1994 and for intercensus 1986–91 experimental estimates provided by the demographers Benham and Howe (1994) or by extrapolation from the 1991 census.

The Aboriginal population differs markedly from the general Australian population in that they are significantly younger, live in larger households (with more dependents), are less likely to own a home, have much higher levels of unemployment, and are more likely to reside in rural areas. Their average income is two-thirds the national average, and high school and higher education retention is well below national participation rates. Life expectancy is estimated to be between fifteen and seventeen years less than that of the whole population, with significantly increased risks of infant and perinatal mortality, hospital admission, diabetes, eye disease, and other morbidities. Moreover, Aboriginal lifestyles, customs, and worldview differ in important respects from those of Europeans with direct consequences for the administration of justice.[3]

[3] Fuller discussion of the characteristics of Aboriginal law is not attempted here. Conceptually, it is fundamentally different from English law, especially in distinguishing between secular and sacred areas. The roles of kinship, restitution, and private versus collective action are striking, as are aspects such as strict liability and the character of punishments. See the Australian Law Reform Commission (1986) for fuller discussion and coverage of civil matters like property, marriage, child custody, gaming, and fishing rights.

The Aboriginal population is significantly more rural, with only 27 percent living in major urban centers compared to 63 percent of all Australians. Nearly a third (32 percent) of Aborigines reside in rural or remote districts compared to 15 percent of all Australians. Significant differences in the extent that Aborigines reside in major urban centers (cities over 100,000 persons) occur according to state. The NT is the least "urbanized" state, with 65 percent of its Aboriginal population living in rural areas (see Australian Bureau of Statistics 1994*a*).

B. Explanations of Aboriginal Crime

Before examining the data, it is necessary to consider the explanations usually given to account for differences in Aboriginal and non-Aboriginal representation in crime statistics. Until relatively recently, the main explanations were based on heredity ("born" criminal), later deprivation (strain/stress), labeling (cultural or racial stereotypes), conflict (different values), and multifactorial and synthesized theories of crime causation.

The hereditary thesis with its origins in phrenology is now fully discredited (Fink 1938). It remains, one suspects, a popular notion among large segments of the Australian public, especially when blended with the other "causes." The notion of biological causes of Aboriginal crime is now more likely to be explained in terms of vulgarized cultural heritage: the tendency to go "walkabout" (interrupts employment), communal sharing and an absence of personal property (leads to a disregard for property), the lack of cultural wisdom or control regarding European imports such as drinking (cannot handle alcohol), and "payback" (an example of lawlessness).

The appeal of deprivation or strain theory explanations rests on the manifest poverty, alienation, all-pervading anxiety, stressed conditions, and "dispossession and powerlessness" of Aboriginal people. An extension of this idea argues that the frustrations caused by deprivation, especially those caused by dispossession, often turn inward on the self and behavior loses meaning and becomes self-destructive. Dispossession is particularly destructive because it breaks the symbiosis between land and culture, past and present; more important, it interdicts the association between the material and the spiritual culture. Because of this, deviance or criminal behavior is one of the few ways open to those deprived of the normal capacity to assert identity or acquire the material benefits of the Australian lifestyle or to escape the stigmatization of poverty and low self-esteem through alcohol abuse.

High rates of unemployment, poor education, poor health, and high crime all testify to the extent of deprivation and thwarted opportunity. The poverty cycle is associated with race and crime; hence Aborigines become associated with crime and are "labeled" and then are expected to confirm the stereotype characterized above. In practice this means all Aborigines come under more intensive surveillance, especially by police, because of their "lawlessness" or "dangerousness," and a self-fulfilling prophecy is generated (see New South Wales Anti-discrimination Board 1982).

Interest in conflict theory has also been revived by the stimulus of revisionist history that has documented the struggle or "warfare" between the races over land use (e.g., Gill 1977; Green 1981; Reynolds 1981; Rose 1991). This reevaluation of Aboriginal-settler relations destroyed the myth of settlement without conquest and culminated in the celebrated 1992 High Court case of *Regina v. Mabo*, which established common-law native land title, overturning the long-established doctrine of *terra nullias* (Bartlett 1993; Rowse 1994). The essential theme of conflict theory, whether applied to minorities or social class, is that the legitimacy of the law is rejected by the "deviant" group on the grounds that it fails to recognize or represent their values. Conflict theory can be applied to Aboriginal aspirations for land versus the imperative to exploit the land in the national interest.

Direct reference to the economic nature of the struggle in contemporary times has been neglected in criminological accounts. Aboriginal overinvolvement in arrest and imprisonment appears very closely related to, and coincides with, economic expansion—and renewed competition over land use in the hitherto remote and "unsettled" parts of North West Australia (Broadhurst 1987, 1988).

Another neglected possibility, often ignored, describes crime as a form of resistance or proto-revolution. Cunneen (1988), however, uses the idea to describe "race riots" in northern NSW. Thus the "criminal" behavior of some Aborigines, while not organized and disciplined in the conventional manner or sense of a "revolutionary" or millennial movement, spontaneously has all the requisite ingredients of political struggle—anger is not directed randomly but at the state and the symbols of authority for limited political purpose.

Undoubtedly, some Aboriginal crimes have elements of rebellion and protest. This is most obvious in the occasional melee or "riot" in country towns (or the inner city) mostly directed at police and publicans. This resistance has been acknowledged by police in some communities as amounting to "aggressive resistance towards police" (Police Inspector Rippon, quoted in Hazelhurst 1987, p. 243). This is the explanation that most frightens the propertied classes of provincial centers and perhaps accounts for intense agitation for more "law and order."

It has been argued that self-help strategies (i.e., Aboriginal courts and community policing) and depolicing of Aboriginal communities may have prospects of reintroducing stronger civil (and by definition more appropriate and legitimate) mechanisms of social control that will ultimately reduce overuse of imprisonment. At the same time withdrawal of policing would allow a rapprochement in the practice of law enforcement for "the relationship between law and self-help is inverse, it follows that the larger and more intrusive a police force is, the weaker self-help will be, a pattern that in the long term exacerbates the problem of crime" (Black 1980, p. 195). Extensive policing of Aboriginal communities has contributed to the demise of effective self-regulation or internalized controls and inevitably intensifies state intervention.

Under the rubric of "self-determination," there is now considerable agreement among many experts (e.g., Australian Law Reform Commission 1986; Hazelhurst 1987; RCIADIC 1991*a*, 1991*b*) that greater involvement of Aboriginal people in their "own" policing and criminal justice processing should be encouraged.

C. *Racial Bias*

Despite the interest generated by the RCIADIC in Aboriginal justice issues, there have been few specific efforts empirically to test for evidence of racial bias in the administration of justice. The RCIADIC systematically measured disparity but was not able to carry out rigorous quantitative studies of racial bias among police, courts, or correctional authorities. Generally, it was assumed that the huge differential risks between Aborigines and non-Aborigines in imprisonment were, if not the direct result of racial prejudice, at least the indirect result of the "underlying issues" of poverty, unemployment, disenfranchisement, and dispossession.

One of the few specific attempts to test racial "bias" by police was undertaken by Gale and Wundersitz (1987) and also by Gale, Bailey-Harris, and Wundersitz (1990) who studied differences in the arrest rates of Aboriginal and non-Aboriginal juveniles in Adelaide for the year 1983–84. They found in their matched study (drawing on some 7,156 cases of whom 289 were Aborigines) that there was "no statistical evidence to indicate that, at the point of arrest, police overtly discriminate against Aborigines on racial grounds" (Gale and Wundersitz 1987, p. 92). Instead, they found unemployment was "independently associated with the likelihood of arrest" (Aborigines were more likely to be unemployed), and the pattern of arrest (as opposed to being cautioned or summoned) did differ significantly for Aboriginal youths. Limitations in the official data available did not enable them to explore the issues with adequate rigor, and they concluded: "Whatever the root causes, Aboriginal youths continue to be disadvantaged by the discretionary process operating at the point of entry into the juvenile justice system" (Gale and Wundersitz 1987, p. 93). In a later account Gale, Bailey-Harris, and Wundersitz (1990) found from direct observation and other sources that police/Aboriginal contacts were highly affrontive, hostile, and presumptive on both sides. The consequences are to heighten the likelihood of arrest even in those situations where no manifest offense or public disturbance has occurred.

A subsequent detailed reanalysis of the Gale and Wundersitz study by Duguid (unpublished, 1992), confirmed strong differences in the probabilities of arrest for the races; that is, higher risks of rearrest for Aborigines. Duguid's study was able to draw on extended data from the period 1980–84 and to control for all variables available from children's court and panel appearances (age, sex, race, offense, arrest or summons, neighborhood, employment, family structure, address, previous appearances, and number of charges), as well as to address the problem of sparse data.

Like Gale and Wundersitz (1987) and Gale, Bailey-Harris, and Wundersitz (1990), Duguid was unable to demonstrate that this higher risk was the result of unfairness (harshness in the case of police). This was because key factors in legitimate application of police discretion to arrest—such as ensuring the appearance of the offender, preventing the continuation of further offenses, and the hindrance of justice (e.g., destruction of evidence)—are not measured by the more general variables used in the inferential statistical analysis. Duguid maintained, nevertheless, that while "Gale, Bailey-Harris, and Wundersitz (1990) found no statistical evidence that Aborigines were more likely to be arrested rather than reported, after taking into account the nine variables identified by them and also used . . . I have found overwhelming evidence for this. On this point we have reached opposite conclusions" (Duguid 1992, p. 4).[4]

[4] "Reported" in this context means summonsed or cautioned instead of being arrested and taken into custody.

Duguid's less well known but equally important follow-up of the study by Gale, Bailey-Harris, and Wundersitz (1990) provides clear statistical support for the proposition that "race" or Aboriginality increases the risk of arrest for Adelaide juveniles. However, "Aboriginality" may be a factor or variable that catches a number of stigmatizing characteristics (such as truancy, unemployment, substance abuse) and in this sense operates as a shorthand "predictive" model for police as to who is a high-risk juvenile.

Supportive quantitative studies on police interaction with Aborigines, which would enable precise tests of bias, are notably absent (see, however, the qualitative studies of New South Wales Anti-discrimination Board 1982; Foley 1984; Roberts, Chadbourne, and Murray 1986; RCIADIC 1991*b*). The available work shows an interaction between unemployment and increased chances of involvement with the law and consequently suggests that poverty mediates the response to Aborigines. However, given Duguid's important reanalysis, calculating exactly the probabilities and accounting for the problems of sparse data and the assumptions of logistic regression combined with the qualitative field data, we know that "Aboriginality" is a powerful discriminator. Thus without contrary data on how discretion is practiced, action is needed to make the system fairer for Aborigines.

II. Crime Victimization

Although three National Crime and Safety (NCS) surveys (and several state surveys) have been conducted in Australia in 1975, 1983, and 1993 by the Australian Bureau of Statistics, there has been no comprehensive attempt to estimate the proportion of victims who are Aborigines (Australian Bureau of Statistics 1979, 1983, 1992*b*, 1994*b*). The relatively small proportion of Aborigines in the Australian population has prevented separate estimates for them. Consequently, the only data available on the "race" of victims is derived from WA police records of citizen reports of crime (and only in relation to offenses against the person), available on a regular basis since 1991 (Broadhurst, Ferrante, and Susilo 1992).

A. Victim Surveys

This dearth of data has been partly rectified by the 1994 NATSI survey (Australian Bureau of Statistics 1995*a*). This is the first comprehensive survey of Aboriginal society (outside the population census) conducted in Australia that yielded information on a range of subjects, including language and culture, family, land use, education and training, employment and income, health, diet, alcohol use and health services, and law and justice.

Of the questions related to crime and justice, importantly, one replicating the 1993 NCS question on assault was asked. "In the last year has anyone attacked or verbally threatened you?" appeared regularly in previous crime victim surveys conducted by the ABS both nationally and in WA in 1991, SA in 1991, and NSW from 1990 to 1994.[5]

The survey found that 12.9 percent of the Aboriginal population said they were the victim of an attack or verbal threat. The 1993 NCS estimated 2.5 percent of all Australians were the victims of such assaults, and thus the NATSI survey found assault approximately five times more prevalent among Aborigines than all Australians.[6] For WA the NATSI survey found a slightly higher estimate of assault at 13.5 percent due to a higher rate of verbal threats reported by males. The 1993 NCS estimated 2.2 percent of Western Australians were the victims of assault, and thus Aborigines are about six times more at risk of assault than all Western Australians. This is similar to the differential risk calculated from official police records of offenses against the person discussed below.

Nearly three-fifths of WA Aboriginal assault victims (7.9 percent) reported being physically attacked. Males (9.4 percent) were more likely to be physically assaulted than females (6.3 percent), and young adults (18.7 percent of those aged 20–24) were more at risk than older age groups (6.2 percent of those aged 44 and over). Assaults were more likely to be reported to the police if they involved a physical attack rather than a verbal threat, and males were less likely than females to report an assault. For example, 45.6 percent of females reported a physical assault to police compared to only 24.6 percent of males. Moreover, males were more likely not to report because the assault was not considered serious enough (17.9 percent of males compared to 5.7 percent of females) or they did not wish to involve police (23.5 percent of males compared to 4.4 percent of females). Similar differences in the willingness of victims to report to the police were observed by age,

[5] Other questions dealt with family violence, police performance, and legal aid and are reported when relevant below. The survey contacted 17,500 respondents or approximately 6.6 percent of the Aboriginal and Torres Strait Islander population.

[6] The NATSI and 1993 NCS are not directly comparable. The NATSI survey was conducted face-to-face, while the NCS was a drop-off/mail-back strategy. The NATSI included all persons over the age of thirteen years, while the NCS applied only to those fifteen years and over. The NATSI survey is likely to encourage more reporting than the NCS.

with older offenders more likely to report to police and less likely to say that the assault was not serious.

Interestingly, WA Aborigines appear less willing to report a physical assault to police than do Aborigines elsewhere. The NATSI survey estimated that overall, 43.6 percent of Aborigines reported a physical assault (30.6 percent reported verbal threats) to police but only 33.4 percent of WA Aborigines did so (29.8 percent reported verbal threats). The lower rate of reporting applied across sex and age groups. It appears that the least willing to report (in any jurisdiction) were the youngest age group.[7] However, the proportion of Aboriginal assault victims willing to report to police does not appear to differ from the reporting rate of non-Aborigines. The 1993 NCS found that 32.1 percent of respondents Australia-wide and 35.3 percent of those in WA reported their assault (physical or verbal) to police (Australian Bureau of Statistics 1994*b*).

It is often speculated that ethnicity or minority group status will affect the willingness of victims to report crimes to police. But comparing the NCS and NATSI survey estimates of the willingness of victims to report shows (at least for assault) that, in this respect, generally differences between Aborigines and non-Aborigines are small. For specific groups, disaggregated by sex, age, and race, some variations in reporting rates and in the severity or injuries may occur.

B. Crime Victims—Crimes Reported to Western Australia Police in 1993

In 1993 the WA police recorded 13,620 offenses (5.6 percent of all reported offenses) against the person (homicide, assault, sex offenses, robbery, kidnapping, and other "violent" offenses), involving 11,283 separate victim reports, of which 56 percent were reported as being cleared by police by charge or other means including unfounding of the alleged offense. Victim reports, which may loosely be referred to as "distinct" victims, are used as the basis for describing the relationship between victim and offender, where known (including sex and race). Each "victim report" may include more than one victim and more than one alleged offender, but for present purposes only the first victims' and the first offenders' details were recorded.

After adjustment for missing records (12.5 and 2.7 percent, respec-

[7] Reporting rates are based on the last incident and in the case of WA are complicated by a high "not stated" response. Nationally, the nonresponse rate for this question (physical assault) was 3.9 percent, but in WA it was 10.3 percent with young males accounting for most of the nonresponse.

TABLE 1

Rates per 100,000 Relevant Population of Victimization for Offenses against the Person, 1993

Group	Against Person	Homicide
Aborigines	3,699.0	33.28
Non-Aborigines	570.5	2.02
All	677.1	2.86

SOURCE.—Harding et al. (1995).

tively, lacked sex and race data), Aborigines were victims in 15.2 percent of offenses reported to police. Aborigines make up about 2.63 percent of the WA population, and thus are 5.78 times more likely to be a victim of violence than would be expected. As table 1 shows, differential risks of victimization for the races can be calculated for all offenses against the person.[8] For non-Aborigines the rate of reported violent crime is estimated to be 570.5 per 100,000 and for Aborigines 3,699.0 per 100,000, and therefore Aborigines are 6.5 times more likely to be a victim of a violent crime than non-Aborigines.

In relation to homicide (excluding driving-caused deaths) forty-eight homicides were reported in 1993 to police at a rate of 2.9 per 100,000 population. Of these forty-eight cases, fifteen were Aborigines, yielding a rate of 33.3 per 100,000, and 33 were non-Aborigines at a rate of 2.0 per 100,000—a differential risk of homicide of 16.5 : 1. Thus Aborigines were over sixteen times more likely to be a victim of homicide than were non-Aborigines.

Sex- and age-specific rates of "violent" victimization reveal that Aboriginal females were substantially more at risk than any other group. Female Aborigines' risk of victimization peaked at 10,255 per 100,000 or about one in ten for those aged 20–24 years. Male Aborigines risk peaked at 3,688 per 100,000 for those aged 25–29. Non-Aborigines risk of victimization peaked in the 15–19 years group for either sex with rates of 1,386 per 100,000 for teenage males and 1,101 per 100,000 for teenage females. The data show that risks of victimization decline with age for all groups, but intriguingly the differential risks (the ratio of Aborigine/non-Aborigine) tend to increase with age so

[8] Of the 11,283 offense reports, 310 did not contain data on race, and allocating these to either race on a pro rata basis permits rates of violent crime to be estimated.

that middle-aged Aborigines are ten times more at risk than are middle-aged non-Aborigines. The age-specific rates of victimization for those aged 10–14 years were 1,506 per 100,000 for Aborigines and 687 per 100,000 for non-Aborigines, a differential risk of 2.2. But by age 35–39, the rate for Aborigines was 5,257 per 100,000 and that for non-Aborigines was 422 per 100,000, a differential risk of 12.4 (Harding et al. 1995).

Aboriginal victims were significantly more likely to sustain serious injury—a factor that may account for their relatively high level of reporting to police. While 37.1 percent of non-Aborigines reported no physical injuries as a result of their victimization, only 14.3 percent of Aboriginal victims reported no injury (Harding et al. 1995).

1. *Victim-Offender Relationships.* The availability of detailed information from the Offence Information System (OIS) makes it possible to determine the proportion of offenses against the person that occur in interpersonal or domestic relationships. Such offenses, sometimes called incidents of "domestic violence," can be approximately determined by reference to information on the relationships of victims to offenders, if this is known. This information also allows the incidence of so-called stranger violence to be estimated.

Patterns of relationships differ markedly by the nature of the offense and the sex and race of the victim. Table 2 reports victim-offender relationships by race for five broad categories of victim-offender relationship and several serious offenses against the person. Robbery is not included since there is usually no relationship between the victim and the offender recorded by police. Women are more likely to be victimized by someone known or related to them, whereas men are more prone to "stranger" violence. For males, "sex assault" and "homicide" are the only offenses where the victim knew the offender more often than not. Table 2 shows that Aborigines (like females) were also more likely to be victimized by someone known or related to them than non-Aborigines. Aboriginal victims are more likely to be offended against in domestic or "family" situations or by someone they know.

For assault offenses the proportion of family members or spouses who offended against the victim provides some guide to the extent of reported offenses of "wife-bashing" and other "domestic violence." The available data, of course, cannot be a guide to unreported offenses, but permit an estimate of the prevalence of "domestic violence" from known (recorded) offenses against the person.

Based on the 750 offenses against the person in which the offender

TABLE 2

Victim-Offender Relationship (by Race of Victim)—Selected Offenses against the Person, Western Australia, 1992–93 (in Percent)

Offense	*N*	None	Spouse	Family	"Friend"	"Other"
Homicide:*						
Aboriginal victim	31	29.0	22.6	22.6	16.1	9.7
Other victim	73	41.1	17.8	12.3	9.6	19.2
Serious assault:†						
Aboriginal victim	1,322	26.3	30.3	16.9	10.2	16.3
Other victim	3,285	61.7	5.3	4.4	8.2	20.4
Common assault:						
Aboriginal victim	1,587	33.8	22.7	16.8	7.8	18.9
Other victim	9,279	63.9	4.6	3.6	6.2	21.8
Sex assault:‡						
Aboriginal victim	232	34.0	3.1	32.8	19.0	12.1
Other victim	1,685	36.4	.8	25.3	17.3	20.2

Source.—Ferrante, Loh, and Broadhurst (1994).
* Includes attempted murder but excludes driving as cause of death.
† Includes grievous and aggravated bodily harm.
‡Includes sex offenses against children.

was the spouse of the victim, Harding et al. (1995) calculated crude estimates of the prevalence of reported domestic violence in the WA adult population for adult Aboriginal females of 3,075 per 100,000 compared with a rate of 58.9 per 100,000 for adult non-Aboriginal females.[9] Adult Aboriginal females were fifty times more at risk of spousal violence than adult non-Aboriginal females.

2. *Cross-Race Violence.* Data collected by the OIS on the race of the victim and the race of the alleged offender (where known) enable us to examine to what extent these offenses of violence are inter- or intraracial. The classification of race is collapsed into Aboriginal and non-Aboriginal. Consequently, the extent to which victims and offenders interact from Asian and non-English-speaking backgrounds is not detailed. The description is also limited to offenses against the person where the relevant data are most complete for 1993.[10]

Data are reported when both victim and offender information are

[9] The category "domestic" includes wife or husband, de facto and estranged spouse.

[10] Of the 176,921 offense reports recorded by police in 1993, descriptive information on 33,042 alleged offenders was obtained. Of these, 19.9 percent were females and 30.8 percent were Aborigines. For a large number of cases the victim's sex (48.1 percent) or race (51.0 percent) was not recorded because the offenses were not against persons.

TABLE 3

Relationship between Race of Victim and Race of Offender, 1993 (in Percent)

	Assault	Sex Offenses	Robbery	Homicide
Intraracial	77.4	94.2	75.0	88.7
Interracial	22.6	5.8	25.0	11.3
N	4,191	703	324	53

Source.—Ferrante, Loh, and Broadhurst (1994).
Note.—Missing race cases are excluded.

available on the offense report; in about half of the reported cases data on the race of the victim or offender are missing. Table 3 summarizes the extent to which robbery, assault, sex offenses, and homicide offenses are cross-racial. For these offenses, victim and alleged offender information is absent in 48.2 percent of assault, 56.8 percent of sex, and 75.6 percent of robbery offenses. Considering only those cases where both victim and offender race were present, interracial offenses against the person occur in about one in seventeen sex offenses, about one in five assaults, one in four robberies, and about one in nine homicide offenses. Except for the rarer offenses of homicide and kidnap, these ratios appear stable, with little year-to-year variation. For example, in 1992 a larger proportion of homicides (36.2 percent) were interracial.

Information is based on the victim's report of the offense and thus is subject to error by misidentification of the alleged offender's race. Moreover, the nature of official records limits ability to generalize about interracial offenses because of the underreporting of offenses (similar difficulties occur with the victim-offender relationship data). Caution needs to be exercised, therefore, in interpreting the data because differential rates of reporting to the police by Aborigines and non-Aborigines cannot be ruled out even though NCS and NATSI survey data indicate few differences. Ethnic minorities may be more likely to underreport offenses when the alleged offender is from the majority ethnic group, and ethnic majority victims may be more likely to report offenses when the alleged offender(s) is from a minority group. Such differential rates of reporting offenses are likely to accentuate interracial offenses against the person.

Interracial violence reported to police is mostly characterized by a non-Aboriginal victim assaulted by an Aboriginal offender. Of the 945 victims (22.6 percent of all assaults) of cross-race assault, 93.3 percent were non-Aborigines and 6.7 percent Aborigines. For the other offenses summarized in table 3, a similar pattern is apparent. For example, of the forty-one victims of cross-race or interracial sex offenses, 75.6 percent were non-Aborigines, and 24.4 percent Aborigines; of the eighty-one victims of interracial robbery offenses (or 25.0 percent of robbery offenses), only one (1.2 percent) was an Aboriginal victim of non-Aboriginal offenders; and of the six interracial homicides, five (83.3 percent) were non-Aboriginal victims, and one (16.7 percent) was an Aboriginal victim.

The predominant pattern of interracial offending is Aboriginal offenders against non-Aboriginal victims, while almost all Aborigines were victimized by Aboriginal offenders. It is important to stress that these data do not indicate the degree to which race itself was a motive in offending. The extent to which such offending represents racial conflict requires detailed research not attempted here. Given the conflictual nature of most Aboriginal police relations it would also be unwise to conclude that these statistics reflect an accurate picture of the nature of interracial offending.

III. Police and Aborigines—Arrests

Information about police apprehensions or arrests is a crucial measure of law enforcement activity. For offenders it is the gateway to further involvement in the criminal justice system. Arrest data are the basic official measure of offending behavior and in Australia are available by race only from WA police. This section describes Aboriginal and non-Aboriginal apprehensions or offenses charged by police during 1990–94 and probabilities of rearrest and briefly summarizes the NATSI survey estimates of the prevalence of arrest. Large differences in the risk of arrest between Aborigines and non-Aborigines are observed, and contrary to expectations that the recommendations of the RCIADIC would decrease the relative risks between the races, there have been increases. Based on 1994 WA police records, Aborigines were 9.2 times more likely to be arrested than non-Aborigines.

A distinction between arrests (or all offenses charged, but not multiple counts of those offenses) and individual persons arrested is made. This distinction provides a more detailed description of the data. Reference is also made to "counts." These are all alleged offenses, inclu-

TABLE 4
Trends in Recorded Arrests, 1990–94

	1990	1991	1992	1993	1994
Persons arrested:	39,178	40,539	37,463	34,602	35,328
Aborigine	6,490	7,212	6,970	6,919	7,262
Non-Aborigine	30,995	32,479	30,059	27,273	27,571
Unknown race	1,693	848	434	410	495
All apprehensions (arrests)	86,079	91,680	83,517	78,859	77,987
All offenses charged (counts)	109,779	115,495	107,360	101,528	99,549

Source.—Ferrante, Loh, and Broadhurst (1994); and personal communication with N. Loh, August 1995, for 1994 arrest data.

sive of multiple incidents of the same type of offense, for which charges have been laid.

Individuals arrested during the counting period are counted once, even though they may have been arrested on more than one occasion or for more than one offense or charge. By counting distinct persons we can tell how many people were involved in alleged offending ("prevalence," rather than how many alleged offenses had been brought to charge, "incidence"). To describe distinct persons, I count only the charge that was the most serious, if there was more than one during the period.[11]

A. Arrest Data by Aboriginality

The 1993 police data record 34,602 distinct persons, charged with 78,859 separate alleged offenses (an average of 3.4 for Aborigines, 2.0 for non-Aborigines, and overall 2.3 charges per person) involving a total of 101,528 counts. Compared to previous years, as table 4 shows, these figures represent significant decreases in apprehensions. The number of distinct persons arrested compared to 1992 fell by 7.6 percent, the number of apprehensions by 5.6 percent, and the number of total charges by 5.4 percent. The total decreases from 1991 to 1994 were larger. Most of the decline can be attributed to reductions in non-Aboriginal, particularly juvenile, arrests. A significant 42.5 percent re-

[11] Although apprehensions involving minor traffic offenses (e.g., speeding and parking offenses) are not included, the data include other traffic-related offenses not usually regarded as crimes. The data do not include juvenile first offenders who appear before the children's (suspended proceedings) panel or who are cautioned. Thus it excludes apprehensions of young offenders who are diverted to alternative procedures.

TABLE 5

Prevalence of Arrest by Race for Western Australia, 1994

	Population	Number of Arrests	Population Arrested (Percent)	Rate per 100,000	Risk Ratio
Aboriginal population	47,251	7,364	15.58	15,584	9:22
Non-Aboriginal population	1,654,649	27,964	1.69	1,690	. . .
Western Australia population	1,701,900	35,328	2.07	2,075	. . .

SOURCE.—Personal communication with N. Loh, August 1995, for 1994 data. Population estimates: Western Australia estimated resident population at June quarter, 1994 (preliminary estimates) are from Australian Bureau of Statistics (1995*b*); Aboriginal population June 1994 is from table C of Australian Bureau of Statistics (1995*a*).

NOTE.—Cases of unknown race are allocated on a pro rata basis.

duction in juvenile arrests from 6,321 or 16.2 percent of all arrests in 1990 to 3,633 or 10.5 percent of all arrests in 1993 is mostly attributed to the introduction of cautioning from August 1991 onward, and the extension of eligibility to appear before a children's (suspended proceedings) panel to juveniles aged seventeen.

In 1.2 percent of cases in 1993, race was not recorded. After adjustment for these unknown cases, one in five distinct persons arrested (20.2 percent) was an Aborigine. However, while 17.9 percent of adults arrested were Aborigines, 30.9 percent of juveniles arrested were Aborigines. The proportion of Aborigines among total arrests has increased since 1990 from 17.1 percent to 20.6 percent in 1994 despite a general decline in arrests and charges.

Differences in the risks of arrests between Aborigines and non-Aborigines are striking. Although as noted, Aborigines make up an estimated 2.63 percent of the WA population, they comprise one-fifth of all individuals arrested. Estimates of the annual prevalence of arrests for 1994 are shown in table 5. Nearly 16 percent of the Aboriginal population was arrested at least once compared to just under 2 percent of the non-Aboriginal population.

Aboriginal estimates of the prevalence of arrest were obtained from the NATSI survey, which asked respondents (over the age of thirteen) if they had been arrested (and how often) in the last five years. Over a quarter (25.4 percent) of WA Aborigines reported being arrested compared to 20.4 percent of Aborigines nationally. About two-thirds of those arrested (15.8 percent) of WA Aborigines reported being arrested more than once in the past five years. By recalculating the estimates of prevalence in table 5 based on the denominator population aged over thirteen years, a comparison with the NATSI estimates can be made. On this basis the annual prevalence rate of recorded arrest is approximately 22 percent and close to the 25.4 percent (over five years) estimated by the NATSI self-report survey.

Variations in the prevalence of arrest by jurisdiction were observed; for example, in Tasmania only 12.6 percent of the Aborigines reported an arrest, whereas 28.5 percent of Aborigines in SA did so. Factors such as age, sex, and employment status also varied the risks of arrest, especially for those who reported being arrested more than once (Australian Bureau of Statistics 1995*a*, NATSI table 53).

Arrest rates declined significantly from 1990 to 1994 for both races and overall. However, decreases were much larger for non-Aborigines than for Aborigines, and relative differences in the risks of arrest for the races have increased. In 1990, Aborigines were 7.7 times (risk ratio) more likely than non-Aborigines to be arrested, but by 1994 Aborigines were 9.2 times more likely to be arrested. From a policy point of view it appears that diversionary schemes (such as cautioning) have had a more substantial impact on non-Aboriginal rates of arrest than on Aboriginal rates (see Broadhurst and Ferrante 1993). Age-specific rates for the races highlight the substantially higher risks of arrest for Aboriginal youth, especially those ten to fourteen years of age. The age-specific rate for this group was estimated to be about 263 per 100,000 for non-Aborigines but 7,240 per 100,000 for Aborigines.

The mean age of those arrested was 27.4 years, although females tended to be slightly older (28.1 years) and Aborigines somewhat younger (25.8 years). Age-standardized rates for arrest peak at 6,985.1 per 100,000 among those nineteen to twenty-four years of age, irrespective of race. For non-Aborigines, rates of arrest for this age group were 5,870 per 100,000 but for Aborigines they were an incredible 42,182 per 100,000.

Differential risks of arrest are greatest for the ten-to-fourteen age group (27.5 : 1) and lowest for the fifteen-to-eighteen (6.9 : 1) and nineteen-to-twenty-four (7.2 : 1) age groups The high rate of arrest for the younger Aboriginal age groups is also reflected in very high rates of juvenile detention (see below). Although significant declines in rates of arrest have occurred for juvenile Aborigines since the introduction of cautioning, these have been offset by only modest declines (even increases) for older age groups.

Police arrest records strongly suggest extremely high levels of contact and conflict with Aboriginal youth, which is borne out by the

TABLE 6

All Charges involving Aborigines, Females, and Juveniles, by Offense Group, 1993 (in Percent)

Offense Group	Aboriginal	Juvenile	Female
Against the person	40.3	15.8	12.2
Break and enter/theft	29.8	32.9	21.3
Property damage	39.2	29.4	13.1
Good order	45.3	16.4	17.7
Drugs	5.4	9.6	16.0
Driving	21.1	9.5	10.9
Other offenses	38.3	14.5	19.1
Unknown	24.1	20.3	15.3
Total	28.6	17.7	15.8

Source.—Ferrante, Loh, and Broadhurst (1994).
Note.—Missing race, sex, and age cases are excluded.

NATSI survey questions relating to police harassment and assault. Of the WA Aborigine sample, 10.2 percent stated they were "hassled by police," and 3 percent claimed they were physically assaulted by police in the last year. Young men made up the bulk of complainants: 31.1 percent of males aged fifteen to nineteen years said they were "hassled" and 8 percent claimed they had been physically assaulted, and for males aged twenty to twenty-four years 23.1 percent claimed they were "hassled" and 8.8 percent assaulted (Australian Bureau of Statistics 1995*a*, NATS1 table 57).

B. Race and Offense Type

Aborigines were least likely to be charged with fraud offenses (only 7.7 percent of charges) but more likely to be charged with vehicle theft (50.8 percent of charges) and break and enter offenses (40.7 percent). One-fifth (20.8 percent) of receiving charges and 24.8 percent of other thefts involved Aborigines.

Table 6 summarizes data for the proportions of Aborigines, juveniles, and females arrested for various offenses. For example, 40.3 percent of offenses against the person were laid against Aborigines, while 59.7 percent were against others; 15.8 percent of such charges were against juveniles, while 84.2 percent were against adults; and 88.2 percent of these offenses were allegedly committed by males, while 12.2 percent were by females.

Aborigines are more likely to be charged with offenses against the person, property damage, and good order offenses and less likely to be charged with driving/motor vehicle and, in particular, drug offenses than their overall representation in the data. Juveniles are more likely to be charged with break-and-enter/theft and property damage than other offenses. Female offenders are more likely to be charged with break-and-enter/theft offenses.

C. *Police Custody in Western Australia and the National Survey of Police Custody*

Of the 34,602 persons arrested or apprehended in 1993, fourteen per cent were held in custody, three-fifths were bailed (52.8 percent), and one-fifth (21.8 percent) were issued with a summons. Custody information was not recorded for eleven percent of arrests. Aborigines are more likely to be held in custody (20.3 percent; 13.0 percent of non-Aborigines) and significantly less likely to be summonsed (10.6 percent; 24.9 percent of non-Aborigines). Slightly more Aborigines (56.4 percent) than non-Aborigines (52.5 percent) were admitted to bail. These data underestimate incidents of police custody because they exclude multiple incidents of custody and detention for drunkenness.

The second National Police Custody (NPC) survey of August 1992 shows WA had the highest rate of Aboriginal detention followed by SA and the NT, whereas Tasmania and Victoria had the lowest. Over-representation ratios varied from a low of 3 : 1 for Tasmania to a high of 52 : 1 for WA (see table 7). The NT had the highest non-Aboriginal police custody rates, and Victoria the lowest.

D. *Rearrest Probabilities*

Estimates of the risk of rearrest for persons arrested are based on apprehension records of the Western Australian Police Service collected over the period April 1, 1984, to June 30, 1993 (Broadhurst and Loh 1995). About 757,000 charges were found, involving 518,915 arrests and 208,059 individuals.[12] As the aim was to estimate probabilities of rearrest, it was important to establish the order and timing of arrest.

[12] An arrest was defined as a charge laid on a given date. If more than one charge was laid on the same day, it was counted as only one arrest. The rule assumed that an individual would not be arrested more than once a day. Finding an arrest record prior to the initial collection start date (April 1, 1984) depended on determining the sequential fingerprint-based identification numbers that were issued prior to that date by the Bureau of Crime Intelligence.

TABLE 7

National Police Custody Rates per 100,000, by State, 1992

State	Total Rate	Aboriginal Rate	Non-Aboriginal Rate	Over-representation Ratio
Northern Territory	1,001	3,628	253	14:3
Western Australia	310	7,001	135	51:9
South Australia	226	3,720	178	20:9
Queensland	205	2,094	157	13:3
New South Wales	98	1,246	79	15:8
Victoria	80	772	76	10:2
Tasmania	86	242	82	3:0
Australian Capital Territory	105	452	103	4:4
Australia	152	2,801	107	26:2

SOURCE.—McDonald (1993).

Thus the sample was refined to exclude all individuals who had an arrest record prior to the start date. Some 62,000 cases were for that reason excluded, leaving 146,038 individuals in the database; twenty-one cases were arrested on the censor date. Those individuals had acquired 313,308 arrests by the cutoff date. Cases arrested in 1984 were followed a maximum of 9.25 years, those in 1985 for 8.25 years, and so on until the cutoff date. Subjects, on average, were followed up for 4.9 years.

Because the probability of arrest is dependent on the follow-up time, the data are said to be censored, since insufficient time had elapsed in some cases between arrest and the chances of rearrest. At the extreme, an individual arrested on June 30, 1993, would have had no opportunity to be rearrested, and ordinarily including such cases would seriously bias estimates of rearrest. A statistical method, known as failure or survival rate analysis, is used to account for such bias and permits accurate estimates of the ultimate probability of arrest (see Broadhurst and Loh 1995).

An important caveat is that the data are not adjusted for time spent in custody. Linked data containing prison records will enable the follow-up time to be corrected to count only the time that an offender is at liberty. Consequently, estimates are conservative since, for the more serious offenders, "time out" caused by imprisonment is not taken into account. In addition, arrests that occur outside the jurisdiction are not included and for some cases a full history of police charges is therefore not available.[13] Although WA is a relatively isolated and closed jurisdiction, compared to others, considerable interstate travel occurs. At present, no adequate national database exists for tracking offenders across jurisdictions. These missing arrest data tend to produce underestimates of the probability of rearrest.

Data were available only for a few items for each arrest event: race, sex, age, bail status, place of birth, occupation (including a partial record of those "unemployed"), offense, and offense count. Thus while the data refer to a large population of arrested persons, they do not contain many factors (e.g., education, employment, mental health, marital status, and drug or alcohol use) often found to be associated with differential risks of rearrest.

Overall, male non-Aborigines made up 66.8 percent of the "first time" arrest population, male Aborigines 3.8 percent, female non-Aborigines 21.5 percent, female Aborigines 2.3 percent, and unknown race or gender 5.6 percent. Females accounted for 24.4 percent of non-Aboriginal arrestees, 37.6 percent of Aboriginal arrestees, and 21.6 percent of those of unknown race. Thus, after adjusting for missing or unknown race, 6.4 percent of the population arrested for the first time since 1984 were Aborigines. Excluding those with arrests prior to 1984 underestimates the proportion of Aborigines in the arrest population at any time. One in five (20.2 percent) of the individuals apprehended annually are Aborigines, and approximately 2.63 percent of the WA population is of Aboriginal descent. Aborigines are therefore overrepresented in the first arrest population by a factor of about 2.4 and by a factor of about 7.7 in the general arrest population.[14] The very high recycling suggested by these differences is confirmed for Aboriginal arrestees.

Table 8 shows the probabilities of rearrest were 0.52 for male non-Aborigines, 0.36 for female non-Aborigines, 0.88 for male Aborigines, and 0.85 for female Aborigines. The difference between female and male Aboriginal rearrests was not significant, but differences between the races and non-Aborigines were statistically significant.[15]

[13] For a comprehensive discussion of the center's offender-tracking data collection and data-linking process, see Ferrante (1993).

[14] The 1994 Aboriginal population estimate in WA was 47,251 and we found at least 18.7 percent of this population arrested for the first time between 1984–93.

[15] As judged by the 95 percent confidence intervals reported for the Aboriginal sex groups.

TABLE 8

Probabilities of Rearrest by Sex and Race, 1984–93

	Non-Aborigine	Aborigine	Unknown
Males:			
Probability of rearrest	.518	.883	. . .
Confidence interval	.51, .52	.85, .90	. . .
Median time to rearrest (years)	17.2	10.7	. . .
Number of individuals	97,572	5,518	6,076
Number of individuals rearrested	38,013	4,042	340
Females:			
Probability of rearrest	.361	.849	. . .
Confidence interval	.34, .38	.79, .89	. . .
Median time to rearrest (years)	26.9	18.7	. . .
Number of individuals	31,440	3,323	1,672
Number of individuals rearrested	7,233	1,958	94

SOURCE.—Broadhurst and Loh (1995).
NOTE.—Arrestees of "unknown race" omitted.

Rearrest probabilities were calculated for the major offense classification groups; while differences were observed for non-Aborigines, offense type did not significantly vary rearrest probabilities for Aborigines. Age, occupation, bail status, place of birth, and number of arrests also varied the probability and speed of rearrest for either race. Younger offenders, those in "blue-collar" occupations, offenders born in WA,[16] and those held in custody were likely to have higher risks of rearrest than others. In addition, the more often one is arrested the greater the risk of rearrest.

1. *Criminal Careers and Race.* The number of subsequent arrests to the cutoff date gives a rough indication of the proportion of the population who persisted with offending. For example, of the 5,518 male Aborigines arrested for the first time, 2,251 (40.8 percent) had been arrested at least five times by the cutoff date, and 8,262 (or 8.5 percent) of the 97,572 male non-Aborigines had been arrested at least five times. The proportions of females with at least five arrests were 2.9 percent of non-Aborigines and 23.8 percent of Aborigines.

A prior record of offending substantially increases the risk of subsequent offending. Given further arrests in this population the probabil-

[16] "Natives" of WA had higher chances of rearrest because they were less subject to processes of attrition which led some offenders (especially those born in the United States and New Zealand) to disappear from the sample by leaving the state.

TABLE 9

Probabilities of Rearrest by Number of Arrests, 1984–93

	Non-Aborigines		Aborigines	
Number of Arrests	Probability of Rearrest	Individuals Arrested	Probability of Rearrest	Individuals Arrested
Males:				
1	.52	97,572	.88	5,518
2	.68	38,013	.92	4,042
3	.78	20,033	.94	3,244
4	.84	12,268	.95	2,649
5	.86	8,262	.96	2,251
6	.89	5,818	.97	1,942
7	.89	4,259	.98	1,691
8	.92	3,229	.98	1,493
9	.94	2,538	.98	1,311
10	.94	2,045	.99	1,175
11	.94	1,658	.98	1,049
12	.96	1,357	.99	943
13	.97	1,156	.98	860
14	.98	979	.99	789
Females:				
1	.36	31,440	.85	3,323
2	.56	7,233	.89	1,958
3	.70	2,814	.88	1,366
4	.77	1,496	.94	1,026
5	.82	907	.91	792
6	.81	593	.93	633
7	.89	416	.95	519
8	.83	311	.96	440
9	.90	228	.97	366
10	.92	183	.95	312
11	.90	154	.97	274
12	.92	119	.96	234
13	.97	94	.98	209
14	.95	85	.97	183

SOURCE.—Broadhurst and Loh (1995).

ity of rearrest increases. In the case of Aboriginal offenders, rearrest probabilities approach absolute certainty of arrest after several episodes. Table 9 shows that given one prior arrest, the probabilities of each successive arrest increase rapidly for non-Aborigines to the point where differences in recidivism by race and sex disappear. In the case of male non-Aborigines, the time to fail falls rapidly from nearly a year-and-a-half for the first rearrest to a few months by the seventh arrest. However, relatively large proportions of non-Aboriginal offenders, even those with three or four arrests, desist from offending. Although probabilities approach certainty of arrest, given several prior arrests, small numbers continue to desist (or perhaps die or leave the jurisdiction).

In contrast, male Aboriginal offenders reach virtual certainty of rearrest very rapidly (after three or four arrests), and the time to fail falls from less than a year to a couple of months. Although far fewer females persisted with offending than males, their reoffending behavior (in terms of the risks of recidivism) was more similar to their male counterparts than dissimilar. In rough terms, female probabilities of rearrest (given one to *n* arrests) are about one step behind the males. Eventually, females reach near certainty of rearrest, coupled with rapidly declining failure times.

2. *Rearrest and Reimprisonment.* Rearrest patterns are very similar to reimprisonment patterns (see Broadhurst and Maller 1990*b;* and Broadhurst 1993). The similarity raises the possibility that imprisonment or other penal interventions may have little direct bearing on the probabilities of rearrest.

IV. Aborigines and the Courts

National adult court data are not available, and WA data sources are limited by incomplete coverage (especially of lower courts) and poor identification of race and other information. In WA there have also been breaks in the published annual statistics produced, thus prohibiting useful trend analysis. Consequently, the latest summary data are available only for the 1992 (Broadhurst, Ferrante, and Loh 1993) and 1991–92 reporting years (Australian Bureau of Statistics 1994*c*). Detailed breakdowns of penalties by race were not available from the ABS.

For all courts (including juvenile courts) in 1991–92, as table 10 shows, the ABS recorded 120,938 convictions of which 24.6 percent involved Aborigines and 16.9 percent of individuals convicted were Aborigines. Aborigines at each appearance at court averaged 4.2 charges compared to 2.6 for non-Aborigines.

Nearly all persons charged were convicted (if not of all charges laid), and this did not vary with race (92.5 percent of Aborigines and 92.3 percent of non-Aborigines). Of all convictions, 14.9 percent resulted in a penalty of imprisonment, but 21.9 percent of Aboriginal convictions led to imprisonment.

Since comprehensive breakdowns by race and penalty are not avail-

TABLE 10

Australian Bureau of Statistics Summary, All Courts, by Race, 1991–92

Court	Aborigines	Aborigine (Percent)	All*
Charges	30,242	24.5	123,465
Distinct persons charged	13,601	23.1	58,821
Individuals charged	7,147	16.9	42,323
Convictions	29,816	24.6	120,938
Distinct persons convicted	13,400	23.2	57,822
Individuals convicted	7,058	16.9	41,672

SOURCE.—Australian Bureau of Statistics (1994*d*).

NOTE.—"Distinct persons" refers to a person appearing in court on a given day, that is, a person may appear many times in the counting period. "Individuals" refers to the number of separate persons appearing in court by the most serious offense with which they are charged/convicted regardless of the number of times they appear in court during the counting period.

* Of all charges, 7.2 percent did not contain information on race—unknown race is included in this category.

able for all courts, differences between the races in relation to disposition must be estimated from lower court outcomes derived from police records for the 1992 counting period. According to ABS estimates, 70.2 percent of charges are dealt with by magistrate or lower courts, 5.2 percent by higher courts, and 24.6 percent in children's courts. Since the bulk of adult matters (93 percent) are heard by the lower courts, outcomes and dispositions by race from this source can be assumed to give a reliable guide to differences between Aborigines and non-Aborigines. Before doing so, the penalty outcomes for juvenile convictions dealt with by the children's courts are briefly summarized (for details, see Harding et al. 1995).

A. Penalties for Juvenile Offenders—1993

A highly significant decline in the workload of the children's courts has been observed since the introduction of police cautioning in 1991. Between 1990 and 1993, the number of juveniles convicted fell 44 percent from 10,513 to 5,889. For 1993, the proportion of juvenile Aborigines was estimated by the ABS at around 23.7 percent of distinct persons convicted (after adjusting for unknown race). Juvenile Aborigines were on average significantly younger (mean age 15.3) than non-Aborigines (mean age 16.1).

TABLE 11

Outcome in Children's Courts by Sex and Race, 1992—Distinct Persons (in Percent)

Outcome	All	Males	Females	Aborigines	Non-Aborigines
Dismissed	44.4	42.3	52.9	27.9	50.3
Fine	17.2	17.9	14.0	13.1	16.4
Noncustodial	31.3	31.9	29.2	44.0	28.2
Custodial	5.8	6.4	3.1	14.5	3.5
Other	1.3	1.4	.7	.5	1.6

Source.—Broadhurst, Ferrante, and Loh (1993).
Note.—Percents sum to 100.0.

The outcome of alleged offenses heard by the children's courts is summarized in table 11 into four broad groups of penalties: dismissed (various forms of dismissal, including discharged with no penalty and dismissed with no conviction record), fines, noncustodial orders (probation, community service orders, combined orders, good behavior bonds, and suspended sentences), custodial orders of imprisonment or detention, and others, including loss of motor driver's license and restitution or compensation.

Table 11 shows that the disposition varied considerably depending on the sex or race of the child or juvenile (after adjustment for missing cases). Females were more likely to be dealt with by way of dismissal and very much less likely to be placed in custody. For the sex-race subgroups, differences are greater than shown in table 11 since Aboriginal male juveniles are more likely to be placed in custody (16.6 percent compared to 4.0 percent) or to receive a noncustodial order (42.9 percent compared to 29.2 percent), but less likely to be fined (13.4 percent compared to 17.1 percent). For females, the race differences are even more marked: Aborigines are less likely to be dealt with by way of dismissal (31.9 percent compared to 61.8 percent) and consequently more likely to receive other penalties. For example, 8.1 percent of female Aborigines received detention compared to 1.4 percent of non-Aboriginal females, and 47.2 percent of female Aborigines received noncustodial orders compared to 23 percent of non-Aborigines. Thus Aborigines convicted by the children's court are about 4.1 times more likely to be imprisoned than are non-Aborigines.

Aborigines were more frequently convicted of offenses against the person and driving or traffic offenses and non-Aborigines of drug and fraud offenses, which suggests that differences in the severity of offenses may account for the greater use of custody for Aborigines. Controlling for offense (a crude measure of severity) did not change the finding that Aborigines were more likely to receive a custodial sentence. For example, in respect to convictions for offenses against the person, 52.8 percent of Aborigines received a custodial sentence compared to 36.2 percent of non-Aborigines, 36.2 percent of Aborigines received a community supervision order compared to 39.4 percent of non-Aborigines, 3.5 percent of Aborigines were fined compared to 5.5 percent of non-Aborigines, and 7.3 percent of Aborigines were dismissed compared to 16.8 percent of non-Aborigines. However, the absence of data about prior convictions makes it impossible to conclude that differences in disposition arise from bias by the courts.

B. Western Australia Courts of Petty Sessions—1992

Detailed information about the activities of summary courts or courts of petty sessions is not readily available in WA. Summary courts are also referred to as police courts, lower courts, or magistrate's courts. They are usually presided over by a stipendiary (paid) magistrate, but in country areas they are often constituted by two lay magistrates (or justices of the peace) sitting together or occasionally a single lay magistrate with restricted powers to imprison. These lay tribunals are more likely to deal with Aboriginal offenders. The majority of cases (61.9 percent) were heard in metropolitan Perth by legally trained magistrates. Country courts of petty sessions dealt with three-quarters of Aboriginal defendants (75.3 percent). The data do not provide details on the makeup of these courts, that is, whether constituted by a stipendiary magistrate, two justices of the peace, or a justice of the peace sitting alone.

During 1992, 81,880 police charges involving 32,175 distinct persons were heard by lower courts—an average of about 2.5 charges per person. Of persons dealt with, 19 percent were females and 17.3 percent were Aborigines, but 22.6 percent of all charges involved Aborigines. Information about the pleas of defendants was not available. However, most charges (96.1 percent) resulted in convictions, 2.3 percent led to an acquittal, and 1.6 percent were withdrawn.

The most frequent offenses were fraud and theft (29.6 percent), followed by driving and motor vehicle offenses (25.1 percent—mostly driving under the influence [DUI] and driver's license breaches), good order offenses (23.3 percent), drug offenses (13.5 percent—mostly

TABLE 12

Penalty by Race—Distinct Persons, Lower Courts, 1992
(in Percent)

Penalty	All	Aborigines	Non-Aborigines
Dismissed	2.8	2.7	2.8
Fine	71.4	64.8	73.0
Noncustodial	10.3	11.7	9.8
Custodial	4.9	16.1	2.6
Other*	10.6	4.7	11.9

Source.—Broadhurst, Ferrante, and Loh (1993).
Note.—Percents sum to 100.0.
* Other penalties include loss or suspension of motor driver's license and restitution.

possession or use), offenses against the person (5 percent—mostly common assault), property damage offenses (2.4 percent), and other sundry offenses (1.1 percent). Aborigines were more likely to be charged with good order offenses and assault, whereas non-Aborigines were more often charged with drug, fraud, and DUI offenses.

Penalties for distinct persons convicted in lower courts are summarized in table 12. Fines (71.4 percent) and noncustodial orders (probation, community service orders, and work orders—10.3 percent) were the most common outcomes imposed overall and on each of the groups represented. Only 4.9 percent of distinct persons were sent to prison, although 9.3 percent of charges resulted in imprisonment. Dismissals (where a person is convicted but no penalty is given or recorded) accounted for 2.8 percent of outcomes. Table 12 also shows that dispositions varied considerably depending on the race of the individual. Of Aborigines convicted some 16.1 percent were placed in custody, as compared to 2.6 percent of convicted non-Aborigines. Thus, once convicted, Aborigines were six times (6.2 : 1) more likely to be incarcerated than non-Aborigines.

Although some differences were found when examining penalty outcomes by offense, especially for public order offenses, the general pattern shown in table 12 did not vary greatly due to offense. As with juvenile conviction it should be emphasized that these data, while showing that Aborigines are more likely to be imprisoned (especially by lower courts), still cannot help us to determine if invidious bias produces more punitive responses for Aborigines. In the absence of data on prior record and inadequate control of offense seriousness, an effective test of bias is not possible.

C. Judicial Bias—Disposition and Penalty Quantum

The RCIADC (1991*b*) found that Aborigines are more likely to be incarcerated than non-Aborigines but was unable to establish (for lack of data) if this was due to the proportion of Aborigines arrested or to the role of the courts (or both). However, they assumed an overuse of imprisonment by the courts and attributed this to the absence of community-based correctional services in remote areas, an inability or unwillingness by Aborigines to pay fines, and the attitudes and practices of the police and justices, especially lay justices in rural areas (see also Martin and Newby 1984).

The implication that justices and Eurocentric court processes discriminate against Aborigines in sentencing thus relied on obvious disadvantages of language and culture and on an overwhelming overrepresentation of Aborigines in prison. Such assumptions are not evidence of discrimination since there is also evidence (although inconsistent) that for more serious offenses substantial discounting of sentence length occurs because of Aborigines' nomadic or "tribal" life (Australian Law Reform Commission 1986; Broadhurst 1987; Royal Commission into Aboriginal Deaths in Custody 1991*b*), including the attitude among some WA higher court judges that "informally at least . . . the tariff for Aboriginal offenders is approximately half that in relation to non-Aboriginal offenders" (Heenan 1991, p. 44).

For example, based on the 1984 national census of prisoners, Walker (1987) found Aborigines on average spent nearly half as much time in prison (42.6 months vs. 86.4 months) as non-Aborigines. This large difference persisted after accounting for prior imprisonment and offense seriousness, although the interaction between offense seriousness and prior imprisonment was only partially examined. While Aboriginal prisoners were on average younger and their offenses appeared less serious than non-Aborigines, Walker did not consider these sufficient to account for the difference but rather it was "more likely that in fact the courts are bending over backwards to keep Aborigines out of prison for lengthy periods" (Walker 1987, p. 113).

Since Walker compared averages at census but did not analyze sentence distributions using conventional analysis of variance or by tabulating medians and quartiles or control for all interactions between the factors considered (or all factors relevant), his method was limited and oversimplified. In most jurisdictions (except WA and the NT) the number of Aboriginal cases was so small as to have virtually no impact on overall average sentence lengths (see Walker 1987, pp. 113–14).

Nevertheless, because the differences in sentence averages were very large between the races, Walker was confident the descriptive data reflected race differences, at least as they applied to terms of imprisonment.

Walker's analysis proved highly controversial but did render simplistic assertions about judicial bias highly suspect and prompted Broadhurst (1993) to conduct an analysis of sentence length by race using a large sample of WA prisoners sentenced between 1975 and 1987. Broadhurst's analysis attempted to control for age, employment at arrest, offense type, marital status, year of sentence, number of terms of imprisonment, and the number of prior (same) offenses. Generally, the sentence length distributions were not normal and highly skewed (despite log transformations), and although several offenses (drunkenness, assault, rape, robbery, and motor vehicle theft) were examined, only assault was found sufficiently normal to employ conventional analysis of variance (ANOVA) methods.[17] The ANOVA for assault showed race alone was not a significant factor in accounting for the variance found in sentence length. While interactions between race and employment, marital status, and prior offense accounted for a small but significant amount of variance, year of sentence and particularly employment were highly significant and accounted for most of the variance.

Because the data were not amenable to analysis by conventional ANOVA and regression techniques, the effects of various factors on sentence-length distributions for several offenses were examined by descriptive methods based on means and quartiles. Broadly, the effect of race on sentence variation was small (for Aborigines sometimes longer or shorter than for non-Aborigines) and complicated by potential interactions and dependent on the nature of the offense. In short, general claims of leniency or harshness in sentence length due to Aboriginality could not be sustained, and "conclusions about the court's leniency towards Aborigines are not always supported by the evidence" (Broadhurst 1993, p. 422). Broadhurst argued that concentrating on sentencing policy would not make a substantial impact on differential risks of imprisonment since the differences in sentence length were relatively minor compared to the risks of arrest. The analysis of sentencing disparity and race is described in the next section and reveals the

[17] The ANOVA procedure was undertaken using the forward stepwise regression method using the statistical package GLIM (General Linear Modeling). The first factor and interaction was entered into the equation in an order determined by the highest *F*-ratio score.

TABLE 13

Higher Court Dispositions by Aboriginality, 1990 (in Percent)

	N	Noncustodial	Prison
Aborigine	298	40.3	59.7
Non-Aborigine	1,177	54.8	45.2
Unknown	125	58.4	41.6

SOURCE.—Broadhurst (1993).
NOTE.—$\chi^2 = 22.1$, df = 2; $p < 0.001$.

complexity and marginality of the effects of discrimination in higher courts.

1. *Higher Court Penalties.* Drawing on convicted persons data for 1990 from WA higher courts (district and supreme courts) provides some indication of the extent to which bias occurs at disposition.[18] That is, given arrest and conviction, to what extent is disparity evident in the choice between a noncustodial and prison disposition?

Under a fifth (18.6 percent) of the 1,600 individuals convicted by higher courts in 1990 were Aborigines, 73.6 percent were non-Aborigines, and a small number were unknown (7.8 percent). This small sample (all of whom were represented by legal counsel) could be described in terms of race, sex, offense, plea, and age but not prior record. Offenses are selected on the basis of the most serious offense of conviction (determined by the quantum and the intrusiveness of the sanction)[19] for each individual whose case was finalized during 1990. Because the numbers of cases was small, discrete analysis of offenses by chi-square was limited to those offenses where sufficient cases were present.[20]

Table 13 shows that Aborigines were more likely to be incarcerated than non-Aborigines for all convictions (irrespective of the offense). Nearly 60 percent of Aboriginal dispositions resulted in imprisonment compared to 45 percent of non-Aboriginals. For this and subsequent

[18] These courts deal with indictable matters and represent only a small (less than 5 percent), albeit more serious, proportion of the criminal matters dealt with by the courts.

[19] The selection of offense is based on the following hierarchy: imprisonment, community service orders, probation orders, fines, and good behavior bonds.

[20] The same analysis was conducted on all charges resulting in conviction, since the number of charges was much larger. However, this did not always improve the cell size and resulted in similar outcomes as found for distinct persons.

TABLE 14

Selected Serious Offenses by Race and Disposition, 1990 (in Percent)

	N	Noncustodial	Prison
Robbery:			
Aborigines	14	21.4	78.6
Non-Aborigines	55	20.0	80.0
Unknown	5	20.0	80.0
Assault:			
Aborigines	58	46.6	53.4
Non-Aborigines	87	51.7	48.3
Unknown	9	11.1	88.9
Break and enter dwelling:			
Aborigines	99	53.5	46.5
Non-Aborigines	301	60.8	39.2
Unknown	21	61.9	38.1
Sexual assault:*			
Aborigines	40	12.5	87.5
Non-Aborigines	80	35.0	65.0
Unknown	8	50.0	50.0

Source.—Broadhurst (1993).
* $\chi^2 = 8.4$, df = 2; $p < 0.05$.

analysis, fines, good-behavior bonds, probation, and community service orders are combined into noncustodial sentences.

Analyzing other cross-tabulations such as gender, plea, and age showed that for all convictions gender was highly significant (the small number of females rendered analysis by offense unreliable); age was not significant but close to significance (at the 5 percent level), with very young offenders more likely to receive a noncustodial penalty. Plea (guilty or not) did not significantly affect the disposition of cases. Offense, not surprisingly, was highly significant, with offenses against the person being more likely to receive a custodial sentence than property offenses.

Table 14 shows disposition by race and offense group (robbery, assault, break and enter dwelling, and sexual assault). Only sexual assault showed Aborigines were significantly more likely to receive a custodial sentence. Age was also significant in sexual assault, with very young offenders less likely to be jailed. For assault and break and enter, sex was highly significant, with females more likely to receive a noncustodial sentence, and age approached significance in assault (younger offenders less likely to receive a custodial sentence). For robbery, none

TABLE 15

Sentence Length (in Days) by Offense, Sex, and Race, 1990

	N	First Quartile	Median	Third Quartile
Males:				
Aborigines:	331	180	365	730
Against person	152	360	730	1,460
Property	123	180	360	540
Good order	56	30	90	180
Non-Aborigines:	1,896	360	540	848
Against person	534	365	730	1,460
Property	1,070	360	480	730
Good order	162	240	365	540
Drugs	98	360	540	1,095
Other offenses	32	180	180	180
Females:				
Aborigines:	28	270	365	519
Against person	3	90	180	4,380
Property	17	225	365	540
Good order	8	270	348	429
Non-Aborigines:	340	360	420	674
Against person	14	365	730	1,460
Property	240	420	540	674
Good order	66	360	360	360
Drugs	20	365	635	730

SOURCE.—Broadhurst (1993).

of the available factors (race, sex, age, or plea) were found significant by chi-square analysis.

2. *Higher Court—Length of Imprisonment.* In order to assess the impression of some judges that the "tariff" is adjusted downward for Aborigines, sentence length can be compared by race. For this exercise all sentences (rather than the major offense of each individual) were converted into days, and the group means, medians, and standard deviations were calculated. The descriptive analysis suggests that a one-third discount does appear to operate for property offenses but overall the difference is slight.

Table 15 summarizes average sentence lengths for broadly grouped offense categories and shows that non-Aborigines receive sentences about 11 percent longer but that non-Aboriginal females receive much longer sentences than Aborigines (about 50 percent longer). Most differences can be explained in terms of differences in the relative severity of offenses. For example, there is a large difference in the average for females sentenced for offenses against the person because in this sample a few homicide offenses by non-Aboriginal females drastically increased the overall average sentence length for that group. As there is only a small number of female Aborigines in the sample it would be unwise to draw any strong conclusions about differences arising from sex-race in this sample.

The statistical interpretation of apparent differences in table 15 is also complicated by the highly skewed distribution of sentence lengths and the consequent difficulties in making valid comparisons between groups. The standard deviations of the sentences for the different groups are large, sometimes approaching the mean.

Overall, the race of the individual appears to have an effect on the decision to dispose of a case by imprisonment, but of the four offense groups with sufficient cases for analysis, only one, sexual assault, was found to be significant in terms of differences in race (and in a later analysis for 1993 data by Harding et al. 1995, it was not found significant). Without the ability to control for prior conviction, these data cannot provide convincing evidence that there is a differential effect of race on the decision to incarcerate. Differences are just as likely to be the result of the greater frequency of arrest rather than judicial preference to incarcerate Aborigines. It is clear, however, that once convicted Aborigines have a greater likelihood (especially in lower courts) of being incarcerated, but this does not necessarily translate into longer terms of imprisonment.

Thus it was found that Aborigines were four times more at risk in the children's court (table 11), six times more at risk in the high-volume lower courts (table 12), and about one-third more at risk in the low-volume higher courts (table 13). Once imprisoned, Aborigines are not generally likely to receive longer sentences, and for offenses against property, shorter sentences are observed. Somewhat imprecisely, the overall differential risk of a custodial disposition is therefore about 5:1.

V. Aborigines and Imprisonment

Imprisonment and community-based correctional programs in Australia are managed by states, with federal prisoners serving sentences in the jurisdiction in which they were charged. Distinctions between "jails" and prisons are not commonly made, although significant numbers of prisoners serve short sentences in police "lockups" in remote areas. Imprisonment includes the confinement of juvenile offenders in detention centers and adults serving sentences in state prisons or police lockups, including persons remanded in custody. Those persons detained by police as intoxicated persons, arrested on charges, or held on warrants pending trial are excluded.

Reception history sheets, police property sheets, warrant summaries, and exit forms are the principal sources of data on prisoners in WA. These data are used to describe annual prison receptions (admissions) of individuals and census (on December 31) through the reform period 1990–93 associated with the RCIADIC.

A. Imprisonment in Western Australia

For summary offenses in WA, imprisonment is infrequently used compared to other penalties and represents about 5 percent of all dispositions. The use of very short sentences of imprisonment by summary courts has been the focus of efforts to limit the use of imprisonment, but there is little evidence that lower courts have done so (Dixon 1981; Broadhurst 1987; Harding 1992).

Prisoners convicted of indictable offenses in higher courts represent an insignificant proportion of all prisoners but the bulk of the long-term imprisoned. The use of imprisonment by higher courts significantly declined during 1983–89 from 59.5 percent to 45.3 percent of persons convicted, assuming a constancy in the relative seriousness of the offenses dealt with. Further analysis by offense attributed most of this decline to reductions in the use of imprisonment for offenses such as break and enter (58 percent to 35 percent) and fraud (41 percent to 26 percent), but not for offenses against the person or drug offenses (Australian Bureau of Statistics 1987, 1988*a*, 1988*b*, 1989, 1990, 1992*a*). The most recent data show a reversal of this trend, with the proportion of persons imprisoned increasing from 47 percent of dispositions in 1990 to 55.7 percent in 1993 (Ferrante, Loh, and Broadhurst 1994).[21]

1. *Aborigines and Imprisonment.* The race of prisoners admitted to prison and in census-date populations is summarized in table 16 for 1990–93. In 1993, 41.5 percent of the admitted population were Aborigines.

[21] Trend analysis is complicated by the discontinuation of the ABS Higher Court statistical series in 1989–91 and from 1993 onward. In addition, significant changes in jurisdiction between courts occurred in 1989 when some offenses were transferred to summary jurisdictions and more defendants became eligible to elect to be tried in lower courts.

TABLE 16

Prison Population by Race, 1990–93

Year	All Persons	Aborigines	Non-Aborigines
Admissions:			
1990	6,717	3,139	3,578
		(46.7)	(53.3)
1991	6,212	2,685	3,527
		(43.2)	(56.8)
1992	5,622	2,358	3,264
		(41.9)	(58.1)
1993	6,042	2,505	3,537
		(41.5)	(58.5)
Distinct persons:			
1990	5,122	2,184	2,938
		(42.6)	(57.4)
1991	4,814	1,884	2,930
		(39.1)	(60.9)
1992	4,409	1,725	2,684
		(39.1)	(60.9)
1993	4,818	1,859	2,959
		(38.6)	(61.4)
Census-date population (December 31):			
1990	1,620	548	1,072
		(33.8)	(66.2)
1991	1.809	581	1,228
		(32.1)	(67.9)
1992	1,852	613	1,239
		(33.1)	(66.9)
1993	2,078	654	1,424
		(31.5)	(68.5)

Source.—Ferrante, Loh, and Broadhurst (1994).
Note.—Numbers in parentheses are percentages.

Trends by race for admissions and census counts show declines since 1990; however, 1993 data show a sharp reversal of this trend. Despite increases in 1993, the number of Aborigines admitted to prison has fallen 20 percent since 1990 compared to a slight decrease of 1.1 percent for non-Aborigines. Similarly, a 14.9 percent decline is observed for Aboriginal persons compared to a slight increase of 0.7 percent for non-Aborigines. In contrast, the number of persons incarcerated on census dates has increased by 28.3 percent since 1990; however, the increase was less for Aborigines than for non-Aborigines (19.3 percent compared to 32.8 percent).

These trends show that the general decrease in the frequency of im-

TABLE 17

Distinct Sentenced Prisoners by Sentence Type, Sex, and Race, 1993 (in Percent)

Group	Fine Default	Prison Only	Prison plus Parole
Female:			
Aborigine	76.3	17.3	6.4
Non-Aborigine	50.8	14.1	35.1
Male:			
Aborigine	45.1	32.0	22.9
Non-Aborigine	45.7	14.5	39.8
All	48.2	20.6	31.2
N	1,788	765	1,157

SOURCE.—Ferrante, Loh, and Broadhurst (1994).
NOTE.—*N* = 3,710. Percents sum to 100.0.

prisonment has not reduced the numbers on census dates. The most likely reasons are the diversion of minor offenders from prison (especially alternatives for fine defaulters and public drunkenness) and longer stays (the proportion of sentenced prisoners with a maximum prison term of one year or more) have increased from 15.4 percent in 1990 to 28.6 percent in 1993.

2. *Offenses, Sentence Type, and Aboriginality.* Table 17 examines differences in the type of sentence of imprisonment received by Aborigines and non-Aborigines. Aborigines are less likely to receive sentences of imprisonment followed by parole supervision in the community because they generally serve relatively short sentences (or sentences in lieu of fines) and because their high rates of recidivism make them less likely to be eligible for early release under parole supervision. Aborigines are also more likely to be released into the community without supervision after completion of a fixed term of imprisonment (less remission) because of shorter sentences (a sentence of greater than one year is usually necessary for parole) and the frequency of minor offenses such as "public order" offenses and property damage.

Table 18 shows the proportion of Aborigines received in prison for the broad offense categories compared to the proportion charged by police at arrest. In all cases the proportion received exceeds that of the proportion charged, suggesting that offense mix or seriousness may have less bearing on the increase in Aboriginal overrepresentation the further one proceeds into the system.

TABLE 18

Prison Admissions and Police Charges Involving Aborigines, by Major Offense Group, 1993 (in Percent)

Offense	Aborigines, Admissions	Aborigines, Police Charges
Against the person	45.2	40.3
Break and enter/theft	40.0	29.8
Property damage	57.9	39.2
Good order	52.6	45.3
Drugs	9.6	5.4
Driving	44.3	21.1
Other offenses	51.9	38.3
Total	41.5	28.6

Source.—Ferrante, Loh, and Broadhurst (1994).

3. *Prevalence of Imprisonment and Racial Disparity.* An approximate prevalence rate of imprisonment based on the number of individuals admitted can be calculated for the races. Overall, the prevalence of persons imprisoned in WA has declined marginally from 317 per 100,000 of population in 1990 to 289 per 100,000 in 1993. For Aborigines the rate of incarceration was 5,055 per 100,000 in 1990 but had fallen to 4,147 per 100,000 in 1993 compared to 187 per 100,000 in 1990 and 177 per 100,000 of the non-Aboriginal population.[22]

After applying these rates to measure relative overrepresentation, in 1990, Aborigines were 27 times more likely to be incarcerated than non-Aborigines and in 1993, 23.4 times. The disparity for imprisonment has decreased, indicating a reduction in the extent that disparity is amplified from arrest to imprisonment. In 1990, Aborigines were 7.7 times more likely to be arrested and 27 times more likely to be imprisoned than non-Aborigines. Three years later Aborigines were 9.2 times more likely to be arrested but less (23.4:1) likely than previously to be imprisoned. Thus substantial reductions in the relative use of im-

[22] The population denominators used to calculate per capita rates of arrest in table 5 are applied here (see also table 3.2 in Harding et al. 1995). Exclusion of sentenced prisoners serving time in police lockups is unlikely to affect Aboriginal rates substantially because of the high congruence between those serving time in lockups and prisons. However, for non-Aborigines evidence of high interchangeability of lockup and imprisonment is less clear. Admissions and exit data from lockups are insufficiently precise to permit a reliable estimate of the prevalence of incarceration in both lockups and prisons.

prisonment have occurred which suggests some effective diversion, perhaps in the wake of the RCIADIC's general efforts to reduce imprisonment.

B. National Imprisonment Rates and Trends

National trends in rates of imprisonment are published by the Australian Institute of Criminology based on census of prisoners (annually as of June 30 and at the first day of each month) and therefore differ from the above prevalence rate based on individuals admitted during the year. Western Australia has always had a significantly higher rate of incarceration than Australia as a whole. For example, at national census March 1994, WA's total rate was 126.4 per 100,000, while Australia's was 86 per 100,000.

Since the mid-1970s, Australia's census-estimated imprisonment rate per 100,000 total population has increased by about 35 percent from 63 per 100,000 to 86 per 100,000 currently. Western Australia's rate has fluctuated, and the longer-term trend is complex.[23] In the mid-to-late 1980s the rate abated (at around 98 per 100,000 in 1989) before sharply rising in the latest reporting period (to 126 per 100,000 in 1994).

General explanations for the increases and fluctuations in WA include rapid increases in Aboriginal involvement since the 1960s following frontier expansion, declines in non-Aboriginal recidivism, and changes in the law criminalizing and decriminalizing some offenses. In addition, new sentencing options and practices in the 1980s and 1990s, especially efforts to minimize short periods of imprisonment, had very substantial impacts on the prison population. To illustrate, the advent in 1990 and rapid expansion of work and development orders designed to divert fine defaulters from prison and the provision of "sobering-up shelters" (i.e., the decriminalization of public drunkenness) provide some explanation for the recent decline in prisoners received but not in daily averages or census. Since these diversions affected prisoners serving very short sentences (mostly less than thirty days and mostly Aborigines) they substantially affected the "flow" (admissions) but had less effect on the census-date counts.

The underuse of community-based sanctions for Aboriginal offenders was highlighted by the RCIADIC as a significant cause of the high

[23] Western Australia prison data between 1969 and 1978 excluded sundry lockups and did not record race of the prisoner. It is likely estimates of the rate of incarceration are underreported during this period in the national series.

rate of Aboriginal imprisonment. However, this does not account for the higher rates of imprisonment in WA since Harding et al. (1995) found that the per capita *community-based* sanctions rate for WA was consistent with the national rate in 1991 (351 per 100,000 for WA compared to the national rate of 332 per 100,000). In 1993, the WA community-based sanction rate for Aborigines was 7,289 per 100,000 and 615 per 100,000 for non-Aborigines. Thus Aborigines were twelve times more likely to receive a community-based sanction than non-Aborigines. By comparing Aboriginal and non-Aboriginal community-based sanction and imprisonment rates (the community-based/custody ratio), it was shown that non-Aborigines were 3.4 times more likely to receive a community-based sanction than prison, whereas Aborigines were only 1.8 times more likely to receive these sanctions in lieu of prison. Harding et al. (1995) also found that there was a significant shift toward the greater use of community-based sanction since the late 1980s but argued the greater use of community-based sanctions probably both produced some net widening and contributed to a reduction of imprisonment.

These systemwide changes are reflected in a radically altered prison population, as an examination of annual prison census populations over the ten-year period 1982–91 in WA illustrates (see Walker 1992). For example, the proportion of violent offenders imprisoned at census increased from 26.8 percent in 1982 to 45.5 percent in 1991, while the proportion of property offenders fell from 36.3 percent to 29.2 percent and driving offenses from 13.3 percent in 1982 to 6.4 percent in 1991. Moreover, the number sentenced to less than a year in prison has also fallen from 30.2 percent in 1982 to 24.5 percent in 1991, and those sentenced to more than five years has increased from 26.9 percent to 36.2 percent. These results suggest that the character of prison "stock" has changed significantly as other options to imprisonment have become available to the courts.

These longer-term changes reflect two trends. First, the preeminence of imprisonment as the primary response to crime no longer has the unconditional support of elites in the criminal justice system. Second, there has been a trend to "bifurcate" penalty severity scales so as to increase penalties for the more serious but rarer offenses and decrease penalties for the more common but less serious offenses (Rutherford 1986). This is reflected in a greater use of alternatives and amendments to the WA criminal code which require that imprison-

TABLE 19

Rate per 100,000 Total Population of Imprisonment by Jurisdiction, on Census Date, March 1, 1994

	Total *N* at Census*	Total Rate†	Aboriginal Rate	Non-Aboriginal Rate	Disparity Ratio
New South Wales	6,430	101.3	963.5	90.2	10.7
Victoria	2,425	54.2	641.2	51.7	12.4
Queensland	2,322	73.2	613.7	59.5	10.3
Western Australia	2,136	126.2	1,453.9	88.0	16.5
South Australia	1,277	87.1	1,204.9	72.9	16.5
Tasmania	248	52.4	237.3	48.4	4.9
Northern Territory	490	289.9	760.2	113.8	6.7
Australia	15,328	86.3	880.7	72.4	12.2

SOURCE.—Australian Bureau of Statistics (1995*a*, 1995*c*); Dagger (1995).
* Census on March 1, 1994.
† Rates per 100,000 total population.

ment be used only "as a last resort" and recognized in sentencing policy as the principle of parsimony.[24]

C. *Interstate Comparisons*

Differences between Australian jurisdictions in Aboriginal imprisonment are estimated from census data collected by the Australian Institute of Criminology on the first day of each month for both adults and juveniles.[25] The latest national data based on the census for March 1, 1994, are compared by race in table 19 for all jurisdictions. Western Australia ranks second to the NT in rates of imprisonment, but WA far exceeds the NT and all other states in Aboriginal rates of imprisonment. However, in terms of overrepresentation WA and SA share the same high disparities, while Tasmania and the NT are the lowest.

[24] Section 19A of the Criminal Code of Western Australia was amended (Acts Amendment no. 70, 1988) to insert this principle.

[25] This series is now published by the ABS. Cross-state comparisons and estimates of overrepresentation vary considerably depending on the reliability of the population denominator and whether the source of imprisonment data is June census, "daily average muster," census on the first day of the month, or other measures such as persons and receptions—see Biles and McDonald (1992, pp. 417–52) and Chan and Zdenkowski (1986) for more details.

TABLE 20

International Comparison of Rates of Imprisonment by Race, 1990

Country	United States, 1990*	United Kingdom, 1990*	Australia, 1990†	Western Australia, 1990†
All	474.3	89.3	83.9	106.6
"Black" or Aboriginal	1,860.0	547.0	754.6‡	1,342.2
"Nonblack" or non-Aboriginal	284.4	80.9	72.7	72.3
"White"§	289.0	77.0	N.A.	N.A.
"Other"‖	241.0	164.0	N.A.	N.A.
Black/nonblack ratio	6.5	6.8	10.4	18.6

SOURCE.—All rates are per 100,000 persons. Australian and Western Australia estimated populations for June 1990 are from Australian Bureau of Statistics (1991); Aboriginal intercensus populations are from Benham and Howe (1994), table 11.

NOTE.—N.A. = not available.

* Tonry (1994), p. 103, table 1.

† Walker (1991).

‡ Of the national prison census, 3.1 percent were of unknown race and have been allocated on a pro rata basis. No missing race records were found for Western Australia.

§ "White" refers to Europeans in the U.S. and U.K. context, but in Australia the category non-Aboriginal includes this group and the category defined "other" for U.S. and U.K. data. Consequently, rates have been recalculated to permit more direct comparison between "black" and "nonblack" and Aboriginal and non-Aboriginal.

‖ "Other" refers to Hispanic and other groups in the United States and in the United Kingdom, predominantly immigrants from the Indian subcontinent. No such category is defined or available from Australian sources.

D. *International Comparisons*

Tonry (1994) calculated per capita incarceration rates for different "race" groups based on 1990 prison census data for England and Wales and for the United States, and these are compared with Australian and WA June 1990 prison census data in table 20. Overall, Australia's imprisonment rate per 100,000 persons is slightly lower than that of the United Kingdom but less than one-fifth of that of the United States. Western Australia's per capita rate of imprisonment for non-Aborigines is the same as for Australia, but its Aboriginal rate of imprisonment is nearly double that of Australia's Aboriginal rate. This higher rate of Aboriginal imprisonment accounts for much of WA's elevated rate of incarceration.

Australian rates of Aboriginal imprisonment are two-fifths the rate of "black" Americans, and U.K. rates of "black" incarceration are under a third those of "black" Americans. Moreover, "nonblack" rates of imprisonment in the United States are nearly four times those of Australian non-Aborigines and three and one-half times those of U.K. "nonblacks." Compared to the United States, Australia and the United Kingdom have much lower rates of incarceration for both "race" groups, but ironically the U.S. high rate of "nonblack" incarceration generates lower differential risks between "blacks" and "nonblacks."

Disparity ratios calculated in table 20 show that although differential risks of imprisonment for "blacks" in the United States and United Kingdom are about the same at 6.5 to 6.8:1, Aborigines are about 50 percent more at risk in Australia at 10.4:1 and almost three times more at risk in WA than blacks in either the United States or United Kingdom. Cross-national differences in disparity ratios highlight contrasts between groups and show that risks, including differential risks of incarceration, vary across cultures. Such relative differences invite detailed analysis of legal, social, and cultural variations rather than simply to establish that Australian or WA criminal justice systems are necessarily 50 percent or three times "worse" than other countries in their treatment of minority groups.

VI. Policy and Race Bias

The many causes of the "disproportionate criminalization" experienced by Aborigines are "related factors that describe a self-perpetuating spiral of criminalization and victimization of Aboriginal people. Numerous studies indicate that the relatively greater incidence of serious crime within the Aboriginal community is linked to the marginal status and alienated character of the Aboriginal people within Australian society" (Amnesty International 1993, pp. 15–16). The government's general remedy is a "commitment to social justice and a recognition of the importance of equal participation of Aboriginal people in the social, economic and cultural life of Western Australia" (Western Australia Department of Aboriginal Affairs 1994) and specifically to support policies of Aboriginal development by raising the socioeconomic status of indigenous people. The "underlying issues" of unemployment, poverty, ill-health, dispossession, and disenfranchisement are seen as the causes of the overinvolvement of Aborigines in prison. These same factors generate racism in Australia. The bias, therefore, in the criminal justice system is the product of indirect discrimination reflecting the outcome of treating unequals equally (RCIADIC 1991*a*).

Equality, it has been argued, will be achieved in the longer term by the economic benefits of granting native land title and, in the political realm, by a process of conciliation and self-determination (RCIADIC 1991*a*, 1991*b*; Amnesty International 1993; Bartlett 1993). However, the colonial legacy of racism cannot be "corrected" by overt positive discrimination or like measures within the justice system because these are resisted on doctrinaire legal grounds or by other means. Instead, consultative and educative processes, the "all-purpose solvent of cultural contradiction" (Rowse 1992, p. 102), are used to guide reforms and enlist Aboriginal communities in the struggle for more equitable or appropriate applications of that ultimate cultural artifact—punishment. But the emphasis on "political correctness" and training is unlikely to change the underlying causes of Aboriginal criminalization, and tactical reforms of criminal justice practices are futile if they rely on co-option. An overconcentration on the race-crime problem is unproductive and narrows the scope for reform by distorting and deflecting attention away from problems of real disparities in health, income, and status (La Prairie 1990).

The key general cause of the disproportionate criminalization of Aborigines is universally perceived (at least at governmental level) to be socioeconomic deprivation and consequential exclusion. Thus the "approved" cause of Aboriginal overrepresentation is low socioeconomic status coupled with some recognition of the historical and cultural origins of Aboriginal marginalization. In the analysis that follows, differences between Australian states in the socioeconomic status and cultural independence of Aborigines are compared with differences in the scale of punishment. In this way the explanatory power of orthodox strain or deprivation theories of crime causation are tested against rival conflict theories that draw on the persistent and substantial differences between the dominant "white" and Aboriginal cultures. The cross-jurisdictional comparison provides support for both culture-conflict and socioeconomic theories. Conflict theory is persuasive because the process of colonization continues in a society that retains, especially in some regions, elements of a literal and metaphorical frontier.

A. The Scale of Punishment

Table 21 shows that Australia's rate of imprisonment between 1987 and 1994 increased from 75 to 86 per 100,000 population, largely because of dramatic increases in NSW arising from the adoption of "truth in sentencing" legislation which restored "just desert" penalties by abolishing good-time (remissions) and early release. In the NT, Tasmania, and Queensland, there have been decreases in the rate due to substantial increases in the use of noncustodial and "community" order sentences. The comparisons also conceal differences in various jurisdictions' administrative practices reflected in the large variations in the average amount of time prisoners spend in custody, the compo-

TABLE 21

Imprisonment Rates for Australian States, per 100,000, in 1987 and 1994

	1994		1987	
	All	Non-Aboriginal	All	Non-Aboriginal
New South Wales	101	90	77	71
Victoria	54	52	46	45
Queensland	73	60	89	77
Western Australia	126	88	110	78
South Australia	87	73	63	53
Tasmania	52	48	62	54
Northern Territory	290	114	311	115
Australia	86	72	75	64

Source.—Table 19; Biles and McDonald (1992).

sition of the remand population, differences in the treatment of fine defaulters, minor offenders, remission, and approaches to diversion from prison (Walker 1992).

These differences were analyzed by a government inquiry into the high rate of imprisonment in WA (Dixon 1981). This inquiry was unable to explain all the variance between the states, even after controlling for the proportion of young males (the NT has an especially high proportion of young males) or Aborigines in the population, the quantity and severity of crime, and unemployment. Controlling for the size of the Aboriginal population, which was highly correlated with the imprisonment rate, did nevertheless account for a substantial amount of the variation (see also Biles and McDonald 1992, p. 97 and table 26). Dixon concluded that differences in administrative traditions and the punitiveness of community attitudes may account for the unexplained variance in imprisonment between the jurisdictions.

Later Babb (1992) compared Victoria and NSW, low and high imprisonment states, respectively. He found the demographic characteristics of NSW and Victoria roughly similar in terms of urbanization, unemployment, age group (fifteen years to thirty-four years), and single-parent families. He also controlled for conviction rates, police strength, length of stay, and the proportion of prisoners on remand and concluded that the frequency of cases brought to courts or the greater demand for punishment in NSW compared to Victoria accounted for the differences. Babb oddly neglected to control for the differences in the proportion of Aborigines found in either jurisdiction, so it is open to suggest that the larger Aboriginal population in NSW contributed to the greater frequency of cases.

Harding (1992) also concluded that the high rate of imprisonment in WA compared to other states could mostly be attributed to the higher frequency of cases resulting in imprisonment. The most incarcerated group were Aborigines sentenced by lay magistrates in rural and remote WA. Harding argued that administrative traditions, particularly in WA lower courts, led to less use of noncustodial sanctions than in other states. Although subsequent research (Harding et al. 1995) found WA use of noncustodial sanctions by 1990 above the national average, Aborigines were still less likely to be given these orders relative to imprisonment. This led Harding to urge curtailment of the power of lay magistrates to imprison, proactive review by superior courts of summary court sentencing practice, and application of a radical quota scheme, restricting the number of prison beds (akin to the queuing practices found in the Netherlands), in order to reduce the rate of imprisonment. All but the last were endorsed in 1995 by the state legislature's amendments to sentencing laws.

B. *Toward a General Theory of Aboriginal Imprisonment*

While variations in Aboriginal imprisonment and administrative factors contribute to differences between jurisdictions, other intangible factors such as community attitudes may be relevant. For example, Broadhurst and Indermaur (1982) found public opinion to be more punitive in WA than in comparable jurisdictions.

1. *The Frontier and Aboriginal Crime.* The high level of punitiveness indicated by imprisonment rates and punitive attitudes in WA may both be associated with a "frontier" culture (Keen 1988; Tyler 1993). That is, a settler society perceives itself as vulnerable and threatened by outsiders of whom the indigenous Aborigines—the "exotic other"—represent a traditional and recurring example. A literal frontier is also implied because vast areas remain "wilderness" and settlers or immigrants and the surviving indigenous people contest the social, economic, and moral domains, especially at the geographic and cross-cultural margins. In such a society the "frontier" metaphor justifies a more punitive response to crime and deviance since social order and

solidarity is conditional and constantly redefined to meet evolving circumstances.

Drawing in part from Erikson's (1966) thesis that once a settler society subdues the wilderness, its sense of social solidarity weakens and "deviance" is internalized and redefined to recreate social order, it follows that severe repression of crime or deviance is a normal consequence of establishing cultural solidarity. In Erikson's thesis, social control in Puritan New England was reaffirmed through the "discovery" of witchcraft which acted to supplant the declining influence of the frontier on settler solidarity and morality. In this way cultural boundaries are exemplified by definitions of deviance, and in Australia's "frontier" states Aboriginal culture provides an inexhaustible source of deviant possibilities. In contrast to the dominant materialist, time-governed, politically cohesive, and largely Protestant Anglo-Australian culture, the Aboriginal cultural domain is characterized by the preservation of unique cultural practices, intense reciprocal relations, supreme individual sovereignty, and "the relatively unfettered consumption of time" (Rowse 1922, pp. 22–35).

In postcolonial Australia, subjugation of the "wilderness" is incomplete, and the literal and metaphorical frontier is defined along the axis of natural resource exploitation. The continuing process of colonization increases social interaction between the races, changes the nature of economic relations and governance (from assimilation to self-determination), and provokes contests over land use and definitions of deviance. Coupled with the revival of Aboriginal land rights and the renaissance of Aboriginal culture, even marginal threats such as those posed by the "moral" disorder of Aboriginal social life (as perceived by the dominant non-Aborigines) intensify conflict. Frontier states such as WA and the NT with large Aboriginal populations who retain or claim substantial areas of "undeveloped" land maintain strong elements of cultural authority and resist the drive for development and "progress" may be especially conducive to a punitive approach.

Table 22 attempts to show the relationship between punitiveness and a "frontier" culture. Frontier is defined in this context by a generally low level of urbanization and population density, a large and independent Aboriginal population, and a sizable proportion of land in Aboriginal hands. The NT and WA best illustrate "frontier" jurisdictions, while Victoria and Tasmania are the least. South Australia, Queensland, and NSW fall between. On the six general measures

TABLE 22

Aboriginal Population, Land Occupation, Language Retention, Imprisonment Rate, and Proportion of Aboriginal Prisoners by State (Ranked High to Low)

	Aboriginal Population (Percent)	Rank	Land Area (Percent)	Rank	Language Retention (Percent)	Rank	1987 Prison Rate (per 100,000)				Aborigines in Prison at Census (Percent)	Rank	Overall Rank
							All	Rank	Aborigine	Rank			
Northern Territory	22.4	1	36.1	1	68.0	1	311	1	962	3	71.5	1	1
Western Australia	2.7	2	12.1	3	23.6	2	110	2	1,331	1	30.9	2	2
Queensland	2.4	3	2.0	4	8.6	4	89	3	578	5	15.1	4	4
Tasmania	1.5	4	.0	6	.2	7	62	6	104	7	2.8	6	7
New South Wales	1.1	5	.1	5	1.1	6	78	4	613	4	8.2	5	5
South Australia	1.1	5	18.8	2	21.2	3	63	5	1,029	2	16.8	3	3
Victoria	.3	6	.0	6	2.2	5	47	7	412	6	2.7	7	6
Australia	1.5		13.1		18.4		75		776		14.8		

SOURCE.—Broadhurst (1993).

NOTE.—The overall rank assuming equal weight summarizes the rankings over all six measures. The 1987 prison data are used for comparability with population, land area, and language estimates derived from the 1986 census.

provided in table 22, those jurisdictions with the highest frontier profile have the highest rates of imprisonment.[26]

Tasmania, Victoria, and NSW have average or below-average Aboriginal populations, negligible proportions retaining traditional languages, little or no land under Aboriginal "control" or claim, and relatively low Aboriginal participation in imprisonment. Western Australia and the NT have well-above-average Aboriginal populations, language retention, and large areas under Aboriginal control—both have high rates of imprisonment and very high Aboriginal participation in imprisonment. South Australia has a below-average Aboriginal population, but higher language retention and significant areas under Aboriginal control, whereas Queensland has an above-average Aboriginal population but below-average language retention and only a small area of land under Aboriginal control. Both have levels of Aboriginal participation in imprisonment that fall in between the extremes.

The situation in Tasmania is especially instructive since it has an average size Aboriginal population but the lowest level of overrepresentation in the prison population. Cove (1992, p. 156) has suggested that one important explanation for the lower participation rate of Aborigines is the high degree of "cultural homogeneity, both among Tasmanian Aborigines and between them and the wider Tasmanian population." A clear indicator of homogeneity "is the predominance of Tasmanian Aborigines who are English only speakers—98.3 percent as compared to the national average of 76.8 percent."

2. *Socioeconomic and Conflict Theories.* The "frontier" proposition requires more than the general relationships described in table 22 for convincing demonstration. The RCIADIC, for example, while recognizing cultural conflicts, gave primary emphasis to the overwhelming deprivation of Aborigines. Thus the "underlying issues" of poverty and subculture produce the exceedingly high overrepresentation of Aborigines in prison. These notions of causation are generally similar to orthodox strain or conflict explanations of crime, and their cogency can be examined by using data from the 1994 NATSI survey.

The NATSI survey data enabled broad indexes of Aboriginal socio-

[26] Calculation of Spearman's rank-order correlation coefficients for the rankings in table 22 also lends support to the discussion that follows. In this method, tied rankings are allocated half scores; following this procedure changes the overall rankings marginally, by reversing the ranking of Tasmania and Victoria—Victoria has the lowest overall rank. Of the fifteen possible correlations between the rankings, we would expect a small number to be significant even if there were no relationships between the variables. However, more than ten correlations were significant at the 5 percent level.

economic and cultural status to be created and compared with various measures of punitiveness including the prevalence of arrest among Aborigines for each Australian jurisdiction. Jurisdictions with high Aboriginal socioeconomic deficits are also those with strong Aboriginal cultures and consequently the highest levels of punitiveness as measured by imprisonment and arrest rates.

Thus the NATSI survey enables us to examine by jurisdiction the relationship of crime with Aboriginal cultural integrity or "strength" and socioeconomic or "stress" factors. The "cultural strength" index was based on data collected on the proportion of Aborigines who identified with a geographical area or "homeland," related to a clan or skin group, spoke an Aboriginal language, saw elders as important, voted in Aboriginal and Torres Strait Islander Council elections, and participated in various cultural activities and ceremonies. Similarly, a socioeconomic "stress" index was created by such factors as the proportion of single-parent families, the amount of unemployment (especially long-term employment), the extent of unsatisfactory housing and service access, the proportion on low incomes (less than $A 12,000), the extent that alcohol is considered the main health problem, and postschool qualifications rates. In addition, for each jurisdiction a crime or punitiveness index was created and operationalized as the proportion of the Aboriginal population arrested in the last five years (1994 NATSI survey), Aboriginal and overall police custody rates (1992 National Custody Survey, table 7), and Aboriginal and overall imprisonment rates (1994 National Prison Census, table 19). A combined measure comprised the punitiveness index because the "prevalence of arrest" measure was less reliable than others, and overall rates (including Aborigines and non-Aborigines) are more accurate indicators of the relative punitiveness of jurisdictions.

For this exercise the proportion of each jurisdiction's population who reported assault victimization were given either a positive or negative valence depending on the index. Thus the proportion of the Aboriginal population not victimized was treated as a "cultural strength," while the proportion victimized was treated as a "stress" indicator. The values in each index are scored and treated as additive, permitting the simple ranking of the jurisdictions according to their cultural "strength," socioeconomic "stress," and punitiveness. Based on the average score for Australia, four jurisdictions (NT, WA, SA, and to a lesser extent NSW) are classed as having both high "cultural strength" and "stress"; two (Victoria and Tasmania) have low "cultural strength" and "stress," and one (Queensland) has high "cultural strength" and low "stress." No jurisdiction is found with a high "stress" and low "cultural strength" pattern, although NSW borders on this classification (see table 23).

Theoretically, "cultural strength" indicates a degree of resistance and potential conflict with the dominant society, while socioeconomic "stress" is an indicator of relative deprivation. Thus a high "cultural strength" ranking presumably associated with culture conflict should be related to a higher punitive rank, and similarly a high "stress" ranking would simulate deprivation or strain and should also be associated with a high punitive ranking. Consequently, those jurisdictions with high "cultural strength" *and* socioeconomic "stress" ranks would also be those most likely to have a high punitiveness rank. A series of rank-order correlation tests conducted on the three indices generally showed this to be the case and is consistent with those found in the above "frontier" analysis.[27] That is, the "frontier" states NT and WA have the highest "strength" and "stress" scores and the highest police or prison custody rates and high overall punitiveness ranks, while Tasmania and Victoria with low "strength" and low "stress" ranks were found with the lowest custody rates and punitiveness ranks. Although slight variations were observed depending on the combination of punitive indicators employed, these did not sufficiently alter the general relative order of jurisdictions (for detailed results and discussion, see Broadhurst 1996).

These analyses support the proposition that cultural strength and socioeconomic stress are associated with higher punitiveness. Most striking was the high correlation between "cultural strength" and "stress" such that either index could be regarded as interchangeable and arguably support a conflict-stress model of Aboriginal criminalization. An exception appears to be the case of the NT which has the highest "cultural strength" and socioeconomic "stress" rank, but Aboriginal arrest and imprisonment modestly, or only poorly, correlated with these factors. Nevertheless, the NT has the highest rank when *overall* police and prison custody rates are correlated and a moderately

[27] Spearman rank-order correlation tests were conducted on the "strength" and "stress" indices and on the arrest, police custody, prison census indices, and the combined "punitive index." In all, fifteen tests were conducted of which all but four were significant at the 95 percent (*) or 99 percent (**) confidence level. Strength and stress were highly correlated (r_s = 0.96**), and both were significantly correlated with all indices except NATSI arrest.

TABLE 23

Rankings by Jurisdiction on Indexes of "Cultural Strength," "Socioeconomic Stress," "Punitiveness," and Various Crime Measures

	Cultural Strength Index		Socioeconomic Stress Index		Police Arrest, NATSI Survey		Policy Custody*		Prison Census*		
	Average	Rank	Average	Rank	Population (Percent)	Rank	Rate	Rank	Rate	Rank	Punitive Index Rank†
Northern Territory	589	1	321	1	19.6	5	1,001	1	290	1	3
Western Australia	468	2	316	2	25.4	2	310	2	126	2	1
South Australia	450	3	295	3	28.5	1	226	3	87	4	2
Queensland	436	4	264	5	14.9	6	205	4	73	5	5
New South Wales	379	5	290	4	22.5	4	96	5	101	3	4
Victoria	364	6	253	6	22.6	3	80	7	54	6	6
Tasmania	263	7	211	7	12.6	7	86	6	52	7	7
Australia	367		284		20.4		152		86		

Source.—Broadhurst (1996).

* Policy Custody Survey-August 1992 and National Prison Census-March 1994; all rates per 100,000 population.

† Combined index comprises overall and Aborigional rates for the 1992 Policy Custody Survey and 1994 National Prison Census, plus percent of Aboriginal population reporting arrest in 1994 National Aboriginal and Torres Strait Islander (NATSI) survey.

high (3) punitiveness index rank. The lower correlation with Aboriginal arrest and custody and "culture"/"stress" indexes in the NT raises the possibility that, given its exceptionally large Aboriginal population and high land and language retention, high cultural strength provides immunity to excessive criminalization. This hypothesis is strengthened by the fact that culturally strong states like the NT, Queensland, and to a lesser extent WA have lower assault victimization rates. Tasmania complies entirely with expectations by having both the lowest "strength" and "stress" rank and the lowest crime rank on all measures. Moreover, WA and SA which have a very high "cultural strength" and "stress" index also have the highest arrest rankings and very high overall punitiveness rank.

C. Conclusion

Diverse rates of imprisonment between jurisdictions can usually be "attributed to fundamental differences in the character of a society over long time periods or significant differences in society or government" (Zimring and Hawkins 1991, p. 222). Punishment could be a sensitive indicator of cultural differences, and in turn sensibilities about the infliction of pain a better indicator of the scale of imprisonment than the actual amount of crime. Moreover, differential rates of imprisonment for minority and disenfranchised groups might also reflect the extent to which contested cultural boundaries are defined by deviance and remain unresolved by legalistic solutions. Finding convincing data to explain why some states have scales of imprisonment widely different from others is difficult (once account is taken of variation in the amount of and responses to recorded crime), but differences arising from the "frontier" character of some Australian states suggests the usefulness of culture-conflict explanations.

However, swift changes in imprisonment rates over short periods of time, as have recently occurred in the United States and in some Australian states, suggest penal "reforms" are not mere captives to more or less stable sociocultural factors. That the scale of imprisonment appears to be somewhat insensitive to the amount of crime also suggests that questions of the effectiveness of imprisonment are less important to the scale of imprisonment than the demand for punishment. Arguably, the scale of punishment responds more to "market forces" than to strictly rational purposes, and thus the effectiveness of punishment will be less relevant than issues about "for whom" and "for what" imprisonment is used (Wilkins 1991).

It has been popular to dramatize and criticize the high level of Aboriginal overrepresentation because "when imprisonment does not deter but is shouldered by the Aboriginal as an inevitable yoke to be carried as a consequence of his residence in white society, we would be moronic to go on using it punitively and ineffectively" (Clifford 1982, p. 11). This criticism assumes that imprisonment should work to reduce or affect crime. However, reductionist goals may be incidental to the symbolic role of punishment (Garland 1990). Given the economy of imprisonment as a means of regulating the disorder represented by Aboriginal deviance, its deployment may be useful in managing the stress of race conflict and cross-cultural inequalities. Efforts to reduce Aboriginal involvement in imprisonment by mechanistic means may therefore be limited since these do not address the demand for punishment.

REFERENCES

Amnesty International. 1993. *Australia: A Criminal Justice System Weighted against Aboriginal People.* Sydney: Australian Section Office.

Australian Bureau of Statistics. 1979. *General Social Survey Crime Victims—May 1975.* Canberra: Australian Bureau of Statistics, catalog no. 3201.0.

———. 1983. *Victims of Crime: Australia 1983.* Catalog no. 3201.0. Canberra: Australian Bureau of Statistics.

———. 1987. *Court Statistics: Higher Criminal Courts Western Australia, 1985–86.* Catalog no. 4501.5. Perth: Australian Bureau of Statistics.

———. 1988*a*. *Court Statistics: Courts of Petty Sessions Western Australia, 1986–87.* Catalog no. 4502.5. Perth: Australian Bureau of Statistics.

———. 1988*b*. *Court Statistics: Higher Criminal Courts Western Australia, 1986–87.* Catalog no. 4501.5. Perth: Australian Bureau of Statistics.

———. 1989. *Court Statistics: Higher Criminal Courts Western Australia, 1987–88.* Catalog no. 4501.5. Perth: Australian Bureau of Statistics.

———. 1990. *Court Statistics: Higher Criminal Courts Western Australia, 1988–89.* Catalog no. 4501.5. Perth: Australian Bureau of Statistics.

———. 1991. *Estimated Resident Population by Sex and Age, States and Territories of Australia: June 1990.* Catalog no. 3201.0. Canberra: Australian Bureau of Statistics.

———. 1992*a*. *Court Statistics: Higher Criminal Courts Western Australia, 1989–90.* Catalog no. 4501.5. Perth: Australian Bureau of Statistics.

———. 1992*b*. *Crime Victims: Western Australia, 1991.* Catalog no. 4506.5. Perth: Australian Bureau of Statistics.

———. 1994*a*. *Australian Social Trends, 1994*. Catalog no. 4102.0. Canberra: Australian Bureau of Statistics.

———. 1994*b*. *Crime and Safety: Australia 1993*. Catalog no. 3201.0. Canberra: Australian Bureau of Statistics.

———. 1994*c*. *Summary of Criminal Court Proceedings—Western Australia, 1991–1992*. Catalog no. 4504.5. Perth: Australian Bureau of Statistics.

———. 1995*a*. *National Aboriginal and Torres Strait Islander Survey 1994:Detailed Findings*. Catalog no. 4190.0. Canberra: Australian Bureau of Statistics.

———. 1995*b*. *Monthly Summary of Statistics, June 1995: Western Australia*. Catalog no. 1305.1. Perth: Australian Bureau of Statistics.

———.1995*c*. *Estimated Resident Population by Sex and Age: States and Territories of Australia, June 1994*. Catalog no. 3201.0. Canberra: Australian Bureau of Statistics.

Australian Law Reform Commission. 1986. *The Recognition of Aboriginal Customary Law*, vols. 1 and 2. Canberra: Australian Government Printing Service.

Babb, L. 1992. "Imprisonment Rates in NSW and Victoria: Explaining the Difference." *Crime and Justice Bulletin*, no. 14. Sydney: New South Wales Bureau of Crime Statistics and Research.

Bartlett, R. 1993. *The Mabo Decision*. Sydney: Butterworth.

Benham, D., and A. Howe. 1994. "Experimental Estimates of the Aboriginal and Torres Strait Islander Population 1986–1991: States and Territories and Australia." Demography Working Paper no. 94/2. Canberra: Australian Bureau of Statistics.

Biles, D., and D. McDonald. 1992. *Deaths in Custody Australia, 1980–1989*. Canberra: Australian Institute of Criminology.

Black, D. 1980. *The Manners and Customs of the Police*. New York: Academic Press.

Broadhurst, R. 1987. "The Imprisonment of the Aborigine in Western Australia: 1957–1987." In *Ivory Scales: Black Australians and the Law*, edited by K. Hazelhurst. Sydney: University of New South Wales Press.

———. 1988. "Legal Control and the Aboriginal Struggle for Law." *Wakuri* 16:188–208.

———. 1993. "Evaluating Imprisonment and Penal Policy in Western Australia: An Analysis of Return to Prison." Ph.D. thesis, University of Western Australia, Department of Law.

———. 1996. "Toward a General Theory of Aboriginal Crime and Punishment: An Empirical Test of Socio-economic, Conflict and Frontier Theories." Paper presented to the eleventh annual conference of the Australian and New Zealand Society of Criminology, Victoria University, Wellington, January 29–February 2.

Broadhurst, R., and A. Ferrante. 1993. "Trends in Juvenile Crime and Justice, 1990–1992." In *Repeat Juvenile Offenders: The Failure of Selective Incapacitation in Western Australia*, edited by R. W. Harding. Crime Research Centre Report no. 10. Nedlands: University of Western Australia.

Broadhurst, R., A. Ferrante, and N. Loh. 1993. *Crime and Justice Statistics for Western Australia: 1992*. Nedlands: University of Western Australia, Crime Research Centre.

Broadhurst, R., A. Ferrante, and N. Susilo. 1992. *Crime and Justice Statistics for Western Australia: 1991.* Nedlands: University of Western Australia, Crime Research Centre.

Broadhurst, R., and D. Indermaur. 1982. "Crime Seriousness Ratings: The Relationship of Information Accuracy and General Attitudes in Western Australia." *Australian and New Zealand Journal of Criminology* 15:219–34.

Broadhurst, R., and N. Loh. 1993. "The Phantom of Deterrence: The Crime (Serious and Repeat Offenders) Sentencing Act." *Australian and New Zealand Journal of Criminology* 26:251–71.

———. 1995. "Rearrest Probabilities for the 1984–1993 Apprehended Western Australian Population: A Survival Analysis." *Journal of Quantitative Criminology* 11:289–313.

Broadhurst, R., and R. Maller. 1990*a*. "White Man's Magic Makes Black Deaths in Custody Disappear." *Australian Journal of Social Issues* (December): 279–89.

———. 1990*b*. "The Recidivism of Prisoners Released for the First Time: Reconsidering the Effectiveness Question." *Australian and New Zealand Journal of Criminology* 23:88–104.

Brunton, R. 1993. *Black Suffering, White Guilt?* Perth: Institute of Public Affairs.

Chan, J., and G. Zdenkowski. 1986. "Just Alternatives." *Australian and New Zealand Journal of Criminology* 19(2/3):63–90, 131–54.

Clifford, W. 1982. "An Approach to Aboriginal Criminology." *Australian and New Zealand Journal of Criminology* 15:9–17.

Cove, J. J. 1992. "Aboriginal Over-representation in Prisons: What Can Be Learned from Tasmania." *Australian and New Zealand Journal of Criminology* 25:156–68.

Cunneen, C. 1988. "Constructing a Law and Order Agenda: Conservative Populism and Aboriginal People in North West N.S.W." Paper presented at the fourth annual conference of the Australian and New Zealand Society of Criminology, University of Sydney, August.

———. 1992. "Commentary on the Report of the Aboriginals and the Law Mission, International Commission of Jurists, Australian Section." *Australian and New Zealand Journal of Criminology* 25:186–91.

Dagger, D. 1995. *Australian Prison Trends no. 214: March 1994.* Canberra: Australian Institute of Criminology.

Dixon, O. 1981. *Committee of Inquiry into the Rate of Imprisonment.* Perth: Western Australia Government Printer.

Duguid, A. M. 1992. "Police and Aboriginal Youth—Arrest or Report? Are Aboriginal Youth Treated Differently?" Paper presented to the conference on Measurement and Research in Criminal Justice, Griffith University, Mt. Gravatt, August.

Erikson, K. T. 1966. *Wayward Puritans: A Study in the Sociology of Deviance.* New York: Wiley & Sons.

Ferrante, A. 1993. "Developing an Offender-Based Tracking System: The Western Australia INOIS project." *Australian and New Zealand Journal of Criminology* 26:232–50.

Ferrante, A., N. Loh, and R. Broadhurst. 1994. *Crime and Justice Statistics for Western Australia: 1993*. Nedlands: University of Western Australia, Crime Research Centre.

Fink, A. E. 1962. *Causes of Crime: Biological Theories in the United States, 1800–1915*. New York: Perpetual. (Originally published 1938).

Foley, M. 1984. "Aborigines and the Police." In *Aborigines and the Law*, edited by P. Hanks and B. Keon-Cohen. Sydney: Allen & Unwin.

Gale, F., R. Bailey-Harris, and J. Wundersitz. 1990. *Aboriginal Youth and the Criminal Justice System: The Injustice of Justice?* Melbourne: Cambridge University Press.

Gale, F., and J. Wundersitz. 1987. "Police and Black Minorities: The Case of Aboriginal Youth in South Australia." *Australian and New Zealand Journal of Criminology* 20:78–94.

Garland, D. 1990. *Punishment and Modern Society: A Study in Social Theory*. London: Clarendon Press.

Geis, G., and P. Jesilow. 1988. "Australian Immigrants and Crime: A Review Essay." *Australian and New Zealand Journal of Criminology* 21:179–85.

Gill, A. 1977. "Aboriginal, Settlers and Police in the Kimberleys, 1887–1905." *Studies in Western Australian History*, vol. 1 (June). Nedlands: University of Western Australia Press.

Green, N. 1981. *Broken Spears*. Nedlands: University of Western Australia Press.

Harding, R. W. 1992. "The Excessive Scale of Imprisonment in Western Australia: The Systemic Causes and Some Proposed Solutions." *University of Western Australia Law Review* 22:72–93.

Harding, R., R. Broadhurst, A. Ferrante, and N. Loh. 1995. *Aboriginal Contact with the Criminal Justice System and the Impact of the Recommendations of the Royal Commission into Aboriginal Deaths in Custody*. Sydney: Federation Press.

Heenan, D. 1991. "Prison the Last Option." In conference proceedings, Social Responsibilities Commission, Anglican Church, Perth.

Hazelhurst, K. 1987. "Widening the Middle Ground: The Development of Community Based Options." In *Ivory Scales: Black Australians and the Law*, edited by K. Hazelhurst. Sydney: New South Wales University Press.

Hood, R. 1992. *Race and Sentencing: A Study in the Crown Court*. Oxford: Clarendon.

Junger, M., and W. Polder. 1992. "Some Explanations of Crime among Four Ethnic Groups in the Netherlands." *Journal of Quantitative Criminology* 8:51–78.

Keen, I. 1988. "Aboriginal Cultures in Settled Australia." In *Being Black*, edited by I. Keen. Canberra: Aboriginal Studies Press.

LaPrairie, C. 1990. "The Role of Sentencing in the Over-representation of Aboriginal People in Correctional Institutions." *Canadian Journal of Criminology* 32:429–40.

Martin M., and L. Newby. 1984. "Aborigines in Summary Courts in Western Australia. A Regional Study: Preliminary Report on Selected Findings." In *Aborigines and Criminal Justice*, edited by B. Swanton. Conference Proceedings, Australian Institute of Criminology, Canberra.

McDonald, D. 1993. *National Police Custody Survey, 1992.* Canberra: Australian Institute of Criminology.

New South Wales Anti-discrimination Board. 1982. *A Study of Street Offences by Aborigines.* Sydney: New South Wales Anti-discrimination Board.

Reynolds, H. 1981. *The Other Side of the Frontier.* Ringwood: Penguin.

Roberts, L., R. Chadbourne, and R. Murray. 1986. "Aboriginal/Police Relations in the Pilbara: A Study of Perceptions." Report to the Australian Criminology Research Council and Western Australian Special Cabinet Committee on Aboriginal/Police and Community Relations, Perth.

Rose, D. 1991. *Hidden Histories: Black Stories from Victoria River Downs, Humbert River and Wave Hill Stations.* Canberra: Aboriginal Studies Press.

Rowse, T. 1992. *Remote Possibilities: The Aboriginal Domain and the Administrative Imagination.* Darwin: Australian National University, North Australian Research Unit.

———. 1994. *After Mabo.* Melbourne: Melbourne University Press.

Royal Commission into Aboriginal Deaths in Custody. 1991*a. Regional Report of Inquiry into Underlying Issues in Western Australia.* Commissioner: P. Dodson. Vol. 1. Canberra: Australian Government Printing Service.

———. 1991*b. National Report.* Commisioner: Elliot Johnston. Canberra: Australian Government Printing Service.

Rutherford, A. 1986. *Prisons and the Process of Justice.* Oxford: Oxford University Press.

Tonry, M. 1994. "Racial Disproportion in U.S. Prisons." *British Journal of Criminology* 34:97–115.

Tyler, W. 1993. "Conceptions of Community in Post Colonial Criminal Justice Reforms in the Northern Territory: A Sociological Critique." Paper presented to the ninth annual conference of the Australian and New Zealand Society of Criminology, Sydney University, September 1993.

Walker, J. 1987. "Prison Cells with Revolving Doors." In *Ivory Scales: Black Australians and the Law*, edited by K. Hazelhurst. Sydney: New South Wales University Press.

———. 1991. *Australian Prisoners, 1990.* Canberra: Australian Institute of Criminology.

———. 1992. "Basic Indicators of Imprisonment Trends by Jurisdiction, 1981–82 to 1990–91; Changes in the Composition of the Prison Populations, 1981–82 to 1990–91; Derived Indicators of Imprisonment Trends by Jurisdiction, 1981–82 to 1990–91." *Facts and Figures in Crime and Criminal Justice.* Canberra: Australian Institute of Criminology.

Western Australia Department of Aboriginal Affairs. 1994. *Royal Commission into Aboriginal Deaths in Custody: Government of Western Australia Implementation Report, 1994.* Perth: Western Australia Department of Aboriginal Affairs.

Wilkins, L. 1991. *Punishment, Crime and Market Forces.* Aldershot: Dartmouth.

Zimring, F., and G. Hawkins. 1991. *The Scale of Imprisonment.* Chicago: University of Chicago Press.

Julian V. Roberts and Anthony N. Doob

Race, Ethnicity, and Criminal Justice in Canada

ABSTRACT

The relationship between crime and race or ethnicity has important implications for Canada. The constitution affirms the country's multicultural heritage. As in other Western nations, certain minorities are overrepresented in the prison population. Aboriginal and black offenders account for a disproportionate number of admissions. There has not been much research on why such disproportions exist, except concerning Aboriginal Canadians. Canada is not immune to problems of discrimination. Compared with whites, black accuseds are significantly more likely to be denied pretrial release on bail and, for certain offenses, to be incarcerated.

Although Canadians pride themselves on the tolerant and law-abiding nature of their society, the relationship between race or ethnicity and crime has provoked important debate in recent years. Relations between the police and certain ethnic groups in Canada's major cities have become increasingly strained as a result of certain high-profile incidents. These problems gave rise in 1993 to the creation of a major public inquiry in the province of Ontario into allegations of systemic racism in the Ontario criminal justice system. There have been calls for greater vigilance in terms of immigration in order to prevent an increase of crime. There has also been a heated (and as yet unresolved) debate as to whether criminal justice statistics should record the race

Julian V. Roberts is professor of criminology at the University of Ottawa. Anthony N. Doob is professor of criminology at the University of Toronto. We gratefully acknowledge the cooperation of the Canadian Centre for Justice Statistics and the research staff and members of the Commission on Systemic Racism in the Ontario Criminal Justice System.

0192-3234/97/0021-0008$01.00

or ethnicity of suspects or accuseds. In short, many of the issues that have arisen in other jurisdictions, and which are explored by other essays in this volume, have confronted Canadians. In some respects Canada's experience and response have been unique.

Public and professional concern about crime and ethnicity in Canada focuses on two groups: Aboriginal Canadians and blacks. Both tend to be overrepresented in prison admissions, although in different parts of the country. There has been a great deal of attention paid to Aboriginal Canadians, far less to the black population. That is now changing, as the percentage of the population accounted for by visible minorities rises, and as a result of problems between the black communities and the police in Toronto and Montreal. There are accordingly similarities and discontinuities. Although both minorities are overrepresented in correctional statistics, their experiences are quite different. We explore the issues relating to both groups in this essay. It is clear from previously published research, as well as a large-scale new study reported here for the first time, that discriminatory treatment of both populations accounts in part at least for the overrepresentation of Aboriginals and blacks in the country's correctional institutions. However, the discrimination effect is not of the consistency or magnitude observed in other jurisdictions. Thus at the sentencing stage, an offender's race affects the disposition imposed only for a small number of offenses.

In this essay, we summarize race, ethnicity, and crime issues in the Canadian criminal justice system. We begin, in Section I, with an introduction to the constitutional context and the current ethnographic profile of the country. This section also includes a discussion of recent events in Canada and a summary of statistics relating to the disproportions of racial and ethnic minorities in the prison population. Section II discusses research on victimization and offending patterns of racial minorities. Section III presents a summary of research findings on the processing of racial and ethnic minorities by the criminal justice system. For Aboriginal Canadians, we review the considerable literature on this topic that has accumulated to date. For the black minority, we discuss the findings from the first major empirical study on the treatment of black accuseds. The focus of this study was on the bail and sentencing stages. We offer evidence to show that black accuseds are subject to differential treatment by the criminal justice system in Ontario. In Section IV we draw some conclusions relating to the issues of disparity and discrimination.

I. Canada's Ethnic Profile

Canada prides itself as being a "multicultural" society. The popular image held by many Canadians is that Canada represents a "mosaic" of ethnic backgrounds rather than the "melting pot" image more popular, in some periods, in the United States. Careful observers have suggested that this mosaic is, of course, hierarchical—a "vertical mosaic" to quote the title of a highly acclaimed book (Porter 1972). Though it is a bit difficult to know how to interpret it, Canada's multicultural heritage is written into its 1982 Constitution. Section 27 of the Charter of Rights and Freedoms indicates: "This Charter shall be interpreted in a manner consistent with the preservation and enhancement of the multicultural heritage of Canadians." Canada's Constitution guarantees all of the normal civil liberties and legal rights that are part of Western democratic tradition. Interpreting these in the context of a "multicultural heritage" is likely to be a challenge.

The Constitution also guarantees certain Aboriginal rights—though these rights are hard to enumerate because they refer to other documents that are, themselves, somewhat ambiguous. The Constitution guarantees, in Section 15: (1) every individual is equal before and under the law and has the right to the equal protection and equal benefit of the law without discrimination and, in particular, without discrimination based on race, national or ethnic origin, color, religion, sex, age, or mental or physical disability. (2) Subsection (1) does not preclude any law, program, or activity that has as its object the amelioration of conditions of disadvantaged individuals or groups including those that are disadvantaged because of race, national or ethnic origin, color, religion, sex, age, or mental or physical disability.

These are the constitutional guarantees, but the "rights" laid out in the Constitution are quite different from the realities in society, as will be seen in the course of this essay.

A. Race, Ethnicity, and Immigration in Canada

It has been suggested (Breton 1988) that in order to understand the nature of ethnicity in Canada, one has to realize that ethnic differentiation can be described on three important—and historically very different—axes: between Aboriginal and non-Aboriginal people; between French and English; and between the original colonizing groups (the "French" and the "English") and the other immigrant groups.

Breton (1988) points out that the issues—whether they be language issues or criminal justice issues—play out differently depending on which "ethnicity" axis one looks at. Thus, for example, one cannot assume that the issues related to Aboriginal people in the criminal justice system and those related to black people have any particular characteristics in common.

Talking about issues of "race" in Canada becomes more complicated since even the word "race" has, at various points in Canadian history, referred to quite different phenomena. At various times, the French and the English in Canada have been referred to as being different races. At other times, "the French" and "the English" have been referred to as being of different "cultures." Similarly, treating Aboriginal people as a single "race" in contrast with "non-Aboriginal" people has a tendency to lump together within each category of people some rather heterogeneous groups. Finally, the experience of the various "other immigrant groups" ("other" than the "English" and "French") is enormously varied in some ways.

Recently, a legal category has been created (in employment equity legislation, for example) called "visible minorities." Who is "visible" is sometimes a complex issue. But when "facts" are cited suggesting that, as a group, "visible minorities" are better educated and have higher-status jobs than "nonvisible minorities," one has to remember that the "mean educational level" of the "visible minorities" consists of the mixing of groups with quite different experiences. The "average" may not, therefore, describe members of any single group.

Canadian provinces vary enormously in terms of the origin of their residents. Canada's most populous province, Ontario, has seen large demographic changes over the past ninety years. It is estimated that, in the beginning of the twentieth century, 86 percent of Ontario's population was of either British or French origin (Breton 1988). By 1986, only 50 percent listed their ethnic origins as solely English (44 percent) or French (6 percent).

But "ethnicity" is only one part of the "race" story. It is estimated that in 1986, 9 percent of the Ontario population were "racial minorities"—a term that the Ontario government defines as "non-white and/ or non-Caucasian" (Ontario Ministry of Citizenship 1991). Seventy percent of this group were born outside Canada. By 1991, 10.5 percent of the Ontario population consisted of (single-origin) racial minorities. The proportion of Ontario residents who are "racial minorities" is expected to increase to about 15 percent by the year 2011. According to the 1986 census, the largest single "racial" group in Ontario were those described as "black," making up about 29 percent of the racial minority population. In 1991, the single-origin black (African, Caribbean, "black") population made up 2.3 percent of the Ontario population, 1.3 percent of the Canadian population, and 4.9 percent of the Toronto population. Aboriginal people are estimated to be about 2 percent of the Ontario population (Ontario Ministry of Citizenship 1991).

The origin of Canada's black population has changed dramatically in the past thirty years (Walker 1988). Until the 1960s, most of Canada's black population came from the United States. In the 1960s, changes to Canada's immigration rules, among other things, resulted in increased numbers of black immigrants from Africa and the West Indies; the black population changed from being overwhelmingly American in origin to becoming overwhelmingly West Indian and African (Walker 1988). Eighty percent of the English-speaking West Indian immigrants settled in Ontario, primarily in Toronto (Labelle, Larose, and Piché 1988). The majority of recent West Indian immigrants to Ontario are, relative to the population as a whole, underrepresented among those who are wealthy and have high levels of education and overrepresented among those from the lower educational and economic strata (Labelle, Larose, and Piché 1988).

Part of the difficulty in writing about "race" or "ethnicity" in Canada is that Canada, like some other countries (Statistics Canada and the U.S. Bureau of the Census 1992), has had some difficulty arriving at a method of assessing race or ethnicity. In the major national census that takes place every ten years, different questions have been used in each administration of the census between 1951 and 1991. Thus it is not surprising to learn that the questions will be changed once again in the next census.

The changes are not trivial and can be seen as social indicators in and of themselves. From 1901 through 1941, for example, "racial origins" were asked (and those with non-European or non-Aboriginal origins were described as being "Negro or Mongolian [Chinese or Japanese] as the case may be" [White, Badets, and Renaud 1992, p. 225]). Looking at more recent censuses, in 1951, 1961, and 1971, respondents were asked only about their paternal ancestry countries (White, Badets, and Renaud 1992, p. 239). Furthermore, the characterization of a person as being of a specific ethnic group was performed by the census taker until 1971 (White, Badets, and Renaud 1992, p. 227). The 1961 published definition of "ethnicity," for example, reveals a fair amount about Canada's view at that time of this characteristic: "In the census, a person's ethnic group is traced through his father. In 1961, each person was asked the question, 'To what ethnic or cultural group did you or your ancestors (on the male side) belong on coming to this continent?' The language spoken at the time by the person was used as an aid in determining the person's ethnic group. Special instructions were provided in cases where the language criterion was not applicable" (Dominion Bureau of Statistics 1963).

Until 1981, only one descriptor was allowed. In 1981, the number of descriptors of a single person increased dramatically, and by the 1991 census people were able to check off any or all of fifteen "ethnic or cultural groups" to which "this person's ancestors belong" (including such diverse descriptors as English, Italian, black, Jewish, and Métis). People were also allowed to write in choices. Such is multiculturalism. In the next census, Statistics Canada has received federal cabinet approval to ask respondents if they fit into one or more "racial" groups including white, black, Chinese, South Asian, and so forth, in order to get baseline data needed to fulfill government employment equity laws (Mitchell 1995). However, even this is controversial. Canada's national newspaper, the *Globe and Mail*, carried its story about the decision to measure "race" on the front page of its newspaper, complete with criticisms of the decision by academic anthropologists.

The result of these changes in the measuring instrument is that it is impossible to have comparable estimates of the proportion of Canadians who were not "white" across different censuses. Nevertheless, one can estimate the number who might not be considered to be "white" by those varying definitions. Our estimate, for the past few decades of the proportion of Canadians who are Aboriginal or of "non-European" origins, is contained in table 1. These data are *very* rough estimates, but give a flavor of the changes that have occurred in the past thirty years.

Canada's immigration policy reflects, in many ways, shifting economic concerns and social attitudes. In the late nineteenth century, immigration was largely from Europe and from the United States. At the close of the nineteenth and the beginning of the twentieth century, policy was driven explicitly by the goal of inducing experienced (largely European) farmers to move to the Canadian prairies to develop agriculture. Recruitment and inducements to come to Canada, therefore, focused on (white) Europeans. Restrictions in the latter part of the century reflected racist Canadian attitudes. For example, in 1885, the federal government imposed a "head tax" on Chinese immigrants in

TABLE 1

Percentage Change in the "Ethnic Origins" of Canadians, 1961–91

	Non-European Origin	Aboriginal
1961	2.0	1.2
1971	5.6	1.4
1981	4.2	2.0
1991	8.5	3.7

Source.—Data derived from Dominion Bureau of Statistics (1963, 1973); Statistics Canada (1984, 1993).

an attempt to discourage immigration. Such taxes lasted for over sixty years and were not imposed on any other ethnic group. After World War I, additional restrictions were added which lasted until the 1960s. At that point, country of origin, economic status, and employment background of immigrants became somewhat less important than they had been in the past.

Canada's Aboriginal population is also changing. It is now estimated that more than half of Canada's native people live "off reserve," often in large urban centers. In Ontario, it is estimated that about two-thirds of the Aboriginal population lives off reserve. But the size of the Aboriginal population has increased dramatically due in part to social and legal changes rather than birthrates. In the mid-1980s, for example, the federal government changed the legal definition of a "status Indian" (one who could claim rights under the federal Indian Act). The result was that thousands of people living off reserves who prior to that time had not been legal Indians were, all of a sudden, full- (or in some instances, almost full-) status Indians who could live on reserves. More interesting were the changes that were revealed in the 1991 national census. The number of people identifying themselves as Aboriginal people in that census increased dramatically over five and ten years earlier, presumably as a result of changing perceptions of the connotation and value of being an Aboriginal person. Nevertheless, even this number underestimates the number of Aboriginal people in Canada since, in recent censuses, a number of Indian reserves ("about 55" in 1991, according to White, Badets, and Renaud 1992, p. 247) did not "participate" in the census for a number of complex political reasons.

Given the ambivalence that Canadians have apparently felt toward measuring race and ethnicity, it is not surprising that we have very few data on these dimensions for those in the criminal justice system. In general, such data are not collected, the main exception being data related to Aboriginal people and, sometimes, correctional data. In the early 1990s, as part of a large change in the way in which Canadian "Uniform Crime Reports" data were reported, it had been proposed that the police collect race data on suspects and victims. Public opposition forced the police and Canada's national statistical agency to rethink this policy. The issue of collecting "race crime statistics," however, was debated publicly and in academic journals (see, e.g., Doob 1991; and the various articles in the special issue of the *Canadian Journal of Criminology:* Roberts 1994*c*).

B. Commission on Systemic Racism in the Ontario Criminal Justice System

Although Canadians may talk a great deal about the issue, little is known about the relationship between "race" (or ethnicity) and "crime" or decisions in the criminal justice system in Canada. This is about to change, at least in the province of Ontario. The commission was established in 1992 to inquire into and make recommendations about the extent to which the criminal justice system in Ontario reflects systemic racism. In early 1996 it released its final report containing seventy-seven recommendations. The commission found evidence of differential treatment of black persons at several stages in the criminal process, although the strength of the effect was stronger at some stages than others. Both of us were involved in one of the major empirical research projects, and in Section III of this essay we summarize the principal findings from that research.

The Commission on Systemic Racism in the Ontario Criminal Justice System had the responsibility, among other things, to look into the treatment of "blacks and other racial minorities" in the criminal justice system. "Blacks and other racial minorities" packs a lot of meaning into five words. The working presumption appeared to be that issues involving racism in the criminal justice system would be most pronounced with respect to blacks. Although "Asian" or "Vietnamese" gangs make news from time to time, in Ontario at least blacks are the focus of the largest attention. Public concern about "black" (or "Jamaican") crime is often discussed in the newspapers and in the electronic media. Furthermore, a number of shootings of black people by the police in Toronto and Montreal over the past few years have focused concern about the manner in which the police, in particular, treat black people.

The commission decided not to look at the treatment of Aboriginal people. The immediate reason for this is simple and clear: Aboriginal people in Canada, because of their special constitutional status, are reluctant to have their concerns about treatment be seen simply as a form of "racism" or "unfair treatment" accorded to "visible minorities." Indeed, definitions of "groups" for certain legal purposes clearly differentiate between Aboriginal people and "visible minorities." In employment equity legislation, for example, they form separate legally defined groups.

C. Definitions

Throughout this essay, we have had to live with various definitions of race and ethnicity. The difficulty for Canadian researchers is that current census data allow respondents to classify themselves in a large number of different ways, while the criminal justice system either imposes a much simpler classification of its own or allows offenders to classify themselves using a system that does not correspond to the census scheme.

In our discussion of the research on racial disproportions in Canada's penal institutions, we draw on the census data, which we have sometimes had to simplify by including only those persons who report a single ethnic origin. We generally use three principal categories: Aboriginals, blacks, and whites. For the original research, described in Section III, we are concerned with processing rather than disproportion. There we use a binary breakdown (black, white), which simply represents a skin-color judgment made by a police officer at the time of the arrest. We are in a sense interested in what the police consider black to be, rather than a self-classification of black. Clearly though, these variable definitions and classifications are unsatisfactory. For the present, however, they provide sufficient information to answer some of the basic questions raised by this essay.

D. Racial Disproportions in Canada's Prisons

As Michael Tonry notes, a significant racial disproportion exists in U.S. prisons: in 1991, blacks made up 12 percent of the general population, but accounted for almost half (48 percent) of the population of prison and jail inmates (Tonry 1994*a*, p. 97; Tonry 1994*b*). Similar findings exist in England and Wales (see Smith 1994). To what extent is this racial disproportion a problem in Canada?

Researchers working on race in Canada face a somewhat more complex database than their counterparts in the United States. The picture is further complicated by the federal-provincial split in criminal justice jurisdiction. According to the constitution, Canada's criminal laws are within the jurisdiction of the federal government. The administration of justice, however, is a provincial responsibility. Those with sentences totaling less than two years are imprisoned by the provinces. Those with aggregate sentences of two years or more are placed in federal penitentiaries.

Given the provincial administration of most criminal justice matters, and of most prison sentences, it should come as no surprise that data are not available on the racial origin of inmates in all provinces and territories. The type of ethnic-racial data collected by correctional systems varies considerably across Canada and usually reflects the parochial interests of each jurisdiction. In Ontario, for example, the correctional system records the ethnicity of inmates (as seen and recorded by the intake officer), and these data are available (although not routinely published). British Columbia, however, has detailed, comprehensive statistics on inmates broken down by whether they are native or nonnative. Thus we know that 16 percent of adult admissions in British Columbia are Aboriginals. But there is no information available on visible minorities *other* than Aboriginals, even though there is significant proportion of Asians in the province, particularly in Vancouver. In the province of Quebec, where there are significant numbers of blacks and Aboriginals, the correctional system classifies admissions as one of four categories: Francophones, Anglophones, Amerindian, Inuit. Clearly then, Canada needs better information on the ethnic composition of the custodial population.

It is hard, therefore, to make statements about the racial disproportion of various ethnic groups in Canada by relying on provincial corrections data. It can be said that to date at least, the focus on racial disproportion in prison populations has almost always been on Aboriginals, rather than on blacks, or South or East Asians.

1. *Federal Penitentiaries (Sentences of Two Years or Longer).* The federal government has responsibility for Canada's penitentiaries, which house all offenders sentenced to terms of two years or longer. On an average day in 1993–94, federal prisoners accounted for about 48 percent of the 27,573 sentenced prisoners (Reed 1995). In this long-term

prison environment, Aboriginal Canadians and blacks are overrepresented, although the disproportion is more striking for the former. Aboriginals can be considered to account for approximately between 3.7 percent of the general population. Of the 14,823 inmates in the federal system on an average day in 1993, 12 percent were Aboriginal (Correctional Services Canada 1994, p. 19). Admission data are much the same: 12 percent of the sentenced admissions to federal custody were described in 1993–94 as being Aboriginal—a proportion that has not changed dramatically in the previous five years. Blacks account for about 2 percent of the general Canadian population and 5 percent of the federal inmate population (Correctional Services Canada 1994, p. 19).[1]

2. *Provincial Jails (Sentences under Two Years).* The picture changes considerably at the provincial level, however. Across Canada as a whole, 17 percent of provincial prison admissions were described as being Aboriginal in 1993–94. This figure is similar to what it was in 1989–90 (18 percent) and 1990–91 (19 percent). Unfortunately, daily prison census data are not available on a national basis for provincial prisons.[2] The proportion of Aboriginal inmates in the provincial jail populations varies from 2 percent in Quebec to 90 percent in the Northwest Territories. Several provinces have very high proportions of Aboriginal people admitted to prison. In 1993–94 in Saskatchewan they represented 72 percent of sentenced admissions, and in Manitoba 47 percent of the sentenced admissions to provincial prisons (Canadian Centre for Justice Statistics 1994).

Table 2 gives a rough description, province by province, of the overrepresentation of Aboriginal people admitted to provincial institutions. It should be remembered that the population estimates of Aboriginal people for each province were created using different methods from the assessments of being Aboriginal by the provincial correctional authorities.[3] We have, as a result, very little confidence in the *exact* num-

[1] By this term we mean people who classify themselves as such in response to a census questionnaire.

[2] Because the average daily prison census data are not available broken down by race for provincial prisons, we were not able to calculate imprisonment rates for Aboriginal and other prisoners.

[3] Each time we went to a different Statistics Canada source for estimates of the Aboriginal population in Canada, we came up with different estimates. The reasons have been described elsewhere but relate to such problems as different definitions of "Aboriginal" (e.g., single ethnicity vs. multiple ethnicity) or different estimates of the number of those who refused, for political reasons, to participate in the census. Estimates are unstable because at different times different assumptions are made about the transient lives of some Aboriginal people in urban settings. Recently shifting sensibilities of people

TABLE 2

Percentage of Overrepresentation of Aboriginal People in Provincial Prison Admissions (1993–94)

	General Population: Proportion Aboriginal	Sentenced Admissions: Proportion Aboriginal
Newfoundland and Labrador	2	4
Prince Edward Island	.4	4
Nova Scotia	1.0	4
New Brunswick	1	6
Quebec	1	2
Ontario	1–2	7
Manitoba	9	47
Saskatchewan	9	72
Alberta	4	34
British Columbia	3	16
Yukon	16	62
Northwest Territories	57	90
Canada	2.2–4.0	17

Source.—Estimates on the Aboriginal people in each province are derived from the Aboriginal people's survey, "Language, Tradition, Health, Lifestyle, and Social Issues," in Statistics Canada (1993). Population estimates, with the year 1991 used as a base, are derived from Statistics Canada (1993), app. B. See also Canadian Centre for Justice Statistics (1994), table 17. The data reported for 1993–94 are very similar to those for 1990–91.

bers presented in the table. However, they give a rough picture of what is, undoubtedly, the case: Aboriginal people are vastly overrepresented in provincial admissions (and probably, as a result, in the prison population generally).[4]

Although not all provincial and territorial correctional authorities record or publish statistics relating to visible minorities other than Aboriginals, it is clear that in some provinces, there is a disproportion of black inmates. In fact, in some regions, the racial disproportion of

of Aboriginal and mixed Aboriginal ancestry have apparently led more people to identify themselves as being Aboriginal. Finally, changes that came into place in the mid-1980s in the legal definition of what constitutes an "Indian" under the Indian Act may well have affected the likelihood that a person would identify himself or herself as having Aboriginal origins. The range of the estimated size of the "Aboriginal" population of Canada does not approach, however, the range of the estimated prison population of "Aboriginal people."

[4] Because we have so little confidence in the meaning of the exact published numbers in this and other tables that involve population estimates (or Aboriginal and other "visible minorities" such as blacks), we are reluctant to reify these numbers further by turning them into imprisonment rates.

blacks matches that of Aboriginals. Recent data from Ontario bear this out. Blacks and "Arabians"[5] accounted for over 16 percent of admissions in the same year, a substantial overrepresentation relative to their incidence in the general Ontario population (Ontario Ministry of the Solicitor General and Correctional Services 1994) estimated by another Ontario Ministry to be about 2.4 percent of the population (Ontario Ministry of Citizenship 1991).

When the Ontario correctional admission data are converted to rates, the black-white comparisons become striking. Using 1991 census data from Ontario, and 1992–93 admissions data from Ontario correctional facilities, analyses reveal a prison admission rate of 705 per 100,000 residents for whites, compared to 3,686 for blacks. The rate for Aboriginals is 1,993 per 100,000. When the male data are analyzed separately, the black admission rate rises to 6,796 per 100,000, compared to 1,326 for whites and 3,600 for Aboriginals. These incarceration statistics show the same pattern as the data from the United States cited by Tonry (1994*a*, table 4). Clearly, then, when we talk about racial disproportions in Canada's correctional institutions, we are not talking only about Aboriginal Canadians. This may seem obvious, but unlike the data for Aboriginals, these data are not part of the public discourse about crime and the criminal justice system in Canada. The Canadian Centre for Justice Statistics publishes, on a regular basis, the "percent Aboriginal" who are admitted to provincial custody under the category "selected inmate characteristics," but there is no mention of blacks or other visible minorities.

E. Discrimination as a Public Issue

The intersection of race, ethnicity, and crime has, with one important exception, only recently become an important public issue in this country. There are several reasons for this: the changing ethnographic profile of the country, combined with fears that crime is rising, may have focused attention on recent immigrants.

The exception is the case of Aboriginal Canadians. It has long been acknowledged by criminal justice officials and politicians of all levels that a disproportionate number of Aboriginals occupy Canada's prisons. It is further recognized that this disproportion is likely to be a consequence of some combination of the following: higher rates of of-

[5] This is the term employed in data releases from the Ontario Ministry of Correctional Services; it is not necessarily the term provided by inmates at the time of admission when they are asked to identify their ethnic origins.

fending by the Aboriginal population, higher use of the criminal justice system in some Aboriginal communities to deal with certain types of crime, direct and indirect discrimination by the criminal justice system, and the socially disadvantaged role occupied by Aboriginals in Canadian society. Awareness of the problem is to be found in the proliferation of government inquiries and commissions that have studied the treatment of Aboriginal offenders. These include the inquiry into the wrongful conviction of Donald Marshall,[6] and, most recently, a royal commission into the role of Aboriginals in Canadian society. As well, there has been a great deal of empirical research into the treatment of Aboriginal offenders. Discrimination toward Aboriginal offenders is a social issue which receives considerable media attention. More recently, however, public attention has focused on serious crimes of violence committed by other visible minorities, particularly blacks and recent immigrants to Canada. One consequence has been a debate over the use of criminal justice statistics that include the race or ethnic origin of the suspect or accused.

1. *Criminal Justice Statistics and Race/Ethnicity of the Suspect/Accused.* As with other countries, the issue of "who commits crimes" is not simply an empirical question that is difficult to answer. It is a question that elicits an intensely political debate. In the days before computers, those keeping statistics about crime and the criminal justice system apparently thought nothing of recording the "national origin" of people who became entangled in the criminal justice system. Thus in 1929, when J. C. McRuer (who subsequently became a chief justice of the Supreme Court of Ontario and author of a royal commission report on civil rights) was giving a speech in Toronto on the nature of Canadian crime, he responded to those commentators who blamed crime on immigrants by citing court and prison statistics on who was apprehended for committing crime. He pointed out that although the foreign-born (mostly, of course, from the United States and Europe) committed some crimes, the vast majority of crime in Ontario was committed by those born in Canada (McRuer 1929).

The kind of statistics reviewed by McRuer are no longer available in Canada. The formalization of a national effort to collect police, court, and corrections statistics led to a decline in the quantity of information collected on any individual case or person. The introduction

[6] Donald Marshall was a Mik'Maq Indian in Nova Scotia who spent eleven years in prison for a crime committed by another person.

of computerization of the statistics collecting system led to a further reduction in information. Indeed, the attempt to computerize court statistics in the early 1970s killed off the collection of all court statistics for over twenty years. Canada is only now beginning to publish court statistics gathered from some courts in some provinces (Turner 1993). On the "information highway" of the 1990s, those working on Canadian adult court statistics are in the garage trying desperately to reinvent the wheel.

The current situation then is that Statistics Canada does not collect data on the racial or ethnic origin of suspects, accuseds, or convicted persons, though it does publish correctional statistics on Aboriginal people. Statistics Canada asked police forces to submit data on the ethnic origin of suspects for a trial period in 1990. As well, a consultation exercise was held with criminal justice professionals. The exercise was terminated, and the request for such data abandoned, it would appear, for two principal reasons. First, only a minority of police forces were submitting the information to Statistics Canada. Police forces were unwilling, or unable, to provide data on the racial or ethnic origin of suspects. Second, there was a negative response from black community groups and many academics, all of whom had reservations about the utility of collecting and publishing such data. Following that experiment, Statistics Canada decided not to collect such information. Measures of race and ethnicity are not at present on the official "wish list" of data to be collected, although this could change in the future, as several influential pressure groups such as the Canadian Association for Chiefs of Police are advocating the collection and publication of such data.

The issue of collecting crime statistics with "race" as one of the variables is, itself, an issue that is almost as hotly debated as the issue of who, actually, is committing crime. The term "race-crime statistics" became a topic, in itself, that was publicly debated: one was often labeled as being "for" or "against" race-crime statistics. A great deal of public and media attention focused on the issues of race-crime statistics in 1991. This arose after several "leaks" of "statistics" purporting to show that blacks, Vietnamese, and Chinese refugees were particularly active in committing crimes in Toronto. (These "statistics" were little more than rough guesses based on the personal experiences of some Toronto police officers.) It was the controversy surrounding these data and the "discovery" by the newspapers that the police were planning on collecting these data routinely that led to the political decision not to collect the data on a national basis. Before the national decision was made, some police forces had been ordered by their (civilian) boards not to forward such data to the national statistical agency and not to code the information from original "occurrence reports."

The debate surrounding race-crime statistics reemerged in 1994 when the *Globe and Mail* (Canada's principal newspaper) ran a long front-page feature story on the issue of collecting "race-crime statistics," complete with an edited transcript of a panel discussion on the topic. They also, rather laboriously, coded the race of suspects contained in the reports prepared by the police for the news media on crimes occurring each day.[7] These data were then used to illustrate the difficulties in drawing inferences from such race-crime statistics. Finally, Canada's only popular afternoon TV talk show had a panel discussion with participation from a live audience on the issue of "race-crime statistics." News media interest in race-crime issues intensified in April 1994, when several homicides in Canadian cities were committed by black youths. Politicians have been involved in the issue as well. Several municipal officials have called for the collection of race-crime data.

2. *Role of the Academic Community.* The Centre of Criminology, University of Toronto, in response to a request from the Ministry of the Solicitor General, Canada, ran a workshop on the issue, the report of which became a Canadian minor criminological best-seller (Doob 1991). The issue of race-crime statistics also attracted the attention of academics, and there has been a vigorous debate in the academic community, sometimes spreading into the newspapers, regarding the utility of collecting and publishing such data (e.g., Gabor 1994; Roberts 1994*a*).

The arguments in favor of collecting race-crime statistics are straightforward. Given that Canadians, like members of most societies, use "race" as a variable on which to discriminate among people, it is important to know whether "race" is also entering into the decision-making process in criminal justice. Within the black community in Toronto, for example, there has been concern expressed about the way in which black people on the street are treated by police officers and the manner in which black defendants are treated by the criminal jus-

[7] The police do not record the race of the suspect in their information systems, but this information is available on the occurrence reports completed by the investigating officer.

tice system. The arguments against collecting statistics on race relate most directly to the problem of blaming crime on certain groups. In addition, the black community in Canada is more heterogeneous than the black population in some other countries. Black immigrants to Canada do not come principally from one Caribbean island, or even exclusively from that general area. There has been significant immigration from Anglophone and Francophone islands in the Caribbean, but also from several African countries.

The classification system tested by Statistics Canada proved to be of little assistance in capturing the multiple identities of members of different ethnic minorities. Aggregating "Aboriginals" or "blacks" made little sense from the perspective of the individual. Members of racial or ethnic minorities are concerned that "overrepresentation" in the criminal justice system will lead these groups to be blamed for society's problems generally, or at least its crime problem. They are concerned that a focus on "race" will lead to discriminatory immigration policies. Their fear has some basis. Tom Gabor, a criminologist, suggests that in addition to using individual characteristics to determine whether a person would make a good immigrant to Canada: "Just as a professional group may be placed in a higher or less favoured category at a given time, national groups could be ranked as more or less favoured based on the danger they have posed to public safety. Groups could be reclassified every few years according to the level of their criminal involvement during a specified period of time" (Gabor 1994, p. 162).

3. *Public Views.* All this discussion has left the public with an ambivalent attitude toward the collection of race-crime statistics. A recent national poll found the public equally divided over whether these data should be collected and published. It is clear that most Canadians believe that visible minorities are responsible for a disproportionate amount of serious crime in Canada. One recent poll (Angus Reid Group 1995) demonstrates the clear link between race and criminality in the minds of almost half the population. Respondents were asked whether they believed that certain racial or ethnic groups were "more likely, on average, to be involved in crime than people from other racial or ethnic groups." Forty-five percent believed that there was a link between ethnicity and criminal activity. Of this group, two-thirds identified blacks as the group more likely to be involved in criminal activity. This finding can be explained, presumably, by news media reports of violent crimes in which the race of the suspect or accused appears

to be more likely to be mentioned if the individual is black. This news media practice has been condemned by various black groups in Ontario for several years now.

A number of polls in recent years have suggested that an important component of Canadians' attitudes to immigration policies is the issue of crime by new immigrants (Palmer 1996). The major explanation for this appears to be increased attention to the problem of "immigrant" crime by the media. For example, in the early 1990s, there was considerable coverage of crimes by "gangs" of immigrants from China and Vietnam now operating in Toronto and Vancouver. More recently, the emphasis has shifted to Somali refugees in Toronto and Ottawa. It is worth noting that a major review that demonstrated that the foreign-born were highly underrepresented in the population of those incarcerated for violent crimes (see Thomas 1993) received little publicity in the news media.

4. *Perceptions of Systemic Racism.* One of the research activities of the Ontario Commission on Racism was to survey the general public in Canada's largest city, Toronto. The survey found that many residents believed that racial minorities are treated with discrimination by the criminal justice system. This perception was particularly strong among members of racial minorities, but a significant number of white residents shared the view. Thus fully 58 percent of the black respondents to the survey and more than three in ten whites (36 percent) believed that judges do not treat black people in the same way as they do whites (Commission on Systemic Racism in the Ontario Criminal Justice System 1995). A significant minority of criminal justice professionals were of the same opinion: 40 percent of defense counsel and 33 percent of judges surveyed perceived differential treatment of white versus black accuseds in the criminal justice system (Commission on Systemic Racism in the Ontario Criminal Justice System 1995). Whatever the research shows, the perception of racial injustice is widespread.

5. *Crime by Immigrants.* The debate over race and crime also affects the issue of immigration. Recent events suggest that something of a moral panic is spreading about crimes committed by immigrants, or nonresidents awaiting deportation. This issue has arisen in the wake of a well-publicized homicide in April 1994 (known locally as the "Just Desserts Murder" because the murder took place during a robbery in a café "Just Desserts") and the murder of a police officer a month later. Although the individuals arrested have yet to be tried, let alone convicted, it has emerged that both were awaiting the execution of depor-

tation orders at the time the homicides occurred. The widespread publicity devoted to this has promoted further unease among a public that already feels Canada's immigration policy is too generous. Most recently, it has become clear that this issue will continue to be in the news since the nation's largest police union has launched a multimillion dollar civil lawsuit against the federal immigration department for not acting more expeditiously in deporting these two accuseds.

Most recently, in June 1994, the federal minister of immigration introduced a bill that would amend the Immigration Act in various ways. These changes would tighten procedures of appeal against deportation. The bill was a direct response to the murder of a police officer in Toronto. The accused was a black immigrant from Jamaica who had been ordered deported three years prior to the killing although the immigration department had not succeeded in having him deported.

Canada's immigration policies in this regard have also attracted international attention recently on account of an appeal to the UN Human Rights Committee. The act permits the deportation of immigrants for crimes committed years after they arrived in Canada. Thus an immigrant arriving here as a child, who is convicted of a crime as an adult, may be deported to a country he or she left years before.

II. Victimization and Offending

In Section II, we focus exclusively on Aboriginals, on account of the dearth of data relating to blacks or other groups. Data on the race or ethnicity of victims are not routinely collected in Canada. For example, Canada carried out its first national victimization survey in 1988 (Sacco and Johnson 1990) with a long-term plan to repeat the survey at five-year intervals. This was done in 1993 (Gartner and Doob 1994). In neither survey were any race or ethnicity questions asked about either the victim or the offender. There are no plans that we are aware of to add them in future surveys.

While the controversy concerning whether or not race-crime statistics should be collected in Canada has carried on for the past five years or so, data on Aboriginal people have been collected quite routinely. Data about Aboriginals have not routinely been captured in the Uniform Crime Reporting system. However, in the provincial and federal correctional systems, these data have been collected. Interestingly enough, they have also been captured and analyzed in Canada's homicide reporting system. In addition, there have been a number of smaller-scale studies of Aboriginal crime.

Probably the clearest finding in the Aboriginal crime literature is the enormous variability in the incidence of crime across communities. To some extent such variation in recorded crime can be seen as reflecting variation in the nature of policing in the communities and variation in the likelihood of the police recording incidents that are reported to them. Brodeur and LaPrairie (1992), for example, note that many incidents reported to the police in the (Quebec) James Bay Cree communities do not get recorded as official incidents. Nevertheless, when members of communities are asked about the prevalence of certain kinds of problems, communities which, on the surface, might appear to be quite similar to one another differ dramatically. In one study, for example (Auger et al. 1992), 73 percent of surveyed residents in one community saw drugs as being a problem that surfaced frequently. In another Aboriginal community which is part of the same treaty organization, the figure was 21 percent. "Stealing something" was seen as occurring frequently by the majority of residents (67 percent) in one community and by only about a quarter (24 percent) of the residents in another.

A similar pattern emerges in officially recorded "crime rates," yet the relationship between officially recorded crime and public estimates of the size of the problem was much less than perfect. Recorded violence rates (per 100 residents) in one year in one community were approximately four times the rate in another community. Equally dramatic were the differences over time, particularly relating to matters that go to court. In one community, there was an 83 percent drop in charges involving violence (part of a 79 percent drop in total adult charges) over a two-year period, whereas during the same two-year period in another community, there was a 3 percent increase (part of a 46 percent overall increase in criminal charges). Such variation is not unusual, particularly in some of the smaller isolated communities where local policies (law enforcement, enforcement of liquor control bylaws, etc.) can change dramatically almost overnight.

Although there is a great deal of variation in the type and rates of crimes involving Aboriginal people, there seems to be little question that the overall level of crime among Aboriginal people is considerably higher than that for non-Aboriginal people. This is particularly true for violent crime. The violent crime rate for Aboriginal bands is approximately four times the national rate (see Wolff 1991; Griffiths and Verdun-Jones 1994). Interestingly enough, unlike crimes involving other groups within Canadian society, there seems to have been relatively little political concern within the Aboriginal community or

TABLE 3

Representation of Aboriginal People in Reported Crime in Three Canadian Cities (in Percent)

City	Estimated Percent of Aboriginals in CMA	Violent Offenses	Property Offenses	Drug Offenses	Other Criminal Code Offenses	Total
Calgary	2.3	10	8	10	11	9
Regina	5.5	47	42	30	45	43
Saskatoon	6.1	36	29	31	49	37

SOURCE.—Data are derived from Trevethan (1993).
NOTE.—CMA = central metropolitan area.

within the criminal justice policy community about public discussion of apparently high rates of Aboriginal crime.

In a Canadian Centre for Justice Statistics (1993) report, for example, a sentence appeared that could not have been written about any group in Canada other than Aboriginal people: "The disproportionate involvement of Aboriginal persons in the criminal justice system has been recognized for a long time. . . . Although aboriginal people represent only 2% of Canada's population, they represent 10% of the nation's federal penitentiary population" (Trevethan 1993, p. 9).

Trevethan (1993) reported that in three western Canadian cities, Aboriginals are disproportionately represented among those accused of various forms of criminal offenses. There are some serious limitations of these data including, in some instances, a fair amount of missing data in the measurement of race. In addition, the estimates of the Aboriginal population in each city may be low. Nevertheless, as shown in table 3, for all three cities, Aboriginal people were overrepresented in all of the listed forms of reported crime. These data deal solely with urban off-reserve Aboriginal people. Data from reserves appear, in many instances, to show similar patterns. However, there are large differences in reported crime across reserve communities in part because of variation in policing styles.

On a national scale, however, what few data we have are consistent with these more limited data. In 1988, approximately 2–4 percent of Canada's population was Aboriginal, and yet Aboriginal people made up 22.2 percent of all homicide suspects and 17.6 percent of homicide victims. A study of on- and off-reserve homicides in Ontario for the years 1980–90 (Doob, Grossman, and Auger 1994) suggested that in both of these settings the rate of homicides by or to Aboriginal people was considerably higher than the rates for non-Aboriginal people in the province.

The high rate of Aboriginal involvement in crime (both as accused and victims) is not as interesting as the differences in the nature of Aboriginal as compared to non-Aboriginal crime. The data in table 4, for example, suggest that Aboriginal women are much more likely (relative to men) to be involved as accuseds and as victims in reported crime than are non-Aboriginal women. The data for suspects in Ontario homicides are similar. About 10 percent of non-Aboriginal homicide suspects were female compared to 21 percent of the off-reserve Aboriginal homicide suspects and 28 percent of the on-reserve homicide suspects. Homicide victims among Aboriginals (on- and off-reserve) were, however, less likely to be women (26 percent of Aboriginal homicide victims were women compared to 38 percent of non-Aboriginal victims). Not surprisingly, the vast majority of Aboriginal crimes are intraracial. In Ontario, all of the on-reserve homicides (of Aboriginal people) were committed by Aboriginals. Roughly two-thirds of the off-reserve Aboriginal homicides were committed by other Aboriginals. Non-Aboriginal victims were, of course, almost always killed by other non-Aboriginals.

To turn to violent crime, it is clear that Aboriginal victims (in the one Canadian city where data were available) were considerably more likely to have been assaulted by someone they knew than were non-Aboriginal victims (table 5). This is similar to what is known about homicides: Aboriginal homicide victims are less likely to be killed by strangers than are non-Aboriginal victims.

These data are important since they suggest that the difference between Aboriginal and non-Aboriginal crime may be not only a question of degree but also of kind. Aboriginal victims, for example, are less likely to have been killed with a firearm than are non-Aboriginal victims. During the 1980s, about 30 percent of non-Aboriginal victims of homicide in Ontario were killed with a firearm. This compares to 23 percent of the on-reserve Aboriginal homicides and 19 percent of the off-reserve Aboriginal homicides. These data are particularly notable for one reason: it is likely that the level of firearms availability on Ontario Aboriginal reserves in Canada is extremely high.

The differences in the nature of Aboriginal crime can be demonstrated in other ways. Table 6 presents the data on alcohol use in crime in Calgary and Regina. In every comparison that was possible, Aborigi-

TABLE 4

Proportion of Accused and Victims Who are Female

	Percent of Accused Who Are Females (in Percent)										Female Victims of Violence (in Percent)	
	Violent Offenses		Property Offenses		Drugs		Other Criminal Code		Total			
	Aboriginal	Non-Aboriginal	Aboriginal	Non-Aboriginal	Aboriginal	Non-Aboriginal	Aboriginal	Non-Aboriginal	Aboriginal	Non-Aboriginal	Aboriginal	Non-Aboriginal
Calgary	24	10	32	24	13	11	35	18	30	20	69	47
Regina	21	11	25	19	27	15	38	10	27	18	68	48
Saskatoon	25	16	37	31	N.A.	N.A.	36	13	34	23	N.A.	N.A.

Source.—Data are derived from Trevethan (1993).
Note.—N.A. = not available.

TABLE 5

Relationship of Accused to Victim of Violent Crimes (Regina)

	Aboriginal (in Percent)	Non-Aboriginal (in Percent)
Spouse/ex-spouse	24	13
Other/extended family	21	10
Friend/business/casual acquaintance	28	33
Stranger	12	35
Unknown	14	8
Victim living with accused	28	15

Source.—Data are derived from Trevethan (1993).

nal accuseds (and in the case of violent crime, Aboriginal victims) were more likely—in some cases considerably more likely—to have been reported to have been using alcohol prior to the crime. The data on alcohol use (by victim and offender) in Ontario homicides are similarly dramatic. More than half of the homicides involving Aboriginal victims (54 percent of those occurring on reserve and 52 percent of those occurring off reserve) were described by the police in their report of the incident as involving alcohol on the part of both the victim and the offender. The comparable figure for non-Aboriginal Ontario homicides was 11 percent.

To look at the social situation leading up to the homicide it is, once again, quite clear that the immediate precursors to homicides were different within the Aboriginal communities. Table 7 demonstrates this quite starkly. Events leading up to the killing of an Aboriginal person were considerably more likely to have begun with a more benign social interaction. Considering this, and the fact that alcohol use was more likely among Aboriginal accuseds, it is not at all surprising that Aboriginal people accused of a homicide offense were less likely than non-Aboriginal accuseds to be charged with first-degree (premeditated) murder.

The differences between Aboriginal and non-Aboriginal crime are important in that they suggest that we should focus less on the differences in the amount of crime between groups and more on the possible different factors responsible for crime in different communities.

III. Criminal Justice Processing Cases Involving Visible Minorities

We noted in Section I that there are more Aboriginal people in Canada's remand facilities, provincial prisons, and federal penitentiaries

TABLE 6

Alcohol Use by Accused and Victim, Calgary and Regina (in Percent)

City	Alcohol Use by the Accused										Alcohol Use by Victim of Violent Crime	
	Violent Crime		Property Crime		Drugs		Other Criminal Code		Total			
	Aboriginal	Non-Aboriginal	Aboriginal	Non-Aboriginal	Aboriginal	Non-Aboriginal	Aboriginal	Non-Aboriginal	Aboriginal	Non-Aboriginal	Aboriginal	Non-Aboriginal
Calgary	47	29	30	7	21	17	37	23	34	14	43	14
Regina	38	23	N.A.	N.A.	N.A.	N.A.	N.A.	N.A.	N.A.	N.A.	30	11

SOURCE.—Data are derived from Trevethan (1993).
NOTE.—N.A. = not available.

TABLE 7

Situation in Which the Homicide Occurred (Ontario, 1980–90)

	Victim and Location of the Homicide		
	Aboriginal Victim, on Reserve	Aboriginal Victim Off Reserve	Non-Aboriginal
Victim and suspect were socializing together	36.5	34.6	10.8
Verbal argument was part of the sequence leading to the death	48.1	51.9	24.3
Fight was involved at some stage which escalated, or the accused was seeking revenge	34.6	34.6	18.3
One or more of the above three occurred (socializing, argument, fight)	69.2	66.7	35.5
Of those socializing, fighting, arguing, how many were drinking?			
Suspect drinking	80.6	66.7	33
Victim drinking	83.3	70.4	34.9
Both suspect and victim were drinking	77.8	63	28.3

Source.—Data are derived from Doob, Grossman, and Auger (1994).

than would be expected given the portion of the population that they constitute. Why this is, however, is not clear. In Section III, we briefly summarize some recent data relating to the processing of ethnic minorities in Canada. For Aboriginal offenders, we summarize research findings from several provinces. For blacks, however, we discuss a single recent study in some detail, as it is the only major research initiative in this area.

A. Aboriginal Offenders

As LaPrairie (1990) points out, those who look solely to the Canadian courts when trying to understand the overrepresentation of Aboriginal people in prison are likely to be ignoring a wide range of possible explanations. The problem in assessing the causes of Aboriginal overrepresentation in Canada's prisons, however, is that we do not have adequate data that pertain to cases as they travel through the criminal justice system. Nevertheless, we do know that there are some differences in the way in which justice is administered that almost certainly have an impact on imprisonment. This is particularly true in the area of policing. We also know that differences exist in the treatment accorded Aboriginals after the sentencing stage, namely, in terms of parole.

1. *Policing.* Regarding the policing of Aboriginals, Landau (1994) found that what is normally thought of as "pretrial custody" (holding an accused in a cell after arrest but before a finding of guilt has been made) has a quite different meaning and purpose in many Aboriginal communities. In reading police occurrence reports, it was not uncommon to find descriptions of people being "lodged in a cell" overnight without charges being laid or even ever being contemplated. In some communities, many more people are placed in custody for short times than are charged with offenses. The police cell is seen as a service facility, the purpose of which is to "lodge" someone who is intoxicated until such time as they are no longer perceived as a threat to themselves or others. Most such incarcerations do not make it into formal counts. The number that can occur at one time in a community is also limited by the number of jail cells.

Griffiths and Verdun-Jones (1994) summarized the findings of a number of royal commissions and studies on Aboriginal peoples and the police in Canada and reached the following conclusion: "A consistent finding of many commissions of inquiry and research studies is that the relations between the police and Aboriginals are often characterized by mutual hostility and distrust, increasing the likelihood of conflict and high arrest rates" (Griffiths and Verdun-Jones 1994, p. 641).

Few who have had any contact with Aboriginal communities in Canada would question their conclusion. At the same time, however, there is some evidence that the police may be called by Aboriginal people to deal with problems in some Aboriginal communities that would not be seen as "police property" in non-Aboriginal communities. Part of the reason for this is that the police may be the only "service" available in the community to deal with a problem. The problem of whether Aboriginal people are "overpoliced," therefore, is a complex one.

2. *Courts and Corrections.* At the sentencing stage, it is clear that in remote Aboriginal communities sentencing options are quite limited. In many instances, there are, in fact, two choices: prison or nothing. "Nothing" may technically be a term of probation; however, in many communities there are no probation officers to enforce orders. In addition, in many instances, sending an accused to prison means trans-

porting him hundreds of kilometers by air. Comparing the sentencing of Aboriginals in such settings to the sentencing of non-Aboriginals in cities, therefore, tells us little about the reasons for differences. LaPrairie concluded that for many remote Aboriginal communities: "Existing data, although limited and incomplete, would suggest the disproportionate sentencing of aboriginal people to periods of incarceration [is due to] the absence of other sentencing options" (LaPrairie 1990, p. 437). More generally, however, LaPrairie pointed out that existing data do not allow us to rank the relative importance of a number of factors in explaining the overrepresentation of Aboriginal people that exists in Canada's federal and provincial prisons. She noted that there are data that suggest that police and prosecutorial decisions as well as different sentencing decisions could account for some of the high numbers of Aboriginal people in prisons in Canada. One could also add discretionary release (e.g., parole) decisions.

The problem of attributing the overrepresentation of Aboriginal people in prisons to simple racism is challenged by some data suggesting that for certain offenses, Aboriginal people given sentences involving incarceration may receive shorter sentences than comparable non-Aboriginal people (LaPrairie 1990, p. 435). More important, LaPrairie notes that many of the problems facing Aboriginal people in sentencing in Canada may relate to problems of "treating unequals equally, that is applying the same criteria to all offenders in disposition considerations. This phenomenon may have more adverse consequences for Aboriginal accused if, for example, judges make dispositions decisions and/or probation officers make recommendations regarding dispositions based on the presence or absence of certain structural factors such as employment, education, or family and community supports" (p. 437).

It also appears clear that part of the explanation for the high proportion of Aboriginal inmates in some provincial prisons is their failure to pay fines. This is true despite the existence of fine option programs specifically tailored to the needs of Aboriginal offenders. In Saskatchewan, for example, Aboriginal offender admissions were placed in custody for nonpayment of fines at a rate which was more than twice that of non-Aboriginal offenders (Moyer et al. 1985). Finally, it is worth noting that research into the treatment of Aboriginal offenders by provincial parole boards has also found significant differences between Aboriginals and non-Aboriginals. One recent study found lower rates of day parole and full parole for Aboriginal inmates in the prairie provinces (Cawsey 1991).

Several recent studies of decision making at a single point in the justice system in urban settings have examined differences in the treatment of Aboriginal and non-Aboriginal accused people. One of the more comprehensive is a study of over 1,500 cases in a youth court in Edmonton (Schissel 1993). There is no simple way of summarizing the findings of this study. However, being Aboriginal appeared to be at least a factor in the decisions of the youth court. The analytic problem becomes evident when the offenses that brought offenders to court are isolated. There were complex interactions involving race (white, Aboriginal, and "other"), age, and whether a youth had a criminal record. There were, in addition, differences in plea decisions. Aboriginal youth whose parents were with them in court were less likely to plead guilty than those whose parents were not in court. For whites, the presence of a parent was not related to the plea; for the "others," the presence of a parent increased the likelihood of a guilty plea.

As with any such study, the meaning of a variable is open to question. For example, the presence of a parent in court may, in effect, be a proxy for different constellations of variables across different (racial) groups. Hence it may not be the presence of a parent per se that is important as much as it is other correlated factors. In the end, however, Aboriginal youth were less likely to win "unconditional release" than were members of other groups. Having a parent present appeared to be beneficial for native youth but not for white or "other" youth.

Although the author of the study concludes that "it is apparent from this research that youth courts apply the law with discretion and prejudice," it would appear to us that this may overstate the clarity of the findings. What is clear is that cases are dealt with differently when they involve Aboriginal youth in this court. Judges, in fact, are often quite open in admitting that they look at the family and social situation of the young person when handing down dispositions. If for example, the youth court judge is operating at least in part on a rehabilitative model of dispositions, it would not be surprising that the family and social situation of the young person would have a large—and perhaps unpredictable—impact on dispositions.

B. Black Offenders: Race, Bail, and Imprisonment in Ontario[8]

1. *Background.* In this section we review findings from the first major study of criminal justice processing of black accuseds in Canada. As

[8] This section of our report summarizes findings described in two separate documents (Doob 1994; Roberts 1994*b*). Of necessity, we have had to omit a great deal of information.

noted earlier, the vast majority of previous research has been directed at the treatment of Aboriginal offenders. A series of fortuitous events is responsible for the genesis of the present research. First, the Commission on Systemic Racism in the Ontario Criminal Justice System had the resources and interest to conduct a large-scale study of this kind. Second, the study received the support of the provincial Ministry of the Attorney General. Third, the Canadian Centre for Justice Statistics (located in Statistics Canada, a federal government department) was able to undertake the collection of the data. Finally, although race-crime statistics are no longer collected by police forces across the country, they had been recorded by the Toronto police force in Toronto in 1989–90. Accordingly, the data described in this section of the report come from that period. Since this is the first major study that has examined the processing of blacks and whites by Canadian courts, we describe the results in some detail.

2. *Previous Research on the Treatment of Racial Minorities by the Court System.* Very little research has been conducted on bail decision making involving members of visible minorities.[9] Research by the Ontario Commission on Systemic Racism has demonstrated a significant relation between bail and race for young offenders: black youth were less likely to be released immediately by the police by means of an appearance notice. As well, a greater proportion of black young offenders were detained to the point of a show-cause hearing (Commission on Systemic Racism in the Ontario Criminal Justice System 1994*b*). The research described in the following paragraphs represents the first step toward understanding the treatment in the adult system of visible minorities at this stage of the criminal justice process.

Unlike bail, there are a few studies on the treatment of blacks at the sentencing stage. One of these was conducted by Clairmont, Barnwell, and O'Malley (1989) for the royal commission which studied the wrongful conviction of Marshall. Clairmont, Barnwell, and O'Malley were following up earlier work by Renner and Warner (in 1989), which had found that black defendants in Nova Scotia courts were less likely than white accuseds to receive discharges, the least severe penalties available under Canadian criminal law. Renner and Warner found that 23 percent of white accuseds received a discharge, but that none of the black accuseds did. However, the sample size was small (only

[9] There is little research on bail decision making in general, the few studies on bail for adults being now quite old. See, e.g., Koza and Doob 1975*a*, 1975*b*.

twenty-eight black defendants), and when a multiple regression analysis was conducted, race was not a significant predictor of sentence severity (see Renner and Warner 1981, p. 71).

Clairmont, Barnwell, and O'Malley (1989) generated a sample of only 51 blacks and 126 whites and were restricted to a single, minor offense (theft; most of the cases in the sample involved shoplifting). The Clairmont study found some marginal evidence of disparity of treatment between blacks and whites, but for the primary analyses no race effect emerged. For example, a regression analysis examined the extent to which sentencing patterns can be predicted by variables such as criminal record, education, race, and socioeconomic status. The only variables found to predict sentence outcome were criminal record, education, and age (see Clairmont, Barnwell, and O'Malley 1989, p. 155). However, with only a single offense, and such a small sample, this research cannot be considered more than a case study. The Nova Scotia study focused exclusively on sentencing and did not include information on court decisions that precede the sentencing stage (such as whether the accused is denied bail).

Another study by Clairmont (1989), which examined sentencing patterns for assault, constituted a better test of the hypothesis that race affects sentencing patterns. A slightly larger sample was used, but the results were no different. Clairmont concluded (p. 183): "The findings overall are consistent with earlier research conducted in the same locale but focusing on convictions for theft. Essentially there is little support for the proposition that on the average the race of an offender directly affects the sentencing he will receive."

The research literature in this country regarding race and sentencing can be summarized by saying that there is no convincing evidence to date of disparity in sentencing as a result of an offender's race. At the same time, however, there has been no large-scale attempt to test the hypothesis until now, and it is possible that the offenses previously selected for analysis were ones for which the race of the accused was an important factor.

3. *The Sample.* The sampling procedure is described elsewhere (Morrison and Armstrong 1993). Essentially, the goal was to produce two equal-sized samples of defendants comparable in terms of the offenses with which they were charged. Information was available on 1,653 cases (821 blacks and 832 whites). There were two racial categories (black and white) and five offense categories: robbery, sexual assault, drugs, serious assault, and bail violations. An attempt was made

to control for age by equating the number of older and younger accused in the sample for each race-offense combination. The original intention had been to capture information on 2,200 defendants, but records were not available for 547 cases.

An obvious problem is that the range of available data is limited. A limited number of offense categories was sampled. Neither of us was involved with the project during the planning and data collection, and, therefore, we do not know how sampling decisions were made. However, given concerns about drugs and violence, the rationale for four of the five offenses chosen is evident. The choice of "bail offenses" is a bit more mysterious, but presumably reflects the belief held by some that blacks may be treated more harshly than whites in administration of bail violations in particular. A more serious problem with these data is that we do not have much information on how the cases may differ. For example, we have little information about most aspects of the offense itself or details of its seriousness. And, in terms of understanding the role of the police, we have no data on the nature of the initial police-suspect interaction. Even on matters such as criminal record, we are restricted to the limited number of ways in which criminal records were coded and categorized. The result is, of course, that differences between racial groups might be either created or obscured by differences in the cases that we were not able to "control for" adequately. Such qualifications hold in any study involving correlational data such as these; however, we are at a particular disadvantage with these data because they were gathered by others solely from written records created for quite different purposes than research. Nevertheless, we believe that they give a glimpse of the relative treatment of black and white accuseds in Toronto. And, they are the only data that were available on this topic.

4. *Results.* If a police officer arrests someone for a minor offense without a warrant, the presumption is that the accused should be released immediately after issuing an appearance notice to the accused person. If the offense is not very serious, the police officer in charge (e.g., a sergeant at a police station) is expected to release the accused unless there are reasons to hold him or her for a formal bail ("judicial interim release") hearing. For more serious charges, or those where the police have decided not to release the accused, a formal "judicial interim release" hearing is held, normally before a justice of the peace (typically, a person without legal training). In some places, judges will preside over such hearings, and in the case of the most serious charges

TABLE 8

Criminal Record and Bail (in Percent)

	No Prior Convictions	One to Five Prior Convictions	Six or More Prior Convictions
Released by police when charged	11	8	5
Released by police at station	23	13	5
Released at show-cause hearing	54	52	45
Detained	12	27	45

Source.—Each column sums to 100 percent. The information in this and in tables 9–18 comes from the study carried out for the Commission on Systemic Racism in the Ontario Criminal Justice System by the Canadian Centre for Justice Statistics. The information in these tables derives from the reports produced for that commission by Doob (1994) and Roberts (1994*b*).

Note.—$\chi^2 = 68$, df $= 6$, $p < .01$.

(e.g., murder) a superior court judge must preside. Such hearings must be held soon after the arrest, typically within twenty-four hours.

Race and Criminal Record. With some important exceptions, the burden of proof is on the prosecutor to demonstrate that pretrial detention is justified. Otherwise, the accused person is to be released. A prosecutor can justify detention if "detention is necessary to ensure his attendance in court" or if "detention is necessary in the public interest or for the protection or safety of the public, having regard to all circumstances including any substantial likelihood that the accused will, if he is released from custody, commit a criminal offence or interfere with the administration of justice" (Criminal Code § 515[10]). These two provisions—in particular the second—give enormous scope to the prosecutor to argue for the detention of those accused of offenses. In some cases the legal burden is on the accused to demonstrate why release is justified. The "reverse onus" provisions apply if the alleged offense is said to have occurred while the accused was on release for another offense, had escaped from prison, or was facing a charge of trafficking or importing narcotics. This last provision is very relevant in relation to bail decisions for narcotic offenses.

Criminal record is very highly correlated with bail decisions. This can be seen in table 8 (showing the combined data for blacks and whites). If blacks have longer or more serious criminal records, this may explain a race-bail differential. However, contrary to some stereotypes, the black accuseds in our sample were *less* likely to have a serious

TABLE 9

Criminal Record Percentage Breakdown of White and Black Accuseds (Total Sample)

Criminal Record Category	White	Black
No prior convictions	35 (288)	40 (325)
One to five prior convictions	33 (273)	34 (278)
Six or more prior convictions	33 (270)	26 (216)
Total	100 (831)	100 (819)

NOTE.—$\chi^2 = 8$, df $= 2$, $p < .01$; sample sizes are in parentheses.

criminal record (defined as six or more previous convictions). Thus 33 percent of the white accuseds had a record of six or more priors compared to only 26 percent of the black sample. Similarly, the black sample contained a higher percentage of first offenders (40 percent) than did the white sample (35 percent). These differences are statistically significant and are presented in table 9. It is not surprising, therefore, that white accuseds were significantly more likely to have been sentenced to longer periods in custody than were black accuseds (14 percent of white accuseds had, in their lifetimes, accumulated custodial sentences totaling more than three years as compared to 7 percent of black accuseds).

Among those who had a criminal record, black accuseds were significantly more likely than whites (25 percent vs. 15 percent) to have been convicted in the previous three months. Blacks and whites had a similar likelihood of having a criminal record that included violence: 28 percent of the white defendants and 33 percent of the black defendants had one or more previous convictions involving violence (a nonsignificant difference). Fourteen percent of the white accuseds and 16 percent of the black accuseds (a difference that was not significant) had one or more previous convictions of a type similar to that of the main offense for which they had been charged.

Race and Bail Decision Making. Table 10 provides information about the relationship between race and bail decision making. As can be seen from that table, white accuseds are more likely to be released

TABLE 10

Percentage of Race and Bail Release (Total Sample)

	White Accused	Black Accused
Released by police when charged	10	6
Released by police at station	19	12
Released at show-cause hearing	48	52
Detained	23	30

NOTE.—$\chi^2 = 30$, df = 3, $p < .01$; each column sums to 100 percent.

when charged, and less likely, at the end of the show cause, to be detained. Overall then, we can see that the two samples, comparable in many important respects, are treated differently by the criminal justice system at the pretrial stage. It would appear, on the basis of this preliminary table, that blacks are the object of harsher treatment.

This effect is not uniform across the five offenses included in this research. When we examine the specific offenses individually, we find that the effect is strongest for offenders charged with drug offenses, sexual assault, and serious assault and is absent for bail violators and those charged with robbery. Table 11 shows the race-bail effect for the drug offenders alone. Here the race differential is strongest of all: almost one-third of the white accuseds are released when charged, compared to 14 percent of the black sample. Not surprisingly, 31 percent of the black sample are detained prior to trial, compared to just under 10 percent of the white sample (see table 11).

Whether an offender is released or detained is not a decision taken on a single occasion. An accused may be detained at the police station and then released by a court following a show-cause hearing. Bail is a

TABLE 11

Percentage of Race and Bail Release (Drug Offenses Only)

	White Accused	Black Accused
Released by police when charged	31	14
Released by police at station	30	16
Released at show-cause hearing	29	39
Detained	10	31

NOTE.—$\chi^2 = 40$, df = 3, $p < .01$; each column sums to 100 percent.

TABLE 12

Percentage of Race and Release (Total Sample)

	White Accused	Black Accused
At first contact with the police:*		
Released by police when charged	9	6
Detained by the police	91	94
By the police at the police station:†		
Released by the police at the police station	20	11
Detained by police	80	89
At the show-cause hearing:‡		
Released at the show-cause hearing	68	63
Detained	32	37

Note.—Percentages in each group sum to 100 percent.
* $\chi^2 = 6.4$, df = 1, $p < .05$.
† $\chi^2 = 18.7$, df = 1, $p < .05$.
‡ $\chi^2 = 3.4$, df = 1, $p > .05$.

multistage process involving different actors. While all decisions affect whether the accused is in detention or at liberty, there are also important distinctions among the various stages. At this point we present bail release decision making across three stages: events occurring when the individual is charged at the scene (phase 1), events at the police station (phase 2), and the show-cause hearing itself (phase 3).

Decision making in phase 1 is taken by the individual police officer (within certain statutory limits); phase 2 is the outcome of discretion exercised by the officer in charge of the station (although there are limits on this discretion), while phase 3 is a judicial proceeding, adversarial in nature and adjudicated by a member of the judiciary. It is also important to separate the show cause from the decisions that precede it for the reason that different criminal justice professionals are involved. Although the police have an interest in the outcome of the show cause, their influence on the accused's detention status is obviously greatest at first contact with the suspect.

When release decisions are analyzed sequentially, rather than as a single variable with seven levels, it becomes clear that differentials exist at the scene, and also at the police station, but not once a show-cause hearing is held. Table 12 lays out three cross-tabulations between race and release at three stages: arrest, police station, and show cause. (For the purposes of this analysis, all decisions have been classified as released or detained.)

Multivariate Analyses. The results presented so far have been bivariate in nature. Before concluding that there is a direct relationship between race and bail status, however, it is necessary to conduct multivariate analyses. Multiple regression analyses were conducted using thirteen "control" variables: (1) whether the accused was on bail when charged; (2) whether the accused was under some other kind of warrant (e.g., parole); (3) whether the accused had a criminal record, and if so, how many convictions were recorded; (4) the number of previous convictions for a similar offense; (5) the number of previous convictions for a violent offense; (6) the length of time since the most recent conviction; (7) the nature of the most serious previous conviction; (8) the length of any previous custodial term; (9) whether the accused was on welfare; (10) whether the accused had a fixed address; (11) whether the accused was employed; (12) the type of employment; and (13) the marital status of the accused.

In the multiple analyses, these thirteen "control" variables were first entered into the equation predicting whether the accused was released or detained. Then the race of the accused was added. The critical question was whether race added anything above and beyond the other thirteen predictors to the prediction of the bail decision. Table 13 shows the results of the multiple regression analyses. The results are relatively straightforward. For all the offenses combined (the total sample), the race of the accused had an effect on the bail decision above and beyond the combined effect of the other predictors. For drug offenses, the effect of race was particularly striking: it had the largest "weight" of all fourteen predictors in the final multiple regression equation. Another way of stating the effect is to say that the effect of race on bail decisions that emerged in the bivariate analyses is replicated using standard multivariate techniques. Controlling for other variables—social and legal—did not make the "race" effect disappear.

The Plea and the Outcome of the Case. At the point in the proceedings where an accused would be expected to be entering a plea, it appeared from the records that a substantial number of the cases were completed because all charges were withdrawn (24 percent of cases). In an additional 14 percent of cases, it appeared that the main charge was withdrawn, but other charges remained. In all, it appears that 41 percent of the black defendants had their main charge withdrawn, in comparison with 34 percent of white defendants, a difference which was statistically significant (chi-square = 7.55, df = 1, $p < .05$).

In close to 15 percent of cases, it was impossible, from the records,

TABLE 13

Summary of Multiple Regression Results: Bail Decisions

	All Offenses	Drugs	Sexual Assault	Bail Violations	Serious Assaults	Robbery
R^2 change when race is added	.014	.059	.011	.004	.013	.000
Significance of R^2 change	.001	.001	N.S.	N.S.	.023	N.S.
Final multiple R	.485	.577	.512	.351	.521	.506
Predictors:						
Accused on bail	−.186	−.147	. . .	. . .	. . .	−.156
Accused on warrant	−.052	. . .	. . .	. . .	. . .	. . .
Criminal record	. . .	. . .	. . .	. . .	. . .	. . .
Has conviction for similar offense	. . .	.120	. . .	. . .	. . .	. . .
Has conviction for violent offense	. . .	. . .	. . .	. . .	. . .	. . .
Time since last conviction	−.118	−.179	. . .	. . .	. . .	. . .
Most serious previous conviction	. . .	. . .	. . .	. . .	. . .	. . .
Previous custodial term	.088	. . .	. . .	. . .	. . .	. . .
On welfare when charged	. . .	. . .	. . .	. . .	. . .	. . .
Has fixed address	.177	.251	.158	. . .	.211	. . .
Employed	.266	.218	. . .	.308	.283	.280
Status of employment	−.149	−.124	. . .	−.269	−.280	. . .
Marital status	−.052	. . .	. . .	. . .	. . .	. . .
Race	.122	.258	. . .	. . .	.118	. . .

Note.—Cell entries are included *only* for those predictors with significant ($p < .05$) weight in the final regression equation. N.S. = not significant.

to determine exactly what had happened at the plea stage. However, of those where the main charge did go to trial, and where a plea on it was unambiguously recorded, more whites (77 percent) than blacks (62 percent) entered a plea of guilty. To the extent that a "discount" is available for a plea of guilty, it would appear that at this stage of the proceedings, more blacks were taking a chance with a not-guilty plea.

Looking at the outcome of the trial, then, given the tendency of whites to be more likely to plead guilty, it is not surprising that more whites than blacks were, in fact, found guilty (89 percent vs. 79 percent of those who went to trial; chi-square = 19.27, df = 1, $p < .01$).

Race and Incarceration: Sample Attrition. Before proceeding to the results of the analyses, it is important to note that the sample size diminishes considerably once we analyze the sentenced sample, rather than the total sample of defendants. There were 871 cases in which a sentence was recorded as having been imposed. This represents slightly over half (53 percent) of the entire sample. The other cases were dismissed, withdrawn, never got to trial for some other reason, or resulted in acquittals.

The degree of case attrition introduces an important constraint into the subsequent analyses: it eliminates the possibility of conducting detailed analyses *within* offense categories, because the sample sizes for individual categories become so small. For example, there were only twenty-five black defendants and fifty-one whites in the sexual assault category.

Before proceeding to the results of the multivariate analyses, we first examine differences that may exist between the two types of defendants on variables *other* than the offense of conviction. We begin with demographic variables. There were no significant differences on any demographic variables (on which data were collected),[10] with one exception: the sample of black defendants had a higher percentage of unemployed individuals than the white sample (56 percent compared to 38 percent). The two samples were comparable on a number of characteristics associated with the crime.[11] These findings suggest that the two black and white samples were still comparable by the time they were sentenced.

Criminal Record. After the seriousness of the offense, criminal record is the most powerful determinant of sentence severity. This is true

[10] See table 13 for the list of variables available to us.

[11] There were no significant differences on the following variables that can relate to the seriousness of the incident: number of victims, extent of injury to the victim, relationship between victim and accused, amount of property loss, sex of victim, nature of drug, quantity of drug.

TABLE 14

Percentage of Criminal Record Breakdown (Sentenced Sample)

Criminal Record Category	White	Black
No prior convictions	28 (139)	35 (132)
One to five prior convictions	35 (172)	37 (143)
Six or more prior convictions	36 (177)	28 (108)
Total	100 (488)	100 (383)

NOTE.—$\chi^2 = 7$, df $= 2$, $p < .04$; sample sizes are in parentheses.

in Canada and in other countries such as the United Kingdom and the United States (see Roberts 1996). Support for this finding comes from empirical research on sentencing (e.g., Hogarth 1971) and case law decisions relating to sentencing (see Nadin-Davis 1982; Ruby 1994). As well, the literature on race and sentencing has demonstrated the importance of controlling for the number of previous convictions (e.g., Hagan 1974, p. 378; Hagan and Bumiller 1983). Several researchers have found that an apparent sentencing differential in favor of whites sometimes disappears when analyses are conducted to take into account criminal histories of black defendants (see Brown and Hullin 1992). For this reason a number of different measures of previous criminal conduct were included in the study. Before presenting the sentencing data, then, we examine the criminal histories of the black and white samples, using a number of different measures.

The race breakdown in terms of number of previous convictions is presented in table 14, from which it is clear that as a group, the black defendants have a *less* serious history of previous offending. This is surprising since earlier research in Canada has shown that sentenced offenders from visible minorities tend to have longer criminal records than whites convicted of comparable crimes. For example, in the study conducted by Don Clairmont for the Marshall Commission, the black sample had a significantly more serious pattern of prior offending (see Clairmont, Barnwell, and O'Malley 1989).

One of the criticisms of research finding a sentencing differential in favor of whites has been that this difference can be explained by differences in criminal history between racial samples. In our study, this was not the case: on this variable at least, whites had a more serious pattern of previous offending. Thus 28 percent of white accuseds had no priors, compared to 35 percent of blacks. In addition, a higher percentage (36 percent) of whites had six or more convictions (compared to 28 percent of blacks). These differences are statistically significant (see table 14).

Sentences usually consider issues such as whether the previous offending included crimes of violence, whether the previous offenses were similar to the current conviction, and how much time has elapsed since the previous convictions (see Nadin-Davis 1982; Ruby 1994). It is to these that we now turn. The differences for those who got to the sentencing stage of proceedings were similar to the whole sample. There were no significant differences between the black and white samples on the number of violent priors. Nor were there differences between the black and white samples in terms of the number of priors that were similar to the current offense or between the percentage of blacks and whites that had served a prior term of custody.

There was a statistically significant difference in the aggregate *length* of previous sentences for those who had previously been sentenced to prison. However, the difference was in the direction of whites having built up longer aggregate custodial time: the average number of days of custody from previous sentences was 752 for whites compared to only 271 for blacks. The only measure on which blacks clearly did "worse" was in terms of "clean time," that is, the amount of time that had elapsed since the most recent previous conviction. For blacks being sentenced, twenty-three months had elapsed (on average) since the most recent conviction, compared to thirty-four months for the white sample.

To summarize the data on criminal record, there is no evidence from the criminal history information to suggest that the black sample had a more serious history of prior offending. On the contrary, with a single exception ("clean time") the black sample had comparable, or less serious, criminal records than the white offenders.

Sentencing and Bail. Before taking up the multivariate analysis of *sentencing* data, it is worth returning briefly to the question of bail release. It will be recalled that the analyses of bail decisions described earlier revealed a significant relationship between race and release: blacks were more likely to be detained (or more likely to be released later) than whites. The releasing decision was also highly predictive of

TABLE 15

Relationship between Race and Incarceration for Accuseds Released on Bail (in Percent)

	Prison	Other Sentence
White	41	59
Black	53	47

NOTE.—Includes accused persons released when charged, at the station, or following a show-cause hearing. $\chi^2 = 7$, df $= 1$, $p = .01$.

the decision to incarcerate following conviction: accused persons denied bail were more likely to be imprisoned. This was true for blacks and whites.

The question addressed at this point is the following: if blacks are more likely to be denied bail, and being denied bail heightens the chance of imprisonment, is there any additional discrimination at the sentencing stage? Is there a "double discrimination" effect in operation? If the race-prison effect (blacks being more likely to be incarcerated) is *totally* explained by the effect of bail, equating the two racial groups in terms of their bail status should have the effect of equating their incarceration rates. This does not occur. Instead, when we compared the imprisonment rates of blacks and whites with similar bail histories, we observed that a sentencing differential persists between the two groups. This finding can be demonstrated in the following way. Table 15 shows the different incarceration rates for blacks and whites who obtained pretrial release at some point. As can be seen, there is still a substantial, statistically significant incarceration rate differential: 41 percent of the whites were sent to prison, compared to 53 percent of the blacks. So there does seem to be some evidence pointing toward discrimination, above and beyond the bail decision.

These findings suggest, but do not conclusively establish, a racial bias in sentencing independent of the bail decision. To be more certain of this, we need to conduct additional, multivariate analyses.

Incarceration Rates. Are incarceration rates different for black and white defendants with similar profiles? Using univariate analyses, aggregating across offenses, the incarceration rate for black accuseds was higher than the incarceration rate for whites, and this difference was statistically significant: the incarceration rates for the total sample were

TABLE 16

Race and Imprisonment (Percentage of All Offenses Combined)

	Noncustodial Disposition	Prison
White	43	57
Black	31	69

NOTE.—$\chi^2 = 13$, df = 1, $p < .01$; percentages for each group sum to 100 percent.

69 percent for blacks and 57 percent for whites (see table 16). Two additional observations are in order. First, as with the bail data, these aggregate statistics mask a high degree of variability from one offense category to another: the incarceration rate differential as a function of race varied from +30 percent for the drug offenses to −2 percent for robbery cases. That is, the incarceration rate was 30 percent higher for blacks convicted of drug crimes compared to whites and 2 percent lower for blacks convicted of robbery.

Later we present multivariate analyses based on three offense categories. In order to keep comparable analyses together, table 17 provides the race-by-incarceration cross-tabulation for three offense groups: drugs, sexual assault, and bail violations. As can be seen when these three offenses are examined, the sentencing differential is even more striking: less than half (47 percent) of the white sample were incarcerated for one of these offenses, compared to over two-thirds of the black sample (see table 17).

TABLE 17

Percentage of Race and Imprisonment (Drugs, Sexual Assault, and Bail Offenses Only)

	Noncustodial Disposition	Prison
White	53	47
Black	32	68

NOTE.—$\chi^2 = 25$, df = 1, $p < .01$; percentages for each group sum to 100 percent.

TABLE 18

Offense-Specific Incarceration Rates, by Race (in Percent)

	White	Black
Drugs:*		
Prison	36	66
Noncustodial	64	34
Sexual assault:†		
Prison	62	76
Noncustodial	38	24
Bail violation:‡		
Prison	56	69
Noncustodial	44	31
Assault:§		
Prison	50	56
Noncustodial	50	44
Robbery:‖		
Prison	93	91
Noncustodial	7	9

NOTE.—Percentages in each group sum to 100 percent.

* $\chi^2 = 29$, df = 1, $p < .001$.

† $\chi^2 = 1.5$, df = 1, not significant.

‡ $\chi^2 = 3$, df = 1, $p < .10$.

§ $\chi^2 = .7$, df = 1, not significant.

‖ $\chi^2 = .9$, df = 1, not significant.

Table 18 summarizes the individual offense incarceration patterns for the two samples of offenders. The statistically significant effect is restricted to drug offenders, although there is a marginal ($p < .10$) effect for those convicted of bail violations. These relative incarceration rates do not take into account the effect of other variables related to the accused, the crime, and the criminal justice response to the case. It would be a mistake to interpret the incarceration rate differential noted above as a direct estimate of racial discrimination in sentencing. It is possible that a combination of legally relevant factors explain the sentencing differential between blacks and whites. For this reason, at this time we now shift our attention to the multivariate analyses.

Multivariate Analyses. The purpose of the multivariate analyses was to establish whether race is a significant predictor of the incarceration decision having controlled for other variables. In the present case, this means controlling for the impact of, among other variables, bail status and criminal record. Several models were constructed, which attempted to explain variance in the incarceration decision. These models differed from the models used to predict whether the accused is released on bail, because the legally relevant factors differ for the two decisions. For example, the primary ground for continued detention of the accused is that it is necessary to ensure the accused's attendance at trial. In considering this issue, a broad range of personal circumstances such as whether the accused has a fixed address, his or her employment status, and general social networks are likely to be considered by the justice adjudicating the bail hearing. Previous convictions will play a less important role. However, those convictions are likely to be critical to the sentencing judge, particularly if they were related to the current charge.

As well, there are decisions taken after the bail decision that need to be considered. Thus the accused's plea is likely to have a strong impact on the sentencing decision, with accuseds who enter a guilty plea receiving a sentencing "discount" (particularly if the plea is entered early in the judicial proceedings). This factor can have no bearing on the decision as to whether to release the accused at a show-cause hearing.

Race emerged only inconsistently as a significant predictor of imprisonment when multiple regressions were conducted on the entire sample of all five offense categories. From this we concluded that the relationship between race and incarceration is rather inconsistent. One problem with comparing black and white incarceration rates for a category of offenses is that the racial groups may be disproportionately distributed across specific offenses of varying seriousness. If black accuseds were facing possession for the purposes of trafficking charges while whites had been charged with simple possession, this could explain a sentencing differential. Although missing data became a factor, 67 percent of the black sample were charged with mere possession compared to 90 percent of the white sample. However, internal analyses conducted on a sample of blacks and whites charged only with possession revealed the same effect: a sentencing differential in the direction of higher custody rates for blacks (chi-square (1) = 15.1, $p < .001$). These findings suggest that the incarceration differential between blacks and whites is not likely to be simply a function of differences in the seriousness of the offense of charge within a particular offense category.

In an attempt to localize the effect, a second series of multiple regression analyses was conducted, using the same set of predictors but with one important change. On this occasion, only three of the five offense categories were included, those in which the univariate cross-tabulations indicated the race-incarceration effect was strongest: drugs, sexual assault, and bail violations. Now the results become clearer, and the effect more stable.[12] The effect of the bail decision is clear: all three pretrial release variables are highly significant predictors of the incarceration decision. The criminal record variables are also significant, as well as whether the crown proceeds by way of summary conviction or indictment and whether the accused pleaded guilty or not. The only characteristic of the offender that emerged as a significant predictor of the imprisonment decision is the one noted at the beginning of the report, employment status.

What happens when race is added to the equation? The addition of race leads to a small but statistically significant ($p < .02$) increase in the amount of variance explained. In addition to several other predictor variables (such as amount of previous time served and whether the offender had been released or detained on bail), race was a significant predictor. It is important to note, however, that the race effect was restricted to this subset of offense categories, and the statistical magnitude of the effect did not approach the effect of race on bail decisions (see earlier sections of this essay).[13]

Discussion: Restrictions on the Study. It is important to point out two limitations on the research reported here. First, a limited number of offenses was used. The offenses selected by the commission were chosen because there had been assertions that sentencing differentials existed for these offenses. In order to make statements about bail and sentencing in general, it would have been necessary to have studied a

[12] One of the problems with case file analyses is missing data. For a variety of reasons, data were missing for a number of cases. For this reason we repeated the analyses using different strategies, including pairwise deletion and mean substitution. The only change was a slight nonsignificant shift in beta weights. Accordingly, we are confident that the race effects are unaffected by the absence of data for some variables in some cases.

[13] Additional analyses were conducted on the effect of race on sentence length. Race did not affect the length of custody imposed, with the exception of the drug category. Here, results showed that on average the black sample were sentenced to slightly shorter terms of imprisonment than the white sample. This simply reflects the incarceration differentials. That is, since a number of the black cases would, had they been white, have received a noncustodial sentence, their profiles generate a less punitive judicial response, and hence a shorter term of custody.

random sample of black and white defendants. The Criminal Code contains over 500 offenses; this study examined only a small number of these at one point in history in one Ontario city.

We cannot therefore conclude that sentencing discrimination exists across a wide spectrum of offenses. But there do appear to be bail release and sentencing differentials for the offenses examined in this study, even after eliminating the influence of a significant number of "control" variables, such as the offender's criminal record. Second, for pragmatic reasons relating to the amount of time and resources available for the research, only one visible minority group was studied. We do not have information on other visible minorities such as Aboriginal Canadians or Asians.

There are parallels between the Canadian literature and the British research on race and sentencing. That is, while some earlier research in England (e.g., McConville and Baldwin 1982; Crow and Cove 1984) found little evidence of racial bias in sentencing trends, the most recent (and the most comprehensive) study to date in that jurisdiction (Hood 1992) did uncover evidence of variation in sentencing across race that could not be attributed to offense, criminal record, or other legally accepted case processing variables (see also Cook and Hudson 1993). The results from this research project are consistent with previous research in another respect: the sentencing differential as a function of the race of the accused is not a characteristic of all offenses, but in this case is a characteristic of the offenses of sexual assault, bail violations, and drugs.

In this research project, we examined the impact of race on bail decisions and sentencing patterns. Two critical areas were studied: the decision to detain an accused under the bail provisions of the Criminal Code, and the decision to imprison convicted offenders. It seems clear that race plays an important role in the area of bail, although the effect seems restricted to events preceding the show-cause hearing, or what we have referred to as police bail. Some black offenders were denied bail when white accuseds with apparently comparable profiles were released.

As for sentencing, the impact of race is somewhat less clear-cut. We would draw two conclusions. First, that the effect of race is statistically weaker at the sentencing stage than at the bail stages. Second, that the sentencing differential only emerges when analyses are conducted on a subset of the five offenses included in this research. The size of the race-incarceration effect is not great in comparison to other predictors of sentence outcome and is less pronounced than the race-bail effect, but it is nonetheless statistically significant.

IV. Disparity and Discrimination

What can be concluded on the basis of this research about the processing of cases involving visible minority offenders? Researchers have to be rather more circumspect about the issue of discrimination in Canada as it relates to blacks, because, as noted earlier in this document, the necessary research is only now beginning to be conducted. We shall be in a much better position to draw inferences about discrimination once the research program of the Ontario Commission on Racism is published, early in 1996. Nevertheless, some tentative conclusions about the issues of disparity and discrimination can be offered.

Bail appears to be the critical decision point. As earlier research shows (Friedland 1965; Koza and Doob 1975*b*), being detained prior to trial can have important adverse effects on the accused's progress through the criminal process. It seems clear that visible minority accuseds are disadvantaged from the outset. The research reported here supports inferences of direct discrimination against members of visible minorities. Whether the discrimination at the stage of proceedings where the accused is interacting with the police is transmitted further through the criminal process is not known. What is clear is that blacks spend more time in detention prior to trial than one would expect on the basis of the legally relevant characteristics of their cases.

We would further argue that the locus of discrimination is strongest at the point of contact involving police officers. Once the judicial hearing (the show cause) is under way, the differential in release rates between blacks and whites disappears, with one important exception: accuseds facing drug-related charges. Drug offenders appear to constitute a special case. We do not know why. It may have to do with stereotypical attributions about black persons charged with drug-related crimes. Police officers may believe that a black person found in possession of a quantity of an illegal drug is likely to be a drug trafficker.

In many respects this report is about what we need to know, as well as what we have learned, about the processing of visible minority suspects, accuseds, and offenders in Canada. The drug accuseds are a good example of this. We do not know why the bail release and sentencing differentials are greatest for this category of offense. Nor at present do we know what proportion of drug offenders are members of visible minorities. We also need to know more about differential rates of offending. In the absence of criminal justice statistics relating to the race of the suspect, we do not know how differential offending or differential apprehension rates affect differential processing. We do know that certain members of visible minorities account for significant proportions of persons charged with criminal offenses. Some data from the study we have just described make this clear. For example, over one-third of the cases of bail violations in Toronto during the period when the sample was drawn involved black accused persons. Blacks accounted for a similar percentage of drug cases from the same period.

Largely because we lack the data, we are, then, less able to make concrete suggestions similar to those made by Tonry (1995) with respect to policies that have a discriminatory effect in the United States. Canada's sentencing "policy" endorses virtually all of the standard purposes of sentencing, and recent changes to that policy are very unlikely to make the sentencing process more predictable (Roberts and Von Hirsch 1995). Hence it is not possible in Canada to point to obvious discriminatory policies at sentencing such as those identified by Tonry (1995). This is not to suggest that such policies do not exist. It is only to suggest that they are implicit rather than explicit.

A. Treatment of Racial Minorities in Prison

In addition to the racial disproportions noted in Section I of this essay, research is beginning to suggest that racial discrimination of various forms is experienced by both black and Aboriginal inmates. In its study of corrections in Ontario, the Commission on Systemic Racism in the Ontario Criminal Justice System concluded that: "It is clear from our evidence that *racist language and attitudes plague the environments of many Ontario prisons*" (Commission on Systemic Racism in the Ontario Criminal Justice System 1994*a*, p. 27; emphasis in original). The commission's inquiry was restricted to the province of Ontario. However, there is no reason to suspect that the treatment of visible minority inmates would be very different in other parts of the country.

B. Criminal Justice Response to Racial Disproportions in Custodial Populations

Few Canadians would be surprised to learn that Canada's native population is overrepresented in the prison population. This fact has been brought to the attention of the public through news media reports for many years now. Criminal justice professionals have long been aware of the disproportion of Aboriginal Canadians in the country's penal institutions. This said, little has been done to alleviate the problem. The sentencing reform bill (C-41) introduced in June 1994 and which is scheduled to take effect in 1996 contains one brief mention of the problem. The bill contains a statutory statement of the purposes and principles of sentencing. The last of the five principles of sentencing enunciated by the bill states the following: "(e) all available sanctions other than imprisonment that are reasonable in the circumstances should be considered for all offenders, *with particular attention to the circumstances of aboriginal offenders*" (House of Commons Canada 1994, p. 9, emphasis added). It is unlikely that many judges are ignorant of the overrepresentation of Aboriginal Canadians in Canada's prisons. It is also unlikely that this statute alone will change much. The bill contains no concrete sentencing guidelines that might address the problem in a more effective way. Finally, the wording of the bill also reflects the nature of the concern about minorities in prison: almost all the emphasis to date has been on Aboriginals in prison. There has been no discussion of the racial disproportion of other visible minorities, and yet as we have noted, Canada's most populous province (Ontario) has a relatively high proportion of blacks in its custodial population.

Although there are significant gaps in our knowledge of the criminal justice system as it relates to visible minorities (particularly blacks), we believe that a number of broad conclusions can still be drawn.

1. Canada is a multiracial society with significant numbers of visible minorities. The percentage of the Canadian population that classify themselves as a member of a visible minority has been growing in recent years and will continue to grow in the future.

2. The Aboriginal population in Canada occupies a clearly subordinate stratum in Canadian society. This is reflected in a much higher unemployment rate and high levels of substance abuse, as well as many other indicators of the social and economic disadvantage suffered by Canadian Aboriginal people.

3. Aboriginals and blacks in Canada are overrepresented in the country's prison populations. The exact disproportion varies considerably across the country.

4. While Aboriginals have to date been the principal focus of attention and policy making, this is now changing, at least in Ontario and Quebec, provinces that are home to almost two-thirds of the Canadian population.

5. In Ontario, there has been a dramatic surge in prison admissions for blacks, particularly for drug offenses.

6. For Aboriginals at least, the racial disproportion in prison can be explained in part by higher rates of crime and/or higher rates of police attention to Aboriginal areas. For blacks, the data on rates of participation in crime are not yet available.

7. Systematic research on Aboriginal accuseds has demonstrated discrimination within the criminal justice system, particularly at the level of policing, but also with regard to sentencing and early release from prison.

8. More recent research on black accuseds in Ontario demonstrates a discrimination effect in the pretrial release of suspects by the police. Analysis of sentencing decisions revealed some residual discrimination, although not of the magnitude observed at the level of bail.

9. Common to the research on Aboriginals and blacks is the finding that discrimination effects are probably strongest at the policing stage.

REFERENCES

Angus Reid Group. 1995. *The CFRB-Angus Reid Group Poll: Crime.* Ottawa: Angus Reid Group.

Auger, D., A. N. Doob, P. Auger, and P. Driben. 1992. "Crime and Control in Three Nishnawbe-Aski Nation Communities: An Exploratory Investigation." *Canadian Journal of Criminology* 34:317–38.

Breton, Raymond. 1988. "Ethnic and Race Relations." In *The Canadian Encyclopedia,* vol. 2, 2d ed. Edmonton: Hurtig.

Brodeur, Jean-Paul, and Carol LaPrairie. 1992. *Justice for the Cree: Final Report.* Grand Council of the Crees of Quebec and the Cree Regional Authority, August.

Brown, I., and R. Hullin. 1992. "A Study of Sentencing in the Leeds Magistrates' Courts." *British Journal of Criminology* 32:41–53.

Canadian Centre for Justice Statistics. 1993. *Adult Correctional Services in Canada, 1992–1993.* Ottawa: Statistics Canada.

———. 1994. *Adult Correctional Services in Canada, 1993–1994.* Ottawa: Statistics Canada.

Cawsey, R. A. 1991. *Justice on Trial: Report of the Task Force on the Criminal Justice System and Its Impact on the Indian and Metis People of Alberta.* Edmonton: Attorney General and Solicitor General of Alberta.

Clairmont, D. 1989. *Discrimination in Sentencing: Patterns of Sentencing for Assault Convictions.* Halifax: Royal Commission on the Donald Marshall, Jr., Prosecution.

Clairmont, D., W. Barnwell, and A. O'Malley. 1989. *Sentencing Disparity and Race in the Nova Scotia Criminal Justice System.* Halifax: Royal Commission on the Donald Marshall, Jr., Prosecution.

Commission on Systemic Racism in the Ontario Criminal Justice System. 1994*a*. *Racism behind Bars: The Treatment of Black and Other Racial Minority Prisoners in Ontario Prisons. Interim Report.* Toronto: Queen's Printer for Ontario.

———. 1994*b*. *Racial Minority Youth Processing in the Criminal Justice System.* Toronto: Commission on Systemic Racism in the Ontario Criminal Justice System.

———. 1995. *Report of the Commission on Systemic Racism in the Ontario Criminal Justice System.* Toronto: Queen's Printer for Ontario.

Cook, D., and B. Hudson. 1993. *Racism and Criminology.* London: Sage.

Correctional Services Canada. 1994. *Basic Facts about Corrections in Canada,* 1993 ed. Ottawa: Minister of Supply and Services Canada.

Crow, I., and J. Cove. 1984. "Ethnic Minorities and the Courts." *Criminal Law Review* (July), pp. 413–17.

Dominion Bureau of Statistics. 1963. *1961 Census of Canada. Population Bulletin SP-2: Ethnic Groups.* Canada: Queen's Printer.

———. 1973. *1971 Census of Canada. Special Bulletin. Population: Specific Ethnic Groups.* Canada: Queen's Printer.

Doob, A. 1991. *Workshop on Collecting Race and Ethnicity Statistics in the Criminal Justice System.* Toronto: University of Toronto, Centre of Criminology.

———. 1994. *Race, Bail and Imprisonment.* Report for the Commission on Systemic Racism in the Ontario Criminal Justice System. Toronto: University of Toronto, Centre of Criminology.

Doob, A. N., M. G. Grossman, and R. Auger. 1994. "Aboriginal Homicides in Ontario." *Canadian Journal of Criminology* 36:29–62.

Friedland, M. 1965. *Detention before Trial.* Toronto: University of Toronto Press.

Gabor, T. 1994. "The Suppression of Crime Statistics on Race and Ethnicity: The Price of Political Correctness." *Canadian Journal of Criminology* 36:153–65.

Gartner, R., and A. N. Doob. 1994. "Special Issue: Trends in Criminal Victimization: 1988–1993." *Juristat* 14(13).

Griffiths, C., and S. Verdun-Jones. 1994. *Canadian Criminal Justice,* 2d ed. Toronto: Harcourt Brace.

Hagan, J. 1974. "Extra-legal Attributes and Criminal Sentencing: An Assessment of a Sociological Viewpoint." *Law and Society Review* 8:357–83.

Hagan, J., and K. Bumiller. 1983. "Making Sense of Sentencing: A Review and Critique of Sentencing Research." In *Research on Sentencing: The Search for Reform,* vol. 2, edited by A. Blumstein, J. Cohen, S. Martin, and M. Tonry. Washington, D.C.: National Academy Press.

Hogarth, John. 1971. *Sentencing as a Human Process.* Toronto: University of Toronto Press.

Hood, R. 1992. *Race and Sentencing: A Study in the Crown Court.* Oxford: Clarendon Press.

House of Commons Canada. 1994. *Bill C-41: An Act to Amend the Criminal Code (Sentencing) and Other Acts in Consequence Thereof.* Ottawa: House of Commons Canada.

Koza, P., and A. N. Doob. 1975*a*. "Some Empirical Evidence on Judicial Interim Release Proceedings." *Criminal Law Quarterly* 17:258–72.

———. 1975*b*. "The Relationship of Pretrial Custody to the Outcome of a Trial." *Criminal Law Quarterly* 17:391–400.

Labelle, M., S. Larose, and V. Piché. 1988. "West Indians." In *The Canadian Encyclopedia*, vol. 4, 2d ed. Edmonton: Hurtig.

Landau, Tammy C. 1994. "Policing and Security in Four Remote Aboriginal Communities: A Challenge to Coercive Models of Police Work." Ph.D. thesis, University of Toronto, Centre of Criminology.

LaPrairie, C. 1990. "The Role of Sentencing in the Over-representation of Aboriginal People in Correctional Institutions." *Canadian Journal of Criminology* 32:429–40.

McConville, M., and J. Baldwin. 1982. "The Influence of Race on Sentencing in England." *Criminal Law Review* (October), pp. 652–58.

McRuer, J. 1929. "The Attitude of the Citizen toward the Crime Problem." In *Proceedings of the 59th Annual Congress of the American Prison Association.* Toronto: American Prison Association.

Mitchell, Alanna. 1995. "1996 Census to Ask about Race: Statscan Says Laws Need Equity Data." *Globe and Mail* (September 11), p. 1.

Morrison, P., and M. Armstrong. 1993. *Research File for the Commission on Systemic Racism in the Ontario Criminal Justice System.* Ottawa: Canadian Centre for Justice Statistics.

Moyer, S., F. Kopelman, C. LaPrairie, and B. Billingsley. 1985. *Native and Non-Native Admissions to Provincial and Territorial Correctional Institutions.* Ottawa: Ministry of the Solicitor General Canada.

Nadin-Davis, P. 1982. *Sentencing in Canada.* Ottawa: Carswell.

Ontario Ministry of Citizenship. 1991. *Ontario: A Diverse and Changing Society: A Report on Selected Demographic Changes.* Toronto: Queen's Printer for Ontario.

Ontario Ministry of the Solicitor General and Correctional Services. 1994. *Racial Composition of Ontario's Adult Institutional Population.* North Bay: Ministry of the Solicitor General and Correctional Services, Research Services.

Palmer, D. 1996. "Determinants of Canadian Attitudes toward Immigration: More than Just Racism?" *Canadian Journal of Behavioural Science* (forthcoming).

Porter, J. 1972. *The Vertical Mosaic.* Toronto: University of Toronto Press.

Reed, Micheline. 1995. "Special Issue: Correctional Services in Canada: Highlights for 1993–94." *Juristat* 15(5).

Renner, K., and A. Warner. 1981. "The Standard of Social Justice Applied to an Evaluation of Criminal Cases Appearing before the Halifax Courts." *Windsor Yearbook of Access to Justice* 1:62–80.

Roberts, Julian V. 1994*a*. "Crime and Race Statistics: Toward a Canadian Solution." *Canadian Journal of Criminology* 36:175–85.

———. 1994*b*. *The Influence of Race on Sentencing Patterns in Toronto*. Toronto: Commission on Systemic Racism in the Ontario Criminal Justice System.
———. 1994*c*. "Special Issue: Crime and Race Statistics." *Canadian Journal of Criminology*, vol. 36 (April).
———. 1996. "The Role of Criminal Record in the Sentencing Process." In *Crime and Justice: A Review of Research*, vol. 22, edited by M. Tonry. Chicago: University of Chicago Press (forthcoming).
Roberts, Julian V., and Andrew von Hirsch. 1995. "Statutory Sentencing Reform: The Purpose and Principles of Sentencing." *Criminal Law Quarterly* 37:220–42.
Ruby, C. 1994. *Sentencing*. 4th ed. Toronto: Butterworths.
Sacco, V., and H. Johnson. 1990. *Patterns of Criminal Victimization in Canada*. Ottawa: Statistics Canada.
Schissel, Bernard. 1993. *Social Dimensions of Canadian Youth Justice*. Toronto: Oxford University Press.
Smith, D. 1994. "Race, Crime and Criminal Justice." In *The Oxford Handbook of Criminology*, edited by M. Maguire, R. Morgan, and R. Reiner. Oxford: Clarendon.
Statistics Canada. 1984. *1981 Census of Canada: Ethnic Origins*. Ottawa: Statistics Canada.
———. 1993. *1991 Census: Ethnic Origin: The Nation*. Ottawa: Statistics Canada.
Statistics Canada and the U.S. Bureau of the Census. 1992. *Challenges of Measuring an Ethnic World: Science, Politics and Reality*. Proceedings of the Joint Canada–United States Conference on the Measurement of Ethnicity, April 1–3. Ottawa: Statistics Canada.
Thomas, D. 1993. *The Foreign Born in the Federal Prison Population*. Ottawa: Carleton University, Canadian Law and Society Association Conference, June 8.
Tonry, M. 1994*a*. "Racial Disproportion in U.S. Prisons." *British Journal of Criminology* 34:97–115.
———. 1994*b*. "Racial Disparities Getting Worse in U.S. Prisons and Jails." *Overcrowded Times* 5(2):1, 16–17.
———. 1995. *Malign Neglect: Race, Crime, and Punishment in America*. New York: Oxford University Press.
Trevethan, Shelly. 1993. *Police-Reported Aboriginal Crime in Calgary, Regina, and Saskatoon*. Ottawa: Canadian Centre for Justice Statistics.
Turner, J. 1993. *Sentencing in Adult Criminal Provincial Courts: A Study of Six Canadian Jurisdictions*. Ottawa: Statistics Canada.
Walker, James W. St. G. 1988. "Blacks." In *The Canadian Encyclopedia*, vol. 1, 2d ed. Edmonton: Hurtig.
White, Pamela M., Jane Badets, and Viviane Renaud. 1992. "Measuring Ethnicity in Canadian Censuses." In *Challenges of Measuring an Ethnic World: Science, Politics and Reality*. Proceedings of the Joint Canada–United States Conference on the Measurement of Ethnicity, April 1–3. Ottawa: Statistics Canada and the U.S. Bureau of the Census.
Wolff, L. 1991. *Crime in Aboriginal Communities: Saskatchewan 1989*. Ottawa: Canadian Centre for Justice Statistics.

Pierre Tournier

Nationality, Crime, and Criminal Justice in France

ABSTRACT

Except for some prison statistics, official data in France distinguish only between French citizens and "foreigners." Foreigners are overrepresented among persons suspected of offending and among those admitted to and held in prison. Disparities are greatest among pretrial detainees whose cases are dealt with summarily. A sizable proportion of foreigners' offenses involve immigration; when these are deleted from the data, disparities are considerably lower. In addition, disparities would be lower still if it were possible to adjust the data to exclude all offenses by nonresident foreigners. Because this is not possible, all ratios of disproportion are overstated. Little research has been done to test discrimination hypotheses, and it is accordingly difficult to reach firm conclusions on the degree to which bias or xenophobia cause or increase disproportions.

Most Western countries face challenging policy issues related to racial and ethnic disparities in offending and justice system processing and are wrestling with other issues relating to immigration and foreign minorities. This volume, with its focus on ethnicity, crime, and immigration, is testament to the ubiquity of these issues. In like vein, in 1994, an international network funded by the European Community and entitled "Law, Crime, Control Policies and Racial, Ethnic, or Foreign Minorities in European Countries" was established at the initiative of Françoise Tulkens and Fabienne Brion of the University of Louvain-La-Neuve, Belgium. The framework is similar to that for this volume but gives explicit emphasis to "foreign minorities."

Pierre Tournier is senior research officer, specializing in correctional demographics, at the Centre de Recherches Sociologiques sur le Droit et les Institutions Pénales (CESDIP, Ministry of Justice, Paris) and teaches at the University of Paris I Panthéon Sorbonne.

0192-3234/97/0021-0009$01.00

France is a state governed by the rule of law. The only distinction made in statutory language is between French citizens and foreigners (a "foreigner" is someone who cannot claim French nationality). Administrative and statistical operations and records respect this citizenship-based division. The Constitution stipulates that French citizens are not to be differentiated on the base of race, origin, or religion. This egalitarian proviso, inherited from the Declaration of the Rights of Man, forms the basis of the "French model for integration" (Haut Conseil à l'Intégration 1993).

The January 6, 1978, law on "computerization, records, and civil liberties," for instance, prohibits the recording of data on racial origins or participation in any trade union, political, philosophical, or confessional activity (art. 31). A permanent national committee, Commission Nationale Informatique et Libertés (CNIL), is charged with making sure this law is enforced; any breach constitutes a criminal offense (arts. 41–44).

For this reason, French statistics do not make distinctions based on the notions of "race" or "ethnic group." This is true of administrative statistics and of studies and surveys in the social sciences. Some specialists in immigration and integration criticize this situation on grounds that the criterion of nationality is irrelevant in attempts to account for social phenomena involving alleged discrimination tied to individuals' origins (Simon 1993; Tribalat 1993).

Two distinct concepts—of "foreigner" and "immigrant"—are often confused in debates on social policy issues (insecurity, unemployment, education, health, etc.). This is true even at the highest governmental levels as evidenced in a statement by Mr. Balladur, prime minister at the time, printed in the daily paper *Le Monde* on April 20, 1993: "The Prime Minister notes a connection between insecurity and immigration, in view of the fact that half of drug-linked offences are committed by foreigners."

In both 1982 and 1990, slightly fewer than five million people in France, around nine percent of the total population, were "foreigners" or "immigrants." According to the definition adopted by the Haut Conseil à l'Intégration, an "immigrant" is someone who was born a foreigner, in a foreign country, and who resides in France. This status does not vary over the course of a lifetime because it refers to the place of birth. At the last census (1990), there were 3.6 million foreigners and 4.1 million immigrants in metropolitan France (table 1). Foreigners constituted 6.3 percent of the population. Of the 3.6 million for-

TABLE 1

Foreigners and Immigrants in France at the 1982 and 1990 Censuses

	1982	1990
Population in metropolitan France	54,270,000	56,630,000
A. French by Birth and French by acquisition born in France	49,420,000	51,760,000
B. French by acquisition born outside of France	1,170,000	1,290,000
C. Foreigners born outside of France	2,850,000	2,840,000
D. Foreigners born in France	830,000	740,000
C + D: Foreigners	3,680,000	3,580,000
B + C: Immigrants	4,020,000	4,130,000

SOURCE.—Haut Conseil à l'Intégration (1992).

eigners, 650,000 were Portuguese, 614,000 Algerian, 570,000 Moroccan, 250,000 Italian, 216,000 Spanish, 210,000 Tunisian, and 200,000 Turkish.

Between the 1982 and 1990 censuses, the number of foreigners dropped by 3 percent and the number of immigrants increased by 3 percent. These opposite trends led to controversies in the mass media, since the extreme right is always anxious to accuse the government of attempting to conceal the truth about immigration. The government attempted at the time to enlighten citizens on the definitions of these categories (*Le Monde*, September 26, 1991).

In its work on immigration, the Institut National d'Études Démographiques (INED, National Institute for Demographic Studies) also makes use of two other quite different notions. The "population of households headed by an immigrant" is composed of all individuals living in a household for which the reference person is an immigrant; 6.1 million people lived in such households in 1990 (Tribalat 1993). The "population of foreign origin" is composed of all people born in France and having at least one immigrant among his or her parents or grandparents, irrespective of the date of immigration. This population has been estimated at around 10 million individuals (Tribalat 1991).

Contrary to what these successive increments seem to suggest (3.6 million, 4.1 million, 6.1 million, 10 million), these successively larger subgroups do not each encompass the smaller ones that precede them. The population of foreigners is not a subset of the population of immigrants: 31 percent of immigrants are not foreigners, and 21 percent of foreigners are not immigrants (1990). As Michèle Tribalat (1993) has shown, the notion of "population of households headed by an immigrant" opens the path to new analyses on integration.

Whatever the analytical or empirical benefits of all of these different categories, only one of them—nationality, or more specifically alien status (the distinction between French and non-French)—is used to measure criminality in France. It may be deemed regrettable and the distinction found much too simplified for the study of relations between immigration and crime and the establishment of indicators of integration through measurement of deviant behavior. Or, again, it may be celebrated for the defense of civil liberties by the elimination in records maintained by the criminal justice system of any distinctions among French citizens on the basis of the way in which they acquired their citizenship. The official policy does not, however, prevent recourse to sociodemographic field surveys. They remain to be done.

To further complicate matters, the category "foreigners" shown in police, judicial, and prison statistics is not a subgroup of the alien population counted by the French census (the 3.6 million people). Suspected, sentenced, or imprisoned foreigners may be people whose papers are not in order, tourists, or seasonal workers, none of which categories is counted by the national statistics agency (Institut National de la Statistique et des Études Économiques [INSEE]). This must be taken into account in determining the terms of comparison (for the calculation of rates). The numerator, based on numbers of people arrested, imprisoned, and so on, whether they are legal or illegal residents, tourists, or refugees, often does not match up with the denominator, people counted as foreigners in the relevant census year.

Moreover, comparison between rates for French nationals and foreigners can be misleading because all naturalized citizens, including first- and second-generation immigrants, are counted as French. Thus, for example, persons born in Morocco or to Moroccan parents who are naturalized are counted in the French national data and rates while persons born in Morocco or to Moroccan parents who are legal residents but not naturalized are counted in the data and rates for foreigners.

Some penal data do take the nationality of suspects into consideration. However, nothing comparable is available for victims. This is a major gap in French criminal statistics. A number of victimization surveys have been conducted (Zauberman 1990), but they are not useful for purposes of this essay, since they include data on sex, age, occupation or social category, and size of the town or city, but not the nationality of the victim or any other variables pertaining to his or her origins.

I. Offending

In French law, offenses are divided into three categories on the basis of their seriousness: *crimes* or major offenses, judged by a *cour d'assises*, at which a jury sits; *délits* or moderately serious offenses, judged by a *correctionnel cour*; and *contraventions* or minor offenses, judged by police courts. Only *crimes* and *délits* are punishable by prison sentences: at least ten years for a *crime* and ten years at most for a *délit*. The French terms are used in this essay.

Since 1972, the Ministry of the Interior has published a yearly report on major and minor crimes recorded by the police and *gendarmerie*. The data refer primarily to three kinds of measures: reported acts, elucidated acts, and suspects.

"Reported acts" are *crimes* and *délits* for which a police report was completed and transmitted to the public prosecutor's office by the police or *gendarmerie*. Excluded from these reports are offenses of which the police have knowledge but for which no report was filed, offenses handled by other administrations, *contraventions*, homicides or injuries by negligence, motoring offenses, and last, of course, offenses of which public agencies lack knowledge. "Reported acts" data to some degree overstate the volume of crime because of exaggerated or imaginary complaints (mostly connected with loss claims against property insurance) and redundant reports resulting from the same act being recorded by several agencies.

"Elucidated acts" are *crimes* and *délits* attributed by the police or gendarmerie to one or several identified individuals. "Elucidation" is equivalent to "clearance" in English-speaking countries.

"Suspects" are individuals who are believed, on the basis of sufficient evidence, to be the perpetrators or accomplices of an act. The only sociodemographic features recorded for suspects are sex, age ("of age" and "under age"), and alien status ("French" and "foreign"), the last variable not being cross-tabulated to sex and age.

Reported acts, elucidated acts, and suspects are concepts used in Ministry of the Interior statistics since their inception (1949). They have no legal meaning. Often the facts underlying reported acts are

TABLE 2

Reported Acts and Police Suspects, 1993

Offense	Reported Acts		Suspects	
	Number	Percentage	Number	Percentage
All thefts (including receiving and concealing):	2,640,417	68.1	275,726	39.9
Those involving cars and motor bikes	1,386,703	*35.7**	71,595	*10.4**
White-collar crimes:	409,246	10.5	86,528	12.5
Those involving bad checks	162,401	*4.2**	18,177	*2.6**
Intentional personal offenses	95,092	2.4	66,711	9.7
Morals offenses	26,569	.7	15,521	2.2
Breaches of domestic and parental duties	31,103	.8	25,124	3.6
Narcotics	64,841	1.7	59,852	8.7
Immigration laws	49,777	1.3	45,415	6.6
Destruction and deterioration of property:	419,961	10.8	39,891	5.8
Those involving private vehicles	269,931	*7.0**	14,142	*2.0**
Miscellaneous *délits*	144,888	3.7	75,687	11.0
Total	3,881,894	100.0	690,455	100.0

Source.—Ministère de l'Intérieur (1993).
*Percentages in italic are subsets of more inclusive categories.

not ascertained; simply, a complaint was filed. Elucidation is provisional and awaits corroboration by the justice system. Finally, the suspect is not someone against whom legal charges are brought but a person suspected by the police who may subsequently be exonerated.

A. The Three Levels of Police Statistics

The 3,881,894 *crimes* and *délits* reported in 1993 (in metropolitan France) are primarily property offenses (68 percent are thefts or receiving and concealing), as table 2 shows. The number of offenses connected with motor vehicles is noteworthy: over one-third of all reported acts and over half of all thefts involve motor vehicles. Eleven percent of recorded acts involve destruction and deterioration of property, the same as for white-collar crimes. Personal offenses represent only 4 percent of total *crimes* and *délits.* Fewer than 2 percent involve violation of narcotics laws. *Délits* concerning immigration laws constituted only 1 percent of all reported acts.

In 1993, there were 1,250,293 elucidated acts (an elucidation rate of 32 percent). This overall rate of fewer than three acts elucidated for ten reported obscures considerable variations depending on the nature of the case.

The elucidation rate exceeds nine out of ten recorded acts for shoplifting, receiving and concealing, white-collar crime (especially for cases involving checks), narcotics cases, and délits involving immigration laws. It ranges from seven to eight out of ten for most personal offenses and breaches of domestic or parental duties. It ranges between one of ten for thefts involving cars and motorbikes and other simple larcenies affecting private individuals, and one of five for theft with violence, with intermediate rates for housebreaking, and theft with entry by trickery, and so on.

Thus the composition of elucidated acts differs substantially from the composition of reported acts. Thefts and receiving and concealing are only 29.5 percent of the total (compared with 68.1 percent of reported acts). They are exceeded by white-collar crime in general (36 percent of elucidated acts). Intentional personal offenses double from 4.2 percent of reported acts to 9 percent, and the proportion of immigration offenses increase by three (4 percent), as does the number of narcotics-related cases (5.5 percent).

Finally, there were 690,455 suspects in 1993, or 100 suspects for every 180 elucidated acts. This average also conceals major variations depending on the nature of the crimes, but these are difficult to analyze. Several individuals may be suspected of the same *crime* or *délit* if there are co-offenders and accomplices. Reciprocally, several reported cases may be attributed to the same individual.

Thus, the shift in focus from reported acts to suspects yields not only a considerable change in magnitude (in 1993, from 3.9 million acts to 690,000 suspects) but also basic changes in the composition of offenses involved.

B. *Suspects*

Of the 690,455 suspects counted in 1993, 136,799, or 20 percent, were foreigners, although this percentage is distorted by inclusion of immigration and related offenses. The percentage ranges from 96.3 percent for violation of immigration laws to 3.5 percent for housebreaking involving second homes (table 3). This compares with the 6.3 percent of the population officially counted as "foreign."

In 1993, nearly one out of three foreign suspects (32 percent) was

TABLE 3

Individuals Suspected by the Police, by Foreign Nationality and Selected Offenses, 1993

	Percentage Foreign
Immigration laws	96.3
Forged identification papers or other documents	70.4
Pickpocketing	42.6
Trafficking in narcotics	34.1
Coinage offense	27.9
Shoplifting	21.5
Theft with violence without firearm	20.9
Narcotics use/resale	19.0
Housebreaking in second home	3.5
Bad checks	4.8
Forgery and use of stolen checks	10.3
Housebreaking (exclusive of second homes)	11.4

SOURCE.—Ministère de l'Intérieur (1993).

accused of violation of the immigration laws—an offense that almost by definition involves few nationals. If immigration offenses are excluded, foreigners represent only 14.4 percent of all suspects (instead of 20 percent).

If the category "forged identification papers and other administrative documents," which involves foreigners in seven of ten cases, is excluded, the proportion of foreigners among suspects drops to 13.8 percent.

Between 1972 and 1993, the number of suspects annually varied from a high of 925,000 in 1985 to a low of 515,000 in 1976. As a whole, there were fewer suspects at the end of the period than at its onset: 690,000 in 1993 compared with 727,000 in 1972. The foreign proportion among suspects increased steadily during those years irrespective of sharp year-to-year changes in the total number. The foreign proportion began at around 10 percent in the early 1970s, fluctuated around 15 percent from 1976 to 1985, and rose to 20 percent in 1992 and 1993.

Both in absolute numbers and as a proportion of foreign suspects, immigration offenses involving foreigners increased steadily from 1973 to 1993. In 1973, there were 81,846 foreign suspects, of which 5,699, or 7 percent, involved immigration laws. By 1993, there were 136,799 foreign suspects, of which 43,723, slightly more than 25 percent, involved immigration laws. The absolute number of foreign suspects in immigration law cases thus increased by a factor of eight.

In 1993, the Ministry of the Interior counted 45,415 suspects for violation of immigration laws, over 96 percent of whom were foreigners. When this type of offense is excluded from aggregate data on suspects, the proportion of foreigners among suspects increased from 10 percent in 1973 to 14 percent in 1976 and fluctuated between 13 and 15 percent from then to 1993.

The suspect rate is the ratio between the number of individuals suspected during a year and the average number of inhabitants for that same year. Denominators are taken from the French censuses conducted by INSEE.

Census figures show the proportion of foreigners to be 5.3 percent in 1968, 6.5 percent in 1975, 6.8 percent in 1982, and 6.4 percent in 1990. These percentages are much lower than those found for police suspects.

However, use of the INSEE data to calculate the suspect rate with respect to nationality raises two sorts of methodological problems: the census does not include all those categories of foreigners liable of being suspected, and for those categories that are included, the level of omissions is much higher for foreigners than for nationals.

Foreigners who reside habitually in metropolitan France should in theory be included in the census. The figures do not, however, include tourists, seasonal workers, asylum seekers, or any other person residing in France for a short period of time. Illegal aliens also are not included.

The only way to obtain meaningful rates is to subtract from the numerator all categories of foreigners who are not counted in the denominator. In practice, this correction can only be made for "illegal aliens" (or more specifically, those foreigners suspected of violation of the immigration laws).

The second problem is only mentioned here, because it has been discussed at length elsewhere. For a variety of reasons, the official census undercounts foreigners just as in the United States the decennial censuses undercount members of minority groups: "Omissions in data collection are mostly due to the poor integration of certain categories of foreigners, evidenced by their illiteracy, precarious housing conditions, and high geographic mobility, not to mention the suspicion with which they regard an operation of this type, and even their deliberate abstention" (INSEE 1984).

Depending on whether immigration offenses are included in the calculation, and relying on the official census data and official data on suspects, foreigners are 2.5 (excluding immigration offenses) to 3.6 (including them) times more likely than French nationals to be suspects. This is, of course, the upper-bound estimate since the census undercounts reduce the denominator and the presence of illegals, tourists, and other nonresidents increases the numerator.

II. Processing of Cases

The penal process may be divided into three broad phases: the prosecutorial decisions by whether to prosecute and for what, the preliminary investigation, and the court decision about sentence. Unfortunately, reliable national data on prosecution and investigation are not available. Thus only at the sentencing stage can meaningful analyses be made.

Each year, the prosecutors' offices deliver reports of their main activities to the Ministry of Justice. These include information on complaints, assignment of cases, and investigations. These data, however, indicate neither sociodemographic characteristics nor the nationality of individual suspects.

Until recently, the situation was the same for the preliminary investigation stage. However, an investigations data system established in January 1985 yields some information about defendants, including nationality. Analysis of these data shows that the proportion of defendants placed in pretrial detention is much higher for foreigners than for nationals. Conversely, foreigners are less often granted pretrial surveillance (a measure that avoids incarceration by placing a number of constraints on the suspect). Unfortunately, these data are not disaggregated for the nature of the offense (distinguishing only between *crimes* and *délits*), which limits their value. Proposals to enrich data collection at this level are under consideration.

A. Sentencing

Decisions about sentencing are better documented in statistical systems than are decisions at earlier stages, although formidable problems have been encountered in constructing homogeneous chronological series integrating the most recent data (Tournier et al. 1989). The analysis here concerns the year 1991, the most recent year for which published figures are available.

Some points of law must be clarified by way of introduction. Sentences involving personal restraint are divided into two categories: *ré-*

clusion criminelle, in English, penal detention (for *crimes*); and imprisonment (for *délits*). A sentence to imprisonment may be totally suspended, partly suspended (a portion of the sentence is suspended and the balance is executed), or unsuspended. Suspension may be "simple" (without surveillance by a probation officer), "on probation" (with surveillance by a probation officer), or "involve the obligation to do community service work" (a community service order is the main sentence and is considered an alternative sentence).

The 557,832 sentenced individuals counted in 1991 on the basis of their criminal record (*crimes*, *délits*, and the most serious *contraventions*, called "5th class *contraventions*") include 435,652 French nationals (78.1 percent), 81,737 foreigners (14.7 percent), and 40,443 "nationality unknown" and "stateless" (together, 7.3 percent). The large figure for the last category is noteworthy. If this last category is excluded (as in the tables below), the proportion of persons sentenced who were foreigners is 15.8 percent.

Table 4 shows the percentages of foreigners among people sentenced in 1991 for *crimes*, high volume *délits*, and 5th class *contraventions*. Immigration offenses by themselves powerfully influence the overall disproportion since 93.6 percent of those sentenced are foreigners. If this offense is excluded, the proportion of foreigners sentenced drops from 15.8 percent to 13.6 percent. The highest disproportions among the offenses shown are the immigration offenses, forgery (40.6 percent foreigners), and narcotics offenses (28.2 percent foreigners). These three offenses always (immigration) or often (forgery, involving entry or similar documents, and narcotics trafficking) have transnational features. For other offenses shown in table 4, the largest foreign disproportions are considerably lower. Nineteen percent of rape and assault and battery *crimes* and 18 percent of assault and battery *délits* involve foreigners.

Generally speaking, offenses in which foreigners are more frequently involved are more often punished by sentences to confinement than are *crimes*, *délits*, and 5th class *contraventions* taken as a whole. For instance, the proportions of executed (that is, unsuspended) sentences—20 percent for the entire group—are 62 percent for immigration law violations, 29 percent for forgery, 46 percent for narcotics offenses, 83 percent for assault and battery *crimes*, 94 percent for rape, and 25 percent for assault and battery *délits*.

This may partly explain why, overall, foreigners are more likely to receive the severer forms of sentences than are French citizens and less

TABLE 4

Proportion of Foreigners among Sentenced Individuals, by Type of *Crimes*, *Délits* for Which at Least 2,000 Sentences Were Ordered, and 5th Class *Contraventions*, 1991

Offenses	Total*	Foreigners	Percentage Foreigners
Crimes:			
Rape	886	165	18.6
Theft, receiving and concealing, destruction	843	117	13.9
Intentional manslaughter	534	79	14.8
Intentional assault and battery	304	58	19.1
Attack on public safety and other	34	4	11.8
Total crimes	2,601	423	16.3
Délits:			
Theft, receiving and concealing	132,638	22,328	16.8
Road offenses	108,524	8,624	7.9
Intentional assault and battery	22,452	3,975	17.7
Checks	21,927	2,291	10.4
Narcotics offenses	18,849	5,321	28.2
Embezzlement, breach of trust	15,231	2,133	14.0
Immigration laws	14,026	13,129	93.6
Administrative and judiciary order	13,993	2,125	15.2
Unintentional injury	12,700	994	7.8
Destruction deterioration	11,133	1,485	13.3
Breach of domestic duties	8,949	702	7.8
Military offenses	7,648	442	5.8
Occupational and medical insurance	6,385	1,120	17.5
Forgery of public or private documents	6,126	2,485	40.6
Morals offenses	6,037	812	13.5
Trade and transportation of weapons	4,959	828	16.7
Attack on the environment	3,510	207	5.9
Unintentional homicide	2,915	232	8.0
Other personal offenses	2,881	340	11.8
Fraud and counterfeiting	2,135	228	10.7
Total *délits*†	431,232	71,178	16.5
5th class *contraventions*	83,556	10,136	12.1
Total offenses*	517,389	81,737	15.8

Source.—Ministère de la Justice (1991).

* Excluding "nationality unknown" and stateless individuals.

† *Délits* total includes offenses not listed for which fewer than 2,000 individuals were sentenced.

TABLE 5

Proportion of Foreigners among Sentenced Individuals, by Nature of Sentence, 1991

Offenses	Total*	Foreigners	Percentage Foreigners
Life sentence	87	28	32.2
Penal detention, for limited term	1,764	269	15.2
Imprisonment, unsuspended	86,489	26,725	30.9
Imprisonment, partly suspended:	18,766	2,773	14.8
Simple	8,211	1,535	18.7
On probation	10,555	1,238	11.7
Imprisonment, suspended:	195,874	23,255	11.9
Simple	166,643	20,646	12.4
On probation	22,494	1,949	8.7
Community service order	6,737	660	9.8
Fine:	149,802	19,906	13.3
Unsuspended or partly	137,122	18,541	13.5
Suspended	12,679	1,365	10.8
Alternative sentence	35,253	5,151	14.6
Rehabilitation measure	19,884	2,604	13.1
Exemption from punishment	9,471	1,026	10.8
Total*	517,389	81,737	15.8

Source.—Ministère de la Justice (1991).
* Excluding "nationality unknown" and stateless.

likely to receive less severe sentences. For example, although foreigners make up 15.8 percent of all individuals sentenced, they receive 31 percent of the executed (unsuspended) sentences imposed, as table 5 shows. Conversely, they represent fewer than 11 percent of those exempted from punishment altogether and fewer than 10 percent of those given suspended sentences on probation or with community service obligations.

A similar pattern is evident in data on the lengths of sentences imposed in 1991, as table 6 shows. This table reports data on executed (unsuspended) and partly suspended confinement sentences. Although only 15.8 percent of sentenced individuals were foreigners, they constitute 27.8 percent of those sentenced to confinement, including 30 percent, or higher, of those sentenced to terms of imprisonment between three months and five years and 32 percent of those sentenced to life imprisonment.

We were able to take the analysis a step further by comparing the

TABLE 6

Proportion of Foreigners among Sentenced Individuals, by Length of Confinement, 1991

	Total*	Foreigners	Percentage Foreigners
Penal detention:			
Five to less than ten years	891	159	17.8
Ten to less than twenty years	797	98	12.3
Twenty years and over (excluding life)	76	12	15.8
Life	87	28	32.2
Imprisonment:			
Less than one month	9,873	1,292	13.1
One month to less than three months	33,219	7,673	23.1
Three months to less than six months	26,340	8,706	33.1
Six months to less than one year	18,987	6,185	32.6
One year to less than three years	13,032	4,000	30.7
Three years to less than five years	2,612	1,022	39.1
Five years and over	1,192	620	52.0
Total*	107,106	29,795	27.8

SOURCE.—Ministère de la Justice (1991).
* Excluding "nationality unknown" and stateless.

sentences pronounced against nationals and foreigners for some offenses. We used the most disaggregated level of nomenclature used in Ministry of Justice publications and examined the sixteen *délits* for which at least 4,000 sentences were handed down following trial in 1991.

These data are based on the "main offense," that is, the most serious category of offense of which the offender was convicted. This necessarily creates a bias since sentences are generally heavier for multiple offenders. However, this bias is not likely seriously to distort the analyses since the "main offense" was the only offense in 75 percent of *délits* in 1991. The proportion of cases involving only one offense is no doubt lower for foreigners than for nationals because of the violations of immigration laws, but the difference is minor (there are no more than 5,000 sentences for illegal entrance and residence offenses in cases in which other offenses were involved).

The courts have a greater propensity to sentence foreigners to prison, irrespective of the offense considered. The first phase of analysis covered the variations in the proportion of offenders sentenced to a partly suspended or unsuspended prison term. Overall, among individuals convicted of *délits* at trial, and sentenced, 21 percent receive confinement sentences, ranging from 75 percent for illegal entrance or residence of a foreigner to 0.7 percent for unintentional injury by a driver. However, when the *délits* are disaggregated, the percentage of cases involving foreigners that result in confinement penalties (44.1 percent) is more than two-and-a-half times higher than for French citizens. Although the high confinement rate (76 percent) for immigration offenses, of which French citizens are seldom convicted, explains part of the disproportion, for narcotics offenses, foreign offenders are more than twice as likely to be sentenced to confinement. For nearly every offense shown in table 7, the foreign confinement percentage is higher.

In the second part of the analysis, we separated out those *délits* for which the percentage of prison sentences (unsuspended or partly suspended) reached or exceeded 20 percent, and we studied the length of the unsuspended portion. Table 8 shows distribution of sentences to at least one year. For sentencing to long terms, the only significant difference pertains to possession and purchasing of narcotics: 74 percent of the foreigners were given sentences to less than one year as opposed to 50 percent of nationals. Otherwise, the percentages are similar.

We have done similar analyses for executed sentences of less than three months, alternative (community service) sentences, and fines. These analyses are not reported here. The differences are small, and not always favorable to French nationals.

B. *Enforcement of Sentences Involving Personal Restraint*

Data on the nationality of prisoners in pretrial detention or serving a sentence may be found in three sources. Quarterly statistics on the prison population, compiled since 1968, show the situation for the "stock" prison population on the first day of the three-month period, along with admissions and discharges during the previous period. Nationality data are maintained only for the stock population and are cross-tabulated only with sex data. These data are serialized by the CESDIP (SEPT database). To augment these data, the correctional authorities have set up a computerized data system based on the up-to-date National Prisoners File (FND). Monthly statistics are maintained for foreigners imprisoned for violation of article 19 of the November 2, 1945, *ordonnance* on the entrance and residence of foreigners. These statistics indicate the number of "article 19 foreigners," in

TABLE 7

Sentencing following Trial, Percentage of Unsuspended Prison Sentences (With or Without Partial Suspension) for the Most Frequent *Délits*, According to Alien Status, 1991

	Total		French		Foreigners	
	Number	Percentage	Number	Percentage	Number	Percentage
Illegal entrance or residence of a foreigner	8,875	75.0	202	36.6	8,500	75.9
Theft with violence	5,902	57.7	4,369	57.3	1,176	63.5
Possession and purchasing of narcotics	5,642	51.4	3,955	40.8	1,495	80.1
Housebreaking	15,865	37.0	13,046	36.7	1,780	48.5
Illegal use of narcotics	4,686	28.7	3,687	23.3	795	55.8
Simple receiving and concealing	12,259	24.7	9,258	19.9	2,319	46.1
Simple larceny	63,264	23.8	49,592	21.2	9,736	39.7
Intentional assault and battery with TWI, less than one week with aggravating circumstances*	6,186	22.8	5,021	21.3	969	29.4
Destruction of property	6,460	13.7	5,333	12.8	761	23.7
Intentional assault and battery with TWI, more than one week without aggravating circumstances*	8,034	12.6	6,502	12.1	1,190	15.7
Insulting a representative of the public authorities	4,395	8.5	3,787	7.8	449	14.0
Bad checks	6,129	6.7	5,292	6.7	500	7.0
Drunken driving	76,692	5.9	69,830	5.9	4,875	6.5
Desertion of home	4,738	5.6	4,190	5.4	327	6.4
Hit-and-run offense	6,322	4.3	5,519	4.1	571	5.6
Unintentional injury by a driver	6,388	.7	5,758	.6	404	1.5
Total *délits*	325,538	20.8	262,241	16.7	49,255	44.1

SOURCE.—Ministère de la Justice (1991).
*TWI = temporary work incapacitation.

TABLE 8

Sentencing following Trial, Percentage of Unsuspended Prison Sentences (With or Without Partial Suspension) for at Least One Year, According to Alien Status, 1991*

	Total		French		Foreigners	
	Number	Percentage	Number	Percentage	Number	Percentage
Possession and purchasing of narcotics	2,901	60.6	1,615	50.3	1,198	74.1
Theft with violence	3,408	39.9	2,502	39.8	747	42.8
Illegal use of narcotics	1,347	23.5	858	23.8	444	23.9
Housebreaking	5,875	21.3	4,787	21.7	864	20.4
Simple receiving and concealing	3,023	20.2	1,842	19.1	1,069	22.0
Intentional assault and battery with TWI, less than one week with aggravating circumstances†	1,410	14.4	1,073	13.2	285	19.6
Simple larceny	15,033	11.2	10,525	11.3	3,864	11.2

Source.—Ministère de la Justice (1991).

* *Délits* for which at least 20 percent of sentences involved unsuspended imprisonment (with or without partial suspension).

† TWI = temporary work incapacitation.

effect "illegal aliens" as they might be called in other countries, in prison on the first day of each month and the number of article 19 foreigners incarcerated during the previous month, broken down to distinguish between those whose behavior includes "no other offense" and those "including another offense." This data series has been in existence since September 1983.

1. *Evolution of the Number of Prisoners according to Nationality.* The data shown in figure 1 indicate the percentages of French citizens and foreigners imprisoned in metropolitan France between 1968 and 1995. Although the French prison population fell from 34,083 in 1968 to 26,072 in 1975, nearly 24 percent, as a result of changes in legislation or administrative regulations, the population increased steadily thereafter. In twenty years, the number of prisoners went from 26,032 on January 1, 1975, to 51,623 on January 1, 1995—nearly a 100 percent increase—the only exceptions being caused by amnesties following presidential elections and collective pardons granted on national holidays.

The proportion of foreign prisoners oscillated between 14 and 16 percent from 1968 to 1974, after which it rose steadily, to peak at 31.4 percent on January 1, 1993. It declined slightly in 1993 and 1994. The trend was even more marked among female prisoners. Eight percent of female prisoners in 1968 were foreign, half the percentage of foreign male prisoners in that year. By 1995 that number had tripled to 25 percent.

Between 1975 and 1995, the number of foreign prisoners increased by 3.2, compared with an increase of 1.7 times for French prisoners. Furthermore, the periods of declining prison populations are much less marked for foreigners. This differential trend may be partly accounted for by the high figures for pretrial prisoners among the foreign population. However, the data available for "stock" do not enable us to verify this hypothesis.

The increase in the number of foreign prisoners was attended by an equally marked change of structure in terms of nationality. On January 1, 1995, the population of foreigners in prison was broken down as shown in table 9, which disaggregates the data by geographical region and also shows separate national origin data for nationalities that represent more than 1,000 prisoners. Nearly half of foreign prisoners derive from the three Maghreb countries. Algerians constitute the largest category of non-French nationals (4,076 prisoners), followed by Mo-

TABLE 9

Foreign Prison Population, by Nationality, January 1, 1995

	Number	Percentage
Total prisoners	51,623	100
French	36,644	71.0
European Community	2,295	4.4
Other Europe	731	1.4
Algeria	4,076	7.9
Morocco	2,712	5.3
Tunisia	1,096	2.1
Other Africa	2,383	4.6
Americas	443	.9
Asia and Oceania	1,192	2.3
Stateless or unknown	46	.1

Source.—Centre de Recherches Sociologiques sur le Droit et les Institutions Pénales (CESDIP) (1968–95).

roccans (2,712) and Tunisians (1,096). For no other nationality did the number of inmates in French prisons on January 1, 1995, exceed 700.

Figure 2 shows the composition of foreign prisoners in France from 1968 to 1995. The European share fell from two-fifths to one-fifth during that period. The Maghreb percentage (Algeria, Tunisia, Morocco) fluctuated between the high forties and the low fifties. The other categories showed increases by approximately eight times. In 1995, 16 percent of foreign prisoners belonged to the group "Other Africa," 3 percent were from the Americas, and 8 percent from Asia.

2. *Incarceration Flows.* Of the 82,201 prison commitments recorded in metropolitan France in 1993, 26,948 (33 percent) involved foreigners. This is slightly higher than the 29 percent representation of foreigners among the stock prison population on January 1, 1995. This gives us a ratio for "stock/flow," indicative of the average length of detention, which is lower on average for foreigners (6.8 months) than for French citizens (7.4 months). Table 10 shows the composition of prison admissions in 1993 by nationality.

Table 11 shows admissions by five types of detention: "pretrial/summary" (rapid procedure), "pretrial/other" (generally on a committal order issued by an investigating judge), "final sentence," "civil imprisonment" (for debt to the state), and "other cases." The starkest disproportion is among the people incarcerated for a rapid procedure (47

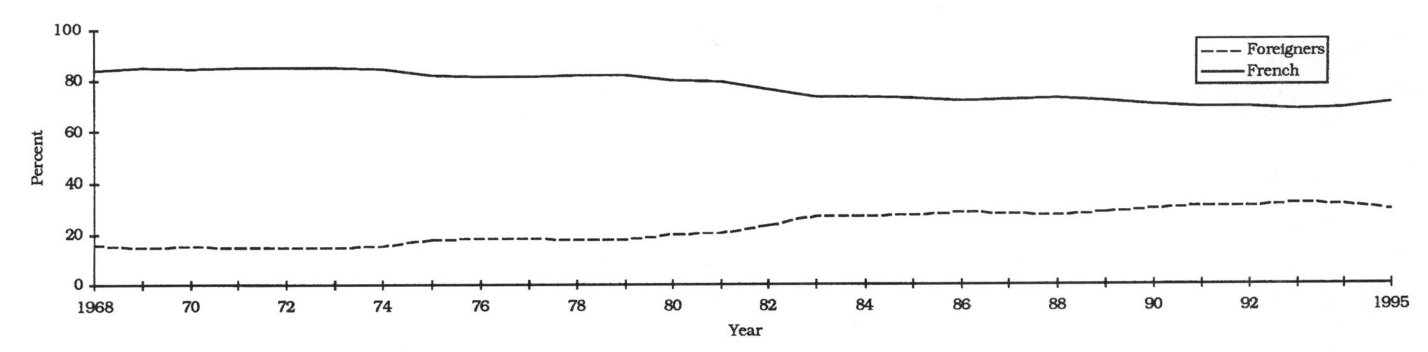

FIG. 1.—Composition of prison population on January 1, French citizens and foreigners, 1968–95. Source: Centre de Recherches Sociologiques sur le Droit et les Institutions Pénales (CESDIP) (1968–95).

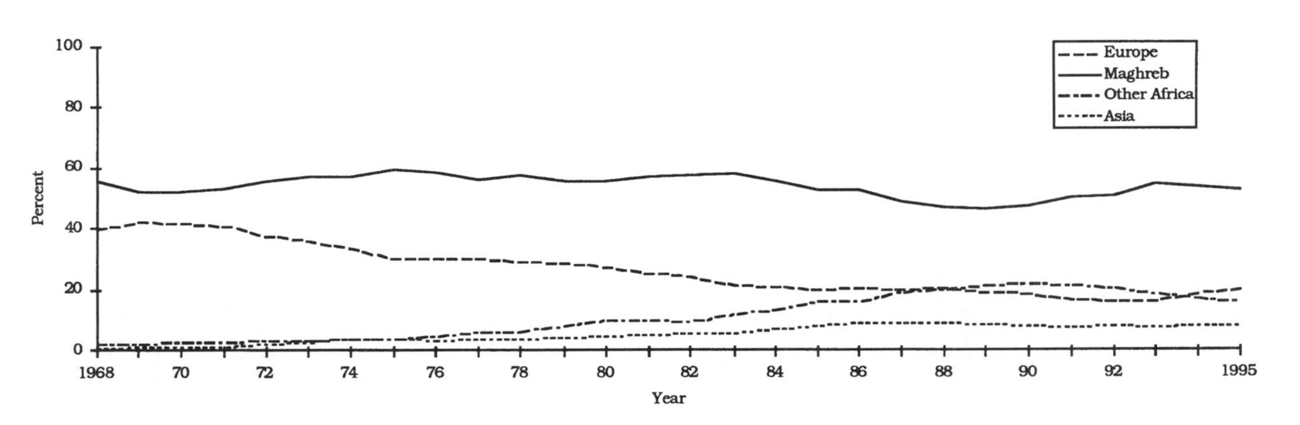

FIG. 2.—Composition of foreign prison population in French prisons on January 1, 1968–95. Source: Centre de Recherches Sociologiques sur le Droit et les Institutions Pénales (CESDIP) (1968–95).

TABLE 10

Admissions, by Nationality, 1993

	Number	Percentage
Total admissions	82,201	100
French	55,253	67.2
Foreigners:	26,891	32.8
European Community countries	2,557	3.1
Non–European Community European countries	1,313	1.6
Maghreb	15,250	18.6
French-speaking Africa except Maghreb	4,496	5.5
Non-French-speaking Africa	1,042	1.3
Asia and Oceania	1,971	2.4
North America	43	*
Central and South America	219	.3
Unknown	18	*
Stateless	39	*

SOURCE.—Ministère de la Justice (1995).
* Less than .05.

TABLE 11

Admissions, by Nationality, 1993

	Total	Number	Percentage Foreigners
A. By admission type:			
Total	82,201	26,948	32.8
Pretrial/summary	34,106	16,114	47.2
Pretrial/other	33,240	8,970	27.0
Final sentence	14,386	1,721	12.0
Civil prison	225	44	19.6
Other	244	99	40.6
B. By offense category:			
Immigration laws	9,364	9,461	98.2
Total (less immigration laws)	72,567	17,487	24.1
Crimes	5,864	1,063	18.1
Délits and contraventions	66,703	16,424	24.6

SOURCE.—Ministère de la Justice (1995).

TABLE 12

Percentage of Admissions by Pretrial Detention and Breakdown of Summary Trials, by Nationality and Offense, 1993

Offense	Total	Foreigners
Immigration laws	90.3	90.5
Simple larceny	69.7	79.5
Drunken driving	83.2	88.7
Theft with violence and other aggravated thefts	49.9	56.8
Intentional assault and battery	47.6	53.6
Receiving and concealing	39.4	46.0
Trafficking in narcotics	22.2	27.3
Morals offenses	22.0	25.9
Embezzlement, swindling, breach of trust	20.8	26.1

Source.—Ministère de la Justice (1995).

percent), that is, with no investigation. This may be related to the nature of the offense. Considering that foreigners make up only 6.3 percent of the French population, they are heavily overrepresented within all admission categories, especially the pretrial detention categories which make up the vast majority of all admissions.

Part B of table 11 shows admissions by offense type. Overall, foreign persons constituted 32.8 percent of all admissions but 98.2 percent of immigration offenses. If immigration offenses are excluded, the proportion of admissions of foreigners falls to 24.1 percent. Among the most serious offenses—*crimes*—the foreign percentage is 18.1 percent. By offense category (data not shown) the greatest foreign disproportions were for narcotics trafficking (42.8 percent of admissions) and "receiving and concealing" (33.2 percent).

Table 12 breaks down pretrial admissions in 1993 by nationality and offense, showing the percentages of French nationals and foreigners detained for summary trials. The figure varies considerably with the offense: from 90 percent for violation of immigration laws to 21 percent for embezzlement, swindling, and breach of trust. This partly accounts for the overrepresentation of foreigners in this type of procedure. For each offense shown, the proportion of summary trials is higher for foreigners than for entering prisoners as a whole.

3. *Illegal Entrance or Residence.* Since 1983, statistics have been available that distinguish between foreign persons incarcerated for "no legal status" (violation of article 19 of the November 2, 1945, *ordon-*

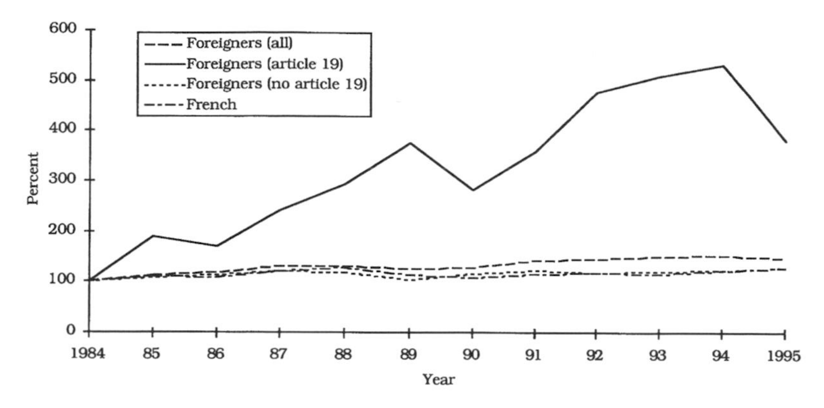

Fig. 3.—Prison population on January 1, by nationality and, among foreigners, by "illegal presence," 1984–95. Source: Monthly statistics on foreign prisoners with no legal status.

nance on the entrance and residence of foreigners in France) and for other reasons. On January 1, 1995, "article 19 foreign prisoners" made up 5.6 percent of all prisoners and other foreign prisoners made up an additional 23.4 percent.

Figure 3 shows prison population trends from 1984 to 1995 broken down to isolate article 19 prisoners. Although the number of foreign prisoners increased by 48 percent overall, a larger increase than for French prisoners (up 29 percent), most of the increase is caused by an increase in article 19 foreign prisoners (up 280 percent). For other foreign prisoners, though the trend varies slightly in comparison with French prisoners, the eleven-year increase of 29 percent is exactly the same.

4. *Incarceration Rate by Nationality.* The incarceration rate is determined by comparing the number of prisoners on a specific date with the number of inhabitants on the same date. Table 13 provides summary data on the disproportionate presence of foreign persons among those admitted to prison in 1993 or held there on January 1, 1995. Relative to population, foreigners are heavily overrepresented in both populations. In 1990, they constituted 6.37 percent of the population, but they were 32.8 percent of admissions in 1993 and 27.0 percent of the confined population in 1995.

Earlier parts of this essay which showed that foreign defendants were overrepresented among suspects and were likelier than French citizens to be incarcerated make the findings of overrepresentation not surprising.

TABLE 13

Overrepresentation of Foreign Persons among Prison Admissions in 1993 and among Prisoners on January 1, 1995

	Percentage
Proportion of foreigners in March 1990:	6.4
In admissions, 1993	32.8
In prison, January 1, 1995	29.0
Disproportion in admissions (1993):	
Total rate per 100,000 population	142.5
French nationals	102.3
Foreigners	733.7
Ratio, French/foreign	7.2
Ratio, French/foreign (without article 19)	3.0
Disproportion in prison populations:	
Total rate per 100,000 population (1995)	89.0
French nationals	67.4
Foreigners	405.2
Ratio, French/foreign	6.0
Ratio, French/foreign (without article 19)	4.9

Source.—Ministère de la Justice (1991, 1995).

Table 13 shows admission and incarceration rates per 100,000 same-group population. The ratios of disproportion are much higher than for the ratios among suspects that were mentioned earlier (relative to population, foreigners were 3.6 times more likely than French nationals to be suspects if immigration offenses are counted and 2.5 times if they are not).

Relative to population, foreigners are six times more likely than French nationals to be in confinement and 7.2 times more likely to be sent there. As this essay has repeatedly shown, however, article 19 offenses are by definition almost exclusively committed by foreign persons, and those offenses exaggerate overrepresentation. Even when they are omitted from the analysis, the disproportions remain substantial. Not counting article 19 offenses, foreign persons were three times likelier than French nationals to be admitted to prison and 4.9 times likelier to be confined on January 1, 1995.

These admission and confinement rates are not directly comparable to police statistics because the latter do not include homicide and injury by neglect and road traffic *délits.* These offenses represent 7 percent of all incarcerations in 1993, and the proportion of foreigners involved is low (9 percent) but still slightly larger than their population share.

III. Disparity and Discrimination

A number of inferences can be drawn from the various findings presented above. The questions to be considered are the existence of nationality-linked disparities in involvement in crime and of discrimination against foreigners by the criminal justice system.

A. Control of Illegal Immigration

Taken as a whole, these data show that the key question is control of illegal immigration. Without this offense, the proportion of foreigners in police statistics would have been stable (at 14 percent) since 1976. During that year, the police suspected 7,000 foreigners of illegal entrance or residence in France. In 1993 the figure for the same offense was 44,000. For these cases, an unsuspended prison sentence is the rule (75 percent of cases in 1993). If the accused person is French (and therefore tried for collusion), the proportion receiving unsuspended prison sentences drops to 37 percent. Of the sixteen *délits* most frequently punished by the courts (taking foreigners and French nationals as a whole), the highest percentage of unsuspended prison sentences is for illegal entrance or residence in France, far ahead of theft with violence (58 percent) and possession or purchase of narcotics (51 percent).

This deliberate decision to punish illicit immigration by imprisonment is the primary cause of the overrepresentation of foreigners in prison. As a result, the exclusion of foreigners incarcerated for illegal entrance or residence in France brings the coefficient of overrepresentation of foreigners among admissions down from seven to three (1993). The fact remains, however, that foreigners are three times more likely than nationals to be admitted to prison.

B. More Serious Offenses

Aside from violations of immigration laws, statistics for sentencing show that the offenses for which foreigners are prosecuted (forgery of public or private documents, rape, intentional assault and battery, violation of the narcotics laws, etc.) are, by their very nature and without consideration of the nationality of the suspect, more frequently punished by unsuspended prison sentences than are *crimes*, *délits*, and 5th class *contraventions* as a whole. If foreigners are punished more severely on the whole (12 percent are given totally suspended sentences, 31 percent unsuspended sentences), it is to a significant degree because the acts of which they are accused are more serious—according to the criteria of the criminal justice system, at any rate.

C. Greater Use of Imprisonment

In itself, however, the type of offense cannot account for this differential treatment. Using sentencing statistics again, for a given offense, recourse to unsuspended prison sentences is more frequent when a foreigner is involved. This analysis demands elaboration by analysis of findings restricted to sentencing for single offenses. While alternative sentences or fines are meted out equally frequently to foreigners and nationals, totally suspended sentences are largely reserved for nationals, as are exemptions from punishment altogether. In comparison with French nationals, the probability that a foreigner will receive an unsuspended prison sentence is 2.4 times higher for illegal use of narcotics, 2.3 times higher for receiving and concealing, twice as high for possession and purchasing of narcotics or illegal entrance and residence, 1.9 times higher for simple larceny, and 1.8 times higher for insulting a representative of the public authority. There is just a short way to go from these findings to an inference that they evidence xenophobic attitudes among judges, but that step should not be taken too hastily (although such attitudes may exist, of course). As a rule, the sentences meted out to foreigners are not longer than those for French nationals, despite the fact that short sentences (less than three months) are definitely less frequent. This may be influenced by pretrial detention.

D. Decisions Are Partly Predetermined Upstream in the Process

We must look back to what went on before the sentencing stage. The sentencing decisions—and especially the choice between an unsuspended and a completely suspended prison term—may be influenced by the way in which a case was processed, that is to say, by earlier decisions made by other police or judicial agencies, including *garde à vue* (police custody), *déférement au parquet* (suspect conducted to the prosecutor's office under police escort), *comparution immédiate* (sentencing following a summary procedure in case of flagrant violation, with no investigation), or pretrial detention in the framework of an investigation. The question of "guarantees against defaulting" is constantly in the forefront throughout this filtering process. Foreigners and nationals are often not similarly situated with respect to residential stability, family status, and employment and as a result may appear more likely to abscond. Because of that apparent higher likelihood, they may be more likely to be held in pretrial detention.

E. Is There More Criminality among Foreigners?

If violations of immigration laws are excluded, the proportion of foreigners among police suspects was 14 percent in 1993, when foreigners represented only 6 percent of the French population according to the 1990 INSEE census (INSEE 1992). Do these figures mean that foreigners are overrepresented among offenders? Here, too, such a conclusion would be jumping to conclusions. First, we have seen that these two percentages were not directly comparable, since the census does not include all those categories of foreigners potentially containing suspects. This is true of a foreigner arriving at the Paris-Roissy airport, suspected of trafficking in narcotics, and taken in for questioning, and of a supporter of a foreign football team, taken in for intentional assault and battery after a game at the Parc des Princes stadium. This results in an overestimation of the foreign suspect rate per 1,000 inhabitants.

Furthermore, we lack knowledge of the entire group of offenders liable to punishment. There is no justification for the assertion that the proportion of foreigners within that population, impossible to determine, would still be 14 percent. There are some reasons to suspect the percentage may be lower. The battle to control clandestine immigration leads the police to intervene more frequently in areas with a high density of foreigners, and these policies facilitate the detection of offenses committed by foreigners. For this kind of "proactive" policing, manpower and the amount of time invested are the crucial elements. Where "reactive policing" is concerned, much depends on how the victim behaves. In violent offenses, for example (offenses often involving foreigners), the more familiar the victim is with the offender, the more he or she is reluctant to treat an assault as a criminal offense (Zauberman 1990). Conversely, when the aggressor is a stranger, the victim is more likely to file a complaint. That a nonnegligible portion of the French population is susceptible to evidencing racist and xenophobic attitudes could mean that French citizens would be especially likely to report offenses in which the apparent assailant was a foreigner. There is reason to believe, then, that the proportion of foreigners would be lower if all perpetrators of aggressions were identified.

This is, however, but one of many questions to which current data and research can provide no clear answers.

REFERENCES

Centre de Recherches Sociologiques sur le Droit et les Institutions Pénales (CESDIP). 1968–95. Base de données SEPT (séries pénitentiaires temporelles). Paris: CESDIP.

Haut Conseil à l'Integration. 1992. *La connaissance de l'immigration et de l'intégration.* Paris: La Documentation Française, Collection des Rapports Officiels.

———. 1993. *L'intégration à la française.* Ed. 10/18, Collected Documents. Paris: Union Générale d'Éditions.

Institut National de la Statistique et des Études Économiques (INSEE). 1984. *Recensement général de la population de 1982, les étrangers.* Paris: La Documentation Française.

———. 1992. *Recensement général de la population de 1990, les étrangers.* Paris: La Documentation Française.

Le Monde. 1991. Untitled article. September 26.

———. 1993. Untitled article. April 20.

Ministère de l'Intérieur. 1972–93. *Direction générale de la police nationale, direction centrale de la police judiciaire, division des études et de la documentation générale: Rapports annuels sur la délinquance et la criminalité constatées en France.* Paris: La Documentation Française.

Ministère de la Justice. 1991. *Direction de l'administration générale et de l'équipement, sous direction de la statistique, des études et de la documentation.* Statistique annuelle, no. 10, les condamnations. Paris: La Documentation Française.

———. 1995. "Direction de l'administration pénitentiaire, Service de la communication, des études et des relations internationales (SCERI), statistique issue du fichier national des détenus (FND)." Paris: Ministère de la Justice.

Simon, P. 1993. "Nommer pour agir." *Le Monde* (April 2), p. 2.

Tournier, P., Ph. Robert, B. Leconte, and P.-J. Couton. 1989. *Les étrangers dans les statistiques pénales—constitution d'un corpus et analyse critique des données,* p. 256. Déviance et contrôle social, no. 49. Paris: Centre de recherches sociologiques sur le droit et les institutions pénales (CESDIP).

Tribalat, M. 1991. "Combien sont les français d'origine étrangère?" *Economie et statistique* INSEE, no. 242(April):17–29.

———. 1993. "Les immigrés au recensement de 1990 et les populations liées à leur installation en France." *Population* 6:1911–46.

Zauberman, R., et al. 1990. *Les victimes, comportements et attitudes, enquête nationale de victimation.* Paris: Centre de recherches sociologiques sur le droit et les institutions pénales (CESDIP).

ADDITIONAL READINGS

For further information the reader is referred to the following works.

Bernard, Ph. 1993. *L'immigration.* Paris: Le Monde/Marabout.

Levy, R. 1987. *Du suspect au coupable: Le travail de police judiciaire.* Geneva and Paris: Librairie des Méridiens, Médecine & Hygiène.

Robert, Ph., B. Aubusson de Cavarlay, M.-L. Pottier, and P. Tournier. 1994. *Les comptes du crime, les délinquances et leurs mesures,* p. 329. Paris: Les Éditions l'Harmattan.

Tournier, P. 1993. "Les étrangers dans les statistiques pénitentiaires: Le cas français et aperçu européen." In *Ausländer, Kriminalität und Strafrechtspflege—Etrangers, criminalité et système pénal,* edited by Stefan Bauhofer and Nicolas Queloz, pp. 323–46. Schweizerische Arbeitsgruppe für Kriminologie—Groupe Suisse de Travail de Criminologie, Reihe Kriminologie—Collection Criminologie, vol. 11. Chur: Verlag Rüegger.

———. 1993. "Etrangers et délinquances: Des chiffres en liberté très peu surveillée." *Plein Droit* 21:36–40.

———. 1993–94. "Que faire des statistiques pénales en matière d'extranéité?" *Loi, criminalité, politiques de contrôle social et minorités raciales, ethniques ou étrangères dans les pays européens,* p. 8. Brussells: Séminaire.

Tournier, P., and Ph. Robert. 1991. *Etrangers et délinquances, les chiffres du débat,* p. 263. Paris: Les Éditions l'Harmattan.

———. 1992. "Mehr Gefangene als Täter." *Neue Kriminalpolitik, forum für Praxis, Politik und Wissenschaft* 2:38–40.

———. 1993. "Etrangers: Police, Justice, Prison." In *La connaissance de l'immigration et de l'intégration,* pp. 133–70. Rapport 1992 du Haut Conseil à l'Intégration. Paris: La Documentation Française, Collection des Rapports Officiels.